Undergraduate Topics in Computer Science

T0259918

Series editor

Ian Mackie

Advisory Board

Samson Abramsky, University of Oxford, Oxford, UK
Karin Breitman, Pontifical Catholic University of Rio de Janeiro,
    Rio de Janeiro, Brazil
Chris Hankin, Imperial College London, London, UK
Dexter Kozen, Cornell University, Ithaca, USA
Andrew Pitts, University of Cambridge, Cambridge, UK
Hanne Riis Nielson, Technical University of Denmark, Kongens Lyngby, Denmark
Steven Skiena, Stony Brook University, Stony Brook, USA
Iain Stewart, University of Durham, Durham, UK

Undergraduate Topics in Computer Science (UTiCS) delivers high-quality instructional content for undergraduates studying in all areas of computing and information science. From core foundational and theoretical material to final-year topics and applications, UTiCS books take a fresh, concise, and modern approach and are ideal for self-study or for a one- or two-semester course. The texts are all authored by established experts in their fields, reviewed by an international advisory board, and contain numerous examples and problems. Many include fully worked solutions.

More information about this series at http://www.springer.com/series/7592

Dana Vrajitoru · William Knight

Practical Analysis
of Algorithms

 Springer

Dana Vrajitoru
William Knight
Indiana University
South Bend, IN
USA

ISSN 1863-7310   ISSN 2197-1781   (electronic)
Undergraduate Topics in Computer Science
ISBN 978-3-319-09887-6   ISBN 978-3-319-09888-3   (eBook)
DOI 10.1007/978-3-319-09888-3

Library of Congress Control Number: 2014946382

Springer Cham Heidelberg New York Dordrecht London

Printed on acid-free paper

Springer is part of Springer Science+Business Media (www.springer.com)

Preface

Analysis of algorithms plays an essential role in the education and training of any serious programmer preparing to deal with real world applications. It provides the tools for understanding which algorithm might yield better performance for solving a particular aspect of an application, or adapt best to the problem specifications. The goals of this field are: to provide a solid basis for the comparison of two or more algorithms available for the same problem, to give programmers an idea of how efficient a program is, and to allow them to estimate how well an algorithm will scale up with the data. Even if the students do not directly apply the knowledge acquired in such a class to the problems they need to solve for their professional work, they acquire structured thinking and deep understanding of the mechanism of an algorithm, which are always necessary to write good code. For this reason, algorithm analysis is typically included in the core curriculum of most bachelor's degrees in computer science or informatics.

The subject is a non-trivial one, however, and many students find it difficult to grasp. Part of the problem is the substantial mathematical background that is needed to understand the material. In order to provide a solid analysis of an algorithm, one must use rigorous proofs and other tools that can be challenging even for someone with good training. This is an aspect that makes a course like Analysis of Algorithms particularly demanding of both the students and the teacher.

This textbook addresses the needs of collegiate computing programs without assuming a strong mathematical background. Thus, our purpose is to provide proofs and explanations where all the steps are carefully detailed. We hope that they can be valuable assets for the student with the patience to read them and the will to understand them. For each of the topics discussed, many practical and detailed examples are provided, as well as similar exercises to allow the readers to test their comprehension.

Approach

We approach the field of analysis of algorithms on two fronts that are connected but can be studied separately. The first front concerns the fundamental notations in the big-Oh family, their definition, and how to prove that they apply to various functions. Chapters 2 and 3 of the book focus on this aspect. Chapter 2 provides the tools for it, and Chap. 3 applies these tools to proofs and exercises related to these notations.

The second front concerns the study of algorithms to find the time and space complexities, and then determining the order of complexity in the best, worst, and average case. The next four chapters are focused on this aspect. We start with a chapter dedicated to recurrence relations, preparing the readers with a major tool for the remaining chapters. Then we follow with deterministic algorithms and study the best and worst cases for them. The following chapter introduces the role of probability theory in this field, and how it is used for finding the average complexity of some algorithms. The related topic of probabilistic algorithms is also covered in this chapter. The last chapter follows with graph theory, where various techniques seen before are applied.

We aimed for this book to be sufficient for an analysis of algorithms course without extensive references to other textbooks. It covers all the tools directly applied to analysis of algorithm in detail. It provides methods and examples to understand these tools and their use, such as the summation notation or recurrence relations. We dedicate a whole chapter to the latter and provide recipes to solve the major types encountered in analysis of algorithms. While most books on the topic discuss them, extensive coverage of recurrence relations can mostly found in discrete mathematics and related textbooks. Our goal is to be able to understand them fully for use within algorithms analysis and be able to derive complete solutions systematically. An appendix on probability theory reviews the major definitions and theorems that we use in the chapter Algorithms and Probabilities to make reading this chapter more seamless.

An aspect that we also try to attend to is the gap between theory and practice, a difficulty that many students encounter in courses of this nature. They understand the theory relatively well, but they are mystified when it comes to applying it to practical examples. Most textbooks on the subject are written at a level of abstraction that makes them difficult for the average computer science student to understand completely and to put them into practice. Many of the presented proofs are sketchy and leave the details to the self-study of the reader. Methods for solving related problems are introduced with few practical examples of how they are applied. These are mostly useful reference books for the class instructors, or for the computer science professionals who might need a quick access to an algorithm outline.

To address this, our book contains many fully worked examples and provides many of the proofs with enough details to be followed step by step. The chapter Fundamental Notations shows many examples of practically proving that a function is in one of the big-Oh relationship with another. For the same purpose, the previous chapter, Mathematical Preliminaries, covers the major functions that appear in proofs of the fundamental notations, such as the logarithms. We review properties of these functions that play a role in connection with the fundamental notations and show how they are used through many examples and exercises. In the chapter Recurrence Relations we compute many solutions down to the value of the coefficients, and the same is done afterwards with recurrence relations emerging from analyzing specific algorithms. The graph theory algorithms are given with justification and with examples of execution on practical problems.

We present the material in order of difficulty, starting from the chapter that the students are probably the most familiar with. Each new chapter builds on the knowledge acquired in the previous ones and raises the bar higher with a new topic.

Book Outline

The book teaches the concepts of analysis of algorithms required in core courses in many undergraduate and graduate computer science degrees, as well as provides a review of the fundamental mathematical notions that are necessary to understand these concepts. For all of the chapters, the explanations are aimed to the level of understanding of the common upper level student, and not only the teacher. All the materials are accompanied by many examples explained in much detail and by exercises.

An introduction explains the purpose of studying this field and the major ideas behind the notion of complexity of algorithms. We make the connection between the execution time and the count of operations, and continue towards the more abstract notion of order of complexity. This leads the way to understanding the need for the fundamental notations, such as the big-Oh.

The second chapter, Mathematical Preliminaries, reviews the fundamental mathematical notions that the students need to understand analysis of algorithms. Even though these concepts are most likely taught in mathematical classes, the knowledge level may be non-uniform and this chapter serves the purpose of bringing them to a common ground. It also prepares the reader to understand the proofs and exercises in the Fundamental Notations chapter. We cover several functions that play a role in analysis of algorithms, as well as the summation operation, which is essential to loop counting.

The third chapter, Fundamental Notations, lays the foundation of the analysis of algorithms theory in terms of the big-Oh, Omega, and Theta notations. It also covers the related topics of the little-Oh and asymptotic functions. We use the properties of the functions introduced in the previous chapter to prove the relationships defined by the fundamental notations for a variety of expressions.

The fourth chapter, Recurrence Relations, introduces a very important tool used in analysis of algorithms. We go in further detail than other algorithms textbooks over the definition, properties, and procedures for solving various types of recurrence relations. We cover the major types of recurrence relations that occur often from analyzing algorithms and provide systematic procedures for solving them.

The next chapter introduces the students to the core of the analysis of algorithms theory, explaining the concept of basic operation, followed by traditional loop counting, and the ideas of best case and worst case complexities. We then provide a detailed analysis for the classes of algorithms that are most commonly seen in a data structures textbook or course. This chapter also provides a section on the theorem setting the lower bound for the worst-case complexity of comparison-based sorting algorithms. It also discusses algorithms with unusual and interesting proofs of their complexity, such as Euclid's algorithm or KMP for pattern matching.

The chapter that follows, Algorithms and Probabilities, accomplishes two goals. First, it introduces the students to a number of algorithms of a probabilistic nature. Second, it uses elements of probability theory to compute the average complexity of some algorithms such as Quicksort. Textbooks rarely discuss the computation of the expected value of algorithms in such detail; many of them only cover the best and worst case complexities of Quicksort, for example.

The last chapter introduces a variety of classical finite graph algorithms, such as are taught in upper level computer science classes, together with an analysis of their complexity. These algorithms have many applications and provide an excellent playground for applying the various ideas introduced before.

Contents

Introduction

1

Analysis of algorithms is the science of determining the amounts of time and space required by computers to carry out various procedures. The aims of this theoretical part of computer science are twofold. First, to give programmers mathematical tools for choosing intelligently from among competing algorithms available for performing a task. Second, to provide an informed idea of how efficiently an algorithm is solving a problem and how well it will scale with the size of the problem.

Programmers who have assimilated the concepts and understood the analysis of the major types of algorithms will acquire an intuition for how efficient an algorithm is and find it easier to choose the appropriate algorithm for any given task, or even invent a new one. They will know how avoid simple programming traps that can transform a linear function into a quadratic one. Similarly, they will be able to distinguish between appropriate and inappropriate use of recursion. With the emergence of very large databases containing millions of records to be processed, it is more important than ever to be able to write efficient algorithms.

It is an unfortunate fact of life in computing that algorithms that use computer memory space quite efficiently are often among the slowest to execute, while algorithms that execute extremely rapidly often require exorbitant amounts of memory space. Thus "choosing intelligently" requires us to understand the well-known space-time trade-off dilemma in algorithm design. Program designers must frequently make choices that balance the need for speed of execution against the limitations of computer memory in the systems on which their programs will run.

In the early days of computing, when main memory in a computer system was pitifully small and hideously expensive, a great deal of attention was given to inventing algorithms that ran in as little main memory space as possible. Today's gigantic computer memories have rendered many of those algorithms obsolete. Nowadays, algorithm designers tend to focus on creating algorithms that run faster than previously known algorithms, ignoring space costs. After all, the amount of main memory available in a typical computer system has gone up by a factor of 10 every few years throughout the computer age.

With the increase of available memory came the increase in amount of data to process. We see a shift of interest from merely providing a correct answer in a

© Springer International Publishing Switzerland 2014
D. Vrajitoru and W. Knight, *Practical Analysis of Algorithms*,
Undergraduate Topics in Computer Science, DOI 10.1007/978-3-319-09888-3_1

reasonable amount of time to being able to provide an answer quickly for a large amount of data to process. The question we often have to ask now is not "can we solve this problem?" but rather "can we solve it fast enough for this huge collection of objects?" Thus, it is important to know what we can expect to happen to the execution time and amount of memory needed when the problem size increases by a large factor.

1.1   Measuring Execution Time

When several computer algorithms are available for solving problems of a particular type, you will almost always find that the more efficient algorithms will be more difficult to understand and to code than the simpler, more intuitive algorithms. To take a familiar example, a very large number of algorithms are available for sorting the objects in an array. Algorithms such as Bubble Sort, Selection Sort, and Insertion Sort are very easy to understand and to code, but the average amount of time required by these algorithms to sort an array of n objects in random order is proportional to n^2, which makes them very slow on large arrays. By contrast, fast algorithms such as Quicksort, Heap Sort, and Merge Sort are significantly more difficult to understand and to code correctly,[1] but the average amount of time that they require to sort an array of n objects in random order is proportional to $n \log(n)$. It is tempting for a human programmer to believe that if an algorithm requires complicated code then it will be "hard" for the computer to perform the operations correctly and efficiently, and that simple code will be easier and (therefore) quicker for the computer. Not so. A computer is not "confused" and slowed down by intricate, non-intuitive algorithms in the way that human beings are when they attempt to carry out such algorithms on paper. A computer executes code tirelessly and flawlessly, and with blinding speed. If you give it a correct implementation of an efficient algorithm, it will perform the algorithm without mental fatigue. The moral here is that you should never judge the efficiency of an algorithm by how difficult and confusing it is for you to carry out the algorithm on paper. The way to judge an algorithm's efficiency is to subject it to a careful mathematical analysis.

So how do we judge whether an algorithm is efficient? We start by attempting to describe the amounts of time and space that the algorithm requires as functions of the size of the problem. But what is the size of the problem? In many cases this is easy to determine. For example, if we are performing an operation on a collection of n objects, then n can be considered the size of the problem. What about a function determining whether a number is prime? In that case the number itself can be considered to be the size of the problem, or if we want to be more precise, the number of digits in its decimal or binary representation.

---

[1] The Quicksort algorithm is notorious for its sensitivity to minor changes in its implementation in code. The slightest change will almost certainly make the code perform incorrectly on some data. Many erroneous versions of Quicksort have been published in journals and texts on programming.

The next question is how do we proceed to measure the execution time? What kind of measurement is precise and reliable enough? We could simply run the algorithm with examples of various sizes on a given platform and measure the execution time with a stopwatch. However, the results will depend significantly on the speed of the processor, on the available memory and type of CPU, on the operating system and other applications running in the background. Thus, this is not a method that we can seriously consider.

A better idea is to look at the set of operations that are necessary to complete the algorithm. To give a practical example, let us suppose that an algorithm applied to a problem of size n, requires $n + 2$ comparisons and $n - 1$ assignments, and that each of them involve expressions that do not require more than a limited number of assembly instructions to be completed. We must be able to assume that such operations are not affected by the size of the problem. We can call any operation that fits this description a *basic operation*. On any specific platform, a comparison will require approximately a constant amount of time that we can denote by c_1. Similarly, the time required by an assignment can be approximated by a second constant c_2. Then on the whole, the algorithm will take $c_1(n + 2) + c_2(n - 1)$ time. This can be expressed as $(c_1 + c_2)n + (2c_1 - c_2)$. This is a linear expression in the variable n, or more precisely, a polynomial of first degree in this variable. This description of the execution time is more informative than any specific measurement. Thus, it is wiser to count the number of basic operations performed by the algorithm than to measure the execution time.

1.2   Classes of Algorithms

As a side effect of the ideas in the previous paragraph, the actual constant multiplied by n in the expression we obtain is not especially important because it can vary from one platform to another. Thus, what matters most in the expression describing the execution time is the largest term in n. Furthermore, when the value of n becomes large, the constants or the terms of a lower degree that are added to the largest term will not contribute in a significant way to the overall value, and can be ignored. This way we can move from the simple idea of execution time to a more evocative notion of "order of complexity" of the algorithm. This abstract description leads to categories of algorithms with similar behavior. Algorithms of "the same order of complexity" show similarities in the way their execution time changes when the problem size increases. We will call this the "growth rate" of the algorithm.

Let us examine some of these categories of algorithms based on the order of complexity. One variety that many programmers are quite happy with consists of *linear algorithms*. They are called linear because their execution time is a linear function of the size of the problem, as in the practical example we discussed. As a consequence, their execution time increases approximately by the rate of the size of the problem. Thus, when the problem size doubles, the execution time also doubles. In general, a linear algorithm performs some operation on each (or almost each) object in the collection, but does not need to perform more than a limited number of operations for each object. To be more precise, the execution time of a linear algorithm has an upper bound that can be described as a constant multiplied by n.

Are linear algorithms efficient enough? In most situations they are sufficient. In particular, if the algorithm cannot ignore any object in the collection in order to accomplish its goal, then linear is the best that we can hope for. However, if we are searching for a particular record in a very large database, a linear algorithm may not be acceptable. This is particularly true for online search engines that are used extensively and whose users will not have the patience to wait for more than a few seconds for an answer.

Another category that we can look at is *quadratic algorithms*. The execution time for these algorithms grows approximately with the square of the rate of the size of the problem. Thus, if the problem size doubles, we can expect the execution time to grow by a factor of four. As mentioned before, some sorting algorithms are quadratic, which makes them impractical for problems of large size. Sorting algorithms that have a growth rate of $n \log(n)$ are much closer to linear algorithms than they are to quadratic ones and thus are preferable to the latter. As a side note, why don't we design a linear sorting algorithm? As it turns out, there are limitations to how fast a sorting algorithm can be and still work on an array containing any kind of data in a random order.

As long as the largest term in n in the time complexity function is a constant power of n, the algorithm is in the *polynomial* family. These are the good guys. These are the algorithms that we can run on problems of a large size and still expect them to complete within a reasonable amount of time. For such problems, we can expect that by increasing the computation speed and available memory, we can solve problems of a significantly larger size. For all polynomial algorithms, if the size of the problem doubles, the execution time grows by a multiplicative constant. Naturally, the higher the power of n, the higher the constant is. In general, problems for which we do not have a polynomial algorithm are considered solved only for small size problems.

Let's look at an algorithm in a non-polynomial category, such as one where the largest term in the execution time is 2^n. We can call this algorithm *exponential*. What happens when we double the size of the problem? The execution time will be multiplied by 2^n. As we see, it doesn't simply grow by a constant factor, as happens with a polynomial algorithm. The larger the value of n, the more the cost for doubling it will increase. An example of such an algorithm is one that needs to examine every subset of a set of n elements.

As a practical approach, programmers have been developing less-than-perfect-but-fast algorithms for such difficult problems, called *heuristics*. These alternative solutions provide a good answer in polynomial time within an acceptable margin of error or with a high probability. They are not guaranteed, however, to give the correct answer 100 % of the time, or to always be fast enough.

To use a different approach in comparing these categories of algorithms, we can ask the following: let's suppose that we move from a computer of a given speed to one that is twice as fast. If in one minute an algorithm would solve a problem of size n, what size problem can the algorithm solve in the same amount of time on the faster computer? If the algorithm has the largest term $\log(n)$, then we can solve a problem of size n^2. If the algorithm is linear, then we can solve a problem of size $2n$. If the algorithm is quadratic, then we can solve a problem of size $\sqrt{(2)}n$. But if the algorithm is exponential of base 2, then we can only solve a problem of size $n + 1$ by doubling the speed of the computer. This may be the best argument against such algorithms.

1.3 Order of Complexity

The description we have offered so far does not mention the fact that the size of the problem is not the only factor in deciding the complexity of the algorithm. For any given size, the arrangement of the objects in the collection or other properties of the data can cause the algorithm to complete faster in some cases, and to take more time in others. We can ask in this case what are the conditions under which the algorithm will provide the fastest execution time for a size n, and what are the conditions under which the algorithm will take the longest. These are known as the *best case* and the *worst case* for the algorithm, and the order of complexity for them can be quite different. We may also want to know what we can expect on the *average* from an algorithm.

When we are looking at a particular algorithm to solve a problem, these are the ideas that we must consider in order to decide whether it is efficient enough for the needs of an application we are developing. If we are comparing two algorithms that solve the same problem, then we can first look at their order of complexity. The best measure of comparison is the average, if available. For example, Merge Sort is faster than Quicksort in the worst case, but Quicksort is faster on the average, which explains its popularity.

If two algorithms have the same order of complexity, then to compare them we must be more precise in our analysis. This is where we would look not only for the largest term in the execution time function, but also for the specific value of its coefficient. For a realistic measurement, we need to count the basic operations in the same way in the two algorithms. For example, we can count each comparison and each assignment as 1 for both of them. If necessary, we can also look in detail at each arithmetic operation involved in comparisons and assignments.

1.4 Book Organization

This descriptive notion of order of complexity for an algorithm must be defined in precise mathematical terms to be of any use. The formal definition involves three major notations, that we introduce in this book in Chap. 3. The first one, the big-Oh, provides an upper bound for the growth rate of the algorithm. Thus, if we say that $f(n)$ is $O(g(n))$, then f will grow no faster than g with the size of the problem.

In general, we use the worst-case situations to decide on the big-Oh order for an algorithm. The second one, the big-Omega, provides a lower bound for the growth rate of an algorithm. Thus, if we say that $f(n) = \Omega(g(n))$, then f will grow at least as fast as g. The big-Omega notation is generally related to the best-case complexity. Finally, if the function g provides both a lower bound and an upper bound for the growth rate for f, then we can say that f is big-Theta of g, or $f(n) = \Theta(g(n))$. In this case, we can say that f and g have the same growth rate with the size of the problem. It is important to note that we do not compare the actual values of these functions, but only how they react to the changes in size of the problem.

Chapter 2 focuses on the major mathematical functions that appear often in functions describing the complexity of algorithms. We examine their basic properties and look at examples of using them to prove facts about them or to solve various exercises. These properties are then used separately and together in the fundamental notations chapter to show how various functions can be compared to each other. Fundamentally we would like to be able to determine whether two functions are in one or more of the relationships described by the big-letter notations. Oftentimes we would like to find the closest simple expression that satisfies the big-Oh, big-Omega, or even big-Theta notations for a complicated expression we may have obtained from analyzing an algorithm.

Chapter 3 introduces a major tool in analysis of algorithms, *recurrence relations*. Basically a recurrent expression is one that is defined in some way in terms of itself. In this chapter we examine functions of integer variables, such as the ones describing the complexity of an algorithm, that are defined for the value of n in terms of their value for $n - 1$, $n - 2$, and so on. These relations are directly connected to recursive functions and are the most natural way to describe their behavior. However, their application to algorithms analysis is not limited to recursion. We will see in the subsequent chapters how ubiquitous their use is in this field. We classify recurrence relations by various features and provide recipes for solving several common types, along with many examples and exercises.

In Chap. 4 we start to look at major algorithms and categories of algorithms. We begin with deterministic algorithms, which are algorithms that do not involve any randomized quantities or behaviors, and that always provide the same answer when run again on the same data. We use the knowledge accumulated thus far to find the best-case and worst-case complexities for each algorithm as precisely as we can.

Chapter 5 is dedicated both to non-deterministic algorithms and to complexity analysis that involves probability theory. This means that we will examine the tools for determining the average algorithms complexity. We also look at several useful algorithms that involve the use of random number generators. Such algorithms are called probabilistic, as they can provide a different answer when run again on the same data. Alternatively, if the answer is always the same, then a probabilistic algorithm might take a different set of steps to find it.

Finally, a special chapter is dedicated to graph theory. This topic is an important building block in the theory of computer science and has a great variety of applications, which justifies the special treatment. Additionally, the subject provides several algorithms that are interesting to discuss as programming challenges and constitute a good practice exercise for the algorithm analysis tools introduced in the book.

We hope that by the end of the book, the reader will have a good idea both of what the complexity of an algorithm is, and how we can prove it in a rigorous way.

Mathematical Preliminaries

2

In this chapter we'll review some mathematical concepts that will be used throughout this course. We'll also learn some new mathematical notations and techniques that are important for analysis of algorithms.

2.1 Floors and Ceilings

In doing computer computations, we sometimes have to discard the fractional part of a real number x, while in other cases we may have to round upward to the first integer larger than or equal to x. It is convenient to have simple mathematical notations that indicate these operations. The "floor" and "ceiling" notations were invented for this purpose.

Notations. We shall use $\mathbf{N}$ for the set of cardinal or natural numbers, $\mathbf{N} = \{0, 1, 2, \ldots\}$, $\mathbf{Z}$ for the set of integers, $\mathbf{Q}$ for the set of rational numbers, and $\mathbf{R}$ for the set of real numbers.

Definition 2.1.1 The *floor* of a real number x, denoted by $\lfloor x \rfloor$, is the largest integer that is less than or equal to x. The *ceiling* of a real number x, denoted by $\lceil x \rceil$, is the smallest integer that is greater than or equal to x. We can express these definitions in the following way:

$$\lfloor x \rfloor = \max\{k : k \in \mathbf{Z}, k \le x\};$$
$$\lceil x \rceil = \min\{k : k \in \mathbf{Z}, k \ge x\}.$$

Examples 2.1.2

$$\lfloor 3.7 \rfloor = 3; \ \lfloor 0.04 \rfloor = 0; \ \lfloor -0.04 \rfloor = -1; \ \lfloor 6 \rfloor = 6; \ \lfloor 22.104 \rfloor = 22;$$
$$\lceil 3.7 \rceil = 4; \ \lceil 0.04 \rceil = 1; \ \lceil -0.04 \rceil = 0; \quad \lceil 6 \rceil = 6; \ \lceil 22.104 \rceil = 23.$$

© Springer International Publishing Switzerland 2014
D. Vrajitoru and W. Knight, *Practical Analysis of Algorithms*,
Undergraduate Topics in Computer Science, DOI 10.1007/978-3-319-09888-3_2

In a C or C++ program, an expression of the form n/m indicates *integer division* when n and m are of an integer data type. The mathematical expression $\left\lfloor \dfrac{n}{m} \right\rfloor$ denotes the exact value of the C/C++ expression n/m when n and m are positive. Thus, when reasoning about programs in which integer division is performed, we will make repeated use of expressions such as $\left\lfloor \dfrac{n}{m} \right\rfloor$.

If you consult the documentation for the C/C++ "math.h" or "cmath" library header file, you will find that it contains the following two prototypes:

```
double ceil (double x);
double floor(double x);
```

Note that the values returned by these two functions are of type double, not long. This may surprise you until you realize that floating point real numbers can be *far* larger than the integer LONG_MAX, and so in order to have expressions such as floor(3.182e19) return a sensible value, the function must return the integer 31820000000000000 in floating point form.

The following lemma gives us a property of integers that we will use often in this chapter.

Lemma 2.1.3 *Let n and m be any integer numbers. If $n < m$, then $n + 1 \leq m$ and $n \leq m - 1$.*

Proof Suppose $n < m$. If $n + 1$ were greater than m, then m would be an integer strictly between n and $n + 1$. That is impossible. Thus $n + 1$ must be less than or equal to m. It follows from $n + 1 \leq m$ that $n \leq m - 1$.   ∎

The following theorem lists some properties of floor and ceiling that we will use throughout in this book. It gives us a better idea about how the floor and the ceiling relate to their argument and to each other.

Theorem 2.1.4 *Let x and y be any real numbers. Let n, m, and k be any integers.*

(a) $\lfloor x \rfloor \leq x < \lfloor x \rfloor + 1$*; equivalently,* $x - 1 < \lfloor x \rfloor \leq x$.
(b) $\lceil x \rceil - 1 < x \leq \lceil x \rceil$*; equivalently,* $x \leq \lceil x \rceil < x + 1$.
(c) *If* $n \leq x < n + 1$ *(or* $x - 1 < n \leq x$*), then* $n = \lfloor x \rfloor$*; similarly, if*
    $n - 1 < x \leq n$ *(or* $x \leq n < x + 1$*), then* $n = \lceil x \rceil$.
(d) *If* $x \leq y$*, then* $\lfloor x \rfloor \leq \lfloor y \rfloor$ *and* $\lceil x \rceil \leq \lceil y \rceil$*. Similarly for* $x \geq y$.
(e) *If* $n \leq x$*, then* $n \leq \lfloor x \rfloor$*. If* $n \geq x$ *then* $n \geq \lceil x \rceil$.
(f) *If x has an integer value, then* $\lfloor x \rfloor = x = \lceil x \rceil$*. If x has a non-integer value, then*
    $\lceil x \rceil = \lfloor x \rfloor + 1$.
(g) $\lfloor (-1)x \rfloor = (-1)\lceil x \rceil$ *and* $\lceil (-1)x \rceil = (-1)\lfloor x \rfloor$.

Proof (a) Take any real number x. The inequality $\lfloor x \rfloor \leq x$ is true because the floor of x is an element of a set of integers less than or equal to x. The inequality $x < \lfloor x \rfloor + 1$ is true because $\lfloor x \rfloor$ is the *largest* of the integers less than or equal to x, and $\lfloor x \rfloor + 1$ is an integer larger than $\lfloor x \rfloor$, so $\lfloor x \rfloor + 1$ *cannot* be in the set of integers less than or equal to x. Thus $\lfloor x \rfloor + 1$ is greater than x. This completes the proof that $\lfloor x \rfloor \le x < \lfloor x \rfloor + 1$. To prove that $x - 1 < \lfloor x \rfloor \le x$, we need only prove that $x - 1 < \lfloor x \rfloor$ because we have already proved that $\lfloor x \rfloor \le x$. Take the inequality $x < \lfloor x \rfloor + 1$, which we have already proved, and subtract 1 from both sides. This gives $x - 1 < \lfloor x \rfloor$.

(b) Take any real number x. The inequality $x \le \lceil x \rceil$ is true because the ceiling of x is an element of a set of integers greater than or equal to x. To prove the inequality $\lceil x \rceil - 1 < x$, first note that $\lceil x \rceil$ is the *smallest* of the integers greater than or equal to x, and $\lceil x \rceil - 1$ is smaller than $\lceil x \rceil$, so $\lceil x \rceil - 1$ *cannot* be in the set of integers greater than or equal to x. Thus $\lceil x \rceil - 1$ is smaller than x. This completes the proof that $\lceil x \rceil - 1 < x \le \lceil x \rceil$. The inequalities $x \le \lceil x \rceil < x + 1$ are proved by taking apart the inequalities above, adding 1 to both sides of $\lceil x \rceil - 1 < x$, and then putting the pieces back together again in a different order.

(c) Let x be any real number, and let n be an integer satisfying $n \le x < n + 1$. Then n must be the largest of the integers that are less than or equal to x because by Lemma 2.1.3 every integer greater than n is at least $n + 1$. By definition of $\lfloor x \rfloor$, it follows that $n = \lfloor x \rfloor$. The second assertion has a similar proof.

(d) Suppose $x \le y$. We'll prove that $\lfloor x \rfloor \le \lfloor y \rfloor$ and leave the other assertions as exercises. First note that either $x < \lfloor y \rfloor$ or $\lfloor y \rfloor \le x$. If $x < \lfloor y \rfloor$, then we can combine this with the inequality $\lfloor x \rfloor \le x$ (see part (a)) to conclude that $\lfloor x \rfloor < \lfloor y \rfloor$. If, instead, $\lfloor y \rfloor \le x$, we can combine this with $x \le y$ and $y < \lfloor y \rfloor + 1$ to obtain $\lfloor y \rfloor \le x < \lfloor y \rfloor + 1$. Since $\lfloor y \rfloor$ is an integer, it follows from part (c) that $\lfloor x \rfloor = \lfloor y \rfloor$.

(e) Suppose $n \le x$. Then by (d), $\lfloor n \rfloor \le \lfloor x \rfloor$. Since n has an integer value, $\lfloor n \rfloor = n$, which means that $n \le \lfloor x \rfloor$.

The proof of the second part is similar.

(f) Suppose x has an integer value. Then trivially x belongs to the set $\{k : k \in \mathbf{Z}, k \le x\}$ and is the largest element of the set, so $x = \lfloor x \rfloor$. Similarly, $x = \lceil x \rceil$. Now suppose x is not an integer. We will prove that $\lceil x \rceil = \lfloor x \rfloor + 1$ by showing that $\lceil x \rceil \le \lfloor x \rfloor + 1$ and $\lceil x \rceil \ge \lfloor x \rfloor + 1$. Since x is not an integer, then $\lfloor x \rfloor < x < \lceil x \rceil$, from which we get $\lfloor x \rfloor < \lceil x \rceil$. Since both $\lfloor x \rfloor$ and $\lceil x \rceil$ are integers, we can use Lemma 2.1.3 to conclude that $\lfloor x \rfloor + 1 \le \lceil x \rceil$. By part (a): $x < \lfloor x \rfloor + 1$. Since $\lfloor x \rfloor + 1$ is an integer, we can apply (e) to deduce that $\lceil x \rceil \le \lfloor x \rfloor + 1$. From the two inequalities that we have proved, we can conclude that $\lceil x \rceil = \lfloor x \rfloor + 1$.

(g) Let us start with the second inequality from (a): $\lceil x \rceil - 1 < x \le \lceil x \rceil$. Multiply through by -1 to reverses the inequalities:

$$(-1)(\lceil x \rceil - 1) > (-1)x \ge (-1)(\lceil x \rceil).$$

This can be rewritten from right to left as

$$(-1)\lceil x \rceil \le (-1)x < (-1)\lceil x \rceil + 1.$$

We can see that the integer $(-1)\lceil x \rceil$ satisfies the first part of (c) with respect to the real number $(-1)x$, and thus it must be the floor of this number: $(-1)\lceil x \rceil = \lfloor (-1)x \rfloor$. The second part is proved in a similar way. ∎

The following theorem shows some properties of the floor and ceiling functions in relation to arithmetic operations applied to their arguments.

Theorem 2.1.5 *Let x and y be any real numbers. Let n, m, and k be any integers.*

(a) $\lfloor x \pm n \rfloor = \lfloor x \rfloor \pm n$ *and* $\lceil x \pm n \rceil = \lceil x \rceil \pm n$; *but in general,* $\lfloor nx \rfloor \neq n \lfloor x \rfloor$ *and* $\lceil nx \rceil \neq n \lceil x \rceil$ *and* $\lfloor x + y \rfloor \neq \lfloor x \rfloor + \lfloor y \rfloor$ *and* $\lceil x + y \rceil \neq \lceil x \rceil + \lceil y \rceil.$

(b) $\left\lfloor \dfrac{n}{2} \right\rfloor + \left\lceil \dfrac{n}{2} \right\rceil = n.$

(c) $\left\lfloor \dfrac{n+1}{2} \right\rfloor = \left\lceil \dfrac{n}{2} \right\rceil$; *equivalently,* $\left\lfloor \dfrac{n-1}{2} \right\rfloor + 1 = \left\lceil \dfrac{n}{2} \right\rceil.$

(d) *If* $k > 0$, *then* $\left\lfloor \dfrac{\lfloor y \rfloor}{k} \right\rfloor = \left\lfloor \dfrac{y}{k} \right\rfloor$ *and* $\left\lceil \dfrac{\lceil y \rceil}{k} \right\rceil = \left\lceil \dfrac{y}{k} \right\rceil.$ *In particular, if* $m \neq 0$ *we can put* $y = \dfrac{n}{m}$ *to get these identities:* $\left\lfloor \dfrac{\lfloor \frac{n}{m} \rfloor}{k} \right\rfloor = \left\lfloor \dfrac{n}{mk} \right\rfloor$ *and* $\left\lceil \dfrac{\lceil \frac{n}{m} \rceil}{k} \right\rceil = \left\lceil \dfrac{n}{mk} \right\rceil.$

Proof (a) Take any particular integer n. We'll prove that $\lfloor x + n \rfloor = \lfloor x \rfloor + n$. Since $\lfloor x \rfloor + n$ is an integer, by Theorem 2.1.4 (c) it suffices to prove that $(\lfloor x \rfloor + n) \leq x + n < (\lfloor x \rfloor + n) + 1$. These two inequalities are logically equivalent to $(\lfloor x \rfloor + n) - n \leq x + n - n < (\lfloor x \rfloor + n) + 1 - n$, which are in turn equivalent to $\lfloor x \rfloor \leq x < x + 1$, which are true for all x (see Theorem 2.1.4 (a)). This completes the proof for floors.

The proof for ceilings is similar. The equation $\lfloor x - n \rfloor = \lfloor x \rfloor - n$ is proved by noting that $\lfloor x - n \rfloor = \lfloor x + (-n) \rfloor = \lfloor x \rfloor + (-n) = \lfloor x \rfloor - n$ because $-n$ is an integer.

The assertions involving $\lfloor nx \rfloor$ and $\lceil nx \rceil$ are demonstrated by using examples: $\lfloor 4 \cdot 0.5 \rfloor \neq 4 \lfloor 0.5 \rfloor$ and $\lceil 4 \cdot 0.5 \rceil \neq 4 \lceil 0.5 \rceil$.

(b) Take any integer n and real number x. If n is even, then $n = 2m$ for some integer m, and thus $\left\lfloor \dfrac{n}{2} \right\rfloor + \left\lceil \dfrac{n}{2} \right\rceil$

$= \left\lfloor \dfrac{2m}{2} \right\rfloor + \left\lceil \dfrac{2m}{2} \right\rceil = \lfloor m \rfloor + \lceil m \rceil = m + m = 2m = n.$

If n is odd, then $n = 2m + 1$ for some integer m, and thus $\left\lfloor \dfrac{n}{2} \right\rfloor + \left\lceil \dfrac{n}{2} \right\rceil =$

$\left\lfloor \dfrac{2m+1}{2} \right\rfloor + \left\lceil \dfrac{2m+1}{2} \right\rceil = \left\lfloor m + \dfrac{1}{2} \right\rfloor + \left\lceil m + \dfrac{1}{2} \right\rceil.$ By part (a) of this theorem,

this last expression equals $m + \left\lfloor \dfrac{1}{2} \right\rfloor + m + \left\lceil \dfrac{1}{2} \right\rceil = m + 0 + m + 1 = 2m + 1 = n.$

(c) Take any integer n. If n is even, then $n = 2m$ for some integer m, so $\left\lfloor \dfrac{n+1}{2} \right\rfloor = \left\lfloor \dfrac{2m+1}{2} \right\rfloor = \left\lfloor m + \dfrac{1}{2} \right\rfloor = m + \left\lfloor \dfrac{1}{2} \right\rfloor = m + 0 = m$ and $\left\lceil \dfrac{n}{2} \right\rceil = \left\lceil \dfrac{2m}{2} \right\rceil = \lceil m \rceil = m$ also, so $\left\lfloor \dfrac{n+1}{2} \right\rfloor = \left\lceil \dfrac{n}{2} \right\rceil.$

If n is odd, then $n = 2m + 1$ for some integer m, and thus $\left\lfloor \dfrac{n+1}{2} \right\rfloor =$

$\left\lfloor \dfrac{2m+2}{2} \right\rfloor = \lfloor m+1 \rfloor = m + 1$, and $\left\lceil \dfrac{n}{2} \right\rceil = \left\lceil \dfrac{2m+1}{2} \right\rceil = \left\lceil m + \dfrac{1}{2} \right\rceil =$

$m + \left\lceil \dfrac{1}{2} \right\rceil = m+1$ also, and thus $\left\lfloor \dfrac{n+1}{2} \right\rfloor = \left\lceil \dfrac{n}{2} \right\rceil$. The fact that $\left\lfloor \dfrac{n-1}{2} \right\rfloor + 1 =$

$\left\lfloor \dfrac{n+1}{2} \right\rfloor$ follows from part (a) and simple algebra.

(d) Take any real number y and any integer $k > 0$. By definition of the floor, $\left\lfloor \dfrac{y}{k} \right\rfloor$

is an integer. To prove that $\left\lfloor \dfrac{\lfloor y \rfloor}{k} \right\rfloor = \left\lfloor \dfrac{y}{k} \right\rfloor$ it suffices by Theorem 2.1.4 (c) to

prove that the integer $\left\lfloor \dfrac{y}{k} \right\rfloor$ satisfies the inequalities $\left\lfloor \dfrac{y}{k} \right\rfloor \leq \dfrac{\lfloor y \rfloor}{k} < \left\lfloor \dfrac{y}{k} \right\rfloor + 1$

(take x to be $\dfrac{\lfloor y \rfloor}{k}$ and n to be $\left\lfloor \dfrac{y}{k} \right\rfloor$).

First, let's prove $\left\lfloor \dfrac{y}{k} \right\rfloor \leq \dfrac{\lfloor y \rfloor}{k}$. By Theorem 2.1.4 (a), $\left\lfloor \dfrac{y}{k} \right\rfloor \leq \dfrac{y}{k}$, so $\left\lfloor \dfrac{y}{k} \right\rfloor k \leq y$.

Since $\left\lfloor \dfrac{y}{k} \right\rfloor k$ is the product of two integers, it is an integer, and it is less or equal

to y, so $\left\lfloor \dfrac{y}{k} \right\rfloor k \leq \lfloor y \rfloor$ by Theorem 2.1.4 (e). That proves $\left\lfloor \dfrac{y}{k} \right\rfloor \leq \dfrac{\lfloor y \rfloor}{k}$.

To prove that $\dfrac{\lfloor y \rfloor}{k} < \left\lfloor \dfrac{y}{k} \right\rfloor + 1$, we note that $\left\lfloor \dfrac{y}{k} \right\rfloor + 1 > \dfrac{y}{k}$ by Theorem 2.1.4 (a),

and $\dfrac{y}{k} \geq \dfrac{\lfloor y \rfloor}{k}$ because $y \geq \lfloor y \rfloor$ by Theorem 2.1.4 (a). Thus $\left\lfloor \dfrac{y}{k} \right\rfloor + 1 > \dfrac{\lfloor y \rfloor}{k}$,

which is what we wanted to prove (in turned-around form). The proof of the
assertion about ceilings is quite similar and will be omitted here. ∎

As an example of where some of the formulas in Theorems 2.1.4 and 2.1.5 are useful,
consider what happens during a binary search of a subarray a[first..last].
Here is a fragment of the code for the search (for the complete function see Fig. 5.3,
p. 176):

```
while (first <= last && !found) // The value parameters first and last will
{     // be modified during execution of this code
   int mid = (first + last)/2;
   if (target < a[mid])
      ......
```

A similar calculation of mid = (first + last)/2 occurs during the Merge
Sort algorithm, which splits an array into two pieces, sorts them recursively, and then
merges them back together.

When analyzing such algorithms, it is useful to have mathematical expressions
for the lengths of the following three smaller subarrays

```
a[first..mid-1]     a[first..mid]     a[mid+1..last]
```

in terms of the length of the larger subarray a[last].

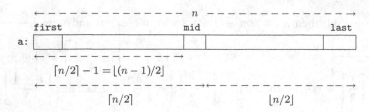

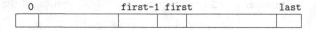

Fig. 2.1 Theorem 2.1.6

Fig. 2.2 Theorem 2.1.6 a

Theorem 2.1.6 *Consider a subarray* a[first..last] *of some array* a, *where* $0 \le$ first $\le$ last. *Let n denote the length of the subarray, and let* mid *denote the quantity* (first + last) / 2 *(this is the average of the subscripts at the ends of the subarray). Then*

(a) *n is the value of the expression* last - first + 1
(b) *the length of the subarray* a[first..mid] *is* $\left\lceil \dfrac{n}{2} \right\rceil$;
(c) *the length of the subarray* a[first..mid-1] *is* $\left\lceil \dfrac{n}{2} \right\rceil - 1 = \left\lfloor \dfrac{n-1}{2} \right\rfloor$;
(d) *the length of the subarray* a[mid+1..last] *is* $\left\lfloor \dfrac{n}{2} \right\rfloor$.

See Fig. 2.1 for a graphical representation.

Proof Part (a) is proved by considering the full array that starts at location 0 and ends at location last. There are last + 1 cells in that subarray. If we then remove the cells in the subarray a[0..first-1] we produce the sub-array a[first..last]. We are removing (first-1)+1 = first cells from last + 1 cells, leaving (last+1)-first = last-first+1 cells. See Fig. 2.2.

For the proof of statement (b), we begin by noting that the subarray a[first.. mid] contains mid-first+1 cells, and mid = $\lfloor$(first+last)/2$\rfloor$. Then we can write

$$\text{mid} - \text{first} + 1 = \left\lfloor \frac{\text{first} + \text{last}}{2} \right\rfloor - \text{first} + 1$$

$$= \left\lfloor \frac{\text{first} + \text{last}}{2} - \text{first} + 1 \right\rfloor \quad \text{(by Theorem 2.1.5 (a))}$$

$$= \left\lfloor \frac{\text{first} + \text{last} - 2\,\text{first} + 2}{2} \right\rfloor = \left\lfloor \frac{\text{last} - \text{first} + 2}{2} \right\rfloor$$

$$= \left\lfloor \frac{(\text{last} - \text{first} + 1) + 1}{2} \right\rfloor$$

$$= \left\lfloor \frac{n+1}{2} \right\rfloor = \left\lceil \frac{n}{2} \right\rceil.$$

To prove part (c), note that the subarray a[first..mid-1] has one less cell than a[first..mid]. By part (b), the length of a[first..mid] is $\lceil n/2 \rceil$, so the length of a[first..mid-1] is

$$\left\lceil \frac{n}{2} \right\rceil - 1 = \left\lfloor \frac{n+1}{2} \right\rfloor - 1 = \left\lfloor \frac{n-1}{2} \right\rfloor$$

by Theorem 2.1.5 (c).

To prove part (d), subtract the number of cells in a[first..mid] from n to obtain the number of cells in a[mid+1..last]. We get $n - \left\lceil \frac{n}{2} \right\rceil = \left\lfloor \frac{n}{2} \right\rfloor$ by Theorem 2.1.5 (b). ∎

2.1.1 Further Examples

Example 2.1.7 (a) $\left\lfloor \dfrac{26}{7} \right\rfloor = ?$ (b) $\left\lceil \dfrac{26}{7} \right\rceil = ?$ (c) $\left\lfloor \dfrac{7}{26} \right\rfloor = ?$ (d) $\left\lceil \dfrac{7}{26} \right\rceil = ?$

Solution (a) $\left\lfloor \dfrac{26}{7} \right\rfloor = \lfloor 3 + 5/7 \rfloor = 3$ (b) 4   (c) 0   (d) 1

Example 2.1.8 Use part (a) of Theorem 2.1.4 to prove that $0 \le x - \lfloor x \rfloor < 1$ for all real numbers x.

Solution By Theorem 2.1.4 (a) we know that $\lfloor x \rfloor \le x < \lfloor x \rfloor + 1$ for all real x. We can pull this expression apart into the following pair of inequalities: $\lfloor x \rfloor \le x$ and $x < \lfloor x \rfloor + 1$ for all real x. From the first of these it follows that $0 \le x - \lfloor x \rfloor$ (subtract $\lfloor x \rfloor$ from both sides of the inequality); from the second it follows similarly that $x - \lfloor x \rfloor < 1$. Thus we have $0 \le x - \lfloor x \rfloor$ and $x - \lfloor x \rfloor < 1$ for all x. Putting these back together gives the desired expression: $0 \le x - \lfloor x \rfloor < 1$.

Example 2.1.9 Verify part (a) of Theorem 2.1.5 in the case where $x = 12.46$ and $n = -5$.

Solution $\lfloor x + n \rfloor = \lfloor 12.46 + (-5) \rfloor = \lfloor 7.46 \rfloor = 7$, and $\lfloor x \rfloor + n = \lfloor 12.46 \rfloor + (-5) = 12 - 5 = 7$. Thus we have verified in this one particular case that $\lfloor x + n \rfloor = \lfloor x \rfloor + n$. Similarly, $\lceil x + n \rceil = \lceil 12.46 + (-5) \rceil = \lceil 7.46 \rceil = 8$ and $\lceil 12.46 \rceil + (-5) = 13 - 5 = 8$.

Example 2.1.10 Verify part (c) of Theorem 2.1.5 for some odd integer n and also for some even integer n.

Solution For $n = 13$, is it true that $\left\lfloor \dfrac{13+1}{2} \right\rfloor = \left\lceil \dfrac{13}{2} \right\rceil$, i.e., that $\lfloor 7 \rfloor = \lceil 6.5 \rceil$? Yes: both are equal to 7. For $n = 14$, is it true that $\left\lfloor \dfrac{14+1}{2} \right\rfloor = \left\lceil \dfrac{14}{2} \right\rceil$, i.e., that $\lfloor 7.5 \rfloor = \lceil 7 \rceil$? Yes: both are equal to 7.

Example 2.1.11 For each of the assertions below, cite one or more parts of Theorems 2.1.4 and 2.1.5 to help you justify the assertion.

(a) For all integers p and q, $\left\lfloor \dfrac{p+q}{2} \right\rfloor + \left\lceil \dfrac{p+q}{2} \right\rceil = p+q$.

(b) For all integers m, $\lfloor 2m + \sqrt{m} \rfloor = 2m + \lfloor \sqrt{m} \rfloor$.

(c) For all integers n, p, and q, if $p = \left\lfloor \dfrac{n}{2} \right\rfloor$ and $q = \left\lfloor \dfrac{p}{2} \right\rfloor$, then $q = \left\lfloor \dfrac{n}{4} \right\rfloor$. More generally, if $p_1 = \left\lfloor \dfrac{n}{2} \right\rfloor$, $p_2 = \left\lfloor \dfrac{p_1}{2} \right\rfloor$, $p_3 = \left\lfloor \dfrac{p_2}{2} \right\rfloor$, ..., $p_n = \left\lfloor \dfrac{p_{n-1}}{2} \right\rfloor$, then $p_n = \left\lfloor \dfrac{n}{2^n} \right\rfloor$.

(d) For all integers n, $\left\lfloor \dfrac{n}{2} \right\rfloor = \left\lceil \dfrac{n+1}{2} \right\rceil - 1$.

Solution (a) Use part (b), with $n = p + q$.

(b) Use part (a), with $x = \sqrt{m}$ and $n = 2m$.

(c) Use part (d) with $m = 2$ and $k = 2$. That is, $q = \left\lfloor \dfrac{p}{2} \right\rfloor = \left\lfloor \dfrac{\left\lfloor \frac{n}{2} \right\rfloor}{2} \right\rfloor = \left\lfloor \dfrac{n}{2 \cdot 2} \right\rfloor = \left\lfloor \dfrac{n}{4} \right\rfloor$. The second sentence in (c) is proved by induction.

(d) Use part (c), with $m = 2$.

Example 2.1.12 In the C++ loop given below, assume that the variable n has some positive integer value. When the loop is executed, how many times will the body of the loop be executed? (In this loop, the body of the loop consists of just the cout statement.) Express your answer as a mathematical formula in terms of the variable n.

```
int k; for (k = 1; (3*k)+1 <= n; ++k)
   cout << k << endl;
```

Solution First note that the initial value computed for (3*k)+1 is 4, so if the value of n is 3 or less, the body of the loop will be executed 0 times. So now let's look at the cases where the value of n is at least 4. In these cases the body of the loop will be executed at least once.

Since the variable k starts with the value 1 and is incremented by 1 each time the body of the loop is executed, k is a loop counter. That is, when its value is 1 in the cout statement, the body of the loop is being executed for the first time. When its value is 2 in the cout statement, the body of the loop is being executed for the second time. Etc. Let L denote the value of k in the cout statement the last time the body of the loop is executed. Then that number L is the total number of times the body of the loop is executed. That is, L is the number we want to compute.

Let n denote the value of the program variable n. Then $3L + 1 \leq$ n because when k has the value L, the loop control condition (3*k) +1 <= n must be true. (If that were not so, the body of the loop would not be executed when k gets the value L.) Also note that when k is then incremented to $L + 1$ (in the expression k++), the loop control condition must then be false in order to make the loop halt. Thus $3(L + 1) + 1 >$ n. We now have the following two inequalities involving L and n :

$$3L + 1 \leq n < 3(L + 1) + 1.$$

Subtracting 1 from each the part of this expression, and then dividing each part by 3 gives the inequalities

$$L \leq \frac{n - 1}{3} < L + 1$$

It follows that the integer L must be the floor of the fraction (n-1) /3 (see Theorem 2.1.4 (c)). That is, $L = \left\lfloor \dfrac{n - 1}{3} \right\rfloor$. This is the number of times the body of the loop is executed when $n \geq 4$. In fact, this formula gives the correct number of times even in the case where n is 1, 2, or 3.

Example 2.1.13 Prove that for all real numbers x and y we have $\lceil x \rceil + \lceil y \rceil \leq \lceil x + y \rceil + 1$.

Solution Take any real numbers x and y. By Theorem 2.1.4 (b), $\lceil x \rceil < x + 1$ and $\lceil y \rceil < y + 1$. It follows that $\lceil x \rceil + \lceil y \rceil < x + y + 2$. By Theorem 2.1.4 (b), $x + y \leq \lceil x + y \rceil$, so $x + y + 2 \leq \lceil x + y \rceil + 2$. Putting together the inequalities in the two preceding sentences we get $\lceil x \rceil + \lceil y \rceil < \lceil x + y \rceil + 2$. Note that the left and right sides of this inequality are integers. If $i < j$ for integers i and j, then we know that $i \leq j - 1$, so $\lceil x \rceil + \lceil y \rceil \leq \lceil x + y \rceil + 1$.

2.1.2 Exercises

2.1.14 Let a be the name of an array of length n > 0 in a C or C++ program. Explain why the expression a [n/2] will be accepted by the compiler (even though n may be an odd integer) but a [floor (n/2.0)] will not compile.

2.1.15 Use part (b) of Theorem 2.1.4 to prove that $0 \leq \lceil x \rceil - x < 1$ for all real numbers x.

2.1.16 Is it always true that $\lceil x \rceil = 1 + \lfloor x \rfloor$? If so, prove this fact. If not, give a counterexample, i.e., an example of a real number for which the equation is not true.

2.1.17 Theorem 2.1.4 (d) says that if $x \leq y$ then $\lfloor x \rfloor \leq \lfloor y \rfloor$ for all real numbers x and y. Can we conclude that if $x < y$ then $\lfloor x \rfloor < \lfloor y \rfloor$?

2.1.18 (a) Give an example of an integer n and a real number x for which $\lfloor nx \rfloor \neq n \lfloor x \rfloor$. (See part (a) of Theorem 2.1.5.)
(b) Give an example of two real numbers x and y for which $\lfloor x + y \rfloor \neq \lfloor x \rfloor + \lfloor y \rfloor$. (See part (a) of Theorem 2.1.5.)

2.1.19 Verify part (b) of Theorem 2.1.5 for the odd integer $n = 11$ and also for the even integer $n = 12$.

2.1.20 (a) Verify part (d) of Theorem 2.1.5 in the case where $n = 37$, $m = 8$, and $k = 3$.
(b) Verify part (d) of Theorem 2.1.5 in the case where $n = 26$, $m = 7$, and $k = 2$.

2.1.21 Is it true that $\lfloor x \rfloor - n = \lfloor x - n \rfloor$ for all integers n and real numbers x? Answer the same question for the equation $n - \lfloor x \rfloor = \lfloor n - x \rfloor$.

2.1.22 For each of the assertions below, cite one or more parts of Theorems 2.1.4 and 2.1.5 to help you justify the assertion.

(a) For all integers n, $\left\lfloor \dfrac{n}{2} \right\rfloor + \left\lfloor \dfrac{n+1}{2} \right\rfloor = n$.
(b) For all non-negative real numbers x, $\lfloor \sqrt{x} - 1 \rfloor = \lfloor \sqrt{x} \rfloor - 1$.
(c) For all integers n, $\left\lceil \dfrac{n+1}{2} \right\rceil + \left\lceil \dfrac{n}{2} \right\rceil = n + 1$.
(d) For all real numbers x and non-negative integers p, $\lfloor x^2 + 2^p \rfloor = \lfloor x^2 \rfloor + 2^p$.
(e) For all real numbers x, $\lfloor x + \lfloor x \rfloor \rfloor = 2 \lfloor x \rfloor$.

2.1.23 In the C++ loop given below, assume that the integer variable n has some positive value. How many times is the *body* of the loop executed? Express your answer as a mathematical expression in terms of the value of n. Justify your answer by an argument similar to the one in Example 2.1.12 on p. 17. Also check your answer carefully by determining what integers are sent to output when n = 50.

```
int k;
for (k = 1; k*k <= n; ++k)
    cout << k << endl;
```

2.1.24 In the C++ loop given below, assume that the integer variable n has some positive value. How many times is the *body* of the loop executed? Express your answer as a mathematical expression in terms of the value of n. Justify your answer by an argument similar to the one in Example 2.1.12 on p. 17. Also check your answer carefully by determining what integers are sent to output when n = 10 and also when n = 11.

```
int k;
for (k = 1; 2*k < n; ++k)
    cout << k << endl;
```

2.1.25 (a) Prove that for all real numbers x and y we have $\lfloor x \rfloor + \lfloor y \rfloor \leq \lfloor x + y \rfloor \leq \lfloor x \rfloor + \lfloor y \rfloor + 1$.

(b) Prove that for all real numbers x and y we have $\lceil x \rceil + \lceil y \rceil - 1 \leq \lceil x + y \rceil \leq \lceil x \rceil + \lceil y \rceil$.

(c) Prove that for all non-negative real numbers x and y, $\lfloor x \rfloor \lfloor y \rfloor \leq \lfloor xy \rfloor \leq \lfloor x \rfloor \lfloor y \rfloor + (\lfloor x \rfloor + \lfloor y \rfloor)$.

2.1.26 Let n and m be two positive integer numbers. Prove that $\dfrac{n - m + 1}{m} \leq \left\lfloor \dfrac{n}{m} \right\rfloor \leq \dfrac{n}{m}$ and $\dfrac{n}{m} \leq \left\lceil \dfrac{n}{m} \right\rceil \leq \dfrac{n + m - 1}{m}$.

2.1.27 Let n be an integer number. If n is odd, then $\left\lfloor \dfrac{n}{2} \right\rfloor = \dfrac{n - 1}{2}$ and $\left\lceil \dfrac{n}{2} \right\rceil = \dfrac{n + 1}{2}$.

2.2 Logarithms

Definition 2.2.1 For a fixed real number $b > 1$, the *logarithm base b function* is defined on positive real numbers x as follows: $\log_b(x) =$ "the power on b that produces x". In other words, $\log_b(x) = y$ if and only if $b^y = x$.

Examples:
$\log_3(9) = 2$ because $3^2 = 9$.
$\log_5(125) = 3$ because $5^3 = 125$.
$\log_4(4) = 1$ because $4^1 = 4$.
$\log_6(1) = 0$ because $6^0 = 1$.
    Two important equations follow instantly from this definition.

Theorem 2.2.2 *For any fixed real number $b > 1$,*

(a) $b^{\log_b(x)} = x$ *for all real* $x > 0$;
(b) $\log_b(b^y) = y$ *for all real* y.

Logarithms were invented nearly 400 years ago because they have several important properties that could be used to simplify certain difficult arithmetic calculations: they convert products to sums, they convert quotients to differences, and they convert powers to products. Here is a precise statement of these properties.

Theorem 2.2.3 *For any fixed real number $b > 1$,*

(a) $\log_b(s \cdot t) = \log_b(s) + \log_b(t)$ *for all positive real numbers s and t;*
(b) $\log_b(s/t) = \log_b(s) - \log_b(t)$ *for all positive real numbers s and t;*
(c) $\log_b(t^p) = p \, \log_b(t)$ *for all real numbers p and all positive real numbers t.*

Proof The proofs are given in algebra or pre-calculus textbooks and will not be repeated here.   ∎

Example 2.2.4 Most of us met logarithms base 10 in our high school algebra class.
$\log_{10}(1000) = 3$; $\log_{10}(100) = 2$; $\log_{10}(10) = 1$; $\log_{10}(1) = 0$ because $10^0 = 1$;
$\log_{10}(0.01) = -2$ because $0.01 = 10^{-2}$;
$\log_{10}(-100)$ is undefined because $10^x > 0$ for all real x;
$1 < \log_{10}(25) < 2$ because $10^1 < 25 < 10^2$; by calculator, $\log_{10}(25) \approx 1.4$;
$\log_{10}(1/t) = -\log_{10}(t)$.

Example 2.2.5 Here is the logarithm you met in calculus; it's called the *natural logarithm*:

$$\log_e(x) = \ln(x) = \int_1^x \frac{1}{t} \, dt \quad \text{for all real } x > 0, \quad \text{where } e \approx 2.71828.$$

Of course, $e^{\ln(x)} = x$ if $x > 0$, and $\ln(e^y) = y$ for all real numbers y.

In computer science, the logarithm that we encounter more often than any other is the *logarithm base 2 function*, denoted by "$\lg(x)$" or $\log_2(x)$. Here are some easily computed values of this function:

$\lg(32) = 5$; $\lg(8) = 3$; $\lg(1024) = 10$; $\lg(1) = 0$; $\lg(2) = 1$; $\lg(1/16) = -4$.

What is the numerical value of $\lg(100)$? We can see that it must be between 6 and 7 because $2^6 < 100 < 2^7$. If we want a more exact answer we will need to consult a table of logarithms or use an electronic calculator. Most pocket calculators, however, don't have a "lg" button. This is not a problem because, as we will now prove, *all logarithm functions are just constant multiples of each other.*

Theorem 2.2.6 *For all real numbers a and b greater than 1 and all positive real numbers x,*

$$\log_b(x) = \frac{\log_a(x)}{\log_a(b)}.$$

Proof Take the logarithm, base a, of both sides of the identity $b^{\log_b(x)} = x$.   ∎

Example 2.2.7 $\ln(x) = \dfrac{\log_{10}(x)}{\log_{10}(e)} \approx 2.303 \log_{10}(x)$ by using a calculator.

Similarly, $\lg(x) = \dfrac{\ln(x)}{\ln(2)} \approx \dfrac{\ln(x)}{0.693} \approx 1.44 \ln(x)$; also, $\lg(x) = \dfrac{\log_{10}(x)}{\log_{10}(2)} \approx 3.32 \log_{10}(x)$.

In analysis of algorithms, we seldom have occasion to compute $\lg(x)$ when x is a non-integer real number. Mostly we will encounter $\lg(n)$ where n is a positive integer. Moreover, the "lg" usually appears in connection with the floor or ceiling function. The following theorem gives a number of useful identities involving the lg function combined with floors and ceilings.

Theorem 2.2.8 *Let n be a positive integer.*

(a) $2^{\lfloor \lg(n) \rfloor} \le n < 2^{\lfloor \lg(n) \rfloor + 1}$; *equivalently,* $\dfrac{n}{2} < 2^{\lfloor \lg(n) \rfloor} \le n$.

(b) $\left\lfloor \dfrac{n}{2^{\lfloor \lg(n) \rfloor}} \right\rfloor = 1$ *and* $\left\lfloor \dfrac{n}{2^{\lfloor \lg(n) \rfloor + 1}} \right\rfloor = 0$. *Moreover, the only integer k for which*
$\left\lfloor \dfrac{n}{2^k} \right\rfloor = 1$ *is $k = \lfloor \lg(n) \rfloor$.*
We can interpret this as saying that $\lfloor \lg(n) \rfloor$ is the number of "integer divisions by 2" that are required to reduce n down to 1.

(c) $\lceil \lg(n+1) \rceil = 1 + \lfloor \lg(n) \rfloor$ *for all $n \ge 1$.*

(d) $\lfloor \lg(\lfloor n/2 \rfloor) \rfloor = -1 + \lfloor \lg(n) \rfloor$ *for all $n \ge 2$.*

(e) $\lceil \lg(\lceil n/2 \rceil) \rceil = -1 + \lceil \lg(n) \rceil$ *for all $n \ge 2$.*

(f) $\lfloor \lg(\lceil n/2 \rceil) \rfloor = -1 + \lfloor \lg(n+1) \rfloor$ *for all $n \ge 1$.*

(g) $\lceil \lg(\lfloor n/2 \rfloor) \rceil = -1 + \lceil \lg(n-1) \rceil$ *for all $n \ge 3$.*

Proof To prove part (a), we can start from the fact that

$$\lfloor \lg(n) \rfloor \le \lg(n) < \lfloor \lg(n) \rfloor + 1,$$

which is an instance of Theorem 2.1.4 (a), with $x = \lg(n)$. From this it follows that

$$2^{\lfloor \lg(n) \rfloor} \le 2^{\lg(n)} < 2^{\lfloor \lg(n) \rfloor + 1}.$$

Since $2^{\lg(n)} = n$, this proves that $2^{\lfloor \lg(n) \rfloor} \le n < 2^{\lfloor \lg(n) \rfloor + 1}$.

To prove the first of the two equations in part (b), divide the first double inequality in part (a) through by $2^{\lfloor \lg(n) \rfloor}$ to obtain

$$1 \le \dfrac{n}{2^{\lfloor \lg(n) \rfloor}} < 2.$$

By Theorem 2.1.4 (c), this immediately implies that the integer 1 is the floor of $\dfrac{n}{2^{\lfloor \lg(n) \rfloor}}$; that is $\left\lfloor \dfrac{n}{2^{\lfloor \lg(n) \rfloor}} \right\rfloor = 1$.

To prove the second part we start from the double inequality above and divide it through by 2 to obtain $\dfrac{1}{2} \le \dfrac{n}{2^{\lfloor \lg(n) \rfloor + 1}} < 1$. Since $0 < \dfrac{1}{2}$, we can deduce that $0 < \dfrac{n}{2^{\lfloor \lg(n) \rfloor + 1}} < 1$, which implies that $\left\lfloor \dfrac{n}{2^{\lfloor \lg(n) \rfloor + 1}} \right\rfloor = 0$.

To prove the last assertion in part (b), let's start with n and divide it repeatedly by 2, discarding remainders. We'll give names to the integers we produce along the way:

$n_0 = n = \left\lfloor \dfrac{n}{2^0} \right\rfloor$ (here we are using the fact that $\lfloor n \rfloor = n$ and $2^0 = 1$)

$n_1 = \left\lfloor \dfrac{n_0}{2} \right\rfloor = \left\lfloor \dfrac{n}{2^1} \right\rfloor$

$n_2 = \left\lfloor \dfrac{n_1}{2} \right\rfloor = \left\lfloor \dfrac{n}{2^2} \right\rfloor$ (here we are using Theorem 2.1.5 (d); note we've divided by 2 twice)

$n_3 = \left\lfloor \dfrac{n_2}{2} \right\rfloor = \left\lfloor \dfrac{n}{2^3} \right\rfloor$ (again we're using Theorem 2.1.5 (d); note we've divided by 2 three times) etc. For any positive integer k, after k divisions by 2 we obtain

$n_k = \left\lfloor \dfrac{n_{k-1}}{2} \right\rfloor = \left\lfloor \dfrac{n}{2^k} \right\rfloor$.

In particular, when $k = \lfloor \lg(n) \rfloor$, we see by the first equation in part (b) that we will arrive at the value 1. That is, by dividing n by 2 (discarding remainders) $\lfloor \lg(n) \rfloor$ times, we reduce n to 1.

To prove the equation in part (c), it suffices by Theorem 2.1.4 (c) to prove that the integer $1 + \lfloor \lg(n) \rfloor$ satisfies the inequalities

$$(1 + \lfloor \lg(n) \rfloor) - 1 < \lg(n + 1) \le 1 + \lfloor \lg(n) \rfloor,$$

which are equivalent to

$$\lfloor \lg(n) \rfloor < \lg(n + 1) \quad \text{and} \quad \lg(n + 1) \le 1 + \lfloor \lg(n) \rfloor.$$

The first one is easy because $\lfloor \lg(n) \rfloor \le \lg(n) < \lg(n + 1)$. For the second, start with the inequality $n < 2^{\lfloor \lg(n) \rfloor + 1}$ that we proved in part (a). Both sides of the inequality are integers, so it must be true that $n + 1 \le 2^{\lfloor \lg(n) \rfloor + 1}$. Taking logarithms on both sides gives the desired inequality above.

To prove part (d) we begin with the first inequalities in part (a) and divide by 2 to obtain

$$2^{\lfloor \lg(n) \rfloor - 1} \le n/2 < 2^{\lfloor \lg(n) \rfloor} \quad \text{for all positive integers } n.$$

If $n \ge 2$, then $2^{\lfloor \lg(n) \rfloor - 1}$ and $2^{\lfloor \lg(n) \rfloor}$ are both integers, and thus

$$2^{\lfloor \lg(n) \rfloor - 1} \le \lfloor n/2 \rfloor < 2^{\lfloor \lg(n) \rfloor} \quad \text{for all integers } n \ge 2.$$

Taking the logarithm of every term gives

$$\lfloor \lg(n) \rfloor - 1 \le \lg(\lfloor n/2 \rfloor) < \lfloor \lg(n) \rfloor,$$

which is exactly what is needed to show that $\lfloor \lg(n) \rfloor - 1 = \lfloor \lg(\lfloor n/2 \rfloor) \rfloor$ (see Theorem 2.1.4 (c)).

To prove part (e), note that

$$\lceil \lg(\lceil n/2 \rceil) \rceil = \left\lceil \lg\left(\left\lfloor \dfrac{n-1}{2} \right\rfloor + 1\right) \right\rceil \quad \text{(by Theorem 2.1.5 (c))}$$

$$= 1 + \left\lfloor \lg\left(\left\lfloor \dfrac{n-1}{2} \right\rfloor\right) \right\rfloor \quad \text{(by part (c) above)}$$

$$= 1 + (-1 + \lfloor \lg(n - 1) \rfloor) \quad \text{(by part (d) above)}$$

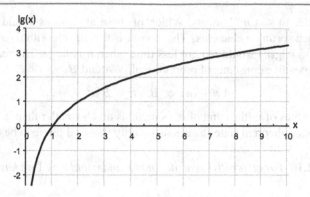

Fig. 2.3 Plot for the function $y = \lg(x)$

$$= \lfloor \lg(n-1) \rfloor = -1 + \lceil \lg((n-1)+1) \rceil \quad \text{(by part (c) above, with } n \text{ replaced by } n-1)$$
$$= -1 + \lceil \lg(n) \rceil.$$

The proofs of parts (f) and (g) are similar, and left as an exercise. ∎

Example 2.2.9 To illustrate part (b) of Theorem 2.2.8, take $n = 100$. Then

$$\lfloor 100/2 \rfloor = 50; \quad \lfloor 50/2 \rfloor = 25; \quad \lfloor 25/2 \rfloor = 12; \quad \lfloor 12/2 \rfloor = 6; \quad \lfloor 6/2 \rfloor = 3; \quad \lfloor 3/2 \rfloor = 1.$$

There are 6 integer divisions by 2 in that sequence, and indeed, $\lfloor \lg(100) \rfloor = 6$ because $2^6 < 100 < 2^7$, so $6 < \lg(100) < 7$.

Since we encounter many "divide and conquer" algorithms that involve continually splitting a list of length n into two roughly equal pieces, Theorem 2.2.8 (b) gives us some insight into why these algorithms often have running times that involve $\lg(n)$ in one way or another.

The most important thing to understand about $\lg(n)$ is how very slowly it grows as n increases. Even when n gets extremely large, $\lg(n)$ tends to remain relatively small. The reason is this: doubling the argument in $\lg(n)$ just adds 1 to the value of the logarithm $\lg(2n) = 1 + \lg(n)$. This is illustrated in the graph of $y = \lg(x)$ shown in Fig. 2.3.

You might wonder whether there is some horizontal asymptote for this graph, i.e., a horizontal line that the graph approaches as $n \to \infty$. In fact, there is *no such asymptote*. If we draw a horizontal line at height h, the graph of $y = \lg(x)$ will intersect that line when x reaches the value 2^h, and will continue to rise slowly above the line thereafter. In mathematical notation,

$$\lim_{x \to \infty} \lg(x) = +\infty \tag{2.1}$$

Later in this book we will analyze methods for sorting data into key order. Some sorting algorithms require an amount of time proportional to n^2 in order to sort n elements, while certain other algorithms require an amount of time proportional to

$n \lg(n)$ in order to sort n elements. Which of these algorithms would require the least time when sorting n elements? The answer is that the algorithm requiring time proportional to $n \lg(n)$ would require less time when n is large. The reason is this: for any fixed positive constants of proportionality A and B,

$$A\, n\, \lg(n) \ll B\, n\, n = B\, n^2$$

for all large values of n (the symbol $\ll$ is read "is much smaller than").

The following theorem states a curious identity that will prove to be useful.

Theorem 2.2.10 *For all positive real numbers x and y and $b > 1$ we have $x^{\log_b(y)} = y^{\log_b(x)}$.*

Proof Since the logarithm function is inductive (one-to-one) on its domain (the set of all positive real numbers), we can prove that two positive numbers are equal by proving that their logarithms (in any base) are equal. Thus the formula in the theorem is true if and only if $\log_b(x^{\log_b(y)}) = \log_b(y^{\log_b(x)})$ which is equivalent to $\log_b(y) \cdot \log_b(x) = \log_b(x) \cdot \log_b(y)$. The latter is surely true for any positive x and y.   ∎

2.2.1 Further Examples

Example 2.2.11 For all positive integers n, $3^{\lg(n)} = n^{\lg(3)} \approx n^{1.58} \approx n\sqrt{n}$.

Example 2.2.12 Do the following multiple choice exercises *without using a calculator.*

(a) $\ln(e^{7x}) =$ Choose one: (i) $7\ln(x)$ (ii) $7x$ (iii) $7e^x$ (iv) $\ln(7) + \ln(x)$

(b) $\ln(x^7) =$ Choose one: (i) $7\ln(x)$ (ii)$7x$ (iii)$7e^x$ (iv) $\ln(7) + \ln(x)$

(c) $\ln(7x) =$ Choose one: (i) $7\ln(x)$ (ii) $7x$ (iii) $7e^x$ (iv) $\ln(7) + \ln(x)$

(d) $e^{\ln(7x)} =$ Choose one: (i) $7\ln(x)$ (ii) $7x$ (iii) $7e^x$ (iv) $7 + x$

(e) $e^{x+\ln(7)} =$ Choose one: (i) $7\ln(x)$ (ii) $7x$ (iii) $7e^x$ (iv) $7 + x$

(f) $\lg(2^{-n}) =$ Choose one: (i) $-n$ (ii) $1/n$ (iii) $1 - n$ (iv) $(1/2)\lg(n)$

(g) $\lg(8n) =$ Choose one: (i) $3n$ (ii) $8n$ (iii) $3 + n$ (iv) $3 + \lg(n)$

(h) $\lg(8 + n) =$ Choose one: (i) $3n$ (ii) $8n$ (iii) $3 + n$ (iv) $3 + \lg(n)$

(i) $\lg(n/32) =$ Choose one: (i) $n/5$ (ii) n^5 (iii) $5 - n$ (iv) $\lg(n) - 5$

(j) $2^{\lg(18)} =$ Choose one: (i) 2^9 (ii) 18 (iii) 11 (iv) 36

(k) $2^{3\lg(3)} =$ Choose one: (i) 27 (ii) 64 (iii) 18 (iv) 81

(l) $2^{-\lg(n^2)} =$ Choose one: (i) n^{-2} (ii) $n^{-1/2}$ (iii) 2^{-n} (iv) $2n^2$

(m) $\lg(2^{18}) =$ Choose one: (i) 18 (ii) 36 (iii) $2\lg(18)$ (iv) 18^2

(n) $\lg(\sqrt{2}) =$ Choose one: (i) 1 (ii) 0.5 (iii) $\sqrt{\lg(2)}$ (iv) $2^{0.5}$

(o) $\ln(e^{x^2}) =$ Choose one: (i) $2\ln(x)$ (ii) $e^{2\ln(x)}$ (iii) x^2 (iv) $2x$

(p) $e^{\ln(n+1)} =$ Choose one: (i) $n + e$ (ii) en (iii) n (iv) $n + 1$

(q) $e^{n\ln(x)} =$ Choose one: (i) x^n (ii) n^x (iii) nx (iv) $n^{\ln(x)}$

(r) $e^{\ln(n)-\ln(m)} =$ Choose one: (i) $n - m$ (ii) n/m (iii) $\ln(n - m)$ (iv) $e^{\ln(n-m)}$
(s) $2^{4\lg(3)} =$ Choose one: (i) 12 (ii) 24 (iii) 48 (iv) 81
(t) $\lg(32^{20}) =$ Choose one: (i) 25 (ii) 52 (iii) $5\lg(20)$ (iv) 100

Solution (a) (ii) because $\ln(e^r) = r$ for any real number r
(b) (i) because $\ln(x^p) = p\ln(x)$ for any real number p
(c) (iv) because $\ln(st) = \ln(s) + \ln(t)$ (d) (ii) because $e^{\ln(t)} = t$
(e) (iii) because $e^{a+b} = e^a \cdot e^b$ by the properties of exponents
(f) (i) because $\lg(2^p) = p$
(g) (iv) because $\lg(8n) = \lg(8) + \lg(n) = 3 + \lg(n)$
(h) There is no correct answer. It was a trick question.
(i) (iv) because $\lg(n/32) = \lg(n)g(n) - 5$
(j) (ii) because $2^{\lg(x)} = x$
(k) (i) because $2^{3\lg(3)} = 2^{\lg(3^3)} = 2^{\lg(27)} = 27$
(l) (i) because $2^{-\lg(n^2)} = \dfrac{1}{2^{\lg(n^2)}} = \dfrac{1}{n^2} = n^{-2}$
(m) (i) (n) (ii) because $\sqrt{2} = 2^{0.5}$ (o) (iii) (p) (iv)
(q) (i) because $n\ln(x) = \ln(x^n)$
(r) (ii) because $\ln(n) - \ln(m) = \ln(n/m)$
(s) (iv) because $4\lg(3) = \lg(3^4) = \lg(81)$
(t) (iv) because $\lg(32^{20}) = 20\lg(32)$

Example 2.2.13 Show how to compute the value of $\lfloor\lg(1500)\rfloor$ without using a calculator.

Solution $2^{10} = 1024 < 1500 < 2048 = 2^{11}$, so $10 < \lg(1500) < 11$, so $\lfloor\lg(1500)\rfloor = 10$.

Example 2.2.14 In the block of C++ code shown below, assume that the variable n has a positive integer value. When the code is executed, how many times is the body of the loop executed? Express the answer in terms of the value of n.

```
int k = 1;
int k, p;
for (k = 1, p = 2;  p <= n;  p *= 2)   // Double p after body of loop is executed.
{
  cout << k << endl;
  ++k;
}
```

Solution First consider the special case where n has the value 1. In that case, the loop control condition n <= n is immediately false, so the body of the loop is executed 0 times. Now let's look at the cases where the value of n is at least 2, so that the body of the loop will be executed at least once. As in Example 2.1.12 on p. 17, the variable k is a loop counter. Let L denote the value of k in the cout statement the last time the body of the loop is executed. Then L is the number we want to compute.

When the body of the loop is executed, the initial value 1 of k is sent to output and then k is incremented to 2. Next, the value of p is doubled to 4 (= 2^2) and then the loop control condition p <= n is tested. If it is found to be true, then the value 2 of k will be sent to output, k will be incremented to 3, and p will be doubled to 8 (= 2^3). Again the loop control condition will be tested. When k gets the value L (which we want to compute), the variable p will then get the value 2^L, and the loop control condition will be true for the last time. The number L will be sent to output, the variable k will be incremented to $L+1$, and p will be doubled to 2^{L+1}. The loop condition will now be found to be false. If we let n denote the (fixed) value of the program variable n, then the following inequalities must be true:

$$2^L \le n < 2^{L+1}.$$

Taking the logarithm base 2 of each part gives us

$$L \le \lg(n) < L + 1.$$

As we know from Theorem 2.1.4 (c), this means that $L = \lfloor \lg(n) \rfloor$. This is the number of times the body of the loop is executed. Note that this formula is valid even when n has the value 1, for in that case $\lg(n) = 0$.

In the solution of the preceding example, the key observation was that there exists a simple mathematical relationship between the values k and p of the program variables k and p each time the loop control condition is tested. That relationship is $p = 2^k$, and it is true even when the loop control is tested for the last time and found to be false (at that point $k = L + 1$ and $p = 2^{L+1}$). Any condition that's true for the program variables every time a loop control condition is tested is called a *loop invariant* for the loop. In the block of code in Example A.2.14, the loop invariant $p = 2^k$ is easy to spot, and seeing it was the key to solving the given problem. There are other loop invariants for the block of code in Example 2.2.14. Examples are $p > 1$ and $k < p$, but these invariants are not useful in solving the problem that we were given.

2.2.2 Exercises

2.2.15 Do the following multiple choice exercises *without* using an electronic calculator.

   (a) $2^{5+\lg(t)} =$ Choose one: (i) $32 + t$ (ii) $32t$ (iii) $5 + t$ (iv) $5t$
   (b) $\lg(2^{5n}) =$ Choose one: (i) $5 + n$ (ii) $32 + n$ (iii) $5n$ (iv) $32n$
   (c) $\lg(32p) =$ Choose one: (i) $5\lg(p)$ (ii) $32\lg(p)$ (iii) $5p$ (iv) $5 + \lg(p)$
   (d) $\lg(n^8) =$ Choose one: (i) $8\lg(n)$ (ii) $3\lg(n)$ (iii) $3n$ (iv) $3 + \lg(n)$
   (e) $2^{3\lg(k)} =$ Choose one: (i) $8\lg(k)$ (ii) $8k$ (iii) k^3 (iv) $3k$
   (f) $\lg(8^{-k}) =$ Choose one: (i) $8/k$ (ii) $-3k$ (iii) $1/(3k)$ (iv) $3\lg(k)$

(g) $\lfloor \lg(32x) \rfloor =$ Choose one: (i) $5 + \lfloor \lg(x) \rfloor$ (ii) $5x$ (iii) $32 + x$ (iv) $5 \lfloor \lg(x) \rfloor$
(h) $\lg(a\, b\, c) =$ Choose one: (i) $a + b + c$ (ii) $2^{a\, b\, c}$ (iii) 2^{a+b+c}
                                    (iv) $\lg(a) + \lg(b) + \lg(c)$
(i) $\lg(8/n^2) =$ Choose one: (i) $6 - \lg(n)$ (ii) $3/\lg(n^2)$ (iii) $3/n^2$
                                    (iv) $3 - 2\lg(n)$
(j) $2^{\lg(5)} =$ Choose one: (i) 5 (ii) 32 (iii) 25 (iv) $\lg(25)$
(k) $2^{3\lg(5)} =$ Choose one: (i) 13 (ii) 15 (iii) 40 (iv) 125
(l) $2^{-\lg(8n)} =$ Choose one: (i) $-8n$ (ii) $1/(8n)$ (iii) $8/n$ (iv) $64n^2$
(m) $\lg(2^8) =$ Choose one: (i) 256 (ii) 3 (iii) 8 (iv) 6
(n) $\lg(\sqrt{38}) =$ Choose one: (i) 19 (ii) $\frac{1}{2}\lg(38)$ (iii) $\sqrt{\lg(38)}$ (iv) 2^{38}
(t) $\lg(8^5) =$ Choose one: (i) 15 (ii) 40 (iii) $8\lg(5)$ (iv) $3 + \lg(5)$

2.2.16 For each of the following, give a single numerical value without using a calculator.
(a) $\lg(36) - \lg(9)$ (b) $\lg(56) - \lg(7)$ (c) $\lg(\sqrt{128})$ (d) $\lg(\sqrt[3]{32})$

2.2.17 (a) Show how to compute the value of $\lfloor \lg(1500) \rfloor$ without using a calculator.
(b) Show how to compute the value of $\lceil \lg(1900) \rceil$ without using a calculator.

2.2.18 (a) Express $\log_3(x)$ as some constant C times $\log_{10}(x)$. Use a pocket calculator to determine the numerical value of the constant C.
(b) Express $\log_5(x)$ as some constant C times $\ln(x)$. Use a pocket calculator to determine the numerical value of the constant C.

2.2.19 (a) Use Theorem 2.2.10 to express $2^{\ln(n)}$ as a power of n. Use a calculator to find the numerical value of the power.
(b) Use Theorem 2.2.10 to express $5^{\ln(2n)}$ as some constant times a power of n. Use a calculator to find the numerical value of the power.

2.2.20 We noted that the first of the two equations in Theorem 2.2.8 (b) can be interpreted as saying that $\lfloor \lg(n) \rfloor$ is the number of "integer divisions by 2" that are required to reduce n down to 1. Give a similar interpretation for the second of the two equations in Theorem 2.2.8 (b).

2.2.21 Consider the following block of C++ code in which n is a positive integer.

```
int k;
for (k = n; k > 1; k = k/2)
  cout << "Hello" << endl;
```

(a) How many times will the cout statement be executed if the value of n is 1 when the loop begins?
(b) How many times will the cout statement be executed if the value of n is 2 when the loop begins?

(c) How many times will the cout statement be executed if the value of n is 3 when the loop begins?

(d) Give an expression involving the variable n for the number of times that the code above will send "Hello" to output. Cite one of the theorems in this section to justify your answer.

2.2.22 (a) Use (among other things) Theorem 2.1.4 on floors and ceilings to prove that for all positive integers n, $n \leq 2^{\lceil \lg(n) \rceil} < 2n$. Warning: in general, $2^{\lceil \lg(n) \rceil} \neq \lceil 2^{\lg(n)} \rceil$. *Hint:* look at the proof for Theorem 2.2.8 (a).

(b) Use (among other things) Theorem 2.1.4 on floors and ceilings to prove that for all positive integers n, $\dfrac{n}{10} < 10^{\lfloor \log_{10}(n) \rfloor} \leq n$. Warning: in general, $10^{\lfloor \log_{10}(n) \rfloor} \neq \lfloor 10^{\log_{10}(n)} \rfloor$. *Hint:* look at the proof for Theorem 2.2.8 (a).

2.2.23 (a) Use Theorem 2.1.5 (c) and part (d) of Theorem 2.2.8 to prove part (f) of Theorem 2.2.8.

(b) Use Theorem 2.1.5 (c) and part (e) of Theorem 2.2.8 to prove part (g) of Theorem 2.2.8.

2.2.24 (a) How many many times is the body of the loop below executed? (Note: the block differs from the code in Example 2.2.14 only in the initial value of p.) Justify your answer by using a loop invariant. Assume that n has a positive integer value.

```
int k, p;
for (k=1, p = 1; p <= n; p *= 2) // Double p after body is executed.
{
  cout << k << endl;
  ++k;
}
```

(b) How many many times is the body of the loop below executed? Assume that n has a positive integer value. You may base your answer on your answer for part (a).

```
int p;
for (p = 1; p <= n; p *= 2) // Double p after body is executed.
  cout << p << endl;
```

(c) How many times is the body of the loop below executed? Assume that n has a positive integer value.

```
int p;
for (p = 1;  p < n;  p *= 2)   // Double p each time body of loop is executed.
  cout << p << endl;
```

Hint. Imagine that a loop-counting variable k with initial value 1 is introduced into the code. Give a loop invariant involving the values k and p of the program variables k and p. Let L denote the value of k the last time the body of the loop is executed. Use your loop invariant to calculate L. You will need to cite Theorem 2.1.4 (c) at some point.

2.3   Sums and Summation Notation

What is the value of the sum

$$1^2 + 3^2 + 5^2 + 7^2 + \cdots + 19^2?$$

To answer this question, you first have to fill in the missing terms that are indicated by the "3 dots" in the sum. In this case that's not hard to do. The 3 dots must surely stand for

$$9^2 + 11^2 + 13^2 + 15^2 + 17^2.$$

What about the sum

$$2 + 6 + 12 + 20 + 30 + \cdots + 90?$$

Here we may or may not see that the terms can be written as

$$1 \cdot 2 + 2 \cdot 3 + 3 \cdot 4 + 4 \cdot 5 + 5 \cdot 6 + \cdots + 9 \cdot 10,$$

in which case the missing terms are $42 + 56 + 72 = 6 \cdot 7 + 7 \cdot 8 + 8 \cdot 9$. It is useful to have a notation that lets us express sums in a more precise way that eliminates the guesswork associated with the 3 dots notation. The sigma summation notation was invented for this purpose. The two sums given above can be written this way:

$$\sum_{k=1}^{10}(2k - 1) \quad \text{and} \quad \sum_{k=1}^{9} k(k + 1)$$

More generally, suppose a real function $f(k)$ is defined on integers k in the range $m, \ldots, n$. The expression

$$\sum_{k=m}^{n} f(k)$$

where $\sum$ is the upper case Greek letter "sigma", is a precise and concise way of writing the sum

$$f(m) + f(m + 1) + \cdots + f(n).$$

The numerical value represented by these expressions is exactly the value that would be produced in the variable sum by executing the following fragment of C code:

```
sum = 0;
for (k = m; k <= n; ++k)
  sum += f(k);
```

In particular, by convention, $\sum_{k=m}^{n} f(k)$ has the value 0 if $n < m$ (look at the loop above).

Examples 2.3.1 (a) $\sum_{k=2}^{5} \dfrac{k}{k+1} = \dfrac{2}{3} + \dfrac{3}{4} + \dfrac{4}{5} + \dfrac{5}{6} = \dfrac{183}{60}$

(b) $\sum_{k=0}^{7} k 2^{k-1} = 0 \cdot 2^{-1} + 1 \cdot 2^{0} + 2 \cdot 2^{1} + 3 \cdot 2^{2} + 4 \cdot 2^{3} + 5 \cdot 2^{4} + 6 \cdot 2^{5} + 7 \cdot 2^{6} = 769$

(c) $\sum_{k=4}^{4} \lfloor 15/k \rfloor = \lfloor 15/4 \rfloor = 3$

(d) $\sum_{k=10}^{25} 3 = 3 + 3 + 3 + \cdots + 3 = 48$ (because there are $15 + 1$ terms here, not just 15). More generally, $\sum_{k=m}^{n} c = c(n - m + 1)$ for any fixed real number c and integers $m \le n$.

(e) $\sum_{j=1}^{3} \left(\sum_{k=1}^{j} (j-k)^2 \right) = \left(\sum_{k=1}^{1} (1-k)^2 \right) + \left(\sum_{k=1}^{2} (2-k)^2 \right) + \left(\sum_{k=1}^{3} (3-k)^2 \right)$
$= (0^2) + (1^2 + 0^2) + (2^2 + 1^2 + 0^2) = 6$

The variable k in the expression $\sum_{k=m}^{n} f(k)$ is called the *summation index*. It is important to understand that it is a "dummy index" that can be replaced by any other letter that has no pre-assigned meaning. Thus, for example, all four of the following expressions have the same value:

$$\sum_{k=2}^{7} k(k+1) \qquad \sum_{i=2}^{7} i(i+1) \qquad \sum_{t=2}^{7} t(t+1) \qquad \sum_{a=2}^{7} a(a+1).$$

Another important fact is that summation is a "linear operator"; that is,

$$\sum_{k=m}^{n} c \cdot f(k) = c \left(\sum_{k=m}^{n} f(k) \right) \quad \text{and} \quad \sum_{k=m}^{n} [f(k) \pm g(k)] = \sum_{k=m}^{n} f(k) \pm \sum_{k=m}^{n} g(k).$$
$$(2.2)$$

Occasionally we have to "interchange the order of summation" in a double sum. That is, we have to use the fact that

$$\sum_{k=m}^{n} \left(\sum_{j=p}^{q} f(j,k) \right) = \sum_{j=p}^{q} \left(\sum_{k=m}^{n} f(j,k) \right).$$

This equation simply says that if we sum over each row separately in the following array, and then add up the sums we get, we obtain the same answer as if we sum over each column separately and then add up those sums. We can do this as long as the boundaries p and q for the interior sum are independent of the index variable of the exterior sum k.

$$
\begin{array}{llll}
f(p,m) & f(p+1,m) & f(p+2,m) & \ldots f(q,m) \\
f(p,m+1) & f(p+1,m+1) & f(p+2,m+1) & \ldots f(q,m+1) \\
f(p,m+2) & f(p+1,m+2) & f(p+2,m+2) & \ldots f(q,m+2) \\
\ldots & \ldots & \ldots & \ldots \\
f(p,n) & f(p+1,n) & f(p+2,n) & \ldots f(q,n)
\end{array}
$$

We are now going to look at several types of sums that occur frequently in analysis of algorithms. Our goal will be to find some shortcuts for computing the values of these sums.

Our first example is the simple sum $1 + 2 + 3 + \cdots + n$, where n is a positive integer. (When n is 1 or 2 or 3, then by $1 + 2 + 3 + \cdots + n$ we mean simply 1 or $1 + 2$ or $1 + 2 + 3$ respectively.) We can write this sum in the sigma summation notation this way: $\sum_{k=1}^{n} k$. This is called a *triangular sum* because if we draw a bar graph with bars of heights $1, 2, 3, \ldots, n$, they form a rough triangle. It turns out that there is a simple formula for the value of the triangular sum. It can be obtained by the following algebraic trick. Let $S(n)$ denote the sum $\sum_{k=1}^{n} k$. Then

$$
\begin{array}{ll}
& S(n) = 1 \quad +2 \quad +3 \quad +\cdots + (n-1) + n. \\
\text{In reverse order we have} & S(n) = n \quad + (n-1) + (n-2) + \cdots + 2 + \quad 1. \\
\text{Adding them gives} & 2S(n) = (n+1) + (n+1) + (n+1) + \cdots + (n+1) + (n+1) = n(n+1) \\
\text{so} & S(n) = \dfrac{n(n+1)}{2}.
\end{array}
$$

Theorem 2.3.2 *For any positive integer n we have*

$$
1 + 2 + 3 + \cdots + n = \frac{n(n+1)}{2}.
$$

More generally, for any integers m and n satisfying $m \le n$ we have

$$
m + (m+1) + (m+2) + \cdots + n = (n-m+1)\frac{m+n}{2}.
$$

Proof We have already proved the first of these summation formulas. The second can be proved in a similar way. ∎

These formulas should be memorized. It will help you to note that in both formulas above the first factor on the right side is the *number of terms* on the left side, while the second factor on the right side is the *average* of the first and last numbers on the left side.

In general, when we are confronted with an expression X involving a sigma-summation symbol or a 3-dots ellipsis we like to have a **closed form** for the expression, by which we mean a mathematical expression Y whose value is the same as that of X, but Y is compact and easily computed with a fixed number of operations including exponentiation and formation of logarithms. (We regard 2^n as a closed form because it can be evaluated in two steps: let $x = n \ln(2)$; then $2^n = \exp(x)$.) The calculation in Theorem 2.3.2 shows that $\dfrac{n(n+1)}{2}$ is a closed form for the expressions

$$1 + 2 + 3 + \cdots + n \text{ and } \sum_{k=1}^{n} k.$$

Our next example of a frequently occurring sum looks like this: $1 + t + t^2 + t^3 + \cdots + t^n$, where t is any real number and n is any non-negative integer. We can write the sum in sigma notation this way: $\displaystyle\sum_{k=0}^{n} t^k$. Note that the lower limit of the summation is $k = 0$. By convention, in sigma sums of this form, t^0 is understood to stand for 1, *even when* $t = 0$. (Normally in mathematics the expression 0^0 is considered to be undefined.) Sums of this form are called *(finite) geometric sums*. We can find a closed form for the sum by a trick similar to the one used for triangular sums. Let $G(t, n)$ denote $\displaystyle\sum_{k=0}^{n} t^k$. Then

$$G(t, n) = 1 + t + t^2 + t^3 + \cdots + t^n.$$

Multiplying by t gives $t\, G(t, n) = t + t^2 + t^3 + t^4 + \cdots + t^{n+1}$.

Subtracting them gives $G(t, n) - t\, G(t, n) = 1 - t^{n+1}$ (other terms cancel).

Factoring gives $G(t, n)(1 - t) = 1 - t^{n+1}$. If $t \neq 1$, then we obtain $G(t, n) = \dfrac{1 - t^{n+1}}{1 - t}$.

That is, $1 + t + t^2 + t^3 + \cdots + t^n = \dfrac{1 - t^{n+1}}{1 - t} = \dfrac{t^{n+1} - 1}{t - 1}$. when $t \neq 1$.

Theorem 2.3.3 *For all real numbers t and non-negative integers n,*

$$\sum_{k=0}^{n} t^k = \begin{cases} \dfrac{1 - t^{n+1}}{1 - t} & \text{if } t \neq 1; \\ n + 1 & \text{if } t = 1. \end{cases}$$

Proof See paragraphs preceding this theorem.   ∎

Our third example of a frequently occurring sum looks like this: $1 + \dfrac{1}{2} + \dfrac{1}{3} + \cdots + \dfrac{1}{n}$, which can be written in sigma summation notation this way: $\displaystyle\sum_{k=1}^{n} \dfrac{1}{k}$. We call a sum of this form a *harmonic sum* and denote it by H(n). (In music, if strings of like material, diameter, and torsion have lengths 1, 1/2, 1/3, etc., then when set in vibration they produce harmonic tones.) Sadly, there is no closed form for harmonic sums. Nevertheless, we can approximate their values very closely by using a technique that is applicable both here and in other similar situations. The technique is given by the following theorem.

Theorem 2.3.4 *Let $f(x)$ be a strictly decreasing function defined over an interval $[m, n]$, where m and n are integers such that $m < n$. Then*

$$f(n) + \int_m^n f(x)dx \; < \; \sum_{k=m}^n f(k) \; < \; f(m) + \int_m^n f(x)dx.$$

Similarly, if $f(x)$ is strictly increasing on $[m, n]$, then

$$f(m) + \int_m^n f(x)dx \; < \; \sum_{k=m}^n f(k) \; < \; f(n) + \int_m^n f(x)dx.$$

Proof The proof is easier if we begin by assuming that $f(x) \geq 0$ for all x in $[m, n]$. At the end of the proof we will see how to take care of the cases where $f(x)$ has some negative values.

For the proof when $f(x) \geq 0$ and decreasing we use a graph of the equation $y = f(x)$ on $[m, n]$, draw some rectangles, and compare their areas with the area of the region under the curve $y = f(x)$ shown in Fig. 2.4.

Note that the area of the left-most rectangle in Fig. 2.4 is $1 \times f(m) = f(m)$, the area of the next rectangle is $1 \times f(m + 1) = f(m + 1)$, and so on to the last one, which has area $1 \times f(n - 1) = f(n - 1)$. Now consider the region R bounded by the x-axis, the curve $y = f(x)$, and the vertical lines at $x = m$ and $x = n$. This region R lies inside the collection of rectangles shown, and thus the sum of areas of

Fig. 2.4 Theorem 2.3.4

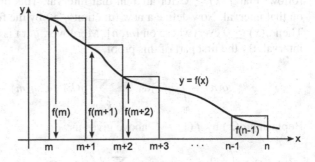

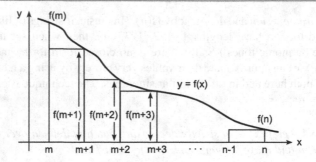

Fig. 2.5 Theorem 2.3.4

these rectangles is greater than the area of R. This can be expressed as follows:

$$\text{area of region } R = \int_m^n f(x)\,dx \; < \; f(m) + f(m+1) + \cdots + f(n-1) = \sum_{k=m}^{n-1} f(k).$$

Adding $f(n)$ to both sides of the inequality above gives the first of the inequalities about decreasing functions.

For the second of the inequalities about decreasing functions, consider the graph shown in Fig. 2.5. All the rectangles in Fig. 2.5 lie inside the region S bounded by the x-axis, the curve $y = f(x)$, and the vertical lines at $x = m$ and $x = n$, so the sum of the areas of the rectangles is less than the area of S. This can be expressed as follows:

$$f(m+1) + f(m+2) + \cdots + f(n) \; < \; \text{area of region } S = \int_m^n f(x)\,dx.$$

Adding $f(m)$ to both sides of the inequality above gives the second of the inequalities about decreasing functions.

Now let's take care of the case where some or all of the values of $f(x)$ are negative. Let C denote the value of $f(n)$. Since $f(x)$ is decreasing on the interval $[m, n]$, it follows that $f(x) \geq C$ for all x in that interval. This implies that $f(x) - C \geq 0$ on that interval. Now define a new function $g(x)$ by the formula $g(x) = f(x) - C$. Then $g(x) \geq 0$ everywhere on $[m, n]$. Moreover, $g(x)$ is strictly decreasing on that interval. By the first part of this proof,

$$g(n) + \int_m^n g(x)\,dx \; < \; \sum_{k=m}^n g(k) \; < \; g(m) + \int_m^n g(x)\,dx.$$

Replacing $g(x)$ by $f(x) - C$ above gives us

$$f(n) - C + \int_m^n [f(x) - C]\,dx \; < \; \sum_{k=m}^n [f(k) - C] \; < \; f(m) - C + \int_m^n [f(x) - C]\,dx.$$

Now we use properties of summation mentioned in Examples 2.3.1 (d) and in formula (2.3) on p. 29, together with standard integration formulas to produce the following inequalities:

$$f(n) - C + \int_m^n f(x)dx - C(n-m) < \sum_{k=m}^n f(k) - C(m-n+1) < f(m) - C$$

$$+ \int_m^n f(x)dx - C(n-m).$$

Adding $C(n-m+1)$ to each part of the inequalities above gives the inequalities for $f(x)$ stated in the theorem.

The proofs for the inequalities involving increasing functions are similar and will be left as an exercise. ∎

Theorem 2.3.5 (Approximation for Harmonic Sums). *For all integers $n > 1$ we have*

$$\frac{1}{n} + \ln(n) < H(n) < 1 + \ln(n).$$

Proof We want to approximate $H(n) = \sum_{k=1}^n \frac{1}{k}$ for $n > 1$.

To do this we apply Theorem 2.3.4 to the strictly decreasing function $f(x) = \frac{1}{x}$, with $m = 1$ and $n > 1$. We get

$$\frac{1}{n} + \int_1^n \frac{1}{x}dx < \sum_{k=1}^n \frac{1}{k} < \frac{1}{1} + \int_1^n \frac{1}{x}dx \quad \text{for all } n > 1,$$

which immediately yields the inequalities stated in the theorem. ∎

The important thing to remember from Theorem 2.3.5 is that for all large n we have $H(n) \approx \ln(n)$. In rare cases where we want a more accurate approximation for $H(n)$ when n is large, we can use the following theorem discovered by Leonhard Euler.

Theorem 2.3.6 (Euler) $\lim_{n\to\infty} [H(n) - \ln(n)] = 0.5772$ *approximately and therefore* $H(n) \approx 0.5772 + \ln(n)$ *for all large n.*

Proof See almost any advanced calculus textbook. The number 0.5772 given in this theorem is an approximation to the actual limit, which is known to be an irrational number. ∎

When $n \geq 15$, Euler's approximation is correct to within 1 % of the actual value. Of course, for small values of n, we can calculate H(n) very accurately with a pocket calculator.

Closed forms for several other types of sums are occasionally needed in analysis of algorithms. They do not, however, occur with sufficient frequency to make them worth memorizing. We give four such sums below.

Theorem 2.3.7 *For all positive integers n and real numbers $t \neq 1$,*

$$1 + 2t + 3t^2 + \cdots + nt^{n-1} = \frac{1 + nt^{n+1} - (n+1)t^n}{(t-1)^2}.$$

Proof The left side is just the derivative with respect to t of the finite geometric sum $1 + t + t^2 + t^3 + \cdots + t^n$. Thus we can obtain the formula above simply by differentiating both sides of the formula given in Theorem 2.3.3 with respect to t.   ∎

Theorem 2.3.8 *For all positive integers n,*

$$\sum_{k=2}^{n} \lceil \lg(k) \rceil = n \lfloor \lg(n) \rfloor + (n+1) - 2^{\lfloor \lg(n) \rfloor + 1}$$

and

$$\sum_{k=2}^{n} \lfloor \lg(k) \rfloor = (n+1) \lfloor \lg(n+1) \rfloor + 2 - 2^{\lfloor \lg(n+1) \rfloor + 1}.$$

Proof When $k = 2$ we have $\lceil \lg(k) \rceil = 1$. When $k = 3$ or $k = 4$ we have $\lceil \lg(k) \rceil = 2$. When $k = 5$ or 6 or 7 or 8 we have $\lceil \lg(k) \rceil = 3$. Etc. Thus, the terms in $\sum_{k=2}^{n} \lceil \lg(k) \rceil$ can be grouped as follows

$$\underbrace{1}_{\substack{k=2 \\ 2^0 \text{ term}}} + \underbrace{(2+2)}_{\substack{k=3,4 \\ 2^1 \text{ terms}}} + \underbrace{(3+3+3+3)}_{\substack{k=5,6,7,8=2^3 \\ 2^2 \text{terms}}} + \underbrace{(4+4+\cdots+4)}_{\substack{k=9,10,\ldots,16=2^4 \\ 2^3 \text{terms}}} + \cdots + \underbrace{(\lfloor \lg(n) \rfloor \cdots + \lfloor \lg(n) \rfloor)}_{\substack{k=2^{\lfloor \lg(n) \rfloor -1}+1,\ldots,2^{\lfloor \lg(n) \rfloor} \\ 2^{\lfloor \lg(n) \rfloor -1} \text{terms}}} + more$$

The *"more"* (above) gives the remaining terms, corresponding to $k = 2^{\lfloor \lg(n) \rfloor} + 1$ up to $k = n$ (this set of terms is empty if n is a power of 2). Each of these terms is equal to $\lfloor \lg(n) \rfloor + 1$. Thus we have

$$\sum_{k=2}^{n} \lceil \lg(k) \rceil = \sum_{p=1}^{\lfloor \lg(n) \rfloor} 2^{p-1} p + \left(n - 2^{\lfloor \lg(n) \rfloor} \right) (\lfloor \lg(n) \rfloor + 1). \qquad (2.3)$$

The sigma sum on the right side is just the sum given in Theorem 2.3.7, but with k replaced by p, n replaced by $\lfloor \lg(n) \rfloor$, and t replaced by 2. Thus we get

$$\sum_{p=1}^{\lfloor \lg(n) \rfloor} 2^{p-1} p = \frac{1 + \lfloor \lg(n) \rfloor 2^{\lfloor \lg(n) \rfloor + 1} - (\lfloor \lg(n) \rfloor + 1) 2^{\lfloor \lg(n) \rfloor}}{(2-1)^2}.$$

Inserting this into Eq. (2.3) gives us

$$\sum_{k=2}^{n} \lceil \lg(k) \rceil = 1 + \lfloor \lg(n) \rfloor 2^{\lfloor \lg n \rfloor + 1} - (\lfloor \lg(n) \rfloor + 1) 2^{\lfloor \lg n \rfloor} + n\lfloor \lg(n) \rfloor + n - \lfloor \lg(n) \rfloor 2^{\lfloor \lg n \rfloor} - 2^{\lfloor \lg n \rfloor},$$

which reduces to the first of the two sums in the statement of the theorem.

To prove the second identity in this theorem, begin by replacing the symbol n by the symbol $n + 1$ everywhere in the first equation stated in the theorem. This gives

$$\sum_{k=2}^{n+1} \lceil \lg(k) \rceil = (n+1)\lfloor \lg(n+1) \rfloor + (n+2) - 2^{\lfloor \lg(n+1) \rfloor + 1} \quad \text{for all positive integers } n.$$

By Theorem 2.2.8 (c), with n replaced by $k - 1$, we get $\lceil \lg(k) \rceil = 1 + \lfloor \lg(k-1) \rfloor$, so the sum above is

$$\sum_{k=2}^{n+1} (1 + \lfloor \lg(k-1) \rfloor) = (n+1)\lfloor \lg(n+1) \rfloor + (n+2) - 2^{\lfloor \lg(n+1) \rfloor + 1}. \quad (2.4)$$

The left side can be expressed as

$$\sum_{k=2}^{n+1} 1 + \sum_{k=2}^{n+1} \lfloor \lg(k-1) \rfloor = n + 0 + \lfloor \lg(2) \rfloor + \lfloor \lg(3) \rfloor + \cdots + \lfloor \lg(n) \rfloor = n + \sum_{k=2}^{n} \lfloor \lg(k) \rfloor.$$

Putting this into Eq. (2.4) gives

$$n + \sum_{k=2}^{n} \lfloor \lg(k) \rfloor = (n+1)\lfloor \lg(n+1) \rfloor + (n+2) - 2^{\lfloor \lg(n+1) \rfloor + 1}.$$

Subtracting n from both sides of this equation gives the desired equation. ∎

Example 2.3.9 Many computer science textbooks discuss the representation of positive integers using various bases. For example, the integer 6029_{10} (base 10 notation) can also be written in binary notation (base 2 notation) as 1011110001101_2 or in octal notation (base 8) as 13615_8 or in hexadecimal notation (base 16) as $178D_{16}$. Of course, it is also possible to write this integer in these bases with one or more leading zeroes: 006029_{10}, 0000010111100011101_2, 013615_8, $178D_{16}$. Let's agree to use the phrase *standard representation of n base b* to describe the representation of a positive integer n without leading zeroes in base b notation. Note that the number of digits required by the standard representation of n depends on the base used as well as on the size of n. For example, the standard representations of the number discussed in the second sentence of this paragraph require 4, 13, 5, and 4 digits, respectively, in base 10, base 2, base 8, and base 16.

How many digits are there in the standard decimal (i.e., base 10) representation of the integer 34^{295}? How many bits (binary digits) does its standard binary representation contain? More generally, given any positive integers n and b, can we find a formula for the number of digits that will be required for the standard representation of n base b?

Solution Let's solve the general case first. Assume we are given positive integers n and b. Let k denote the (unknown) number of digits in the standard representation of n base b. Denote those digits by $d_0, d_1, d_2, \ldots, d_{k-1}$, where d_0 is the least significant digit and d_{k-1} is the most significant (and is therefore not zero). Each of these digits lies in the range from 0 to $b - 1$. (For example, if b is 10, then each digit lies in the range from 0 to 9.) Moreover, d_{k-1} is at least 1. Then

$$n = d_{k-1}\, b^{k-1} + \cdots + d_2\, b^2 + d_1\, b^1 + d_0\, b^0.$$

Since $d_{k-1} \geq 1$ and all other $d_i \geq 0$, it follows that

$$n \geq 1\, b^{k-1} + \cdots + 0 + 0 + 0.$$

That is, $n \geq b^{k-1}$. Similarly, since every $d_i \leq b - 1$, it follows that

$$n \leq (b - 1)b^{k-1} + \cdots + (b - 1)b^2 + (b - 1)b^1 + (b - 1)b^0$$
$$n \leq (b - 1)[b^{k-1} + \cdots + b^2 + b + 1]$$
$$n \leq (b - 1)\frac{b^k - 1}{b - 1}$$
$$n \leq b^k - 1.$$

From this it follows that $n < b^k$. We have now established the inequalities

$$b^{k-1} \leq n < b^k,$$

where k is the number of digits in the standard representation of n base b. Taking logarithms base b of each of the quantities above gives us these inequalities:

$$k - 1 \leq \log_b(n) < k.$$

Since $k - 1$ is an integer, it follows from Theorem 2.1.4 (c) that $k - 1 = \lfloor \log_b(n) \rfloor$, or equivalently, $k = 1 + \lfloor \log_b(n) \rfloor$. By Theorem 2.2.8 (c), $k = \lceil \log_b(n + 1) \rceil$. Thus we have proved the following useful fact:

Theorem 2.3.10 *Let n and b be positive integers with $b \geq 2$. The number of digits in the standard representation of n base b is*

$$1 + \lfloor \log_b(n) \rfloor = \lceil \log_b(n + 1) \rceil.$$

Proof This formula is derived in Example 2.3.9.   ■

Now we can answer the question we asked in Example 2.3.9 about the number of digits in the standard decimal representation of the integer 34^{295}. The answer, obtained with the aid of a calculator, is

$$1 + \lfloor \log_{10}(34^{295}) \rfloor = 1 + \lfloor 295 \log_{10}(34) \rfloor = 1 + \lfloor 295 \times 1.5315 \rfloor = 1 + \lfloor 451.79 \rfloor = 452.$$

The number of bits in the standard binary representation of 34^{295} is

$$1 + \lfloor \log_2(34^{295}) \rfloor = 1 + \lfloor 295 \log_2(34) \rfloor = 1 + \lfloor 295 \times 5.087 \rfloor = 1 + \lfloor 1500.80 \rfloor = 1501.$$

The sum in the following theorem appears here and there in analysis of algorithms. Unfortunately it has no simple closed form, so it is helpful to have good lower and upper bounds for it.

Theorem 2.3.11 *The sum* $\displaystyle\sum_{k=1}^{\lfloor \lg(n) \rfloor} \left\lfloor \frac{n}{2^k} \right\rfloor$ *is asymptotic to n. In particular, it satisfies the inequalities*

$$n - 2 - \lfloor \lg(n) \rfloor \; < \; \sum_{k=1}^{\lfloor \lg(n) \rfloor} \left\lfloor \frac{n}{2^k} \right\rfloor \; \le \; n - 1. \tag{2.5}$$

Proof Using the fact that $x - 1 < \lfloor x \rfloor \le x$ for all real numbers x, we can write that

$$\sum_{k=1}^{\lfloor \lg(n) \rfloor} \left(\frac{n}{2^k} - 1 \right) \; < \; \sum_{k=1}^{\lfloor \lg(n) \rfloor} \left\lfloor \frac{n}{2^k} \right\rfloor \; \le \; \sum_{k=1}^{\lfloor \lg(n) \rfloor} \frac{n}{2^k}.$$

These inequalities are equivalent to

$$\sum_{k=1}^{\lfloor \lg(n) \rfloor} \frac{n}{2^k} - \lfloor \lg(n) \rfloor \; < \; \sum_{k=1}^{\lfloor \lg(n) \rfloor} \left\lfloor \frac{n}{2^k} \right\rfloor \; \le \; \sum_{k=1}^{\lfloor \lg(n) \rfloor} \frac{n}{2^k}. \tag{2.6}$$

The sum $\displaystyle\sum_{k=1}^{\lfloor \lg(n) \rfloor} \frac{n}{2^k}$ that appears in these inequalities can be computed by factoring out the n that occurs in every term and then using the geometric sum formula. Note that the term for $k = 0$ is missing from the sum and must therefore be subtracted from it:

$$\sum_{k=1}^{\lfloor \lg(n) \rfloor} \frac{n}{2^k} = n \sum_{k=1}^{\lfloor \lg(n) \rfloor} \left(\frac{1}{2} \right)^k = n \left(\frac{1 - \left(\frac{1}{2} \right)^{\lfloor \lg(n) \rfloor + 1}}{1 - \frac{1}{2}} - 1 \right) = n \left(\frac{2^{\lfloor \lg(n) \rfloor + 1} - 1}{2^{\lfloor \lg(n) \rfloor}} - 1 \right)$$

$$= n \left(2 - \frac{1}{2^{\lfloor \lg(n) \rfloor}} - 1 \right)$$

$$= n - \frac{n}{2^{\lfloor \lg(n) \rfloor}}.$$

Inserting this last formula into line 2.6 we get

$$n - \frac{n}{2^{\lfloor \lg(n) \rfloor}} - \lfloor \lg(n) \rfloor \; < \; \sum_{k=1}^{\lfloor \lg(n) \rfloor} \left\lfloor \frac{n}{2^k} \right\rfloor \; \le \; n - \frac{n}{2^{\lfloor \lg(n) \rfloor}}. \tag{2.7}$$

To get from inequation (2.7) to the desired inequation (2.5) we must estimate the term $-\dfrac{n}{2^{\lfloor \lg(n)\rfloor}}$. Theorem 2.2.8 (a) gives us these useful inequalities:

$$2^{\lfloor \lg(n)\rfloor} \le n < 2^{\lfloor \lg(n)\rfloor+1}.$$

Dividing all terms by $2^{\lfloor \lg(n)\rfloor}$ and then multiplying throughout by -1 gives

$$-1 \ge -\frac{n}{2^{\lfloor \lg(n)\rfloor}} > -2.$$

It follows that

$$n - 2 - \lfloor \lg(n)\rfloor < n - \frac{n}{2^{\lfloor \lg(n)\rfloor}} - \lfloor \lg(n)\rfloor \quad \text{and} \quad n - \frac{n}{2^{\lfloor \lg(n)\rfloor}} \le n - 1.$$

Combining this pair of inequalities with inequality (2.7) gives the desired result (2.5).
∎

2.3.1 Further Examples

Example 2.3.12 Evaluate the following sums. In each case, give a single numerical answer.

(a) $\displaystyle\sum_{k=1}^{5} \frac{1}{k(k+1)}$ (b) $\displaystyle\sum_{r=0}^{3} \frac{r+1}{2^r}$ (c) $\displaystyle\sum_{p=1}^{4} \left(\sum_{q=1}^{p} \frac{p}{q} \right)$ (d) $\displaystyle\sum_{k=100}^{50} \frac{\lfloor \lg(k)\rfloor}{2k}$

Solution (a) $\dfrac{1}{2} + \dfrac{1}{6} + \dfrac{1}{12} + \dfrac{1}{20} + \dfrac{1}{30} = \dfrac{5}{6}$ (b) $\dfrac{1}{1} + \dfrac{2}{2} + \dfrac{3}{4} + \dfrac{4}{8} = \dfrac{13}{4}$

(c) $\displaystyle\sum_{j=1}^{1} \frac{1}{j} + \sum_{j=1}^{2} \frac{2}{j} + \sum_{j=1}^{3} \frac{3}{j} + \sum_{j=1}^{4} \frac{4}{j} \quad = \quad 1 + \left(\frac{2}{1} + \frac{2}{2} \right) + \left(\frac{3}{1} + \frac{3}{2} + \frac{3}{3} \right)$

$+ \left(\dfrac{4}{1} + \dfrac{4}{2} + \dfrac{4}{3} + \dfrac{4}{4} \right) = \dfrac{107}{6}$

(d) The value of this sum is 0 because the lower limit of summation (100) is larger than the upper limit (50).

Example 2.3.13 Write each of the following sums in sigma summation notation:

(a) $\dfrac{2}{(1)^2} + \dfrac{3}{(2)^2} + \dfrac{4}{(3)^2} + \dfrac{5}{(4)^2}$ (b) $1 + \dfrac{1}{3} + \dfrac{1}{9} + \dfrac{1}{27} + \cdots + \dfrac{1}{3^{10}}$

Solution (a) $\displaystyle\sum_{k=1}^{4} \frac{k+1}{k^2}$ or $\displaystyle\sum_{j=0}^{3} \frac{j+2}{(j+1)^2}$ or $\displaystyle\sum_{r=2}^{5} \frac{r}{(r-1)^2}$ (b) $\displaystyle\sum_{k=0}^{10} \frac{1}{3^k}$

Example 2.3.14 For each of the following sums, evaluate it numerically or express it in an algebraic closed form.

(a) $1000 + 999 + 998 + 997 + \cdots + 1$ (b) $100 + 101 + 102 + \cdots + 349 + 350$

(c) $5 + 10 + 15 + \cdots + 745 + 750$ (d) $5 + 8 + 11 + 14 + \cdots + 98 = \sum_{k=1}^{32}(3k+2)$

(e) $1 + 2 + 3 + \cdots + (2n - 1) + 2n$ (Express your answer in terms of n.)

(f) $\sum_{r=1}^{2^n} r$ (g) $\sum_{t=1+m^2}^{m^3} t$

Solution (a) Triangular Sum: $1 + 2 + 3 + \cdots + 1000 = \dfrac{1000 \cdot 1001}{2} = 500500$.

(b) A Generalized Triangular Sum: $100 + 101 + 102 + \cdots + 349 + 350 =$

$$= (350 - 100 + 1)\tfrac{100+350}{2} = 251 \cdot 225 = 56,475.$$ Alternatively, the sum is

$$(1+2+3+\cdots+350) - (1+2+3+\cdots+99) = \frac{350 \cdot 351}{2} - \frac{99 \cdot 100}{2} = 56,475.$$

(c) Factor out 5: $5(1 + 2 + 3 + \cdots + 150) = 5\dfrac{150 \cdot 151}{2} = 56,625.$

(d) $\displaystyle\sum_{k=1}^{32}(3k+2) = \sum_{k=1}^{32} 3k + \sum_{k=1}^{32} 2 = 3\sum_{k=1}^{32} k + 2 \cdot 32 = 3\frac{32 \cdot 33}{2} + 64 = 1648.$

(e) Replace n by $2n$ in the Triangular Sum formula: $1 + 2 + \cdots + 2n = \dfrac{2n(2n+1)}{2}$
$= 2n^2 + n.$

(f) Replace n by 2^n in the Triangular Sum formula: $\displaystyle\sum_{r=1}^{2^n} r = \frac{2^n(2^n+1)}{2}.$

(g) A Generalized Triangular Sum: $(m^3 - (1 + m^2) + 1)\dfrac{1 + m^2 + m^3}{2} =$
$m^2(m - 1)\dfrac{1 + m^2 + m^3}{2}.$

Example 2.3.15 Consider the following nested pair of loops:

```
int j, k;
for (k = 2; k <= 50; ++k)
  for (j = 1; j < k; ++j)
    cout << "hello" << endl;
```

How many times, exactly, will the word "hello" be sent to output by the block of code shown above?

Solution When k is given the value 2 in the outer loop, the inner loop then outputs "hello" just once because j is initialized to 1 and then the body of the loop is executed only while j < 2. Next, k is incremented to the value 3 in the outer loop; then the inner loop outputs "hello" twice. Next, k is incremented to the value 4 in the outer loop; then the inner loop outputs "hello" three times. Etc. When k is given the value 50, the inner loop outputs "hello" 49 times. Then k is incremented once more, but now the outer loop exits. The total number of times that "hello" is sent to output is

$$1 + 2 + 3 + \cdots + 49 = \frac{49 \cdot 50}{2} = 1225.$$

Example 2.3.16 Suppose a block of high-level language computer code has 26 instructions, one after another. The *2-way complexity* of the block is the number of 2-way interactions that are possible between different instructions in the block. Assuming that any two instructions can give rise to an interaction, what is the 2-way complexity of the block of 26 instructions? *Hint:* suppose we label the instructions A through Z. Then A can interact with B, C, D, ..., Z, which is 25 possible interactions. Moreover, B can interact with C, D, ..., Z, which is 24 more possible interactions. Etc. How many are there altogether? More generally, if a block of code has n instructions in sequence, what is the 2-way complexity of the block?

Solution The total number of possible interactions is $25 + 24 + 23 + \cdots + 1 = \frac{25 \cdot 26}{2} = 325$. More generally, there are $\frac{(n-1)n}{2} \approx \frac{1}{2}n^2$ possible 2-way interactions in a block of n instructions. This is why we modularize our programs, to keep the complexity from growing as the square of the number of instructions.

Example 2.3.17 For each of the following sums, evaluate it or express it in closed form:

(a) $1 + 4 + 16 + 64 + \cdots + 4^7$ (b) $1 + \frac{1}{3} + \frac{1}{9} + \frac{1}{27} + \cdots + \frac{1}{3^{10}}$ [Hint: $\frac{1}{3^k} = (1/3)^k$]

(c) $1 + x + x^2 + \cdots + x^{n-1}$ (d) $\sum_{p=7}^{30} t^p$ (e) $\sum_{r=0}^{2n-1} 3^r$

(f) $1 + x^3 + x^6 + x^9 + \cdots + x^{3n}$ [Hint: $x^{3k} = (x^3)^k$.]   (g) $\sum_{k=1}^{n} (\lfloor \lg(t) \rfloor)^k$

Solution (a) Geometric: $1 + 4^1 + 4^2 + \cdots + 4^7 = \frac{4^8 - 1}{4 - 1} = 21{,}845$, obtained using a calculator.

(b) $1 + (1/3)^1 + (1/3)^2 + \cdots + (1/3)^{10} = \frac{(1/3)^{11} - 1}{(1/3) - 1} = \frac{-.999994355}{-2/3} \approx 1.5$, by using a calculator.

(c) $\frac{x^{n-1+1} - 1}{x - 1} = \frac{x^n - 1}{x - 1}$ if $x \neq 1$. The sum is n if $x = 1$.

(d) Factor out t^7 : $t^7(1 + t + t^2 + \cdots + t^{23}) = t^7 \frac{t^{24} - 1}{t - 1} = \frac{t^{31} - t^7}{t - 1}$ if $t \neq 1$. The sum is 24 if $t = 1$.

(e) $\sum_{r=0}^{2n+1} 3^r = 1 + 3 + 3^2 + \cdots + 3^{2n+1} = \frac{3^{2n+2} - 1}{3 - 1} = \frac{(3^2)^{n+1} - 1}{2} = \frac{9^{n+1} - 1}{2}$.

(f) $1 + x^3 + (x^3)^2 + (x^3)^3 + (x^3)^4 + \cdots + (x^3)^n = \dfrac{(x^3)^{n+1} - 1}{x^3 - 1}$ if $x \neq 1$; the sum
is $n + 1$ is $x = 1$.

(g) $(\lfloor \lg(t) \rfloor)^1 + (\lfloor \lg(t) \rfloor)^2 + (\lfloor \lg(t) \rfloor)^3 + \cdots + (\lfloor \lg(t) \rfloor)^n = \lfloor \lg(t) \rfloor \left(1 + (\lfloor \lg(t) \rfloor)^1 + (\lfloor \lg(t) \rfloor)^2 + \cdots + (\lfloor \lg(t) \rfloor)^{n-1} \right)$ if $t \neq 2$; the sum is n if $t = 2$ because $\lg(2) = 1$.
$= \lfloor \lg(t) \rfloor \dfrac{(\lfloor \lg(t) \rfloor)^n - 1}{\lfloor \lg(t) \rfloor - 1}$

Example 2.3.18 (With apologies to Mother Goose.) As I was coming from St. Ives, I met a man with 7 wives. Each wife had 7 sacks, each sack had 7 cats, each cat had 7 kits, each kit had 7 ticks. Ticks, kits, cats, sacks, wives, man. How many were *going to* St. Ives?

Solution $1(\text{man}) + 7(\text{wives}) + 7^2(\text{sacks}) + 7^3(\text{cats}) + 7^4(\text{kits}) + 7^5(\text{ticks}) = \dfrac{7^6 - 1}{7 - 1} = 19,608.$

Example 2.3.19 For each of the following sums, tell which variable the sum is a function of.

(a) $\displaystyle\sum_{k=1}^{n} \dfrac{k^2}{k+1}$ (b) $\displaystyle\sum_{n=1}^{p} 2^{n+p}$ (c) $\displaystyle\sum_{j=1}^{100} j^k$

Solution (a) $\displaystyle\sum_{k=1}^{n} \dfrac{k^2}{k+1}$ is a function of the variable n; we can assign any positive integer value to n in the sum. For example, assigning n the value 25 produces $\displaystyle\sum_{k=1}^{25} \dfrac{k^2}{k+1}$. The given sum is NOT a function of k; we are not allowed to assign any value we choose to k; the values of k are determined by the value of n; whatever value of n we pick, the values of k will then be $1, \ldots, n$.

(b) $\displaystyle\sum_{n=1}^{p} 2^{n+p}$ is a function of the variable p; we can assign any positive integer value to p in the sum. For example, if we assign p the value 4 we get the sum $\displaystyle\sum_{n=1}^{4} 2^{n+4} = 2^5 + 2^6 + 2^7 + 2^8$. The given sum is NOT a function of n; we cannot assign any values we choose to n; instead, the values of n are determined by the value of p; whatever value of p we pick, the values of n will be $1, 2, \ldots, p$.

Fig. 2.6 A perfect tree with 5 levels

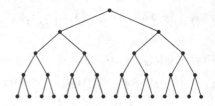

(c) $\displaystyle\sum_{j=1}^{100} j^k$ is a function of k; we can assign any positive integer value to k. For example, if we assign k the value 3 we get $\displaystyle\sum_{j=1}^{100} j^3$. The given sum is NOT a function of j. The values of j must be $1, 2, \ldots, 100$.

Example 2.3.20 A *perfect binary tree* is one in which every node has either no children (i.e., is a leaf) or 2 children, and all leaves of the tree are at the same level. In other words, every non-empty level in the tree is completely filled. It has 5 levels, numbered 0 (root level), 1, 2, 3, and 4 (bottom level). See Fig. 2.6 for an example.

(a) How many nodes are there in the level number k of a perfect binary tree?
(b) How many nodes are there altogether in a perfect binary tree with levels $0, 1, 2, \ldots, n$? Solve this by adding up the numbers in all the various levels.
(c) Do parts (a) and (b) over again, this time with a perfect ternary tree, i.e., a tree in which every non-leaf node has 3 children, and all leaves are at the same level.

Solution (a) 2^k (b) $2^0 + 2^1 + 2^2 + \cdots + 2^n = \dfrac{2^{n+1} - 1}{2 - 1} = 2^{n+1} - 1$

(c) 3^k, $\dfrac{3^{n+1} - 1}{2}$

Example 2.3.21 For each of the following sums, evaluate it or express it in a closed form.

(a) $1 + 2 \cdot 2 + 3 \cdot 2^2 + 4 \cdot 2^3 + \cdots + 10 \cdot 2^9$ (b) $\displaystyle\sum_{k=0}^{11} \frac{k+1}{2^k}$ *Hint:* $\dfrac{1}{2^k} = (1/2)^k$

(c) $t + 2t^2 + 3t^3 + \cdots + nt^n$ (Express your answer in terms of t and n.)

Solution (a) Take $t = 2$ and $n = 10$ in Theorem 2.3.7: $\dfrac{1 + 10 \cdot 2^{11} - 11 \cdot 2^{10}}{(2 - 1)^2} =$ 9217.

(b) The sum is $1 + 2(1/2) + 3(1/2)^2 + 4(1/2)^3 + \cdots + 12(1/2)^{11}$

$$= \frac{1 + 12(1/2)^{13} - 13(1/2)^{12}}{((1/2) - 1)^2} = 4(1 + 12/2^{13} - 13/2^{12}) = 4 + \frac{6}{2^{10}} - \frac{13}{2^{10}} =$$

$$4 - \frac{7}{1024} \approx 4 - 0.007 = 3.993.$$

(c) Factor out $t : t(1 + 2t + 3t^2 + \cdots + nt^{n-1}) = \dfrac{nt^{n+2} - (n+1)t^{n+1} + t}{(t-1)^2}$ if $t \neq 1$.

The sum is n if $t = 1$.

Example 2.3.22 Use Theorem 2.3.4 to find lower and upper bounds for the sum $\displaystyle\sum_{k=1}^{n} \sqrt{k}$. The bounds will be functions of n.

Solution We apply Theorem 2.3.4 to the function $f(x) = \sqrt{x}$ on the interval $[1, n]$. Since this $f(x)$ is strictly increasing on $[1, n]$ for every positive integer n, Theorem 2.3.4 gives us

$$\sqrt{1} + \int_1^n \sqrt{x}\, dx \; < \; \sum_{k=1}^{n} \sqrt{k} \; < \; \sqrt{n} + \int_1^n \sqrt{x}\, dx \quad \text{for all integers } n > 1.$$

Since $\displaystyle\int \sqrt{x}\, dx = \int x^{1/2}\, dx = \frac{2}{3} x^{3/2}$ the inequalities above yield

$$1 + \frac{2}{3} n^{3/2} - \frac{2}{3} \; < \; \sum_{k=1}^{n} \sqrt{k} \; < \; n^{1/2} + \frac{2}{3} n^{3/2} - \frac{2}{3} \quad \text{for all integers } n > 1.$$

Example 2.3.23 Explain why $\displaystyle\sum_{k=1}^{2^n} \frac{1}{k}$ is *roughly* equal to $n \ln(2) \approx \frac{7}{10} n$. Also give a more precise approximation.

Solution $\displaystyle\sum_{k=1}^{n} \frac{1}{k} = H(n) \approx \ln(n)$ (roughly), so $\displaystyle\sum_{k=1}^{2^n} \frac{1}{k} = H(2^n) \approx \ln(2^n) =$ $n \ln(2) \approx 0.693n \approx \frac{7}{10} n$. A more accurate approximation uses Euler's constant:

$$\sum_{k=1}^{n} \frac{1}{k} = H(n) \approx \ln(n) + 0.5772, \text{ so } \sum_{k=1}^{2^n} \frac{1}{k} = H(2^n) \approx \ln(2^n) + 0.5772 =$$
$$n \ln(2) + 0.5772 \approx 0.693n + 0.5772.$$

Example 2.3.24 Use the inequalities we have derived and a pocket calculator to find a numerical lower bound and a numerical upper bound for the harmonic sum $1 + \frac{1}{2} + \frac{1}{3} + \cdots + \frac{1}{100}$. Also give the best estimate you can using Euler's approximation.

Solution As shown in Theorem 2.3.5, $\frac{1}{100} + \ln(100) < H(n) < 1 + \ln(100)$. Using a calculator we get 4.615 as a lower bound and 5.605 as an upper bound for H(100). Euler's approximation says that a very good estimate for H(100) is $0.5772 + \ln(100)$ ≈ 5.182.

Example 2.3.25 How many bits are there in the standard binary representation of the integer
725194 × 386011?

Solution As shown in Example 2.3.9, the answer is $1 + \lfloor \log_2(725194 \times 386011) \rfloor$. Using the fact that $\log_b(xy) = \log_b(x) + \log_b(y)$ and the fact that $\log_2(x) = \frac{\log_{10}(x)}{\log_{10}(2)}$, we obtain the answer

$$1 + \left\lfloor \frac{\log_{10}(725194)}{\log_{10}(2)} + \frac{\log_{10}(386011)}{\log_{10}(2)} \right\rfloor = 1 + \lfloor 19.468 + 18.588 \rfloor = 39$$

with the aid of a calculator.

2.3.2   Exercises

2.3.26 In each of these two problems, show the computations leading to a single numerical answer.

(a) If $f(x) = \lfloor \lg(x) \rfloor$, then $\sum\limits_{k=1}^{7} f(k) = ?$ (b) If $f(x) = \lceil \lg(x) \rceil$, then $\sum\limits_{k=1}^{9} f(k) = ?$

2.3.27 Write the following sums in sigma summation notation:

(a) $1 + 4 + 7 + 10 + \cdots + 97 + 100$ (b) $\dfrac{2}{\sqrt{1}} + \dfrac{4}{\sqrt{3}} + \dfrac{6}{\sqrt{5}} + \dfrac{8}{\sqrt{7}} + \cdots + \dfrac{1000}{\sqrt{999}}$

2.3.28 (a) Write the following sums in "3 dot" notation. Note that despite superficial resemblances, they are actually different sums: $\sum\limits_{k=1}^{n} k^n$ and $\sum\limits_{n=1}^{k} k^n$.

(b) Write the following sums in "3 dot" notation. Note that despite superficial resemblances, they are actually different sums: $\sum\limits_{k=1}^{n} \dfrac{k+1}{n+1}$ and $\sum\limits_{n=1}^{k} \dfrac{k+1}{n+1}$.

2.3.29 Suppose a positive integer n is given in binary representation by a sum of the form

$$n = b_k 2^k + b_{k-1} 2^{k-1} + \cdots + b_2 2^2 + b_1 2^1 + b_0 2^0.$$

where the numbers $b_0, b_1, b_2, \ldots, b_k$ denote the binary digits (the bits) in the *standard* binary representation of n (i.e., no leading zeroes; see Example 2.3.9). Express the value of the number k here in terms of the integer n. Then write the equation above in sigma summation notation.

2.3.30 There is a well-known algorithm for deriving the binary representation of a positive integer n from its decimal (base 10) representation. Using the notation in Exercise 2.3.29 above, the least significant bit b_0 is calculated as the remainder of n after division by 2. That is, $b_0 = 0$ if n is even, but $b_0 = 1$ if n is odd. That is, $b_0 = \text{parity}(n)$, so $b_0 = n - 2\lfloor n/2 \rfloor$. Then we divide n by 2 and discard the remainder to produce a smaller integer, call it n_1, which is given by the equation

$$n_1 = \left\lfloor \frac{n}{2} \right\rfloor = b_k 2^{k-1} + b_{k-1} 2^{k-2} + \cdots + b_2 2^1 + b_1 2^0$$

(the b_0 term has been discarded). Using the same procedure, we can now calculate the value of b_1 : it's the remainder after n_1 is divided by 2; that is,

$$b_1 = \text{parity}(n_1) = n_1 - 2\left\lfloor \frac{n_1}{2} \right\rfloor = \left\lfloor \frac{n}{2} \right\rfloor - 2\left\lfloor \frac{n}{2^2} \right\rfloor.$$

Now we divide n_1 by 2 and discard the remainder to produce a smaller integer n_2:

$$n_2 = \left\lfloor \frac{n_1}{2} \right\rfloor = b_k 2^{k-2} + b_{k-1} 2^{k-3} + \cdots + b_2 2^0.$$

(a) Express b_2 as a difference of two floor expressions involving n.
(b) Express b_3 in a similar way as a difference of two floor expressions involving n. Generalize.
(c) For all positive integers n let $B(n)$ denote the number of 1s in the standard binary representation of n. Then $B(1) = 1$, $B(2) = 1$, $B(3) = 2$, $B(4) = 1$, $B(5) = 2$, $B(6) = 2$, $B(7) = 3$, and so on. In the notation we have used in this exercise and Exercise 2.3.29,

$$B(n) = b_0 + b_1 + b_2 + \cdots + b_{k-1} + b_k$$

Into this sum, substitute the formulas for b_0, b_1, b_2, b_3, b_4 etc. derived in earlier parts of this exercise, and simplify a little to derive this formula:

$$B(n) = n - \sum_{p=1}^{\lfloor \lg(n) \rfloor} \left\lfloor \frac{n}{2^p} \right\rfloor. \quad \text{You will need to use the fact that for all positive}$$

integers n, $\left\lfloor \dfrac{n}{2^{\lfloor \lg(n) \rfloor + 1}} \right\rfloor = 0$ (Theorem 2.2.8 (b)).

2.3.31 For each of the following sums, tell what variable the sum is a function of. In other words, if you computed each of those sums, what would the resulting expression be a function of? See Example 2.3.19 for a similar exercise.

(a) $\displaystyle\sum_{k=1}^{m} \frac{m-k}{m+k}$ (b) $\displaystyle\sum_{p=1}^{20} \lfloor \lg(p+t) \rfloor$ (c) $\displaystyle\sum_{i=1}^{v} v^i$ (d) $\displaystyle\sum_{r=p}^{2^p} r^3$ (e) $\displaystyle\sum_{n=i}^{100} i^n$

2.3.32 Evaluate the following sums or express them in closed form.

(a) $50 + 49 + 48 + 47 + \cdots + 10$

(b) $100 + 102 + 104 + 106 + 108 + \cdots + 200$

(c) $1 + 2 + 3 + \cdots + (n-3) + (n-2)$

(Express your answer in terms of n.)

(d) $n + (n+1) + (n+2) + \cdots + (3n-1) + 3n$ (Express your answer in terms of n.)

(e) $\sum_{k=1}^{1000}(2k+7)$

(f) $\sum_{i=n}^{n^2} i$ (Express your answer in terms of n.)

(g) $\frac{1}{n} + \frac{2}{n} + \frac{3}{n} + \cdots + \frac{n}{n}$ (in terms of n)

(h) $n + 2n + 3n + \cdots + n^2$ (express in terms of n)

2.3.33 Evaluate the following sums or express them in closed form.

(a) $25 + 26 + 27 + \ldots + 75$

(b) $100 + 99 + 98 + 97 + \cdots + 31$

(c) $1 + 2 + 3 + \cdots + (n+1) + (n+2)$

(Express your answer in terms of n.)

(d) $2n + (2n+1) + (2n+2) + \cdots + (5n-1) + 5n$ (Express your answer in terms of n.)

(e) $\sum_{k=1}^{100}(7k+2)$

(f) $\sum_{j=\lfloor\sqrt{n}\rfloor}^{2\lfloor\sqrt{n}\rfloor} j$ (Express your answer in terms of n.)

(g) $n^2 + 2n^2 + 3n^2 + \cdots + 100n^2$

(Express your answer in terms of n.)

(h) $\frac{1}{n+1} + \frac{2}{n+1} + \frac{3}{n+1} + \cdots + \frac{n}{n+1}$

(Express your answer interms of n.)

2.3.34 Consider the block of code in Example 2.3.15.

(a) How many times, exactly, will the initialization "$j = 1$" be executed in that block of code?

(b) How many times, exactly, will the inequality "$j < k$" be tested (i.e., evaluated)?

(c) How many times, exactly, will the increment operation "$++j$" be executed?

2.3.35 Give a closed form for each of the following sums.

(a) $2^p + 2^{2p} + 2^{3p} + 2^{4p} + \cdots + 2^{mp} = \sum_{k=1}^{m} 2^{kp}$, where p is a non-zero real constant.
Hint: $2^{xy} = (2^x)^y = (2^y)^x$.

(b) $(a+b)^2 + (a+b)^3 + (a+b)^4 + \cdots + (a+b)^n = \sum_{k=2}^{n}(a+b)^k$, where a and b are real constants with $a+b \neq 1$.

(c) $n + 2n + 4n + 8n + \cdots + n2^n = \sum_{k=0}^{n} n2^k$, where n is a positive integer.

2.3.36 Give a closed form for each of the following sums.

(a) $3^{p+1} + 3^{p+2} + 3^{p+3} + \cdots + 3^{p+m} = \sum_{k=1}^{m} 3^{p+k}$, where p is a non-zero real constant. Hint: $3^{x+y} = 3^x \cdot 3^y$.

(b) $(1+x)^2 + (1+x)^3 + (1+x)^4 + \cdots + (1+x)^n = \sum_{k=2}^{n} (1+x)^k$, where x is a non-zero real constant.

(c) $\dfrac{1}{n} + \dfrac{2}{n} + \dfrac{4}{n} + \dfrac{8}{n} + \cdots + \dfrac{2^n}{n} = \sum_{k=0}^{n} \dfrac{2^k}{n}$, where n is a positive integer.

2.3.37 (a) Let t be a real number not equal to -1. Give a closed form for the following sum:

$$1 + \left(\frac{t}{t+1}\right) + \left(\frac{t}{t+1}\right)^2 + \left(\frac{t}{t+1}\right)^3 + \cdots + \left(\frac{t}{t+1}\right)^n = \sum_{p=0}^{n} \left(\frac{t}{t+1}\right)^p$$

Your answer should be one of the following:

$(i) \dfrac{(t+1)^{n+1} - t^{n+1}}{(t+1)^n}$ $(ii) \dfrac{(t+1)^n - t^{n+1}}{(t+1)^n}$ $(iii) \dfrac{t^n + t^{n+1}}{(t+1)^n}$

(b) Let x be a real number not equal to 1. Give a closed form for the following sum:

$$1 + \sqrt[9]{x} + (\sqrt[9]{x})^2 + (\sqrt[9]{x})^3 + \cdots + (\sqrt[9]{x})^9 = \sum_{r=0}^{9} (\sqrt[9]{x})^r$$

2.3.38 A clever man has done the sultan a tremendous favor, and the sultan asks the man to name his own payment. The man says, "Oh, I don't really want very much. Just place a grain of corn on one square of this chessboard, then 2 grains on another square, and twice 2 grains on another square, and so on, doubling the number of grains each time, until all the squares of the board are filled." How many grains of corn has the man asked to be paid? Express the answer in closed form. (Note: for those who don't know, there are 64 squares on a chessboard.) How many decimal digits will be required to express the answer in base 10?

2.3.39 Prove the part of Theorem 2.3.4 that deals with *increasing* functions.

2.3.40 (a) Prove that if $f(x)$ is a strictly decreasing function defined over an interval $[m-1, n+1]$, where m and n are integers such that $m \leq n$, then

$$\int_{m}^{n+1} f(x)dx < \sum_{k=m}^{n} f(k) < \int_{m-1}^{n} f(x)dx.$$

(b) Prove that if $f(x)$ is a strictly increasing function defined over the interval $[m-1, n+1]$, then

$$\int_{m-1}^{n} f(x)dx < \sum_{k=m}^{n} f(k) < \int_{m}^{n+1} f(x)dx.$$

2.3.41 Use Theorem 2.3.4 to prove that for all real numbers $p > 0$,

$$1 + \frac{1}{p+1}n^{p+1} < \sum_{k=1}^{n} k^p < n^p + \frac{1}{p+1}n^{p+1}$$

2.3.42 Evaluate each of the following sums by computing the values of all the fractions in the sum and adding them all up (use a calculator to do this). In each case, compare your answer with the Euler approximation given in Theorem 2.3.6 (use a calculator for this also).

(a) $\frac{1}{1} + \frac{1}{2} + \frac{1}{3} + \frac{1}{4} + \cdots + \frac{1}{17}$ (b) $\frac{1}{1} + \frac{1}{2} + \frac{1}{3} + \frac{1}{4} + \cdots + \frac{1}{15}$.

2.3.43 (a) Use a calculator to help you compute a fairly exact numerical value for the sum

$$1 + \frac{1}{2} + \frac{1}{3} + \cdots + \frac{1}{1500} = \sum_{k=1}^{1500} \frac{1}{k}.$$

(b) Use a calculator to help you compute a fairly exact numerical value for the sum

$$1 + \frac{1}{2} + \frac{1}{3} + \cdots + \frac{1}{2000} = \sum_{k=1}^{2000} \frac{1}{k}.$$

2.3.44 (a) Use a calculator to help you compute a fairly exact numerical value for the sum

$$\frac{1}{250} + \frac{1}{251} + \frac{1}{252} + \cdots + \frac{1}{700} = \sum_{k=250}^{700} \frac{1}{k}.$$

(b) Use a calculator to help you compute a fairly exact numerical value for the sum

$$\frac{1}{400} + \frac{1}{401} + \frac{1}{402} + \cdots + \frac{1}{650} = \sum_{k=400}^{650} \frac{1}{k}.$$

2.3.45 (a) Explain why $\sum_{k=1}^{mn} \frac{1}{k}$ is roughly equal to $\sum_{k=1}^{m} \frac{1}{k} + \sum_{k=1}^{n} \frac{1}{k}$ for all large positive integers m and n.

(b) Explain why $\sum_{k=1}^{100n} \frac{1}{k}$ is approximately equal to $5.18 + \sum_{k=1}^{n} \frac{1}{k}$ for all large positive integers n. You may use a calculator.

2.3.46 (a) Show that for all large positive integers n the sum $\frac{1}{2n+1} + \frac{1}{2n+2} + \frac{1}{2n+3} + \cdots + \frac{1}{3n}$ is approximately equal to 0.405. You may use a calculator.

(b) Show that for all large positive integers n the sum $\dfrac{1}{n+1} + \dfrac{1}{n+2} + \dfrac{1}{n+3} +$
$\cdots + \dfrac{1}{2n}$ is approximately equal to 0.693. You may use a calculator.

2.3.47 Find an approximate closed form for the sum $\dfrac{n}{1} + \dfrac{n}{2} + \dfrac{n}{3} + \dfrac{n}{4} + \cdots + \dfrac{n}{n}$.

2.3.48 (Index Shifting in Sigma Sums) In Example 2.3.13, p. 41, the instruction is
to write the sum $\dfrac{2}{1^2} + \dfrac{3}{2^2} + \dfrac{4}{3^2} + \dfrac{5}{4^2}$ in sigma summation notation. Three answers
were given:

$$\sum_{k=1}^{4} \frac{k+1}{k^2} \quad \text{or} \quad \sum_{j=0}^{3} \frac{j+2}{(j+1)^2} \quad \text{or} \quad \sum_{r=2}^{5} \frac{r}{(r-1)^2}$$

It is possible to pass from one of these answers to another by a mechanical process
of substitution.

For example, starting from the first sum, which we write in the form $\displaystyle\sum_{k=1}^{k=4} \frac{k+1}{k^2}$
(emphasizing that the upper limit 4 is the last value of k), replace k everywhere
by $j + 1$ to obtain $\displaystyle\sum_{j+1=1}^{j+1=4} \frac{j+1+1}{(j+1)^2}$. Simplification reduces this to the answer

$\displaystyle\sum_{j=0}^{j=3} \frac{j+2}{(j+1)^2}$. Alternatively, replace k everywhere by $r-1$ to obtain $\displaystyle\sum_{r-1=1}^{r-1=4} \frac{r-1+1}{(r-1)^2}$,

which simplifies to $\displaystyle\sum_{r=2}^{r=5} \frac{r}{(r-1)^2}$.

(a) What sum is obtained if you replace k everywhere by $k+a$ in the sum $\displaystyle\sum_{k=a}^{b} \frac{k-a}{k+a}$?

(b) The sum $\displaystyle\sum_{m=2}^{21} \lfloor \lg(m+3)\rfloor)$ is equal to the sum $\displaystyle\sum_{p=?}^{?} \lfloor \lg(p)\rfloor)$ (give the correct limits
of summation in the second sum).

2.3.49 (a) Calculate the exact number of digits in the standard decimal representation of 7702914^5.

(b) Calculate the exact number of bits in the standard binary representation of
1024^{99}.

2.3.50 Use mathematical induction to prove that for every positive integer n,

$$\sum_{k=1}^{n} k^2 = \frac{n(n+1)(2n+1)}{6}.$$

2.3.51 (This exercise requires a knowledge of combinatorial counting techniques.) Let n denote a positive integer. Consider any set S that contains exactly n elements. Label the elements of S by $x_1, x_2, \ldots, x_n$. Now take k to be any positive integer somewhat less than n.

(a) How many ways can we construct a subset of S of size k?
(b) How many ways can we construct a subset of S of size k that contains the last element x_n?
(c) How many ways can we construct a subset of S of size k that contains x_{n-1} but not x_n?
(d) How many ways can we construct a subset of S of size k that contains x_{n-2} but not x_{n-1} and not x_n?
(e) How many ways can we construct a subset of S of size k that contains x_{k+1} but not any of the elements $x_{k+2} \ldots x_n$?
(f) How many ways can we construct a subset of S of size k that contains x_k but not any of the elements $x_{k+1} \ldots x_n$?
(g) Use parts (a) through (f) above to help explain why

$$\binom{n-1}{k-1} + \binom{n-2}{k-1} + \binom{n-3}{k-1} + \cdots + \binom{k+1}{k-1} + \binom{k}{k-1} + \binom{k-1}{k-1} = \binom{n}{k}.$$

(h) Show that if you divide both sides of the equation in part (g) by $\binom{n}{k}$ and perform a lot of cancellations you produce the following summation formula:

$$\frac{k}{n} + \frac{(n-k)k}{n(n-1)} + \frac{(n-k)(n-k-1)k}{n(n-1)(n-2)} + \cdots + \frac{(n-k)(n-k-1)(n-k-2)\ldots(1)k}{n(n-1)(n-2)(n-3)\ldots(k)} = 1.$$

(i) Show that by factoring out a common factor on the left side and then performing a little bit of algebra, you can produce the following summation formula:

$$1 + \frac{n-k}{n-1} + \frac{(n-k)(n-k-1)}{(n-1)(n-2)} + \cdots + \frac{(n-k)(n-k-1)(n-k-2)\ldots(1)}{(n-1)(n-2)(n-3)\ldots(k)} = \frac{n}{k}.$$

(j) Let b denote the integer $n - 1$, and let a denote the integer $n - k$. (Note that $a \le b$.) Then

$$1 + \frac{a}{b} + \frac{a(a-1)}{b(b-1)} + \frac{a(a-1)(a-2)}{b(b-1)(b-2)} + \cdots + \frac{a!}{b(b-1)(b-2)\ldots(b-a+1)} = \underline{\quad\quad}.$$

(fill in the blank on the right side of the equation)

2.4   Factorials

Definition 2.4.1 The *factorial function* is defined on the non-negative integers as follows:

$$0! = 1, \quad 1! = 1, \quad \text{and} \quad n! = 1 \cdot 2 \ldots (n-1) \cdot n = n \cdot (n-1) \ldots 2 \cdot 1 \quad \text{for all } n \ge 2,$$

where "$n!$" is read "n factorial". Alternatively, one can define factorials recursively as follows:

$$0! = 1, \text{ and } n! = (n-1)! \cdot n \quad \text{for all } n \geq 1.$$

Examples 2.4.2 (a) Is $(2n)! = 2(n!)$ in general?

No. The left side is $(2n)! = (2n)(2n-1)(2n-2)\ldots 2 \cdot 1$. The right side is $2[n(n-1)\ldots 2 \cdot 1]$.

(b) Express the following product in terms of factorials: $2 \cdot 4 \cdot 6 \cdot 8 \ldots (2n)$.

The solution involves noticing that each factor is divisible by 2, so we could factor out all the 2s and leave $1 \cdot 2 \cdot 3 \cdot 4 \ldots n$. There are n 2s, so we find that $2 \cdot 4 \cdot 6 \cdot 8 \ldots (2n) = 2^n \cdot n!$.

(c) Express the following product in terms of factorials: $1 \cdot 3 \cdot 5 \cdot 7 \ldots (2n-1)$.

The solution for this involves introducing "missing" factors that could give us a factorial, and then compensating by dividing the expression by the introduced factors. That is,

$$1 \cdot 3 \cdot 5 \cdot 7 \ldots (2n-1) = \frac{1 \cdot 2 \cdot 3 \cdot 4 \cdot 5 \cdot 6 \cdot 7 \cdot 8 \ldots (2n-1)(2n)}{2 \cdot 4 \cdot 6 \cdot 8 \ldots (2n)} = \frac{(2n)!}{2^n \cdot n!}.$$

The factorial function $n!$ grows extremely rapidly as n increases; e.g. $10! \approx 3,000,000$. In fact, with most C/C++ compilers, the value of $13!$ overflows a `long int` variable. Thus, when computing with factorials in a C/C++ program, you'll almost always need to use double precision floating point variables instead of integer or long integer variables.

We can get some idea of how fast the factorial function grows by using our theorem on approximation of sums by integrals. We start by deriving a valuable approximation for $\ln(n!)$, which turns up from time to time in the analysis of algorithms.

Theorem 2.4.3 *For all integers $n \geq 2$,*

$$n \ln(n) - n + 1 < \ln(n!) < (n+1) \ln(n) - n + 1. \tag{2.8}$$

Proof Use Theorem 2.2.3 (a) to write

$$\ln(n!) = \ln(1) + \ln(2) + \ln(3) + \cdots + \ln(n) = \sum_{k=1}^{n} \ln(k).$$

This identity allows us to use Theorem 2.3.4 to obtain lower and upper bounds for $\ln(n!)$. The function $\ln(x)$ is strictly increasing on the open interval $(0, +\infty)$, so Theorem 2.3.4 gives us

$$\ln(1) + \int_{1}^{n} \ln(x)dx < \sum_{k=1}^{n} \ln(k) < \ln(n) + \int_{1}^{n} \ln(x)dx \quad \text{for all } n > 1.$$

From an integral table or integration by parts we find that $\int \ln(x)dx = x\ln(x) - x$, so

$$0 + \left[x\ln(x) - x\right]_{x=1}^{x=n} < \sum_{k=1}^{n} \ln(k) < \ln(n) + \left[x\ln(x) - x\right]_{x=1}^{x=n} \text{ for all } n > 1,$$

and thus

$$[n\ln(n) - n] - [0 - 1] < \ln(n!) < \ln(n) + [n\ln(n) - n] - [0 - 1].$$

This simplifies to the inequalities stated in the theorem.   ∎

Corollary 2.4.4 *For all integers $n > 1$,*

$$e\left(\frac{n}{e}\right)^n < n! < ne\left(\frac{n}{e}\right)^n.$$

Proof Starting from the inequality (2.8) in Theorem 2.4.3, we find that

$$\ln(n^n) - n + 1 < \ln(n!) < \ln(n^n) + \ln(n) - n + 1.$$

Exponentiating gives

$$e^{\ln(n^n)-n+1} < e^{\ln(n!)} < e^{\ln(n^n)-n+\ln(n)+1},$$

which in turn gives

$$n^n e^{-n} e^1 < n! < n^n e^{-n} n e^1 .$$ ∎

If you think of $n!$ as growing roughly at the same rate as n^n you'll be in the right ballpark. When we need an even more accurate estimate for the growth of $n!$ we can use an approximation discovered several hundred years ago by the English mathematician John Stirling.

Theorem 2.4.5 Stirling's Formula: $n! \approx \left(\frac{n}{e}\right)^n \sqrt{2\pi n}$ *for all large values of n. More precisely,*

$$\lim_{n\to\infty} \frac{n!}{(n/e)^n\sqrt{2\pi n}} = 1.$$

Proof This can be found in most books on advanced calculus. The proof is somewhat lengthy.   ∎

In Stirling's approximation, the *percent error* approaches zero as $n \to \infty$. This is the meaning of the formulation involving the limit of 1. By contrast, the *absolute error*, i.e., the difference between the left and right sides of the approximation formula, grows without bound as $n \to \infty$.

2.4.1 Further Examples

Example 2.4.6 Compute $\dfrac{13!}{4!\,9!}$ and $\dfrac{20!}{15!\,5!}$ as efficiently as possible without using a calculator.

Solution $\dfrac{13!}{4!\,9!} = \dfrac{10\cdot 11\cdot 12\cdot 13}{2\cdot 3\cdot 4} = 5\cdot 11\cdot 13 = 715;$

$\dfrac{20!}{15!\,5!} = \dfrac{16\cdot 17\cdot 18\cdot 19\cdot 20}{2\cdot 3\cdot 4\cdot 5} = 8\cdot 17\cdot 6\cdot 19 = 15504.$

Example 2.4.7 In each case below, write out the three largest factors of the product indicated. Assume that n is a positive integer of size at least 6.
(a) $(n^2)!$ (b) $(\lfloor n/2\rfloor)!$ (c) $(2^n)!$

Solution (a) $(n^2)(n^2-1)(n^2-2)\ldots(1)$
(b) $\lfloor n/2\rfloor(\lfloor n/2\rfloor-1)(\lfloor n/2\rfloor-2)\ldots(1)$
(c) $2^n(2^n-1)(2^n-2)\ldots(1)$

Example 2.4.8 Simplify the expressions $\dfrac{(n+1)!}{n!}$, $\dfrac{n!}{(n+2)!}$, and $\dfrac{(n-1)!}{(n+1)!}$, where n is a positive integer.

Solution $\dfrac{(n+1)!}{n!} = n+1;$

$\dfrac{n!}{(n+2)!} = \dfrac{n!}{(n+2)(n+1)\cdot n!} = \dfrac{1}{(n+2)(n+1)}$

$\dfrac{(n-1)!}{(n+1)!} = \dfrac{(n-1)!}{(n-1)!\,n(n+1)} = \dfrac{1}{n(n+1)}$

Example 2.4.9 Calculate $12!$ exactly, and then compare with the value you get using Stirling's approximation and a calculator.

Solution $12! = 479,001,600;$ $\left(\dfrac{12}{e}\right)^{12}\sqrt{2\pi\cdot 12} \approx 475,687,500.$

The percent error in the approximation is $\dfrac{479001600 - 475687500}{479001600}\cdot 100 \approx 0.7\,\%,$ i.e., the error is less than $1\,\%$ (even though the magnitude of the error is more than 3 million).

2.4.2 Exercises

2.4.10 Without using a calculator, find the exact value of
(a) $\dfrac{82!}{3!\,79!}$ (b) $\dfrac{42!}{3!\,39!}.$

2.4.11 In each case below, write out the four largest factors of the product indicated. Assume that n is a positive integer of size at least 16.
(a) $(2n + 3)!$ (b) $(\lfloor \lg(n) \rfloor)!$

2.4.12 In each case below, write out the four largest factors of the product indicated. Assume that n is a positive integer of size at least 3.
(a) $(5n + 2)!$ (b) $(n!)!$

2.4.13 Simplify the following expressions in which n is a positive integer:
(a) $\dfrac{(3n + 1)!}{(3n - 1)!}$ (b) $\dfrac{(2n - 1)!}{(2n + 1)!}$

2.4.14 Use the multiplication key on your calculator to compute 15! (don't use the ! key if your calculator has one). Then use the calculator to compute Stirling's approximation for 15!. Calculate the percent error in the approximation.

2.5   Remainders in Integer Division

In this section we'll explore an arithmetic concept that plays an important role in a number of interesting algorithms. We begin with the mathematical definition of a "remainder" in integer division.

Definition 2.5.1 Let n be any integer and let m be a strictly positive integer. Then the *remainder of n divided by m* (also called the *residue of n modulo m*) is defined to be the integer

$$n - m \left\lfloor \frac{n}{m} \right\rfloor.$$

We denote this integer by the expression $n \bmod m$.

Examples 2.5.2 27 mod 12 = 3 because $27 - 12 \left\lfloor \dfrac{27}{12} \right\rfloor = 27 - 12\lfloor 2.25 \rfloor = 27 - 12(2) = 3$.

33 mod 7 = 5 because $33 - 7 \left\lfloor \dfrac{33}{7} \right\rfloor = 33 - 7\lfloor 4.714 \rfloor = 33 - 7(4) = 5$.

72 mod 9 = 0 because $72 - 9 \left\lfloor \dfrac{72}{9} \right\rfloor = 72 - 9\lfloor 8 \rfloor = 72 - 9(8) = 0$.

6 mod 10 = 6 because $6 - 10 \left\lfloor \dfrac{6}{10} \right\rfloor = 6 - 10\lfloor 0.6 \rfloor = 6 - 10(0) = 6$.

-27 mod 12 = 9 because $-27 - 12 \left\lfloor \dfrac{-27}{12} \right\rfloor = -27 - 12\lfloor -2.25 \rfloor = -27 - 12(-3) = 9$.

-33 mod 7 = 2 because $-33 - 7 \left\lfloor \dfrac{-33}{7} \right\rfloor = -33 - 7\lfloor -4.714 \rfloor = -33 - 7(-5) = 2$.

$$-72 \bmod 9 = 0 \text{ because } -72 - 9 \left\lfloor \frac{-72}{9} \right\rfloor = -72 - 9\lfloor -8 \rfloor = -72 - 9(-8) = 0.$$

$$-6 \bmod 10 = 4 \text{ because } -6 - 10 \left\lfloor \frac{-6}{10} \right\rfloor = -6 - 10\lfloor -0.6 \rfloor = -6 - 10(-1) = 4.$$

Integers of the form $n \bmod 12$ can be visualized in a simple way involving a clock. Imagine that the hours on the face of a clock are labeled $1, 2, 3, \ldots, 11$, and 0 (instead of the usual 12). Then for any positive integer n the integer $n \bmod 12$ will turn out to be the label we stop at if we advance the hour hand clockwise by n hours, starting at label 0. In Examples 2.5.2 we saw that $27 \bmod 12 = 3$ and indeed, advancing the hour hand by 27 h, starting at 0, takes the hand past 0 twice (24 h go by) and brings it to the label 3. As a second example, $60 \bmod 12 = 0$ because advancing the hour hand by 60 h moves it full circle 5 times. For a negative integer n we can obtain $n \bmod 12$ by turning the hour hand backward (counter-clockwise) by $|n|$ hours, starting at label 0. in Examples 2.5.2 we saw that $-27 \bmod 12 = 9$ and now we see that turning the hour hand backward by 27 h brings it to the label 9. As still another example, $-5 \bmod 12 = 7$ because turning the hour hand backward by 5 h brings it to the label 7. And of course $-36 \bmod 12 = 0$.

It is easy to generalize this clock interpretation to expressions of the form $n \bmod m$, where m is any positive integer. Just replace the standard 12 h clock with a clock whose circular face is divided into m periods of time with labels $\{0, 1, 2, \ldots, m - 1\}$.

You might ask whether the integer $n \bmod m$, as we've specified it in Definition 2.5.1, always turns out to belong to the set $\{0, 1, 2, \ldots, m - 1\}$. The following theorem says that it does.

Theorem 2.5.3 *For every integer n and positive integer m the remainder $n \bmod m$ satisfies the inequalities $0 \leq n \bmod m < m$. Furthermore, if $0 \leq n < m$, then $n \bmod m = n$.*

Proof By Theorem 2.1.4 (a), with $\frac{n}{m}$ in place of x, we have $\frac{n}{m} - 1 < \left\lfloor \frac{n}{m} \right\rfloor \leq \frac{n}{m}$. Multiplying throughout by the positive integer m yields $n - m < m \left\lfloor \frac{n}{m} \right\rfloor \leq n$. Subtracting n from each part yields $-m < -n + m \left\lfloor \frac{n}{m} \right\rfloor \leq 0$. Multiplying all parts by -1 reverses the directions of the inequalities to produce $m > n - m \left\lfloor \frac{n}{m} \right\rfloor \geq 0$. This is equivalent to the double inequality stated in the theorem.

For the second part, $0 \leq n < m$ implies $0 \leq \frac{n}{m} < 1$, and so $\left\lfloor \frac{n}{m} \right\rfloor = 0$. It follows that $n \bmod m = n - m \left\lfloor \frac{n}{m} \right\rfloor = n$. ∎

Algorithms that make use of "modular arithmetic" typically involve addition and multiplication of integers followed by a "mod" operation. For example, most encryption algorithms involve computing many remainders of the form $n^p \bmod m$ for positive integers n, p, and m that are several hundred digits long. If the only way this computation could be performed was to first raise n to the power p and afterward carry out the "mod" operation, the computation of n^p would generate integers having trillions of trillions of digits—far too many to be stored in a computer's memory. Fortunately, the computation can be accomplished using the following useful facts about modular arithmetic.

Theorem 2.5.4 *For all integers n and q and positive integers m,*

$$(n + m\,q) \bmod m = n \bmod m.$$

Proof By the formulas in Definition 2.5.1,

$$(n + m\,q) \bmod m = n + m\,q - m \left\lfloor \frac{n + m\,q}{m} \right\rfloor = n + m\,q - m \left\lfloor \frac{n}{m} + q \right\rfloor.$$

Since q is an integer, it can be extracted from the floor by Theorem 2.1.5 (a), which results in

$$n + m\,q - m\,q - m \left\lfloor \frac{n}{m} \right\rfloor = n - m \left\lfloor \frac{n}{m} \right\rfloor.$$

We recognize this last expression as $n \bmod m$ by Definition 2.5.1.   ■

Theorem 2.5.5 Division Theorem. *For every integer n and and positive integer m, there exist unique integers q and r such that $n = q\,m + r$ and $0 \leq r < m$.*

Proof If we denote $\left\lfloor \dfrac{n}{m} \right\rfloor$ by the letter q and $n \bmod m$ by the letter r, then by Definition 2.5.1 and Theorem 2.5.3 the integers q and r satisfy the properties in the theorem. We still must prove that they are unique.

Suppose that we have q_1, q_2, r_1, r_2, $0 \leq r_1, r_2 < m$ such that $n = q_1 m + r_1$ and $n = q_2 m + r_2$. Then

$$q_1 m + r_1 = q_2 m + r_2$$

which can be rewritten as

$$(q_1 - q_2)m = r_2 - r_1$$

which yields

$$q_1 - q_2 = \frac{r_1 - r_2}{m}.$$

This shows that $\dfrac{r_1 - r_2}{m}$ is an integer.

We know that $0 \leq r_2 < m$. From $0 \leq r_1 < m$ we deduce that $-m < -r_1 \leq 0$. By combining these inequalities we get $-m < r_2 - r_1 < m$, which yields $-1 < \dfrac{r_1 - r_2}{m} < 1$. Since we have shown that $\dfrac{r_1 - r_2}{m}$ is an integer, and we now see that is lies strictly between -1 and 1, we must conclude that $\dfrac{r_1 - r_2}{m}$ is 0. This implies that $r_1 = r_2$, which then yields $q_1 = q_2$.   ■

Example 2.5.6 As an example of the usefulness of the Division Theorem 2.5.5, let's use it to prove the following: for all integers n and positive integers m,

$$\left\lfloor \frac{n}{m} \right\rfloor = \left\lceil \frac{n+1}{m} \right\rceil - 1.$$

The proof goes as follows: let q and r denote the unique integers for which $n = qm + r$ and $0 \le r < m$. Then $\left\lfloor \dfrac{n}{m} \right\rfloor = q$. We'll now proceed to prove that $\left\lceil \dfrac{n+1}{m} \right\rceil - 1 = q$. We note that

$$\left\lceil \frac{n+1}{m} \right\rceil - 1 = \left\lceil q + \frac{r+1}{m} \right\rceil - 1 = q + \left\lceil \frac{r+1}{m} \right\rceil - 1.$$

Now $1 \le r + 1 \le m$, so $\dfrac{1}{m} \le \dfrac{r+1}{m} \le 1$, from which it follows that $\left\lceil \dfrac{r+1}{m} \right\rceil = 1$.

Thus,

$$q + \left\lceil \frac{r+1}{m} \right\rceil - 1 = q + 1 - 1 = q$$

as desired. This completes the proof.

Theorem 2.5.7 *Let a and b be any integers, and let m be a positive integer. The remainder $(a+b)$ mod m can be computed by first computing the separate remainders of a and b, adding those remainders together, and then computing the remainder of their sum. In symbols,*

$$(a + b) \bmod m = ((a \bmod m) + (b \bmod m)) \bmod m.$$

Similarly for the difference $a - b$ and the product ab :

$$(a - b) \bmod m = ((a \bmod m) - (b \bmod m)) \bmod m,$$

$$(ab) \bmod m = ((a \bmod m)(b \bmod m)) \bmod m.$$

Proof We start by using Theorem 2.5.5 to express a as $q_1 m + r_1$ and b as $q_2 m + r_2$, where $0 \le r_1, r_2 < m$. In particular, the proof of this theorem tells us that $a \bmod m = r_1$ and $b \bmod m = r_2$. Then

$$(a + b) \bmod m = (q_1 m + r_1 + q_2 m + r_2) \bmod m.$$

We can use Theorem 2.5.4 to reduce the above expression to

$$(r_1 + r_2) \bmod m.$$

The right hand side of the equation in the theorem is equal to

$$((a \bmod m) + (b \bmod m)) \bmod m = (r_1 + r_2) \bmod m$$

The proofs of the equations for the difference $a - b$ and the product ab are very similar and left as an exercise. ∎

As an example, let's use Theorem 2.5.7 to compute the remainder 75^6 mod 11 without first computing 75^6. We begin by computing the remainder 75 mod 11 = 9. Then by Theorem 2.5.7,

$$75^2 \text{ mod } 11 = ((75 \text{ mod } 11)(75 \text{ mod } 11)) \text{ mod } 11 = (9)(9) \text{ mod } 11 = 81 \text{ mod } 11 = 4.$$

Again by Theorem 2.5.7 and the values we've already computed, we find that

$$75^3 \text{ mod } 11 = ((75 \text{ mod } 11)(75^2 \text{ mod } 11)) \text{ mod } 11 = (9)(4) \text{ mod } 11 = 36 \text{ mod } 11 = 3.$$

Finally,

$$75^6 \text{ mod } 11 = ((75^3 \text{ mod } 11)(75^3 \text{ mod } 11)) \text{ mod } 11 = (3)(3) \text{ mod } 11 = 9 \text{ mod } 11 = 9.$$

You may wonder how n mod m is defined when $m < 0$. The answer is that we seldom find it useful to have that operation defined, so we will not give a definition in this text.

2.5.1 Implementation of the Mod Operator in C and C++

We now consider the problem of using C or C++ to compute remainders of pairs of integers. Suppose that n and m are program variables of some integer data type, and let n and m denote the mathematical values of those variables. Assume in what follows that $m > 0$. How can we use the program variables n and m to compute n mod m, the remainder of n divided by m?

By our mathematical definition, $n \text{ mod } m = n - m \left\lfloor \dfrac{n}{m} \right\rfloor$. As we noted in Sect. 2.1, if n is positive, the value of the C/C++ expression n/m is $\left\lfloor \dfrac{n}{m} \right\rfloor$, so the C/C++ expression

$$\text{n} - \text{m} * (\text{n/m}) \tag{2.9}$$

can be used as the remainder n mod m when $n > 0$. Trivially, this expression also gives the correct value when n is 0.

The C and C++ languages have a "modulus" operator, which is denoted by the symbol %. The standards for the C and C++ languages require that the expression n % m have exactly the same value as the expression in formula 2.9 for all non-zero values of m. Thus n % m returns n mod m when $n \geq 0$. (Keep in mind that we are assuming $m > 0$.)

When $n < 0$ the expression n % m will return n mod m if and only if the integer division expression n/m returns $\left\lfloor \dfrac{n}{m} \right\rfloor$. Some C and C++ compilers implement n/m that way. However, the majority of C and C++ compilers implement it as the result of the function truncate applied to the real number $\dfrac{n}{m}$. This function eliminates the fractional part of the real number. The result is that n/m will return $\left\lfloor \dfrac{n}{m} \right\rfloor$ when $n \geq 0$ and $\left\lceil \dfrac{n}{m} \right\rceil$ when $n < 0$. For these compilers the expression n % m does *not* return $n \bmod m$ when $n < 0$, except in those cases where the fractional part of the real number $\dfrac{n}{m}$ is 0.

It would be legal for a compiler to implement the integer division expression n/m as the value obtained by applying the function $\texttt{round}$ to the real number $\dfrac{n}{m}$ when $n < 0$. With this function, the integer division expression n/m will return $\left\lfloor \dfrac{n}{m} \right\rfloor$ if $\dfrac{n}{m} - \left\lfloor \dfrac{n}{m} \right\rfloor > \left\lceil \dfrac{n}{m} \right\rceil - \dfrac{n}{m}$, and will return $\left\lceil \dfrac{n}{m} \right\rceil$ otherwise.

The possibilities for n/m described above are the only sensible choices when $n < 0$, because they are the only ones that produce values for $n \; \% \; m$ that lie strictly between $-m$ and m, which is where we expect "remainders" to fall. Note that for each of these possibilities, n/m returns either $\left\lfloor \dfrac{n}{m} \right\rfloor$ or $\left\lceil \dfrac{n}{m} \right\rceil$.

If the value returned is $\left\lfloor \dfrac{n}{m} \right\rfloor$ then, as we noted earlier, $n \; \% \; m$ will return $n \bmod m$, which by Theorem A.5.3 is non-negative.

If the value returned by n/m is not $\left\lfloor \dfrac{n}{m} \right\rfloor$, then it must be returning $\left\lceil \dfrac{n}{m} \right\rceil$, in which case Theorem 2.1.4 (f) tells us that $\dfrac{n}{m}$ is not an integer and

$$\left\lceil \dfrac{n}{m} \right\rceil = 1 + \left\lfloor \dfrac{n}{m} \right\rfloor.$$

It follows that $n \; \% \; m$ returns the value

$$n - m \left\lceil \dfrac{n}{m} \right\rceil = n - m \left(1 + \left\lfloor \dfrac{n}{m} \right\rfloor\right) = n - m - m \left\lfloor \dfrac{n}{m} \right\rfloor = n \bmod m - m.$$

From this we can deduce that $n\%m + m$ will return $n \bmod m$. By Theorem 2.5.3 we can also see that the value returned by $n\%m$ is negative.

The preceding paragraph implies the following: if $n\%m$ returns a non-negative value, then the value returned by n/m must be $\left\lfloor \dfrac{n}{m} \right\rfloor$, so by the paragraph before that, $n\%m$ returns $n \bmod m$. Similarly, if $n\%m$ returns a negative value, the value of n/m cannot be $\left\lfloor \dfrac{n}{m} \right\rfloor$, so it must be $\left\lceil \dfrac{n}{m} \right\rceil$, and thus $n \; \% \; m \; + \; m$ returns $n \bmod m$. From these observations we can write the following portable function implementing the mathematical mod function.

```
// This function assumes that the parameter m has a strictly positive value.
// It returns n mod m, i.e., the remainder (or residue) of n divided by m,
// which is defined mathematically as n - m * floor(n/m).
// The function has been written so as to be portable among
// C/C++ compilers.
int mod(int n, int m)
{
    if (m <= 0)                    // We do not define n mod m for m <= 0.
      "error; throw an exception"

    int n_percent_m = n % m; // Store it for multiple use

    if (n_percent_m >= 0) // The % operator correctly implements the
      return n_percent_m;          // mathematical mod operator in this case.
    else
      return n_percent_m + m;      // This is when n % m < 0.
}
```

2.5.2 Exercises

2.5.8 Evaluate the following: 3 mod 2;   2 mod 3;   17 mod 5;   34 mod 6; 63 mod 7;   −3 mod 2;   −2 mod 3;   −17 mod 5;   −34 mod 6;   −63 mod 7.

2.5.9 Evaluate n mod 1 for all integers n. Evaluate n mod 2 for all integers n. What are the possible values of n mod 100, where n can be any integer (positive, negative, or zero)?

2.5.10 Prove the identity $(a\,b)$ mod $m = ((a \bmod m)(b \bmod m))$ mod m stated in Theorem 2.5.7.

2.5.11 Prove the following variants of the identities in Theorem 2.5.7:

(a) $(a + b)$ mod $m = (a + (b \bmod m))$ mod m.
(b) $(a\,b)$ mod $m = ((a \bmod m)b)$ mod m.
   These identities are examples of the rule that says when we want to calculate the remainder modulo m of any expression involving addition, subtraction, and multiplication, we can apply the "mod" operator at any or all stages of the evaluation process. For example

$$(a - bc + d) \bmod\ m = ((a \bmod\ m) - b(c \bmod\ m) + d) \bmod\ m.$$

2.5.12 Without using an electronic calculator, compute 21436597^8 mod 11. Show the steps in your computation. Hint: $n^8 = n^4 \times n^4$; $n^4 = n^2 \times n^2$.

2.5.13 Use a similar idea to Example 2.5.6 to prove that for all integers n and m and all positive integers k,

$$\left\lfloor \frac{m}{k} \right\rfloor + \left\lfloor \frac{n - 1 - m}{k} \right\rfloor \geq \left\lfloor \frac{n}{k} \right\rfloor - 1.$$

[*Hint:* express m in terms of its integer quotient and remainder when divided by k, and substitute that expression for m into the left side of the inequality above. Make use of Theorem 2.1.5 (a).]

2.5.14 Prove that for all integers n, $(-n)$ mod $2 = n$ mod 2. Give an example to show that it is not always true that $(-n)$ mod $3 = n$ mod 3.

Fundamental Notations in Analysis of Algorithms

3

In this chapter we introduce the mathematical definition of the fundamental notations used to describe the complexity of an algorithm.

3.1 Little-Oh Notation

When we analyze an algorithm, we typically study the amount of time and space it will require to solve a problem having input of size n, where n can be any positive integer. The amounts of time and space required will typically be functions of n, and we will compare two algorithms by comparing their time and space functions. For this it is important to know the relative growth rates of various standard functions such as $\lg(n)$, $\sqrt{n}$, n^2, 2^n, and so on. In this section we will study these growth rates.

Definition 3.1.1 Let $f(n)$ and $g(n)$ be positive functions defined on the positive integers. We say $f(n)$ *is little-oh of* $g(n)$ as $n \to \infty$ if and only if $\lim\limits_{n\to\infty} \dfrac{f(n)}{g(n)} = 0$, or, equivalently, $\lim\limits_{n\to\infty} \dfrac{g(n)}{f(n)} = +\infty$. In this case we write $f(n) = o(g(n))$ as $n \to \infty$. We will often omit the phrase "as $n \to \infty$" when context makes it clear that "$n \to \infty$" is intended.

It is important to understand that the expression "$f(n) = o(g(n))$" is not an equation in the usual mathematical sense of saying that two numerical quantities are equal. Indeed, the right hand side is not a numerical quantity at all, nor should it be thought of as a function. Instead, we must interpret the little-oh expression as simply a short, convenient way of stating that $\lim\limits_{n\to\infty} \dfrac{f(n)}{g(n)} = 0$, and nothing more.

The expression $= o()$ represents a relation between f and g. We can think of $o(g(n))$ as representing an entire category of functions for which the limit of the

© Springer International Publishing Switzerland 2014

D. Vrajitoru and W. Knight, *Practical Analysis of Algorithms*,

Undergraduate Topics in Computer Science, DOI 10.1007/978-3-319-09888-3_3

fraction with denominator g is 0. The function f belongs to this category or set, but it is customary to use the equal sign instead of $\in$.

Intuitively, $f(n) = o(g(n))$ means that $f(n)$ **grows at a slower rate than** $g(n)$ as $n \to \infty$, or to put it the other way around, $g(n)$ **grows at a faster rate than** $f(n)$ as $n \to \infty$. These phrases, however, do not *define* the little-oh property. Whenever we want to prove any little-oh relationship, we must do it either by using the limit definition or by citing some theorem that we have proved using the limit definition.

On rare occasions we might encounter a situation in which $\lim\limits_{n \to \infty} \dfrac{f(n)}{g(n)} = 0$, where $g(n)$ is always positive but $f(n)$ is negative, or perhaps of mixed sign (positive for some n, negative for others, like $(-1)^n$). In such cases, we will still allow ourselves to write $f(n) = o(g(n))$.

Example 3.1.2 (a) Let's prove that $n^2 = o(n^3)$. In the little-oh definition above, take $f(n) = n^2$ and $g(n) = n^3$. We must prove that $\lim\limits_{n \to \infty} \dfrac{n^2}{n^3} = 0$. This is trivially true because $\dfrac{n^2}{n^3} = \dfrac{1}{n}$ for all positive integers n, and thus $\lim\limits_{n \to \infty} \dfrac{n^2}{n^3} = \lim\limits_{n \to \infty} \dfrac{1}{n} = 0$.

(b) What does it mean if we write $f(n) = o(1)$?
Answer: $\lim\limits_{n \to \infty} f(n) = 0$.

(c) Is it true that the function $3n$ is little-oh of $10n$? You might think so if you believe that $3n$ grows at a slower rate than $10n$. But let's check the definition. Take $f(n) = 3n$ and $g(n) = 10n$. Is it true that $\lim\limits_{n \to \infty} \dfrac{3n}{10n} = 0$? No: $\dfrac{3n}{10n} = \dfrac{3}{10}$ for all positive integers n, so $\lim\limits_{n \to \infty} \dfrac{3n}{10n} = \lim\limits_{n \to \infty} \dfrac{3}{10} = \dfrac{3}{10} \neq 0$.

The way to think about the growth rates of $3n$ and $10n$ is to notice that when n is doubled, $3n$ is doubled and $10n$ is also doubled, so doubling the variable causes each of the functions to grow by the same percent. By contrast, consider what happens with the functions n^2 and n^3 in part (a) above when the variable n is doubled. The function n^2 increases by a factor of 4, while n^3 increases by a factor of 8, so the percent change in n^3 is much greater than the percent change in n^2 when n is doubled.

(d) When we studied logarithms, we said that $\lg(n)$ grows much more slowly than n. Does this mean that $\lg(n) = o(n)$? To find out, we must examine $\lim\limits_{n \to \infty} \dfrac{\lg(n)}{n}$. Both the numerator and denominator approach $+\infty$ as $n \to \infty$, so this limit expression is an "indeterminate form". We can apply L'Hospital's Rule to evaluate this limit. First recall that $\lg(n) = \dfrac{\ln(n)}{\ln(2)} = C \ln(n)$, where C is the constant $1/\ln(2)$. Thus $\lim\limits_{n \to \infty} \dfrac{\lg(n)}{n} = \lim\limits_{n \to \infty} \dfrac{C \cdot \ln(n)}{n} = \lim\limits_{n \to \infty} \dfrac{C/n}{1} = 0$.

(e) We saw in example (a) that n^2 is little-oh of n^3. Is it true that $\lg(n^2)$ is little-oh of $\lg(n^3)$? To find out, we must examine $\lim\limits_{n \to \infty} \dfrac{\lg(n^2)}{\lg(n^3)}$. Since $\lg(n^p) = p \lg(n)$ for all constants p, it follows that $\dfrac{\lg(n^2)}{\lg(n^3)} = \dfrac{2 \cdot \lg(n)}{3 \cdot \lg(n)} = \dfrac{2}{3}$ for all positive integers

n, so $\lim\limits_{n\to\infty} \dfrac{\lg(n^2)}{\lg(n^3)} = \lim\limits_{n\to\infty} \dfrac{2}{3} \neq 0$. We must conclude that $\lg(n^2)$ is not little-oh of $\lg(n^3)$.

When we use the little-oh notation, we usually suppress all multiplicative constants inside the little-oh's parentheses. That is to say, we generally do not write statements such as

$$n^3 = o(5n^7) \quad \text{or} \quad \lg(n) = o(0.3\sqrt{n}),$$

even though both of these statements turn out to be true by the little-oh definition. Instead, we "suppress" the multiplicative constants and write simply

$$n^3 = o(n^7) \quad \text{and} \quad \lg(n) = o(\sqrt{n}).$$

This can always be justified on the basis of the following theorem.

Theorem 3.1.3 *If* $f(n) = o(c\, g(n))$ *for some positive constant* c, *then* $f(n) = o(g(n))$. *Conversely, if* $f(n) = o(g(n))$, *then for every positive constant* c, $f(n) = o(c\, g(n))$ *and* $c\, f(n) = o(g(n))$.

Proof Suppose $f(n) = o(c\, g(n))$ for some positive constant c. By definition, this means that $\lim\limits_{n\to\infty} \dfrac{f(n)}{c\, g(n)} = 0$. We want to prove that $\lim\limits_{n\to\infty} \dfrac{f(n)}{g(n)} = 0$. This is done by noting that $\lim\limits_{n\to\infty} \dfrac{f(n)}{g(n)} = \lim\limits_{n\to\infty} c\dfrac{f(n)}{c\, g(n)} = c \lim\limits_{n\to\infty} \dfrac{f(n)}{c\, g(n)} = c \cdot 0 = 0$. The proof of the second half of this theorem is similar. ∎

Note that the statement of Theorem 3.1.3 violates the convention that we suppress multiplicative constants in the little-oh expressions. It is better, however, to just go ahead and violate the convention than to turn oneself inside-out while following the convention slavishly.

Whenever a logarithm appears in a little-oh expression, we generally write simply "log" instead of "lg" or "ln" or "$\log_{10}$". The reason for this is that all logarithm functions are constant multiples of each other (see Theorem 2.2.6), so in a sense we are suppressing constants of proportionality by simply writing "log".

In the proof of Theorem 3.1.3 we used the fact that for all constants c, $\lim\limits_{n\to\infty} c A(n) = c \lim\limits_{n\to\infty} A(n)$. This is a standard property of limits. Here are some other standard properties.

Theorem 3.1.4 (Facts about Limits): *Suppose* $\lim\limits_{n\to\infty} F(n) = L$ *and* $\lim\limits_{n\to\infty} G(n) = M$ *where* L *and* M *are real numbers (not infinite). Then*

(a) $\lim_{n \to \infty} cF(n) = cL$ for all constants c; that is, $\lim_{n \to \infty} cF(n) = c \lim_{n \to \infty} F(n)$.

(b) $\lim_{n \to \infty} [F(n) + G(n)] = L + M$; i.e., $\lim_{n \to \infty} [F(n) + G(n)] = \lim_{n \to \infty} F(n) + \lim_{n \to \infty} G(n)$.

(c) $\lim_{n \to \infty} [F(n)G(n)] = LM$; i.e., $\lim_{n \to \infty} [F(n)G(n)] = [\lim_{n \to \infty} F(n)][\lim_{n \to \infty} G(n)]$.

(d) $\lim_{n \to \infty} \dfrac{F(n)}{G(n)} = \dfrac{L}{M}$ provided $M \neq 0$; i.e., $\lim_{n \to \infty} \dfrac{F(n)}{G(n)} = \dfrac{\lim_{n \to \infty} F(n)}{\lim_{n \to \infty} G(n)}$.

(e) $\lim_{n \to \infty} [F(n)]^p = L^p$; i.e., $\lim_{n \to \infty} [F(n)]^p = [\lim_{n \to \infty} F(n)]^p$, except when $L = 0$ and $p < 0$.

(f) If $\lim_{n \to \infty} F(n) = +\infty$, then $\lim_{n \to \infty} [b + cF(n)] = +\infty$ provided $c > 0$, and $\lim_{n \to \infty} [b + cF(n)] = -\infty$ if $c < 0$, and $\lim_{n \to \infty} \dfrac{c}{F(n)} = 0$ regardless of the value of c.

(g) If $\lim_{n \to \infty} F(n) = 0$, then $\lim_{n \to \infty} \dfrac{c}{F(n)} = +\infty$ provided $c > 0$ and $F(n) > 0$.

(h) If $\lim_{n \to \infty} F(n) = \lim_{n \to \infty} G(n) = +\infty$, or if $\lim_{n \to \infty} F(n) = \lim_{n \to \infty} G(n) = 0$, then $F(n) + G(n)$ and $F(n) \cdot G(n)$ have the same limit as the individual functions, but $\lim_{n \to \infty} \dfrac{F(n)}{G(n)}$ cannot be determined without further calculation (e.g., by using algebra or L'Hospital's Rule).

(i) If $L > 0$, then for any logarithm function, $\lim_{n \to \infty} \log(F(n)) = \log(L)$. If $F(n) > 0$, then $L = 0$ if and only if $\lim_{n \to \infty} \log(F(n)) = -\infty$.

(j) If b is a real number satisfying $0 < b < 1$, then $\lim_{n \to \infty} b^n = 0$.

(k) **(Sandwich Principle)** If $f(n) \leq g(n) \leq h(n)$ for all large n and $\lim_{n \to \infty} f(n) = \lim_{n \to \infty} h(n) = L$ then $\lim_{n \to \infty} g(n) = L$.

Proof See any calculus text.   ∎

Theorem 3.1.5 Let $P(n) = a_p n^p + a_{p-1} n^{p-1} + \cdots + a_1 n + a_0$ and $Q(n) = b_q n^q + b_{q-1} n^{q-1} + \cdots + b_1 n + b_0$ where $a_p \neq 0$ and $b_q \neq 0$. Then

$$\lim_{n \to \infty} \frac{P(n)}{Q(n)} = \begin{cases} 0 & \text{if } p < q \\ \dfrac{a_p}{b_q} & \text{if } p = q \\ \infty & \text{if } p > q \text{ and } a_p b_q > 0 \\ -\infty & \text{if } p > q \text{ and } a_p b_q < 0 \end{cases}$$

Proof Each of these limits can be proved by applying l'Hospital Rule until one of the sides of the fraction has become a constant.

If $p < q$, then we have the limit of a constant divided by a polynomial of degree $p - q$, which has the limit 0.

If $p = q$, then we are left with the fraction $\dfrac{a_p \, p!}{b_q \, q!} = \dfrac{a_p}{b_q}$.

If $k > m$, then we are left with a simple polynomial of degree $p - q$ that has the limit plus or minus infinity depending on the sign of its coefficient.   ∎

Here are some useful properties of functions having little-oh behavior.

Theorem 3.1.6 *Let $f(n)$, $g(n)$, $h(n)$, $A(n)$, and $B(n)$ be positive functions defined on the positive integers.*

(a) *If $f(n) = o(g(n))$ and $g(n) = o(h(n))$, then $f(n) = o(h(n))$. ("Transitivity of little-oh".)*

(b) *If $f(n) = o(g(n))$, then $f(n)h(n) = o(g(n)h(n))$, and conversely.*

(c) *If $f(n) = o(g(n))$, then for all positive constants c, $c f(n) = o(g(n))$ and $f(n) = o(c\, g(n))$.*

(d) *If $f(n) = o(h(n))$ and $g(n) = o(h(n))$, then $[af(n) + bg(n)] = o(h(n))$ for all constants a and b.*

(e) *If $f(n) = o(A(n))$ and $g(n) = o(B(n))$, then $f(n)g(n) = o(A(n)B(n))$ and $f(n) + g(n) = o(A(n) + B(n))$.*

(f) *If $f(n) \le g(n)$ for all large n and $g(n) = o(B(n))$, then $f(n) = o(B(n))$.*

Proof Let's prove part (f). Suppose $f(n) \le g(n)$ for all large n and $g(n) = o(B(n))$. It follows from these hypotheses that $0 < \dfrac{f(n)}{B(n)} \le \dfrac{g(n)}{B(n)}$ for all large n, and

$$\lim_{n\to\infty} \frac{g(n)}{B(n)} = 0.$$ By the Sandwich Principle (Theorem 3.1.4(k)), $\lim_{n\to\infty} \dfrac{f(n)}{B(n)} = 0.$

This proves that $f(n) = o(B(n))$. Proofs of the other parts are similar.   ∎

The following theorem gives the most important little-oh facts about specific functions. We will use these facts repeatedly in this book.

Theorem 3.1.7 (a) *If p and q are constants such that $p < q$, then $n^p = o(n^q)$. (Small powers of n grow more slowly than larger powers.) In particular, $n^{-r} = o(1)$ and $1 = o(n^r)$ for every positive constant r.*

(b) *For every constant $q > 0$ and every constant $b > 1$, $\log_b(n) = o(n^q)$, but $1 = o(\log_b(n))$. More generally, for all positive constants p and q and every constant $b > 1$, $[\log_b(n)]^p = o(n^q)$.*
   (Logarithm functions grow more slowly than positive power functions.)

(c) *For all constants $p > 0$ and $b > 1$, $n^p = o(b^n)$.*
   (A power function will always grow more slowly in the long run than an increasing exponential function.)

(d) *For all positive constants a and b, if $a < b$ then $a^n = o(b^n)$.*
   (The larger the base of an exponential function, the faster it grows.)

(e) *For all constants $b > 1$, $b^n = o(n!)$.*
   (All exponential functions grow more slowly than the factorial function.)

Proof (a) Assume that p and q are constants such that $p < q$. Let $r = p - q$. Then $\lim\limits_{n\to\infty} \dfrac{n^p}{n^q} = \lim\limits_{n\to\infty} \dfrac{1}{n^r} = 0$ because $r > 0$ and thus $\lim\limits_{n\to\infty} n^r = +\infty$ (Theorem 3.1.4(g)).

(b) Use L'Hospital's Rule:

$$\lim_{n\to\infty} \frac{\log_b(n)}{n^q} = \lim_{n\to\infty} \frac{c\ln(n)}{n^q} = \lim_{n\to\infty} \frac{c/n}{q\,n^{q-1}} = \lim_{n\to\infty} \frac{c/q}{n^q} = 0.$$

More generally,

$$\lim_{n\to\infty} \frac{[\log_b(n)]^p}{n^q} = \lim_{n\to\infty} \left[\frac{\log_b(n)}{n^{q/p}}\right]^p = \left[\lim_{n\to\infty} \frac{\log_b(n)}{n^{q/p}}\right]^p = 0^p$$

by the line above.

(c) Take any constants $p > 0$ and $b > 1$. To prove that $\lim\limits_{n\to\infty} \dfrac{n^p}{b^n} = 0$, it suffices by Theorem 3.1.4(i) to prove that $\lim\limits_{n\to\infty} \ln\left(\dfrac{n^p}{b^n}\right) = -\infty$. Now $\ln\left(\dfrac{n^p}{b^n}\right) = \ln(n^p) - \ln(b^n) = p\ln(n) - n\ln(b)$, and $\lim\limits_{n\to\infty} [p\ln(n) - n\ln(b)] = \lim\limits_{n\to\infty} n\left[p\dfrac{\ln(n)}{n} - \ln(b)\right]$. As $n \to \infty$, $p\dfrac{\ln(n)}{n}$ approaches 0 and $-\ln(b)$ remains a negative constant, so the n in front takes the product to $-\infty$.

(d) Take any positive constants a and b for which $a < b$. Then $0 < a/b < 1$, so $\lim\limits_{n\to\infty} \dfrac{a^n}{b^n} = \lim\limits_{n\to\infty} (a/b)^n = 0$ by Theorem 3.1.4(j).

(e) Take any positive constant $b > 1$. To prove that $\lim\limits_{n\to\infty} \dfrac{b^n}{n!} = 0$, it suffices by Theorem 3.1.4 to prove that $\lim\limits_{n\to\infty} \ln(b^n/n!) = -\infty$. Now

$$\ln\left(\frac{b^n}{n!}\right) = n\ln(b) - \ln(n!) < n\ln(b) - [n\ln(n) - n + 1]$$

by Theorem 2.4.3, so

$$\lim_{n\to\infty} \ln\left(\frac{b^n}{n!}\right) \le \lim_{n\to\infty} n\ln(n)\left[\frac{\ln(b)}{\ln(n)} - 1 + \frac{1}{\ln(n)} - \frac{1}{n\ln(n)}\right].$$

The quantity inside the square brackets approaches -1 as $n \to \infty$, and the quantity $n\ln(n)$ approaches ∞. ∎

Example 3.1.8 (a) $\sqrt{n} = o(n)$ by Theorem 3.1.7(a) because $\sqrt{n} = n^{1/2}$ and $n = n^1$ and $1/2 < 1$. It then follows from Theorem 3.1.6(b) that $n\sqrt{n} = o(n^2)$ and $\sqrt{n}\lg(n) = o(n\log(n))$.

(b) $\lg(n) = o(\sqrt{n})$ by Theorem 3.1.7(b).

(c) $n^{100} = o(2^n)$ by Theorem 3.1.7(c) (take p to be 100 and b to be 2). Also, $2^n = o(n!)$ by Theorem 3.1.7(e). It then follows from Theorem 3.1.6(a) that $n^{100} = o(n!)$.

(d) $10^{1.5n} = o(n!)$ by Theorem 3.1.7(e) because $10^{1.5n} = (10^{1.5})^n = o(n!)$.

(e) Sort the following list of functions into increasing order by rate of growth; i.e., arrange them into a list in which each function is little-oh of the function that follows it:

$$n^2 \quad 2^n \quad \sqrt{n} \quad \sqrt{n}\lg(n) \quad n! \quad 4^n \quad \ln(n) \quad 10n \quad n\lg(n)$$

Solution of part (e)

(1) $\ln(n) = o(\sqrt{n})$ by Theorem 3.1.7(b).
(2) $1 = o(\lg(n))$ by Theorem 3.1.7(b), so $\sqrt{n} = o(\sqrt{n}\lg(n))$ by Theorem 3.1.6(b). (Note that once again we are violating a little-oh convention by writing $o(\lg(n))$ instead of $o(\log(n))$. But how else can we follow the instructions for this example problem?)
(3) $\lg(n) = o(\sqrt{n})$ by Theorem 3.1.7(b), so $\sqrt{n}\lg(n) = o(\sqrt{n}\sqrt{n}) = o(n)$ by Theorem 3.1.6(b), so $\sqrt{n}\lg(n) = o(10n)$ by Theorem 3.1.3.
(4) $1 = o(\lg(n))$ by Theorem 3.1.7(b), so $10 = o(\lg(n))$ by Theorem 3.1.3, so $10n = o(n\lg(n))$ by Theorem 3.1.6(b).
(5) $\lg(n) = o(n)$ by Theorem 3.1.7(b), so $n\lg(n) = o(n \cdot n) = o(n^2)$ by Theorem 3.1.6(b).
(6) $n^2 = o(2^n)$ by Theorem 3.1.7(c).
(7) $2^n = o(4^n)$ by Theorem 3.1.7(d).
(8) $4^n = o(n!)$ by Theorem 3.1.7(e).

The required ordering of the list of functions is

$$\ln(n) \quad \sqrt{n} \quad \sqrt{n}\lg(n) \quad 10n \quad n\lg(n) \quad n^2 \quad 2^n \quad 4^n \quad n!.$$

The following theorem will be very useful in the next section of these notes. It says that if $f(n)$ is little-oh of $g(n)$, then any small multiple of $g(n)$ dominates $f(n)$ when n is large.

Theorem 3.1.9 *If $f(n)$ and $g(n)$ are positive functions defined on the positive integers, and if $f(n) = o(g(n))$, then for every positive number ϵ, no matter how small,*

$$f(n) < \epsilon g(n) \quad \text{for all sufficiently large } n.$$

More precisely, for every positive number ϵ there exists a positive integer n_0 such that for every integer $n > n_0$ we have $f(n) < \epsilon g(n)$.

Proof We are given that $f(n)/g(n) > 0$ and $\lim_{n \to \infty} f(n)/g(n) = 0$. In an xy-plane, draw the horizontal line at height ϵ above the x-axis. Then if we graph $y = f(n)/g(n)$ we know that the graph will lie above the x-axis, but it will approach the x-axis as $n \to \infty$, so eventually the graph will go below the line at height ϵ and stay there for all large n.   ∎

Here is a slight generalization of the little-oh notation.

Definition 3.1.10 Let $f(n)$, $g(n)$, and $A(n)$ be non-negative functions defined for all large integers n. We write $f(n) = g(n) + o(A(n))$ if and only if $f(n) - g(n) = o(A(n))$.

Example 3.1.11 Let's prove that $\lg(2^n + n) = n + o(1)$.

By the definition above, we are required to show that $\lg(2^n + n) - n = o(1)$. That is, we must show that $\displaystyle\lim_{n\to\infty} \frac{\lg(2^n + n) - n}{1} = 0$. We note that $n = \lg(2^n)$, and thus $\lg(2^n + n) - n = \lg(2^n + n) - \lg(2^n) = \lg\left(1 + \dfrac{n}{2^n}\right)$. Since we know that $\displaystyle\lim_{n\to\infty} \frac{n}{2^n} = 0$, it follows that $\displaystyle\lim_{n\to\infty} \lg\left(1 + \dfrac{n}{2^n}\right) = \lg(1+0) = 0$. This completes the proof.

3.1.1 Further Examples

Example 3.1.12 In each case below, state which part(s) of Theorem 3.1.4 justify the given equation.

(a) $\displaystyle\lim_{n\to\infty} \sqrt{F(n)} = \sqrt{\lim_{n\to\infty} F(n)}$ (b) $\displaystyle\lim_{n\to\infty} \frac{3}{\lg(n)} = 0$

(c) $\displaystyle\lim_{n\to\infty} \lfloor\lg(7)\rfloor (2/3)^n = 0$ (d) $\displaystyle\lim_{n\to\infty} \frac{2}{(9/10)^n} = +\infty$

(e) $\displaystyle\lim_{n\to\infty} \ln\left(\frac{2}{n} + \frac{3}{n^2}\right) = -\infty$

Solutions

(a) Use Theorem 3.1.4(e), with $p = 1/2$.
(b) First recall from p. 66 that $\displaystyle\lim_{n\to\infty} \lg(n) = +\infty$. Then use Theorem 3.1.4(f).
(c) By Theorem 3.1.4(j), $\displaystyle\lim_{n\to\infty} (2/3)^n = 0$. Then use Theorem 3.1.4(a).
(d) By Theorem 3.1.4(j), $\displaystyle\lim_{n\to\infty} (9/10)^n = 0$. Then use Theorem 3.1.4(g).

(e) $\displaystyle\lim_{n\to\infty} n = +\infty$ and $\displaystyle\lim_{n\to\infty} n^2 = +\infty$, so $\displaystyle\lim_{n\to\infty} \left(\frac{2}{n} + \frac{3}{n^2}\right) = 0$ by Theorem

3.1.4(b) and (f). Then $\displaystyle\lim_{n\to\infty} \ln\left(\frac{2}{n} + \frac{3}{n^2}\right) = -\infty$ by Theorem 3.1.4(i).

Example 3.1.13 In each case below, demonstrate whether the given expression is true or false.

(a) $\dfrac{1}{10}n^3 = o(n^3)$ (b) $2^n = o(3^n)$ (c) $2^n = o(2^{n+1})$ (d) $6[\ln(n)]^3 = o(n)$

(e) $n^2 \lg(n) = o(n^3)$ (f) $\lg(n^3) = o((1.5)^n)$ (g) $[n \lg(n)]^2 = o(n^2 \sqrt{n})$

Solutions

(a) False: $\lim\limits_{n\to\infty} \dfrac{n^3/10}{n^3} = \lim\limits_{n\to\infty} \dfrac{1}{10} = \dfrac{1}{10} \neq 0$

(b) True by Theorem 3.1.7(d).

(c) False: $\lim\limits_{n\to\infty} \dfrac{2^n}{2^{n+1}} = \lim\limits_{n\to\infty} \dfrac{1}{2} = \dfrac{1}{2} \neq 0$

(d) True: by Theorem 3.1.7(b) we have $[\ln(n)]^3 = o(n)$, so by Theorem 3.1.3, $6[\ln(n)]^3 = o(n)$.

(e) True: we know $\lg(n) = o(n)$ by Theorem 3.1.7(b), so by Theorem 3.1.6(b), $n^2 \lg(n) = o(n^2 n)$, so $n^2 \lg(n) = o(n^3)$. Alternatively, $\lim\limits_{n\to\infty} \dfrac{n^2 \lg(n)}{n^3} = \lim\limits_{n\to\infty} \dfrac{\lg(n)}{n} = 0$ because $\lg(n) = o(n)$.

(f) True: $\lg(n^3) = 3\lg(n)$; by Theorem 3.1.7(b), $\lg(n) = o(n)$; by Theorem 3.1.7(c), $n = o((1.5)^n)$; thus by Theorem 3.1.6(a), $\lg(n) = o((1.5)^n)$; it then follows from Theorem 3.1.6 that $3\lg(n) = o((1.5)^n)$.

(g) True: $[n\lg(n)]^2 = n^2[\lg(n)]^2$; by Theorem 3.1.7(b), $[\lg(n)]^2 = o(\sqrt{n})$, so by Theorem 3.1.6(b) it follows that $n^2[\lg(n)]^2 = o(n^2\sqrt{n})$.

3.1.2 Exercises

3.1.14 In each case below, demonstrate whether the given expression is true or false.

(a) $3n^2\sqrt{n} = o(n^3)$ (b) $\lg(n) = o(\lg(2n))$ (c) $3^n = o(3^{2n})$

(d) $n^4\sqrt{n} = o(n!)$ (e) $\sqrt{\lg(n)} = o(\sqrt[5]{n})$ (f) $n! = o((n+1)!)$

3.1.15 In each case below, demonstrate whether the given expression is true or false.

(a) $5n^2 = o(n\sqrt{n})$ (b) $e^n = o(\pi^n)$ (c) $\lg(e^n) = o(\lg(\pi^n))$

(d) $10\lg(n) = o(2^n)$ (e) $\sqrt{n\lg(n)} = o(n)$ (f) $\ln(n!) = o(n\ln(n))$

3.1.16 Arrange the following functions into a list in which each function is little-oh of the function that follows it.

$$\sqrt{n}\lg(n) \quad \lg(n^{10}) \quad \sqrt{n!} \quad 3 \quad \dfrac{1}{\lg(n)} \quad n^2\lg(n) \quad n^{5/2} \quad 2^{1+\lg(n)} \quad [\lg(n)]^2 \quad \lfloor\lg(10)\rfloor^n$$

The 3 in the list above denotes the constant function whose value is 3 for all n.

3.1.17 (a) Prove Theorem 3.1.6(a). State explicitly where you are using part(s) of Theorem 3.1.4.

[Hint: Use the simple algebraic equation $\dfrac{f(n)}{h(n)} = \dfrac{f(n)}{g(n)} \dfrac{g(n)}{h(n)}$.]

(b) Prove Theorem 3.1.6(b).

(c) Prove Theorem 3.1.6(c). State explicitly where you are using part(s) of Theorem 3.1.4.

(d) Prove Theorem 3.1.6(d). State explicitly where you are using part(s) of Theorem 3.1.4.

3.1.18 (a) Prove that $\dfrac{n^4}{n^2 - 1} = n^2 + o(n)$.

(b) Prove that $\dfrac{n^5 + 3n^3}{n^3 + 5} = n^2 + o(n)$.

3.1.19 Recall that $H(n)$ denotes the n-th harmonic sum and that $H(n) \approx \ln(n)$ for all large n. Is it true that $H(n) = \ln(n) + o(1)$? Justify your answer by citing a theorem stated in Sect. 2.3.

3.1.20 (a) Prove that $\lg(n^2 + n) = 2\lg(n) + o(1)$.
(b) Prove that $\lceil n/3 \rceil = n/3 + o(\lg(n))$. *Hint:* Theorems 2.1.4(b) and 3.1.4(k).

3.2   Big-Oh, Big-Omega, and Big-Theta Notations

When we are analyzing an algorithm to determine its running time $T(n)$ as a function of input size n, we may find that the algorithm is so complicated that the best we can do is find an upper bound for $T(n)$. We now introduce a notation that allows us to express the fact that one function is bounded above by a constant multiple of another.

Definition 3.2.1 Let $f(n)$ and $A(n)$ be positive functions defined on the positive integers. We say $f(n)$ *is big-oh of* $A(n)$ as $n \to \infty$ if and only if there exists a positive constant C such that $f(n) \le CA(n)$ for all large values of n. We denote this by writing $f(n) = O(A(n))$ as $n \to \infty$. We will often omit the phrase "as $n \to \infty$".

When we resort to this notation, it will always be the case that the function $A(n)$ will be something relatively simple, and as with the little-oh notation, we usually do not include a multiplicative constant inside the big-oh parentheses. The whole idea is to suppress irrelevant constants.

When we say "$f(n) \le C A(n)$ for all large values of n" we mean that there exists an n_0 such that for all $n \ge n_0$, $f(n) \le C A(n)$.

Intuitively speaking, an equation of the form $f(n) = O(A(n))$ says that the growth rate of $f(n)$ is *no faster than* (but may be slower than) the growth rate of $A(n)$.

On rare occasions we might encounter a situation in which we wish to compare the growth rate of a function $f(n)$ that's negative or of mixed sign with a positive function $A(n)$. In that case we work with $|f(n)|$. That is, in such a case we write $f(n) = O(A(n))$ if and only if $|f(n)| = O(A(n))$.

Example 3.2.2 (a) Let's prove that $3n + 7 = O(n)$. Here we are taking $f(n) = 3n + 7$ and $A(n) = n$ in the big-oh definition above. Using a little creativity, we see that

$$3n + 7 \leq 3n + 7n = 10n \quad \text{for all positive integers } n,$$

so we can take the constant C in the big-oh definition to be 10.

(b) Let's prove that $7n^2 - 6n = O(n^2)$. This is easy: $7n^2 - 6n < 7n^2$ for all positive integers n, so we can take C in the big-oh definition to be 7.

(c) Let's prove that $\lg(7n^2 + 4n) = O(\log(n))$, where $\log(n)$ can be a logarithm with any base greater than 1.

$$\lg(7n^2 + 4n) < \lg(7n^2 + 4n^2) = \lg(11n^2) = \lg(11) + 2\lg(n) < \lg(n) + 2\lg(n) = 3\lg(n)$$

for all $n > 11$. We can take C in the big-oh definition to be 3 and n_0 to be 12.

(d) Let's prove that $\ln(n!) = O(n\log(n))$. Recall from Theorem 2.4.3 that

$$\ln(n!) < (n + 1)\ln(n + 1) - (n + 1) + 1 \text{ for all } n \geq 2.$$

Observe that when $n \geq 2$ we have $n + 1 < n + n = 2n$ and $-(n + 1) + 1 < 0$, so

$$(n+1)\ln(n+1) - (n+1) + 1 < 2n\ln(2n) = 2n\ln(n) + 2n\ln(2) \leq 2n\ln(n) + 2n\ln(n).$$

Putting this together with the first inequality gives $\ln(n!) < 4n\ln(n)$ when $n \geq 2$. We can take C in the big-oh definition to be 4 to give us $\ln(n!) = O(n\ln(n))$. Since all logarithms are constant multiples of each other, we can write this as $\ln(n!) = O(n\log(n))$ without specifying the base of the logarithm term.

(e) Let's prove that $4\lg(n) = O(n)$. We already know that $\lg(n) = o(n)$. It then follows from Theorem 3.1.9, with ϵ chosen to be 1, that $\lg(n) < n$ for all large values of n. From this it follows that $4\lg(n) < 4n$ for all large values of n, and thus $4\lg(n) = O(n)$.

Example (e) above suggests a general rule, stated as part of the following theorem.

Theorem 3.2.3 *If a function $f(n)$ is little-oh of a positive function $g(n)$, then $f(n)$ is also big-oh of $g(n)$, but $g(n)$ is definitely not big-oh of $f(n)$.*

Proof Suppose $f(n) = o(g(n))$. By Theorem 3.1.9, with $\epsilon = 1$, we have $f(n) \leq g(n)$ for all large n, and thus $f(n) = O(g(n))$ (take $C = 1$ in the definition of big-oh). Is it possible that there also exists a positive constant K such that $g(n) \leq Kf(n)$ for all large n? Suppose so. Then $f(n) \geq (1/K)g(n)$ for all large n, which contradicts Theorem 3.1.9 with $\epsilon = 1/K$. This proof by contradiction shows that no such K can exist. ∎

The big-oh notation gives us a simple way of indicating an *upper bound* for the growth rate of a function. There is an analogous notation for indicating a *lower bound* for a function's growth rate.

Definition 3.2.4 Let $f(n)$ and $A(n)$ be positive functions defined on the positive integers. We say that $f(n)$ *is big-omega of* $A(n)$ as $n \to \infty$ if and only if there exists a positive constant C such that $f(n) \geq CA(n)$ for all large values of n. We denote this by writing $f(n) = \Omega(A(n))$ as $n \to \infty$. We will often omit the phrase "as $n \to \infty$".

As with the little-oh and big-oh notations, we seldom include a multiplicative constant inside the big-omega parentheses. We want to suppress irrelevant constants.

Intuitively speaking, an equation of the form $f(n) = \Omega(A(n))$ says that the growth rate of $f(n)$ is *at least as fast as* (and may even be faster than) the growth rate of $A(n)$.

On those rare occasions when we want to say that $f(n) = \Omega(A(n))$, where $A(n)$ is positive but $f(n)$ is negative or of mixed sign, we interpret this to mean that $|f(n)| = \Omega(A(n))$.

Example 3.2.5 (a) Let's prove that $3n + 7 = \Omega(n)$. This is easy because $3n+7 > 3n$ for all positive integers n, so we can take the constant C in the big-omega definition to be 3.

(b) Let's prove that $3n - 7 = \Omega(n)$. The minus sign makes this a little harder than the problem in part (a) above. Note however that $3n - 7 = 2n + (n - 7) > 2n$ when $n > 7$. Thus for all sufficiently large n, $3n - 7 > 2n$, and this suffices to prove that $3n - 7 = \Omega(n)$ (take the constant C in the definition to be 2).

(c) Let's prove that $\frac{1}{2}n - 6\lg(n) = \Omega(n)$. Begin by writing $\frac{1}{2}n - 6\lg(n) = \frac{1}{4}n + \frac{1}{4}n - 6\lg(n)$. Now we can see that it suffices to prove that $\frac{1}{4}n - 6\lg(n) > 0$ for all large n. This is equivalent to $\frac{1}{4}n > 6\lg(n)$, which is equivalent to $6\lg(n) < \frac{1}{4}n$, which is equivalent to $\lg(n) < \frac{1}{24}n$. We know that $\lg(n) = o(n)$, and so by Theorem 3.1.9 with $\epsilon = 1/24$ we know that $\lg(n) < \frac{1}{24}n$ for all large n.

(d) Let's prove that $\ln(n!) = \Omega(n \log(n))$. Recall from Theorem 2.4.3 that

$$\ln(n!) > n \ln(n) - n + 1 \quad \text{for all } n \geq 2.$$

We begin by writing

$$n\ln(n) - n + 1 = \frac{1}{2}n\ln(n) + \frac{1}{2}n\ln(n) - n + 1 > \frac{1}{2}n\ln(n) + n[\ln(\sqrt{n}) - 1] + 0.$$

When $n > e^2$ we have $\sqrt{n} > e$, so $\ln(\sqrt{n}) > 1$, so $\ln(\sqrt{n}) - 1 > 0$, and thus

$$\frac{1}{2}n\ln(n) + n[\ln(\sqrt{n}) - 1] + 0 > \frac{1}{2}n\ln(n).$$

Putting all this together shows that when $n > e^2$ we have $\ln(n!) > \frac{1}{2}n\ln(n)$. This proves that $\ln(n!) = \Omega(n \log(n))$.

(e) Suppose $f(n)$ and $g(n)$ are two positive functions such that $f(n) = \Omega(g(n))$. Intuitively this means the rate of growth of $f(n)$ is at least as fast as the rate of growth of $g(n)$. This ought to mean that the rate of growth of $g(n)$ is no faster than the rate of growth of $f(n)$, and therefore we ought to be able to say that $g(n) = O(f(n))$. Can we prove that from the definitions of big-oh and big-omega? Yes, it's quite easy.

Since we know that $f(n) = \Omega(g(n))$, we know from the definition of big-omega that there exists a positive constant C such that $f(n) \geq Cg(n)$ for all large n. It follows that $\dfrac{1}{C} f(n) \geq g(n)$ for all large n. Stating this inequality in an equivalent way we see that $g(n) \leq \dfrac{1}{C} f(n)$ for all large n. Since $\dfrac{1}{C}$ is a positive constant, it follows from the definition of big-oh that $g(n) = O(f(n))$.

Sometimes it happens that a function $f(n)$ is both big-oh and big-omega of some other function $A(n)$. Intuitively what this means is that $f(n)$ is growing *at the same rate* as $A(n)$. When this happens, we have a special notation for it.

Definition 3.2.6 Let $f(n)$ and $A(n)$ be positive functions defined on the positive integers. We say $f(n)$ *is big-theta of* $A(n)$ as $n \to \infty$ if and only if $f(n) = O(A(n))$ and $f(n) = \Omega(A(n))$, that is, if and only if there exist positive constants C_1 and C_2 such that $C_1 A(n) \leq f(n) \leq C_2 A(n)$ for all large n. We denote this by writing $f(n) = \Theta(A(n))$ as $n \to \infty$. We will often omit the phrase "as $n \to \infty$".

Example 3.2.7 In Example 3.2.2(d) we showed that $\ln(n!) = O(n \log(n))$. In Example 3.2.5(d) we showed that $\ln(n!) = \Omega(n \log(n))$. It then follows from the definition of big-theta that $\ln(n!) = \Theta(n \log(n))$. Since all logarithms are constant multiples of each other, we can see that $\log_b(n!) = \Theta(n \log(n))$ for any log function $\log_b$ with $b > 1$. Since $\log_b(n!) = \sum_{k=1}^{n} \log_b(k)$ for all positive integers n, we can now state the following important fact (memorize it!), which will often prove useful in analysis of algorithms:

$$\log_b(n!) = \sum_{k=1}^{n} \log_b(k) = \Theta(n \log(n)) \text{ for any logarithm function "} \log_b \text{" with } b > 1.$$

Example 3.2.8 When analyzing nested loops we often find ourselves dealing with sums of the form

$$\sum_{k=1}^{n} k, \qquad \sum_{k=1}^{n} k^2, \qquad \sum_{k=1}^{n} k^3, \qquad \sum_{k=1}^{n} k^4, \qquad \text{and so on.}$$

The first of these sums is an old friend, the Triangular sum, but the others are not familiar to us. Exercise 2.3.41, however, gives a useful upper and lower bound for

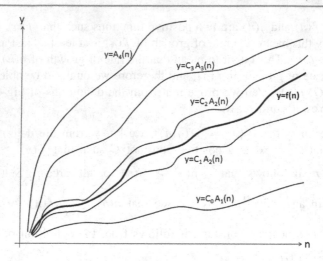

Fig. 3.1 Illustration for $f(n) = \Omega(A_1(n))$; $f(n) = \Theta(A_2(n))$; $f(n) = O(A_3(n))$; $f(n) = o(A_4(n))$

such sums:

$$1 + \frac{n^{p+1}}{p+1} - \frac{1}{p+1} < \sum_{k=1}^{n} k^p < \frac{(n+1)^{p+1}}{p+1} - \frac{1}{p+1} \quad \text{for any real number } p > 0.$$

Thus, for example, $1 + \frac{1}{3}n^3 - \frac{1}{3} < \sum_{k=1}^{n} k^2 < \frac{1}{3}(n+1)^3 - \frac{1}{3}$. Since $\frac{1}{3}(n+1)^3 - \frac{1}{3} < \frac{1}{3}(2n)^3 = \frac{8}{3}n^3$ and $1 + \frac{1}{3}n^3 - \frac{1}{3} > \frac{1}{3}n^3$, we see that $\sum_{k=1}^{n} k^2 = \Theta(n^3)$. It is easy to generalize this argument to obtain the following useful fact:

$$\sum_{k=1}^{n} k^p = \Theta(n^{p+1}) \quad \text{for every real number } p > 0.$$

This is important enough that you should memorize it.

The diagram in Fig. 3.1 illustrates some of the concepts that we have defined up to this point. The functions in Fig. 3.1 are drawn as if they are continuous, but we are assuming only that they are defined for integers n.

The following theorem is the one we most often use to show that a function $f(n)$ is big-theta of a function $A(n)$.

Theorem 3.2.9 *Suppose $f(n)$ and $A(n)$ are positive functions such that*

$$f(n) = bA(n) + b_1 h_1(n) + b_2 h_2(n) + \cdots + b_k h_k(n),$$

where b is a positive constant, the b_i's are non-zero constants, k is a positive constant, and each of the $h_i(n)$ functions satisfies $h_i(n) = o(A(n))$ for $i = 1, 2, \ldots, k$. Then $f(n) = \Theta(A(n))$.

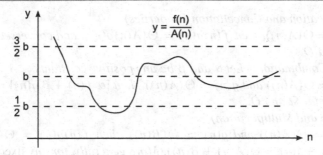

Fig. 3.2 Illustration for $\lim\limits_{n\to\infty} \dfrac{f(n)}{A(n)} = b$

Proof Note first that

$$\frac{f(n)}{A(n)} = b + b_1 \frac{h_1(n)}{A(n)} + b_2 \frac{h_2(n)}{A(n)} + \cdots + b_k \frac{h_k(n)}{A(n)}.$$

By the little-oh hypothesis for each $h_i(n)$ function, we know that $\lim\limits_{n\to\infty} \dfrac{h_i(n)}{A(n)} = 0$

for each of the k functions $h_i(n)$. It follows that $\lim\limits_{n\to\infty} \dfrac{f(n)}{A(n)} = b$. If we draw a graph

of the ratio $\dfrac{f(n)}{A(n)}$ we know that it is going to be something like Fig. 3.2. In this figure,

the graph of $\dfrac{f(n)}{A(n)}$) is drawn as if n could have fractional values, but in actuality the

ratio is defined only for integer values of n.

What we see is that for all large values of n we must have $\dfrac{1}{2}b < \dfrac{f(n)}{A(n)} < \dfrac{3}{2}b$,

which implies that $\dfrac{b}{2}A(n) < f(n) < \dfrac{3b}{2}A(n)$ for all large values of n. By Definition
3.2.6, $f(n) = \Theta(A(n))$.   ∎

Example 3.2.10 (a) Suppose $f(n) = 3\lg(n) - 7\sqrt{n} + \dfrac{1}{2}n\lg(n) - 10n$. Then
   $f(n) = \Theta(n\log(n))$.
(b) Suppose $f(n) = 2n - 7n^2 + 4n\lg(n) + n!$. Then $f(n) = \Theta(n!)$.

The following theorem lists a number of fairly straightforward criteria that one
can use when trying to prove that some function is big-oh, big-omega, or big-theta
of some other function.

Theorem 3.2.11 *Let $f(n)$, $g(n)$, $A(n)$, and $B(n)$ be positive functions defined on
the positive integers.*

(a) *(Transitivity Properties)*
   *If $f(n) = \Theta(A(n))$ and $A(n) = \Theta(B(n))$, then $f(n) = \Theta(B(n))$. Similarly for
   Ω and O.*

(b) *(Multiplication and Cancellation Properties)*
   *If $f(n) = \Theta(A(n))$, then $f(n)g(n) = \Theta(A(n)g(n))$, and conversely. Similarly
   for Ω and O.*

(c) *(Linear Combinations) Let α and β be any positive constants.*
   *If $f(n) = \Theta(A(n))$ and $g(n) = \Theta(A(n))$, then $[\alpha\, f(n) + \beta\, g(n)] = \Theta(A(n))$.
   Similarly for Ω and O.*

(d) *(Addition and Multiplication)*
   *If $f(n) = \Theta(A(n))$ and $g(n) = \Theta(B(n))$, then $f(n)g(n) = \Theta(A(n)B(n))$
   and $f(n) + g(n) = \Theta(A(n) + B(n))$. More generally, for any fixed number of
   functions $f_1(n), \ldots, f_p(n)$ and $A_1(n), \ldots, A_p(n)$, if $f_k(n) = \Theta(A_k(n))$ for
   each pair f_k and A_k, then the product $f_1(n) \ldots f_p(n) = \Theta(A_1(n) \ldots A_p(n))$*

   $$and \sum_{k=1}^{p} f_k(n) = \Theta\left(\sum_{k=1}^{p} A_k(n)\right).\ Similarly\ for\ \Omega\ and\ O.$$

(e) *If $f(k) = \Theta(A(k))$, then* $\displaystyle\sum_{k=1}^{n} f(k) = \Theta\left(\sum_{k=1}^{n} A(k)\right).$ *Similarly for Ω and O.*

   More generally, if $a(n)$ and $b(n)$ are functions whose values are positive integers,

   $$then \sum_{k=a(n)}^{b(n)} f(k) = \Theta\left(\sum_{k=a(n)}^{b(n)} A(k)\right).\ Similarly\ for\ \Omega\ and\ O.$$

(f) *(Division for Big-theta)*
   *If $f(n) = \Theta(A(n))$ and $g(n) = \Theta(B(n))$, then $f(n)/g(n) = \Theta(A(n)/B(n))$.
   (Warning: this statement is not true for O and Ω.)*

(g) *(Using Inequalities)*
   If $f(n) \leq g(n)$ for all large n and $g(n) = O(A(n))$, then $f(n) = O(A(n))$.

   If $f(n) \geq g(n)$ for all large n and $g(n) = \Omega(A(n))$, then $f(n) = \Omega(A(n))$.

   If $g(n) \leq f(n) \leq h(n)$ for all large n and $g(n) = \Theta(A(n))$ and $h(n) = \Theta(A(n))$, then $f(n) = \Theta(A(n))$.

(h) *(Dominant Term)*
   *Suppose $f(n) = \Phi(n) + \psi_1(n) + \cdots + \psi_k(n)$, and $\Phi(n) = \Theta(A(n))$ and
   each $\psi_i(n) = \Theta(h_i(n))$ and each $h_i(n) = o(A(n))$. Then $f(n) = \Theta(A(n))$.
   Similarly for Ω and O.*

Proof For part (a), suppose first that $f(n) = O(A(n))$ and $A(n) = O(B(n))$.
Then by definition, we know that there exist positive constants C_1 and C_2 such that
$f(n) \leq C_1 A(n)$ and $A(n) \leq C_2 B(n)$ for all large n. It follows that $C_1 A(n) \leq C_1 C_2 B(n)$ for all large n, and thus $f(n) \leq (C_1 C_2) B(n)$ for all large n. This proves
that $f(n) = O(B(n))$. Similarly if $f(n) = \Omega(A(n))$ and $A(n) = \Omega(B(n))$.

   The proofs of parts (b) and (c) of the theorem are also similar (and therefore quite
straightforward). So is the proof of the first sentence of part (d). The extension of
part (d) to 3 functions f_1, f_2, f_3 and 3 functions A_1, A_2, A_3 is then trivial, and the
general case for $p > 3$ proceeds by induction on p.

The proof of part (e) is more challenging. By hypothesis, there exist positive constants C and N such that $f(k) \leq CA(k)$ for all $k \geq N$. This leaves open the possibility that $f(k) > CA(k)$ for one or more values of $k < N$. For each k for which that occurs, choose a constant C_k larger than C such that $f(k) \leq C_k A(k)$, and then let C_* denote the largest of all the numbers C and C_k. Then we have found a positive constant C_* such that $f(k) \leq C_* A(k)$ for all integers $k \geq 1$. It follows that for all $n \geq N$ we have $\displaystyle\sum_{k=1}^{n} f(k) \leq \sum_{k=1}^{n} C_* A(k) = C_* \sum_{k=1}^{n} A(k)$ which proves that $\displaystyle\sum_{k=1}^{n} f(k) = O\left(\sum_{k=1}^{n} A(k)\right)$. The proof for Ω and Θ is similar.

To prove part (f) of the theorem, suppose $f(n) = \Theta(A(n))$ and $g(n) = \Theta(B(n))$. Then there exist positive constants C_1, C_2, C_3, and C_4 such that $C_1 A(n) \leq f(n) \leq C_2 A(n)$ and $C_3 B(n) \leq g(n) \leq C_4 B(n)$. It follows that $\dfrac{1}{C_3 B(n)} \geq \dfrac{1}{g(n)} \geq \dfrac{1}{C_4 B(n)}$, or equivalently, $\dfrac{1}{C_4 B(n)} \leq \dfrac{1}{g(n)} \leq \dfrac{1}{C_3 B(n)}$. Combining this with the inequalities involving $A(n)$ and $f(n)$ gives $C_1 A(n)\dfrac{1}{C_4 B(n)} \leq f(n)\dfrac{1}{g(n)} \leq C_4 A(n)\dfrac{1}{C_3 B(n)}$, or $\dfrac{C_1}{C_4}\dfrac{A(n)}{B(n)} \leq \dfrac{f(n)}{g(n)} \leq \dfrac{C_2}{C_3}\dfrac{A(n)}{B(n)}$. This can be written as $D\dfrac{A(n)}{B(n)} \leq \dfrac{f(n)}{g(n)} \leq E\dfrac{A(n)}{B(n)}$, where D is the constant C_1/C_4 and E is the constant C_2/C_3. This proves that $\dfrac{f(n)}{g(n)} = \Theta\left(\dfrac{A(n)}{B(n)}\right)$.

The proofs of the various assertions in part (g) of the theorem are fairly easy to prove, so the proofs will be omitted here. For part (h), we see that there are positive constants C and $c_1, \ldots, c_k$ such that $f(n) \leq CA(n) + c_1 h_1(n) + \cdots + c_k h_k(n)$ for all large n. By Theorem 3.2.9, the sum on the right hand side of this inequality is $\Theta(A(n))$, so it is $O(A(n))$, and thus by part (g), $f(n) = O(A(n))$. ∎

Example 3.2.12 Let's use Theorem 3.2.11 to prove that $(n + 1)\lg(n + 1) = \Theta(n \log(n))$.

Solution We'll show that $n + 1 = \Theta(n)$ and $\lg(n + 1) = \Theta(\log(n))$ and then invoke part (d) of Theorem 3.2.11. By Theorem 3.2.9, $n+1 = \Theta(n)$. For the logarithm part, we'll look at some inequalities involving $\lg(n + 1)$. Clearly $\lg(n) < \lg(n + 1)$, so $\lg(n) = \Omega(\lg(n))$. Also, $lg(n + 1) \leq \lg(n + n) = \lg(2n) = 1 + \lg(n)$. By Theorem 3.2.9, $1 + \lg(n) = \Theta(\lg(n))$, so by Theorem 3.2.11(g), $\lg(n+1) = O(\lg(n))$. We've now shown that $lg(n + 1) = \Omega(\lg(n))$ and $\lg(n + 1) = O(\lg(n))$, which together imply $\lg(n + 1) = \Theta(\lg(n))$. All logarithm functions are constant multiples of each other, so $\Theta(\lg(n))$ is the same as $\Theta(\log(n))$ for any log function.

The following definition extends slightly the notation we have introduced in this section.

Definition 3.2.13 We write $f(n) = g(n) + O(A(n))$ if and only if $f(n) - g(n) = O(A(n))$.
We write $f(n) = g(n) + \Omega(A(n))$ if and only if $f(n) - g(n) = \Omega(A(n))$.
We write $f(n) = g(n) + \Theta(A(n))$ if and only if $f(n) - g(n) = \Theta(A(n))$.

Example 3.2.14 Suppose $f(n) = 2n^2 + n - 3$. Then $f(n) = 2n^2 + \Theta(n)$.

Example 3.2.15 Suppose $f(n) = \dfrac{n^5 + 2}{n^2 + 5}$. Show that $f(n) = n^3 + \Theta(n)$.

Solution We must show that $|f(n) - n^3| = \Theta(n)$. We have

$$|f(n) - n^3| = \left| \frac{n^5 + 2}{n^2 + 5} - n^3 \right| = \left| \frac{n^5 + 2 - n^3(n^2 + 5)}{n^2 + 5} \right| = \left| \frac{n^5 + 2 - n^5 - 5n^3}{n^2 + 5} \right|$$

$$= \left| \frac{2 - 5n^3}{n^2 + 5} \right| = \frac{5n^3 - 2}{n^2 + 5}.$$

By Theorem 3.2.9, $5n^3 - 2 = \Theta(n^3)$ and $n^2 + 5 = \Theta(n^2)$. So by Theorem 3.2.11(f),
$\dfrac{5n^3 - 2}{n^2 + 5} = \Theta(n)$. This completes the argument.

3.2.1 Further Examples

3.2.1.1 Big-Oh Examples

Example 3.2.16 In each case below, demonstrate whether the given expression is true or false.

(a) $5n^3 = O(n^3)$　　　　　　　(b) $100n^2 = O(n^4)$　　(c) $\lg(n^2) = O(\log(n))$
(d) $(n^2 + 7n - 10)^3 = O(n^6)$　(e) $\sqrt{n} = O([\lg(n)]^3)$

Solution

(a) True because $5n^3 \le 5n^3$ for all n. Take C to be 5 in the big-oh definition.
(b) True because $100n^2 \le 100n^4$ for all $n \ge 1$. Take C to be 100 in the big-oh definition.
(c) True because $\lg(n^2) = 2\lg(n) \le 2\log_2(n)$ for all $n \ge 1$. Take C to be 2 in the big-oh definition.
(d) True because $(n^2 + 7n - 10)^3 \le (n^2 + 7n^2)^3 = 8^3 n^6$ for all $n \ge 1$. Take C to be 8^3
(e) False. We can prove this by proving that $[\lg(n)]^3 = o(\sqrt{n})$, for then Theorem 3.2.3 will tell us that $\sqrt{n} \ne O([\lg(n)]^3)$. Theorem 3.1.7 tells us that $[\lg(n)]^3 = o(\sqrt{n})$.

Example 3.2.17 What does it mean to write $f(n) = O(1)$?

Solution The expression $f(n) = O(1)$ means that there exists a positive constant C such that $f(n) \leq C$ for all large n. This implies that $f(n)$ does not grow toward $+\infty$ as $n \to \infty$, but instead $f(n)$ remains bounded above by some constant.

3.2.1.2 Big-Omega Examples

Example 3.2.18 Suppose $f(n) = o(g(n))$, where $f(n)$ and $g(n)$ are positive functions on the positive integers. Prove that $g(n) = \Omega(f(n))$ but $f(n) \neq \Omega(g(n))$.

Solution The proof is similar to the proof for Theorem 3.2.3. Suppose that $f(n) = o(g(n))$. Then by Theorem 3.1.9, with $\epsilon = 1$ we have $f(n) \leq g(n)$ for all large n, and thus $g(n) \geq f(n)$ for all large n, which proves that $g(n) = \Omega(f(n))$. Is it possible that there also exists a positive constant K such that $f(n) \geq K\, g(n)$ for all large n? No, for this would contradict Theorem 3.1.9 with $\epsilon = K$.

Example 3.2.19 In each case below, determine whether the given expression is true or false. You may cite Example 3.2.18 if that is helpful.

(a) $5n^3 = \Omega(n^3)$ $\qquad\qquad$ (b) $100n^2 = \Omega(n^4)$ $\quad$ (c) $\lg(n^2) = \Omega(\log(n))$
(d) $(n^2 + 7n + 10)^3 = \Omega(n^6)$ (e) $\sqrt{n} = \Omega([\lg(n)]^3)$ (f) $\lg(n^2 - 10n) = \Omega(\log(n))$

Solution

(a) True because $5n^3 \geq 5n^3$ for all n. Take C to be 5 in the big-omega definition.
(b) False because $100n^2 = o(n^4)$ by Theorem 3.1.7(a), so by Examples 3.2.18, $100n^2 \neq \Omega(n^4)$.
(c) True because $\lg(n^2) = 2\lg(n) \geq 2\lg(n)$ for all $n \geq 1$. Take C to be 2 in the big-omega definition.
(d) True because $(n^2 + 7n - 10)^3 > (n^2 + 0 + 0)^3 = n^6$ for all n. Take C to be 1 in the big-omega definition.
(e) True. By Theorem 3.1.7(b), $[\lg(n)]^3 = o(\sqrt{n})$. Then invoke the Example 3.2.18.
(f) True because $\lg(n^2 - 10n) = \lg(n(n - 10)) = \lg(n) + \lg(n - 10) \geq \lg(n)$ for $n > 10$.

Example 3.2.20 What does it mean to write $f(n) = \Omega(1)$?

Solution The expression $f(n) = \Omega(1)$ means that there exists a positive constant C such that $f(n) \geq C$ for all large n. In words, this means that $f(n)$ is "bounded away from 0" as $n \to \infty$.

3.2.1.3 Big-Theta Examples

Example 3.2.21 In each case below, determine whether the given expression is true or false. You may cite the solutions to Examples 3.2.16 and 3.2.19 above.

$$(a) 5n^3 = \Theta(n^3) \ (b) 100n^2 = \Theta(n^4) \ (c) \lg(n^2) = \Theta(\log(n))$$

Solution (a) True. See solutions for Examples 3.2.16(a) and 3.2.19(a).
(b) False. See the solution for Examples 3.2.19(b).
(b) True. See solutions for Examples 3.2.16(c) and 3.2.19(c).

Example 3.2.22 What does it mean to write $f(n) = \Theta(1)$?

Solution The expression $f(n) = \Theta(1)$ means that there exist positive constants C_1 and C_2 such that $C_1 \le f(n) \le C_2$ for all large n.

Example 3.2.23 (a) Let $f(n) = 4n^2 + 5n - 8$. Cite theorems to prove that $f(n) = \Theta(n^2)$.
(b) Let $g(n) = 5n^3 + 2^{n-1} - \lg(n^2 + 1)$. Cite theorems to prove that $g(n) = \Theta(2^n)$.

Solution

(a) By Theorem 3.1.7(a), $n = o(n^2)$ and $1 = o(n^2)$, so by Theorem 3.2.9, $f(n) = \Theta(n^2)$.

(b) Write $g(n) = 5n^3 + \frac{1}{2}2^n - \lg(n^2 + 1)$. By Theorem 3.1.7(b), $n^3 = o(2^n)$. Also note that $\lg(n^2 + 1) \le \lg(n^2 + n^2) = \lg(2n^2) = \lg(2) + 2\lg(n) = o(n)$ by Theorem 3.1.7(b), so $\lg(n^2 + 1) = o(n)$. Since $n = o(2^n)$, it follows by Theorem 3.1.6(a) that $\lg(n^2 + 1) = o(2^n)$. Thus by Theorem 3.2.9, $g(n) = \Theta(2^n)$.

Example 3.2.24 In this exercise, refer to the functions f(n) and g(n) defined in Exercise 3.2.23.

(a) By what theorem can we conclude that $f(n)g(n) = \Theta(n^2 2^n)$?
(b) By what theorem can we conclude that $3f(n) + g(n) = \Theta(3n^2 + 2^n)$? Since $3n^2 + 2^n = \Theta(2^n)$, by what theorem can we now conclude that $3f(n) + g(n) = \Theta(2^n)$?
(c) By what theorem can we conclude that $\dfrac{g(n)}{f(n)} = \Theta\left(\dfrac{2^n}{n^2}\right)$?

Solution (a) Theorem 3.2.11(d)   (b) Theorem 3.2.11(d) and (a)   (c) Theorem 3.2.11(f)

Example 3.2.25 Suppose we define a function $f(n)$ by the equation

$$f(n) = \lg(1) + \lg(2) + \lg(3) + \cdots + \lg(n).$$

In Example 3.2.2(d), 3.2.5(d), and 3.2.7(d) we proved that $f(n) = \Theta(n \log(n))$. Now, however, consider applying Theorem 3.2.9 to this function $f(n)$, written "backwards" in the form

$$f(n) = \lg(n) + \cdots + \lg(3) + \lg(2) + \lg(1).$$

Take $A(n)$ in Theorem 3.2.9 to be $\lg(n)$ and the constant b to be 1. Then surely this $A(n)$ "dominates" all the other terms in the sum, so by Theorem 3.2.9, shouldn't we be able to conclude that $f(n) = \Theta(\log(n))$? Of course, this contradicts our earlier proof that $f(n) = \Theta(n \log(n))$. Resolve this paradox.

Solution There are two flaws in the application of Theorem 3.2.9 to the expression $f(n) = \lg(n) + \cdots + \lg(1)$. First, in Theorem 3.2.9, the number k of little-oh functions $h_i(n)$ is *constant*, whereas in the sum above, the number of terms smaller than $\lg(n)$ grows with n. Second, the next term after $\lg(n)$ is $\lg(n-1)$, and this is NOT little-oh of $\lg(n)$. Thus, the hypotheses of Theorem 3.2.9 are not satisfied, so we cannot apply it to prove that $f(n) = \Theta(\log(n))$.

Example 3.2.26 By what theorems and/or examples can we conclude that

$$\sum_{k=1}^{n} (6k^3 - 7k^2 \lg(k) + k\sqrt{k}) = \Theta(n^4)?$$

Solution By Theorems 3.1.7 and 3.2.9, $6k^3 - 7k^2 \lg(k) + k\sqrt{k} = \Theta(k^3)$. It then follows from Theorem 3.2.11(e) that $\sum_{k=1}^{n} (6k^3 - 7k^2 \lg(k) + k\sqrt{k}) = \Theta\left(\sum_{k=1}^{n} k^3\right)$. Next, note that by Example 3.2.8, $\sum_{k=1}^{n} k^3 = \Theta(n^4)$.

Example 3.2.27 Let $f(n)$ denote the number of times the word "hello" will be sent to output by the following code fragment, in which the program variable n has a positive integer value n.

```
int i, j, k;
for (k = 1; k <= n; ++k)
  for (j = 1; j <= k; ++j)
    for (i = 1; i <= j; ++i)
      cout <<"hello"<< endl;
```

Find a simple function $B(n)$ such that $f(n) = \Theta(B(n))$.

Solution Let's begin by examining the two inner loops of the code fragment:

```
for (j = 1; j <= k; ++j)
   for (i = 1; i <= j; ++i)
      cout <<"hello"<< endl;
```

Let k denote the value of the program variable k. When j is 1, the innermost loop will output "hello" 1 time. When j is 2, the innermost loop will output "hello" exactly 2 times. And so on. When j reaches the value k, the innermost loop will output "hello" exactly k times. Thus the two inner loops print "hello" $1 + 2 + \cdots + k$ times, which is exactly $\frac{1}{2}k^2 + \frac{1}{2}k$ times (Triangular Sum).

Now consider the full code fragment we are asked to analyze. When k is 1 the two inner loops output "hello" exactly $\frac{1}{2}1^2 + \frac{1}{2}1$ times. When k is 2, the two inner loops output "hello" exactly $\frac{1}{2}2^2 + \frac{1}{2}2$ times. And so on. When k reaches n, the two inner loops output "hello" exactly $\frac{1}{2}n^2 + \frac{1}{2}n$ times. Altogether then, "hello" will be sent to output exactly this many times:

$$\left(\frac{1}{2}1^2 + \frac{1}{2}1\right) + \left(\frac{1}{2}2^2 + \frac{1}{2}2\right) + \cdots \left(\frac{1}{2}n^2 + \frac{1}{2}n\right) = \sum_{k=1}^{n} \left(\frac{1}{2}k^2 + \frac{1}{2}k\right).$$

Since $\frac{1}{2}k^2 + \frac{1}{2}k = \Theta(k^2)$, it follows from Theorem 3.2.11(e) that $\sum_{k=1}^{n} \left(\frac{1}{2}k^2 + \frac{1}{2}k\right)$

$= \Theta\left(\sum_{k=1}^{n} k^2\right)$. By Example 3.2.8, $\sum_{k=1}^{n} k^2 = \Theta(n^3)$. By Theorem 3.2.11(a) it follows

that $\sum_{k=1}^{n} \left(\frac{1}{2}k^2 + \frac{1}{2}k\right) = \Theta(n^3)$.

The little-oh, big-oh, big-omega, and big-theta ideas can easily be extended to functions of two or more variables. Suppose, for example, that we have positive functions $f(m, n)$ and $A(m, n)$ defined on all pairs of positive integers m and n. We say that $f(m, n) = \Theta(A(m, n))$ as $m \to \infty$ and $n \to \infty$ if and only if there exist positive constants C_1 and C_2 such that $C_1 A(m, n) \leq f(m, n) \leq C_2 A(m, n)$ for all large m and n. Similarly for little-oh, big-oh, and big-omega.

3.2.2 Exercises

3.2.2.1 Big-Oh Exercises

3.2.28 In each case below, demonstrate why the given expression is true.

(a) $2^{n+1} = O(2^n)$ (b) $\sqrt{n^2 + n} = O(n)$ (c) $\lg(\lfloor n^2/2 \rfloor) = O(\log(n))$

3.2.29 In each case below, demonstrate why the given expression is true.

(a) $\lg(n^4) = O(\log(n))$ (b) $(\sqrt{n} + 1)^{10} = O(n^5)$ (c) $\lg(3^{2n}) = O(n)$

3.2.30 Recall that $H(n)$ denotes the n-th harmonic sum and that $H(n) \approx \ln(n)$ for all large n. Prove that $H(n) = O(\log(n))$. Hint: use Theorem 2.3.5.

3.2.31 (a) Prove that $\dfrac{2n}{n+1} = O(1)$. Justify your answer. You may want to review Example 3.2.17.

(b) Prove that $\lg(7 + 1/n) = O(1)$. Justify your answer. You may want to review Example 3.2.17.

3.2.32 Prove that if $f(n) = O(A(n))$ then $\sqrt{f(n)} = O(\sqrt{A(n)})$.

3.2.2.2 Big-Omega Exercises

3.2.33 In each case below, determine why the given expression is true.

(a) $2^{n+1} = \Omega(2^n)$ (b) $\sqrt{n^2 + n} = \Omega(n)$ (c) $\lg(\lfloor n^2/2 \rfloor) = \Omega(\log(n))$

3.2.34 In each case below, demonstrate why the given expression is true.

(a) $\lg(n^4) = \Omega(\log(n))$ (b) $(\sqrt{n} + 1)^{10} = \Omega(n^5)$ (c) $\lg(3^{2n}) = \Omega(n)$

3.2.35 Recall that $H(n)$ denotes the n-th harmonic sum and that $H(n) \approx \ln(n)$ for all large n. Prove that $H(n) = \Omega(\log(n))$. Hint: use Theorem 2.3.5.

3.2.36 (a) Prove that $\dfrac{2n}{n+1} = \Omega(1)$. Justify your answer. You may want to review Example 3.2.20.

(b) Prove that $\lg(7 + 1/n) = \Omega(1)$. Justify your answer. You may want to review Example 3.2.20.

3.2.37 Prove that if $f(n) = \Omega(A(n))$ then $\sqrt{f(n)} = \Omega(\sqrt{A(n)})$.

3.2.2.3 Big-Theta Exercises

3.2.38 Use Exercises 3.2.28 and 3.2.33 to prove (easily) that

(a) $2^{n+1} = \Theta(2^n)$ (b) $\sqrt{n^2 + n} = \Theta(n)$ (c) $\lg(\lfloor n^2/2 \rfloor) = \Theta(\log(n))$

3.2.39 Use Exercises 3.2.29 and 3.2.34 to prove (easily) that

(a) $\lg(n^4) = \Theta(\log(n))$ (b) $(\sqrt{n} + 1)^{10} = \Theta(n^5)$ (c) $\lg(3^{2n}) = \Theta(n)$

3.2.40 Use Exercises 3.2.30 and 3.2.35 to prove (easily) that the harmonic sum function H(n) is $\Theta(\log(n))$.

3.2.41 Use Exercises 3.2.32 and 3.2.37 to prove (easily) that if $f(n) = \Theta(A(n))$ then $\sqrt{f(n)} = \Theta(\sqrt{A(n)})$.

3.2.42 Use Exercises 3.2.31 and 3.2.36 to prove (easily) that

$$\text{(a)} \ \frac{2n}{n+1} = \Theta(1). \qquad \text{(b)} \ \lg(7+1/n) = \Theta(1).$$

3.2.43 By Theorem 2.2.8 (?) we can immediately conclude that $2^{\lfloor \lg(n) \rfloor} = \Theta(?)$. (Replace the question marks appropriately.)

3.2.44 (a) Let $f(n) = 4n^2\sqrt{n} + 6n[\lg(n)]^2 + 7n^2$. Cite theorems to prove that $f(n) = \Theta(n^2\sqrt{n})$.
(b) Let $g(n) = 2^{n+1} + 3(n!) - n^3\sqrt{n}$. Then $g(n) = \Theta(?)$ (replace the question mark by a simple function). Justify your answer by citing appropriate theorems.

3.2.45 In this exercise, refer to the functions $f(n)$ and $g(n)$ defined in Exercise 3.2.44 above.

(a) By what theorem can we conclude that $f(n)g(n) = \Theta(n^2\sqrt{n}\,n!)$?
(b) By what theorem can we conclude that $2f(n) + g(n) = \Theta(2n^2\sqrt{n} + n!)$? Since $2n^2\sqrt{n} + n! = \Theta(n!)$, by what theorem can we now conclude that $2f(n) + g(n) = \Theta(n!)$?
(c) By what theorem can we conclude that $\dfrac{g(n)}{f(n)} = \Theta\left(\dfrac{n!}{n^2\sqrt{n}}\right)$?

3.2.46 Find a simple function $A(n)$ for which $\displaystyle\sum_{k=1}^{n} \frac{k^4 - 2k^2}{5} = \Theta(A(n))$. Justify your answer fully.

3.2.47 Find a simple function $A(n)$ for which $\displaystyle\sum_{k=0}^{n} (2^k + k^2) = \Theta(A(n))$. Justify your answer fully.

3.2.48 Let $g(m)$ denote the number of times the word "hello" will be sent to output by the following code, in which the program variable m is assumed to have some positive integer value m.

```
int i, j, k, n;
for (n = 1; n <= m; ++n)
```

```
for (k = 1; k <= n; ++k)
   for (j = 1; j <= k; ++j)
      for (i = 1; i <= j; ++i)
         cout << "hello" << endl;
```

Find a simple function $D(m)$ such that $g(m) = \Theta(D(m))$. Justify your answer by citing appropriate theorems. You may use the result given in Example 3.2.27.

3.2.49 Let $t(k)$ denote the number of times the instruction "sum += i + j" will be executed by the following code, in which the program variable k is assumed to have some positive integer value k.

```
int i, j, k;
int sum = 0;
for (j = 1; j <= k; ++j)
   for (i = k; i >= j; --i)
      sum += i + j;
```

Find the exact formula for $t(k)$. Find a simple function $A(k)$ such that $t(k) = \Theta(A(k))$. Justify your answer. [Note: you are NOT being asked to compute the final value of the program variable sum.]

3.2.50 Let $f(n)$ denote the number of times the instruction "sum += i + j" will be executed by the following code, in which the program variable n is assumed to have some positive integer value n.

```
int i, j, k;
int sum = 0;
for (k = 1; k <= n; ++k)
   for (j = 1; j <= k; ++j)
      for (i = k; i >= j; --i)
         sum += i + j;
```

Use (among other things) Theorem 3.2.11(e) and Exercise 3.2.49 above to find a simple function $B(n)$ such that $f(n) = \Theta(B(n))$.

3.2.51 Let $g(p)$ denote the number of times the instruction "sum += i + j" will be executed by the following code, in which the program variable p is assumed to have some positive integer value p.

```
int i, j, k, n;
int sum = 0;
for (n = p; n >= 1; --n)
   for (k = 1; k <= n; ++k)
```

```
for (j = 1; j <= k; ++j)
   for (i = k; i >= j; --i)
      sum += i + j;
```

Find a simple function $D(p)$ such that $g(p) = \Theta(D(p))$. You may use Exercise 3.2.50.

3.2.52 Let $f(n)$, $A(n)$, and $B(n)$ be positive functions on the positive integers. Prove that if
$f(n) = \Theta(A(n))$ and $A(n) = o(B(n))$, then $f(n) = o(B(n))$.

3.2.53 Let $f(n)$, $g(n)$, $A(n)$, and $B(n)$ be positive functions on the positive integers. Fill in the blanks in the following statements with the strongest possible answer. You need not give any proof or argument for your answer. (At this point in the chapter, you should have developed such strong intuition about little-oh, big-oh, big-omega, and big-theta, that you can handle these concepts with reasonable confidence and accuracy without the need for lengthy proofs or arguments.)

(a) If $f(n) = \Theta(g(n))$ and $g(n) = \Omega(A(n))$, then $f(n) = $ ___$(A(n))$.
(b) If $f(n) = o(A(n))$ and $A(n) = \Theta(B(n))$, then $f(n) = $ ___$(B(n))$.
(c) If $f(n) = o(A(n))$ and $B(n) = \Theta(A(n))$, then $f(n) = $ ___$(B(n))$.
(d) If $f(n) = o(A(n))$ and $g(n) = O(B(n))$, then $f(n)g(n) = $ ___$($ ___$)$.
(e) If $f(n) = \Theta(A(n))$ and $g(n) = O(B(n))$, then $f(n)g(n) = $ ___$($ ___$)$.

3.2.54 Prove each of the following assertions.

(a) $(1 + 2 + 3 + \cdots + n^3) = \Theta(n^6)$
(b) $1 + (1/2)^2 + (1/2)^3 + \cdots + (1/2)^n = \Theta(1)$
(c) $\dfrac{1}{2} + \dfrac{1}{4} + \dfrac{1}{6} + \ldots + \dfrac{1}{2n} = \Theta(\log(n))$ (You may use Exercise 3.2.40.)
(d) $\sqrt{18n^2 - 1} = \Theta(n)$
(e) $\lfloor \sqrt{n} \rfloor = \Theta(\sqrt{n})$
(f) $(n + 1)^2 = n^2 + \Theta(n)$

3.2.55 Give some justification of the following assertions.

(a) $n^2 + (n^2 + 1) + (n^2 + 2) + \cdots + (n^2 + n^2) = \displaystyle\sum_{k=0}^{n^2}(n^2 + k) = \Theta(n^4)$

(b) $\displaystyle\sum_{k=1}^{n^2} \dfrac{3}{k} = \Theta(\log(n))$ (You may use Theorem 2.3.5.)

(c) $(1 + 3 + 3^2 + \cdots + 3^n) = \Theta(3^n)$
(d) $n\lfloor \lg(n) \rfloor = \Theta(n \log(n))$

(e) (Hard) $\ln(n!) = n \ln(n) + \Theta(n)$ (You may use Theorem 2.4.3.)

3.2.56 The functions listed below are in random order. Order the functions with respect to their growth rates. If two functions have the same growth rate (i.e., each is big theta of the other), then order them based on their difference.

$$n, \quad \ln(n), \quad n \ln(n), \quad n!, \quad 2^n, \quad \ln(n!), \quad n^2, \quad \sqrt{n}, \quad \sqrt{n} \ln(n), \quad n\sqrt{n},$$

$$[\ln(n)]^2, \quad \ln(n^2), \quad n^3, \quad \sqrt{n \ln(n)}, \quad n\sqrt{\ln(n)}, \quad \text{the constant function } 1, \quad n[\ln(n)]^2.$$

3.3   Asymptotic Functions

Occasionally it is useful to have a short way of saying that a function $f(n)$ not only has the same growth rate as a simpler function $A(n)$ but also that $f(n)$ is very nearly equal to $A(n)$ when n is large. The following definition gives us appropriate terminology.

Definition 3.3.1 Let $f(n)$ and $A(n)$ be positive functions defined for all positive integers n. We say that $f(n)$ *is asymptotic to* $A(n)$ *as* $n \to \infty$ if and only if $\lim_{n\to\infty} \dfrac{f(n)}{A(n)} = 1$. We denote this by writing $f(n) \sim A(n)$ as $n \to \infty$. We say that $f(n)$ *is asymptotic to* 0 *as* $n \to \infty$ if and only if $\lim_{n\to\infty} f(n) = 0$. Generally we will omit the phrase "as $n \to \infty$".

Example 3.3.2 $3n^2 + 5n - 12 \sim 3n^2$ because

$$\lim_{n\to\infty} \frac{3n^2 + 5n - 12}{3n^2} = \frac{3}{3} = 1$$

by Theorem 3.1.5. Note that we do NOT suppress the multiplicative constant 3 on the right side of the $\sim$ sign.

Example 3.3.3 $\dfrac{(n+1)2^n}{2^{n+1}+1} \sim \dfrac{n}{2}$ because

$$\lim_{n\to\infty} \frac{\frac{(n+1)2^n}{2^{n+1}+1}}{\frac{n}{2}} = \lim_{n\to\infty} \frac{n+1}{n} \frac{2^{n+1}}{2^{n+1}+1} = \lim_{n\to\infty} \left(1 + \frac{1}{n}\right) \lim_{n\to\infty} \frac{1}{1 + \frac{1}{2^{n+1}}} = 1 \cdot 1 = 1.$$

Example 3.3.4 $H(n) \sim \ln(n)$. The proof uses the Sandwich Principle (Theorem 3.1.4(k)). We proved in Theorem 2.3.5 that $\ln(n) < \ln(n+1) < H(n) < 1 + \ln(n)$. It follows that

$$1 < \frac{H(n)}{\ln(n)} < \frac{1}{\ln(n)} + 1, \text{ and since } \lim_{n\to\infty}\left[\frac{1}{\ln(n)} + 1\right] = 1, \text{ we conclude that } \lim_{n\to\infty} \frac{H(n)}{\ln(n)} = 1.$$

Example 3.3.5 $n! \sim (n/e)^n \sqrt{2\pi n}$ by Stirling's Formula (Theorem 2.4.5).

The following theorem takes care of many cases where we want to prove that one function is asymptotic to another. It is similar to Theorem 3.2.9.

Theorem 3.3.6 *Suppose*

$$f(n) = A(n) + c_1 g_1(n) + c_2 g_2(n) + \cdots + c_k g_k(n),$$

where k is a positive constant, the c_i's are non-zero constants, and $A(n)$ and the $g_i(n)$ functions satisfy $g_i(n) = o(A(n))$ for $i = 1, 2, \ldots, k$. Then $f(n) \sim A(n)$.

Proof Under the hypotheses of this theorem,

$$\lim_{n\to\infty} \frac{f(n)}{A(n)} = \lim_{n\to\infty} \left[1 + c_1 \frac{g_1(n)}{A(n)} + c_2 \frac{g_2(n)}{A(n)} + \cdots + c_k \frac{g_k(n)}{A(n)} \right] = 1 + 0 + 0 + \cdots + 0 = 1.$$

∎

Example 3.3.7 Suppose $f(n) = 3\lg(n) - 6n + 5n^2 + 7n\lg(n)$. Then $f(n) \sim 5n^2$ by Theorem 3.3.6.

Here is an analog for parts of Theorem 3.2.11.

Theorem 3.3.8 *Suppose $f(n) \sim A(n)$ and $g(n) \sim B(n)$ as $n \to \infty$. Then*

(a) $f(n)g(n) \sim A(n)B(n)$ *as $n \to \infty$;*

(b) $\dfrac{f(n)}{g(n)} \sim \dfrac{A(n)}{B(n)}$ *as $n \to \infty$.*

(c) *For all non-zero constants c we have $c\, f(n) \sim c\, A(n)$.*

(d) *If $A(n)$ and $B(n)$ are positive for all large n, then for all positive constants α and β we have*
$\alpha\, f(n) + \beta\, g(n) \sim \alpha\, A(n) + \beta\, B(n)$.

(e) *If $B(n) \equiv A(n)$ (that is, if $f(n)$ and $g(n)$ are asymptotic to the same function), then for all real constants α and β such that $\alpha + \beta \ne 0$ we have $\alpha f(n) + \beta g(n) \sim (\alpha + \beta)\, A(n)$.*

(f) *(Transitivity) If $f(n) \sim A(n)$ and $A(n) \sim D(n)$, then $f(n) \sim D(n)$.*

Proof For part (a) we must prove that $\displaystyle\lim_{n\to\infty} \frac{f(n)g(n)}{A(n)B(n)} = 1$. Since we know

$\displaystyle\lim_{n\to\infty} \frac{f(n)}{A(n)} = 1$ and $\displaystyle\lim_{n\to\infty} \frac{g(n)}{B(n)} = 1$, this is an easy application of Theorem 3.1.4(c).

To prove (b) we use the identity $\dfrac{\left(\dfrac{f(n)}{g(n)}\right)}{\left(\dfrac{A(n)}{B(n)}\right)} = \dfrac{\left(\dfrac{f(n)}{A(n)}\right)}{\left(\dfrac{g(n)}{B(n)}\right)}$ and take the limit as

$n \to \infty$.

The proof of part (c) is trivial.

The proof of part (d) is surprisingly non-trivial. Suppose $A(n)$ and $B(n)$ are positive for all large n. Let any positive constants α and β be given. We must prove that $\lim_{n\to\infty} \dfrac{\alpha f(n) + \beta g(n)}{\alpha A(n) + \beta B(n)} = 1$. This follows from the identity $\dfrac{\alpha f(n) + \beta g(n)}{\alpha A(n) + \beta B(n)} = \dfrac{f(n)}{A(n)} + \left(\dfrac{g(n)}{B(n)} - \dfrac{f(n)}{A(n)}\right) \dfrac{\beta B(n)}{\alpha A(n) + \beta B(n)}$ and the fact that since $\alpha A(n) > 0$ and $\beta B(n) > 0$, the fraction $\dfrac{\beta B(n)}{\alpha A(n) + \beta B(n)}$ is < 1.

Part (e) follows from $\dfrac{\alpha f(n) + \beta g(n)}{(\alpha + \beta) A(n)} = \dfrac{\alpha}{\alpha + \beta} \dfrac{f(n)}{A(n)} + \dfrac{\beta}{\alpha + \beta} \dfrac{g(n)}{A(n)} \to \dfrac{\alpha}{\alpha + \beta} + \dfrac{\beta}{\alpha + \beta} = 1$.

For part (f) we use the identity $\dfrac{f(n)}{D(n)} = \dfrac{f(n)}{A(n)} \cdot \dfrac{A(n)}{D(n)}$ and take the limit as $n \to \infty$. ∎

Example 3.3.9 For an application of the theorem, in Example 3.3.3 we have shown that $f(n) = \dfrac{(n+1)2^n}{2^{n+1}+1} \sim \dfrac{n}{2}$, and in Example 3.3.7 we have shown that $g(n) = 3\lg(n) - 6n + 5n^2 + 7n\lg(n) \sim 5n^2$. Then Theorem 3.3.8(a) tells us that $f(n)g(n) = \dfrac{(n+1)2^n}{2^{n+1}+1}(3\lg(n) - 6n + 5n^2 + 7n\lg(n)) \sim \dfrac{n}{2} 5n^2 = \dfrac{5n^3}{2}$. Theorem 3.3.8(b) tells us that $\dfrac{g(n)}{f(n)} = \dfrac{3\lg(n) - 6n + 5n^2 + 7n\lg(n)}{\frac{(n+1)2^n}{2^{n+1}+1}}$

$= \dfrac{(2^{n+1}+1)(3\lg(n) - 6n + 5n^2 + 7n\lg(n))}{(n+1)2^n} \sim \dfrac{5n^2}{\frac{n}{2}} = 10n$. Theorem 3.3.8(c) tells us that $\dfrac{1}{5}g(n) = \dfrac{3\lg(n) - 6n + 5n^2 + 7n\lg(n)}{5} \sim \dfrac{1}{5}(5n^2) = n^2$. We have used the value $1/5$ for the constant c in the theorem. Theorem 3.3.8(d) tells us that $2f(n) + 3g(n) \sim 2 \cdot \dfrac{n}{2} + 3 \cdot 5n^2 = 15n^2 + n$. We have used the values 2 and 3 for the constants α and β in the theorem respectively. Finally, if we notice that $5n^2 \sim \dfrac{5n^3}{n+1}$, then by Theorem 3.3.8(e) we can conclude that $g(n) \sim \dfrac{5n^3}{n+1}$.

The following theorem connects asymptotic behavior to big-theta behavior.

Theorem 3.3.10 If $f(n) \sim A(n)$, then $f(n) = \Theta(A(n))$ (but not conversely in general).

Proof This is a special case of the following more general theorem, which we will not use in this book. ∎

Theorem 3.3.11 *If* $\lim\limits_{n\to\infty} \dfrac{f(n)}{A(n)}$

(a) *exists and is finite and strictly greater than zero, then* $f(n) = \Theta(A(n))$;
(b) *exists and is zero, then* $f(n) = O(A(n))$, *but* $f(n) \neq \Omega(A(n))$ *and thus* $f(n) \neq \Theta(A(n))$;
(c) *exists and is infinite, then* $f(n) = \Omega(A(n))$, *but* $f(n) \neq O(A(n))$ *and thus* $f(n) \neq \Theta(A(n))$;
(d) *fails to exist, then the test is inconclusive.*

Proof Suppose the limit exists and is finite and strictly greater than zero. Denote it by L. Then for any positive number ϵ the inequality $L - \epsilon < \dfrac{f(n)}{A(n)} < L + \epsilon$ is true for all sufficiently large n (see Fig. 3.2 on p. 77 but replace b by L). By choosing ϵ to be $L/2$ we obtain the inequality $L/2 < \dfrac{f(n)}{A(n)} < 3L/2$ for all sufficiently large n. The numbers $L/2$ and $3L/2$ can serve as the constants C_1 and C_2 in the definition of big-theta. This proves part (a).

For part (b), we can simply cite Theorem 3.2.3.

For part (c), suppose the limit is ∞. This means that no matter what positive constant C we choose, we will have $\dfrac{f(n)}{A(n)} > C$ for all sufficiently large n, so $f(n) > C A(n)$ for all large n. This shows that $f(n) = \Omega(A(n))$. It also shows that there cannot exist a positive constant C such that $f(n) \leq C A(n)$ for all large n.

For part (d) we simply show that when the limit fails to exist we may have various behaviors. First, take $f(n) = n[2 + (-1)^n]$. Then $f(n) = n$ when n is odd and $f(n) = 3n$ when n is even, which means that $f(n) = \Theta(n)$ but $\dfrac{f(n)}{n}$ has no limit as $n \to \infty$. Next, take $f(n) = n[1 + (-1)^n]$. This time $f(n) = O(n)$ but $f(n) \neq \Omega(n)$ because $f(n) = 0$ when n is odd. Note that $\dfrac{f(n)}{n}$ has no limit. Next, take $f(n) = [1 + (-1)^n]n^2 + 3n$. It is not hard to see that $f(n) = \Omega(n)$ but $f(n) \neq O(n)$, and $\dfrac{f(n)}{n}$ has no limit. ∎

The following diagram shows the relationships of the various rates-of-growth that we have studied in this chapter.

$$f(n) = O(A(n)) \quad \leftarrow \quad f(n) = o(A(n))$$

$$f(n) \sim A(n) \quad \rightarrow \quad f(n) = \Theta(A(n)) \nearrow \qquad\qquad \downarrow$$

$$\searrow$$

$$f(n) = \Omega(A(n)) \qquad f(n) \neq \Omega(A(n))$$

3.3.1 Intuitive Analogy

Let us end this chapter with an intuitive analogy for the fundamental notations.

Different species, such as humans and dogs, can have significantly different life spans. A human can be expected to live about 78 years on the average, while for the dogs the average life expectancy is about 12 years, varying quite a lot by breed. Simply comparing the age of a person with that of a dog, elf, turtle, or any other creature, real or imaginary, does not give us much information about their maturity. Even human beings of the same age are not always equally mature.

For a better understanding of the maturity of a creature, we often use "stage of life" terms, such as infant, child, teenager, middle aged, and so on. These terms, although human in nature, are often also applied to other species. Thus, a dog of 2 years of age can be seen as a young adult. To compare the maturity of creatures of different species, we sometimes convert the age using a factor. For example, a commonly used calculation has 1 dog year equal to 7 human years.

If we think of our complexity functions as creatures of various species, and of their value in the variable n as their age at one moment in time, then the fundamental notations are a way to compare their maturity or stage of life. Thus, we can think of the factor 7 in the term "dog years" as the constant c that appears in the definitions of the fundamental notations. Just like the age of a creature needs to be scaled first before it can be compared to that of a creature of a different species, a function can be scaled by a constant to be compared to another one in terms of order of complexity.

Here is a correspondence list of the various notations in terms of maturity, not as a precise mathematical correspondence, but as a way to understand what these notations might mean in terms of comparing the functions.

- $f(n) = O(g(n))$ is analogous to f being *at most* as mature as g.
- $f(n) = \Omega(g(n))$ is analogous to f being *at least* as mature as g.
- $f(n) = \Theta(g(n))$ is analogous to f and g being in the same stage of life, for example, both being young adults.
- $f(n) = o(g(n))$ is analogous to g being more mature than f and in a different generation altogether.
- $f(n) \sim g(n)$ is analogous to f and g being of the same species and current or former classmates in school.

3.3.2 Exercises

3.3.12 (a) Prove that if $f(n) \sim A(n)$ as $n \to \infty$, then $A(n) \sim f(n)$.
(b) Prove that if $g(n) \sim A(n)$ and $h(n) \sim A(n)$ as $n \to \infty$, then $g(n) \sim h(n)$.
(c) Prove that if $f(n) \le g(n) \le h(n)$ and $f(n) \sim A(n)$ and $h(n) \sim A(n)$, then $g(n) \sim A(n)$.

3.3.13 Let $f(n) = 4n^2 + 5n$ and $g(n) = 6n^3 - 7n \lg(n)$ and $h(n) = \dfrac{4n^5 + 1}{n^3 + 4}$.

(a) Verify that $f(n) \sim 4n^2$ and $g(n) \sim 6n^3$ and $h(n) \sim 4n^2$ as $n \to \infty$.

(b) By what theorem can we conclude that $f(n)g(n) \sim 24n^5$?

(c) By what part of Exercise 3.3.12 can we conclude that $f(n) \sim h(n)$?

(d) By what theorem can we conclude that $\dfrac{f(n)}{g(n)} \sim \dfrac{2}{3n}$?

(e) By what theorem can we conclude that $3f(n) + g(n) \sim 6n^2(2+n)$?

(f) By what theorem can we conclude that $\dfrac{3}{2}nf(n) \sim 6n^3$?

3.3.14 Let $f(n) = \dfrac{n^3}{2n-1}$ and $g(n) = 6n^3 + n^2 \lg(n)$ and $h(n) = 6n^3 - n^2$.

(a) Verify that $f(n) \sim \dfrac{n^2}{2}$ and $g(n) \sim 6n^3$ and $h(n) \sim 6n^3$ as $n \to \infty$.

(b) By what theorem can we conclude that $f(n)g(n) \sim 3n^5$?

(c) By what part of Exercise 3.3.12 can we conclude that $g(n) \sim h(n)$?

(d) By what theorem can we conclude that $\dfrac{f(n)}{g(n)} \sim \dfrac{1}{12n}$?

(e) By what theorem can we conclude that $8f(n) + 3g(n) \sim 2n^2(2 + 9n)$?

(f) By what theorem can we conclude that $\dfrac{2}{3}n^3 f(n) \sim \dfrac{1}{3}n^5$?

3.3.15 For each of the assertions below, determine whether it is true or false and justify your answer.

(a) $\lg(n+1) \sim \lg(n)$ *Hint:* $\lg(n+1) = \lg\left(n \cdot \left(1 + \dfrac{1}{n}\right)\right) = \lg(n) + \lg\left(1 + \dfrac{1}{n}\right)$.

(b) $2^{n+1} \sim 2^n$

3.3.16 For each of the assertions below, determine whether it is true or false and justify your answer.

(a) $(n+1)^2 \sim n^2$

(b) $(n+1)! \sim n!$

3.3.17 Suppose $f(n)$ and $g(n)$ are strictly positive functions for which $f(n) \sim g(n)$ as $n \to \infty$. Prove that $\ln(f(n)) = \ln(g(n)) + o(1)$. *Hint:* what can you say about $\ln[f(n)/g(n)]$ as $n \to \infty$?

3.3.18 Suppose $\phi(n) = \psi(n) + o(1)$ as $n \to \infty$. Prove that $2^{\phi(n)} \sim 2^{\psi(n)}$ as $n \to \infty$.

Recurrence Relations

4

In this chapter we introduce the major types of recurrence relations and show how to solve them. Recurrence relations are an important tool in finding the complexity of an algorithm.

4.1   Fundamental Definitions

Example 4.1.1 Suppose you are told that there is a sequence of real numbers $F(0)$, $F(1)$, $F(2)$, ..., whose terms satisfy the following conditions:

$$F(0) = 2 \text{ and } F(n) = \frac{F(n-1)}{1 + F(n-1)} \text{ for all } n \geq 1.$$

How could you use this information to calculate $F(4)$?

Solution The equation that defines $F(n)$ for all $n \geq 1$ is called a *recurrence relation*. It allows us to calculate successive values of $F(n)$, starting with $F(1)$. This method of solving recurrence relations is known as *forward substitution* [14].

$$F(1) = \frac{F(0)}{1 + F(0)} = \frac{2}{1+2} = \frac{2}{3}, \quad F(2) = \frac{F(1)}{1 + F(1)} = \frac{2/3}{1+2/3} = \frac{2}{5},$$

$$F(3) = \frac{F(2)}{1 + F(2)} = \frac{2/5}{1+2/5} = \frac{2}{7}, \quad F(4) = \frac{F(3)}{1 + F(3)} = \frac{2/7}{1+2/7} = \frac{2}{9}.$$

On the basis of these calculations it is natural to conjecture that $F(n) = \dfrac{2}{2n+1}$ for all $n \geq 1$. In fact, it is easy to see that this formula gives the correct value even when $n = 0$. We call this general formula a *solution of the recurrence relation*.

© Springer International Publishing Switzerland 2014
D. Vrajitoru and W. Knight, *Practical Analysis of Algorithms*,
Undergraduate Topics in Computer Science, DOI 10.1007/978-3-319-09888-3_4

To prove that it works for all $n \geq 0$, we substitute the formula $F(n) = \dfrac{2}{2n+1}$ into the recurrence relation $F(n) = \dfrac{F(n-1)}{1 + F(n-1)}$ and see if we get an identity in $n \geq 1$:

$$\frac{2}{2n+1} \overset{?}{=} \frac{\dfrac{2}{2(n-1)+1}}{1 + \dfrac{2}{2(n-1)+1}} = \frac{\dfrac{2}{2n-1}}{1 + \dfrac{2}{2n-1}} = \frac{2}{(2n-1)+2} = \frac{2}{2n+1}.$$

This is, indeed, an identity in $n \geq 1$ (true for all positive integers n), so our conjecture is correct. (*Note* in effect, we have performed the inductive step of a mathematical induction proof here: we showed that if $F(n) = 2/(2n+1)$ for any particular n, then this formula holds for the next larger n. In this instance we were lucky enough to find (by guessing) a nice simple form for the solution of the recurrence relation with the given initial value $F(0) = 2$.)

Now suppose we change the problem so that $F(0) = 5$ but the recurrence relation stays the same. This time we get

$$F(1) = \frac{F(0)}{1+F(0)} = \frac{5}{1+5} = \frac{5}{6}, \qquad F(2) = \frac{F(1)}{1+F(1)} = \frac{5/6}{1+5/6} = \frac{5}{11},$$

$$F(3) = \frac{F(2)}{1+F(2)} = \frac{5/11}{1+5/11} = \frac{5}{16}, \qquad F(4) = \frac{F(3)}{1+F(3)} = \frac{5/16}{1+5/16} = \frac{5}{21},$$

It is easy to guess and to verify that the solution of the problem is $F(n) = \dfrac{5}{5n+1}$ for all $n \geq 0$.

More generally, if $F(0) = a > 0$, then the solution of the problem is $F(n) = \dfrac{a}{an+1}$ for all $n \geq 0$.

This formula is quite typical of the solution of a recurrence relation problem with a given initial value. The solution formula for $F(n)$ depends on the given initial value and on n, but does not explicitly involve $F(n-1)$, $F(n-2)$, etc.

Definition 4.1.2 A *recurrence relation* for a sequence $F(n)$, $n = 0, 1, 2, \ldots$, is an equation of the form

$$F(n) = \Phi(n, F(n-1), F(n-2), \ldots, F(0)),$$

where Φ is a (possibly complicated) formula involving n and some or all of the quantities $F(n-1)$, $F(n-2)$, and so on down to $F(0)$.

A *solution* of the recurrence relation is a formula for $F(n)$, expressed in terms of n, such that the formula satisfies the recurrence relation for all permissible values of n.

The recurrence relation is called a *first order recurrence relation* if and only if it expresses $F(n)$ just in terms of n and $F(n-1)$; for example, the recurrence relation in Example 4.1.1 is first order. Here are a couple more:

$$F(n) = n^2 - F(n-1) \quad \text{and} \quad F(n) = [F(n-1)]^3 + \sqrt{1 + \frac{n}{F(n-1)}}.$$

A *second order recurrence relation* expresses $F(n)$ in terms of n and $F(n-1)$ and $F(n-2)$ only. Here is an example:

$$F(n) = \lfloor \lg(n) \rfloor + F(n-1)[F(n-2) - F(n-1)]^n.$$

Similar definitions hold for *third order, fourth order*, and so on.

A recurrence relation is said to be *linear* if and only if it expresses $F(n)$ in the form

$$F(n) = c_1(n)F(n-1) + c_2(n)F(n-2) + \cdots + c_n(n)F(0) + \phi(n).$$

The functions $c_i(n)$ that appear in the formula above are called the *coefficients* of the various $F(n-i)$'s. Some (or even most) of these coefficient functions may be zero. For example, a second order linear recurrence relation would have the form

$$F(n) = c_1(n)F(n-1) + c_2(n)F(n-2) + \phi(n).$$

If the term $\phi(n)$ is "missing" (more properly, is zero for all values of n), then the linear recurrence relation is said to be *homogeneous*. If the relation is not homogeneous, then we call $\phi(n)$ the *nonhomogeneous term*. The terms "homogeneous" and "nonhomogeneous" are used only when referring to recurrence relations that are linear.

In the definition above of recurrence relation, we assumed that the sequence began with $F(0)$. Of course, some sequences begin with a term $F(1)$ (such a sequence has no $F(0)$ term defined). Others begin with $F(2)$ or $F(3)$ or perhaps even $F(-1)$ (this is rare). The definition of recurrence relation can be extended in an obvious way to cover any such sequence.

It is important not to become "married" to the letters F and n that have been used in the definition of recurrence relation. Thus, for example, an equation of the form

$$T(h) = h\, T(h-1) + \frac{h^2}{T(h-3)} \quad \text{if } h \geq 3$$

is a third order non-linear recurrence relation that defines a sequence $T(3)$, $T(4)$, $T(5)$, ... provided that certain initial values ($T(0)$, $T(1)$, and $T(2)$) are specified. Although we will often use upper case letters such as F and T for the name of a sequence, we are not required to do so. The Fibonacci numbers, which are often discussed in connection with recursion in programming, are usually denoted by lower case letters:

$$f(0) = 0, \quad f(1) = 1, \quad f(n) = f(n-1) + f(n-2) \quad \text{if } n \geq 2.$$

In this chapter we are using function notations for our sequences. Many mathematical texts use *subscript notation* instead of function notation for the terms of an infinite sequence (i.e., a sequence with infinitely many terms). They write

$$x_1,\ x_2,\ x_3,\ x_4,\ \ldots \quad \text{where we write}\quad X(1),\ X(2),\ X(3),\ X(4),\ \ldots$$
$$a_2,\ a_3,\ a_4,\ a_5,\ \ldots \quad \text{where we write}\quad A(2),\ A(3),\ A(4),\ A(5),\ \ldots$$
$$F_0,\ F_1,\ F_2,\ F_3,\ \ldots \quad \text{where we write}\quad F(0),\ F(1),\ F(2),\ F(3),\ \ldots$$

This is merely a notational difference, not a conceptual one. An infinite sequence is defined to be a function whose domain consists of an infinite subset of the integers. Throughout this chapter we could write $F_0, F_1, F_2, F_3, \ldots$ for the terms of a sequence instead of $F(0), F(1), F(2), F(3), \ldots$ The meaning would be exactly the same.

4.1.3 Computational Efficiency: Suppose we want to write a C++ computer program to calculate and print the 10,000th term of the sequence F(n) defined by the recurrence relation

$$F(1) = 1, \quad F(2) = 2, \quad F(n) = F(n-2) - nF(n-1) \quad \text{if } n \geq 3.$$

The lazy way (from the programmer's point of view) would be to write this recursive version:

```
long int F(long int n) // recursive version
{
  if (n <= 2)
    return n;
  else
    return F(n - 2) - n * F(n - 1); // contains 2 recursive calls
}
```

Note The operations in this function will most likely lead to an arithmetic overflow. A careful programmer may want to use a `long long int` type instead, or a custom *software integer* class.

Then the function could be called this way by another function in the program:

```
cout << "10,000th term of the sequence: " << F(10000) << endl;
```

The function calls that would take place as a result of this function call F(10000) can be shown by a tree diagram in which each arrow represents a recursive function call. The top few levels of the tree are shown in Fig. 4.1. This tree is immense and shows that for most integers i less than 10,000, the call $F(i)$ is made over and over again. Thus there is a huge amount of time-consuming, duplicate calculation going on. By contrast, if the code for the function F is written so as to perform its calculations *iteratively*, the function can be quite efficient, despite the fact that the code is somewhat more complicated, as shown in Fig. 4.2.

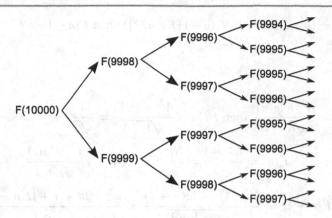

Fig. 4.1 Execution tree

Fig. 4.2 Non recursive version of the function defined in 4.1.3

```
long int F(long int n)    // iterative version
{
    long int last_n     = n,
             F_n         = 2,
             F_n_minus_1 = 1,
             F_n_minus_2;

    if (n <= 2)
        return n;
    for (n = 3; n <= last_n; ++n)
    {
        F_n_minus_2 = F_n_minus_1;
        F_n_minus_1 = F_n;
        F_n = F_n_minus_2 - n * F_n_minus_1;
    }

    return F_n;
}
```

4.1.1   Further Examples

Example 4.1.4 This example is meant to illustrate substitution into formulas for functions.

(a) If $F(n) = \dfrac{n^2 + \lg(n)}{\sqrt{n+1}}$, then $F(1) =?$ $F(8) =?$ $F(t) =?$ $F(n-1) =?$
$F(n) - 1 =?$ $F(\sqrt{n}) =?$ $\sqrt{(F(n))} =?$ $F(\lfloor \lg(n) \rfloor) =?$

(b) If $F(n) = [F(n-1)]^2 - 3F(n-3)$, then $F(t) =?$ $F(n-1) =?$ $F(n+3) =?$
$F(\lfloor n/2 \rfloor) =?$

(c) If $F(n) = (n+2)F(n-2) - (n-1)F(\lfloor n/2 \rfloor)$, then $F(n-1) = ?$ $F(n+3) = ?$
    $F(2n) = ?$ $2F(n) = ?$ $[F(2n)]^2 = ?$

Solutions

(a) If $F(n) = \dfrac{n^2 + \lg(n)}{\sqrt{n+1}}$, then $F(1) = \dfrac{1^2 + \lg(1)}{\sqrt{1+1}} = \dfrac{1}{\sqrt{2}}$,

$$F(8) = \frac{64 + 3}{\sqrt{9}} = \frac{67}{3}, \qquad F(t) = \frac{t^2 + \lg(t)}{\sqrt{t+1}}$$

$$F(n-1) = \frac{(n-1)^2 + \lg(n-1)}{\sqrt{n-1+1}} = \frac{n^2 - 2n + 1 + \lg(n-1)}{\sqrt{n}}$$

$$F(n) - 1 = \frac{n^2 + \lg(n)}{\sqrt{n+1}} - 1, \quad F(\sqrt{n}) = \frac{(\sqrt{n})^2 + \lg(\sqrt{n})}{\sqrt{\sqrt{n}+1}} = \frac{n + (1/2)\lg(n)}{\sqrt{\sqrt{n}+1}},$$

$$\sqrt{F(n)} = \sqrt{\frac{n^2 + \lg(n)}{\sqrt{n+1}}}, \qquad F(\lfloor \lg(n) \rfloor) = \frac{\lfloor \lg(n) \rfloor^2 + \lg(\lfloor \lg(n) \rfloor)}{\sqrt{\lfloor \lg(n) \rfloor + 1}}$$

(b) If $F(n) = [F(n-1)]^2 - 3F(n-3)$, then $F(t) = [F(t-1)]^2 - 3F(t-3)$,
    $F(n-1) = [F(n-2)]^2 - 3F(n-4)$, $F(n+3) = [F(n+2)]^2 - 3F(n)$,
    $F(\lfloor n/2 \rfloor) = [F(\lfloor n/2 \rfloor - 1)]^2 - 3F(\lfloor n/2 \rfloor - 3)$

(c) If $F(n) = (n+2)F(n-2) - (n-1)F(\lfloor n/2 \rfloor)$, then
    $F(n-1) = (n+1)F(n-3) - (n-2)F(\lfloor (n-1)/2 \rfloor)$
    $F(n+3) = (n+5)F(n+1) - (n+2)F(\lfloor (n+3)/2 \rfloor)$,
    $F(2n) = (2n+2)F(2n-2) - (2n-1)F(n)$,
    $2F(n) = 2(n+2)F(n-2) - 2(n-1)F(\lfloor n/2 \rfloor)$,
    $[F(2n)]^2 = [(2n+2)F(2n-2) - (2n-1)F(\lfloor 2n/2 \rfloor)]^2 = [(2n+2)F(2n-2)$
    $- (2n-1)F(n)]^2$

Example 4.1.5 If $F(0) = 2$ and $F(n) = [F(n-1)]^2 - 3F(n-1)$ when $n \geq 1$, find
the numerical value of $F(4)$.

Solution $F(1) = [F(0)]^2 - 3F(0) = 2^2 - 3 \times 2 = -2$,
$F(2) = [F(1)]^2 - 2F(1) = (-2)^2 - 3(-2) = 10$,
$F(3) = [F(2)]^2 - 3F(2) = 10^2 - 3 \times 10 = 70$
$F(4) = [F(3)]^2 - 3F(3) = 70^2 - 3 \times 70 = 4{,}690.$

Example 4.1.6 In each case below, verify by direct substitution that the given formula
for $F(n)$ is a solution of the given recurrence relation. The symbols α and β denote
arbitrary constants.

(a) recurrence relation: $F(n) = F(n-1) + \dfrac{1}{n(n+1)}$; solution: $F(n) = \alpha + \dfrac{n}{n+1}$

(b) recurrence relation: $F(n) = 4F(n-1) + 12F(n-2)$; solution: $F(n) = \alpha(-2)^n + \beta 6^n$

Solutions

(a) We must verify that $\alpha + \dfrac{n}{n+1} = \alpha + \dfrac{n-1}{n-1+1} + \dfrac{1}{n(n+1)}$ for all constants α.

This equation is equivalent to the simpler equation $\dfrac{n}{n+1} = \dfrac{n-1}{n} + \dfrac{1}{n(n+1)}$.

Let's show that the right-hand side of the simpler equation reduces to the left-hand side of the same equation:

$$\frac{n-1}{n} + \frac{1}{n(n+1)} = \frac{(n-1)(n+1)}{n(n+1)} + \frac{1}{n(n+1)} = \frac{n^2-1+1}{n(n+1)}$$

$$= \frac{n^2}{n(n+1)} = \frac{n}{n+1}$$

as desired.

(b) We must verify that

$$\alpha(-2)^n + \beta 6^n = 4[\alpha(-2)^{n-1} + \beta 6^{n-1}] + 12[\alpha(-2)^{n-2} + \beta 6^{n-2}]$$

for all constants α and β. First note that $(-2)^{n-1} = (-2)^n(-2)^{-1} = (-1/2)(-2)^n$ and $(-2)^{n-2} = (-2)^n(-2)^{-2} = (1/4)(-2)^n$. Similarly, $6^{n-1} = (1/6)6^n$ and $6^{n-2} = (1/36)6^n$, so the equation we must verify is logically equivalent to the following equation:

$$\alpha(-2)^n + \beta 6^n = 4[\alpha(-1/2)(-2)^n + \beta(1/6)6^n] + 12[\alpha(1/4)(-2)^n + \beta(1/36)6^n],$$

which is in turn logically equivalent to

$$\alpha(-2)^n + \beta 6^n = \alpha(-2)(-2)^n + \beta(4/6)6^n + \alpha(3)(-2)^n + \beta(12/36)6^n.$$

Combining like terms on the right side gives exactly the expression on the left side.

Example 4.1.7 Find the solution of each of the following problems by computing several terms of the sequence and then making a conjecture. Then verify your conjecture by direct substitution.

(a) $F(0) = 1$, $F(n) = nF(n-1)$ when $n \geq 1$.

(b) $F(0) = 0$, $F(1) = -1$, $F(n) = -2F(n-1) - F(n-2)$ when $n \geq 2$.

Solutions

(a) $F(1) = 1F(0) = 1; F(2) = 2F(1) = 2(1); F(3) = 3F(2) = 3(2)(1) =$
3!, $F(4) = 4F(3) = 4(3)(2)(1) = 4!$; it appears that $F(n) = n!$ for all $n \geq 0$.
Verification by direct substitution: Is $F(0) = 1$? Yes: $0! = 1$. Does the formula
$F(n) = n!$ satisfy the recurrence relation? Yes: $n! = n(n-1)!$ for all $n \geq 1$.
(b) $F(2) = -2F(1) - F(0) = -2(-1) - 0 = 2; F(3) = -2F(2) - F(1) =$
$-2(2) - (-1) = -3; F(4) = -2F(3) - F(2) = -2(-3) - 2 = 4; F(5) =$
$-2F(4) - F(3) = -2(4) - (-3) = -5$; It appears that $F(n) = (-1)^n n$ for all
$n \geq 0$. Verification by direct substitution: Is $F(0) = 0$? Yes: $(-1)^0 0 = 0$.
Is $F(1) = -1$? Yes: $(-1)^1 = -1$. Does the formula $F(n) = (-1)^n n$ satisfy the
recurrence relation? Yes: $(-1)^n n = (-2)[(-1)^{n-1}(n-1)] - [(-1)^{n-2}(n-2)]$
for all $n \geq 2$, as some routine algebra will show (use the fact that $(-1)^{n-2} =$
$(-1)^n$).

Example 4.1.8 State the order of each of the following recurrence relations. Also
state whether the recurrence relation is linear, and if it is, state whether it is homogeneous. If it is linear but non-homogeneous, give the non-homogeneous term.

(a) $F(n) = [F(n-1)]^2 - 3F(n-3)$ 　　　(b) $F(n) = F(n-1) + 2F(n-2) + 3(2^{n-1})$

(c) $F(n) = \dfrac{F(n-1) + F(n-2)}{2}$ 　　　(d) $F(n) = \dfrac{F(n-1) + 1}{2}$

(e) $F(n) = \left(\dfrac{n^2 + \lg(n)}{\sqrt{n+1}}\right) F(n-1) + 3 \times 2^{n-1} F(n-4) - 2 + n + \dfrac{1}{n(n+1)} + \lg\left(\dfrac{n! + 2n}{\sqrt{2\pi n}}\right)$

(f) $\dfrac{2^n F(n) - 2^{n+1} F(n-1)}{F(n-2) + F(n-3)} = 1 + \lfloor \lg(n! + 1) \rfloor$ (g) $F(n) = F(\lfloor n/2 \rfloor) + F(\lceil n/2 \rceil)$

Solutions

(a) Third order, non-linear.
(b) Second order, linear, non-homogeneous; the non-homogeneous term is $3 \times 2^{n-1}$.
(c) Rewriting the relation in the form $F(n) = \dfrac{1}{2}F(n-1) + \dfrac{1}{2}F(n-2)$ makes it
easy to see that is is a second order, linear, homogeneous relation.
(d) Rewriting the relation in the form $F(n) = \dfrac{1}{2}F(n-1) + \dfrac{1}{2}$ makes it easy to
determine that it is first order, linear, non-homogeneous; the non-homogeneous
term is $\dfrac{1}{2}$.
(e) Fourth order, linear, non-homogeneous; the non-homogeneous term is $-2 + n$
$+ \dfrac{1}{n(n+1)} + \lg\left(\dfrac{n! + 2^n}{\sqrt{2\pi n}}\right)$;

(f) The given recurrence relation can be rewritten as

$$2^n F(n) - 2^{n+1} F(n-1) = (1 + \lfloor \lg(n!+1) \rfloor) F(n-2) + (1 + \lfloor \lg(n!+1) \rfloor) F(n-3)$$

which can be rearranged into standard third order, linear, homogeneous form.
(g) This relation does not have a well-defined order; it is linear and homogeneous.

Example 4.1.9 Suppose a programmer wanted to output the first 10,000 terms of the sequence $F(n)$ defined recursively in Example 4.1.3. Why would you advise him/her not to use the following loop, which repeatedly calls the code for function F(n) in Fig. 4.2 on p. 99

```
int n;
for (n = 1; n <= 10000; ++n)
    cout << F(n) << endl;
```

Write an efficient function named output_F for outputting the first m terms of the sequence $F(n)$, where m is the one and only parameter to be passed to the output_F function.

Solution The given loop first calls F(1), which immediately returns 1. Then it calls F(2), which immediately returns 2. Then the loop calls F(3), which sets up F(1) and F(2) before calculating F(3). Then the loop calls F(4), which sets up F(1) and F(2), calculates F(3) again, and then calculates F(4) from F(3) and F(2). Then the loop calls F(5) which repeats the calculation of F(3) and F(4) in order to calculate F(5). Clearly it is inefficient to be calculating the same function values over and over again. The efficient way is to calculate each function value just once *and print it as soon as it is calculated* (Fig. 4.3).

4.1.2 Exercises

4.1.10 If $F(n) = (n!)^{1/n}$, then $F(1) =?$ $F(5) =?$ $F(n+1) =?$ $F(n)+1 =?$ $F(n^2) =?$ $[F(n)]^2 =?$

4.1.11 If $F(n) = \dfrac{n!}{F(n-1)}$, then $F(p) =?$ $F(4k-3) =?$ $F(n^2) =?$ $[F(n)]^2 =?$ $F(5r) =?$ $5F(r) =?$

4.1.12 If $F(n) = \dfrac{n+1}{nF(n-1)}$, then $F(p) =?$ $F(2^n) =?$ $F(n!) =?$ $1/F(n) =?$ $F(3t) =?$ $3F(t) =?$

4.1.13 If $F(n) = F(\lfloor n/2 \rfloor) - 3nF(n-1)$, then $F(2^k) =?$ $F(n^2) =?$ $F(2n) =?$

```
output_F(long int m)
{
  long int n,
          F_n = 2,
          F_n_minus_1 = 1,
          F_n_minus_2;

  if (m  <= 1)
    cout << m << endl;
  else
  {
    cout << 1 << endl;
    cout << 2 << endl;

    for (n = 3; n <= m; ++n)
    {
      F_n_minus_2 = F_n_minus_1;
      F_n_minus_1 = F_n;
      F_n = F_n_minus_2 - n * F_n_minus_1;

      // Output the value of F(n) as soon as it is known.
      cout << F_n << endl;
    }
  }
}
```

Fig. 4.3 Efficient implementation of the function for Example 4.1.9

4.1.14 If $F(0) = 1$ in Exercise 4.1.11 above, find the numerical values of $F(1)$, $F(2)$, and $F(3)$.

4.1.15 If $F(0) = 1$, $F(1) = 5$, and $F(n) = \dfrac{F(n-1) + F(n-2)}{2}$ when $n \geq 2$ (i.e., each term in the sequence is the average of the two preceding terms), find the numerical value of $F(4)$.

4.1.16 If $F(1) = 1$, $F(2) = 2$, and $F(n) = (n+1)F(n-1) + (n+2)F(n-2)$ when $n \geq 3$, find the numerical value of $F(6)$.

4.1.17 If $F(1) = 0$, $F(2) = 1$, and $F(n) = \dfrac{nF(n-1)}{n + F(n-2)}$ for all $n \geq 3$, calculate the exact fractional numerical value of $F(5)$.

4.1.18 Suppose that we try to define a sequence recursively by the equations

$$F(1) = 2, \ \ F(2) = 1, \ \ F(n) = F(n-1) - F(n-3) + 2 \text{ for all } n \geq 3.$$

What difficulty will we encounter? Answer a similar question about the equations

$$G(0) = 1, \ \ G(n) = G(\lfloor n/2 \rfloor) + G(\lceil n/2 \rceil) + 2n \text{ for all } n \geq 1.$$

4.1.19 In each case below, verify by direct substitution that the given formula for $F(n)$ is a solution of the given recurrence relation. The symbols α and β denote arbitrary constants. Give complete details so that it will not appear that you are "fudging".

(a) recurrence relation: $F(n) = F(n-1) + 2F(n-2) + 3(2^{n-1})$; solution: $F(n) = \alpha 2^n + \beta(-1)^n + n2^n$

(b) recurrence relation: $F(n) = \dfrac{n+2}{n(n+1)} + F(n-1)F(n-2)$; solution: $F(n) = \dfrac{n}{n+1}$

(c) recurrence relation: $F(n) = (2n-1)F(n-1) + 2(2n-1)(2n-3)F(n-2)$;

   solution: $F(n) = \dfrac{(2n)!}{n!}$. **Warning**: a common error in trying to do this problem is to conclude that if $F(n) = \dfrac{(2n)!}{n!}$ then $F(n-1) = \dfrac{(2n-1)!}{(n-1)!}$. The correct conclusion is that $F(n-1) = \dfrac{?}{(n-1)!}$.

4.1.20 Find the solution of each of the following problems by computing several terms of the sequence and then making a conjecture. Then verify your conjecture by direct substitution.

(a) $F(1) = 4$, $F(n) = F(n-1) - \dfrac{3}{n(n-1)}$ for all $n \geq 2$

(b) $F(0) = 1$, $F(1) = 2$, $F(n) = 2nF(n-2) - (n-2)F(n-1)$ when $n \geq 2$

4.1.21 For each of the recurrence relations referenced below, state whether the recurrence relation is linear, and if it is, state whether it is homogeneous. If it is linear but non-homogeneous, give the non-homogeneous term.

(a) Example 4.1.6(a)   (b) Exercise 4.1.19(b)   (c) Exercise 4.1.19(c)
(d) Example 4.1.7(a)   (e) Exercise 4.1.20(a)   (f) Exercise 4.1.20(b)
(g) Exercise 4.1.15   (h) Exercise 4.1.17

4.1.22 Suppose, as in Example 4.1.9, a program contains the following loop:

```
int n;
for (n=1; n <= 10000; ++n)
  cout << F(n) << endl;
```

where the function F(n) is the one defined on p. 99. To compute F(1) and F(2), the code for F(n) does not have to perform any arithmetic calculation; instead it just returns 1 and then 2. The remaining 9,998 calls in our loop require the line

```
F_n = F_n_minus_2 - n * F_n_minus_1
```

to be executed at least once. How many times altogether will this line be executed during the 10,000 calls to $F(n)$?

4.1.23 A programmer is given the problem of writing code to calculate values of the function $H(n)$ defined by the following equations:

$$H(0) = 1, \quad H(1) = 3, \quad H(2) = 5,$$
$$H(n) = [1 + H(n-1)][2 + H(n-3)] \text{ for all } n \geq 3.$$

Since the programmer is comfortable with the concept of recursion, she immediately writes the following elegant piece of C++ code:

```
long int H(long int n)
{
    if (n <= 2)      // Base case for the recursive function.
        return 2 * n + 1;
    else
        return (1 + H(n - 1)) * (2 + H(n - 3));
}
```

Despite its elegant simplicity, this is a seriously inefficient algorithm for large values of n.

(a) Draw a tree diagram showing all the calls that will be made to this C++ function when the call H(8) is made. Use the diagram to count the total number of calls that are made to H, starting with the original H(8) call.
(b) Rewrite the code for H so that it is iterative and efficient.
(c) Write an efficient function named output_H that takes a non-negative integer m as its argument and prints all the values of $H(n)$ for $0 \leq n \leq m$.
(d) Each time a function call H(n) is executed, a stack frame (also called an activation record) is placed on the program's runtime stack to keep track of the values of the value parameters and the local variables in the call. Thus, when the initial call H(8) is executed in part (a), a stack frame for that call is placed on the stack. Since H(8) calls H(7), a stack frame for that call is placed just above the stack frame for the H(8) call. Since H(7) calls H(6), a stack frame for that call is placed just above the frame for the H(7) call. And so on to H(2), where no recursive call is made, so the stack frame for H(2) is removed from the stack when execution of H(2) completed. After many calls and completion of calls, execution of H(7) will finally be completed. At that instant its stack

frame and all the frames that were above it will have been removed from the stack, leaving only the frame for H(8) on the stack. Now H(8) "knows" the numerical value of H(7), so it moves on to a call H(5) (that's the call H(n-3) when n has the value 8). A stack frame for H(5) is now placed just above the H(8) frame, and then H(5) begins to execute.

During this lengthy execution of the call H(8), what is the maximum number of stack frames for H that will be on the runtime stack at any one time?

4.2 Linear Homogeneous Recurrence Relations with Constant Coefficients

Look at the definition of "linear recurrence relation" on p. 96. As we remarked there, if the term $\phi(n)$ is missing (i.e., is identically zero), then the equation is called "homogeneous". The $c_i(n)$ functions are called the "coefficients" of the relation, and a special case occurs when all of them are constant (some or most of the constants may be zero). A complete theory has been discovered for the solution of linear homogeneous recurrence relations with constant coefficients and a well-defined order. We will study that theory in this section.

Before we look at the special case of constant coefficients, we need to have in mind one of the most fundamental properties of linear homogeneous equations. The following theorem tells us we can "superimpose" any two solutions of such an equation to obtain still another solution. Note that in this theorem we do not need to assume that the coefficients are constant.

Theorem 4.2.1 (Superposition Theorem): *Suppose $F(n) = g(n)$ and $F(n) = h(n)$ are both solutions of a linear homogeneous recurrence relation*

$$F(n) = c_1(n)F(n-1) + c_2(n)F(n-2) + \cdots + c_n(n)F(0).$$

Then every linear combination $F(n) = \alpha g(n) + \beta h(n)$ is also a solution of the same recurrence relation. In particular, $F(n) = \alpha\, g(n)$ is a solution; this is true even if $\alpha = 0$.

Proof The hypotheses of the theorem give us the following equations:

$$g(n) = c_1(n)g(n-1) + c_2(n)g(n-2) + \cdots + c_n(n)g(0) \qquad \text{and}$$
$$h(n) = c_1(n)h(n-1) + c_2(n)h(n-2) + \cdots + c_n(n)h(0).$$

The theorem asserts that

$$\alpha\, g(n) + \beta\, h(n) = c_1(n)[\alpha\, g(n-1) + \beta\, h(n-1)] + c_2(n)[\alpha\, g(n-2)$$
$$+ \beta\, h(n-2)] + \cdots + c_n(n)[\alpha\, g(0) + \beta\, h(0)].$$

This equation is obtained from the previous two by multiplying them by α and β respectively and adding the results. ∎

Now let's look at a first-order recurrence problem with constant coefficient:

$$F(n) = c_1 F(n - 1), \quad \text{where } c_1 \text{ is a non-zero constant.} \qquad (4.1)$$

Linear   Homogeneous   Recurrence   Relations
with Constant Coefficients

Assume we are given the value of the coefficient c_1 and the value of the initial term of the sequence, say $F(0) = a$. Then $F(1) = c_1 a$, $F(2) = c_1 F(1) = c_1^2 a$, $F(3) = c_1 F(2) = c_1^3 a$, etc. Clearly the solution is $F(n) = a c_1^n$ for all $n \geq 0$.

What would be changed in the first order case if the first term of the sequence were $F(1) = b$ (i.e., if $F(0)$ is not defined)? We would then have $F(2) = c_1 b$, $F(3) = c_1 F(2) = c_1^2 b$, $F(4) = c_1 F(3) = c_1^3 b$, etc. In this case the solution is $F(n) = b c_1^{n-1}$ for all $n \geq 1$, which can be rewritten as follows: $F(n) = (b/c_1) c_1^n$. This can be generalized so that we can state that in the first order case, no matter whether the sequence begins with $F(0)$ or with $F(1)$ or with any other choice, the solution of recurrence relation (4.1) must have the form $F(n) = \alpha c_1^n$, where the constant α will be determined by the initial value of the sequence. We summarize these observations in the following theorem.

Theorem 4.2.2 *The solution of a first order recurrence problem of the form*

$$F(n_0) = a, \quad F(n) = c_1 F(n - 1) \quad \text{for } n \geq n_0 + 1,$$

where c_1 is a non-zero constant, must have the form

$$F(n) = \alpha c_1^n \quad \text{for all } n \geq n_0,$$

where the constant α will be uniquely determined by the initial value $F(n_0) = a$.

Proof We have already derived this formula in two special cases ($n_0 = 0$ and $n_0 = 1$). The same derivation works for any starting point of the sequence. ∎

Now let's turn to the more challenging second order relations. We want to solve

$$F(n) = c_1 F(n - 1) + c_2 F(n - 2), \quad \text{where } c_1 \text{ and } c_2 \text{ are constants, with } c_2 \neq 0. \qquad (4.2)$$

Assume we are given the values of the coefficients c_1 and c_2 and two initial values, say $F(0) = a$ and $F(1) = b$. What form would we expect the solution to have? A reasonable conjecture, based on our experience with the first order case, is that $F(n) = r^n$ for some constant r. To find out whether there is indeed a value of r that "works", we make the substitution $F(n) = r^n$ in the recurrence relation (4.2): $r^n = c_1 r^{n-1} + c_2 r^{n-2}$. Excluding the trivial case of the solution obtained by taking $r = 0$, we now divide by r^{n-2} to get

$$r^2 = c_1 r + c_2. \qquad (4.3)$$

What we have found is that by taking r to be a constant that satisfies the equation above, we will have a solution of recurrence relation (4.2), namely $F(n) = r^n$.

The Eq. (4.3) above is called the *characteristic equation* of the second order relation (4.2). It is a quadratic equation, and will therefore have two roots, say r_1 and r_2 (which may or may not be equal). These numbers are called the *characteristic roots* of the relation (4.2). We have shown above that the functions $F_1(n) = r_1{}^n$ and $F_2(n) = r_2{}^n$ are solutions of the relation (4.2). By the Superposition Theorem, we can add these to obtain a still more general solution for the relation (4.2): $F(n) = \alpha_1 (r_1)^n + \alpha_2 (r_2)^n$. If we then impose some initial conditions (e.g. $F(0) = a$ and $F(1) = b$), these two pieces of initial data can be shown to uniquely determine the values of α_1 and α_2. The following theorem gives the full story.

Theorem 4.2.3 *A second order recurrence problem of the form*

$$F(n_0) = a, \quad F(n_0 + 1) = b, \quad F(n) = c_1 F(n - 1) + c_2 F(n - 2) \quad \text{for all } n \geq n_0 + 2,$$
$$(4.4)$$

where c_1 and c_2 are constants, with $c_2 \neq 0$, has a unique solution, which can be derived as follows. First find the roots, call them r_1 and r_2, of the characteristic equation

$$r^2 = c_1 r + c_2$$

of the relation (4.4). The solution of the relation (4.4) must then have the form

$$\alpha_1 (r_1)^n + \alpha_2 (r_2)^n \text{ for all } n \geq n_0 \text{ if } r_1 \neq r_2 \quad \text{or}$$
$$(\alpha_1 + \alpha_2 n)(r_1)^n \text{ for all } n \geq n_0 \text{ if } r_1 = r_2$$

where the constants α_1 and α_2 will be uniquely determined by the two initial values $F(n_0) = a$ and $F(n_0 + 1) = b$.

Proof We have already derived the fact that if r_1 and r_2 are roots of Eq. (4.3), then the formula $F(n) = \alpha_1 r_1{}^n + \alpha_2 r_2{}^n$ satisfies the recurrence relation (4.2) for all choices of α_1 and α_2. This is true even if $r_1 = r_2$, although in that case the formula reduces to $\alpha r_1{}^n$, where $\alpha = \alpha_1 + \alpha_2$. Now let's verify that if $r_1 = r_2$ in Eq. (4.3), then the formula $F(n) = n r_1{}^n$ satisfies the recurrence relation (4.2). It is a well-known fact from elementary algebra that if r_1 and r_2 are the roots of Eq. (4.3) then the equivalent equation $r^2 - c_1 r - c_2 = 0$ can be written in the form $(r - r_1)(r - r_2) = 0$. If it happens that $r_1 = r_2$ then the equation takes the form $(r - r_1)^2 = 0$. This can be rewritten as $r^2 = 2 r_1 r - r_1{}^2$, so the recurrence relation itself must have the form $F(n) = 2 r_1 F(n - 1) - r_1{}^2 F(n - 2)$. That is, $2 r_1 = c_1$ and $-r_1{}^2 = c_2$. Since $c_2 \neq 0$ it follows that $r_1 \neq 0$. We must show that the function $F(n) = n r_1{}^n$ satisfies this recurrence relation. This means we must prove that

$$n r_1{}^n = 2 r_1 (n - 1) r_1{}^{n-1} - r_1{}^2 (n - 2) r_1{}^{n-2}$$

for all n. It is easy to see, after a little multiplication, that $r_1{}^n$ can be factored out on the right side, giving us the equivalent equation

$$n r_1{}^n = r_1{}^n[2(n - 1) - (n - 2)]$$

to be proved. Trivial algebra now shows that the right side reduces to the left side.

Now let's prove that if $r_1 \neq r_2$ in Eq. (4.2), then for any integer n_0 and any real numbers a and b there exist unique numbers α_1 and α_2 such that $\alpha_1 r_1^{n_0} + \alpha_2 r_2^{n_0} = a$ and $\alpha_1 r_1^{n_0+1} + \alpha_2 r_2^{n_0+1} = b$. This will prove the existence of a solution of the form promised for the recurrence problem (4.4) in the case where $r_1 \neq r_2$. We must show that the pair of simultaneous equations $\alpha_1 r_1^{n_0} + \alpha_2 r_2^{n_0} = a$ and $\alpha_1 r_1^{n_0+1} + \alpha_2 r_2^{n_0+1} = b$ has a unique solution for the "unknowns" α_1 and α_2. A necessary and sufficient condition for this is that the determinant $\begin{vmatrix} r_1^{n_0} & r_2^{n_0} \\ r_1^{n_0+1} & r_2^{n_0+1} \end{vmatrix}$ be non-zero. That is, we must show that $r_1^{n_0} r_2^{n_0+1} - r_1^{n_0+1} r_2^{n_0} \neq 0$. The left side can be written as $r_1^{n_0} r_2^{n_0}(r_1 - r_2)$. Neither r_1 nor r_2 can be zero, for this would make $c_2 = 0$; also $r_1 - r_2 \neq 0$ because $r_1 \neq r_2$. Thus the determinant is non-zero, as we wished to show.

Next we'll prove that if $r_1 = r_2$ in Eq. (4.3), then for any integer n_0 and any real numbers a and b there exist unique numbers α_1 and α_2 such that $(\alpha_1 + \alpha_2 n_0)r_1^{n_0} = a$ and $(\alpha_1 + \alpha_2(n_0 + 1))r_1^{n_0+1} = b$. This will prove the existence of a solution of the form promised for the recurrence problem (4.4) in the case where $r_1 = r_2$. We must show that the pair of simultaneous equations $(\alpha_1 + \alpha_2 n_0)r_2^{n_0} = a$ and $(\alpha_1 + \alpha_2(n_0 + 1))r_2^{n_0+1} = b$ has a unique solution for the "unknowns" α_1 and α_2. A necessary and sufficient condition for this is that the determinant $\begin{vmatrix} r_1^{n_0} & n_0 r_1^{n_0} \\ r_1^{n_0+1} & (n_0 + 1)r_1^{n_0+1} \end{vmatrix}$ be non-zero. That is, we must show that $r_1^{n_0}(n_0 + 1)r_1^{n_0+1} - r_1^{n_0+1} n_0 r_1^{n_0}$ is non-zero. This expression can be written as $r_1^{2n_0+1}(n_0 + 1 - n_0)$, which reduces to $r_1^{2n_0+1}$. By the first paragraph of this proof, $r_1 \neq 0$, so the determinant is non-zero, as we wished to show.

In the two preceding paragraphs we have proved that the recurrence relation (4.4) does have a solution. Now let's prove the uniqueness of solutions for relation (4.4). That is, let's prove that if any two functions $F_1(n)$ and $F_2(n)$ are solutions of relation (4.4), then it must be true that $F_1(n) = F_2(n)$ for all $n \geq n_0$. We'll do this by using the strong form of mathematical induction.

Before we set up the induction argument, note that when we say that a function $F_1(n)$ is a solution of relation (4.4) we mean that

$$F_1(n_0)=a, \quad F_1(n_0 + 1)=b, \quad F_1(n) = c_1 F_1(n-1) + c_2 F_1(n-2) \quad \text{for all } n \geq n_0 + 2.$$

Similarly, when we say that a function $F_2(n)$ is a solution of relation (4.4) we mean that

$$F_2(n_0)=a, \quad F_2(n_0 + 1)=b, \quad F_2(n) = c_1 F_2(n-1) + c_2 F_2(n-2) \quad \text{for all } n \geq n_0 + 2.$$

Thus these equations are true by the hypothesis that $F_1(n)$ and $F_2(n)$ are solutions of relation (4.4).

Let $S(n)$ denote the following predicate: "$F_1(n) = F_2(n)$". Then $S(n_0)$ denotes the proposition "$F_1(n_0) = F_2(n_0)$", which is true because sides are equal to a. Similarly, $S(n_0 + 1)$ denotes the proposition "$F_1(n_0 + 1) = F_2(n_0 + 1)$", which is true because both sides are equal to b. Now take any integer $k \geq n_0 + 1$ such that $S(n)$ is true for all $n \leq k$. That is, k is an integer at least as large as $n_0 + 1$ such that $F_1(n) = F_2(n)$ for all n satisfying $n_0 \leq n \leq k$. We shall prove that $S(k + 1)$ is true. That is, we shall prove that $F_1(k+1) = F_2(k+1)$. Since $k+1 \geq n_0 + 2$, we are given that $F_1(k+1) = c_1 F_1(k+1-1) + c_2 F_1(k+1-2)$ and $F_2(k+1) = c_1 F_2(k+1-1) + c_2 F_2(k+1-2)$, so

$$F_1(k+1) = c_1 F_1(k) + c_2 F_1(k-1) \quad \text{and} \quad F_2(k+1) = c_1 F_2(k) + c_2 F_2(k-1). \tag{4.5}$$

By the inductive hypothesis, $F_1(k) = F_2(k)$ and $F_1(k-1) = F_2(k-1)$. Thus the right sides of Eq. (4.5) are equal, so the left sides must be equal as well.   ∎

Example 4.2.4 Find the solution of the following recurrence problem:

$$F(0) = 3, \quad F(1) = 5, \quad F(n) = -F(n-1) + 2F(n-2), \quad \text{when } n \geq 2.$$

Solution First we write down the characteristic equation of the recurrence relation:

$$r^2 = -1 \cdot r + 2,$$

which we rewrite in the form $r^2 + r - 2 = 0$. This quadratic equation can be solved by factoring:
$(r-1)(r+2) = 0$, which gives us the "characteristic roots" $r_1 = 1$ and $r_2 = -2$. By Theorem 4.2.3, the solution of the recurrence problem must have the form

$$F(n) = \alpha_1 (r_1)^n + \alpha_2 (r_2)^n \quad \text{for all } n \geq 0.$$

By Theorem 4.2.3, this equation is valid for all $n \geq 0$, not just for all $n \geq 2$. We can determine the values of the constants α_1 and α_2 by using the initial values $F(0) = 3$ and $F(1) = 5$. We must have

$$3 = F(0) = \alpha_1 (1)^0 + \alpha_2 (-2)^0 \quad \text{and} \quad 5 = F(1) = \alpha_1 (1)^1 + \alpha_2 (-2)^1.$$

Simplifying and rewriting these equations gives us

$$\alpha_1 + \alpha_2 = 3 \quad \text{and} \quad \alpha_1 - 2\alpha_2 = 5.$$

Subtracting the first equation from the second gives $-3\alpha_2 = 2$, so $\alpha_2 = -2/3$. Back substituting this into either of the two equations above gives $\alpha_1 = 11/3$. We can now state the solution of the given problem:

$$F(n) = \frac{11}{3} - \frac{2}{3}(-2)^n \quad \text{for all } n \geq 0.$$

Let's check this answer by calculating $F(2)$ and $F(3)$ in two different ways: first by using the recurrence relation and the given initial values, and second by plugging $n = 2$ and $n = 3$ into the solution we have derived for $F(n)$. By the recurrence relation we must have $F(2) = -5 + 2 \times 3 = 1$ and $F(3) = -1 + 2 \times 5 = 9$. Our solution for $F(n)$ gives the same values: $F(2) = \frac{11}{3} - \frac{2}{3}(-2)^2 = \frac{11}{3} - \frac{8}{3}$, and $F(3) = \frac{11}{3} - \frac{2}{3}(-2)^3 = \frac{11}{3} + \frac{16}{3} = 9$. These calculations do not *prove* that our formula is correct for all $n \geq 0$, but they give us considerable confidence that we have not made some algebraic or arithmetic error in the derivation of our solution.

Sometimes the roots of the characteristic equation are complex numbers, that is, numbers that involve the square root of -1. The rules for solving linear recurrence relations are valid even when the roots are complex. For example, the recurrence relation

$$F(0) = 0, \quad F(1) = 1, \quad F(n) = 4F(n-1) - 5F(n-2) \quad \text{for } n \geq 2$$

has characteristic equation $r^2 - 4r + 5 = 0$. The roots can be found using the quadratic formula:

$$r = \frac{-(-4) \pm \sqrt{(-4)^2 - 4 \times 1 \times 5}}{2 \cdot 1} = \frac{4 \pm \sqrt{16 - 20}}{2} = \frac{4 \pm 2\sqrt{-1}}{2} = 2 \pm i,$$

where i is the complex number such that $i^2 = -1$. The roots are $r_1 = 2 + i$ and $r_2 = 2 - i$, so

$$F(n) = \alpha_1(2 + i)^n + \alpha_2(2 - i)^n \quad \text{for all } n \geq 0.$$

The constants α_1 and α_2 are obtained from the initial conditions:

$$0 = F(0) = \alpha_1 + \alpha_2, \quad 1 = F(1) = \alpha_1(2 + i) + \alpha_2(2 - i).$$

Solving these simultaneous equations gives $\alpha_1 = \dfrac{1}{2i}$ and $\alpha_2 = \dfrac{-1}{2i}$. Thus

$$F(n) = \frac{1}{2i}[(2 + i)^n - (2 - i)^n] \quad \text{for all } n \geq 0.$$

Third order linear homogeneous recurrence relations are solved by a method similar to that of second order relations. The solution of a recurrence relation of the form

$$F(n) = c_1 \, F(n-1) + c_2 \, F(n-2) + c_3 \, F(n-3),$$

where the c_i's are constants and $c_3 \neq 0$, can be derived by finding the roots, call them r_1, r_2, and r_3, of the characteristic equation:

$$r^3 = c_1 r^2 + c_2 r + c_3.$$

The solution of the recurrence relation must then have the form

$$\begin{array}{ll} F(n) = \alpha_1 \, (r_1)^n + \alpha_2 \, (r_2)^n + \alpha_3(r_3)^n & \text{if all three roots are different,} \\ F(n) = (\alpha_1 + \alpha_2 n)(r_1)^n + \alpha_3(r_3)^n & \text{if } r_1 = r_2 \neq r_3, \\ F(n) = (\alpha_1 + \alpha_2 n + \alpha_3 n^2)(r_1)^n & \text{if } r_1 = r_2 = r_3, \end{array}$$

where the constants α_1, α_2, and α_3 will be determined by the three initial values of the sequence.

Third order linear homogeneous recurrence relations are generally quite a lot harder to solve than first and second order ones because the roots of a cubic characteristic equation are usually not easy to compute. Fourth order linear homogeneous recurrence relations with constant coefficients are solved in an analogous way using a quartic (4th degree) characteristic equation, which is even harder to solve than a cubic one. These higher order relations are much less frequently encountered in analysis of algorithms than the first and second order equations. In this textbook we will have no occasion to try to solve one.

4.2.1 Further Examples

Example 4.2.5 Give just the form of the general solution of each of the following linear homogeneous recurrence relations. (Since no initial values are given in these problems, we cannot give unique solutions; all we can do is give the general form that a solution must have.)

(a) $F(n) = 5F(n-1)$

(b) $F(n) = \dfrac{2F(n-1)}{3}$

(c) $F(n) = F(n-1)$

(d) $F(n) = F(n-1) + 2F(n-2)$

(e) $F(n) = F(n-1) - \dfrac{F(n-2)}{4}$

(f) $F(n) = -3F(n-1) + F(n-2)$

Solution

(a) Every solution has the form $F(n) = \alpha \, 5^n$ for some constant α.

(b) $F(n) = \dfrac{2}{3}F(n-1)$; every solution has the form $F(n) = \alpha \, (2/3)^n$ for some constant α.

(c) Every solution has form $F(n) = \alpha \, 1^n = \alpha$ (a constant sequence) for some constant α.

(d) $F(n) = F(n-1) + 2F(n-2)$; the characteristic equation is $r^2 = r + 2$, which has roots $r_1 = -1$ and $r_2 = 2$; it follows that every solution has the form $F(n) = \alpha_1 (-1)^n + \alpha_2 \, 2^n$ for some constant α.

(e) $F(n) = F(n-1) - \dfrac{1}{4}F(n-2)$; the characteristic equation is $r^2 = r - \dfrac{1}{4}$, which has roots $r_{1,2} = \dfrac{1}{2}$ (identical roots), so by Theorem 4.2.3 every solution has the form $F(n) = (\alpha_1 + \alpha_2 n)(1/2)^n$.

(f) The characteristic equation is $r^2 = -3r + 1$, which has roots $r_1 = \dfrac{-3 + \sqrt{9+4}}{2}$ and $r_2 = \dfrac{-3 - \sqrt{9+4}}{2}$; every solution has form $F(n) = \alpha_1 \left(\dfrac{-3 + \sqrt{13}}{2} \right)^n + \alpha_2 \left(\dfrac{-3 - \sqrt{13}}{2} \right)^n$.

Example 4.2.6 Solve the following first order linear homogeneous recurrence problems. In each case, check your answer by computing one or more values beyond the initial value by two different methods.

(a) $F(0) = 1$, $F(n) = 2F(n-1)$ when $n \geq 1$

(b) $F(1) = 3$, $F(n) = -F(n-1)$ when $n \geq 2$

(c) $F(2) = 7$, $F(k) = F(k-1)$ when $k \geq 3$

(d) $T(0) = 3$, $T(n) = \dfrac{T(n-1)}{2}$ when $n \geq 1$

Solution

(a) The solution must have the form $F(n) = \alpha\, 2^n$ for all $n \geq 0$. The unknown constant α is determined by the initial value that we are given: $F(0) = 1$. Setting n to 0 in the solution gives us $F(0) = \alpha\, 2^0$, so $1 = \alpha \cdot 1$, which implies $\alpha = 1$. Thus the solution is $F(n) = 2^n$ for all $n \geq 0$. [Check: $F(1) = 2$ by the recurrence relation and also by the final formula for the solution.]

(b) The recurrence relation can be written as $F(n) = (-1)F(n-1)$. The solution therefore must have the form $F(n) = \alpha(-1)^n$ for all $n \geq 1$. The unknown constant α is determined by the initial value we are given: $F(1) = 3$. Setting n to 1 in the solution gives us $F(1) = \alpha(-1)^1$, so $3 = \alpha(-1)$, which implies $\alpha = -3$. Thus the solution is $F(n) = -3\,(-1)^n$, which can be written as $F(n) = 3\,(-1)^{n+1}$. The solution is valid for all $n \geq 1$. [Check: $F(2) = -3$ by the recurrence relation and also by the final formula for the solution.]

(c) The recurrence relation can be written as $F(k) = 1 \cdot F(k-1)$. The solution therefore has the form $F(k) = \alpha \cdot 1^k$ for all $k \geq 2$. The unknown constant α is determined by the initial value we are given: $F(2) = 7$. Setting k to 2 in the solution gives us $F(2) = \alpha \cdot 1^2$, so $7 = \alpha$. Thus the solution is $F(k) = 7 \times 1^k$, that is, $F(k) = 7$ for all $k \geq 2$. (This surely makes sense if $F(k) = F(k-1)$ for all $k \geq 3$. All the terms of the sequence have exactly the same value.)

(d) The recurrence relation can be written as $T(n) = \dfrac{1}{2}T(n-1)$. The solution therefore has the form $T(n) = \alpha(1/2)^n$ for all $n \geq 0$. The unknown constant α is determined by the initial value we are given: $T(0) = 3$. Setting n to 0 in the solution gives us $T(0) = \alpha(1/2)^0$, so $3 = \alpha(1/2)^0$, which implies that $\alpha = 3$. Thus the solution is $T(n) = 3\,(1/2)^n$; an alternative algebraic form is $F(n) = \dfrac{3}{2^n}$. The solution is valid for all $n \geq 0$. [Check: $T(1) = \dfrac{3}{2}$ by the recurrence relation and also by the final formula for the solution.]

Example 4.2.7 Solve the following second order linear homogeneous recurrence problems. In each case, check your answer by computing one or more values beyond the initial value by two different methods.

(a) $F(1) = 2$, $F(2) = 0$, $F(n) = F(n-1) + 6F(n-2)$ when $n \geq 3$
(b) $F(0) = 1$, $F(1) = 1$, $F(n) = 2F(n-1) + F(n-2)$ when $n \geq 2$
(c) $f(0) = 0$, $f(1) = 1$, $f(n) = f(n-1) + f(n-2)$ when $n \geq 2$ (This defines the famous **Fibonacci numbers**, i.e., sequence of integers: 0, 1, 1, 2, 3, 5, 8, 13, 21, 34, 55, 89, …)
(d) $A(0) = -3$, $A(1) = 3$, $A(j) = 6A(j-1) - 9A(j-2)$ when $j \geq 2$

Solution

(a) From the recurrence relation we derive the characteristic equation $r^2 = r + 6$, which we rewrite as $r^2 - r - 6 = 0$, which gives $(r-3)(r+2) = 0$, from which we derive the characteristic roots $r_1 = 3$ and $r_2 = -2$ (or, equally correct, $r_1 = -2$ and $r_2 = 3$). It follows that the solution has the form $F(n) = \alpha_1 3^n + \alpha_2 (-2)^n$ for all $n \geq 1$, where α_1 and α_2 are appropriately chosen constants. To find the values of α_1 and α_2, we use the two initial values we are given: $F(1) = 2$ and $F(2) = 0$. Setting n first to 1 and then to 2 in the solution gives the two equations $F(1) = \alpha_1 3^1 + \alpha_2 (-2)^1$ and $F(2) = \alpha_1 3^2 + \alpha_2 (-2)^2$. Putting in the given initial values gives $2 = 3\alpha_1 - 2\alpha_2$ and $0 = 9\alpha_1 + 4\alpha_2$. Solving simultaneously gives $\alpha_1 = 4/15$ and $\alpha_2 = -3/5$. Thus $F(n) = \dfrac{4}{15}3^n - \dfrac{3}{5}(-2)^n$ for all $n \geq 1$. [Check: $F(3) = 12$ by the recurrence relation and also by the final formula for the solution.]

(b) From the recurrence relation we derive the characteristic equation $r^2 = 2r + 1$, which we rewrite as $r^2 - 2r - 1 = 0$. The quadratic formula gives the solutions $r_1 = \dfrac{-(-2) + \sqrt{4 - 4(-1)}}{2} = 1 + \sqrt{2}$ and $r_2 = 1 - \sqrt{2}$. It follows that the solution has the form $F(n) = \alpha_1(1 + \sqrt{2})^n + \alpha_2(1 - \sqrt{2})^n$ for all $n \geq 1$, where α_1 and α_2 are appropriately chosen constants. To find the values of α_1 and α_2, we use the two initial values we are given: $F(0) = 1$ and $F(1) = 1$. Setting n first to 0 and then to 1 in the solution gives the two equations $F(0) = \alpha_1(1 + \sqrt{2})^0 + \alpha_2(1 - \sqrt{2})^0$ and $F(1) = \alpha_1(1 + \sqrt{2})^1 + \alpha_2(1 - \sqrt{2})^1$. Putting in the given initial values gives $1 = \alpha_1 + \alpha_2$ and $1 = \alpha_1(1 + \sqrt{2}) + \alpha_2(1 - \sqrt{2})$. Solving simultaneously gives $\alpha_1 = 1/2$ and $\alpha_2 = 1/2$. Thus $F(n) = \dfrac{1}{2}(1+\sqrt{2})^n + \dfrac{1}{2}(1-\sqrt{2})^n$ for all $n \geq 0$. [Check: $F(2) = 3$ by the recurrence relation and also by the final formula for the solution.]

(c) From the recurrence relation we derive the characteristic equation $r^2 = r + 1$, which we rewrite as $r^2 - r - 1 = 0$. The quadratic formula gives the solutions $r_1 = \dfrac{-(-1) + \sqrt{1 - 4 \times (-1)}}{2} = \dfrac{1 + \sqrt{5}}{2}$ and $r_2 = \dfrac{1 - \sqrt{5}}{2}$. It follows that the solution has the form $f(n) = \alpha_1 \left(\dfrac{1 + \sqrt{5}}{2} \right)^n + \alpha_2 \left(\dfrac{1 - \sqrt{5}}{2} \right)^n$ for all $n \geq 0$, where α_1 and α_2 are appropriately chosen constants. To find the values of α_1 and α_2, we use the two initial values we are given: $f(0) = 0$ and $f(1) = 1$. Setting n first to 0 and then to 1 in the solution gives the two equations $f(0) = \alpha_1 \left(\dfrac{1 + \sqrt{5}}{2} \right)^0 + \alpha_2 \left(\dfrac{1 - \sqrt{5}}{2} \right)^0$ and

$$f(1) = \alpha_1 \left(\frac{1 + \sqrt{5}}{2} \right)^1 + \alpha_2 \left(\frac{1 - \sqrt{5}}{2} \right)^1.$$ Putting in the given initial values

gives $0 = \alpha_1 + \alpha_2$ and $1 = \alpha_1 \left(\frac{1 + \sqrt{5}}{2} \right) + \alpha_2 \left(\frac{1 - \sqrt{5}}{2} \right).$ Solving simulta-

neously gives $\alpha_1 = 1/\sqrt{5}$ and $\alpha_2 = -1/\sqrt{5}$. Thus the Fibonacci numbers are given by the formula

$$f(n) = \frac{1}{\sqrt{5}} \left[\left(\frac{1 + \sqrt{5}}{2} \right)^n - \left(\frac{1 - \sqrt{5}}{2} \right)^n \right] \text{ for all } n \geq 0. \qquad (4.6)$$

[Check: $f(2) = 1$ by the recurrence relation and also by the final formula for the solution.]

(d) From the recurrence relation we derive the characteristic equation $r^2 = 6r - 9$, which we rewrite as $r^2 - 6r + 9 = 0$, which gives $(r - 3)^2 = 0$, from which we derive the characteristic roots $r_1 = r_2 = 3$ (identical roots). It follows that the solution has the form $A(j) = (\alpha_1 + \alpha_2 j) 3^j$ for all $j \geq 0$, where α_1 and α_2 are appropriately chosen constants. To find the values of α_1 and α_2, we use the two initial values we are given: $A(0) = -3$ and $A(1) = 3$. Setting j first to 0 and then to 1 in the solution gives the two equations $A(0) = (\alpha_1 + \alpha_2 \cdot 0)3^0$ and $A(1) = (\alpha_1 + \alpha_2 \cdot 1)3^1$. Putting in the given initial values gives $-3 = \alpha_1$ and $3 = 3\alpha_1 + 3\alpha_2$. Solving simultaneously gives $\alpha_1 = -3$ and $\alpha_2 = 4$. Thus

$$A(j) = (-3 + 4j) 3^j \text{ for all } j \geq 0.$$

[Check: $A(2) = 45$ by the recurrence relation and by the final formula for the solution.].

4.2.2   Exercises

4.2.8 Solve the following first order linear homogeneous recurrence problems. In each case, check your answer by computing one or more values beyond the initial value by two different methods.

(a) $F(1) = 4, \quad F(n) = \frac{3}{2} F(n - 1)$ when $n \geq 2$

(b) $G(2) = 1, \quad G(m) = 3 G(m - 1)$ when $m \geq 3$

4.2.9 Solve the following second order linear homogeneous recurrence problems. In each case, check your answer by computing one or more values beyond the initial value by two different methods.

(a) $F(0) = 4$, $F(1) = 13$, $F(n) = 3F(n-1) + 10F(n-2)$ for all $n \geq 2$
(b) $G(1) = 2$, $G(2) = 5$, $G(k) = 12G(k-2) - G(k-1)$ for all $k \geq 3$
  Be careful: read the equation closely. The terms may not be in the order you expect.
(c) $F(0) = 1$, $F(1) = 2$, $F(n) = 3F(n-1) + F(n-2)$ for all $n \geq 2$
(d) $F(0) = 1$, $F(1) = 0$, $F(n) = 2F(n-2) - 2F(n-1)$ for all $n \geq 2$
  Be careful: read the equation closely. The terms may not be in the order you expect.
(e) $F(0) = 0$, $F(1) = 2$, $F(n) = 2F(n-1) - 5F(n-2)$ for all $n \geq 2$

4.3 Linear Non-homogeneous Recurrence Relations

Now that we know how to solve homogeneous linear recurrence relations with constant coefficients, let's look at the problem of non-homogeneous linear relations. The following three theorems provide the foundation for solving such relations.

Theorem 4.3.1 *Suppose $F(n) = g(n)$ is a solution of a linear nonhomogeneous relation*

$$F(n) = c_1(n)F(n-1) + c_2(n)F(n-2) + \cdots + c_n(n)F(0) + \phi(n), \quad (4.7)$$

and suppose $F(n) = h(n)$ is a solution of the corresponding homogeneous relation

$$F(n) = c_1(n)F(n-1) + c_2(n)F(n-2) + \cdots + c_n(n)F(0). \quad (4.8)$$

Then for every constant α, $F(n) = g(n) + \alpha h(n)$ is a solution of the nonhomogeneous relation (4.7).

Proof The hypotheses of the theorem give us the following equations:

$$g(n) = c_1(n)g(n-1) + c_2(n)g(n-2) + \cdots + c_n(n)g(0) + \phi(n) \text{ and}$$

$$h(n) = c_1(n)h(n-1) + c_2(n)h(n-2) + \cdots + c_n(n)h(0).$$

It follows that

$$g(n) + \alpha h(n) = c_1(n)g(n-1) + c_2(n)g(n-2) + \cdots + c_n(n)g(0) + \phi(n)$$
$$+ \alpha[c_1(n)h(n-1) + c_2(n)h(n-2) + \cdots + c_n(n)h(0)],$$

$$g(n) + \alpha h(n) = c_1(n)[g(n-1) + \alpha h(n-1)] + c_2(n)[g(n-2)$$
$$+ \alpha h(n-2)] + \cdots + c_n(n)[g(0) + \alpha h(0)] + \phi(n),$$

which proves that $F(n) = g(n) + \alpha h(n)$ is a solution of relation (4.7). ∎

Theorem 4.3.2 *Suppose $F(n) = g(n)$ and $F(n) = h(n)$ are solutions, respectively, of the linear nonhomogeneous relations*

$$F(n) = c_1(n)F(n-1) + c_2(n)F(n-2) + \cdots + c_n(n)F(0) + \phi(n)$$
$$F(n) = c_1(n)F(n-1) + c_2(n)F(n-2) + \cdots + c_n(n)F(0) + \psi(n)$$

(the two relations have the same "linear part" but different nonhomogeneous terms). Then for any real constants α and β, the combination $F(n) = \alpha g(n) + \beta h(n)$ is a solution of the following nonhomogeneous relation

$$F(n) = c_1(n)F(n-1) + c_2(n)F(n-2) + \cdots + c_n(n)F(0) + \alpha\phi(n) + \beta\psi(n).$$

In particular (by taking $\beta = 0$), the quantity $F(n) = \alpha g(n)$ is a solution of the nonhomogeneous relation

$$F(n) = c_1(n)F(n-1) + c_2(n)F(n-2) + \cdots + c_n(n)F(0) + \alpha\phi(n).$$

Proof The proof of this theorem will be an exercise.   ■

Theorem 4.3.3 *Suppose $F(n) = g(n)$ and $F(n) = h(n)$ are solutions of the same linear nonhomogeneous relation*

$$F(n) = c_1(n)F(n-1) + c_2(n)F(n-2) + \cdots + c_n(n)F(0) + \phi(n).$$

Then the difference $F(n) = g(n) - h(n)$ is a solution of the corresponding homogeneous relation

$$F(n) = c_1(n)F(n-1) + c_2(n)F(n-2) + \cdots + c_n(n)F(0).$$

Proof This follows from Theorem 4.3.2 by taking $\psi(n)$ to be $\phi(n)$, α to be 1, and β to be -1.   ■

Example 4.3.4 The purpose of this example is to show how Theorems 4.3.1, 4.3.2, and 4.3.3 can be used in solving a specific problem. Suppose we are asked to find all solutions of the following first order linear nonhomogeneous relation

$$F(n) = 3F(n-1) + 4 \times 5^n + 7 \quad \text{for all } n \geq 1. \tag{4.9}$$

First we could solve the corresponding homogeneous relation

$$F(n) = 3F(n-1), \quad n \geq 1. \tag{4.10}$$

As we know from Theorem 4.2.2, the solutions of this relation must have the form $F(n) = \alpha \cdot 3^n$, where α can be any constant (we would need an initial value $F(0)$ to pin down the value of α). Next, with Theorem 4.3.2 in mind, we can introduce the notations $\phi(n) = 5^n$ and $\psi(n) = 7$ for the two terms that make up the nonhomogeneous part of relation (4.7). Then we can try to solve the simpler nonhomogeneous equations

$$F(n) = 3F(n-1) + 5^n, \quad n \geq 1, \tag{4.11}$$
$$F(n) = 3F(n-1) + 7, \quad n \geq 1. \tag{4.12}$$

A little thought shows that a plausible guess for a solution for relation (4.11) is a function of the form $F(n) = \beta \cdot 5^n$ for some constant β. If we try this out in relation (4.11) we get

$$\beta \cdot 5^n = 3\beta \cdot 5^{n-1} + 5^n.$$

Can we find a β that makes this work? Since $5^n = 5^{n-1} \cdot 5$, the equation above takes the form

$$\beta \cdot 5^{n-1} \cdot 5 = 3\beta \cdot 5^{n-1} + 5^{n-1} \cdot 5.$$

Dividing everywhere by the non-zero quantity 5^{n-1} reduces the equation to $5\beta = 3\beta + 5$, that is, $2\beta = 5$. Thus $F(n) = \dfrac{5}{2}5^n = \dfrac{5^{n+1}}{2}$ is a solution for relation (4.11).

Now let's attack Eq. (4.12). A plausible guess for a solution for Eq. (4.12) is a function of the form $F(n) = \gamma$ for some constant γ. It we try this out in relation (4.12) we get

$$\gamma = 3\gamma + 7,$$

which reduces to $\gamma = -\dfrac{7}{2}$. Thus $F(n) = -\dfrac{7}{2}$ is a solution for relation (4.12).

By Theorem 4.3.2 we know that $F(n) = 4\left(\dfrac{5^{n+1}}{2}\right) + \left(-\dfrac{7}{2}\right) = 2 \times 5^{n+1} - \dfrac{7}{2}$ is a solution for relation (4.9). Are there any other solutions of relation (4.9)? Certainly. By Theorem 4.3.1 and the solutions we obtained for homogeneous relation (4.10), we know that

$$F(n) = 2 \times 5^{n+1} - \frac{7}{2} + \alpha \cdot 3^n \qquad\qquad (4.13)$$

is a solution for every value of α. Are there any other solutions beyond these? By Theorem 4.3.3, any other solution $h(n)$ would differ from $2 \times 5^{n+1} - 7/2 + \alpha \cdot 3^n$ by a solution to the homogeneous relation (4.10). That is, $h(n) - [2 \times 5^{n+1} - 7/2 + \alpha \cdot 3^n]$ would have to be of the form $\delta \cdot 3^n$ for some constant δ, and thus

$$h(n) = 2 \times 5^{n+1} - \frac{7}{2} + \alpha \cdot 3^n + \delta \cdot 3^n = 2 \times 5^{n+1} - \frac{7}{2} + (\alpha + \delta)3^n,$$

which is really no different from relation (4.13). Thus Eq. (4.13) is the most general solution for recurrence relation (4.9). The value of α can be determined when we are given a value for $F(0)$.

Example 4.3.4 illustrates the following general procedure.

4.3.5 General Procedure for Solving Linear Non-homogeneous Recurrence Problems

(a) Find the most general solution for the corresponding homogeneous recurrence relation.
(b) Find a single "particular" solution to the nonhomogeneous recurrence relation.

(c) Add the most general solution for the homogeneous relation to the particular solution for the nonhomogeneous relation to obtain the most general solution for the nonhomogeneous relation.

(d) If initial values are given for the sequence, use these values to determine the values of all "arbitrary constants" in the general solution.

In general, it is not an easy thing to solve a nonhomogeneous linear recurrence relation. When the coefficients of the homogeneous part are constants, however, we can state exact rules for solving two frequently occurring special cases, namely the case where the non-homogeneous term is a polynomial in the sequence variable, and the case where the non-homogeneous term is exponential in the sequence variable. We'll now look at those two special cases.

4.3.6 Polynomial Non-homogeneous Terms in Linear Relations with Constant Coefficients

First Order Case: $F(n) = c_1 F(n-1) + P(n)$, where $P(n)$ is a polynomial.

Solution If $c_1 \neq 1$, then a particular solution is $F(n) = Q(n)$, where $Q(n)$ is an appropriately chosen polynomial with the same degree as $P(n)$.

If $c_1 = 1$, then a particular solution is $F(n) = Q(n)$, where $Q(n)$ is an appropriately chosen polynomial whose degree is 1 greater than the degree of $P(n)$ and whose constant term is zero.

Second Order Case: $F(n) = c_1 F(n-1) + c_2 F(n-2) + P(n)$, where $P(n)$ is a polynomial.

Solution Let r_1 and r_2 denote the characteristic roots for the homogeneous relation.

If neither r_1 nor r_2 is 1, then a particular solution is $F(n) = Q(n)$, where $Q(n)$ is an appropriately chosen polynomial with the same degree as $P(n)$.

If exactly one of the roots r_1 and r_2 is 1, then a particular solution is $F(n) = Q(n)$, where $Q(n)$ is an appropriately chosen polynomial whose degree is 1 greater than the degree of $P(n)$ and whose constant term is zero.

If both of the roots r_1 and r_2 are 1, then a particular solution is $F(n) = Q(n)$, where $Q(n)$ is an appropriately chosen polynomial whose degree is 2 greater than the degree of $P(n)$ and whose constant and first degree terms are zero.

Higher Order Cases: Generalize in the obvious way from the first and second order cases above.

Example 4.3.7 Find the form of a particular solution for each of the following recurrence relations:

(a) $F(n) = 2F(n-1) + 2n^3 - 5n$ (b) $F(n) = F(n-1) + 3n$
(c) $F(n) = F(n-1) + 7$

Solution

(a) Since the coefficient of $F(n-1)$ is not 1, and since the non-homogeneous term $2n^3 - 5n$ is a polynomial of degree 3, there will be a particular solution of the form

$$F_{part}(n) = \beta_3 \, n^3 + \beta_2 \, n^2 + \beta_1 \, n + \beta_0$$

for some appropriately chosen constants β_i. These constants can be determined by plugging this formula into the recurrence relation and matching up the coefficients of the powers of n.

(b) Since the coefficient of $F(n-1)$ is 1, and since the non-homogeneous term $3n$ is a polynomial of degree 1, there will be a particular solution of the form $F_{part}(n) = \beta_2 \, n^2 + \beta_1 \, n$ for some appropriately chosen constants β_i.

(c) Since the coefficient of $F(n-1)$ is 1, and since the non-homogeneous term 7 is a polynomial of degree 0, there will be a particular solution of the form $F_{part}(n) = \beta_1 \, n$ for some appropriately chosen constant β_1.

Example 4.3.8 Find the form of a particular solution for each of the following recurrence relations:

(a) $F(n) = 4\,F(n-1) + 5\,F(n-2) + 2\,n$ (b) $F(n) = -5\,F(n-1) + 6\,F(n-2) + 2\,n$ (c) $F(n) = 2\,F(n-1) - F(n-2) + 2\,n$

Solution In each case we'll need to find the characteristic roots of the homogeneous part of the relation.

(a) The characteristic equation is $r^2 = 4r + 5$, or $r^2 - 4r - 5 = 0$, or $(r+1)(r-5) = 0$, so the characteristic roots are $r_1 = -1$ and $r_2 = 5$. Since neither of these roots is 1 [NOTE: -1 is not 1] and since the non-homogeneous term $2n$ is a polynomial of degree 1, there will be a particular solution of the form $F_{part}(n) = \beta_1 \, n + \beta_0$ for some appropriately chosen constants β_i.

(b) The characteristic equation is $r^2 = -5r + 6$, or $r^2 + 5r - 6 = 0$, or $(r-1)(r+6) = 0$, so the characteristic roots are $r_1 = 1$ and $r_2 = -6$. Since exactly one of these roots is 1, and since the non-homogeneous term $2n$ is a polynomial of degree 1, there will be a particular solution of the form $F_{part}(n) = \beta_2 \, n^2 + \beta_1 \, n$ for some appropriately chosen constants β_i.

(c) The characteristic equation is $r^2 = 2r - 1$, or $r^2 - 2r + 1 = 0$, or $(r-1)^2 = 0$, so the characteristic roots are $r_1 = 1 = r_2$. Since both of these roots are 1, and since the non-homogeneous term $2n$ is a polynomial of degree 1, there will be a particular solution of the form $F_{part}(n) = \beta_3 \, n^3 + \beta_2 \, n^2$ for some appropriately chosen constants β_i.

Example 4.3.9 Find the complete solution of the following recurrence problem:

$$F(0) = 1, \quad F(n) = -2\,F(n-1) + n - 1 \quad \text{when } n \geq 1.$$

Solution The general solution of the corresponding homogeneous relation is $F_{homog}(n) = \alpha(-2)^n$ for any constant α. A particular solution of the non-homogeneous relation has the form $F_{part}(n) = \beta_1 n + \beta_0$ for appropriately chosen constants β_i. To find out what values these constants must have, we substitute this particular solution into the non-homogeneous relation:

$$\beta_1 n + \beta_0 = -2(\beta_1(n-1) + \beta_0) + n - 1$$

which can be rewritten as

$$\beta_1 n + \beta_0 = (-2\beta_1 + 1)n + (2\beta_1 - 2\beta_0 - 1).$$

In order for $F_{part}(n) = \beta_1 n + \beta_0$ to be a solution of the recurrence relation, the equation above must be true for all $n \geq 1$. The only way this can be true is to have the coefficients of the powers of n on the two sides be the same. That is, we must have

$$\beta_1 = (-2\beta_1 + 1) \quad \text{and} \quad \beta_0 = (2\beta_1 - 2\beta_0 - 1).$$

Solving the first of these gives $\beta_1 = 1/3$. Using this in the second equation, we can solve for β_0 to get $\beta_0 = -1/9$. Thus we have found the following particular solution: $F_{part}(n) = (1/3)n - 1/9$. The most general solution for the non-homogeneous equation is

$$F(n) = F_{homog}(n) + F_{part}(n) = \alpha(-2)^n + (1/3)n - 1/9.$$

We now use the prescribed initial value $F(0) = 1$ to solve for α : $1 = \alpha(-2)^0 + 0 - 1/9$, which gives $\alpha = 10/9$. The solution to the given problem is

$$F(n) = \frac{10}{9}(-2)^n + \frac{1}{3}n - \frac{1}{9}.$$

While solving the problem in Example 4.3.9, we tacitly used a special case of the following theorem about polynomials.

Theorem 4.3.10 (Matching Coefficients): *Suppose we are given an equation of the form*

$$a_k n^k + a_{k-1} n^{k-1} + \cdots + a_1 n + a_0 = b_k n^k + b_{k-1} n^{k-1} + \cdots + b_1 n + b_0$$

and suppose we are told that the equation is satisfied by infinitely many values of n. Then, necessarily, $a_0 = b_0$, $a_1 = b_1, \ldots, a_k = b_k$. Similarly, an equation of the form

$$c_1 q_1{}^n + c_2 q_2{}^n + c_3 q_3{}^n + \cdots + c_k q_k{}^n = d_1 q_1{}^n + d_2 q_2{}^n + d_3 q_3{}^n + \cdots + d_k q_k{}^n,$$

where all the q_i's are constants distinct from each other, is satisfied by infinitely many values of n if and only if $c_1 = d_1$, $c_2 = d_2, \ldots, \quad c_k = d_k$.

Proof The first equation can be rearranged into the form

$$(a_k - b_k)n^k + (a_{k-1} - b_{k-1})n^{k-1} + \cdots + (a_1 - b_1)n + (a_0 - b_0) = 0$$

The left side is a polynomial, and the hypotheses of the theorem tell us that there are infinitely many values of n that make it zero, that is, the polynomial has infinitely many roots. But a polynomial cannot have more different roots than the degree of the polynomial, unless all its coefficients are zero, so that must be the case here. The proof of the statement concerning exponential terms is similar, but requires deeper mathematical analysis. It will be omitted here (but see Exercise 4.3.29 for the proof of a special case that illustrates the general idea).   ■

Example 4.3.11 In Theorem 2.3.2 on p. 32 we derived the closed form $\dfrac{n(n+1)}{2}$ for

the triangular sum $\displaystyle\sum_{k=1}^{n} k$. The "trick" we used to obtain that closed form does not work

for the sum $\displaystyle\sum_{k=1}^{n} k^2 = 1^2 + 2^2 + 3^2 + \cdots n^2$. (Try it for yourself and see why it doesn't

work. Also, beware of the naive algebraic error of thinking that $1^2 + 2^2 + 3^2 + \cdots n^2$ is equal to $(1 + 2 + \cdots + n)^2$.)

A closed form for $\displaystyle\sum_{k=1}^{n} k^2$ can be found, however, by using a recurrence relation.

Let $S(n)$ denote this sum for all $n \geq 1$. Then $S(1) = 1$, $S(2) = 5$, $S(3) = 14$, and so on. Note that we can break $S(n)$ down as follows: $S(n) = S(n-1) + n^2$ all $n \geq 2$. This is a first order, linear, non-homogeneous recurrence relation, with initial value $S(1) = 1$. The general solution of the homogeneous relation has the form $S_{homog}(n) = \alpha 1^n = \alpha$. A particular solution of the non-homogeneous relation is $S_{part}(n) = \beta_3 n^3 + \beta_2 n^2 + \beta_1 n$ for all $n \geq 1$. We substitute this into the non-homogeneous recurrence relation to solve for β_3, β_2, and β_1:

$$\begin{aligned}
\beta_3 n^3 + \beta_2 n^2 + \beta_1 n &= \beta_3(n-1)^3 + \beta_2(n-1)^2 + \beta_1(n-1) + n^2 \\
&= \beta_3(n^3 - 3n^2 + 3n - 1) + \beta_2(n^2 - 2n + 1) \\
&\quad + \beta_1(n-1) + n^2.
\end{aligned}$$

By the Matching Coefficients Theorem 4.3.10,
$\beta_3 = \beta_3$ and $\beta_2 = -3\beta_3 + \beta_2 + 1$ and $\beta_1 = 3\beta_3 - 2\beta_2 + \beta_1$ and $\gamma = -\beta_3 + \beta_2 - \beta_1 + \gamma$, so $\beta_3 = 1/3$ and $\beta_2 = 1/2$ and $\beta_1 = 1/6$. A particular solution therefore has the form $S_{part}(n) = (1/3)n^3 + (1/2)n^2 + (1/6)n$ for all $n \geq 1$. The general solution of the non-homogeneous relation is obtained by adding the general solution of the homogeneous relation to a particular solution of the non-homogeneous relation:

$$S(n) = \alpha + \frac{1}{3}n^3 + \frac{1}{2}n^2 + \frac{1}{6}n \quad \text{for all } n \geq 1.$$

We can determine α from the initial value: $1 = S(1) = \alpha + (1/3)1^3 + (1/2)1^2 + (1/6)1$, which gives $\alpha = 0$. Thus the sum $S(n)$ is given by $S(n) = (1/3)n^3 + (1/2)n^2 + (1/6)n$ for all $n \geq 1$. After combining terms and remembering what $S(n)$ stands for, we can write

$$\sum_{k=1}^{n} k^2 = \frac{2n^3 + 3n^2 + n}{6} = \frac{n(n+1)(2n+1)}{6} \quad \text{for all } n \geq 1.$$

The formula is valid for $n = 0$, but we haven't proved it. Of course, it's trivially true. In fact, it's even true for $n = -1$.

4.3.12 Exponential Non-homogeneous Terms in Linear Relations with Constant Coefficients

First Order Case: $F(n) = c_1 F(n-1) + d\,q^n$, where d and q are non-zero constants.

Solution If $c_1 \neq q$, then a particular solution is $F(n) = \gamma\,q^n$ for some appropriately chosen constant γ (Greek letter "gamma").

If $c_1 = q$, then a particular solution is $F(n) = \gamma\,n\,q^n$ for some appropriately chosen constant γ.

Second Order Case: $F(n) = c_1 F(n-1) + c_2 F(n-2) + dq^n$, where d and q are non-zero constants.

Solution Let r_1 and r_2 denote the characteristic roots for the homogeneous relation.

If neither r_1 nor r_2 is equal to q, then a particular solution is $F(n) = \gamma q^n$ for some appropriately chosen constant γ.

If exactly one of the roots r_1 and r_2 is equal to q, then a particular solution is $F(n) = \gamma\,n\,q^n$ for some appropriately chosen constant γ.

If both of the roots r_1 and r_2 are equal to q, then a particular solution is $F(n) = \gamma\,n^2\,q^n$ for some appropriately chosen constant γ.

Higher Order Cases: Generalize in the obvious way from the first and second order cases above.

Example 4.3.13 Find the form of a particular solution for each of the following recurrence relations:

(a) $F(n) = F(n-1) + 3 \times 2^n$ (b) $F(n) = 2F(n-1) + 3 \times 2^n + 2 \times 3^n$

Solution

(a) This is an example of the First Order Case described above, with $c_1 = 1$, $d = 3$, and $q = 2$. Since $c_1 \neq q$ in this case, there is a particular solution of the form $F_{part}(n) = \gamma\,2^n$ for some constant γ.
(b) This is a first order relation, but it does not exactly fit the pattern described in the First Order Case above. Instead, there are two separate exponential terms. We can handle this by using Theorem 4.3.2. First let's look at $F(n) = 2F(n-1) + 3 \times 2^n$. Using the information in the First Order Case above, we know there is a particular solution of the form $F_1(n) = \gamma_1 n 2^n$ for some appropriately chosen constant γ_1. (We could solve for γ_1 by substituting this particular solution into the non-homogeneous relation for which $\gamma_1 n 2^n$ is a solution.) Next, let's look at $F(n) =$

$2F(n-1) + 2 \times 3^n$. This has a particular solution of the form $F_2(n) = \gamma_2 3^n$ for some appropriately chosen constant γ_2. By Theorem 4.3.2 we know that $\gamma_1 F_1(n) + \gamma_2 F_2(n)$ will be a particular solution of the given recurrence relation.

Example 4.3.14 Find the form of a particular solution for each of the following recurrence relations:

(a) $F(n) = 5F(n-1) - 6F(n-2) + (-1)^n$
(b) $F(n) = F(n-1) + 2F(n-2) + (-1)^n$
(c) $F(n) = 6F(n-1) - 9F(n-2) + \dfrac{1}{2^n} + 3^n$

Solution

(a) The characteristic equation of the homogeneous relation is $r^2 = 5r - 6$, or $r^2 - 5r + 6 = 0$, or $(r-2)(r-3) = 0$. The characteristic roots are $r_1 = 2$ and $r_2 = 3$. The non-homogeneous term is exponential, and since -1 is not equal to either of the characteristic roots, the non-homogeneous relation has a particular solution of the form $F_{part}(n) = \gamma(-1)^n$ for some constant γ which can be determined by substituting this formula into the non-homogeneous relation.
(b) The characteristic equation of the homogeneous relation is $r^2 = r + 2$, or $r^2 - r - 2 = 0$, or $(r-2)(r+1) = 0$. The characteristic roots are $r_1 = 2$ and $r_2 = -1$. The non-homogeneous term is exponential, and since -1 is one of the characteristic roots, the non-homogeneous relation has a particular solution of the form $F_{part}(n) = \gamma n(-1)^n$ for some constant γ.
(c) The characteristic equation of the homogeneous relation is $r^2 = 6r - 9$, or $r^2 - 6r + 9 = 0$, or $(r-3)^2 = 0$. The characteristic roots are $r_1 = 3 = r_2$. There are two non-homogeneous terms, $(1/2)^n$ and 3^n. Both are exponential, and the base of one of them is the same as the double characteristic root. Thus the non-homogeneous relation has a particular solution of the form $F_{part}(n) = \gamma_1 (1/2)^n + \gamma_2 n^2 3^n$ for some constants γ_1 and γ_2.

Example 4.3.15 Find the complete solution of the following recurrence problem:

$F(1)=1, \ F(2)=2, \ F(n) = 2F(n-1) + 4F(n-2) - 5n + 2(-1)^{n+1}$ for $n \geq 3$.

Solution Rewrite the problem in the following slightly altered form (only the last term is changed):

$F(1)=1, \quad F(2) = 2, \quad F(n) = 2F(n-1) + 4F(n-2) - 5n - 2(-1)^n$ for $n \geq 3$.

The characteristic equation is $r^2 = 2r + 4$, or $r^2 - 2r - 4 = 0$, which has roots $r = \dfrac{-(-2) \pm \sqrt{4 - 4(-4)}}{2} = \dfrac{2 \pm \sqrt{20}}{2}$, so $r_1 = 1 + \sqrt{5}$ and $r_2 = 1 - \sqrt{5}$. Then the general solution of the homogeneous equation is

$$F_{homog}(n) = \alpha_1(1 + \sqrt{5})^n + \alpha_2(1 - \sqrt{5})^n.$$

To find a particular solution of the non-homogeneous relation, note that the non-homogeneous term $-5n$ will require a first order polynomial solution, say $\beta_1 n + \beta_0$, while the non-homogeneous term $-2(-1)^n$ will require an exponential solution, say $\gamma(-1)^n$. Thus we must have a particular solution of the form $F_{part}(n) = \beta_1 n + \beta_0 + \gamma(-1)^n$. We can solve for the coefficients in this particular solution by substituting into the recurrence relation:

$$\beta_1 n + \beta_0 + \gamma(-1)^n = 2[\beta_1(n-1) + \beta_0 + \gamma(-1)^{n-1}] + 4[\beta_1(n-2) + \beta_0$$
$$+ \gamma(-1)^{n-2}] - 5n - 2(-1)^n.$$

Grouping like terms on the right side of this equation gives

$$\beta_1 n + \beta_0 + \gamma(-1)^n = (2\beta_1 + 4\beta_1 - 5)n + (-2\beta_1 + 2\beta_0 - 8\beta_1 + 4\beta_0)$$
$$+ (-2\gamma + 4\gamma - 2)(-1)^n.$$

(Here we have used the fact that $(-1)^{n-1} = (-1)^n(-1)^{-1} = -(-1)^n$ and $(-1)^{n-2} = (-1)^n(-1)^{-2} = (-1)^n$.) Matching the coefficients on the left with the corresponding coefficients on the right gives $\beta_1 = 6\beta_1 - 5$ and $\beta_0 = -10\beta_1 + 6\beta_0$ and $\gamma = 2\gamma - 2$, which we can solve to obtain $\beta_1 = 1$ and $\beta_0 = 2$ and $\gamma = 2$.

Now that we know the general solution of the homogeneous relation and particular solutions for the two non-homogeneous relations above, we can write the general solution of the original recurrence relation:

$$F(n) = \alpha_1(1 + \sqrt{5})^n + \alpha_2(1 - \sqrt{5})^n + n + 2 + 2(-1)^n \quad \text{for all } n \geq 1.$$

To determine the α constants, we use the initial data:

$$1 = F(1) = \alpha_1(1 + \sqrt{5})^1 + \alpha_2(1 - \sqrt{5})^1 + 1 + 2 + 2(-1)^1$$
$$2 = F(2) = \alpha_1(1 + \sqrt{5})^2 + \alpha_2(1 - \sqrt{5})^2 + 2 + 2 + 2(-1)^2$$

These equations simplify to

$$1 = \alpha_1(1 + \sqrt{5}) + \alpha_2(1 - \sqrt{5}) + 1$$
$$2 = \alpha_1(1 + 2\sqrt{5} + 5) + \alpha_2(1 - 2\sqrt{5} + 5) + 6$$

which simplify further to

$$0 = \alpha_1(1 + \sqrt{5}) + \alpha_2(1 - \sqrt{5})$$
$$-4 = \alpha_1(6 + 2\sqrt{5}) + \alpha_2(6 - 2\sqrt{5}).$$

As it turns out, in systems of this form, rewriting the equations in the following form makes them much easier to solve:

$$0 = (\alpha_1 + \alpha_2) + (\alpha_1 - \alpha_2)\sqrt{5}$$
$$-4 = 6(\alpha_1 + \alpha_2) + 2(\alpha_1 - \alpha_2)\sqrt{5}.$$

Adding -2 times the first equation to the second equation gives $-4 = 4(\alpha_1 + \alpha_2)$, so $\alpha_1 + \alpha_2 = -1$. Substituting this back into the first equation gives $\alpha_1 - \alpha_2 = 1/\sqrt{5}$. Now we'll solve simultaneously

$$\alpha_1 + \alpha_2 = -1$$
$$\alpha_1 - \alpha_2 = 1/\sqrt{5}.$$

This gives us $\alpha_1 = \dfrac{1}{2}\left(-1 + \dfrac{1}{\sqrt{5}}\right)$ and $\alpha_2 = \dfrac{1}{2}\left(-1 - \dfrac{1}{\sqrt{5}}\right)$, which can be rewritten as $\alpha_1 = \dfrac{-\sqrt{5}+1}{2\sqrt{5}}$ and $\alpha_2 = -\dfrac{\sqrt{5}+1}{2\sqrt{5}}$. Thus we now have the complete solution:

$$F(n) = \left(\frac{1-\sqrt{5}}{2\sqrt{5}}\right)(1+\sqrt{5})^n - \left(\frac{\sqrt{5}+1}{2\sqrt{5}}\right)(1-\sqrt{5})^n + n + 2 + 2(-1)^n \quad \text{for all } n \geq 1.$$

Since $(1 - \sqrt{5})(1 + \sqrt{5}) = -4$, the solution above can be written somewhat more neatly and compactly as

$$F(n) = \frac{2}{\sqrt{5}}[(1-\sqrt{5})^{n-1} - (1+\sqrt{5})^{n-1}] + n + 2 + 2(-1)^n \quad \text{for all } n \geq 1.$$

We can check our work by computing $F(3)$ in two different ways: from the recurrence relation and from the solution we have calculated. The recurrence relation gives

$$F(3) = 2F(2) + 4F(1) - 5 \times 3 + 2(-1)^{3+1} = 2 \times 2 + 4 \times 1 - 15 + 2 = -5,$$

while the formula for the solution yields

$$\begin{aligned}
F(3) &= \frac{2}{\sqrt{5}}[(1-\sqrt{5})^2 - (1+\sqrt{5})^2] + 3 + 2 + 2(-1)^3 \\
&= \frac{2}{\sqrt{5}}[(1-2\sqrt{5}+5) - (1+2\sqrt{5}+5)] + 3 + 2 - 2 \\
&= \frac{2}{\sqrt{5}}[-4\sqrt{5}] + 3 \\
&= -8 + 3 \\
&= -5.
\end{aligned}$$

4.3.1 Further Examples

Example 4.3.16 This example is designed to make sure you understand what a polynomial is. In each case below, tell whether the given expression is a polynomial in the specified variable, and if it is, state its degree.

(a) $n^3 + 3n^2 - 2n + 1$; variable $= n$ (b) $3^n - 2^n + 1$; variable $= n$
(c) 2^{10}; variable $= n$ (d) $\sqrt{4n^2 - 3n + 7}$; variable $= n$

(e) $\dfrac{k+1}{2}$; variable $= k$ (f) $\left\lfloor \dfrac{k+1}{2} \right\rfloor$; variable $= k$

(g) $p\lg(m)$; m = variable, p = constant (h) $p\lg(m)$; p = variable, m = constant

Solutions

(a) $n^3 + 3n^2 - 2n + 1$ is a polynomial of degree 3 in the variable n.

(b) $3^n - 2^n + 1$ is not a polynomial in the variable n.

(c) 2^{10} is a polynomial of degree 0 in the variable n (it's a "constant polynomial" in any variable).

(d) $\sqrt{4n^2 - 3n + 7}$ is not a polynomial in the variable n (there is a polynomial under the radical).

(e) $\dfrac{k+1}{2}$ can be rewritten as $\dfrac{1}{2}k + \dfrac{1}{2}$, so it is a polynomial of degree 1 in the variable k.

(f) $\left\lfloor \dfrac{k+1}{2} \right\rfloor$ is not a polynomial in the variable k;

(g) $p\lg(m)$; m = variable, p = constant; this is not a polynomial in the variable m.

(h) $p\lg(m)$; p = variable, m = constant; this is a polynomial of degree 1 in the variable p.

Example 4.3.17 For each recurrence relation below, show just the form of the most general solution.

(a) $F(n) = 3F(n-1) + 3n^2 - 2n + 1$ (b) $F(n) = F(n-1) + 3n^2 - 2n + 1$

(c) $G(k) = G(k-1) - 2$ (d) $T(n) = \dfrac{T(n-1) + n}{3}$

(e) $F(n) = 3F(n-1) - 2F(n-2) - \dfrac{n+1}{5}$ (f) $g(n) = -2g(n-1) + 5g(n-2) - 4n^2 + 6$

(g) $F(n) = 2F(n-1) - F(n-2) - n^3$ (h) $M(k) = 5M(k-1) - 6M(k-2) + k^2$

Solutions

(a) Every solution has the form $F(n) = \alpha 3^n + \beta_2 n^2 + \beta_1 n + \beta_0$, where α can be any constant, and the constants β_2, β_1, and β_0 must be chosen specifically to fit the non-homogeneous recurrence relation.

(b) Every solution has the form $F(n) = \alpha 1^n + \beta_3 n^3 + \beta_2 n^2 + \beta_1 n$, where α can be any constant, and the constants β_3, β_2, and β_1 must be chosen specifically to fit the non-homogeneous recurrence relation.

(c) Every solution has the form $G(k) = \alpha 1^k + \beta_1 k$, where α can be any constant, and the constant β_1 must be chosen specifically to fit the non-homogeneous recurrence relation.

(d) $T(n) = \frac{1}{3}T(n-1)+\frac{1}{3}n$; every solution has the form $T(n) = \alpha(1/3)^n + \beta_1 n + \beta_0$, where α can be any constant, and the constants β_1 and β_0 must be chosen to fit the non-homogeneous recurrence relation.

(e) All solutions have the form $F(n) = \alpha_1 1^n + \alpha_2 2^n + \beta_2 n^2 + \beta_1 n$, where α_1 and α_2 can be any constants, and the constants β_2 and β_1 must be chosen specifically to fit the non-homogeneous recurrence relation.

(f) Every solution has the form $g(n) = \alpha_1(-1+\sqrt{6})^n + \alpha_2(-1-\sqrt{6})^n + \beta_2 n^2 + \beta_1 n + \beta_0$, where α_1 and α_2 can be any constants, and the constants β_2, β_1, and β_0 must be chosen specifically to fit the non-homogeneous recurrence relation.

(g) Every solution has the form $F(n) = (\alpha_1+\alpha_2 n)1^n + \beta_5 n^5 + \beta_4 n^4 + \beta_3 n^3 + \beta_2 n^2$, where α_1 and α_2 can be any constants, and the constants β_i must be chosen specifically to fit the non-homogeneous recurrence relation.

(h) Every solution has the form $M(k) = \alpha_1 2^k + \alpha_2 3^k + \beta_2 k^2 + \beta_1 k + \beta_0$, where α_1 and α_2 can be any constants, and the constants β_i must be chosen specifically to fit the non-homogeneous recurrence relation.

Example 4.3.18 Solve each of the following recurrence problems completely. In each case, check your answer by computing in two different ways the next term in the sequence after the initial data value(s).

(a) $F(0) = 1, \quad F(n) = 2F(n-1) - 3n + 1 \quad \text{for } n \geq 1$

(b) $F(1) = 0, \quad F(n) = n^2 + F(n-1) \quad \text{for } n \geq 2$

(c) $F(0) = 1, \quad F(1) = 3, \quad F(n) = F(n-1) + 2F(n-2) - 3 \quad \text{for } n \geq 2$

(d) $F(1) = 0, \quad F(2) = -1, \quad F(n) = -3F(n-1) + 4F(n-2) + 5n \quad \text{for } n \geq 3$

(e) $F(0) = 1, \quad F(1) = 0, \quad F(n) = F(n-1) + 3F(n-2) + 6n^2 - n + 2 \quad \text{for } n \geq 1$

(f) $T(0) = 0, \quad T(1) = 2, \quad T(m) = 2T(m-1) - T(m-2) - 2 \quad \text{for } m \geq 2$

(g) $h(1) = 0, \quad h(2) = 1, \quad h(n) = h(n-2) + n \quad \text{for } n \geq 3$

Solutions

(a) The general solution of the homogeneous relation is $F_{homog}(n) = \alpha 2^n$ for all $n \geq 0$. A particular solution for the non-homogeneous relation is $F_{part}(n) = \beta_1 n + \beta_0$ for all $n \geq 0$. First we'll determine β_1 and β_0 by substituting the formula for the particular solution into the non-homogeneous recurrence relation:

$$\beta_1 n + \beta_0 = 2[\beta_1(n-1) + \beta_0] - 3n + 1.$$

After some simplification we obtain

$$\beta_1 n + \beta_0 = (2\beta_1 - 3)n - 2\beta_1 + 2\beta_0 + 1,$$

which must be satisfied by infinitely many values of n, namely all $n \geq 1$. By the Matching Coefficients Theorem 4.3.10 we must have

$$\beta_1 = 2\beta_1 - 3 \quad \text{and} \quad \beta_0 = -2\beta_1 + 2\beta_0 + 1.$$

Solving these simultaneous equations gives us $\beta_1 = 3$ and $\beta_0 = 5$. Now we know that the general solution of the original non-homogeneous recurrence relation has the form $F(n) = \alpha 2^n + 3n + 5$ for all $n \geq 0$. We obtain the value of α from the initial value we are given: $F(0) = 1$. Setting n to 0 in the solution gives $F(0) = \alpha 2^0 + 3 \times 0 + 5$, so $1 = \alpha + 5$, and thus $\alpha = -4$. The final solution, therefore is

$$F(n) = -4 \times 2^n + 3n + 5 \text{ for all } n \geq 0.$$

We can write this as $F(n) = -2^{n+2} + 3n + 5$, $n \geq 0$. [Check: $F(1) = 0$ by the recurrence relation and also by the final formula for the solution.]

(b) The general solution of the homogeneous relation has the form $F_{homog}(n) = \alpha 1^n = \alpha$ for $n \geq 1$. That is, all constant functions are solutions of the homogeneous relation. A particular solution of the non-homogeneous relation will have the form $F_{part}(n) = \beta_3 n^3 + \beta_2 n^2 + \beta_1 n$ for all $n \geq 1$. We'll determine the values of β_3, β_2, and β_1 by substituting the formula for $F_{part}(n)$ into the non-homogeneous recurrence relation:

$$\beta_3 n^3 + \beta_2 n^2 + \beta_1 n = n^2 + \beta_3 (n-1)^3 + \beta_2 (n-1)^2 + \beta_1 (n-1).$$

After considerable algebraic expansion and simplification we obtain

$$\beta_3 n^3 + \beta_2 n^2 + \beta_1 n = \beta_3 n^3 + (1 - 3\beta_3 + \beta_2)n^2 + (3\beta_3 - 2\beta_2 + \beta_1)n + (-\beta_3 + \beta_2 - \beta_1),$$

which must be satisfied by infinitely many values of n (i.e., all $n \geq 2$). By the Matching Coefficients Theorem 4.3.10 we must have

$$\beta_3 = \beta_3 \quad \text{and} \quad \beta_2 = 1 - 3\beta_3 + \beta_2 \quad \text{and} \quad \beta_1 = 3\beta_3 - 2\beta_2 + \beta_1 \quad \text{and} \quad 0 = -\beta_3 + \beta_2 - \beta_1.$$

Solving these simultaneous equations gives us $\beta_3 = 1/3$, $\beta_2 = 1/2$, and $\beta_1 = 1/6$. Now we know that $F_{part}(n) = (1/3)n^3 + (1/2)n^2 + (1/6)n$ for all $n \geq 1$. The general solution to the original non-homogeneous relation is then obtained by adding the general solution of the homogeneous relation to the particular solution of the non-homogeneous relation:

$$F(n) = \alpha + (1/3)n^3 + (1/2)n^2 + (1/6)n.$$

We obtain the value of α from the initial value we are given: $F(1) = 0$. Setting n to 1 in the solution gives $F(1) = \alpha + (1/3)1^3 + (1/2)1^2 + (1/6)1$, so $0 = \alpha + 1$, and thus $\alpha = -1$. The final solution is

$$F(n) = (1/3)n^3 + (1/2)n^2 + (1/6)n - 1 \quad \text{for all } n \geq 0.$$

[Check: $F(2) = 4$ by the recurrence relation and also by the final formula for the solution.]

(c) The characteristic equation is $r^2 = r + 2$ with solutions -1 and 2, so the general solution of the homogeneous relation has the form $F_{homog}(n) = \alpha_1 (-1)^n + \alpha_2 2^n$. A particular solution for the non-homogeneous relation is $F_{part}(n) = \beta_0$ for all $n \geq 0$. First we'll determine β_0 by substituting the formula for the particular solution into the non-homogeneous recurrence relation:

$$\beta_0 = \beta_0 + 2\beta_0 - 3,$$

which shows that $\beta_0 = 3/2$. The general solution of the non-homogeneous relation is then obtained by adding the general solution of the homogeneous relation to a particular solution of the non-homogeneous relation: $F(n) = \alpha_1(-1)^n + \alpha_2 2^n + 3/2$ for all $n \geq 0$. To determine α_1 and α_2 we use the given initial values: $F(0) = 1$ and $F(1) = 3$. Setting n to 0 and then to 1 in the solution gives the equations $F(0) = \alpha_1(-1)^0 + \alpha_2 2^0 + 3/2$ and $F(1) = \alpha_1(-1)^1 + \alpha_2 2^1 + 3/2$, so $1 = \alpha_1 + \alpha_2 + 3/2$ and $3 = -\alpha_1 + 2\alpha_2 + 3/2$. Solving these simultaneous equations gives us $\alpha_1 = -5/6$ and $\alpha_2 = 1/3$, so the final solution of the problem we were given is

$$F(n) = (-5/6)(-1)^n + (1/3)2^n + 3/2 \quad \text{for all } n \geq 0.$$

[Check: $F(2) = 2$ by the recurrence relation and also by the final formula for the solution.]

(d) The characteristic equation is $r^2 = -3r + 4$ with solutions -4 and 1, so the solution of the homogeneous relation has the form $F_{homog}(n) = \alpha_1(-4)^n + \alpha_2 1^n$. A particular solution of the non-homogeneous relation has the form $F_{part}(n) = \beta_2 n^2 + \beta_1 n$. We'll determine the values of β_2 and β_1 by substituting the formula for $F_{part}(n)$ into the non-homogeneous recurrence relation:

$$\beta_2 n^2 + \beta_1 n = -3[\beta_2(n-1)^2 + \beta_1(n-1)] + 4[\beta_2(n-2)^2 + \beta_1(n-2)] + 5n,$$

which can be rewritten as

$$\beta_2 n^2 + \beta_1 n = (-3\beta_2 + 4\beta_2)n^2 + (6\beta_2 - 3\beta_1 - 16\beta_2 + 4\beta_1 + 5)n$$
$$+(-3\beta_2 + 3\beta_1 + 16\beta_2 - 8\beta_1).$$

By the Matching Coefficients Theorem 4.3.10 we must have

$$\beta_2 = \beta_2 \quad \text{and} \quad \beta_1 = -10\beta_2 + \beta_1 + 5 \quad \text{and} \quad 0 = 13\beta_2 - 5\beta_1.$$

Solving these simultaneous equations gives us $\beta_2 = 1/2$ and $\beta_1 = 13/10$, so $F_{part}(n) = (1/2)n^2 + (13/10)n$. We obtain the general solution for the non-homogeneous recurrence relation by adding the general solution of the homogeneous relation to a particular solution:

$$F(n) = \alpha_1(-4)^n + \alpha_2 + (1/2)n^2 + (13/10)n \quad \text{for all } n \geq 1.$$

We obtain the values of α_1 and α_2 from the initial values we are given: $F(1) = 0$ and $F(2) = -1$. Setting n to 1 and then to 2 in the solution gives $F(1) = \alpha_1(-4)^1 + \alpha_2 + (1/2)1^2 + (13/10)1$ and $F(2) = \alpha_1(-4)^2 + \alpha_2 + (1/2)2^2 + (13/10)2$, so $0 = -4\alpha_1 + \alpha_2 + 18/10$ and $-1 = 16\alpha_1 + \alpha_2 + 46/10$. Solving these simultaneous equations gives us $\alpha_1 = -19/100$ and $\alpha_2 = -64/25$. Thus the final solution of the given problem is

$$F(n) = (-19/100)(-4)^n + (1/2)n^2 + (13/10)n - 64/25 \quad \text{for all } n \geq 1.$$

[Check: $F(3) = 18$ by the recurrence relation and also by the final formula for the solution.]

(e) The characteristic equation is $r^2 = r + 3$, so the characteristic roots are $\dfrac{1 \pm \sqrt{13}}{2}$.
It follows that the general solution of the homogeneous relation has the form

$$F_{homog}(n) = \alpha_1 \left(\frac{1 + \sqrt{13}}{2} \right)^n + \alpha_2 \left(\frac{1 - \sqrt{13}}{2} \right)^n \qquad \text{for all } n \geq 0.$$

A particular solution of the non-homogeneous relation has the form $F_{part}(n) = \beta_2 n^2 + \beta_1 n + \beta_0$. We'll determine the values of β_2, β_1, and β_0 by substituting the formula for the particular solution into the non-homogeneous recurrence relation:

$$\beta_2 n^2 + \beta_1 n + \beta_0 = [\beta_2(n-1)^2 + \beta_1(n-1) + \beta_0] + 3[\beta_2(n-2)^2 + \beta_1(n-2) + \beta_0] + 6n^2 - n + 2$$

which can be rewritten as

$$\beta_2 n^2 + \beta_1 n + \beta_0 = (\beta_2 + 3\beta_2 + 6)n^2 + (-2\beta_2 + \beta_1 - 12\beta_2 + 3\beta_1 - 1)n + (\beta_2 - \beta_1 + \beta_0 + 12\beta_2 - 6\beta_1 + 3\beta_0 + 2).$$

By the Matching Coefficients Theorem 4.3.10 we must have

$$\beta_2 = 4\beta_2 + 6 \quad \text{and} \quad \beta_1 = -14\beta_2 + 4\beta_1 - 1 \quad \text{and} \quad \beta_0 = 13\beta_2 - 7\beta_1 + 4\beta_0 + 2.$$

Solving these simultaneous equations gives us $\beta_2 = -2$, $\beta_1 = -9$, and $\beta_0 = -13$. Thus $F_{part}(n) = -2n^2 - 9n - 13$. We get the general solution of the non-homogeneous relation by adding the general solution of the homogeneous relation to a particular solution of the non-homogeneous relation:

$$F(n) = \alpha_1 \left(\frac{1 + \sqrt{13}}{2} \right)^n + \alpha_2 \left(\frac{1 - \sqrt{13}}{2} \right)^n - 2n^2 - 9n - 13 \quad \text{for all } n \geq 0.$$

We obtain the values of α_1 and α_2 by using the initial values we are given: $F(0) = 1$ and $F(1) = 0$. Setting n to 0 and then to 1 in the solution gives the equations

$$1 = F(0) = \alpha_1 + \alpha_2 - 13 \quad \text{and} \quad 0 = F(1) = \alpha_1 \frac{1 + \sqrt{13}}{2}$$

$$+ \alpha_2 \frac{1 - \sqrt{13}}{2} - 2 \times 1^2 - 9 \times 1 - 13,$$

which give us $\alpha_1 + \alpha_2 = 14$ and $0 = (\alpha_1 + \alpha_2)(1/2) + (\alpha_1 - \alpha_2)(\sqrt{13}/2) - 24$. The solutions of these equations are $\alpha_1 = 7 + 17/\sqrt{13}$ and $\alpha_2 = 7 - 17/\sqrt{13}$. Thus the final solution of the given problem is

$$F(n) = \left(7 + \frac{17}{\sqrt{13}} \right) \left(\frac{1 + \sqrt{13}}{2} \right)^n + \left(7 - \frac{17}{\sqrt{13}} \right) \left(\frac{1 - \sqrt{13}}{2} \right)^n - 2n^2 - 9n - 13 \quad \text{for } n \geq 0.$$

[Check: $F(2) = 27$ by the recursion relation and by the final formula for the solution.]

(f) The characteristic equation is $r^2 = 2r - 1$, so the characteristic roots are $r_1 = r_2 = 1$. Thus the general solution of the homogeneous relation has the form $T_{homog}(m) = (\alpha_1 + \alpha_2 m)1^m = \alpha_1 + \alpha_2 m$. Since the non-homogeneous part of the recurrence relation is a polynomial of degree 0 (i.e., a constant), a particular solution of the non-homogeneous relation is a polynomial of degree 2 without the terms of degree 1 and 0: $T_{part}(m) = \beta_2 m^2$ for all $m \geq 0$. We solve for β_2 by substituting this formula into the given non-homogeneous recurrence relation:

$$\beta_2 m^2 = 2[\beta_2(m-1)^2] - [\beta_2(m-2)^2] - 2.$$

By the Matching Coefficients Theorem 4.3.10 we must have

$$\beta_2 = 2\beta_2 - \beta_2 \quad \text{and} \quad 0 = -4\beta_2 + 4\beta_2 \quad \text{and} \quad 0 = 2\beta_2 - 4\beta_2 - 2,$$

which gives us $\beta_2 = -1$. Thus $T_{part}(m) = -m^2$ for all $m \geq 0$. We obtain the general solution of the non-homogeneous relation by adding the general solution of the homogeneous relation to a particular solution of the non-homogeneous relation:

$$T(m) = \alpha_1 + \alpha_2 m - m^2 \quad \text{for all } m \geq 0.$$

We determine α_1 and α_2 by using the initial data: $T(0) = 0$ and $T(1) = 2$. This gives us $0 = T(0) = \alpha_1 + \alpha_2 0 - 0^2$ and $2 = T(1) = \alpha_1 + \alpha_2 1 - 1^2$, so $\alpha_1 = 0$ and $\alpha_2 = 3$. The final solution of the problem we were given is

$$T(m) = 3m - m^2 \quad \text{for all } m \geq 0.$$

[Check: $T(2) = 2$ by the recurrence relation and by the solution.]

(g) The characteristic equation is $r^2 = 0r + 1$, so the characteristic roots are $r_1 = -1$ and $r_2 = 1$. The general solution of the homogeneous relation has the form $h_{homog}(n) = \alpha_1(-1)^n + \alpha_2 1^n = \alpha_1(-1)^n + \alpha_2$. A particular solution of the non-homogeneous relation is $h_{part}(n) = \beta_2 n^2 + \beta_1 n$ for all $n \geq 1$. If we substitute this formula into the non-homogeneous recurrence relation we get

$$\beta_2 n^2 + \beta_1 n = \beta_2(n-2)^2 + \beta_1(n-2) + n.$$

By the Matching Coefficients Theorem 4.3.10 we have

$$\beta_2 = \beta_2 \quad \text{and} \quad \beta_1 = -4\beta_2 + \beta_1 + 1 \quad \text{and} \quad 0 = 4\beta_2 - 2\beta_1,$$

which gives us $\beta_2 = 1/4$ and $\beta_1 = 1/2$. Thus a particular solution has the form $h_{part}(n) = (1/4)n^2 + (1/2)n$ for all $n \geq 1$. A general solution of the non-homogeneous relation is obtained by adding the general solution of the homogeneous relation to a particular solution of the non-homogeneous relation:

$$h(n) = \alpha_1(-1)^n + \alpha_2 + (1/4)n^2 + (1/2)n \quad \text{for all } n \geq 1.$$

We can determine α_1 and α_2 by using the initial data we are given: $h(1) = 0$ and $h(2) = 1$. Then $0 = h(1) = \alpha_1(-1)^1 + \alpha_2 + (1/4)1^2 + (1/2)1$ and $1 = h(2) = \alpha_1(-1)^2 + \alpha_2 + (1/4)2^2 + (1/2)2$, so $0 = -\alpha_1 + \alpha_2 + 3/4$ and

$1 = \alpha_1 + \alpha_2 + 2$. Solving gives us $\alpha_1 = -1/8$ and $\alpha_2 = -7/8$. The final solution to the given problem is

$$h(n) = (1/8)(-1)^{n+1} - 7/8 + (1/4)n^2 + (1/2)n \quad \text{for all } n \geq 1.$$

[Check: $h(3) = 3$ by the recurrence relation and also by the final formula for the solution.]

Example 4.3.19 Find just the form of the most general solution for each of the following recurrence relations.

(a) $F(n) = 3F(n-1) + 3^n - 2^n$
(b) $F(n) = 3F(n-1) + 5n^2 - 4 \times 2^n$
(c) $F(n) = -F(n-1) - 3^n + 4^n + 7(-1)^n$
(d) $F(n) = -5F(n-1) - 3^n + 4^n + 7(-1)^n$
(e) $F(n) = 4F(n-1) + 2(-1)^n - n^3 + 5n$
(f) $F(n) = F(n-1) + 6F(n-2) - 3^n$
(g) $T(n) = T(n-1) - 2T(n-2) + 3^n - 4$
(h) $F(n) = 4F(n-1) - 4F(n-2) - 7 \times 2^n$
(i) $F(n) = 4F(n-1) + F(n-2) + 2^n - 6^n$
(j) $F(n) = 4F(n-1) - 3F(n-2) + 2^n - 3^n$

(k) $F(n) = 4F(n-1) - 3F(n-2) + 2^n - 6^n + 1$ (l) $F(n) = F(n-1) + 2F(n-2) + 3(-1)^n + \dfrac{5}{2^n}$

Solutions In the following formulas, the αs are arbitrary constants (i.e., any values we choose are correct). The values of the αs would be determined if initial values for the Fs were given. By contrast, the βs and γs can be determined in every case by substituting the solution formulas for the Fs into the corresponding recurrence relations.

(a) $F(n) = \alpha 3^n + \gamma_1 n 3^n + \gamma_2 2^n$

(b) $F(n) = \alpha 3^n + \gamma 2^n + \beta_2 n^2 + \beta_1 n + \beta_0$

(c) $F(n) = \alpha(-1)^n + \gamma_1 3^n + \gamma_2 4^n + \gamma_3 n(-1)^n$

(d) $F(n) = \alpha(-5)^n + \gamma_1 3^n + \gamma_2 4^n + \gamma_3(-1)^n$

(e) $F(n) = \alpha 4^n + \gamma(-1)^n + \beta_3 n^3 + \beta_2 n^2 + \beta_1 n + \beta_0$

(f) $F(n) = \alpha_1(-2)^n + \alpha_2 3^n + \gamma n 3^n$

(g) $T(n) = \alpha_1 \left(\dfrac{1+\sqrt{7}i}{2}\right)^n + \alpha_2 \left(\dfrac{1-\sqrt{7}i}{2}\right)^n + \gamma 3^n + \beta_0$, where $i^2 = -1$.

(h) $F(n) = \alpha_1 2^n + \alpha_2 n 2^n + \gamma n^2 2^n$

(i) $F(n) = \alpha_1(2+\sqrt{5})^n + \alpha_2(2-\sqrt{5})^n + \gamma_1 2^n + \gamma_2 6^n$

(j) $F(n) = \alpha_1 + \alpha_2 3^n + \gamma_1 2^n + \gamma_2 n 3^n$

(k) $F(n) = \alpha_1 + \alpha_2 3^n + \gamma_1 2^n + \gamma_2 6^n + \beta_1 n$

(l) $F(n) = \alpha_1 2^n + \alpha_2(-1)^n + \gamma_1 n(-1)^n + \gamma_2(1/2)^n$

Example 4.3.20 Solve the following recurrence problems.

(a) $F(0) = 2,\quad F(n) = 3F(n-1) + 3^n - 2^n$ for $n \geq 1$
(b) $F(0) = 0,\quad F(n) = 2F(n-1) + 2n^2 - 2 \times 3^n$ for $n \geq 1$

Solutions

(a) $F_{homog}(n) = \alpha 3^n$; $F_{part}(n) = \gamma_1 n 3^n + \gamma_2 2^n$ for $n \geq 0$; substitute the particular solution into the relation to obtain $\gamma_1 n 3^n + \gamma_2 2^n = 3[\gamma_1(n-1)3^{n-1} + \gamma_2 2^{n-1}] + 3^n - 2^n$ for all $n \geq 1$.

Multiplying out the terms and simplifying yields $\gamma_2 2^n = -\gamma_1 3^n + 3\gamma_2 2^{n-1} + 3^n - 2^n$ for all $n \geq 1$, which we can rewrite as $2\gamma_2 2^{n-1} = (-\gamma_1 + 1)3^n + (3\gamma_2 - 2)2^{n-1}$ for all $n \geq 1$.

Matching the coefficients of the different exponential terms gives $2\gamma_2 = 3\gamma_2 - 2$ and $0 = -\gamma_1 + 1$, which means that $\gamma_1 = 1$ and $\gamma_2 = 2$.

Thus the general solution of the non-homogeneous relation is $F(n) = \alpha 3^n + n3^n + 2 \times 2^n$ for all $n \geq 0$.

We determine α from the initial condition: $2 = F(0) = \alpha + 0 + 2 \times 2^0$, so $\alpha = 0$. Thus

$$F(n) = n3^n + 2^{n+1} \quad \text{for all } n \geq 0.$$

[Check: $F(1) = 7$ by the recurrence relation and also by the formula for the solution.]

(b) $F_{homog}(n) = \alpha 2^n$; $F_{part}(n) = \beta_2 n^2 + \beta_1 n + \beta_0 + \gamma 3^n$ for all $n \geq 0$. Substitute the particular solution into the non-homogeneous relation to obtain

$$\beta_2 n^2 + \beta_1 n + \beta_0 + \gamma 3^n = 2[\beta_2(n-1)^2 + \beta_1(n-1) + \beta_0 + \gamma 3^{n-1}]$$
$$+ 2n^2 - 2 \times 3^n \text{ for all } n \geq 1.$$

Rewriting some of the terms yields

$$\beta_2 n^2 + \beta_1 n + \beta_0 + 3\gamma 3^{n-1} = (2\beta_2 + 2)n^2 + (-4\beta_2 + 2\beta_1)n$$
$$+ (2\beta_2 - 2\beta_1 + 2\beta_0) + (2\gamma - 2 \times 3)3^{n-1}$$

for all $n \geq 1$. Matching up coefficients of like terms gives the equations

$\beta_2 = 2\beta_2 + 2$ and $\beta_1 = -4\beta_2 + 2\beta_1$ and $\beta_0 = 2\beta_2 - 2\beta_1 + 2\beta_0$ and $3\gamma = 2\gamma - 6$,

which in turn give $\beta_2 = -2$ and $\beta_1 = -8$ and $\beta_0 = -12$ and $\gamma = -6$. Thus $F(n) = \alpha 2^n - 2n^2 - 8n - 12 - 6 \times 3^n$ for all $n \geq 0$. Using the initial data we get $0 = F(0) = \alpha - 12 - 6 \times 1$ which means that $\alpha = 18$, so

$$F(n) = 18 \times 2^n - 2n^2 - 8n - 12 - 6 \times 3^n \quad \text{for all } n \geq 0.$$

[Check: $F(1) = -4$ from the recurrence relation and also from the formula for the solution.]

4.3.2   Exercises

4.3.21 For each recurrence relation below, show just the form of the most general solution.

(a) $f(m) = 5f(m-1) - 2m$ (b) $F(n) = n^2 - F(n-1)$

(c) $F(k) = k^2 + F(k-1)$ (d) $S(h) = -2S(h-1) + 3S(h-2) - 7h$

(e) $F(n) = 2F(n-1) + 3F(n-2) - 7$ (f) $N(k) = 2N(k-1) - N(k-2) + k^2$

(g) $T(n) = \dfrac{2T(n-1)}{3} + 3n$ (h) $p(n) = 5p(n-1) + 6p(n-2) + n$

4.3.22 Solve each of the following recurrence problems completely. In each case, check your answer by computing in two different ways the next term in the sequence after the initial data value(s).

(a) $F(1) = 3$, $F(n) = 2F(n-1) - 1$ for all $n \geq 2$

(b) $F(1) = 3$, $F(n) = F(n-1) - 2$ for all $n \geq 2$

(c) $F(0) = 7$, $F(1) = 4$, $F(n) = 2F(n-1) + 3F(n-2) - 2 - n^2$ for all $n \geq 2$

(d) $A(0) = 0$, $A(1) = 1$, $A(m) = -2A(m-1) + 3A(m-2) + 16m$ when $m \geq 2$

(e) $X(1) = 3$, $X(2) = 1$, $X(n) = 2X(n-1) - X(n-2) + 2$ when $n \geq 3$

4.3.23 Using ideas similar to those in Example 4.3.11, write a recurrence relation for the sum

$$T(n) = \sum_{k=1}^{n} k^3, \; n \geq 1,$$ and solve it using an appropriate initial value.

4.3.24 Prove Theorem 4.3.2.

4.3.25 Verify by direct substitution that the function defined by $F(n) = \dfrac{1}{n}$ for all $n \geq 1$ is a solution of the homogeneous linear recurrence relation

$$F(n) = 2\frac{n-1}{n}F(n-1) - \frac{n-2}{n}F(n-2) \quad \text{for all } n \geq 3.$$

Verify by direct substitution that the constant function defined by $F(n) = 1$ for all $n \geq 1$ is a solution of the same recurrence relation. Then verify that the function defined by $F(n) = n$ for all $n \geq 1$ is a solution of the nonhomogeneous linear recurrence relation

$$F(n) = 2\frac{n-1}{n}F(n-1) - \frac{n-2}{n}F(n-2) + \frac{2}{n} \quad \text{for all } n \geq 3.$$

Now, using the three statements you have just verified and Theorems 4.2.3, 4.3.1, 4.3.2, and/or 4.3.3, explain why the function defined by $F(n) = n+2-\dfrac{1}{n}$ for all $n \geq 1$ is also a particular solution of the nonhomogeneous relation above. More generally, explain why the function defined by $F(n) = n + \alpha + \beta\dfrac{1}{n}$ is a particular solution of the same nonhomogeneous relation, regardless of the value of the constants α and β.

4.3.26 Find just the form of the most general solution for each of the following recurrence relations.

(a) $F(n) = 4F(n-1) - 2^n$ (b) $F(n) = 4F(n-1) - 4^n$
(c) $G(n) = 4G(n-1) - 3G(n-2) + 2 \times 4^n$ (d) $H(n) = H(n-1) - 3H(n-2) + 2 \times 3^n$
(e) $M(k) = 4M(k-2) + 3 \times 2^k$ (read carefully)   (f) $P(m) = 4P(m-1) - 4P(m-2) + m + 2^m$

4.3.27 Solve the following recurrence problem:

$$F(0) = 2, \quad F(1) = 1, \quad F(n) = 2F(n-1) - F(n-2) + 6 - 2n + \frac{4}{3^n} \quad \text{for all } n \geq 2.$$

Hint: $\dfrac{4}{3^n} = 4(?)^n$.

4.3.28 Verify each of the following assertions.

(a) The function defined by $F(n) = d\, n\, c^n$ is a solution of the recurrence relation
$$F(n) = c\, F(n-1) + d\, c^n.$$

(b) The function defined by $F(n) = \beta\, n^2\, c^n$, for some appropriately chosen constant β, is a solution of the recurrence relation $F(n) = 2c\, F(n-1) - c^2\, F(n-2) + d\, c^n$, which has c as a repeated characteristic root.

4.3.29 Suppose $c_1 2^n + c_2 3^n = d_1 2^n + d_2 3^n$ for all $n \geq 1$. Prove that $c_1 = d_1$ and $c_2 = d_2$.

Hint: *begin* by dividing through the equation by 3^n and then taking the limit on both sides of the resulting equation.

4.4   Recurrence Relations Involving $\lfloor n/2 \rfloor$ and $\lceil n/2 \rceil$

When analyzing "divide and conquer" algorithms such as Quicksort or Binary Search, we often end up with recurrence relations that express the number of operations on a problem of size n in terms involving the number of operations on a problem of size $\lfloor n/2 \rfloor$ or $\lceil n/2 \rceil$, or both (because $\lfloor n/2 \rfloor + \lceil n/2 \rceil = n$). Usually these recurrence relations have reasonably simple forms, and in many cases we can solve them with a little algebra and knowledge of floors and ceilings. Let's take some examples.

Example 4.4.1 Suppose we want to solve a recurrence problem of the form
$$F(1) = a, \quad F(n) = bF(\lfloor n/2 \rfloor) \quad \text{for all } n \geq 2,$$
where b is some non-zero constant.

This is a linear, homogeneous recurrence relation with constant coefficients, but it has no well-defined order, so the theorems in Sects. 4.2 and 4.3 do not apply here. Thus we need to attack it some other way. So imagine that n is some integer greater than 1 and that we want to work out the value of $F(n)$. We are given that

$$F(n) = bF(\lfloor n/2 \rfloor).$$

If $\lfloor n/2 \rfloor > 1$, then we can take another step: since $F(\lfloor n/2 \rfloor) = bF(\lfloor \lfloor n/2 \rfloor /2 \rfloor)$ it follows that

$$F(n) = b[bF(\lfloor \lfloor n/2 \rfloor /2 \rfloor)] = b^2 F(\lfloor n/2^2 \rfloor)$$

(here we have used Theorem 2.1.5(d) on p. 12). If $\lfloor n/2^2 \rfloor > 1$, we can take still another step:

$$F(n) = b^2 F(\lfloor n/2^2 \rfloor) = b^2 [bF(\lfloor \lfloor n/2^2 \rfloor /2 \rfloor)] = b^3 F(\lfloor n/2^3 \rfloor).$$

Continuing in this way until $\lfloor n/2^p \rfloor = 1$ after p steps, we will have

$$F(n) = b^p F(1) = b^p a = a b^p.$$

For what integer p will it be true that $\lfloor n/2^p \rfloor = 1$. We already know the answer by Theorem 2.2.8(b) on p. 22: $p = \lfloor \lg(n) \rfloor$. Thus we have found this solution to our problem: $F(n) = a b^{\lfloor \lg(n) \rfloor}$ for all $n > 1$. For $n = 1$ we have $b^{\lfloor \lg(n) \rfloor} = b^0 = 1$, and thus the formula above is also valid when $n = 1$. Thus we have shown that the solution to the given problem is the following:

$$F(n) = a b^{\lfloor \lg(n) \rfloor} \quad \text{for all } n \geq 1.$$

It is useful to find a simple big-theta expression for this solution in the cases where $a \neq 0$ and $b > 0$. Since $\lg(n) - 1 < \lfloor \lg(n) \rfloor \leq \lg(n)$, it follows that when $b \geq 1$ we have $b^{\lg(n)-1} \leq b^{\lfloor \lg(n) \rfloor} \leq b^{\lg(n)}$. Using Theorem 2.2.10 on p. 24 we then have $\frac{1}{b} n^{\lg(b)} \leq b^{\lfloor \lg(n) \rfloor} \leq n^{\lg(b)}$, which tells us that $F(n) = \Theta(n^{\lg(b)})$. The inequalities are reversed if $0 < b < 1$, but they still give $F(n) = \Theta(n^{\lg(b)})$.

Example 4.4.2 Next let's vary the problem slightly by adding a simple non-homogeneous term:

$$F(1) = a, \quad F(n) = bF(\lfloor n/2 \rfloor) + 1 \quad \text{for all } n \geq 2.$$

Consider an integer n greater than 1. Using the ideas exploited in Example 4.4.1 we get

$$\begin{aligned} F(n) &= bF(\lfloor n/2 \rfloor) + 1 \\ &= b[b F(\lfloor n/2^2 \rfloor) + 1] + 1 = b^2 F(\lfloor n/2^2 \rfloor) + b + 1 \\ &= b^2 [bF(\lfloor n/2^3 \rfloor) + 1] + b + 1 = b^3 F(\lfloor n/2^3 \rfloor) + b^2 + b + 1 \end{aligned}$$

Continuing in this way until $\lfloor n/2^p \rfloor = 1$ we get

$$F(n) = b^p a + b^{p-1} + b^{p-2} + \cdots + 1 \tag{4.14}$$

where, as in Example 4.4.1, we know that $p = \lfloor \lg(n) \rfloor$. We quickly recognize the term $a \, b^{\lfloor \lg(n) \rfloor}$, which forms the general solution of the homogeneous part of the relation (see Example 4.4.1). The remaining terms in Eq. (4.14) form a finite geometric sum with closed form $\dfrac{b^{\lfloor \lg(n) \rfloor} - 1}{b - 1}$, provided $b \neq 1$. This expression can be split into two pieces, the first being $\dfrac{1}{b - 1} b^{\lfloor \lg(n) \rfloor}$ and the second being $\dfrac{-1}{b - 1}$, or $\dfrac{1}{1 - b}$. The first piece is a constant times $b^{\lfloor \lg(n) \rfloor}$, which is a solution of the homogeneous relation, and can be combined with the term $a \, b^{\lfloor \lg(n) \rfloor}$ to produce a term of the form $\alpha b^{\lfloor \lg(n) \rfloor}$. The second piece, $\dfrac{1}{1 - b}$, should then be a particular solution of the non-homogeneous relation, which we can verify by simple substitution:

$$\frac{1}{1 - b} = b \, \frac{1}{1 - b} + 1,$$

which is easily seen to be valid. Thus we have shown that the solution of our problem has the form

$$F(n) = a \, b^{\lfloor \lg(n) \rfloor} + \frac{1}{1 - b} \quad \text{for all } n \geq 1 \text{ provided } b \neq 1.$$

(*Note* the formula above was derived under the assumption that $n > 1$; its validity when $n = 1$ and $b \neq 1$ is easy to verify.) When $b = 1$, the geometric sum reduces to $\lfloor \lg(n) \rfloor$, and $a \, b^{\lfloor \lg(n) \rfloor} = a$, so in this special case we have

$$F(n) = a + \lfloor \lg(n) \rfloor \quad \text{for all } n \geq 1 \text{ when } b = 1.$$

If $b > 1$, the expression $b^{\lfloor \lg(n) \rfloor}$ is an increasing function of n, and as in Example 4.4.1 we get $F(n) = \Theta(n^{\lg(b)})$. If $b = 1$ we see that $F(n) = \Theta(\log(n))$. If $0 < b < 1$ the term $b^{\lfloor \lg(n) \rfloor}$ decreases toward 0 as $n \to \infty$, so $F(n) \to \dfrac{1}{1 - b}$ in this case, which means $F(n) = \Theta(1)$.

Example 4.4.3 Let's try the same linear relation with a different non-homogeneous term:

$$F(1) = a, \quad F(n) = bF(\lfloor n/2 \rfloor) + n \quad \text{for all } n \geq 2.$$

Consider any integer n greater than 1. Using the ideas exploited in Examples 4.4.1 and 4.4.2 we get

$$\begin{aligned}
F(n) &= b \, F(\lfloor n/2 \rfloor) + n \\
&= b \, [bF(\lfloor n/2^2 \rfloor) + \lfloor n/2 \rfloor] + n = b^2 \, F(\lfloor n/2^2 \rfloor) + b\lfloor n/2 \rfloor + n \\
&= b^2 \, [bF(\lfloor n/2^3 \rfloor) + \lfloor n/2^2 \rfloor] + b\lfloor n/2 \rfloor + n = b^3 \, F(\lfloor n/2^3 \rfloor) \\
&\quad + b^2 \, \lfloor n/2^2 \rfloor + b \, \lfloor n/2 \rfloor + n.
\end{aligned}$$

Continuing in this way until $\lfloor n/2^p \rfloor = 1$, where $p = \lfloor \lg(n) \rfloor$, we get

$$F(n) = a \, b^{\lfloor \lg(n) \rfloor} + \sum_{k=0}^{\lfloor \lg(n) \rfloor - 1} \left\lfloor \frac{n}{2^k} \right\rfloor b^k \quad \text{for all } n \geq 1.$$

(*Note* this formula was derived under the assumption that $n > 1$, but the validity of the formula when $n = 1$ is easy to verify.)

The upper limit on the sigma-sum formula above would look nicer if it were just plain $\lfloor \lg(n) \rfloor$ instead of $\lfloor \lg(n) \rfloor - 1$. We can doctor the formula so that it has the nicer appearance by changing the upper limit and then compensating for the extra term we have added:

$$F(n) = a\,b^{\lfloor \lg(n) \rfloor} + \sum_{k=0}^{\lfloor \lg(n) \rfloor} \left\lfloor \frac{n}{2^k} \right\rfloor b^k - \left\lfloor \frac{n}{2^{\lfloor \lg(n) \rfloor}} \right\rfloor b^{\lfloor \lg(n) \rfloor} \quad \text{for all } n \geq 1.$$

By Theorem 2.2.8 on p. 21 we have $\left\lfloor \dfrac{n}{2^{\lfloor \lg(n) \rfloor}} \right\rfloor = 1$, so our formula takes the form

$$F(n) = (a-1)b^{\lfloor \lg(n) \rfloor} + \sum_{k=0}^{\lfloor \lg(n) \rfloor} \left\lfloor \frac{n}{2^k} \right\rfloor b^k \quad \text{for all } n \geq 1. \tag{4.15}$$

This complicated exact formula is seldom useful. What we generally want to know is some asymptotic formula for $F(n)$. We know from Example 4.4.1 that if $b > 0$ then $b^{\lfloor \lg(n) \rfloor} = \Theta(n^{\lg(b)})$. What about the sigma summation expression in Eq. (4.15)? By using the fact that

$$\frac{n}{2^k} - 1 < \left\lfloor \frac{n}{2^k} \right\rfloor \leq \frac{n}{2^k}$$

it is possible to prove the following:

$$\sum_{k=0}^{\lfloor \lg(n) \rfloor} \left\lfloor \frac{n}{2^k} \right\rfloor b^k \sim \frac{2}{2-b}n \quad \text{if } 0 < b < 2,$$

$$\sum_{k=0}^{\lfloor \lg(n) \rfloor} \left\lfloor \frac{n}{2^k} \right\rfloor b^k \sim n\lg(n) \quad \text{if } b = 2,$$

$$\sum_{k=0}^{\lfloor \lg(n) \rfloor} \left\lfloor \frac{n}{2^k} \right\rfloor b^k = \Theta(n\lg(b)) \quad \text{if } b > 2.$$

For those who are interested, the proofs of these assertions are given next.

Let $S(b; n)$ denote the sum $\displaystyle\sum_{k=0}^{\lfloor \lg(n) \rfloor} \left\lfloor \frac{n}{2^k} \right\rfloor b^k$. Using inequalities from the preceding page, $\displaystyle\sum_{k=0}^{\lfloor \lg(n) \rfloor} \left(\frac{n}{2^k} - 1 \right) b^k < S(b; n) \leq \sum_{k=0}^{\lfloor \lg(n) \rfloor} \frac{n}{2^k} b^k$ for all positive real numbers b.

We can write this as $\displaystyle\sum_{k=0}^{\lfloor \lg(n) \rfloor} \frac{n}{2^k} b^k - \sum_{k=0}^{\lfloor \lg(n) \rfloor} b^k < S(b; n) \leq \sum_{k=0}^{\lfloor \lg(n) \rfloor} \frac{n}{2^k} b^k$. Factoring out n gives

$$n \sum_{k=0}^{\lfloor \lg(n) \rfloor} \left(\frac{b}{2} \right)^k - \sum_{k=0}^{\lfloor \lg(n) \rfloor} b^k < S(b; n) \leq n \sum_{k=0}^{\lfloor \lg(n) \rfloor} \left(\frac{b}{2} \right)^k. \tag{4.16}$$

The sums here are finite geometric sums, so we have no difficulty finding closed forms for them. Note that we will have to consider the special cases where $b/2 = 1$ and $b = 1$ (see Theorem 2.3.3).

First consider the special case where $b = 2$. The inequalities (4.16) can be simplified to

$$n(\lfloor \lg(n) \rfloor + 1) - \frac{2^{\lfloor \lg(n) \rfloor + 1} - 1}{2 - 1} < S(2; n) \leq n(\lfloor \lg(n) \rfloor + 1),$$

$$n\lfloor \lg(n) \rfloor + n - 2^{\lfloor \lg(n) \rfloor + 1} + 1 < S(2; n) \leq n\lfloor \lg(n) \rfloor + n.$$

Since $2^{\lfloor \lg(n) \rfloor} \leq 2^{\lg(n)} = n$, it follows that $-n \leq -2^{\lfloor \lg(n) \rfloor}$, so $-2n \leq -2^{\lfloor \lg(n) \rfloor + 1}$, and thus $n\lfloor \lg(n) \rfloor + n - 2n + 1 \leq n\lfloor \lg(n) \rfloor + n - 2^{\lfloor \lg(n) \rfloor + 1} + 1 < S(2; n) \leq n\lfloor \lg(n) \rfloor + n$, which gives us $n\lfloor \lg(n) \rfloor - n + 1 < S(2; n) \leq n\lfloor \lg(n) \rfloor + n$.

Since $n\lfloor \lg(n) \rfloor \sim n \lg(n)$ and $n = o(n \log(n))$, we quickly see that $S(2; n) \sim n \lg(n)$.

Next consider the special case where $b = 1$. Inequality (4.16) takes the form

$$n \sum_{k=0}^{\lfloor \lg(n) \rfloor} (1/2)^k - \sum_{k=0}^{\lfloor \lg(n) \rfloor} 1^k < S(1; n) \leq n \sum_{k=0}^{\lfloor \lg(n) \rfloor} (1/2)^k,$$

$$n \frac{1 - (1/2)^{\lfloor \lg(n) \rfloor + 1}}{1 - (1/2)} - (\lfloor \lg(n) \rfloor + 1) < S(1; n) \leq n \frac{1 - (1/2)^{\lfloor \lg(n) \rfloor + 1}}{1 - (1/2)},$$

$$2n(1 - (1/2)^{\lfloor \lg(n) \rfloor + 1}) - \lfloor \lg(n) \rfloor - 1 < S(1; n) \leq n \frac{1}{1 - (1/2)},$$

$$2n - \frac{n}{2^{\lfloor \lg(n) \rfloor}} - \lfloor \lg(n) \rfloor - 1 < S(1; n) \leq 2n.$$

By Theorem 2.2.8(a) on p. 21 we have $n < 2^{\lfloor \lg(n) \rfloor + 1}$, from which it follows that $\frac{n}{2^{\lfloor \lg(n) \rfloor}} < 2$, which is equivalent to $-2 < -\frac{n}{2^{\lfloor \lg(n) \rfloor}}$. Folding this into the inequalities for $S(1; n)$ above gives us

$$2n - 2 - \lfloor \lg(n) \rfloor - 1 < 2n - \frac{n}{2^{\lfloor \lg(n) \rfloor}} - \lfloor \lg(n) \rfloor - 1 < S(1; n) \leq 2n.$$

From these inequalities it quickly follows that $S(1; n) \sim 2n = \frac{2}{2 - 1}n$ as stated on p. 140 for $0 < b < 2$.

Now take any b except $b \neq 1$ and $b \neq 2$. Then inequality (4.16) can be written in closed form as

$$n\left(\frac{(b/2)^{\lfloor \lg(n) \rfloor + 1} - 1}{(b/2) - 1}\right) - \left(\frac{b^{\lfloor \lg(n) \rfloor + 1} - 1}{b - 1}\right) < S(b; n) \leq n\left(\frac{(b/2)^{\lfloor \lg(n) \rfloor + 1} - 1}{(b/2) - 1}\right).$$

$$(4.17)$$

First consider the case where $0 < b < 2$. Then $0 < (b/2)^p < 1$ for all $p > 0$, so we rewrite inequality (4.17) as

$$n\left(\frac{1 - (b/2)^{\lfloor \lg(n) \rfloor + 1}}{1 - (b/2)}\right) - \left(\frac{b^{\lfloor \lg(n) \rfloor + 1} - 1}{b - 1}\right) < S(b; n) \le n\left(\frac{1 - (b/2)^{\lfloor \lg(n) \rfloor + 1}}{1 - (b/2)}\right).$$

$$(4.18)$$

Since $(b/2)^{\lfloor \lg(n) \rfloor} \to 0$ as $n \to \infty$, the 1 in the numerator of the first and last fractions of inequality (4.18) dominates the numerator, so we can discard the $(b/2)^{\lfloor \lg(n) \rfloor + 1}$ for asymptotic considerations. That is, the first and last fractions in inequality (4.18) are asymptotic to $n\left(\dfrac{1}{1 - (b/2)}\right) = \dfrac{2}{2 - b}n$.

What about the $b^{\lfloor \lg(n) \rfloor + 1}$ term in the numerator of the second fraction in inequality (4.18)? If $b < 1$, then that term approaches 0 and can be ignored, leaving $\dfrac{1}{b - 1}$, which is dominated by $\dfrac{2}{2 - b}n$. If, however, $1 < b < 2$, then we must examine $b^{\lfloor \lg(n) \rfloor + 1}$ further. We know $\lg(n) - 1 < \lfloor \lg(n) \rfloor \le \lg(n)$, so $b^{\lg(n)} < b^{\lfloor \lg(n) \rfloor + 1} \le b^{\lg(n) + 1} = b^{\lg(n)} b^1$, so $n^{\lg(b)} < b^{\lfloor \lg(n) \rfloor + 1} \le b n^{\lg(b)}$ (using $b^{\lg(n)} = n^{\lg(b)}$). Since $b < 2$ it follows that $\lg(b) < 1$, so $n^{\lg(b)}$ is dominated by n^1. Thus we can conclude that the second fraction in inequality (4.18) is dominated by the first, so $S(b; n) \sim \dfrac{2}{2 - b}n$.

Finally, consider inequality (4.16) in the case where $b > 2$. We first rewrite it as

$$2n\left(\frac{\frac{b^{\lfloor \lg(n) \rfloor + 1}}{2^{\lfloor \lg(n) \rfloor + 1}} - 1}{b - 2}\right) - \left(\frac{b^{\lfloor \lg(n) \rfloor + 1} - 1}{b - 1}\right) < S(b; n) \le 2n\left(\frac{\frac{b^{\lfloor \lg(n) \rfloor + 1}}{2^{\lfloor \lg(n) \rfloor + 1}} - 1}{b - 2}\right),$$

$$\frac{b^{\lfloor \lg(n) \rfloor + 1}\frac{2n}{2^{\lfloor \lg(n) \rfloor + 1}} - 2n}{b - 2} - \frac{b^{\lfloor \lg(n) \rfloor + 1} - 1}{b - 1} < S(b; n) \le \frac{b^{\lfloor \lg(n) \rfloor + 1}\frac{2n}{2^{\lfloor \lg(n) \rfloor + 1}} - 2n}{b - 2}.$$

Since $\dfrac{2n}{2^{\lg(n) + 1}} \le \dfrac{2n}{2^{\lfloor \lg(n) \rfloor + 1}} < \dfrac{2n}{2^{\lg(n)}}$, that is, $1 \le \dfrac{2n}{2^{\lfloor \lg(n) \rfloor + 1}} < 2$, the line above implies that

$$\frac{b^{\lfloor \lg(n) \rfloor + 1} - 2n}{b - 2} - \frac{b^{\lfloor \lg(n) \rfloor + 1} - 1}{b - 1} < S(b; n) \le \frac{2 b^{\lfloor \lg(n) \rfloor + 1} - 2n}{b - 2},$$

which we can rewrite as

$$b^{\lfloor \lg(n) \rfloor + 1}\left(\frac{1}{b - 2} - \frac{1}{b - 1}\right) - \frac{2n}{b - 2} + \frac{1}{b - 1} < S(b; n) \le \frac{2 b^{\lfloor \lg(n) \rfloor + 1} - 2n}{b - 2}.$$

Since $n^{\lg(b)} = b^{\lg(n)} < b^{\lfloor \lg(n) \rfloor + 1} \le b^{\lg(n) + 1} = bn^{\lg(b)}$ we obtain

$$n^{\lg(b)}\left(\frac{1}{b - 2} - \frac{1}{b - 1}\right) - \frac{2n}{b - 2} + \frac{1}{b - 1} < S(b; n) \le \frac{2b}{b - 2}n^{\lg(b)} - \frac{2n}{b - 2} < \frac{2b}{b - 2}n^{\lg(b)}.$$

Since $b > 2$ we know that $\lg(b) > 1$, so $n^{\lg(b)}$ dominates n^1. Since the coefficients for $n^{\lg(b)}$ on the left and right are strictly positive, it follows that $S(b; n) = \Theta(n^{\lg(b)})$.

Example 4.4.4 Let's see if we can guess the solution of the linear homogeneous problem

$$F(1) = a, \quad F(n) = F(\lfloor n/2 \rfloor) + F(\lceil n/2 \rceil) \quad \text{for all } n \geq 2.$$

As it turns out, the approach used in Examples 4.4.1–4.4.3 leads into more and more messy expressions (try it for yourself!). An alternative is to simply compute $F(n)$ for some small integers n and then look for a pattern. We get

$F(1) = a,$
$F(2) = F(1) + F(1) = 2a$
$F(3) = F(1) + F(2) = 3a$
$F(4) = F(2) + F(2) = 4a$
$F(5) = F(2) + F(3) = 5a$
$F(6) = F(3) + F(3) = 6a$
$F(7) = F(3) + F(4) = 7a$

On the basis of these data, it takes about a nanosecond to guess that the solution of this problem is

$$F(n) = an \quad \text{for all } n \geq 1.$$

Verification of this solution uses the well-known fact that $\lfloor n/2 \rfloor + \lceil n/2 \rceil = n$ for all integers n.

Example 4.4.5 Now let's add a simple non-homogeneous term to the relation given above.

$$F(1) = a, \quad F(n) = F(\lfloor n/2 \rfloor) + F(\lceil n/2 \rceil) + 1 \quad \text{for all } n \geq 2.$$

Working out $F(n)$ for small values of n gives

$F(1) = a$
$F(2) = F(1) + F(1) + 1 = 2a + 1$
$F(3) = F(1) + F(2) + 1 = 3a + 2$
$F(4) = F(2) + F(2) + 1 = 4a + 3$
$F(5) = F(2) + F(3) + 1 = 5a + 4$
$F(6) = F(3) + F(3) + 1 = 6a + 5$

It must surely be the case that $F(n) = na + (n - 1)$ for all $n \geq 1$. We recognize the terms $na (= an)$ as forming the general solution of the homogeneous part of the relation, while the terms $n - 1$ form a particular solution.

We can combine the n piece of the particular solution of the non-homogeneous relation with the solution of the homogeneous relation to produce the following general solution:

$$F(n) = (a + 1)n - 1 \quad \text{for all } n \geq 1.$$

The verification of this solution merely requires us to verify that $F(n) = -1$ is a particular solution of the non-homogeneous relation. This is trivial.

Example 4.4.6 How about a more difficult non-homogeneous term?

$$F(1) = a, \quad F(n) = F(\lfloor n/2 \rfloor) + F(\lceil n/2 \rceil) + n \quad \text{for all } n \geq 2.$$

Here are some initial terms of the sequence.

$F(1) = a$

$F(2) = F(1) + F(1) + 2 = 2a + 2$

$F(3) = F(1) + F(2) + 3 = 3a + 5$

$F(4) = F(2) + F(2) + 4 = 4a + 8$

$F(5) = F(2) + F(3) + 5 = 5a + 12$

$F(6) = F(3) + F(3) + 6 = 6a + 16$

$F(7) = F(3) + F(4) + 7 = 7a + 20$

$F(8) = F(4) + F(4) + 8 = 8a + 24$

$F(9) = F(4) + F(5) + 9 = 9a + 29$

$F(10) = F(5) + F(5) + 10 = 10a + 34$

$F(11) = F(5) + F(6) + 11 = 11a + 39$

$F(12) = F(6) + F(6) + 12 = 12a + 44$

$F(13) = F(6) + F(7) + 13 = 13a + 49$

$F(14) = F(7) + F(7) + 14 = 14a + 54$

$F(15) = F(7) + F(8) + 15 = 15a + 59$

$F(16) = F(8) + F(8) + 16 = 16a + 64$

$F(17) = F(8) + F(9) + 17 = 17a + 70$

Here are the differences between successive particular solutions.

2
3
3
4
4
4
4
5
5
5
5
5
5
5
5
6

Again we recognize $na (= an)$ as the general solution of the homogeneous part of the relation. Let $F_p(n)$ denote the particular solution that follows na in each case. The differences tabulated above seem to indicate that $F_p(n) - F_p(n-1) = 1 + \lceil \lg(n) \rceil$ for $n \geq 2$. If this is always true, then

$F_p(n) = F_p(n-1) + 1 + \lceil \lg(n) \rceil$ for all $n \geq 2$, and thus $F_p(2) = 0 + 1 + \lceil \lg(2) \rceil$,

$F_p(3) = F_p(2) + 1 + \lceil \lg(3) \rceil = 1 + \lceil \lg(2) \rceil + 1 + \lceil \lg(3) \rceil$,

$F_p(4) = F_p(3) + 1 + \lceil \lg(4) \rceil = 1 + \lceil \lg(2) \rceil + 1 + \lceil \lg(3) \rceil + 1 + \lceil \lg(4) \rceil$,

$F_p(5) = F_p(4) + 1 + \lceil \lg(5) \rceil = 1 + \lceil \lg(2) \rceil + 1 + \lceil \lg(3) \rceil + 1 + \lceil \lg(4) \rceil + 1 + \lceil \lg(5) \rceil$,

etc.

Thus we seem to have derived the following general solution:

$$F(n) = an + (n - 1) + \sum_{k=2}^{n} \lceil \lg(k) \rceil \quad \text{for all } n \geq 1.$$

In Theorem 2.3.8 on p. 37 it is shown that the sigma sum above has the closed form $n \lfloor \lg(n) \rfloor + (n + 1) - 2^{\lfloor \lg(n) \rfloor + 1}$. Putting this into the formula above gives

$$F(n) = (a + 2)n + n \lfloor \lg(n) \rfloor - 2^{\lfloor \lg(n) \rfloor + 1} \quad \text{for all } n \geq 1.$$

The verification that this is indeed a correct solution will be left as exercise. Note that $F(n) \sim n \lg(n)$.

On pp. 147–149 are tables summarizing the results derived in Examples 4.4.1–4.4.6. These tables also give solutions for several other relations we did not examine. The following example shows how to use the table to look up solutions to certain recurrence problems.

Example 4.4.7 Find the exact solution of the following recurrence problem. Also obtain its asymptotic behavior.

$$F(0) = 1, \quad F(n) = 2F(\lfloor n/2 \rfloor) - 7\lfloor n/2 \rfloor + 5n + 3 \quad \text{for } n \geq 1.$$

Solution Using the Table 4.1, p. 147, and Theorem 4.3.2, p. 118, we see that the function

$$F_{part}(n) = (-7)\left(\sum_{k=1}^{\lfloor \lg(n) \rfloor} \left\lfloor \frac{n}{2^k} \right\rfloor 2^{k-1}\right) + 5\left(\sum_{k=0}^{\lfloor \lg(n) \rfloor} \left\lfloor \frac{n}{2^k} \right\rfloor 2^k\right) + 3\left(\frac{1}{1-2}\right) \quad \text{for all } n \geq 1$$

is a particular solution of the given recurrence relation for all $n \geq 2$. By Theorems 4.3.1 and 4.3.3 on pp. 117 and 118, the most general solution is obtained by adding to a particular solution the general solution of the homogeneous part of the equation. This gives us

$$F(n) = \alpha 2^{\lfloor \lg(n) \rfloor} + (-7)\left(\sum_{k=1}^{\lfloor \lg(n) \rfloor} \left\lfloor \frac{n}{2^k} \right\rfloor 2^{k-1}\right) + 5\left(\sum_{k=0}^{\lfloor \lg(n) \rfloor} \left\lfloor \frac{n}{2^k} \right\rfloor 2^k\right) + 3\left(\frac{1}{1-2}\right), \quad n \geq 1.$$

$$(4.19)$$

To determine the constant α, we use the given initial value: $F(0) = 1$. We cannot use this directly in Eq. (4.19), because that formula is valid only for $n \geq 1$, so we calculate $F(1)$ from the recurrence relation we are given, which we are told is valid for all $n \geq 1$. We get

$$F(1) = 2F(0) - 7(0) + 5(1) + 3 = 2 - 0 + 5 + 3 = 10.$$

Now we set $n = 1$ in Eq. (4.19) to obtain

$$F(1) = \alpha 2^{\lfloor \lg(1) \rfloor} + (-7)\left(\sum_{k=1}^{\lfloor \lg(1) \rfloor} \left\lfloor \frac{1}{2^k} \right\rfloor 2^{k-1}\right) + 5\left(\sum_{k=0}^{\lfloor \lg(1) \rfloor} \left\lfloor \frac{1}{2^k} \right\rfloor 2^k\right) + 3\left(\frac{1}{1-2}\right)$$

$$10 = \alpha 2^0 + (-7) \times 0 + 5\left(\left\lfloor \frac{1}{2^0} \right\rfloor 2^0\right) + 3(-1)$$

$$10 = \alpha + 5 - 3$$

$$\alpha = 8$$

Thus the exact solution to our problem is

$$F(n) = 8 \times 2^{\lfloor \lg(n) \rfloor} + (-7)\left(\sum_{k=1}^{\lfloor \lg(n) \rfloor} \left\lfloor \frac{n}{2^k} \right\rfloor 2^{k-1}\right) + 5\left(\sum_{k=0}^{\lfloor \lg(n) \rfloor} \left\lfloor \frac{n}{2^k} \right\rfloor 2^k\right) + 3\left(\frac{1}{1-2}\right), n \geq 1.$$

If all we want is an asymptotic formula for $F(n)$, then by the Table 4.1 on p. 147 and Theorems 3.3.6 and 3.3.8(d) on p. 90 we have

$$F(n) \sim (-7)\frac{n}{2} \lg(n) + 5n \lg(n) = \frac{3}{2}n \lg(n),$$

because $2^{\lfloor \lg(n) \rfloor} = \Theta(n^{\lg(2)}) = \Theta(n) = o(n \log(n))$. If all we want is a big-theta expression for $F(n)$, then we can write $F(n) = \Theta(n \log(n))$.

The method described in this section can be generalized to other bases than 2 in the following theorem, also known as the *Master Theorem* [3, 4, 14] or *Main Recurrence Theorem* [7].

Theorem 4.4.8 *Let $T(n)$ be a function defined by the following recurrence relation where $a > 0$, $b > 1$, $d \geq 0$:*

$$T(n) = aT\left(\left\lceil \frac{n}{b} \right\rceil\right) + f(n), \quad \text{where } f(n) = O(n^d).$$

Then the function satisfies the property

$$T(n) = \begin{cases} O(n^d) & \text{if } d > \log_b(a) \\ O(n^d \log(n)) & \text{if } d = \log_b(a) \\ O(n^{\log_b(a)}) & \text{if } d < \log_b(a) \end{cases}$$

Proof The proof can be found in [4] and shall not be provided here as it is similar to the case where $b = 2$.   ∎

4.4.1 Special Linear Equations Involving $F(\lfloor n/2 \rfloor)$, $F(\lceil n/2 \rceil)$, etc.

In Table 4.1, b and α are any real constants, and $b > 0$. The recurrence relations are assumed to be valid for all $n \geq 2$, with the value of α determined by $F(1)$. [Note: if the recurrence relation is given to be valid for all $n \geq 1$ and $F(0)$ is given as the initial data, then it is necessary to work out $F(1)$ from the recurrence relation and use $F(1)$ to determine α. That is, the given solutions are not valid at $n = 0$.]

In Table 4.2, b and α are any real constants, and $b > 0$. The value of α will be determined by $F(1)$.

In Table 4.3, the symbol α denotes any real constant.

4.4.2 Further Examples

Example 4.4.9 By using the formulas given in the Tables 4.1, 4.2, and 4.3 on pp. 147–149, find exact solutions of the following problems. Also find asymptotic formulas or big-theta formulas for the solutions.

(a) $F(1) = 3$, $F(n) = F(\lfloor n/2 \rfloor) + 2$ for $n \geq 2$
(b) $F(1) = 1$, $F(n) = 2F(\lceil n/2 \rceil) + 3n$ for $n \geq 2$
(c) $F(0) = 5$, $F(n) = 4F(\lfloor n/2 \rfloor) + \lfloor n/2 \rfloor$ for $n \geq 1$
(d) $F(1) = 0$, $F(n) = F(\lfloor n/2 \rfloor) + F(\lceil n/2 \rceil) + 3n/2$ for $n \geq 2$
(e) $T(1) = 1$, $T(n) = 2(1 + n) + T(\lceil n/2 \rceil)$ for $n \geq 2$
(f) $f(1) = 2$, $f(n) = 6\lfloor n/2 \rfloor + 2f(\lceil n/2 \rceil) - 3$ for $n \geq 2$
(g) $\phi(1) = 0$, $\phi(n) = \phi(\lfloor n/2 \rfloor) + \phi(\lceil n/2 \rceil) + 2n - 3\lfloor n/2 \rfloor + 5$ for $n \geq 2$

Solutions

(a) By Table 4.1, p. 147, the general solution has the form $F(n) = \alpha 1^{\lfloor \lg(n) \rfloor} + 2\lfloor \lg(n) \rfloor$ for all $n \geq 1$, because $b = 1$. Taking $n = 1$ in this formula and using the given initial data shows us that $3 = F(1) = \alpha 1^{\lfloor \lg(1) \rfloor} + 2\lfloor \lg(1) \rfloor = \alpha + 0$,

Table 4.1 Solutions for recurrence relations involving $F(\lfloor n/2 \rfloor)$, $F(\lceil n/2 \rceil)$

Recurrence relation	The solution of the homogeneous part valid for all $n \geq 1$	A particular solution of the non-homogeneous relation valid for all $n \geq 1$	Asymptotic formula for the particular solution	
$F(n) = b\,F(\lfloor n/2 \rfloor) + 1$ for $n \geq 2$	$F_{hom}(n) = \alpha\,b^{\lfloor \lg(n) \rfloor} = \Theta(n^{\lg(b)})$	$F_{part}(n) = \lfloor \lg(n) \rfloor$ if $b = 1$; $\;F_{part}(n) = \dfrac{1}{1-b}$ if $b \neq 1$	$F_{part}(n) \sim \lg(n)$ $F_{part}(n)$ is constant	if $b = 1$ if $b \neq 1$
$F(n) = b\,F(\lfloor n/2 \rfloor) + n$ for $n \geq 2$	$F_{hom}(n) = \alpha\,b^{\lfloor \lg(n) \rfloor} = \Theta(n^{\lg(b)})$	$F_{part}(n) = \displaystyle\sum_{k=0}^{\lfloor \lg(n) \rfloor} \left\lfloor \frac{n}{2^k} \right\rfloor b^k$	$F_{part}(n) \sim \dfrac{2}{2-b}\,n$ $F_{part}(n) \sim n\lg(n)$ $F_{part}(n) = \Theta(n^{\lg(b)})$	if $b < 2$ if $b = 2$ if $b > 2$
$F(n) = b\,F(\lfloor n/2 \rfloor) + \lfloor n/2 \rfloor$ for $n \geq 2$	$F_{hom}(n) = \alpha\,b^{\lfloor \lg(n) \rfloor} = \Theta(n^{\lg(b)})$	$F_{part}(n) = \displaystyle\sum_{k=1}^{\lfloor \lg(n) \rfloor} \left\lfloor \frac{n}{2^k} \right\rfloor b^{k-1}$	$F_{part}(n) \sim \dfrac{1}{2-b}\,n$ $F_{part}(n) \sim \dfrac{n}{2}\lg(n)$ $F_{part}(n) = \Theta(n^{\lg(b)})$	if $b < 2$ if $b = 2$ if $b > 2$
$F(n) = b\,F(\lfloor n/2 \rfloor) + \lceil n/2 \rceil$ for $n \geq 2$	$F_{hom}(n) = \alpha\,b^{\lfloor \lg(n) \rfloor} = \Theta(n^{\lg(b)})$	$F_{part}(n) = n + (b-1) \displaystyle\sum_{k=1}^{\lfloor \lg(n) \rfloor} \left\lfloor \frac{n}{2^k} \right\rfloor b^{k-1}$	$F_{part}(n) \sim \dfrac{1}{2-b}\,n$ $F_{part}(n) \sim \dfrac{n}{2}\lg(n)$ $F_{part}(n) = \Theta(n^{\lg(b)})$	if $b < 2$ if $b = 2$ if $b > 2$

Table 4.2 Solutions for recurrence relations involving $F(\lfloor n/2\rfloor)$, $F(\lceil n/2\rceil)$ (continued)

Recurrence relation	The solution of the homogeneous part valid for all $n \geq 1$	A particular solution of the non-homogeneous relation valid for all $n \geq 1$	Asymptotic formula for the particular solution
$F(n) = b\,F(\lceil n/2\rceil) + 1$ for $n \geq 2$	$F_{hom}(n) = \alpha\,b^{\lceil \lg(n)\rceil} = \Theta(n^{\lg(b)})$	$F_{part}(n) = \lceil \lg(n)\rceil$ if $b = 1$; $F_{part}(n) = \dfrac{1}{1-b}$ if $b \neq 1$	$F_{part}(n) \sim \lg(n)$ if $b = 1$ $F_{part}(n)$ is constant if $b \neq 1$
$F(n) = b\,F(\lceil n/2\rceil) + n$ for $n \geq 2$	$F_{hom}(n) = \alpha\,b^{\lceil \lg(n)\rceil} = \Theta(n^{\lg(b)})$	$F_{part}(n) = \displaystyle\sum_{k=0}^{\lceil \lg(n)\rceil} \left\lceil \frac{n}{2^k}\right\rceil b^k$	$F_{part}(n) \sim \dfrac{2}{2-b}n$ if $b < 2$ $F_{part}(n) \sim n\lg(n)$ if $b = 2$ $F_{part}(n) = \Theta(n^{\lg(b)})$ if $b > 2$
$F(n) = b\,F(\lceil n/2\rceil) + \lceil n/2\rceil$ for $n \geq 2$	$F_{hom}(n) = \alpha\,b^{\lceil \lg(n)\rceil} = \Theta(n^{\lg(b)})$	$F_{part}(n) = \displaystyle\sum_{k=1}^{\lceil \lg(n)\rceil} \left\lceil \frac{n}{2^k}\right\rceil b^{k-1}$	$F_{part}(n) \sim \dfrac{1}{2-b}n$ if $b < 2$ $F_{part}(n) \sim \dfrac{n}{2}\lg(n)$ if $b = 2$ $F_{part}(n) = \Theta(n^{\lg(b)})$ if $b > 2$
$F(n) = b\,F(\lceil n/2\rceil) + \lfloor n/2\rfloor$ for $n \geq 2$	$F_{hom}(n) = \alpha\,b^{\lceil \lg(n)\rceil} = \Theta(n^{\lg(b)})$	$F_{part}(n) = n + (b-1)\displaystyle\sum_{k=1}^{\lceil \lg(n)\rceil} \left\lceil \frac{n}{2^k}\right\rceil b^{k-1}$	$F_{part}(n) \sim \dfrac{1}{2-b}n$ if $b < 2$ $F_{part}(n) \sim \dfrac{n}{2}\lg(n)$ if $b = 2$ $F_{part}(n) = \Theta(n^{\lg(b)})$ if $b > 2$

Table 4.3 Solutions for recurrence relations involving $F(\lfloor n/2 \rfloor)$, $F(\lceil n/2 \rceil)$ (continued)

Recurrence relation	The solution of the homogeneous part valid for all $n \geq 1$	A particular solution of the non-homogeneous relation valid for all $n \geq 1$	Asymptotic formula for the particular solution
$F(n) = F(\lfloor n/2 \rfloor) + F(\lceil n/2 \rceil) + 1$ for $n \geq 2$ if $F(1)$ is given as an initial value; for $n \geq 3$ if $F(1)$ and $F(2)$ are given as initial values; etc.	$F_{hom}(n) = \alpha\,n$	$F_{part}(n) = -1$	$F_{part}(n)$ is constant
$F(n) = F(\lfloor n/2 \rfloor) + F(\lceil n/2 \rceil) + n$ for $n \geq 2$ if $F(1)$ is given as an initial value; for $n \geq 3$ if $F(1)$ and $F(2)$ are given as initial values; etc.	$F_{hom}(n) = \alpha\,n$	$F_{part}(n) = n\lfloor \lg(n) \rfloor - 2^{\lfloor \lg(n) \rfloor + 1}$	$F_{part}(n) \sim n\lg(n)$
$F(n) = F(\lfloor n/2 \rfloor) + F(\lceil n/2 \rceil) + \lfloor n/2 \rfloor$ for $n \geq 2$ if $F(1)$ is given as an initial value; for $n \geq 3$ if $F(1)$ and $F(2)$ are given as initial values; etc.	$F_{hom}(n) = \alpha\,n$	$F_{part}(n) = \dfrac{n(n-1)}{2} - \left(\displaystyle\sum_{p=2}^{n-1} \sum_{k=1}^{\lceil \lg(p) \rceil} \left\lfloor \frac{p}{2^k} \right\rfloor \right)$	$F_{part}(n) \sim \dfrac{n}{2}\lg(n)$
$F(n) = F(\lfloor n/2 \rfloor) + F(\lceil n/2 \rceil) + \lceil n/2 \rceil$ for $n \geq 2$ if $F(1)$ is given as an initial value; for $n \geq 3$ if $F(1)$ and $F(2)$ are given as initial values; etc.	$F_{hom}(n) = \alpha\,n$	$F_{part}(n) = \left(\displaystyle\sum_{p=2}^{n} \sum_{k=1}^{\lceil \lg(p) \rceil} \left\lceil \frac{p}{2^k} \right\rceil \right) - \dfrac{(n-1)(n-2)}{2}$	$F_{part}(n) \sim \dfrac{n}{2}\lg(n)$

so the exact solution is $F(n) = 3 + 2\lfloor \lg(n) \rfloor$ for $n \geq 1$.) [Check: $F(2) = 5$ by the recurrence relation and also by the final formula for the solution.] Asymptotically, $F(n) \sim 2\lg(n)$; less precisely, $F(n) = \Theta(\log(n))$.

(b) By Table 4.2, p. 148, the general solution has the form $F(n) = a2^{\lceil \lg(n) \rceil} +$
$$3 \sum_{k=0}^{\lceil \lg(n) \rceil} \left\lceil \frac{n}{2^k} \right\rceil 2^k \text{ for } n \geq 1.$$

Taking $n = 1$ and using the initial data gives us $1 = F(1) = \alpha 2^{\lceil \lg(1) \rceil} +$
$$3 \sum_{k=0}^{\lceil \lg(1) \rceil} \left\lceil \frac{1}{2^k} \right\rceil 2^k = a2^0 + 3 \left\lceil \frac{1}{2^0} \right\rceil 2^0 = \alpha + 3, \text{ so } \alpha = -2. \text{ Thus the exact}$$
solution is

$$F(n) = -2^{1+\lceil \lg(n) \rceil} + 3 \sum_{k=0}^{\lceil \lg(n) \rceil} \left\lceil \frac{n}{2^k} \right\rceil 2^k \quad \text{for all } n \geq 1.$$

[Check: $F(2) = 8$ by the recurrence relation and also by the final formula for the solution.] Asymptotic formula: by the asymptotic formulas in Table 4.2, p. 148, $2^{\lceil \lg(n) \rceil}$ is $\Theta(n^1)$ and $\sum_{k=0}^{\lceil \lg(n) \rceil} \left\lceil \frac{n}{2^k} \right\rceil 2^k \sim n\lg(n)$, so $F(n) \sim n\lg(n)$. A less precise answer is $F(n) = \Theta(n\lg(n))$.

(c) By Table 4.1, p. 147, the general solution is $F(n) = \alpha 4^{\lfloor \lg(n) \rfloor} + \sum_{k=1}^{\lfloor \lg(n) \rfloor} \left\lfloor \frac{n}{2^k} \right\rfloor 4^{k-1}$

for all $n \geq 1$. Since we are given $F(0)$, we first compute $F(1)$ from the recurrence relation: $F(1) = 4 \times 5 + 0 = 20$.
Then setting $n = 1$ in the general solution gives us $20 = F(1) = \alpha 4^{\lfloor \lg(1) \rfloor} +$
$$\sum_{k=1}^{\lfloor \lg(1) \rfloor} \left\lfloor \frac{1}{2^k} \right\rfloor 4^{k-1} = a4^0 + 0, \text{ so } \alpha = 20. \text{ The exact solution: } F(n) =$$
$$20 \times 4^{\lfloor \lg(n) \rfloor} + \sum_{k=1}^{\lfloor \lg(n) \rfloor} \left\lfloor \frac{n}{2^k} \right\rfloor 4^{k-1} \quad \text{for all } n \geq 1.$$
[Check: $F(2) = 81$ from the recurrence relation and also from the final formula for the solution.]
Asymptotic formula: by the asymptotic formulas in Table 4.1, p. 147, we have $F(n) = \Theta(n^{\lg(4)}) = \Theta(n^2)$.

(d) By Table 4.3, p. 149, the general solution is $F(n) = \alpha n + \frac{3}{2}(n\lfloor \lg(n) \rfloor - 2^{\lfloor \lg(n) \rfloor + 1})$ for all $n \geq 1$. Taking $n = 1$ in this formula gives us $0 = \alpha 1 + \frac{3}{2}(1\lfloor \lg(1) \rfloor - 2^{\lfloor \lg(1) \rfloor + 1}) = \alpha + \frac{3}{2}(0 - 2^1) = \alpha - 3$, so $\alpha = 3$. The exact solution is $F(n) = 3n + \frac{3}{2}(n\lfloor \lg(n) \rfloor - 2^{\lfloor \lg(n) \rfloor + 1})$ for all $n \geq 1$.
[Check: $F(2) = 3$ by the recurrence relation and also by the final formula for the solution.]
Asymptotic formula: $F(n) \sim \frac{3}{2}n\lg(n) = \Theta(n\log(n))$.

(e) By Table 4.2, p. 148, the general solution is $T(n) = \alpha 1^{\lfloor \lg(n) \rfloor} + 2\lceil \lg(n) \rceil +$
$2 \sum\limits_{k=0}^{\lceil \lg(n) \rceil} \left\lceil \dfrac{n}{2^k} \right\rceil 1^k$ for $n \geq 1$. Taking $n = 1$ in this formula gives us $1 = \alpha 1^0 +$
$2 \times 0 + 2 \left\lceil \dfrac{1}{2^0} \right\rceil 1^0 = \alpha + 2$, so $\alpha = -1$. Thus the exact solution is $T(n) =$
$-1 + 2\lceil \lg(n) \rceil + 2 \sum\limits_{k=0}^{\lceil \lg(n) \rceil} \left\lceil \dfrac{n}{2^k} \right\rceil 1^k$ for $n \geq 1$.

[Check: $T(2)$ is 7 by the recurrence relation and also by the final formula for the solution.]

Asymptotic formula: $T(n) \sim 2 \lg(n) + 2(\dfrac{2}{2-1}n)$, which simplifies to $T(n) \sim$
$4n$, so $T(n) = \Theta(n)$.

(f) By Table 4.2, p. 148, the solution is $f(n) = \alpha 2^{\lceil \lg(n) \rceil} + 6$
$\left(n + (2-1) \sum\limits_{k=1}^{\lceil \lg(n) \rceil} \left\lceil \dfrac{n}{2^k} \right\rceil 2^{k-1} \right) + (-3)\dfrac{1}{1-2} = a2^{\lceil \lg(n) \rceil} + 6n + 6$
$\left(\sum\limits_{k=1}^{\lceil \lg(n) \rceil} \left\lceil \dfrac{n}{2^k} \right\rceil 2^{k-1} \right) + 3$ for all $n \geq 1$. Then $2 = f(1) = \alpha 2^0 + 6 \times 1 + 6 \times 0 + 3$,
so $\alpha = -7$.

Thus $f(n) = (-7)2^{\lceil \lg(n) \rceil} + 6n + 6 \left(\sum\limits_{k=1}^{\lceil \lg(n) \rceil} \left\lceil \dfrac{n}{2^k} \right\rceil 2^{k-1} \right) + 3$ for all $n \geq 1$.

[Check: $f(2) = 7$ by the recurrence relation and also by the final formula for the solution.]

Asymptotic formula: $2^{\lceil \lg(n) \rceil} = \Theta(n^{\lg(2)}) = \Theta(n)$ and $\sum\limits_{k=1}^{\lceil \lg(n) \rceil} \left\lceil \dfrac{n}{2^k} \right\rceil 2^{k-1} \sim$
$\dfrac{n}{2} \lg(n)$, so $f(n) \sim 3n \lg(n)$ and thus $f(n) = \Theta(n \log(n))$.

(g) By Table 4.3, p. 149, we have $\phi(n) = \alpha n + 2(n \lfloor \lg(n) \rfloor - 2^{\lfloor \lg(n) \rfloor + 1}) -$
$3 \left[\dfrac{n(n-1)}{2} - \left(\sum\limits_{p=2}^{n-1} \sum\limits_{k=1}^{\lfloor \lg(p) \rfloor} \left\lfloor \dfrac{p}{2^k} \right\rfloor \right) \right] + 5(-1)$ for all $n \geq 1$. Putting $n = 1$
into this formula gives us $0 = \phi(1) = \alpha + 2(0 - 2^1) - 3[0 - 0] - 5 = \alpha - 9$,
so $\alpha = 9$. Thus the exact solution is

$$\phi(n) = 9n - 5 + 2n \lfloor \lg(n) \rfloor - 2^{\lfloor \lg(n) \rfloor + 2} - 3 \left[\dfrac{n(n-1)}{2} - \left(\sum\limits_{p=2}^{n-1} \sum\limits_{k=1}^{\lfloor \lg(p) \rfloor} \left\lfloor \dfrac{p}{2^k} \right\rfloor \right) \right] \quad \text{for all } n \geq 1.$$

[Check: $\phi(2) = 6$ by the recurrence relation and also by the final formula for the solution.]

Asymptotically, $\phi(n) \sim 2n \lg(n) - 3\dfrac{n}{2} \lg(n) = \dfrac{n}{2} \lg(n)$, so $\phi(n) = \Theta(n \log(n))$.

4.4.3 Exercises

4.4.10 By using the formulas given in the Tables 4.1, 4.2, and 4.3 on pp. 147–149, find exact solutions of the following problems. Also find asymptotic formulas or big-theta formulas for the solutions.

(a) $F(1) = 3$, $F(n) = 2F(\lfloor n/2 \rfloor) + 3\lfloor n/2 \rfloor - 1$ for all $n \geq 2$
(b) $F(1) = 0$, $F(n) = 2F(\lceil n/2 \rceil) + \lceil n/2 \rceil + 1$ for all $n \geq 2$
(c) $Y(1) = 5$, $Y(n) = 2 + 3n + Y(\lfloor n/2 \rfloor) + Y(\lceil n/2 \rceil)$ for all $n \geq 2$
(d) $g(1) = 2$, $g(n) = g(\lfloor n/2 \rfloor) + 3 + 2n$ for all $n \geq 2$
(e) $F(1) = 1$, $F(n) = F(\lfloor n/2 \rfloor) + F(\lceil n/2 \rceil) - \lfloor n/2 \rfloor$ for all $n \geq 2$
(f) $F(1) = 2$, $F(n) = F(\lfloor n/2 \rfloor) + F(\lceil n/2 \rceil) + 3\lfloor n/2 \rfloor - 2$ for all $n \geq 2$.

4.4.11 The recurrence relation in the problem
$$F(1) = a, \quad F(n) = F(\lfloor n/2 \rfloor) + \lfloor \lg(n) \rfloor \quad \text{for all } n \geq 2,$$
is not in the Tables 4.1, 4.2, and 4.3. Find an exact solution for it using either the method in Examples 4.4.1–4.4.3 or else the method in Examples 4.4.4–4.4.6.

4.4.12 By substituting the formula $F(n) = n\lfloor \lg(n) \rfloor - 2^{\lfloor \lg(n) \rfloor + 1}$ into the recurrence relation $F(n) = F(\lfloor n/2 \rfloor) + F(\lceil n/2 \rceil) + n$, verify that the formula is a particular solution of the relation. You will need to use some of the formulas in Theorem 2.2.8, p. 21. You will also need to use the fact that for positive integers n the formula $\lfloor \lg(n+1) \rfloor = \lfloor \lg(n) \rfloor$ except for those integers n having the form $n = 2^k - 1$ for some positive integer k. When $n = 2^k - 1$, then it is not hard to see that $\lfloor \lg(n+1) \rfloor = \lfloor \lg(n) \rfloor + 1$.

4.4.13 Many computer science textbooks explain that every positive integer n can be expressed uniquely in a binary representation of the form $n = b_k 2^k + b_{k-1} 2^{k-1} + \cdots + b_1 2^1 + b_0 2^0$, where each "bit" b_i is either 0 or 1, and $b_k = 1$. We customarily abbreviate this expression by writing $n = b_k\, b_{k-1} \ldots b_1\, b_0$.

In Exercise 2.3.29 on p. 47 you were asked to come up with the formula $k = \lfloor \lg(n) \rfloor$ for the subscript of the most significant bit b_k. It follows that the total number of bits in this binary representation is $1 + \lfloor \lg(k) \rfloor$ (because the bits are numbered starting with subscript 0).

Now let's ask how many 1's there are in the binary representation of n. Let $B(n)$ denote this number. Then you can easily check that $B(1) = 1$, $B(2) = 1$, $B(3) = 2$, $B(4) = 1$, $B(5) = 2$, $B(6) = 2$, $B(7) = 3$, $B(8) = 1$, etc. Since
$$\lfloor n/2 \rfloor = b_k 2^{k-1} + b_{k-1} 2^{k-2} + \cdots + b_1 2^0,$$
it follows that $\lfloor n/2 \rfloor$ has either the same number of 1's in its binary representation as n (that's when $b_0 = 0$), or else has one fewer (when $b_0 = 1$). Thus $B(n) = B(\lfloor n/2 \rfloor) + b_0$. Note that b_0 is the "parity" of n, defined in Exercise 2.3.30, p. 47. In that exercise you should have come up with the formula parity $(n) = n - 2\lfloor n/2 \rfloor$. Use these observations to derive an exact formula for $B(n)$.

4.5   Other Recurrence Relations

Many of the recurrence problems that turn up in analysis of algorithms fall into one of the two classes we've examined in the preceding sections:

- linear relations with constant coefficients and polynomial or exponential non-homogeneous parts;
- simple recurrence relations involving $F(\lfloor n/2 \rfloor)$ and/or $F(\lceil n/2 \rceil)$.

When confronted with a problem that does not fall into one of these two categories, you have several choices.

1. Consult reference works on recurrence relations (this calls for a trip to the library).
2. Calculate, one by one, a large number of the terms of the sequence. You may be able to guess the solution, after which you can try to verify your guess algebraically.
3. "Play around" with the equation, using various algebraic manipulations. You may spot a substitution ("change of variable") that will turn it into a problem that you already know how to solve.
4. Simplify the problem by turning the equation into a simple *inequality* that can be solved by a known method. This will typically give an inequality satisfied by the terms of the sequence. For example, by this process you may be able to show that $F(n) = O(n \log(n))$ or $F(n) = \Omega(n \log(n))$, or both, which would imply that $F(n) = \Theta(n \log(n))$.

The following examples are intended to illustrate some of these techniques.

Example 4.5.1 Solve the problem $F(0) = a$, $F(n) = F(n-1) + \phi(n)$ when $n \geq 1$.

Solution Working out terms gives
$$F(1) = F(0) + \phi(1) = a + \phi(1)$$
$$F(2) = F(1) + \phi(2) = a + \phi(1) + \phi(2)$$
$$F(3) = F(2) + \phi(3) = a + \phi(1) + \phi(2) + \phi(3)$$
$$F(4) = F(3) + \phi(4) = a + \phi(1) + \phi(2) + \phi(3) + \phi(4)$$
etc.

Clearly the solution is $F(n) = a + \sum_{k=1}^{n} \phi(k)$ for all $n \geq 0$.

   If a closed form can be found for the sigma-sum, all the better. If not, an approximation using integration (Theorem 2.3.4, p. 33) may give information about the asymptotic behavior of $F(n)$.

Example 4.5.2 Solve the problem $F(1) = 1$, $nF(n) = (n - 1)F(n - 1) + 2n$ when $n \geq 2$.

Solution The pattern $nF(n)$ that appears on the left side of the recurrence relation is duplicated—in shifted form—on the right side of the relation: $(n - 1)F(n - 1)$. If we let $G(n)$ stand for the product $nF(n)$, then $G(n - 1)$ will be $(n - 1)F(n - 1)$, and the recurrence relation will take the form $G(n) = G(n - 1) + 2n$ for all $n \geq 2$. Also note that $G(1) = 1 \cdot F(1) = 1$. The problem has been reduced by a substitution (also called a "change of variable") into a very simple linear, constant coefficients problem (or, if you prefer, to the form discussed in Example 4.5.1). The solution is easily found to be $G(n) = 2^{n+1} - 3$ for all $n \geq 1$. Now we return to the original function F: we have $nF(n) = G(n) = 2^{n+1} - 3$ for all $n \geq 1$, and thus

$$F(n) = \frac{2^{n+1} - 3}{n} \qquad \text{for all } n \geq 1.$$

Example 4.5.3 Solve the problem $F(1) = 1$, $nF(n) = (n+1)F(n-1)+1$ when $n \geq 2$.

Solution Here, unfortunately, the pattern on the left is not duplicated on the right. If, however, we divide through the recurrence relation by n and also by $n + 1$ we produce this relation:

$$\frac{F(n)}{n + 1} = \frac{F(n - 1)}{n} + \frac{1}{n(n + 1)} \qquad \text{when } n \geq 2.$$

Now, if we are observant, we can see the same pattern on the left and right sides. If we write $G(n)$ for the quotient $\dfrac{F(n)}{n + 1}$, then $\dfrac{F(n - 1)}{n}$ is exactly $G(n - 1)$. Also note that $G(1) = \dfrac{F(1)}{1 + 1} = \dfrac{1}{2}$, and thus we have produced this simpler recurrence problem:

$$G(1) = \frac{1}{2}, \quad G(n) = G(n - 1) + \frac{1}{n(n + 1)} \qquad \text{when } n \geq 2.$$

This has the form of the recurrence relation in Example 4.5.1, except that the sequence begins with $G(1)$ instead of $G(0)$. Using the method of solution given in Example 4.5.1 we find that

$$G(n) = \frac{1}{2} + \sum_{k=2}^{n} \frac{1}{k(k + 1)} \qquad \text{for all } n \geq 1.$$

At this point we have two choices: we can try to find a closed form for the sum above, or we can try to approximate it, with some definite integrals perhaps, and then find its asymptotic form, which can be used to give an asymptotic form for $F(n)$. As it turns out in this case, if you work out the first few values of $G(n)$, you will have no trouble guessing a closed form and proving it by mathematical induction. See Exercise 4.5.14.

Example 4.5.4 Solve the problem $F(0) = 5$, $F(n) = F(\lfloor (n-1)/2 \rfloor) + 3$ for $n \geq 1$.

Solution The recurrence relation $F(n) = F(\lfloor (n-1)/2 \rfloor) + 3$ resembles, but does not match, any of those involving $F(\lfloor n/2 \rfloor)$ in the table on pp. 147–149. Instead,

the relation we want to solve gives us
  $F(1)$ in terms of $F(0)$,
  $F(2)$ in terms of $F(0)$,
  $F(3)$ in terms of $F(1)$,
  $F(4)$ in terms of $F(1)$,
  $F(5)$ in terms of $F(2)$,
  $F(6)$ in terms of $F(2)$,
  $F(7)$ in terms of $F(3)$,
  etc.

the relations in Table 4.1, p. 147, give us
  $F(2)$ in terms of $F(1)$
  $F(3)$ in terms of $F(1)$
  $F(4)$ in terms of $F(2)$
  $F(5)$ in terms of $F(2)$
  $F(6)$ in terms of $F(3)$
  $F(7)$ in terms of $F(3)$
  $F(8)$ in terms of $F(4)$
  etc.

This suggests that we "re-label" each $F(n)$ as $G(n+1)$, so that $F(0) = G(1)$, $F(1) = G(2)$, etc.

Making this substitution in the given recurrence problem produces the problem

$$G(1) = 5 \text{ and } G(n+1) = G(\lfloor (n+1)/2 \rfloor) + 3 \quad \text{for } n \geq 1, \tag{4.20}$$

where we have used the relation $F(n) = G(n+1)$ to give us

$$F(\lfloor (n-1)/2 \rfloor) = G(\lfloor (n-1)/2 \rfloor + 1) = G(\lfloor (n+1)/2 \rfloor) \quad \text{for all } n \geq 1,$$

(here the identity $\lfloor x \rfloor + 1 = \lfloor x+1 \rfloor$ has been used). The recurrence relation (4.20) is still not in the form we want (the argument on the left side of the recurrence is $n+1$ instead of n), so we replace n by $n-1$ to obtain

$$G(1) = 5 \text{ and } G(n) = G(\lfloor n/2 \rfloor) + 3 \quad \text{for } n - 1 \geq 1, \quad \text{that is, for } n \geq 2.$$

This problem is one whose solution we can obtain from Table 4.1, p. 147:

$$G(n) = \alpha + 3\lfloor \lg(n) \rfloor \quad \text{for n} \geq 1.$$

Setting $n = 1$ gives us $5 = \alpha$, so $G(n) = 5 + 3\lfloor \lg(n) \rfloor$ for $n \geq 1$. Now, of course, we want to return to the function $F(n)$. Since $G(n) = F(n-1)$, we have $F(n-1) = 5 + 3\lfloor \lg(n) \rfloor$ for $n \geq 1$. Replacing n consistently by $n+1$ gives us $F(n) = 5 + 3\lfloor \lg(n+1) \rfloor$ for $n + 1 \geq 1$, that is,

$$F(n) = 5 + 3\lfloor \lg(n+1) \rfloor \quad \text{for } n \geq 0.$$

On the following page there is a short table of transformations that often prove useful in problems like the one in Example 4.5.4 above.

4.5.1   A Table of Transformations

For relations such as $F(n) = b\,F\left(\left\lceil\frac{n+1}{2}\right\rceil\right) + \phi(n)$ and $F(n) = b\,F\left(\left\lfloor\frac{n-1}{2}\right\rfloor\right) + \phi(n)$, just use the identities $\lfloor (n+1)/2 \rfloor = \lceil n/2 \rceil$ and $\lceil (n-1)/2 \rceil = \lfloor n/2 \rfloor$ to change the relations to ones found in Tables 4.1, 4.2, and 4.3 on pp. 147–149 (Table 4.4).

Example 4.5.5 Solve the problem $F(1) = 2, F(n) = F(\lfloor n/2 \rfloor) + n\lfloor n/2 \rfloor$ for $n \geq 2$.

Solution The homogeneous part of this linear relation matches the homogeneous part of the relations in Table 4.1 on p. 147, but the non-homogeneous term is not in that table. You can try the method we used on pp. 137–144 to derive Tables 4.1, 4.2, and 4.3, pp. 147–149, but when you write out a large number of terms for this problem you will find that there is no pattern that can easily be expressed in formulas with which we are acquainted so far.

In this particular example it pays to consider what happens if we temporarily restrict our attention to values of n for which $n/2$ and $n/4$ and $n/8$ and so on are always integers, which allows us to get rid of the floor symbols that partly account for the difficulty in this problem. That is, we should restrict our attention just to values of n that are powers of 2.

This can be done by making the substitution $n = 2^k$ in the recurrence relation to obtain

$$F(2^k) = F(2^{k-1}) + 2^k 2^{k-1} \quad \text{for } k \geq 1.$$

This form of the recurrence is "deficient" because it defines only the terms $F(2)$, $F(4)$, $F(8), \ldots$ in terms of $F(1) = 2$. However, if we now let $G(k)$ denote $F(2^k)$, the problem takes the form

$$G(0) = 2, \quad G(k) = G(k-1) + 2^{2k-1} = G(k-1) + \frac{1}{2}4^k \quad \text{for } k \geq 1.$$

This is a first order linear recurrence relation with constant coefficients and exponential non-homogeneous part. The solution is quickly found to be $G(k) = \frac{2}{3}(2 + 4^k)$ for all $k \geq 0$, so $F(2^k) = \frac{2}{3}(2 + 4^k)$ for all $k \geq 0$. Replacing 2^k by n gives the formula $F(n) = \frac{2}{3}(2 + n^2)$ for those values of n that are powers of 2. This suggests that the entire solution $F(n)$ may be asymptotic to $(2/3)n^2$. Almost certainly we can expect that $F(n) = \Theta(n^2)$.

How might we prove that $F(n) \sim (2/3)n^2$? A good way to begin is to make a table of values of $F(n)$ and $(2/3)n^2$ to see how these quantities compare. Simple computation gives the results shown in Table 4.5.

The table suggests that $(2/3)n^2$ is neither a lower bound nor an upper bound for $F(n)$. However, $(2/3)(n-1)^2$ shows promise as a lower bound for $F(n)$ and $(2/3)(n+1)^2$ is almost certainly an upper bound. Now let's try to prove these assertions by mathematical induction.

Table 4.4 Table of transformations

The recurrence relation	Is transformed by the substitution	Into the relation
$F(n) = b F\left(\left\lfloor \dfrac{n-1}{2}\right\rfloor\right) + \phi(n)$ for $n \geq n_0$	$F(n) = G(n+1)$	$G(n) = b G\left(\left\lfloor \dfrac{n}{2}\right\rfloor\right) + \phi(n-1)$ for $n \geq n_0 + 1$
$F(n) = b F\left(\left\lceil \dfrac{n+1}{2}\right\rceil\right) + \phi(n)$ for $n \geq n_0$	$F(n) = G(n-1)$	$G(n) = b G\left(\left\lceil \dfrac{n}{2}\right\rceil\right) + \phi(n+1)$ for $n \geq n_0 - 1$
$F(n) = F\left(\left\lfloor \dfrac{n-1}{2}\right\rfloor\right) + F\left(\left\lceil \dfrac{n-1}{2}\right\rceil\right) + \phi(n)$ for $n \geq 1$ or for $n \geq 2$	$F(n) = G(n+1)$	$G(n) = G\left(\left\lfloor \dfrac{n}{2}\right\rfloor\right) + G\left(\left\lceil \dfrac{n}{2}\right\rceil\right) + \phi(n-1)$ for $n \geq 2$ or for $n \geq 3$
$F(n) = F\left(\left\lfloor \dfrac{n+1}{2}\right\rfloor\right) + F\left(\left\lceil \dfrac{n+1}{2}\right\rceil\right) + \phi(n)$ for $n \geq 3$	$F(n) = G(n-1)$	$G(n) = G\left(\left\lfloor \dfrac{n}{2}\right\rfloor\right) + G\left(\left\lceil \dfrac{n}{2}\right\rceil\right) + \phi(n+1)$ for $n \geq 2$

Table 4.5 A few examples of comparing the value of $F(n)$ with $(2/3)n^2$

n	$F(n)$	$(2/3)n^2$	$(2/3)(n-1)^2$	$(2/3)(n+1)^2$
1	2	≈ 1	0	≈ 3
2	4	≈ 3	≈ 1	6
3	5	6	≈ 3	≈ 11
4	12	≈ 11	6	≈ 17
5	14	≈ 17	≈ 11	24
6	23	24	≈ 17	≈ 33
7	26	≈ 33	24	≈ 43
8	44	≈ 43	≈ 33	54
9	48	54	43	≈ 67

First, let $S(n)$ denote the predicate "$F(n) < (2/3)(n + 1)^2$". We'll attempt to prove that $F(n)$ is true for all $n \geq 1$. We know it is true for all positive integers satisfying $1 \leq n \leq 9$ (see the Table 4.5).

Now take any integer $k \geq 10$ such that the predicate $S(n)$ is true for all integers $n = 1, 2, 3, \ldots, k - 1$. We'll prove that $S(k)$ must also be true, i.e., that $F(k) \leq (2/3)(k+1)^2$. By the recurrence relation, $F(k) = F(\lfloor k/2 \rfloor)+k\lfloor k/2 \rfloor$. Since $\lfloor k/2 \rfloor < k$, by the inductive hypothesis we know that $F(\lfloor k/2 \rfloor) \leq (2/3)(\lfloor k/2 \rfloor + 1)^2$. Thus $F(k) \leq (2/3)(\lfloor k/2 \rfloor + 1)^2 + k\lfloor k/2 \rfloor$. Since $\lfloor k/2 \rfloor \leq k/2$, it follows that $F(k) \leq (2/3)(k/2+1)^2 +k(k/2)$. If we can prove that this last expression is $\leq (2/3)(k + 1)^2$, we will have completed the induction proof. So let's try to prove that

$$\frac{2}{3}\left(\frac{k}{2}+1\right)^2 + k \cdot \frac{k}{2} \leq \frac{2}{3}(k+1)^2 \quad \text{for all } k \geq 10.$$

This is equivalent to the inequality

$$\frac{2}{3}\left(\frac{k^2}{4}+k+1\right) + \frac{k^2}{2} \leq \frac{2}{3}(k^2 + 2k + 1) \quad \text{for all } k \geq 10.$$

Some algebra reduces this to the equivalent inequality $(2/3)k \leq (4/3)k$, which is certainly true.

If we try to prove that $F(n) \geq (2/3)(n - 1)^2$ by a similar line of reasoning, the numbers don't quite work out. If, however, we try the less ambitious inequality $F(n) \geq (2/3)(n-2)^2$, this does work out by induction. At one point in the argument it is helpful to use the inequality $\lfloor k/2 \rfloor \geq (k - 1)/2$ given in Exercise 2.1.26, p. 19. Details will be left for the interested student.

Knowing that $(2/3)(n-2)^2 \leq F(n) \leq (2/3)(n+1)^2$ for all n, and also knowing that $(2/3)(n \pm c)^2 \sim (2/3)n^2$ for all constants c allows us to conclude (see Exercise 3.3.4(c), p. 89) that $F(n) \sim (2/3)n^2$.

Example 4.5.6 Solve the problem $F(0) = 1$, $\quad F(n) = \dfrac{n}{n+2}F(n-1) + \lfloor n/2 \rfloor$ for $n \geq 1$.

Solution After playing around with this for a while it might occur to us that the fraction $\dfrac{n}{n+2}$ is always less than 1, and is very nearly equal to 1 when n is large. Also, $\lfloor n/2 \rfloor$ is always less than or equal to just plain $n/2$. Thus the numbers $F(n)$ that we're looking for are all positive (that's clear from the recurrence relation and the initial value) and satisfy the inequality $F(n) < 1 \cdot F(n-1) + \dfrac{1}{2}n$. Now it would be reasonable to ask, "If we solve the problem

$$F(0) = 1, \quad F(n) = F(n-1) + \frac{1}{2}n \quad \text{for all } n \geq 1$$

will we get numbers $F(n)$ that are greater than the numbers $F(n)$ that we're actually looking for?" Asking the question that way sort of makes it unclear what we mean by "$F(n)$". The question might be more cleanly phrased if we introduce a new variable $G(n)$ into the picture. That is, suppose we solve the problem

$$G(0) = 1, \quad G(n) = G(n-1) + \frac{1}{2}n \quad \text{for all } n \geq 1,$$

which we can easily do; the solution is $G(n) = \dfrac{1}{4}(n+2)^2 = O(n^2)$. Then will the inequality $F(n) < G(n)$ be true for all $n \geq 1$? That is, can we conclude that $F(n) = O(n^2)$? The answer is yes, and it depends on the truth of the following theorem.

Theorem 4.5.7 *Suppose the terms of a numerical sequence $F(0)$, $F(1)$, $F(2)$, $F(3)$, ... satisfy a recurrence inequality of the form $F(n) < c(n)F(n-1) + \phi(n)$ for all $n \geq 1$, where $c(n) > 0$ for all $n \geq 1$. Let $G(n)$ be the sequence defined by $G(0) = F(0)$, $\quad G(n) = c(n)G(n-1) + \phi(n)$ for all $n \geq 1$. Then $F(n) < G(n)$ for all $n \geq 1$.*

Proof The proof is by mathematical induction. Let $S(n)$ denote the predicate "$F(n) < G(n)$". We want to prove that $S(n)$ is true for all $n \geq 1$. The base case is established by proving $F(1) < G(1)$, which follows simply from

$$F(1) < c(1)F(0) + \phi(1) = c(1)G(0) + \phi(1) = G(1).$$

For the inductive step in the proof, take any positive integer k such that $S(n)$ is true for all $n \leq k$. We shall prove that $S(k+1)$ is true as well, i.e., that $F(k+1) < G(k+1)$. Since $S(k)$ is true, we know that $F(k) < G(k)$, and since $c(k+1) > 0$ by hypothesis of the theorem, it follows that $c(k+1)F(k) < c(k+1)G(k)$. From this we can conclude that

$$F(k+1) < c(k+1)F(k) + \phi(k+1) < c(k+1)G(k) + \phi(k+1) = G(k+1),$$

which gives the desired inequality, $S(k+1) : F(k+1) < G(k+1)$. ∎

4.5.8 Comments on the Theorem: There are many valid variants of the preceding theorem. For example, if we change the hypotheses in the theorem so that

$$F(n) \le c(n)F(n-1) + \phi(n) \quad \text{for all } n \ge 1, \quad \text{and } c(n) \ge 0 \quad \text{for all } n \ge 1,$$
$$\text{and } F(0) \le G(0),$$

then the conclusion will be that $F(n) \le G(n)$ for all $n \ge 0$. Similarly, if we change the hypotheses so that

$$F(n) > c(n)F(n-1) + \phi(n) \quad \text{for all } n \ge 1, \quad \text{and } c(n) \ge 0 \quad \text{for all } n \ge 1,$$
$$\text{and } F(0) = G(0),$$

then the conclusion will be that $F(n) > G(n)$ for all $n \ge 1$. Also, there is nothing significant about the fact that the sequences have started with the subscript 0. Any other starting subscript will work as well, provided appropriate trivial changes are made in the hypotheses. It is also possible to make a similar theorem with relations that are not of first order. For example, if the hypotheses say that

$$F(n) \le c_1(n)F(n-1) + c_2(n)F(n-2) + \phi(n) \quad \text{for all } n \ge 2,$$

$$c_1(n) \ge 0 \text{ and } c_2(n) \ge 0 \text{ for all } n \ge 2, \quad F(0) \le G(0), \quad F(1) \le G(1),$$

then the conclusion will be that $F(n) \le G(n)$ for all $n \ge 0$. Similar theorems hold for recurrence relations containing terms such as $F(\lfloor n/2 \rfloor)$. Using such theorems, we can derive the results stated in Table 4.6, p. 161. Here is how to use that table. In Example 4.4.7, p. 144, we were asked to find the exact solution of the recurrence problem.

$$F(0) = 1, \quad F(n) = 2F(\lfloor n/2 \rfloor) - 7\lfloor n/2 \rfloor + 5n + 3 \quad \text{for } n \ge 1.$$

If, instead, we are asked to find the rate of growth of $F(n)$, we can note that the initial value is positive and that $5n - 7\lfloor n/2 \rfloor + 3$ is positive and $\Theta(n)$, so the table gives us $F(n) = \Theta(n \log(n))$.

4.5.2   Growth Rates for Solutions of Special Linear Equations Involving $F(\lfloor n/2 \rfloor)$, $F(\lceil n/2 \rceil)$, etc.

In Table 4.6 it is assumed that b is a positive constant. Also, it is assumed that all initial values are non-negative and that all non-homogeneous terms are *eventually* non-negative (i.e., positive for all large n).

Note 1: It is useful to keep in mind that $\lfloor n/2 \rfloor$ and $\lceil n/2 \rceil$ are both $\Theta(n)$.

Note 2: We can validly replace Θ by Ω or O everywhere in the equations above.

Table 4.6 Θ growth rate for a number of recurrence relations involving floor and ceiling of $n/2$

Recurrence relation	Solution rate of growth	
$F(n) = b\,F(\lfloor n/2 \rfloor) + \Theta(1)$	$F(n) = \Theta(1)$	if $0 < b < 1$
$or = b\,F(\lceil n/2 \rceil) + \Theta(1)$	$F(n) = \Theta(\log(n))$	if $b = 1$
	$F(n) = \Theta(n^{\lg(b)})$	if $b > 1$ and $F(1) > \dfrac{1}{1-b}$
$F(n) = b\,F(\lfloor n/2 \rfloor) + \Theta(n)$	$F(n) = \Theta(n)$	if $0 < b < 2$
$or = b\,F(\lceil n/2 \rceil) + \Theta(n)$	$F(n) = \Theta(n \log(n))$	if $b = 2$
	$F(n) = \Theta(n^{\lg(b)})$	if $b > 2$
$F(n) = F(\lfloor n/2 \rfloor) + F(\lceil n/2 \rceil) + \Theta(1)$	$F(n) = \Theta(n)$	if $F(1) \geq 0$
$F(n) = F(\lfloor n/2 \rfloor) + F(\lceil n/2 \rceil) + \Theta(n)$	$F(n) = \Theta(n \log(n))$	

4.5.3   Further Examples

Example 4.5.9 Prove that the recurrence relation $F(n) = b\,F(\lceil (n+1)/2 \rceil) + \phi(n)$ when $n \geq n_0$, can transformed by the substitution $F(n) = G(n-1)$ and another change of variable into the recurrence relation $G(n) = b\,G(\lfloor n/2 \rfloor) + \phi(n+1)$ when $n \geq n_0 - 1$.

Solution The substitution $F(n) = G(n-1)$ into the given recurrence relation yields the relation
$G(n-1) = b\,G(\lceil (n+1)/2 \rceil - 1) + \phi(n)$ when $n \geq n_0$. Now replace n by $n+1$ to get
$G(n) = b\,G(\lceil ((n+1)+1)/2 \rceil - 1) + \phi(n+1)$ when $n+1 \geq n_0$. Since
$\lceil ((n+1)+1)/2 \rceil - 1 = \lceil (n/2)+1 \rceil - 1 = \lceil n/2 \rceil$, it follows that
$G(n) = b\,G(\lceil n/2 \rceil) + \phi(n+1)$ when $n \geq n_0 - 1$.

Example 4.5.10 Solve the problem $F(2) = 5$, $F(n) = 2F(\lfloor n/2 \rfloor + 1) + 3\lfloor n/2 \rfloor$ for all $n \geq 3$. Begin by making the substitution $F(n) = G(n-1)$.

Solution The substitution $F(n) = G(n-1)$ gives $G(n-1) = 2G((\lfloor n/2 \rfloor + 1) - 1) + 3\lfloor n/2 \rfloor$ for all $n \geq 3$. [If this is not clear, try thinking about it this way: $F(7) = G(7-1)$; $F(p) = G(p-1)$; $F(m/2) = G(m/2-1)$; $F(\lfloor x \rfloor) = G(\lfloor x \rfloor - 1)$; and thus $F(\lfloor n/2 \rfloor + 1) = G((\lfloor n/2 \rfloor + 1) - 1)$.] The relation simplifies to $G(n-1) = 2G(\lfloor n/2 \rfloor) + 3\lfloor n/2 \rfloor$ for all $n \geq 3$. Now we replace n by $n+1$ to obtain $G(n) = 2G(\lfloor (n+1)/2 \rfloor) + 3\lfloor (n+1)/2 \rfloor$ for all $n+1 \geq 3$, i.e., all $n \geq 2$. The initial data gives us $5 = F(2) = G(1)$. Now, as described on p. 157, we use the identity $\lfloor (n+1)/2 \rfloor = \lceil n/2 \rceil$ to obtain $G(n) = 2G(\lceil n/2 \rceil) + 3\lceil n/2 \rceil$ for all $n \geq 2$.
By Table 4.1, p. 147, the solution is $G(n) = \alpha\,2^{\lceil \lg(n) \rceil} + 3 \displaystyle\sum_{k=1}^{\lceil \lg(n) \rceil} \left\lceil \frac{n}{2^k} \right\rceil 2^{k-1}$ for

all $n \geq 1$. The initial data yields $5 = G(1) = \alpha \cdot 2^0 + 3 \cdot 0$, so $\alpha = 5$. Thus

$$G(n) = 5 \cdot 2^{\lceil \lg(n) \rceil} + 3 \sum_{k=1}^{\lceil \lg(n) \rceil} \left\lceil \frac{n}{2^k} \right\rceil 2^{k-1} \text{ for all } n \geq 1. \text{ Now we return to the } F \text{ func-}$$

tion: $F(n) = G(n-1) = 5 \cdot 2^{\lceil \lg(n-1) \rceil} + 3 \sum_{k=1}^{\lceil \lg(n-1) \rceil} \left\lceil \frac{n-1}{2^k} \right\rceil 2^{k-1}$ for all $n - 1 \geq 1$,

i.e., all $n \geq 2$. [Check: $F(3) = 2F(1+1) + 3 \cdot 1 = 13$ from the recurrence relation, and $F(3) = 5(2) + 3(1) = 13$ from the formula for the solution.]

Example 4.5.11 Solve each of the problems below by making an appropriate substitution (i.e., change of variable), solving the resulting problem, and then returning to the original function.

(a) $F(1) = 0$, $F(2) = 1$, $nF(n) = (n-1)F(n-1) + 6(n-2)F(n-2) + 2^n$ for all $n \geq 3$

(b) $F(1) = 1$, $F(n) + \lg(n) = F(n-1) + \lg(n-1) + n - 2$ for all $n \geq 2$

(c) $F(0) = 1$, $(n+1)F(n) = nF(n-1) + n^3 - n$ for all $n \geq 1$

(d) $F(2) = 3$, $F(n) = 2F(\lceil (n+1)/2 \rceil) - n$ for all $n \geq 3$

(e) $F(0) = 0$, $F(n) = F(\lfloor (n-1)/2 \rfloor) + F(\lceil (n-1)/2 \rceil) + 2n + 1$ for all $n \geq 1$

(f) $F(0) = 2$, $F(n) = \dfrac{3}{2}F(\lfloor (n-1)/2 \rfloor) + \left\lceil \dfrac{n+1}{2} \right\rceil$ for all $n \geq 1$

(g) $F(1) = 2$, $F(n) = \dfrac{3}{2}F(\lceil (n-1)/2 \rceil) + \left\lceil \dfrac{n}{2} \right\rceil$ for all $n \geq 2$

Solution

(a) Let $G(n)$ denote $nF(n)$. Then the recurrence relation has the form $G(n) = G(n-1) + 6G(n-2) + 2^n$ for all $n \geq 3$. Also note that $G(1) = 1F(1) = 0$ and $G(2) = 2F(2) = 2$. The characteristic equation is $r^2 = r + 6$, i.e., $(r+2)(r-3) = 0$. The general solution for the homogeneous part of the relation has the form $G_{homog}(n) = \alpha_1(-2)^n + \alpha_2 3^n$ for all $n \geq 1$. There is a particular solution of the form $G_{part}(n) = \beta 2^n$ for all $n \geq 1$. We can solve for β by substituting this particular solution into the recurrence relation: $\beta 2^n = \beta 2^{n-1} + 6\beta 2^{n-2} + 2^n$, which we rewrite as $4\beta 2^{n-2} = 2\beta 2^{n-2} + 6\beta 2^{n-2} + 4 \cdot 2^{n-2}$. Combining terms, we find that $\beta = -1$. Thus $G(n) = \alpha_1(-2)^n + \alpha_2 3^n - 2^n$ for all $n \geq 1$. Now we introduce the initial data: $0 = G(1) = \alpha_1(-2)^1 + \alpha_2 3^1 - 2^1$ and $2 = G(2) = \alpha_1(-2)^2 + \alpha_2 3^2 - 2^2$, so $-2\alpha_1 + 3\alpha_2 = 2$ and $4\alpha_1 + 9\alpha_2 = 6$, which yields $\alpha_1 = 0$ and $\alpha_2 = 2/3$. Thus $G(n) = (2/3)3^n - 2^n$ for all $n \geq 1$, which can be simplified to $G(n) = 2(3^{n-1} - 2^{n-1})$ for all $n \geq 1$. Since $F(n) = \dfrac{1}{n}G(n)$, we see that $F(n) = \dfrac{2}{n}(3^{n-1} - 2^{n-1})$ for all $n \geq 1$. [Check: $3F(3) = 2F(2) + 6(1)F(1) + 8 = 10$ by the recurrence relation, which gives $F(3) = 10/3$; by the formula for the solution, $F(3) = \dfrac{2}{3}(3^2 - 2^2) = 10/3$ as well.]

(b) Let $G(n) = F(n) + \lg(n)$ for all $n \geq 1$. Then the recurrence relation becomes $G(n) = G(n-1) + n - 2$ for all $n \geq 2$, and the initial data gives us $G(1) = F(1) + \lg(1) = 1 + 0 = 1$. This can be solved by the method in Example 4.5.1: $G(1) = 1$, $G(2) = 1+0, G(3) = 1+0+1$, $G(4) = 1+0+1+2$, $G(5) = 1+0+1+2+3$, etc. The form is clear: $G(n) = 1+0+1+2+3+\cdots+(n-2) = 1 + \dfrac{(n-2)(n-1)}{2}$ for all $n \geq 1$. Since $F(n) = G(n) - \lg(n)$ for all $n \geq 1$, we see that $F(n) = 1 + \dfrac{(n-2)(n-1)}{2} - \lg(n)$ for all $n \geq 1$. Thus $F(n) = \Theta(n^2)$.
[Check: $F(2) + \lg(2) = F(1) + \lg(1) + n - 2$, so $F(2) + 1 = 1 + 0 + 1 - 2$, so $F(2) = 0$; the same value is obtained by substituting n $= 2$ into the solution for $F(n)$.]

(c) Let $G(n) = (n+1)F(n)$. Then the recurrence relation can be written $G(n) = G(n-1) + n^3 - n$ for all $n \geq 1$, and the initial data gives us $G(0) = (0+1)F(0) = 1$. The general solution of the homogeneous relation is $G_{homog}(n) = \alpha 1^n = \alpha$ for all $n \geq 0$. There is a particular solution of the form $G_{part}(n) = \beta_4 n^4 + \beta_3 n^3 + \beta_2 n^2 + \beta_1 n$ for all $n \geq 0$. Substitution into the recurrence relation gives

$$\beta_4 n^4 + \beta_3 n^3 + \beta_2 n^2 + \beta_1 n = \beta_4(n-1)^4 + \beta_3(n-1)^3 + \beta_2(n-1)^2$$
$$+\beta_1(n-1) + n^3 - n$$

$$= \beta_4(n^4 - 4n^3 + 6n^2 - 4n + 1) + \beta_3(n^3 - 3n^2 + 3n - 1) + \beta_2(n^2 - 2n + 1)$$
$$+\beta_1(n-1) + n^3 - n$$

for all $n \geq 1$. Matching coefficients gives the equations $\beta_4 = \beta_4$ and $\beta_3 = -4\beta_4 + \beta_3 + 1$ and $\beta_2 = 6\beta_4 - 3\beta_3 + \beta_2$ and $\beta_1 = -4\beta_4 + 3\beta_3 - 2\beta_2 + \beta_1 - 1$. Solving these gives us $\beta_4 = 1/4$ and $\beta_3 = 1/2$ and $\beta_2 = -1/4$ and $\beta_1 = -1/2$. Thus $G(n) = \alpha + (1/4)n^4 + (1/2)n^3 - (1/4)n^2 - (1/2)n$ for all $n \geq 0$. The initial data gives $1 = G(0) = \alpha$. Thus $G(n) = (1/4)n^4 + (1/2)n^3 - (1/4)n^2 - (1/2)n + 1$ for all $n \geq 0$. Since $F(n) = \dfrac{1}{n+1}G(n)$ we have $F(n) = \dfrac{1}{n+1}[(1/4)n^4 + (1/2)n^3 - (1/4)n^2 - (1/2)n + 1]$ for all $n \geq 0$.
[Check: putting $n = 1$ in the recurrence relation gives $(1+1)F(1) = 1 \cdot F(0) + 1^3 - 1$, so $F(1) = 1/2$. The same value is obtained by putting $n = 1$ in the solution for $F(n)$.]

(d) By Table 4.4, p. 157, the substitution $F(n) = G(n-1)$ transforms the given recurrence relation into $G(n) = 2G(\lceil n/2 \rceil) - (n+1)$ for all $n \geq 2$, with initial value $3 = F(2) = G(1)$. By Table 4.2, p. 148,

$$G(n) = \alpha \, 2^{\lceil \lg(n) \rceil} - \sum_{k=0}^{\lceil \lg(n) \rceil} \left\lceil \frac{n}{2^k} \right\rceil 2^k - \frac{1}{1-2} \quad \text{for all } n \geq 1. \text{ Initial data gives}$$

$$3 = G(1) = \alpha 2^0 - 1 + 1, \text{ so } \alpha = 3. \text{ Thus } G(n) = 3 \times 2^{\lceil \lg(n) \rceil} - \sum_{k=0}^{\lceil \lg(n) \rceil} \left\lceil \frac{n}{2^k} \right\rceil 2^k + 1$$

for all $n \geq 1$. Then

$$F(n) = G(n-1) = 3 \times 2^{\lceil \lg(n-1) \rceil} - \sum_{k=0}^{\lceil \lg(n-1) \rceil} \left\lceil \frac{n-1}{2^k} \right\rceil 2^k + 1 \text{ for all } (n-1) \geq 1,$$

i.e., for all $n \geq 2$.

[Check: $F(3) = 2F(2) - 3 = 3$ by the recurrence relation, and $F(3) = 3 \cdot 2^1 - (2+2) + 1 = 3$ by the formula for the solution.]

(e) By Table 4.4, p. 157, the substitution $F(n) = G(n+1)$ transforms the given relation into
$G(n) = G(\lfloor n/2 \rfloor) + G(\lceil n/2 \rceil) + 2(n-1) + 1$ for all $n \geq 2$. The initial data is $0 = F(0) = G(1)$. By Table 4.3, p. 149, the solution is $G(n) = \alpha n + 2(n \lfloor \lg(n) \rfloor - 2^{\lfloor \lg(n) \rfloor + 1}) - (-1)$ for all $n \geq 1$. The initial data gives $0 = G(1) = \alpha + 2(0 - 2) + 1$, so $\alpha = 3$. Thus $G(n) = 3n + 2(n \lfloor \lg(n) \rfloor - 2^{\lfloor \lg(n) \rfloor + 1}) + 1$ for all $n \geq 1$. Then $F(n) = G(n+1) = 3(n+1) + 2((n+1) \lfloor \lg(n+1) \rfloor - 2^{\lfloor \lg(n+1) \rfloor + 1}) + 1$ for all $n+1 \geq 1$, i.e., for all $n \geq 0$.

[Check: $F(1) = F(0) + F(0) + 2 \times 1 + 1 = 3$ from the recurrence relation, and $F(1) = 3(1+1) + 2(2 \times 1 - 4) + 1 = 3$ from the formula for the solution.]

(f) By Table 4.4, p. 157, the transformation $F(n) = G(n+1)$ changes the given recurrence relation into the form $G(n) = (3/2)G(\lfloor n/2 \rfloor) + \lceil n/2 \rceil$ for all $n \geq 2$, with initial data $2 = F(0) = G(1)$. By Table 4.1, p. 147, the solution is $G(n) = $

$$\alpha (3/2)^{\lfloor \lg(n) \rfloor} + n + (3/2 - 1) \sum_{k=1}^{\lfloor \lg(n) \rfloor} \left\lfloor \frac{n}{2^k} \right\rfloor (3/2)^{k-1} \text{ for all } n \geq 1. \text{ The initial}$$

value gives us $2 = G(1) = \alpha (3/2)^0 + 1 + (1/2) \sum_{k=1}^{\lfloor \lg(1) \rfloor} \left\lfloor \frac{1}{2^k} \right\rfloor (3/2)^{k-1} = \alpha + 1$,

so $\alpha = 1$, and thus

$$G(n) = (3/2)^{\lfloor \lg(n) \rfloor} + n + (1/2) \sum_{k=1}^{\lfloor \lg(n) \rfloor} \left\lfloor \frac{n}{2^k} \right\rfloor (3/2)^{k-1} \text{ for all } n \geq 1. \text{ Then}$$

$$F(n) = G(n+1) = (3/2)^{\lfloor \lg(n+1) \rfloor} + n + 1 + (1/2) \sum_{k=1}^{\lfloor \lg(n+1) \rfloor} \left\lfloor \frac{n+1}{2^k} \right\rfloor (3/2)^{k-1}$$

for all $n+1 \geq 1$, i.e., $n \geq 0$.

[Check: $F(1) = (3/2)F(0) + 1 = 4$ by the recurrence relation, and $F(1) = (3/2)1 + 1 + 1 + (1/2) \times 1 \times (3/2)^0 = 4$ by the formula for the solution.]

(g) As described on p. 157, we use the identity $\lceil (n-1)/2 \rceil = \lfloor n/2 \rfloor$ to change the relation to $F(n) = (3/2)F(\lfloor n/2 \rfloor) + \lceil n/2 \rceil$ for all $n \geq 2$, with $F(1) = 2$. This is exactly the same as the problem we just solved in part (f) (but with $G(n)$ in place of $F(n)$ in part (f)). Thus

$$F(n) = (3/2)^{\lfloor \lg(n) \rfloor} + n + (1/2) \sum_{k=1}^{\lfloor \lg(n) \rfloor} \left\lfloor \frac{n}{2^k} \right\rfloor (3/2)^{k-1} \text{ for all } n \geq 1.$$

Example 4.5.12 Solve the problem below for values of n that are powers of 2. *Hint:* $\sqrt{t^k} = (\sqrt{t})^k$.

$$F(1) = 5, \quad F(n) = F(\lfloor n/2 \rfloor) + \sqrt{n} \quad \text{for all } n \geq 2$$

What conjecture would you make about the asymptotic behavior of the complete solution?

Solution Write $n = 2^k$ for $k \geq 1$. Then $F(2^k) = F(\lfloor 2^{k-1} \rfloor) + \sqrt{2^k}$ for all $k \geq 1$, that is, $F(2^k) = F(2^{k-1}) + (\sqrt{2})^k$. Let $G(k) = F(2^k)$, so that $G(k) = G(k-1) + (\sqrt{2})^k$ for all $k \geq 1$, and $G(0) = F(2^0) = F(1) = 5$. There is a particular solution of the form $G_{part}(k) = \beta \, (\sqrt{2})^k$ for all $k \geq 0$. We obtain the value of β by substitution into the recurrence relation for $G(k)$: $\beta \, (\sqrt{2})^k = \beta \, (\sqrt{2})^{k-1} + (\sqrt{2})^k$, so $\beta = \dfrac{\sqrt{2}}{\sqrt{2}-1} =$ $2 + \sqrt{2}$. The general solution of the homogeneous part of the relation is $G(k) = \alpha$ (a constant), so $G(k) = \alpha + (2 + \sqrt{2})(\sqrt{2})^k$ for all $k \geq 0$. The initial data gives $5 = G(0) = \alpha + (2+\sqrt{2})$, so $\alpha = 3 - \sqrt{2}$. Then $G(k) = (3 - \sqrt{2}) + (2 + \sqrt{2})\sqrt{2^k}$ for all $k \geq 0$. Now we return to the F function: for values of n that have the form 2^k, we have $F(n) = F(2^k) = G(k) = (3 - \sqrt{2}) + (2 + \sqrt{2})\sqrt{2^k} = (3 - \sqrt{2}) + (2 + \sqrt{2})\sqrt{n}$.

[Check: $F(2) = F(1) + \sqrt{2} = 5 + \sqrt{2}$ by the recurrence relation, and $F(2) = F(2^1) = (3 - \sqrt{2}) + (2 + \sqrt{2})\sqrt{2} = 5 + \sqrt{2}$ by the formula for $F(n)$ when n is a power of 2.]

We can conjecture that $F(n) \sim (2 + \sqrt{2})\sqrt{n}$, although we have not proved that this is true.

Example 4.5.13 Use a recurrence inequality and one of the formulas in Table 4.3 on p. 149 to show that the solution of the problem below is $O(n \log(n))$:

$$F(1) = 0, \quad F(n) = F(\lfloor n/2 \rfloor) + F(\lceil n/2 \rceil) + \sqrt{n^2 - 1} \quad \text{for all } n \geq 2.$$

Solution First note that $\sqrt{n^2 - 1} < \sqrt{n^2} = n$ for all $n \geq 0$, so we have the recurrence inequality
$F(n) < F(\lfloor n/2 \rfloor) + F(\lceil n/2 \rceil) + n$ for all $n \geq 2$. So consider the recurrence problem
$G(1) = F(1) = 0$ and $G(n) = G(\lfloor n/2 \rfloor) + G(\lceil n/2 \rceil) + n$ for all $n \geq 2$. By Table 4.3, p. 149,
$G(n) = \alpha n + n \lfloor \lg(n) \rfloor - 2^{\lfloor \lg(n) \rfloor + 1}$ for all $n \geq 1$. The initial data gives us $0 = G(1) = \alpha + 0 - 2$, so $G(n) = 2n + n \lfloor \lg(n) \rfloor - 2^{\lfloor \lg(n) \rfloor + 1}$ for all $n \geq 1$. By Table 4.3, p. 149, $G(n) \sim n \lg(n)$ as $n \to \infty$, from which it follows that $G(n) = O(n \log(n))$. By Theorem 4.5.7, p. 159, $F(n) < G(n)$ for all $n \geq 2$, so it follows that $F(n) = O(n \log(n))$ (see Theorem 3.2.11 (a), p. 77).

4.5.4   Exercises

4.5.14 In Example 4.5.3 in this section we found that $G(n) = \dfrac{1}{2} + \displaystyle\sum_{k=2}^{n} \dfrac{1}{k(k+1)}$

for all $n \geq 1$. Note that since $\dfrac{1}{2} = \dfrac{1}{1(1+1)}$, we can simplify this expression to

$G(n) = \displaystyle\sum_{k=1}^{n} \dfrac{1}{k(k+1)}$ for all $n \geq 1$.

(a) Work out the exact fractional value of $G(1)$, $G(2)$, $G(3)$, $G(4)$, and $G(5)$.
(b) Make a conjecture about the value of $G(n)$ for all $n \geq 1$.
(c) Use mathematical induction to prove the conjecture you make in part (b).

4.5.15 Prove that the recurrence relation $F(n) = F(\lfloor (n-1)/2 \rfloor) + F(\lceil (n-1)/2 \rceil) + \phi(n)$ when $n \geq 1$, can transformed by the substitution $F(n) = G(n+1)$ and another change of variable into the recurrence relation $G(n) = G(\lfloor n/2 \rfloor) + G(\lceil n/2 \rceil) + \phi(n-1)$ when $n \geq 2$.

4.5.16 Solve each of the problems below by making an appropriate substitution (i.e., change of variable), solving the resulting problem, and then returning to the original function.

(a) $F(1) = 2$, $F(2) = 1$, $(n-1)F(n) = (n-2)F(n-1) + 2(n-3)F(n-2)$ for all $n \geq 3$
(b) $F(1) = -1$, $F(n) + \sqrt{n} = F(n-1) + \sqrt{n-1} + n$ for all $n \geq 2$
(c) $F(0) = 1$, $F(n) = F(\lfloor (n-1)/2 \rfloor) + F(\lceil (n-1)/2 \rceil) + 3n$ for all $n \geq 1$
(d) $T(0) = 3$, $T(n) = 2T(\lfloor (n-1)/2 \rfloor) + n + 1$ for $n \geq 1$
(e) $F(1) = 1$, $\dfrac{F(n)}{\lfloor \lg(n+1) \rfloor} = \dfrac{F(n-1)}{\lfloor \lg(n) \rfloor} + n$ for all $n \geq 2$
(f) $P(0) = 0$, $P(n) = 3\lfloor n/2 \rfloor + P(\lfloor n/2 \rfloor) + P(\lfloor (n-1)/2 \rfloor)$ for $n \geq 1$

4.5.17 Solve the problem $F(0) = 3$, $F(n) = 4F(\lceil n/2 \rceil - 1) - \lceil n/2 \rceil$ for all $n \geq 1$. Begin by making the substitution $F(n) = G(n+1)$.

4.5.18 Solve the problem below for values of n that are powers of 2.

$$F(1) = 1, \quad F(n) = F(\lfloor n/2 \rfloor) + F(\lceil n/2 \rceil) + (\lg(n))^2 \quad \text{for all } n \geq 2$$

What conjecture would you make about the asymptotic behavior of the complete solution?

4.5.19 Use Theorem 4.5.7, Comments 4.5.8, and Theorems 2.1.4 and 2.1.5 on p. 10 and 12 to find precise upper and lower bound functions for the solution of $F(n) = F(\lfloor n/2 \rfloor) + \lfloor n/4 \rfloor$, $F(1) = 2$. The bounds you obtain should allow you to find a function $A(n)$ such that $F(n) \sim A(n)$. (This means you cannot use Table 4.4, p. 157.)

Deterministic Analysis of Algorithms

In this chapter we focus on deterministic algorithms and we analyze the best case and worst case complexities for all the algorithms that we consider. A deterministic algorithm is one that will return the same answer no matter how many times it is called on the same data. Moreover, it will always take the same steps to complete the task when applied to the same data.

5.1   Loop Analysis

As stated in the Introduction, the general goal of *analysis of algorithms* is to estimate the amounts of time and space necessary for an algorithm to complete as a function of the size of the problem. For this, a reliable method is to count the number of *basic operations*—i.e. operations that require a limited number of assembly code instructions after compilation—that the algorithm requires for a problem of size n. Thus, we are examining the time or space complexities of the algorithm, as opposed to the execution time.

Specifically, we are looking for

- the largest such number of operations that can occur for a problem of size n, known as the *worst-case* complexity;
- the smallest number of operations that can occur for a problem of size n, known as the *best-case* complexity;
- the number of operations that we can expect on the average, known as the *average* complexity.

In this chapter we will only analyze the best and worst case complexities. The next chapter will introduce the tools used for the average case.

After expressing the complexity as a function of n, we usually look for a simple function that can provide a big-Oh, big-Omega, or big-Theta for our algorithm in terms of time and space requirements.

© Springer International Publishing Switzerland 2014
D. Vrajitoru and W. Knight, *Practical Analysis of Algorithms*,
Undergraduate Topics in Computer Science, DOI 10.1007/978-3-319-09888-3_5

Starting with the simplest form of analysis, many algorithms involve one or more nested loops. The number of basic operations executed in each iteration is usually bounded by constants. In such situations, the time complexity function is determined by the total number of iterations. In this section, we are examining various ways to count the total number of iterations for loops and develop a strategy to deal with nested loops.

Example 5.1.1 Locating the Maximum Object in an Array in Random Order.
Consider the following problem. An array a contains a subarray whose left-most and right-most subscripts we'll denote by first and last, where first ≤ last. We'll denote this subarray by a[first..last]. The objects in the array a are "directly comparable" in the sense that the relational operators <, <=, >, and >= are defined on them. We want to find the subscript of the cell containing the largest object of the subarray. The function in Fig. 5.1 will examine the array and return that subscript. If several cells of the subarray contain copies of the largest object, then the function will return the subscript of the left-most such cell.

Let's start with an analysis of the amount of memory space required by this function to do its work whenever it is called. Actually, what we will calculate will be the *extra* memory space beyond the amount already allocated by the "client" (i.e., some other function that calls this function). Thus we will not include in our analysis the size of the array argument being passed to the function, because the array is passed by "simulated reference" (what's actually passed is a pointer to the existing array in the client). So what do we count? The answer is one stack frame (see Exercise 4.1.23) for the call to location_of_max. This stack frame contains a return address, all local variables, all the parameter values that have been passed, and space for the value that will be returned by the function. The function has a fixed number of local variables of constant size, and all the parameter values have constant size as well. (By "constant sizes" we mean that the sizes are *independent of the size of the subarray being sorted*.) The return address and the space for the return value are also of constant size. To sum up: the (extra) amount of memory space required by a call to this function is some constant.

Now let's analyze the execution time required when this function is called. We expect that the execution time will depend in some way on the number of cells in the

```
template <class otype>
int location_of_max (const otype a[], int first, int last)
{
    int max_loc = first;              // The first cell of the subarray will contain
                                      // the "largest seen so far".
    for (++first; first <= last; ++first)  // Start at the second cell.
        if (a[first] > a[max_loc])    // The value parameter "first" can be modified
            max_loc = first;          // since its initial value need not be
                                      // preserved.
    return max_loc;
}
```

Fig. 5.1 Function finding the location of the maximum element in an array

subarray a[first..last], so let's introduce the letter n to stand for the value of the expression last-first+1 (see Theorem 2.1.6) at the moment when the function begins execution. The value of n will vary from one call to another. It will always be at least 1 because last $\geq$ first.

Here is a list of the steps that occur during execution of our function and the execution time associated with each step.

(1) First there is the time required to set up the stack frame for the function call. This involves changing the address stored in the run-time stack pointer (a hardware register in the CPU), placing a return address in the stack frame, copying the address of the array argument to the parameter a, copying the values of two integer arguments to the two integer parameters first and last, and placing the address of the function code in the program counter (another CPU register). In computer hardware, each of these individual steps takes "constant time". That is, the amount of time does not in any way depend on the value of n, nor does it depend on the values of the addresses and integers being copied. Let S denote the sum of the execution times for these steps in the stack frame set-up. Then S is a constant that depends on the clock speed of the machine and the number of clock cycles required in the CPU for each step.

(2) The first instruction of the function involves assignment of an integer value to an integer variable. This requires an amount of time, call it A, that includes the time to access the memory location of the variable first (i.e., to retrieve its value) and the time to write that value into the memory location for the variable max_loc. In computer hardware these execution times do not depend on the particular values that are stored in these variables, nor on the particular memory addresses at which the values are stored, so A is a machine-dependent constant. Execution now proceeds to the loop in constant time P (the time required to increment the CPU's program counter and load the next instruction).

(3) The actions in the loop are as follows.

   (a) The integer variable first is incremented. This takes constant time, call it I.

   (b) The value of the integer first is compared with the value of the integer last. Even though the built in integers are of constant size (number of bits) for any particular C++ compiler, the operation of comparing them in computer hardware may depend on the particular values stored in these constant-size variables. For example, in some computers the comparison 999999998 <= 999999999 will take much longer than the comparison 1 <= 2. Nevertheless, there will be a definite (machine dependent) upper bound U for the execution time of an integer comparison and also a definite lower bound L. That is, execution time for an integer comparison is bounded. The bounds U and L do not depend in any way on the number n of cells in the subarray we are processing.

   (c) If the integer comparison evaluates to false, then there will be a branch in the machine code to the return statement (see (4) on the next page). Let B

denote the execution time of the branch statement. If, instead, the comparison evaluates to `true`, then execution proceeds in constant time P to the loop body.

(d) In the loop body a comparison is made between two `otype` objects, namely `a[first]` and `a[max_loc]`. *Here we must confront a question about the nature of the* `otype` *objects*: Are they conceptually of fixed size (number of bits), like the integers in part (b) above, so that execution time for the comparison operation > is bounded? Or are they class objects containing pointers to data structures external to the array `a`, such as strings or linked lists? If that is the case, then from a conceptual point of view the objects are not of fixed size, and if there is no bound on the sizes of these external structures, then there may be no upper bound for the execution time of a single comparison operation between pairs of `otype` objects. In such cases we cannot analyze the execution time of the algorithm we are considering unless we are given further information about the specific objects in the array `a`. For now, however, let's suppose the comparison operation > on `otype` objects requires bounded execution time. Let M and X denote the minimum and maximum execution times.

(e) If the `otype` comparison returns false, then execution will branch to the second of the two `++first` statements in the loop control line. Branch execution time is B. Otherwise, execution will proceed in constant time P to the body of the `if` statement.

(f) The body of the `if` statement is an integer assignment, with execution time A. When it is executed, control then returns via a branch statement (time B) to the second `++first` instruction.

(g) Execution of the second `++first` instruction requires time I, followed by P. Then a branch (time B) transfers control to the integer comparison in step (b) above.

(4) Eventually the loop will cease execution when the branch discussed in step (3)(c) occurs. Then the return statement will be executed. On most machines this involves copying the value of `max_loc` into a space in the stack frame reserved for return values, re-setting the value of the run-time stack pointer, and copying the return address into the program counter. All these are constant time operations, so let R denote the total execution time that they require.

The body of the loop will be executed as many times as the comparison in step (3)(b) evaluates to `true`. Since `first` is already equal to the subscript of the second cell when the comparison is made for the first time, the comparison will evaluate to `true` exactly $n - 1$ times.

Now we are ready to total up all the times that make up the complete execution time for a call to the `location_of_max` function.

- Step (1) occurs only once, with time S.
- Step (2) occurs only once, with time $A + P$.

- Step (3)(a) occurs only once, with time $I + P$.
- Step (3)(b) occurs n times: $n - 1$ times the comparison evaluates to `true`, and 1 time it evaluates to false. The total time here is at least $n L$ and at most $n U$.
- The move to the loop body is step (3) (c) occurs $n - 1$ times, which requires $(n - 1)P$ time. The branch in step (3)(c) occurs only once, with time B.
- Step (3)(d) occurs $n - 1$ times, with total execution time at least $(n - 1)M$ and at most $(n - 1)X$.
- There will be a total of $n - 1$ branches back to the `++first` instruction. Some of these may occur in step (3)(e); all the others occur at the end of step (3)(f). The total time for these $n - 1$ branches is $(n - 1)B$.
- When `a[first > a[max_loc]` evaluates to `true` in step (3)(e), execution will proceed in time P to the integer assignment statement `max_loc = first`. This can happen anywhere from 0 to $n - 1$ times, depending on the ordering of the objects that happen to be in the subarray we are processing. For example, if the largest object happens to reside in the very first cell of the subarray, this assignment will never be executed. At the other extreme, if the objects are in increasing order, each strictly larger than the one before it, then the assignment will occur $n - 1$ times. Thus the total execution time for this statement is at least 0 and at most $(n - 1)(P + A)$.
- Step (3)(g) occurs exactly $n - 1$ times, with total execution time $(n - 1)(B + I)$.
- Step (4) occurs exactly once, with time R.

Adding up these numbers, we find that the *minimum* possible execution time for a call to our `location_of_max` function will be

$$S + (A+P) + (I+P) + nL + (n-1)P + B + (n-1)M + (n-1)B + 0 + (n-1)(B+I) + R$$

and the *maximum* will be

$$S + (A+C) + (I+C) + nU + (n-1)P + B + (n-1)X + (n-1)B + (n-1)A + (n-1)(B+I) + R.$$

Combining terms that involve n gives minimum execution time

$$(L + P + M + 2B + I)n + (S + A + P - B - M + R)$$

and maximum

$$(U + 2P + X + 2B + A + I)n + (S - B - X + R).$$

If we let $T_{min}(n)$ denote the minimum execution time, and $T_{max}(n)$ the maximum executions time, then we have shown that

$$T_{min}(n) = C_1 n + D_1 \quad \text{and} \quad T_{max}(n) = C_2 n + D_2,$$

where C_1, D_1, C_2, and D_2 are constants, with $0 < C_1 < C_2$. It follows that $T_{min}(n) = \Theta(n)$ and $T_{max}(n) = \Theta(n)$, but $T_{min}(n) < T_{max}(n)$.

Note that all the constants in the discussion above depend on the available instruction set for a particular processor, the number of clock cycles required for each separate type of instruction, and the clock speed at which it is driven. They also depend on the way in which the compiler translates the original source code into machine code. A different processor or compiler could produce a somewhat different analysis. In the end, however, the result would be the same: execution time will invariably be $\Theta(n)$.

This is the only time in this book that we will descend to such a low-level, detailed analysis of the execution time for an algorithm. **DO NOT IMITATE THIS ANALYSIS IN ANY OF THE EXERCISES IN THIS CHAPTER.** Experienced computer scientists do the analysis more concisely.

Here is how an experienced practitioner of analysis of algorithms might compute the execution time for the algorithm in Example 5.1.1.

- Introduce the mathematical variable n to denote the length of the subarray to be examined.
- Set-up time and return time for this function are both constant (i.e., independent of n).
- Non-loop operations in the body of this function require constant time.
- Each single operation in the control line of the loop requires execution time that's $\Theta(1)$ as $n \to \infty$. (That is, for each of these operations there are two positive constants A_1 and A_2, which do not depend on n, such that the execution time for that operation is at least A_1 and at most A_2 each time that operation is executed.)
- The body of the loop is executed $n - 1$ times, where n is the length of the array to be scanned. (Note: this is not "execution time", which would be expressed in seconds or milliseconds; instead, it is "number of times"—a pure integer.)
- The code in the body of the loop requires execution time that's $\Theta(1)$ as $n \to \infty$. (That is, there are two positive constants B_1 and B_2, which do not depend on n, such that the execution time for the body of the loop is at least B_1 and at most B_2 each time it is executed.)
- It follows that the total execution time for the loop is $\Theta(n - 1)$, or more properly, $\Theta(n)$.

Theorem 5.1.2 below generalizes the discussion in Example 5.1.1.

Theorem 5.1.2 *Suppose we are given a loop whose execution time we want to analyze. The loop should be such that if m denotes the number of times the body of the loop is to be executed, then there is no theoretical limit on the size of m. Suppose that the execution time for each of the individual loop control operations is bounded by constants, by which we mean that for each operation there are (machine dependent) positive constants A_1 and A_2 such that the execution time for that operation is at least A_1 and at most A_2 each time it is executed. (In the context of this theorem we could express that by saying that the execution time for each operation is $\Theta(1)$ as $m \to \infty$.) Also suppose that the execution time for the body of the loop is $\Theta(1)$ as $m \to \infty$. Then the total execution time for the loop is $\Theta(m)$ as $m \to \infty$.*

```
template <class otype>
int location_by_linear_search (const otype a[], const otype &target,
                               int first, int last)
{
   while ( first <= last  &&  a[first] != target )
      ++first;     // Advance to the next cell if target not found.
   return first;
}
```

Fig. 5.2 Function locating a target by linear search

Proof. See the discussion in Example 5.1.1, in which the number $n - 1$ plays the role of m in this theorem. ∎

Example 5.1.3 Here is an example similar in some ways to the one in Example 5.1.1. The function in Fig. 5.2 performs a straightforward linear search for a prescribed target in a subarray a[first..last]. The code assumes that otype is a data type on which the non-equality operator != is defined.

Note that this function returns the value last + 1 if target is not present in the subarray a[first..last]. This fact would be mentioned in the documentation of the function above if the function appeared in a program.

The analysis of the extra memory space required by a call to this function is the same as in Example 5.1.1. Each of the parameter values passed to the function is of constant size. In particular, the array a is passed by means of a pointer and the same is true for the object target, which is passed by constant reference, not by value. If we introduce the mathematical variable n to denote the size of the subarray to be searched by the function (so that $n = $ last-first+1), and if we use $S(n)$ to denote the number of extra memory cells required by a call to this function, then we can say that $S(n) = \Theta(1)$ as $n \to \infty$.

The analysis of the execution time for a call to this function can go as follows. Assume that $n \geq 1$ (i.e., that first $\leq$ last initially). Also assume that execution of the != operation on otype objects requires only time bounded by constants, independent of n. (We are ruling out situations such as an array a[] of arbitrarily long strings.)

- The set-up time for the function call is constant because only integers and memory addresses (pointers) are passed as parameters.
- The body of the while loop executes at least once and at most n times.
- Execution time for each of the loop control operations is bounded by constants (as in Theorem 5.1.2).
- Execution time for the body of the loop is constant.
- Execution time for the return statement is constant.

Let $T_{\min}(n)$ and $T_{\max}(n)$ denote respectively the minimum and maximum execution times for a call to our function. Then $T_{\min}(n) = \Theta(1)$, and by Theorem 5.1.2, $T_{\max}(n) = \Theta(n)$.

   We can give more information by considering separately the case where the function call succeeds in finding the target and the case where it fails. When it succeeds, the minimum execution time is $\Theta(1)$ and the maximum is $\Theta(n)$. When it fails, execution time is always $\Theta(n)$.

   It would also be possible to give *less precise* information about the execution time for a call to the function by saying that successful search time is $\Omega(1)$ and $O(n)$, while unsuccessful search time is $\Theta(n)$. You should think carefully about why the statement in the preceding sentence is less precise than the statement in the preceding paragraph.

Example 5.1.4 Suppose we want to search a subarray for a prescribed target and we know in advance that the objects in the subarray are arranged in increasing order. Then, as we all know, a binary search, can be used in place of a linear search. A version of this justly famous "divide and conquer" algorithm is shown in Fig. 5.3 on p. 176.

```
template <class otype>
void binary_search (const otype a[], const otype & target, int first,
                    int last, bool & found, int & subscript)
{
    int mid;

    found = false;  // Will remain false until target is found.

    while (first <= last && !found)     // The value parameters "first"
    {                                   // and "last" are modified
        mid = (first + last)/2;         // during loop execution.
        if (target < a[mid])
            last = mid - 1;
        else if (a[mid] < target)
            first = mid + 1;
        else // Only remaining logical possibility: a[mid] matches target.
            found = true;
    }

    if (found)
        subscript = mid;     // The location of "target".
    else
        subscript = first;   // This is the appropriate subscript to
}                            // return if "target" is not present.
```

Fig. 5.3 Binary search algorithm

A call to this binary search function requires a little more memory space for the parameters than the linear search function we examined in Example 5.1.3, but the space requirement is still constant. If we let n denote the length of the subarray a[first..last] to be searched (i.e., $n = $ last-first+1) and $S(n)$ denote the total extra memory space required by a call to the function, then $S(n) = \Theta(1)$.

Now let's analyze the execution time required by a call to the function. As in the earlier examples, assume first $\leq$ last initially and that execution of the $<$ operation on otype objects requires only $\Theta(1)$ time as $n \to \infty$. The set-up time for a call to this function is constant, and all the instructions outside the loop require together only $\Theta(1)$ time as $n \to \infty$. The return from the function requires only constant time. Thus the total execution time for a call to the function depends just on the execution time for the loop. The body of the loop has execution time $\Theta(1)$ as $n \to \infty$, and the same is true for each of the loop control instructions, so by Theorem 5.1.2, the total execution time is big-theta of the number of times the body of the loop will be executed.

That number depends in part on whether the subarray a[first..last] actually contains an object identical to the target. When it does, the very first cell that we examine may contain an object matching the target, in which case the body of the loop will be executed just once. Thus 1 is the minimum number of times the body of the loop can be executed during a successful search, so the minimum execution time, call it $T_{\min}(n)$, for a *successful* binary search is $\Theta(1)$.

What is the maximum number of times the body of the loop can be executed during a successful search on a subarray of length n? When $n > 1$, a matching object will not be found on the first time through the loop body (remember, we're looking for the *maximum* number of times the body can be executed). Then the algorithm modifies the value of either first or last. At that point our search moves into a subarray of size $\lfloor (n-1)/2 \rfloor$ or $\lfloor n/2 \rfloor$, depending on whether the search leads into the left or right "half" of the original subarray (see Fig. 2.1 on p. 14). The maximum will occur in the larger of these two "halves", which has length $\lfloor n/2 \rfloor$. So in the maximum case we are dealing with a subarray whose length is obtained by dividing the original length n by 2 and discarding any remainder. Now we repeat that process, which, in the maximum case, takes us into a subarray whose length is obtained by dividing the preceding length by 2 and discarding any remainder. We continue this process until we reach an array of length 1, at which point the target will be found (in a successful search).

As we know from Theorem 2.2.8 (b) on p. 21, the number of integer-divisions by 2 to bring a positive integer n down to 1 is $\lfloor \lg(n) \rfloor$. When the subarray to be searched has been reduced to a single cell, it is necessary to execute the body of the loop one more time in order to discover that the target really is in that one cell (remember, we are looking at a *successful* search). Thus the body of the loop is executed $\lfloor \lg(n) \rfloor + 1$ times altogether. By Theorem 5.1.2, the maximum execution time during a successful search is $\Theta(\lfloor \log(n) \rfloor + 1)$. More precisely, $T_{\max}(n) = \Theta(\log(n))$.

What about unsuccessful searches? Based on our previous discussion, it suffices to compute the number of times that the body of the loop will be executed during an unsuccessful search of our subarray of length n. As it happens, the minimum number and the maximum number here are not always the same (this can easily be seen in the case of an array of length 2, where the minimum number is 1 and the maximum number is 2). An analysis almost identical to the one in the preceding paragraph tells us that the maximum number is $\lfloor \lg(n) \rfloor + 1$. What about the minimum number? We will compute this using a recurrence relation. The key here will be to introduce a symbol for what we want to compute.

Let $M(n)$ denote the minimum number of times that the body of the loop will be executed during an unsuccessful binary search of a subarray of length $n \geq 1$. Also, for convenience in the analysis, let $M(0)$ denote 0 (this is the number of times the body of the loop will be executed when `last < first`, which we can think of as the case of $n = 0$). It is very easy to see that $M(0) = 0$ and $M(1) = 1$, and as mentioned above, $M(2) = 1$ also. But what about for larger values of n? For $n \geq 3$, the body of the loop is executed once, and then `first` or `last` is modified and we essentially start a new unsuccessful binary search in an array of size either $\lfloor (n-1)/2 \rfloor$ or $\lfloor n/2 \rfloor$, depending on whether the search leads into the left or right "half" of the original subarray. The minimum will occur in the smaller of these two "halves", which has length $\lfloor (n-1)/2 \rfloor$. Thus we see that $M(n)$, the number of times the body of the loop is executed when given a subarray of size $n \geq 3$, is 1 (for that size subarray) plus $M(\lfloor (n-1)/2 \rfloor)$, the number of times the body of the loop will be executed starting with a subarray of size $\lfloor (n-1)/2 \rfloor$. To summarize,

$$M(0) = 0, \ M(1) = 1, \ M(2) = 1, \quad \text{and} \quad M(n) = 1 + M(\lfloor (n-1)/2 \rfloor) \quad \text{for all } n \geq 3.$$
$$(5.1)$$

A little computation shows that the cases $M(1)$ and $M(2)$ can be computed from $M(0) = 0$ and the recurrence relation, so we can simplify our problem to the form

$$M(0) = 0, \quad M(n) = 1 + M(\lfloor (n-1)/2 \rfloor) \quad \text{for all } n \geq 1.$$

This recurrence relation does not appear in the Tables 4.1–4.3 on pp. 147–149, but as discussed in Example 4.5.4, p. 155, and in the table on p. 157, a substitution transforms this into a form we can solve. We write $M(n) = G(n+1)$, or equivalently, $G(n) = M(n-1)$, which transforms the recurrence problem into the form

$$G(1) = 0, \qquad G(n) = 1 + G(\lfloor n/2 \rfloor) \quad \text{for all } n \geq 2.$$

The exact solution is $G(n) = \lfloor \lg(n) \rfloor$ for all $n \geq 1$, so $M(n) = \lfloor \lg(n+1) \rfloor$ for all $n \geq 0$.

We have now shown that in an unsuccessful binary search of an ordered subarray of size n, the body of the loop will be executed at least $\lfloor \lg(n+1) \rfloor$ times and at most $\lfloor \lg(n) \rfloor + 1$ times. If we let $U_{min}(n)$ and $U_{max}(n)$ denote respectively the minimum and maximum execution times for search a call, then by Theorem 5.1.2 we know that $U_{min}(n) = \Theta(\lfloor \lg(n+1) \rfloor)$ and $U_{max}(n) = \Theta(\lfloor \lg(n) \rfloor + 1)$. More properly, $U_{min}(n) = \Theta(\log(n))$ and $U_{max}(n) = \Theta(\log(n))$.

Binary search in a large ordered array is astonishingly efficient. For example, if the array contains a billion objects, then a binary search for a target object will examine no more than $\lfloor \lg(10^9) \rfloor = 30$ objects in the array to discover whether the target is present, and if it is, where it can be found. By contrast, a linear search on the same array might have to examine all billion objects to discover whether the target is present.

It should be noted, however, that for very small ordered arrays, linear search is faster than binary search. The reason is that our code for binary search shown in Fig. 5.3 on p. 176 is considerably more complex than our code for linear search, so even though fewer objects may be examined using our binary search, the process of examining each object requires more than twice as much time as in linear search. As a rough guide, you can assume that linear search will be more efficient on arrays of size about 10 or less.

In our next example we are going to be forming integer products in which there is a possibility of overflow if we fail to guard against it. Suppose a C++ program has two long integer variables p and q that have positive values. How can it test whether their product (as a mathematical value, not a computer generated product) will exceed LONG_MAX? The program should not make the test

```
if (p * q > LONG_MAX) ...
```

because the overflow (if any) in the operation p * q will have occurred before the inequality is tested. The correct test is

```
if (p > LONG_MAX / q) ...
```

You might have some skepticism about whether this is correct on the grounds that computation of LONG_MAX / q discards any remainder from the division operation. Here is a theorem that justifies the claim that performing the operation p * q will produce overflow if and only if the inequality

p > LONG_MAX / q   returns true.

Theorem 5.1.5 *Let p, q, and M be positive integers. Then $pq > M$ if and only if $p > \lfloor M/q \rfloor$.*

Proof. First let's prove the "if" part of the theorem: if $p > \lfloor M/q \rfloor$ then $pq > M$. Assume that $p > \lfloor M/q \rfloor$. Then since p and $\lfloor M/q \rfloor$ are both integers, it follows that $p \geq \lfloor M/q \rfloor + 1$. We know from Theorem 2.1.4 (a), p. 10, that $\lfloor M/q \rfloor > M/q - 1$. Combining the inequalities from the two preceding sentences, we find that $p \geq \lfloor M/q \rfloor + 1 > (M/q - 1) + 1 = M/q$. That is, $p > M/q$. It follows that $pq > M$.

Next let's prove the "only if" part of the theorem: if $pq > M$ then $p > \lfloor M/q \rfloor$. Assume that $pq > M$. Then $p > M/q$. By Theorem 2.1.4 (a), p. 10, we know that $M/q \geq \lfloor M/q \rfloor$. Combining the inequalities of the two preceding sentences, we see that $p > \lfloor M/q \rfloor$.   ∎

Example 5.1.6 There is no library function in C++ that computes an integer power of an integer and *returns the result as an integer*. Figure 5.4 on p. 180 shows a function with that property.

We can pass any two integer values b and n to the function, and it will *try* to return b^n, provided that the mathematical value of b^n is an integer. For example, if we pass the function $b = -3$ and $n = 4$ it will return 81, which is $(-3)^4$, and it will set the reference parameter error to false. (We must always pass a Boolean (bool) variable as a third argument to the function.) If, instead, we pass the function the values $b = 4$ and $n = -3$, we are asking the function to compute the "integer"

```
// Returns b to the power n if that's an integer no larger than LONG_MAX.
// The code uses this expression for absolute value of p:  (p < 0 ? -p : p).
long int power (long int b, long int n, bool & error)
{
    error = false;            // We'll set error to true if an error occurs.
    // First we will handle 3 special cases:  b == 0, b == 1, b == -1.
    if (b == 0)
    {
        if (n > 0)            // 0 to a positive power is 0.
            return 0;
        else                  // 0 to the power n will be mathematically undefined.
        {
            error = true;
            return LONG_MIN;  // Return an unexpected value.
        }
    }
    else if (b == 1)
        return 1;
    else if (b == -1)         // We must determine whether n is even or odd.
        return (n % 2 == 0 ? 1 : -1);
    // If execution reaches this point, then |b| >= 2.
    else if (n < 0)
    {
        error = true;         // b to a negative power cannot be an integer.
        return 0;             // Return an unexpected value.
    }
    // If execution reaches this point, then n >= 0 and |b| >= 2.
    else
    {
        long int p = 1;
        while (n > 0)
        {
            if ( (p < 0 ? -p : p) > LONG_MAX / (b < 0 ? -b : b) )  // abs vals of p, b
            {
                error = true;     // Integer overflow will occur if we try to form
                return 0;         // the product p * b. Return an unexpected value.
            }
            else
            {
                p *= b;           // Multiply p by b.
                --n;
            }
        }
        return p;
    }
}
```

Fig. 5.4 Iterative power function

4^{-3}, which is nonsense, because $4^{-3} = 1/64$ (not an integer). In that case, the function will set error to true and return the nonsense value 0. If we pass $b = 1$ and $n = 475$ to the function, it almost immediately returns the value 1. If we pass $b = -1$ and $n = 475$, the function quickly returns -1. If we pass $b = 5$ and $n = 12$, the function eventually goes into a loop in which it starts with 1 and multiples that by 5 twelve times; it returns the result 244140625. If we pass $b = 5$ and $n = 120$, the function goes into the same loop, but part way through the calculation it detects that an overflow is about to occur, so it sets `error` to `true` and returns 0.

First let's ask how much extra memory space is required by a call to this power function. The answer is the same as in all our preceding examples, namely constant space for the stack frame of the call to the function.

Now let's ask about execution time. As in our earlier examples, each of the statements except the `while` loop requires time bounded by constants. If b is 0, 1, or -1, or if $|b| \geq 2$ and $n < 0$, then the function call will end before reaching the loop, so in all these cases the execution time is bounded above by some constant. Now let's look at the cases where $|b| \geq 2$ and $n \geq 0$. Let $T_b(n)$ denote the execution time for any b and n for which b^n can successfully be calculated (i.e., no overflow occurs). In that case the body of the loop will be executed exactly n times (keep in mind that n denotes the initial value of the program variable n), and execution time for the body of the loop is $\Theta(1)$ as $n \to \infty$. Thus $T_b(n) = \Theta(n)$ by Theorem 5.1.2.

Example 5.1.7 The algorithm used in Example 5.1.6 is a very simple and straight-forward one (after you get past all the special cases). When $|b| \geq 2$ it iteratively calculates b^n one multiplication at a time, until all n multiplications have been done. An alternative approach to computing b^n uses the following recursive formula:

$$b^n = \begin{cases} 1 & \text{if } n = 0 \\ b^{n/2} * b^{n/2} & \text{if } n \text{ is positive and even} \\ b^{\lfloor n/2 \rfloor} * b^{\lfloor n/2 \rfloor} * b & \text{if } n \text{ is positive and odd} \end{cases}$$

In this formula it is assumed that $n \geq 0$ and $b \neq 0$. Using this formula, we can write a recursive function to calculate b^n. To avoid testing for all the special cases every time the recursive function is called, we separate the function into two pieces: a "driver function" that makes all the initial tests, shown in Fig. 5.5, and a recursive function that builds b^n from lower powers, shown in Fig. 5.6.

Let's analyze the memory space and execution time required for a call to the power function in Fig. 5.5. Let b and n denote the integer values passed to the parameters b and n. Let $S_b(n)$ and $T_b(n)$ denote respectively the total amount of memory space and total execution time required for such a call. Since the first part of the code is identical with the code for the function in Fig. 5.4 on p. 180, we see that if $|b| \leq 1$ or $n < 0$, then only one stack frame of size independent of n is required.

Now let's look at any case where $|b| \geq 2$ and $n \geq 0$. In such a case, the recursive function `recur_power` will be called. That call will require an additional stack frame on the run time stack, just above the stack frame for the call to the power function. If $n > 0$, then `recur_power` will call itself recursively, with numeric arguments b and $\lfloor n/2 \rfloor$. That recursive call will require yet another stack frame on the run time stack, just above the one for the initial call to `recur_power`. If $\lfloor n/2 \rfloor > 0$, then the recursive call will make its own recursive call, with numeric arguments b and $\lfloor n/4 \rfloor$. That will put another stack frame on the stack. These recursive calls continue to be made with numeric arguments $\lfloor n/2^k \rfloor$, for $k = 1, 2, 3, \ldots, \lfloor \lg(n) \rfloor + 1$, passed to the function parameter n (see Theorem 2.2.8 (b) on p. 21). Thus recursion

```
// Returns b to the power n if that's an integer no larger than LONG_MAX.
// The code uses this expression for absolute value of p:  (p<0 ? -p : p).
long int power (long int b, long int n, bool & error)
{
    error = false;              // We'll set error to true if an error occurs.

    // First we will handle 3 special cases:  b == 0, b == 1, b == -1.
    if (b == 0)
    {
        if (n > 0)              // 0 to a positive power is 0.
            return 0;
        else                    // 0 to the power n will be mathematically undefined.
        {
            error = true;
            return LONG-MIN;    // Return an unexpected value.
        }

    else if (b == 1)
        return 1;

    else if (b == -1)           // We must determine whether n is even or odd.
        return (n % 2 == 0 ? 1 : -1);

    // If execution reaches this point, then |b| >= 2.
    else if (n < 0)
    {
        error = true;           // b to a negative power cannot be an integer.
        return 0;               // Return an unexpected value.
    }

    // If execution reaches this point, then n >= 0 and |b| >= 2.
    else
        return recur_power (b, n, error);  // Initial call to recursive function.
}
```

Fig. 5.5 Driver function for the recursive power function

puts a total of $\lfloor \lg(n) \rfloor + 1$ stack frames on the stack, each frame of the same fixed size independent of n. Thus when $|b| \geq 2$ we have $S_b(n) = \Theta(\log(n))$. This is true even if overflow eventually occurs because no multiplications take place in the recursive calls until after the base case has been reached and the recursion has started to "unwind".

Now let's compute the execution time $T_b(n)$ for a call to the power function with numeric arguments b and n, in those cases where $|b| \geq 2$ and $n \geq 0$. The statements that are executed before the initial call to the recur_power function require altogether some constant execution time. The set-up time for the call to recur_power, i.e, the time required to construct a stack frame and branch to the first instruction of the new call, is another constant. If $n = 0$, the call ends and total execution time is some constant. If $n > 0$, then there will be $\lfloor \lg(n) \rfloor + 1$ recursive calls. The execution of the instructions in each individual recursive call, exclusive of the recursive call within that recursive call, requires $\Theta(1)$ time, i.e., time independent

```
// Assumes n >= 0 and |b| >= 2 and error = false.  Tries to compute b to the
// power n.  If overflow occurs, "error" is set to true, and the unexpected
// value 0 is returned.  The code uses the expression (k<0 ? -k : k) for absolute
// value of k.
long int recur_power (long int b, long int n, bool & error)
{
  if (n == 0)                  // Base case for the recursion.
    return 1;
  else
  {
    long int k = recur_power (b, n/2, error);
    if (error)                 // Overflow was detected during recursion.
      return 0;
    else if ( ( (k<0 ? -k : k) > LONG_MAX / (k<0 ? -k : k) )
    {
      error = true;            // Overflow will occur if we square k.
      return 0;
    }
    else
    {
      k = k * k;               // Replace k by its square.
      if ( n % 2 == 0 )        // then n is even, so
        return k;
      else if ( (b<0 ? -b : b) > LONG_MAX / (k<0 ? -k : k) )
      {
        error = true;          // Overflow will occur if we multiply b by k.
        return 0;
      }
      else
        return b * k;
    }
  }
}
```

Fig. 5.6 Recursive power function

of n. Thus the total time required to execute all calls to the recur_power function is $\Theta(\log(n))$, and thus $T_b(n) = \Theta(\log(n))$ regardless of whether overflow occurs.

Example 5.1.8 Figure 5.7 shows a function that determines whether a positive integer n is prime, i.e., is greater than 1 and has no factors except itself and 1. The loop uses the fact that if $n = jk$, where j and k are positive integers not equal to n or 1, then either j or k must be $\leq \sqrt{n}$, that is, either $j^2 \leq n$ or $k^2 \leq n$. Thus we can limit our search for factors of n to integers k satisfying $2 \leq k$ and $k^2 \leq n$.

Let n denote the value of the parameter n, and let $S(n)$ denote the amount of extra memory space required by a call to this function with argument n. Then as in earlier examples, $S(n) = \Theta(1)$.

Let $T(n)$ denote the execution time required by a call to this function with argument n. If $n \leq 1$, then the function will return immediately and $T(n)$ will be a very small constant, call it C_1. If $n = 2$ or $n = 3$, then the loop test will be made but the body of the loop will not be executed, so $T(n)$ will be a slightly larger constant C_2. For all $n \geq 4$, the body of the loop will be executed at least once and at most $\lfloor \sqrt{n} \rfloor - 1$

```
bool is_prime (int n)
{
  if (n <= 1)
    return false;

  else
  {
    int k;
    for (k = 2; k * k <= n; ++k)
      if (n % k == 0)  // If  n  is divisible by  k  then  n is not prime.
        return false;
    return true; // If the loop ends without finding a divisor.
  }
}
```

Fig. 5.7 Function checking if an integer is prime

times (see Exercise 2.1.23 on p. 19; there is a -1 here because the loop starts with
k = 2 instead of k = 1). It follows that $T(n) = \Omega(1)$ and $T(n) = O(\lfloor \sqrt{n} \rfloor - 1)$,
or more properly, $T(n) = O(\sqrt{n})$. A little thought tells us that when n is even (i.e.,
divisible by 2), then the loop terminates after the body is executed just once, so there
is some constant C_3 such that $T(n) = C_3$ for all even n. When n is a prime integer
or the square of a prime, then $T(n)$ is roughly $C_4\sqrt{n}$ for some constant C_4. For other
integer values of n, the value of $T(n)$ is somewhere between those extremes. There
is no simple function $A(n)$ for which $T(n) = \Theta(A(n))$. A bar graph of the number
of iterations is shown in Fig. 5.8.

It is worth pointing out a difference between this example and several earlier ones
in this section. Here it makes no sense to introduce notations $T_{\min}(n)$ and $T_{\max}(n)$
for the minimum and maximum executions times when the function is passed the
argument n. For each individual n the execution time is a single (machine dependent)
value that does not depend on the arrangement of some set of data values associated

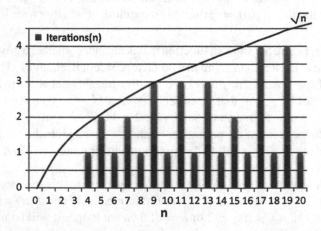

Fig. 5.8 Number of iterations for the function is_prime

```
/******************** S I M P L E   B U B B L E   S O R T ********************
This function rearranges the objects of subarray "a[0..n-1]" into increasing order.
It is assumed that the objects in the subarray are of a data type on which the
comparison operator ">" is defined.
Coded by W. Knight using a well-known algorithm. */

template <class otype>
void simple_bubble_sort (otype a[], int n)
{
  int j, k;
  for (k = n-1;  k >= 1;  --k)
    for (j = 0;  j <= k-1;  ++j)
      if (a[j] > a[j+1])                    // then these 2 objects are out of order
        swap (a[j], a[j+1]);
}
```

Fig. 5.9 Bubble sort function

with n, or on the sizes of those data values. Compare the situation here with the ones described in Examples 5.1.1, 5.1.3 and 5.1.4.

In each of our preceding examples in this section there was a loop, and the execution time for the body of the loop was bounded below and above by positive constants. Often, however, that is not the case, as the following example illustrates.

Example 5.1.9 The algorithm in Fig. 5.9 gives the code for the simplest version of a well-known sorting algorithm called Bubble Sort. We will here assume that a comparison between two otype objects and also an assignment of an otype object to a variable of that type are well defined and in each case require only time bounded by constants. We will also assume that the sorting function can call a swap function to interchange the objects at any two memory locations. Every programmer knows how to write a swap function (but may need to be reminded that the parameters must be *reference parameters* in order for the swap to accomplish its mission). When such a swap function is called, its total execution time for that call will be bounded by constants. This is a consequence of our assumption that assignment is a bounded time operation.

Let n denote the value of the parameter n, and let $S(n)$ denote the amount of extra memory space required by a call to this function with argument n. Since this function calls another function, namely the swap function, we have to think carefully about the stack frames involved. Since the swap function is called inside a loop that executes many times, many stack frames for these calls are created and destroyed. Since each call to swap ends before the next one begins, there is never more than one stack frame for the swap function on the run-time stack at any one time. Each one of the frames occupies exactly the same space as all the ones that are created and destroyed before it and after it. Thus at any one time during the call to the simple_bubble_sort function there are at most two stack frames that are a result of that call, and each one is of constant size. It follows that $S(n) = \Theta(1)$.

Now let's analyze the execution time. The set-up time for the function call and the return time are constants, so the body of the function determines the execution time. The body of the function consists of an *outer loop* governed by the test condition k>= 1. The assignment k = n-1 is performed once. The comparison k >= 1 is performed n times. The operation -k is performed $n - 1$ times. Each of these loop control operations requires time bounded by constants. Thus the total execution time consumed by loop control operations of the outer loop is $\Theta(n)$. We will add that amount to the total time for the repeated executions of the *body* of the outer loop to get the total execution time for the function call.

So now we examine the body of the outer loop. It consists of an *inner loop* governed by the test condition j <= k - 1. The first time the inner loop is executed, k has the value $n - 1$, so the body of the inner loop is executed $n - 1$ times. The second time the inner loop is executed, k has the value $n - 2$, so the body of the inner loop is executed $n - 2$ times. And so on down to the last time, when k has the value 1, so that the body of the inner loop is executed 1 time. Let k denote any of the possible values that the local variable k can assume, and let $I(k)$ denote the execution time required by the inner loop when k has the value k. Then the total time for the repeated executions of the body of the outer loop will be $\sum_{k=1}^{n-1} I(k)$. By a now familiar application of Theorem 5.1.2, it is easy to see that $I(k) = \Theta(k)$, so by Theorem 3.2.11 (e) on p. 77 and the formula for triangular sums,

$$\sum_{k=1}^{n-1} I(k) = \sum_{k=1}^{n-1} k = \Theta(n^2).$$

As stated in the preceding paragraph, we obtain the total execution time for a call to the function by adding the $\Theta(n)$ execution time for the outer loop control instructions to the total time for all the repeated executions of the body of the outer loop. The sum of a $\Theta(n)$ function and a $\Theta(n^2)$ function is a $\Theta(n^2)$ function. This is the total execution time for sorting an array of n objects using Simple Bubble Sort.

It should be noted that Simple Bubble Sort always requires $\Theta(n^2)$ time to sort n objects, even when the objects are already in increasing order! It is properly scorned by all knowledgeable programmers. There is a version of Bubble Sort, however, that keeps track of the location of the last swap on each pass over the array, and when it detects that no swap has occurred during a pass, it knows the array is sorted and it terminates the outer loop. See Exercise 5.1.21.

We can generalize part of the discussion in Example 5.1.9 in the following strategy, which we will illustrate with several additional examples.

Theorem 5.1.10 (Fundamental Strategy) *Suppose we have a loop whose execution time we want to compute as a function of some mathematical variable n, explicit or introduced, whose value determines in some way the number of times the body of the loop is executed. There should be no theoretical upper bound on n, so that we can describe the execution time with some big-oh, big-omega, or big-theta formula that's*

valid as n → ∞. Suppose that each of the loop control operations requires only $\Theta(1)$
time as n → ∞. Suppose moreover that we can associate a mathematical variable,
call it k, with the body of the loop in such a way that each time the body of the loop is
executed, k assumes a different value, and that as the loop is executed repeatedly, the
value of k runs through all the integers between some integer $f(n)$ and some integer
$g(n)$ such that $f(n) \leq g(n)$. (In many cases $f(n)$ will be a constant and $g(n)$ will
simply be n.) The variable k may take its values in increasing or decreasing order.
Finally, suppose that when the body of the loop is executed for the various values of
k, the execution time $T_{body}(k)$ can be shown to have growth rate $\Theta(A(k))$ as k → ∞
for some positive function $A(k)$ such that $A(k) = \Omega(1)$. [1] *Then the total execution*

time for the entire loop is $\Theta\left(\displaystyle\sum_{k=f(n)}^{g(n)} A(k)\right)$ *as n → ∞. Similar statements can*

made for O and Ω.

Proof. For any value of n, the body of the loop will be executed $g(n) - f(n) + 1$ times,
so the total execution time required by the "loop overhead" is $\Theta(g(n) - f(n) + 1)$.

The sum of the execution times for the body of the loop is $\Theta\left(\displaystyle\sum_{k=f(n)}^{g(n)} T_{body}(k)\right)$.

By hypothesis, $T_{body}(k) = \Theta(A(k))$, so by Theorem 3.2.11 (e) on p. 77,

$\Theta\left(\displaystyle\sum_{k=f(n)}^{g(n)} T_{body}(k)\right) = \Theta\left(\displaystyle\sum_{k=f(n)}^{g(n)} A(k)\right)$. Thus the total execution time for the

loop is $\Theta(g(n) - f(n) + 1) + \Theta\left(\displaystyle\sum_{k=f(n)}^{g(n)} A(k)\right)$. Which of the two big-theta

expressions is dominant? Since $A(k) = \Omega(1)$, there is a positive constant c such

that $A(k) \geq c$ for all k, so $\displaystyle\sum_{k=f(n)}^{g(n)} A(k) \geq c[g(n) - f(n) + 1]$. It follows that

$\Theta\left(\displaystyle\sum_{k=f(n)}^{g(n)} A(k)\right)$ dominates $\Theta(g(n) - f(n) + 1)$, and thus the total execution time

is determined by $\Theta\left(\displaystyle\sum_{k=f(n)}^{g(n)} A(k)\right)$.   ∎

How would our Fundamental Strategy be applied to the `simple_bubble_sort`
function in Example 5.1.9? The execution time for the function is determined by the
execution time for the body of the function, which consists solely of a loop, to which
we will now apply our Fundamental Strategy. In that loop the mathematical variables
n and k described in our Strategy can simply be the values of the program variables

---

[1] The assumption $A(k) = \Omega(1)$ is valid provided the body of the loop contains at least one operation.

n and k. The value of n is the integer value passed to n when the function is called. The value of k runs from 1 to $n-1$ (so $f(n) = 1$ and $g(n) = n-1$). Note that k runs through those values in decreasing order. The function $T_{body}(k)$ in our Strategy is exactly the function $I(k)$ in Example 5.1.9. Since $I(k) = \Theta(k)$, the function $A(k)$ in our Strategy is simply $A(k) = k$. Our Strategy says that the total execution time $T(n)$ for the loop is $\Theta(\sum_{k=1}^{n-1} k)$, which gives the same $\Theta(n^2)$ expression that we derived in Example 5.1.9.

The reader who is thinking carefully about the precision of our mathematical analysis of `simple_bubble_sort` may validly object to the introduction of a function expression $T(n)$ for "the total execution time" of this algorithm. If $T(n)$ were a genuine function, its value would depend only on the value of n, which is the length of the array passed to `simple_bubble_sort`. But the total execution time depends not only on n but also on the initial arrangement of the objects in the array. If the objects are already in increasing order (i.e., the array is pre-sorted), then $n(n-1)/2$ object comparisons will be made, but not a single swap will occur. If, instead, the same objects are in decreasing order (i.e., they are "reverse sorted"), then the same $n(n-1)$ object comparisons will be made, but each comparison will be followed by a swap of two objects. The execution time in the second case is bound to be significantly larger than the execution time on a pre-sorted array. Thus we should really introduce two mathematical functions, $T_{\min}(n)$ and $T_{\max}(n)$, to denote respectively the minimum and maximum possible execution times. In this instance, however, $T_{\min}(n) = \Theta(n^2)$ and $T_{\max}(n) = \Theta(n^2)$, so it is customary to be slightly imprecise and say "the execution time is $\Theta(n^2)$", and sometimes even introduce function notation $T(n)$ for "the" execution time. In a later chapter we'll see that $T(n)$ can be regarded as denoting a random variable whose value depends on both n and the initial arrangement of the objects in the array.

The reader may be concerned that the execution time also depends on what type of objects are being sorted and on the instruction set and clock speed of the computer on which the algorithm is executed. In every analysis we perform, however, our point of view is that the analysis applies to a fixed object type and a fixed machine. The mathematical results will remain valid, whatever the object type and the machine may be. All that will change in going from one setting to another is the constants that are hidden in the Θ or O or Ω expressions.

Our Fundamental Strategy supersedes Theorem 5.1.2 on p. 174 because Theorem 5.1.2 is a special case. To see this, assume (as we did in Theorem 5.1.2) that we have a loop, the body of which is executed m times, where m is a variable with no theoretical upper bound. Also assume that the execution time for each of the loop control operations is $\Theta(1)$ as $m \to \infty$, and that the execution time of the body of the loop is $\Theta(1)$ as $m \to \infty$. Then the variable n of our Fundamental Strategy is the variable m in Theorem 5.1.2. We can imagine introducing a mathematical variable k for the loop such that k begins at 1 and increases to m as the body of the loop is executed repeatedly. Since execution time for the body of the loop is $\Theta(1)$ as $m \to \infty$, we can let $A(k)$ in the Fundamental Strategy be the constant function with

```
/*********************** S E L E C T I O N   S O R T ***************************
This function rearranges the objects of subarray "a[first..last]" into increasing
order. It is assumed that the objects in the subarray are of a data type on which
the binary comparison operator ">" is defined.
Coded by W. Knight using a well-known algorithm. */

template <class otype>
void selection_sort (otype a[], int first, int last)
{
  int i;
  while (last > first)
  {
    i = location_of_max (a, first, last);
    if (i != last)
      swap (a[i], a[last]);  // Code not shown for swap function.
    --last;
  }
}
```

Fig. 5.10 Selection Sort function

value 1. Then $T_{body}(k) = \Theta(A(k)) = \Theta(1)$, so by the Fundamental Strategy, the total execution time for the loop is $\Theta(\sum_{k=1}^{m}(1)) = \Theta(m)$, as asserted in Theorem 5.1.2.

In our next example, the integers n and k described in our Fundamental Strategy are not present in some explicit way as they were in Example 5.1.9, but we can introduce them into the analysis fairly easily, as you will see.

Example 5.1.11 Figure 5.10 shows a C++ function that implements a well-known algorithm called Selection Sort on a subarray a[first..last]. As usual, assume that the otype objects have the property that assignment of one such variable to another requires time bounded by constants, and similarly for the operations of comparison between two such objects.

The idea of the selection_sort algorithm is that the largest object in the subarray a[first..last] is located by a call to our location_of_max function (see Example 5.1.1) and is then swapped into the last cell of the subarray, which is exactly the place where is supposed to end up. (If the largest object is already in the last cell, no swap takes place.) After that, the value parameter last is decremented, which reduces by 1 the size of the subarray to be sorted. We repeat this procedure until the subarray to be sorted has shrunk to size 1.

Let n denote the initial length of the subarray to be sorted. This can be computed from the initial values, call them F and L of the parameters first and last: $n = L - F + 1$. We will express the space requirement and execution time of a call to the selection_sort function in terms of the variable n as $n \to \infty$.

First let's look at the space requirement for a call to the selection_sort function. As in the simple_bubble_sort function of Example 5.1.9, such a call will result in placing at most two constant-size stack frames on the run-time stack at any moment during execution. A stack frame for a call to the location_of_max function is always removed from the stack before a frame for a call to swap goes onto the stack. Thus if $S(n)$ denotes the extra memory space required by a call to `selection_sort` with a subarray of length n, then $S(n) = \Theta(1)$.

Now let's look at execution time for a call with a subarray of length n. The set-up time and return time for such a call are constants, so the execution time is determined by the body of the function, which consists entirely of a `while` loop. We can analyze the execution of that loop by using our Fundamental Strategy. We already have a variable n that can grow arbitrarily large. The execution time for the loop control operation (a simple comparison of two subscripts) is $\Theta(1)$ as $n \to \infty$. Now let's introduce a mathematical variable k for the variable length of the subarray `a[first..last]` as last decreases from its initial value L down to its final value F. Then k starts with the value n and decreases by 1 each time the body of the loop is executed, until it reaches the value 1, at which point the body of the loop is not executed. The smallest value of k for which the body of the loop is executed is 2. The function $f(n)$ described in our Fundamental Strategy is the constant 2, and the function $g(n)$ is simply n.

We now need to find an expression for the execution time $T_{body}(k)$ of the body of the loop when it is executed for values of k running (backward) between n and 2. With the exception of the call to the `location_of_max` function, each operation in the body of the loop has execution time $\Theta(1)$ as $k \to \infty$. There is a fixed number of these operations, so they contribute $\Theta(1)$ time to $T_{body}(k)$. What about the `location_of_max` function? By Example 5.1.1, the execution time is big-theta of the length of the array `a[first..last]`, which is exactly our variable k. The function call contributes $\Theta(k)$ time to $T_{body}(k)$. The sum of times that are $\Theta(1)$ and $\Theta(k)$ is $\Theta(k)$, so $T_{body}(k) = \Theta(k)$. In the notation of our Fundamental Strategy, $A(k) = k$. Thus the total execution time for a call to our `selection_sort` function is $\Theta(\sum_{k=2}^{n}(k)) = \Theta(n^2)$.

Let's compare execution times for our `simple_bubble_sort` and `selection_sort` algorithms when they are applied to an array `a[1..n]`. In each case we showed that the execution time is $\Theta(n^2)$. Does this mean that the execution times for the two algorithms are always approximately the same? The answer is no. Often the execution time of `selection_sort` will turn out to be significantly less than the execution time for `simple_bubble_sort`. We can see this by counting the occurrences of the two operations that dominate these algorithms. The two operations are comparison between two objects and swapping of two objects. It is not hard to see that each of these two sorting algorithms makes exactly $(n-1) + (n-2) + \cdots + 3 + 2 + 1 = n(n-1)/2$ comparisons between pairs of objects. (In `selection_sort` these comparisons are hidden in the calls to the `location_of_max` function.) By contrast, the number of object swaps in `simple_bubble_sort` can be any number between 0 and $n(n-1)/2$, while the number of object swaps in `selection_sort` can be any number between 0 and $n-1$. If the objects in the array are already arranged in increasing order when either of our functions is called, then no swaps will occur in either function. If the objects in the array are arranged in decreasing order (the reverse of the desired order), then simple_bubble_sort will make $n(n-1)/2$ swaps (one swap for each comparison), and selection_sort will make only $\lfloor n/2 \rfloor$ swaps (one swap for each of the first $\lfloor n/2 \rfloor$ calls to the location_of_max function, after which the objects will be in increasing order). An initial arrangement of the objects that can force selection_sort to make $n-1$ swaps is the arrangement that puts the largest object in the first array cell and then all the other objects in increasing order in the remaining cells. It is not difficult to prove by induction that selection_sort never makes more swaps than simple_bubble_sort.

Later in this book we will prove that when the objects are arranged initially in random order, the average number of swaps made by simple_bubble_sort is $\Theta(n^2)$, while the average number of swaps made by selection_sort is only $\Theta(n)$. Thus, in general, selection_sort is more efficient than simple_bubble_sort. The moral of this discussion is that when two algorithms have the same big-theta execution time, a more detailed analysis may reveal that one of them is usually (or even always) a better choice than the other.

Example 5.1.12 Figure 5.11 shows a function that outputs all the prime integers between 2 and a prescribed integer z. The function makes repeated calls to the Boolean function is_prime given in Example 5.1.8.

Let's analyze the space and time requirements for a call to this function. We'll express our results in terms of the integer value z passed to the function because the larger z is, the more work the function will have to do.

First let's look at space. The extra space requirements for a call to this function are easily see to be $\Theta(1)$ as $z \to \infty$ because there will be at most two constant-size stack frames on the run-time stack at any point during execution of our function.

Now let's look at execution time. Set-up and return times for a call to the function are constants. The output statements using cout can be assumed to require $\Theta(1)$ time as $z \to \infty$. Thus the entire execution time for a call to the function depends entirely on the for loop in the body of the function. To analyze the loop, we'll use

```
// This function outputs in a column all the prime integers in the range
// from 2 to z provided z is at least 2.

void output_primes_up_to (int z)
{
   int p;

   cout << "Prime integers in the range from 2 to " << z << ':' endl;

   for ( p = 2; p <= z; ++p )
      if ( is_prime(p) )
         cout << p << endl;
}
```

Fig. 5.11 Outputting primes

the Fundamental Strategy in Theorem 5.1.10 on p. 186. The variable z here will play the role of n in the Strategy. Each loop control operation requires only $\Theta(1)$ time as $z \to \infty$. Now let's introduce the mathematical variable p (in place of the variable k in the Strategy) to denote the value of the local variable p in the function as that value runs from 2 to z. In this case the function $f(z)$ in our Strategy is the constant 2 and $g(z) = z$. Now look at the body of the loop. As shown in Example 5.1.8, the execution time for a call to is_prime with argument p requires $O(\sqrt{p})$ time (this is an upper bound on the growth of the execution time as $z \to \infty$) and also can be said to require $\Theta(1)$ time (this is a lower bound on growth). These times dominate other parts of the loop body, so $T_{body}(p) = O(\sqrt{p})$ and also $T_{body}(p) = \Omega(1)$ in the notation of the Fundamental Strategy. Thus the execution time, which we'll denote by $T(z)$, is $O(\sum_{p=2}^{\sqrt{p}}) = O(z^{3/2})$ (see Example 3.2.8 on p. 75), and also $T(z) = \Omega(z)$. Since there is no simple function $A(p)$ such that $T_{body}(p) = \Theta(A(p))$, we cannot use our Strategy to obtain a Θ expression for $T(z)$. This does not prove that no such Θ expression exists for $T(z)$. It's possible that a much more lengthy and sophisticated mathematical argument might establish something like $T(z) = \Theta(z \log(z))$.

In some algorithms, there may be two variables that determine the execution time for the algorithm. This is often the case when analyzing finite graph algorithms, where the execution time will depend on both the number of vertices and on the number of edges.

Here is a simpler example involving two variables.

Example 5.1.13 Suppose we have two arrays, call them a and b, containing data in their initial m and n cells respectively. The following function locates all cells in a whose data matches exactly the data in some cell in b, and it outputs the subscripts of all matching cell pairs. We assume that the equality operator == is defined on otype objects.

```
template <class otype>
void find_matching_entries (otype a[], int m, otype b[], int n)
{
  int i, j;
  for (i = 0;  i < m;  ++i)
    for (j = 0;  j < n;  ++j)
      if ( a[i] == b[j] )
        cout << i << " and " << j << '\n';
}
```

Assume that a test for equality between two otype objects has execution time bounded by constants, and similarly for the output statement in the function. Let m and n denote the values of the parameters m and n. The body of the inner loop is executed the same number of times (n times) for each value assumed by the control variable i in the outer loop, and execution time for the body of the inner loop is bounded by constants, so the total execution time for the inner loop is $\Theta(n)$ as

$n \to \infty$. The body of the outer loop is executed exactly m times, so we have a situation similar to what we had in Examples 5.1.9 and 5.1.11: the total execution time for the body of the function is $\Theta(m\,n)$ as $m \to \infty$ and $n \to \infty$.

5.1.1 Exercises

5.1.14 In this problem, suppose that we are looking at a C++ program in which we have the following definition.

```
template <class otype>
struct node
{
  otype datum;
  node *next;
};
```

The definition has been made to allow the program to create and manipulate linked lists. Suppose also that the program contains the following function, which returns a pointer to the node containing the largest datum object in a NULL-terminated linked list, where we assume that the otype objects have the usual relational operators <, <=, >, and >= defined directly on them. The function returns NULL if the list passed to the function is empty (i.e., if p is NULL).

```
template <class otype>
node * location_of_max (node * p)  // p points to a list of nodes
{
  if (p == NULL)
    return NULL;
  else
  {
    node * max_loc = p;       // The first node of the list will
                              // contain the "largest seen so far".

    for (p = p->next; p != NULL; p = p->next)
      if (p->datum > max_loc->datum)    // The value parameter "p"
        max_loc = p;                    // can be modified since its
                                        // initial value need not be
    return max_loc;                     // preserved.
  }
}
```

As we did in various examples in this section, assume that comparison between two otype objects requires only time bounded by constants. Analyze the space requirement and execution time for a call to the function above. Express your answers in terms of the length, call it n, of the list pointed to by p.

5.1.15 Assume the same definitions and properties as in Exercise 5.1.14 above. Consider the function on the next page that searches a NULL-terminated linked list for a specified target object. If it finds the target, it returns a pointer to the node containing a copy of the target. Otherwise it returns NULL. Assume that the operator != is defined on the otype objects and that this kind of comparison requires only time bounded by constants.

```
template <class otype>
node * location (node * p, const otype &target)
{
  while ( p != NULL  &&  p->datum != target )
    p = p->next;      // Advance to the next node if target not found
  return p;
}
```

(a) Analyze the space requirement and execution time of a call to this function. Consider separately the cases of successful search and unsuccessful search. Express your answers in terms of the length, call it n, of the list pointed to by p.

(b) Now suppose that the relational operators <, <=, >, and >= have been overloaded (if necessary) to allow comparisons between objects of type otype. Rewrite the function above so that the modified version can be applied to (and only to) linked lists in which the objects are arranged in increasing order. Give your modified function the name location_in_ordered_list. The modified code should take advantage of the fact that the datum members are arranged in order, and thus it should produce an improvement in the execution time in one of the cases discussed in part (a) of this exercise. Explain how the analysis of your modified version differs from the analysis you carried out in part (a).

5.1.16 Here is a function that returns the smallest divisor, other than 1, of an integer n greater than 1. It uses the same ideas as those used in Example 5.1.8.

```
int smallest_nontrivial_divisor (int n)
{
  if (n <= 1) // We don't want to deal with integers <= 1, so if
    return 0; // such an integer is given, return a nonsense answer.

  else
  {
    int k;
    for (k = 2; k * k <= n; ++k)
      if (n % k == 0)  // If  n  is divisible by  k  then we have
        return k;      // found the divisor we were hunting for.

    // If the loop ends without finding a divisor less than or
    // equal to the square root of  n, then  n  must be prime,
    // so its only divisor aside from  1  is  n.
    return n;
  }
}
```

Analyze the space requirement and the execution time of a call to this function.

5.1.17 Analyze the execution time for each of the following code fragments. In each case assume that the program variable n has already been declared and given a positive value n. Here, as elsewhere, the phrase "X is bounded by constants" means that there exist positive constants A and B such that $A \leq X \leq B$.

(a)
```
int k;
for (k = 0; k <= n * n; ++k)
{ The execution time for the body of this loop is bounded by constants. }
```

(b)
```
int k, j;
for (k = 0; k < n * n; ++k)
    for (j = n; j >= 1; -j)
    { The execution time for the body of this loop is bounded by constants. }
```

(c)
```
int k, j;
for (k = 0; k < n * n; ++k)
    for (j = k; j >= 1; -j) //This line is different from the 2nd line in (b).
    { The execution time for the body of this loop is bounded by constants. }
```

(d)
```
int k, j; for (k = 1; k <= n; ++k)
    for (j = 1; j * j <= n; ++j)
    { The execution time for the body of this loop is bounded by constants. }
```

(e)
```
int k, j;
for (k = 1; k <= n; ++k)
    for (j = 1; j * j <= k; ++j) //Line is different from the 2nd line in (d).
    { The execution time for the body of this loop is bounded by constants. }
```

(f)
```
int k, j;
for (k = 2; k * k <= n; ++k)
    for (j = k; j >= 1; j = j/2)
    { The execution time for the body of this loop is bounded by constants. }
```

(g)
```
int k, j;
for (k = n * n; k >= 1; -k)
    for (j = k; j >= 1; j = j/2)
    { The execution time for the body of this loop is bounded by constants. }
```

(h)
```
int p, k, i;
for (p = 1, k = 1; k <= n; ++k, p = 2*p) // double p at each iteration
    for (i = 1; i <= p; ++i)
    { The execution time for the body of this loop is bounded by constants. }
```

(i) In this problem it will be useful to review Example 2.2.14 on page 31.
```
int j, k;
for (k = 1; k <= n; ++k)
    for (j = 1; j <= k; j = 2 * j)
    { The execution time for the body of this loop is bounded by constants. }
```

5.1.18 Refer to the Linear Insertion Sort Algorithm shown in Fig. 5.12. Let n denote the value of the parameter n.

(a) Analyze the space requirement and the execution time of a call to this function in terms of n, as $n \to \infty$.

(b) Modify the function in Fig. 5.12 so that it can be used to sort any subarray a[first..last] of a larger array a[]. The prototype for your revised function should be

```
void linear_insertion_sort (otype a[], int first,
int last).
```

(c) Suppose we restrict our attention to the action of linear insertion sort on nearly sorted arrays, more precisely, on arrays in which no object is farther than d cells away from the cell where it will end up after the array is sorted. Here we are regarding d as some known constant such as 10. Referring to Fig. 5.12, explain why for each value of k in the outer for loop, the body of the inner for loop will never be executed more than d times. (This is tricky. It may help to observe that if an object X originally in cell k were to be inserted into a cell j farther than d cells to its left, then some other object farther (originally) to the right of X would have to be inserted later to the left of X in order to push X to the right and therefore closer to its original position.)

(d) Consider the collection of arrays in which no object is more than d cells out of order (i.e., no more than d cells away from the cell where it will end up after the array is sorted), where d is some known constant. Use part (c) to prove that the execution time of linear insertion sort on these nearly sorted arrays of length n is $\Theta(n)$. This demonstrates the important fact that *linear insertion sort is very efficient on nearly sorted arrays (i.e. arrays in which all the objects are close to the cell in which they belong). This is especially true for long arrays.*

5.1.19 A standard programming problem involves being given a sequence of real numbers in an array and asked to find the "maximum subsequence sum" in the sequence. More precisely, suppose we are given an array a[0..n-1] real numbers (floating point numbers), where some (or even all) of the numbers may be negative. The problem is to find the subarray a[j..k] for which the sum $\sum_{i=j}^{k} a[i]$ is as large as possible. A subsequence of length 1 is permissible; that is, we can take j = k in the notation above, in which case the sum reduces just to a[j]. In fact, we'll even permit a subarray of length 0; in this case, by convention, we will take the sum to be 0, but in this case, the starting and ending subscripts j and k of the maximum-sum subarray are not well-defined.

To take an example, suppose the given sequence consists of the following 10 real numbers:

```
/************ L I N E A R   I N S E R T I O N   S O R T ********************
This function accepts an array  a[0..n-1]  of objects on which the operator >
is defined and sorts them into increasing order.*/

template <class otype>
void linear_insertion_sort (otype a[], int n)          // sorts a[0..n-1]
{
    int k;
    for (k = 1; k < n; ++k)
    {
        otype temp = a[k]; // Move a[k] to open a hole in the array.
        // Make a backward linear search, using a subscript i.
        for (int i = k-1; i >= 0 && a[i] > temp; --i)
            a[i+1] = a[i];    // Slide a[i] to the right by one cell
        // Subscript  i  was decremented after correct position was found.
        a[i+1] = temp;      // Move old a[k] value to its correct position.
    }
}
```

Fig. 5.12 Linear insertion sort function

0	1	2	3	4	5	6	7	8	9
4.1	2.7	− 9.9	3.8	6.0	− 2.5	3.1	− 7.9	− 1.6	9.0

Then the maximum subsequence sum turns out to be 10.4, which is the sum of the numbers in the subarray a[3..6], which is therefore the maximum-sum subarray. You can verify this by exhaustive calculation if you are so inclined. Note that if all the numbers in the array are strictly negative, then the maximum subsequence sum is (by our convention) 0, but the maximum-sum subarray is not well-defined in that special case.

Figure 5.13 on p. 198 shows some C++ code to implement the most straightforward, brainless algorithm for solving the Maximum Subsequence Sum Problem. The algorithm simply evaluates every possible subsequence sum $\sum_{i=j}^{k} a[i]$, and then reports the largest sum it was able to find. It also identifies the subarray that gives the maximum sum. Using the example array shown above, it is easy to see that the function below would form the following sums:
4.1,   4.1 + 2.7,   4.1 + 2.7 + (−9.9),   4.1 + 2.7 + (−9.9) + 3.8, etc., 4.1 + 2.7 + (−9.9) +... + 9.0,
2.7, 2.7 + (−9.9), 2.7 + (−9.9) + 3.8,   etc.,   2.7 + (−9.9) + 3.8 +... + 9.0,
(−9.9), (−9.9) + 3.8, (−9.9) + 3.8 + 6.0,   etc.,   (−9.9) + 3.8 + 6.0 +... + 9.0,
etc., etc., etc., 9.0.

The function would discover that the best_j is 4 and the best_k is 7. Note that the code is designed to work on any array a[first..last]; that is, it does not assume that the first subscript of the array is 1.

Analyze the space and time requirements of this simple-minded algorithm in terms of the length, call it n, of the given subarray.

```
/********** M A X I M U M   S U B S E Q U E N C E   S U M ******************
This function accepts an array of real numbers a[first...last] and finds the
subarray a[j...k] whose sum-of-terms is as large as possible.  It returns as
its value this maximum possible sum-of-terms, and it changes the second and
third arguments so that they have the values j and k for the subarray
a[j...k] with maximum sum-of-terms.  If all the entries in a[first...last] are
negative or zero, then the function will return the value 0.0, and in this
case, no particular values are placed in the second and third arguments (that
is, they should be treated as "garbage").  */

double max_subsequence_sum (double a[], int & first, int & last)
{
    double max_sum_so_far = 0.0;
    int i, j, k, best_j, best_k; // Never initialized if max seq sum is 0.0.
    for (j = first; j <= last; ++j)
      for (k = j; k <= last; ++k)
      {
          double new_sum = 0.0;
          for (i = j; i <= k; ++i)    // Add up the cells of a[j...k].
            new_sum += a[i];
          if (new_sum > max_sum_so_far)
          {
              max_sum_so_far = new_sum;
              best_j = j;
              best_k = k;
          }
      }
    first = best_j;  // Change the reference parameter values as
    last  = best_k;  // described in the function documentation.
    return max_sum_so_far;
}
```

Fig. 5.13 Maximum subsequence sum function

5.1.20 If you thoroughly understand how the algorithm shown in Exercise 5.1.19 works, then you have probably realized that the algorithm sums up the same numbers over and over again, but in slightly different combinations. For example, after calculating the sum of the cells in a[j...k] for a particular pair of subscripts j and k, it re-adds the same cells while computing the sum for a[j...k+1]. This idiotic redundancy can easily be removed from the algorithm. Write an improved algorithm similar to the one above, but eliminate redundant summations. Analyze space and time requirements of your improved algorithm, and compare with your results for Exercise 5.1.19.

5.1.21 Figure 5.14 shows a "smarter" version of the bubble sorting strategy. It sorts the objects in an array a[0...n-1] into increasing order. It is smart because when it is making a pass over the array, it keeps track of where the last swap in the pass occurred, and on the next pass it does not examine cells beyond the ones where the last swap occurred. For example, if on the first pass across an array a[0...99] the last swap interchanges the objects at locations 95 and 96, then the objects in

```
template <class otype>
void smart_bubble_sort (otype a[], int n)      //Sorts a[0...n-1].
{
  int j,k;

  k = n-1;
  while (n >= 1)
  {
    for(j=0;j<n-1;++j)          // Each time execution reaches this point,
    {                           // k and n-1 have the same value.
      if (a[j] > a[j+1])
      {
        swap (a[j],a[j+1]);
        k = j;                  // k records position of most recent swap
      }
    }

    if (k == n-1)   // No swap occurred during execution of the inner loop.
      n = 0;        // This will stop the loop.
    else
      n = k+1;      // Last swap in the loop was at cells numbered k and
  }                 // k+1, so all the objects starting at location k
}                   // and going to the right are in increasing order.
```

Fig. 5.14 An efficient version of the bubble sort

the subarray a[96...99] must be increasing order (else there would have been a swap in that subarray). The algorithm stores the number 95 and on the second pass it will examine only the subarray a[0...95]. If, on the second pass, the last swap interchanges the objects at locations 88 and 89, then the third pass will examine only the subarray a[0...88], and so on. The algorithm ends when the subarray to be examined is of size 1 or at the end of a pass in which no swap is made.

Let n denote the initial value of the parameter n and let $T_{min}(n)$ and $T_{max}(n)$ denote the minimum and maximum execution times for smart_bubble_sort. Derive a Θ expression for $T_{min}(n)$ and describe the initial arrangement of the array objects that produces that execution time. Do the same for $T_{max}(n)$.

5.1.22 (A Really Bad Sorting Algorithm) After analyzing a number of different sorting algorithms, some students begin to believe that no sorting algorithm can have execution time greater than $\Theta(n^2)$, where n is the number of objects being sorted. But never underestimate the ability of a beginning programmer to do a thing more inefficiently than anyone would think possible. Here is a sorting algorithm submitted by a student in an elementary programming class.

```
// Sorts the floating point numbers in  a[0..n-1].

int i;
for (i = 0;  i < n - 1;  ++i)
{
  if ( a[i] > a[i+1] )    // These consecutive floating point numbers
  {                       // are out of order relative to each other.
```

```
      swap (a[i], a[i+1]);
      i = 0;                    // NOTE THAT i IS BEING RESET!
   }
}
```

The algorithm turns out to be similar to Linear Insertion Sort (p. 196), but note that it contains only one loop. This may make you doubt that the algorithm actually sorts the numbers. But note that whenever a swap occurs, the loop control variable i is immediately reset to 0 and then immediately incremented to 1 by the ++i in the loop heading. Thus the loop repeatedly "starts over".

Compute the number of *object comparisons* that will be made (i.e., the number of times the inequality a[i] > a[i+1] will be evaluated) when this algorithm is applied to an array of n floating point numbers in *reverse order* (i.e., the numbers in the array decrease as you go from left to right). Hint: because the numbers are in reverse order, each one—starting at the second one and scanning to the right—will be moved from its original position all the way to the left end. For example, when the algorithm is applied to the array

$$1 \quad 2 \quad 3 \quad 4$$

$$\boxed{44 \,|33\, |22\, |11}$$

the 33 is swapped into cell 1, then 22 is gradually moved into cell 1, and finally 11 is tediously moved into cell 1. For each separate item, compute the number of comparisons and swaps required to move that item from its original position all the way to cell 1. You may use Exercise 2.3.50 on p. 52 or the answer to Example 4.3.11 on p. 123 if it is helpful.

5.1.23 In Examples 5.1.3 and 5.1.4 we analyzed search algorithms in terms of the number of times the body of the search loop was executed. In this way we were able to obtain big-theta information about the minimum and maximum execution times for the algorithms. Sometimes, however, this method of analysis fails to distinguish adequately between two competing search algorithms. Both may have the same big-theta expression for their execution time, yet one will run significantly faster than the other because the constants hidden by the big-theta notation are very different.

To take an example, the execution time of a search algorithm is often dominated by the time required for the comparisons between the data objects. (In the two searches we looked at in this section, the "data objects" are the otype objects in the cells of the array.) Thus a standard way of comparing two competing search algorithms is to count the number of data object comparisons that each of them makes.

(a) Let $D_{min}(n)$ and $D_{max}(n)$ denote the minimum and maximum number of data object comparisons that will be made during an unsuccessful search of an ordered array of n objects using the binary search algorithm in Fig. 5.3 on p. 176. Also, for convenience in the analysis, let $D_{min}(0)$ and $D_{max}(0)$ denote 0. Calculate

```
template <class otype>
int different_binary_search (const otype a[], const otype &target,
                            int first, int last)
{
  while (first <= last) // The value parameters first and last may
  {                     // be modified during execution of this code
    int mid = (first + last)/2;
    if (a[mid] < target)
      first = mid + 1;
    else
      last = mid - 1;
  }
  return first;         // The calling function can then examine
}                       // a[first] to see whether target is there.
```

Fig. 5.15 Different version of binary search

0	1	2	3	4	5	6	7	8	9	10	11	12	13
7	25	25	25	38	59	64	70	75	82	82	88	94	97

Fig. 5.16 The list array

$D_{min}(1)$, $D_{max}(1)$, $D_{min}(2)$, $D_{max}(2)$, $D_{min}(3)$, $D_{max}(3)$. Write recurrence relations for $D_{min}(n)$ and $D_{max}(n)$ and solve them exactly. (This will be similar to the problem we solved on p. 179, except that now you are required to count minimum and maximum numbers of *data object comparisons* instead of minimum and maximum numbers of times the body of the loop is executed. Do NOT count subscript comparisons. Those are not "data object comparisons" of the kind we are considering.)

(b) The function in Fig. 5.15 implements a version of binary search that appears in many programming textbooks. On first inspection, this algorithm may appear not to work correctly because when mid arrives at a location containing target, the algorithm does not take special notice of that fact and just sets last to mid - 1 and goes on searching. Nevertheless, it can be proved using loop invariants that the variable first will end up equal to the subscript of a cell containing a copy of the target object if the array contains such an object. It can also be proved that if no copy of target is present in the search array, then the value returned by the function is the subscript of the cell into which a copy of target could properly be inserted (in order) if space were to be made for it by right-shifting the contents of that cell and all cells to its right (cf. the documentation in Fig. 5.3, p. 176).

Now suppose the function call different_binary_search (list, 64, 0, 13); is made on the ordered array named list shown in Fig. 5.16 (the otype here is just int):

Which cells will be probed (i.e., which cells will have their contents compared with the target 64)? What value does the function return in this case? Which cells will be probed when the target is 25 instead of 64? What value does the function return in this case? Which cells will be probed when the target is 80? What value does the function return in this case? Which cells will be probed when the target is 99? What value does the function return in this case?

```
template <class otype>
int alternative_binary_search (const otype a[], const otype &target,
                               int first, int last)
{
  while (first <= last) // The value parameters first and last may
  {                     // be modified during execution of this code
    int mid = (first + last)/2;
    if (target < a[mid])
      last = mid - 1;
    else
      first = mid + 1;
  }
  return last;          // The calling function can then examine
}                       // a[last] to see whether target is there.
```

Fig. 5.17 An alternative version of binary search

(c) Let $E_{\min}(n)$ and $E_{\max}(n)$ denote the minimum and maximum number of data object comparisons that will be made during a search of an ordered array of n objects using the different_binary_search algorithm in part (b). [Note: we make no distinction here between successful and unsuccessful searches because the algorithm itself does not determine whether the search is successful or unsuccessful; that determination is made by the calling function when it receives the returned value.] Also let $E_{\min}(0)$ and $E_{\max}(0)$ denote 0. Calculate $E_{\min}(0)$, $E_{\max}(0)$, $E_{\min}(1)$, $E_{\max}(1)$, $E_{\min}(2)$, $E_{\max}(2)$, $E_{\min}(3)$, $E_{\max}(3)$. Write recurrence relations for $E_{\min}(n)$ and $E_{\max}(n)$ and solve them exactly. Compare your answers with the answer in part (a).

5.1.24 The version of binary search given in Fig. 5.15 has the property that when the array a[first..last] contains more than one copy of the target, the algorithm ends with the subscript first equal to the subscript of the left-most occurrence of the target in the array (this can be proved using loop invariants). For example, if 25 is the target of a search of the array in Fig. 5.16, then the algorithm will end with first having the value 1 (the subscript of the *left-most* occurrence of the number 25).

There is a slightly different version of the algorithm that returns the *right-most* occurrence of the target in the array. It is shown in Fig. 5.17.

Let L denote the value returned by the alternative binary search function in Fig. 5.17. Then loop invariants can be used to prove that if the array contains a copy of target, then L will be the subscript of the right-most occurrence of target in the array. Furthermore, it can be proved that if the array contains no copy of target, then the integer $L + 1$ will be the subscript of the cell into which a copy of target can properly be inserted (in order) if space is made for it by right-shifting the contents of that cell and all cells to its right.

(a) Which cells will be probed by this alternative version when searching the array in Fig. 5.16 for the target 64? (i.e., which cells will have their contents compared with the target 64)? List the cell numbers in the order in which the cells will be probed during the search. What value does this alternative version of the algorithm return at the end of this search? Which cells will be probed when the target is 25 instead of 64? What value does the algorithm return in this case? Which cells will be probed when the target is 80? What value does the algorithm return in this case? Which cells will be probed when the target is 99? What value does the algorithm return in this case?

(b) Let $F_{min}(n)$ and $F_{max}(n)$ denote the minimum and maximum number of data object comparisons that will be made during a search of an ordered array of n objects using the alternative binary search algorithm in Fig. 5.17. [Note: we make no distinction here between successful and unsuccessful searches because the algorithm itself does not determine whether the search is successful or unsuccessful; that determination is made by the calling function when it receives the returned value.] Let $F_{min}(0)$ and $F_{max}(0)$ denote 0. Compute $F_{min}(1)$, $F_{max}(1)$, $F_{min}(2)$, $F_{max}(2)$, $F_{min}(3)$, $F_{max}(3)$. Write recurrence relations for $F_{min}(n)$ and $F_{max}(n)$ and solve them exactly.

5.1.25 Figure 5.18 shows some C++ code for the well-known Binary Insertion Sort algorithm. The idea of the algorithm is that after the first k objects in the array have been sorted, we use binary search to find the cell where the $(k + 1)$-st object should be inserted among the sorted objects, and then if necessary we shift objects to the right to make a place for the $(k + 1)$-st object. For example, if we have sorted the first 10 objects in the array

0	1	2	3	4	5	6	7	8	9	10	11	12	13	14	15	16
Ann	Bob	Don	Eve	Flo	Hal	Joy	Ken	Nat	Pat	Ida	Lee	Cal	Gus	Sue	Zoe	Roy

then the 11-th object is Ida, and a binary search of the sorted subarray a[0..9] will reveal that Ida belongs in cell 7 (between Hal and Joy). Then we can move Ida into a temporary location, shift the objects in a[6..9] to the right by 1 cell each, and then move Ida into cell 7. Then we can repeat this process on the 12-th object (inserting it into cell 9 of a[0..10]) and so on. Initially, to get the algorithm started, we regard the subarray consisting of just one cell (the first cell) to be a trivial sorted array of length 1. The function call to "alternative_binary_search" is a call to the function in Fig. 5.17.

A sorting algorithm is called *stable* if it does not disrupt the order of elements in the array having identical values. The binary insertion sort will be a stable sorting algorithm if it uses the alternative binary search function because when there are multiple copies of the target in the array, this version always finds the right-most one. Also, it cuts down the amount of shifting when the item to be inserted is identical with several items in the sorted subarray.

(a) Consider what happens during one execution of the body of the outer for loop for some value of the loop variable k. First a binary search is made on a subarray

```
template <class otype>
void binary_insertion_sort (otype a[], int first, int last)
{
    int i, k;
    for (k = first; k < last; ++k)
    {
        // Make a binary search of a[first..k] for a[k+1].
        int p = alternative_binary_search (a, a[k+1], first, k);
        // The item in cell a[k+1] should be inserted at position p+1.
        // Move a[k+1] into temporary storage and then shift objects.
        otype temp = a[k+1];
        for (i = k; i > p; --i)
            a[i+1] = a[i];                    // Shift each cell to right.
        a[p+1] = temp;
    }
}
```

Fig. 5.18 Binary insertion sort

of length k - first + 1. Let m denote this length, and note that m is 1 the first time through the body of the outer loop, m is 2 the second time through the body of the outer loop, and so on up to $n - 1$. By Exercise 5.1.24, the binary search on an array of size m requires an amount of time of the form $\Theta(\log(m))$. After each binary search, some objects are shifted to make a space for a[k+1] to be inserted. What are the minimum and maximum possible execution times for the inner for loop (the shifting loop) on this array of length m?

(b) In part (a) we looked at possible execution times for one pass through the body of the outer for loop. Now let $T_{max}(n)$ denote the maximum execution time for this binary_insertion_sort algorithm on an array of length n, so that $T_{max}(n)$ is the sum of all- the maximum execution times for all $n - 1$ passes through the body of the outer loop. Using your answer from part (a) and various inequalities and equations derived in Chapter A, find a big-theta expression for $T_{max}(n)$. What initial arrangement of the objects in the array will produce this maximum execution time?

(c) Let $T_{min}(n)$ denote the minimum execution time for this binary_insertion _ sort algorithm on an array of length n. Find a big-theta expression for $T_{min}(n)$. What initial arrangement of the objects in the array will produce this minimum execution time?

5.2   Euclid's Algorithm for the Greatest Common Divisor

Over 2,000 years ago Greek mathematicians discovered a powerful algorithm for finding the greatest common divisor (g.c.d.) of two positive integers. The geometer Euclid included this algorithm in one of the books he wrote on geometry and number theory. Dasgupta et al. [4] shows how this algorithm can also be the basis of modular division. In recent years, a slight modification of this algorithm has taken on great importance in computing because it is the central computation in the widely used RSA Public Key encryption system [4]. In this section we will derive an upper bound for the running time of the original Euclidean algorithm. This proof is based on a theorem by G. Lamé from 1845, and is related to the theory of continued fractions, as explained by [11].

Suppose we are given two positive integers m and n. Without loss of generality, assume that $m \leq n$. Euclid's algorithm finds the largest positive integer d such that both m and n are divisible by d. The algorithm works like this:

Step 1:

Compute the remainder r when n is divided by m:

$$r = n \bmod m$$

where "mod" denotes the "modulus operation," which returns the remainder of the integer division of the first number by the second one (in C++ we would write r = n % m;). If r is zero, then n is divisible by m, and so the g.c.d. of n and m is m. If, however, r is not zero, then as shown in the theorem at the end of this section, r must also be divisible by the g.c.d., call it d, of m and n, and d must be the g.c.d of m and r. Also, $0 < r < m$. This leads us to

Step 2:

Compute the remainder, call it r_2, when m is divided by r:

$$r_2 = m \bmod r$$

If r_2 is zero, then r is the g.c.d. of m and r, and thus is the g.c.d. of n and m. If r_2 is not zero, then $0 < r_2 < r$, and so we go on to

Step 3:

Compute the remainder, call it r_3, when r is divided by r_2:

$$r_3 = r \bmod r_2$$

If r_3 is zero, then r_2 is the g.c.d. of r and r_2, and thus is the g.c.d. of n and m. If r_3 is not zero, then $0 < r_3 < r_2$, and so we continue these steps until eventually we perform a division and get a remainder of 0. At this point the most recent divisor is the g.c.d. of m and n.

A C++ function to implement this algorithm is shown in Fig. 5.19.

Example 5.2.1 Let's use the Euclidean algorithm to find the g.c.d. of the integers 14 and 34. The result is shown in Table 5.1.

Example 5.2.2 Let's use the Euclidean algorithm to find the g.c.d. of the integers 1,000 and 4,000. The result is shown in Table 5.2.

Example 5.2.3 Let's use the Euclidean algorithm to find the g.c.d. of the integers 66 and 183. The result is shown in Table 5.3.

Table 5.1 Euclidian Algorithm table for 14 and 34

	Dividend	Divisor	Remainder	
1st step	34	14	6	
2nd step	14	6	2	
3rd step	6	2	0	g_c_d (14, 34) = 2

Table 5.2 Euclidian Algorithm table for 1,000 and 4,000

	Dividend	Divisor	Remainder	
1st step	4,000	1,000	0	g_c_d (1,000, 4,000) = 1,000

In the discussion that follows, we will refer to tables such as Tables 5.1, 5.2 and 5.3 as Euclidean Algorithm tables. They are the tables we produce when we write out the steps of the Euclidean algorithm applied to two particular positive integers.

The natural question is this: given two positive integers m and n, what is the execution time of Euclid's Algorithm as a function of m and n? The examples above make it clear that the execution time will not be a simple function of m and n. In Example 5.2.2 we started with fairly large numbers, but the algorithm required only one "modulus" (remainder) operation to obtain the answer. By contrast, in Example 5.2.3, we started with somewhat smaller numbers, but the algorithm required 5 modulus operations. (That's the most expensive operation in each step.)

One useful observation is that at the first step the remainder must be smaller than the divisor (this is always true when you perform division with positive integers),

```
// Euclid's algorithm

int g_c_d (int m, int n) // m and n are assumed to be positive
{
  int dividend = larger (m, n);    // code not shown for "larger"
  int divisor  = smaller (m, n);   // code not shown for "smaller"
  int remainder = dividend % divisor;

  while (remainder != 0)
  {
    dividend = divisor;
    divisor  = remainder;
    remainder = dividend % divisor;
  }

  return divisor;
}
```

Fig. 5.19 Euclid's algorithm for the greatest common divisor

Table 5.3 Euclidian Algorithm table for 66 and 183

	Dividend	Divisor	Remainder	
1st step	183	66	51	
2nd step	66	51	15	
3rd step	51	15	6	
4th step	15	6	3	
5th step	6	3	0	g_c_d (66, 183) = 3

Table 5.4 Euclidian Algorithm table for n and m

	Dividend	Divisor	Remainder	
1st step	n	m	$m - 1$	(assume that $n > m$)
2nd step	m	$m - 1$	$m - 2$	
3rd step	$m - 1$	$m - 2$	$m - 3$	
4th step	$m - 2$	$m - 3$	$m - 4$	
etc.				
$m - 2$ step	4	3	2	
$m - 1$ step	3	2	1	
m-th step	2	1	0	

and then each successive remainder must be smaller than the preceding one because the preceding one is the divisor at the next step. Since the algorithm starts by making the divisor the smaller of m and n, then we can be sure that the remainders decrease by at least 1 at each stage, so conceivably we could have a Euclidean Algorithm table like the one in Table 5.4. This would be a worst case, if it could happen. Note that there are m steps, each of constant time, where m is the smaller of the two given integers. Thus we can say that the execution time is $O(\min\{m, n\})$.

But can the table shown above actually occur when m and n are large? As it turns out, the answer is no. The upper bound we have derived is correct, but a much better (i.e., smaller) upper bound can be derived with some effort.

Note that the more slowly the remainders decrease to zero in a Euclidean Algorithm table, the longer the algorithm takes. Thus we must investigate how slowly the remainders can decrease to zero. This can be done by "working backward": we'll investigate how slowly the remainders can increase from zero (in the last line of a table) to the value obtained in the first line of a table.

Begin by looking at the last three lines in Table 5.4. It is possible for the last two lines to look like that, but when we go one step higher in the table, we see a line that looks like this:

Dividend Divisor Remainder

$m - 2$ step   4   3   2

This is not possible. The remainder when 4 is divided by 3 is 1, not 2. To get a remainder of 2, the dividend would have to be *at least* 5 (the divisor plus the remainder). Thus the last few lines of the table *could* look like this:

Dividend Divisor Remainder

d_4 3   2   where d_4 is at least 5
3   2   1
2   1   0

Now suppose we want to back up to the next line above the top one shown here. It would look like this:

Dividend Divisor Remainder

d_5 d_4 3

By the same reasoning we have used above, the dividend d_5 would have to be at least $d_4 + 3$, and since d_4 is at least 5, it follows that d_5 would have to be at least 8. Thus the last few lines of the table could look like this:

Dividend Divisor Remainder

d_5 d_4 3   where d_5 is at least 8
d_4 3   2   where d_4 is at least 5
3   2   1
2   1   0

Repeating this argument a couple more times, we would see that the last few lines of the table could look like this:

Of course, the last non-zero divisor, call it d_1, does not have to be 1. It could be larger. That is, $d_1 \geq 1$. Similarly, the last non-zero dividend, call it d_2, does not have to be 2. It has to be larger than d_1, so it has to be at least 2. Thus any table at all that has at least six lines will look like this:

Dividend	Divisor	Remainder	
d_7	d_6	d_5	where d_7 is at least 21
d_6	d_5	d_4	where d_6 is at least 13
d_5	d_4	3	where d_5 is at least 8
d_4	3	2	where d_4 is at least 5
3	2	1	
2	1	0	

Dividend	Divisor	Remainder	
d_7	d_6	d_5	where d_7 is at least 21
d_6	d_5	d_4	where d_6 is at least 13
d_5	d_4	d_3	where d_5 is at least 8
d_4	d_3	d_2	where d_4 is at least 5
d_3	d_2	d_1	where d_3 is at least 3
d_2	d_1	0	where d_2 is at least 2
			where d_1 is at least 1

Examine the right-most column of integers in that table $(21, 13, 8, \ldots, 1)$. Each integer above the bottom two is the sum of the two integers below it. That is, these integers are Fibonacci numbers, as defined in Example 4.2.7, p. 114. In the problem we are concerned with at this moment, $d_1 \geq 1 = f(2)$, $d_2 \geq 2 = f(3)$, $d_3 \geq 3 = f(4)$, $d_4 \geq 5 = f(5)$, $d_5 \geq 8 = f(6)$, etc. In general,

$$d_k \geq f(k+1) = \frac{1}{\sqrt{5}} \left[\left(\frac{1 + \sqrt{5}}{2} \right)^{k+1} - \left(\frac{1 - \sqrt{5}}{2} \right)^{k+1} \right],$$

where we have used the Fibonacci formula (Eq. (15)) given on p. 116. The number $\frac{1 - \sqrt{5}}{2}$ is less than 1 in absolute value, so for large values of k the term $\left(\frac{1 - \sqrt{5}}{2} \right)^{k+1}$ is very nearly zero. Thus with negligible error we can say that for the divisor d_k in the k-th line, counting from the bottom, of a Euclidean Algorithm table,

$$d_k \geq \frac{1}{\sqrt{5}} \left(\frac{1 + \sqrt{5}}{2} \right)^{k+1}.$$

The first numeric line of a Euclidean Algorithm table must have the form for some

dividend	divisor	remainder
d_{K+1}	d_K	d_{K-1}

integer K, where d_K is the smaller of the two given integers m and n. Let's suppose

m is the smaller. Thus

$$m \geq \frac{1}{\sqrt{5}}\left(\frac{1+\sqrt{5}}{2}\right)^{K+1},$$

where K is the total number of lines in the Euclidean Algorithm table, i.e., the number of times the Euclidean algorithm must execute the body of its loop. Let's solve this inequality for K. Taking logarithms base 2 on both sides of the inequality gives us

$$\lg(m) \geq -\frac{1}{2}\lg(5) + (K+1)\lg((1+\sqrt{5})/2).$$

A pocket calculator shows that $\lg(5) \approx 2.32$ and $\lg((1+\sqrt{5})/2) \approx 0.694$. Thus

$$\lg(m) \geq -1.16 + 0.694(K+1).$$

Turning this around gives the equivalent inequality

$$0.694(K+1) - 1.16 \leq \lg(m).$$

Simple algebra transforms this into

$$K \leq \frac{1}{0.694}\lg(m) + \frac{1.16}{0.694} - 1 = 1.44\lg(m) + 0.67. \tag{5.2}$$

This shows us that when the Euclidean algorithm is used to find the g.c.d. of two positive integers m and n, the number of times the modulus operation (%) will be executed is

$$O(\log(\min\{m, n\})) \quad \text{(note the big-oh)}.$$

Note that it would be incorrect to assert that the modulus operation will be executed $\Theta(\log(\min\{m, n\}))$ times, because when one of the integers m and n divides the other evenly, the algorithm requires only one modulus operation.

If the Euclidean algorithm is implemented with the built-in integers of bounded size in a language such as C++, then the assignment and modulus operations that make up the algorithm all require time bounded by constants. The number of modulus operations is one greater than the number of times the `while` loop is executed, and so we can say that with built-in integers of bounded size, the execution time of the Euclidean algorithm is $O(\log(\min\{m, n\}))$. If, instead, the algorithm is implemented using software integers of unbounded size (e.g. the soft integer class present in many libraries), then the execution time is somewhat more complicated.

5.2.1   Proof of the Underlying Theorem

Euclid's algorithm depends crucially on the following theorem about divisors.

Theorem 5.2.4 *Let m and n be positive integers, with $m \leq n$. Let r denote the remainder when n is divided by m. Then the g.c.d. of r and m is equal to the g.c.d. of m and n.*

Proof Since r is the remainder after division of n by m, there must exist a positive integer q such that $n = qm + r$ (the number q is the integer quotient when n is divided by m). This equation can be rearranged into the form $r = n - qm$.

Let d denote the g.c.d. of m and n. Then $m = da$ and $n = db$, where a and b are positive integers whose only common divisor is 1. By the last equation in the preceding paragraph,

$$r = db - qda = d(b - qa).$$

Since $b - qa$ is an integer, the equation above shows that the integer d is a divisor of r. Thus d is a common divisor of m and r. All that remains to do in the proof is to shows that d is the greatest common divisor of m and r.

Suppose, for purposes of contradiction, that m and r are both divisible by an integer $e > d$. That is, suppose $m = eu$ and $r = ev$, where u and v are positive integers. Then from the equation $n = qm + r$ in the first paragraph of this proof, we would have

$$n = q(eu) + ev = e(qu + v).$$

Since $qu + v$ is an integer, this would imply that n was also divisible by e. That is, n and m would both be divisible by an integer e *greater than the greatest common divisor d* of n and m. This is logically impossible, so m and r cannot have a common divisor larger than d (which we have already shown is a common divisor of m and r). ∎

5.2.2   Exercises

5.2.5 **(a)** If the Euclidean Algorithm is used to compute the greatest common divisor of the integers 315 and 588, then before the computation begins we can be sure that the table used in the computation will contain no more than how many lines? Show how you got your answer.

(b) Use the Euclidean Algorithm to find the greatest common divisor of the integers 315 and 588. Show your work.

5.2.6 Use the Euclidean Algorithm to prove that for all positive integers n the g.c.d. of n and $n + 1$ is 1. *Hint.* For any two integer numbers p and m, p can be represented uniquely as $km + d$ for an integer k and an integer d satisfying $0 \le d < m$. Furthermore, d must be a multiple of the g.c.d. of p and m.

5.3   Binary Trees

Binary trees appear in many contexts in computing. Among their many applications are the following:

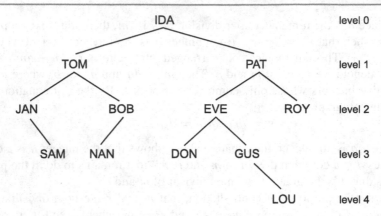

Fig. 5.20 An example of a binary tree

1. storage of data for fast retrieval, insertion, and deletion (AVL trees and splay trees);
2. efficient implementations of priority queues (heaps);
3. representation of the order of operations in complex algebraic expressions (a compiler application);
4. encoding of characters in data compression schemes (e.g., Huffman encoding).

Definition 5.3.1 A *binary tree* is a set of *nodes*. An *empty binary tree* is a binary tree containing no nodes whatsoever. If a binary tree is not empty, then one of its nodes is the *root node*, and the remaining nodes are partitioned into a *left subtree* and a *right subtree*, each of which is a binary tree. Either or both of these subtrees may be empty.

Definition 5.3.2 Relationships Between Nodes

- The root node of a binary tree is considered to be the *parent* of the roots of the left and right subtrees (if these are not empty), and the root of each subtree is a *child* of its parent.
- The *left child* of a node is the root of the left subtree of that node (if that subtree is not empty), and the *right child* of a node is the root (if it exists) of the right subtree of that node.
- *Grandparent* and *grandchild* are defined in the obvious way.
- Two nodes are *siblings* of each other if they have the same parent.
- A *leaf* is a node with no children (i.e., a node whose left and right subtrees are empty).
- The *descendants* of a node are the nodes in its left and right subtrees. The reverse is called an *ancestor node*; more precisely, an ancestor of a node is any node on the path connecting it to the root of the tree.

Fig. 5.21 Trees with 4 nodes
and height equal to 3

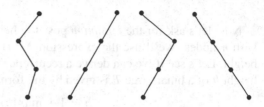

Properties of Binary Trees

- The root of a binary tree is said to be at *level 0* in the tree, its children are at *level 1*, its grandchildren are at *level 2*, and so on.
- The *height* of a binary tree is defined as follows: the height of an empty binary tree is taken to be -1 (a useful convention), the height of a binary tree containing only one node (its root) is 0, and a binary tree with more than one node has height equal to 1 plus the height of the taller of its two subtrees, or their common height if both are of the same height.

The binary tree shown in Fig. 5.20 can be used to illustrate the definitions above. The tree has height 4. Its root is IDA. The left subtree has 5 nodes, and its root is TOM. The right subtree has 6 nodes, and its root is PAT. The left child of PAT is EVE, and GUS is a grandchild of PAT. JAN and BOB are siblings, but SAM and NAN are not siblings. The leaves of the tree are SAM, NAN, DON, LOU, and ROY. The node GUS has an empty left subtree, and its right subtree contains just one node (LOU). The descendants of PAT are EVE, DON, GUS, LOU, and ROY.

The most common way of implementing a binary tree in a computer program is as a linked data structure, with each node represented as an object containing a pointer to the left child, a pointer to the right child, and at least one other member. A NULL pointer indicates an empty tree or subtree. There are other implementations, however. For example, a "heap" is a binary tree whose nodes are stored in the cells of an array. Their arrangement in the array allows the parent-child relationships to be deduced from the subscripts of the cells. We'll discuss heaps in detail later.

Height for a Given Number of Nodes

First let's investigate the relationship between the height h of a binary tree T and the number n of nodes in T. One relationship is fairly obvious: if we are given a certain number of nodes, say n, to build a binary tree with, then the maximum possible height among the trees we can build is $n - 1$. We obtain this height if and only if all but one of the nodes in the tree are "only children", i.e., nodes with no siblings; the only exception is the root of the tree (which is never the child of any other node). For example, if we are given 4 nodes to play around with, then we can build trees such as shown in Fig. 5.21, all of which are of height 3, but no taller trees with exactly 4 nodes are possible. Thus we have the following (equivalent) inequalities, which are valid for all binary trees T (even the empty tree):

$$h \le n - 1 \quad \text{and} \quad h + 1 \le n.$$

Now let's ask for the *minimum* possible height of a binary tree that can be built with n nodes. We'll use the expression $M(n)$ to stand for this minimum possible height. Let's see if we can derive a recurrence relation for $M(n)$. By definition, the height h of a binary tree T is given by the formula

$$h = 1 + \max\{h_L, h_R\}.$$

where h_L and h_R denote respectively the heights of the left and right subtrees of T, call them L_T and R_T. If we build a tree T with n nodes, where $n \geq 1$, then one of those nodes is the root and the remaining $n-1$ nodes must be placed in L_T and R_T. If we put i nodes into L_T, then there will be $n-1-i$ nodes in R_T. We can minimize the height of T by minimizing the heights of its left and right subtrees. That is, the minimum height of an n-node binary tree with i nodes in its left subtree is given by the expression

$$1 + \max\{M(i), M(n-1-i)\}.$$

Now, by allowing i to vary over all possible values from 0 to $n-1$ and selecting the smallest value of the expression above, we obtain the minimum possible height of a binary tree with n nodes:

$$M(n) = \min_{0 \leq i \leq n-1} \{1 + \max\{M(i), M(n-1-i)\}\}. \tag{5.3}$$

This recurrence relation, which is valid for all $n \geq 1$, is unfortunately not of a form that we know how to solve. We might, on the basis of some numerical values, try to conjecture a formula for the solution and then verify our conjecture mathematically. There is, however, a way to simplify the recurrence relation above by thinking a little about the relative sizes of the numbers $M(i)$. Note first the obvious fact that the function $M(n)$ is monotone increasing; that is, $M(1) \leq M(2) \leq M(3) \leq M(4) \leq \ldots$ This is true because the more nodes we put into a binary tree, the more likely it is that we will be forced to use an additional level to store the nodes.

Now consider a numerical example. Let's take $n = 10$ in the example above.

$$M(10) = \min\{1 + \max\{M(0), M(9)\}, \ 1 + \max\{M(1), M(8)\},$$
$$1 + \max\{M(2), M(7)\}, \ 1 + \max\{M(3), M(6)\},$$
$$1 + \max\{M(4), M(5)\}, \ 1 + \max\{M(5), M(4)\},$$
$$1 + \max\{M(6), M(3)\}, \ 1 + \max\{M(7), M(2)\},$$
$$1 + \max\{M(8), M(1)\}, \ 1 + \max\{M(9), M(0)\}\}.$$

The larger of $M(0)$, $M(9)$ is $M(9)$. The larger of $M(1)$, $M(8)$ is $M(8)$. And so on. Throwing out duplicates from the expression above we get

$$M(10) = \min\{1 + M(9), 1 + M(8), 1 + M(7), 1 + M(6), 1 + M(5)\}.$$

By the monotonicity of the $M(n)$ function, the minimum of the terms in braces above is $1 + M(5)$. Thus $M(10) = 1 + M(5)$.

Generalizing the example above, we find that the minimum specified in Eq. (5.3) on p. 214 must be $M(\lceil (n-1)/2 \rceil)$. Thus we need to solve the relation

$$M(n) = 1 + M(\lceil (n-1)/2 \rceil) \quad \text{for all } n \geq 1.$$

We also have the initial value $M(0) = -1$, from which we can derive $M(1) = 0$. Using the properties of the floor and ceiling given in Theorem 2.1.5 (c), but with n replaced by $n - 1$, we get $M(n) = 1 + M(\lfloor n/2 \rfloor)$ for $n \geq 1$. Using Table 4.1, p. 147, we find that $M(n) = \lfloor \lg(n) \rfloor$ for all $n \geq 1$.

Number of Nodes for a Given Height

In the discussion up to this point we have started with a given number of nodes n and asked, "What are the maximum possible height and the minimum possible height of a tree with n nodes?" There is a related question, one that can be regarded as the "inverse" of the question just quoted. It starts with a given height h and asks, "What are the maximum number of nodes and the minimum number of nodes that can be in a tree with height h?" The answer to the minimum problem is easy: just use $h + 1$ nodes in a "string". A formula for the maximum number of nodes is not quite so obvious. Let's call it $N(h)$. A little thought shows us that we can write a recurrence relation for $N(h)$. It is based on the obvious fact that the "fullest" tree of height h is obtained by taking the left and right subtrees both to be of height $h - 1$ and filling those subtrees as full as possible. We have

$$N(-1) = 0, \quad N(h) = 1 + 2N(h - 1) \quad \text{for all } h \geq 0$$

(the leading 1 is there to count the root of the tree). The solution to this is quickly found to be $N(h) = 2^{h+1} - 1$ for all $h \geq -1$.

Every non-empty binary tree contains one or more empty subtrees. If a binary tree has n nodes, what is the maximum number of empty subtrees it can have, and what is the minimum? For example, let's look at some binary trees with 5 nodes and see how many empty subtrees they have (Fig. 5.22).

These examples suggest, but do not prove, that the number of empty subtrees in a binary tree with n nodes is independent of the shape of the tree and depends in a simple way on n. This turns out to be true: the number of empty subtrees is always exactly $n + 1$ no matter how the n nodes of the tree are arranged. There is a simple way to see this if we think of the implementation of a binary tree using nodes and node pointers. A binary tree with n nodes contains $2n$ pointers. The ones that are NULL indicate the empty subtrees in the tree. How many are NULL? We'll count them by counting the complementary set of those that are not NULL. A non-NULL pointer points to exactly one node, and no two pointers point to the same node, so the number of non-NULL pointers is exactly the same as the number of nodes that have a pointer pointing to them. There are $n - 1$ such nodes; only the root node is not pointed to. Thus the number of NULL pointers is $2n - (n - 1) = n + 1$. This is the number of empty subtrees in a binary tree with n nodes. The formula is valid

Fig. 5.22 Trees with 5 nodes

even when n is zero provided we consider the empty tree to be an empty subtree of itself.

We can "invert" the formula we have just derived: since the number of empty subtrees in a binary tree is exactly one more than the number of nodes, it follows that the number of nodes in a binary tree is exactly one less than the number of empty subtrees.

What can we say about the relationship between the number of nodes in a binary tree and the number of leaves? First, it is easy to see that a non-empty binary tree with n nodes can have just one leaf: just put all the nodes in a chain leading down from the root to the one leaf. This is true no matter how large n may be. So now we know the minimum number of leaves in a non-empty binary tree. What is the maximum number of leaves in a non-empty binary tree with n nodes? It turns out to be easier to solve the "inverted" problem: if a non-empty binary tree has λ leaves, what is the minimum number of nodes the tree can contain? Well, each leaf contains two NULL pointers, so we see immediately that the tree must contain at least 2λ empty subtrees. As shown in the preceding paragraph, this means that the tree must contain at least $2\lambda - 1$ nodes. Thus if n is the number of nodes in a non-empty binary tree containing λ leaves, then $n \geq 2\lambda - 1$. By simple algebra, it follows that $\lambda \leq \dfrac{n+1}{2}$. Since λ must be an integer, it follows that $\lambda \leq \left\lfloor \dfrac{n+1}{2} \right\rfloor = \left\lceil \dfrac{n}{2} \right\rceil$. Thus we have derived an upper bound on the number of leaves in a non-empty binary tree with n nodes. Is that upper bound always attainable? That is, given a positive integer n, can we always construct a binary tree with n nodes and exactly $\left\lceil \dfrac{n}{2} \right\rceil$ leaves, or is it the case that for some values of n the number λ of leaves must be strictly less than $\left\lceil \dfrac{n}{2} \right\rceil$ in all trees with n nodes? This question is settled fairly easily by looking at the binary trees in Fig. 5.23.

Table 5.5 summarizes what we were able to prove in the preceding discussion about the relationships of heights of binary trees and number of nodes in binary trees.

5.3.1 Exercises

5.3.3 What is the height of the empty binary tree? What is the height of a binary tree with just one node? What is the height of a binary tree with exactly 2 nodes? What is the maximum possible height of a tree with 1,000 nodes? What is the minimum possible height of a tree with 1,000 nodes?

Fig. 5.23 Binary trees with increasing maximal number of leaves

Table 5.5 Binary tree relationships

Maximum possible height of a binary tree with n nodes:	$n - 1$
Minimum possible height of a binary tree with n nodes:	$\lfloor \lg(n) \rfloor$
Maximum number of nodes in a binary tree of height h:	$2^{h+1} - 1$
Minimum number of nodes in a binary tree of height h:	$h + 1$
In every binary tree with n nodes and height h,	$\lfloor \lg(n) \rfloor \leq h \leq n - 1$ and $h + 1 \leq n \leq 2^{h+1} - 1$
Number of empty subtrees in a binary tree with n nodes:	$n + 1$
Number of nodes in a binary tree with e empty subtrees:	$e - 1$
Minimum number of leaves in any non-empty binary tree:	1
Maximum number of leaves in a non-empty n-node binary tree:	$\left\lceil \dfrac{n}{2} \right\rceil$
Minimum number of nodes in a non-empty binary tree with λ leaves:	$2\lambda - 1$

5.3.4 Use Table 5.5 to show that in a non-empty binary tree with n nodes, the number of parent nodes (i.e., non-leaf nodes) is at least $\lfloor n/2 \rfloor$.

5.3.5 Explain why a binary tree with n nodes contains at least $\lfloor \lg(n) \rfloor - 1$ grandparent nodes and at most $n - 2$ grandparent nodes.
Hint: think of the connection between the height of the tree and the length of the longest path in the tree.

5.3.6 Prove by strong induction that in a binary tree with n nodes there are at least $\lfloor n/4 \rfloor$ grandparent nodes. You may use the result in Exercise 2.5.12.

5.3.7 A binary tree is said to be *perfect* if and only if each non-empty level in the tree is completely filled with nodes. The perfect binary trees of heights 0, 1, 2, and 3 are shown in Fig. 5.24. Note that in a perfect tree of height $h \geq 1$, each of the two subtrees is a perfect tree of height $h - 1$. Let $N(h)$ denote the number of nodes in a

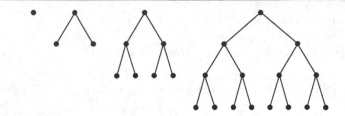

Fig. 5.24 Examples of perfect trees

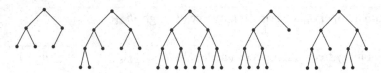

Fig. 5.25 Examples of complete trees (first three) and incomplete (last two)

perfect tree of height h. Write a recurrence relation for $N(h)$ and solve it using an appropriate initial value for $N(0)$.

5.3.8 A binary tree is said to be *complete* if and only if all levels of the tree are completely filled with nodes, except possibly for the lowest level, and in the lowest level all the nodes are located as far to the left side as possible. For the trees shown in Fig. 5.25, the first three are complete, while the last two are not complete. What is the height of a complete binary tree that contains n nodes? HINT: a complete binary tree with n nodes is as short as a binary tree with that number of nodes can be! So just cite one of the results we have derived in this section of the notes.

5.3.9 In this exercise we'll call a binary tree *compact* if and only if all its levels are completely filled with nodes, except possibly the lowest level. This is slightly less restrictive than the definition of "complete" in Exercise 5.3.8. In Fig. 5.26, trees T_1 and T_2 are compact, but T_3 is not. A compact binary tree consists of a perfect tree (see Exercise 5.3.7) to whose leaves some additional nodes may (or may not) have been attached. Find a general formula for the height of the perfect part of a compact binary tree with n nodes. (In Fig. 5.26, the height of the perfect part of T_1 is 2, and the height of the perfect part of T_2 is 3.) *Hint:* by Exercise 5.3.7 we can write the following pair of inequalities involving the unknown height h of the perfect part of a compact tree and the known number of nodes n in the tree: $2^h - 1 < n \leq 2^{h+1} - 1$. Solve for h.

5.3.10 As we have seen, every non-empty binary tree with n nodes has $n + 1$ empty subtrees. It will be useful later to know the level numbers at which those empty subtrees can occur. To be precise, let's agree to say that an empty binary subtree of

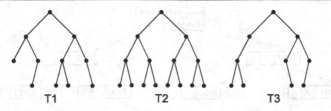

Fig. 5.26 Examples of two compact trees (T_1 and T_2) and one that is not (T_3)

a binary tree T is located at level λ in T if the parent of the subtree is at level $\lambda - 1$. For example, in Fig. 5.20 on p. 212 the right subtree of Bob is empty and it is at level 3 because its parent (Bob) is at level 2. (Remember that the root is considered to be at level 0.) Similarly the empty left subtree of Lou is at level 5. In Fig. 5.21, each of the four trees has one empty subtree at level 1 (just below the root). In fact, for any positive integer n there are many binary trees with n nodes and an empty subtree at level 1. That is, when we are told that a non-empty binary tree T contains n nodes, we can say that the minimum possible level number of an empty subtree of T is 1.

(a) Given a non-empty binary tree T with n nodes and height h, what is the largest level number of an empty binary subtree of T? Give your answer in terms of h.
(b) Let T denote a non-empty binary tree containing n nodes. Explain why there must be at least one empty subtree whose level number is $1 + \lfloor \lg(n) \rfloor$ or less. *Hint:* suppose this were not true. What would have to be true about the top part of T? You may use the answer for Exercise 5.3.7. and Theorem 2.2.8 (a) on p. 21.

5.4   Traversals of Binary Trees

In this section we are going to look at some C++ functions that operate on binary trees. To that end, assume we are working with a program containing the following definitions:

```
template <class otype>
struct node
{
  otype datum;
  node * left, * right;
}

typedef node * node_ptr;
```

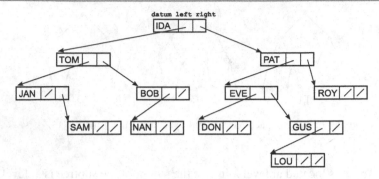

Fig. 5.27 Data structure representation for the tree in Fig. 5.20

Using the definitions above, it would be possible to create a structure that represents the binary tree shown in Fig. 5.20 on p. 212. We can visualize the computer representation like in Fig. 5.27:
where the "datum" members of the nodes are of some string data type.

For the moment, let's set aside the question of how we could construct such a tree from an external data file or an internal array of strings or some other data source. Our goal right now is to study various operations one can perform on such trees.

Many standard operations on a binary tree perform a complete *traversal* of the tree, during which each node is visited at least once and one or more operations are performed at that node. A traversal is typically carried out recursively. To take a well-known and simple example, let's look at a function that accepts a pointer to the root of a binary tree T (or NULL if T is empty) and prints out (i.e., sends to standard output) the datum members of the nodes according to the following rule: *for each node N in the tree T, the* datum *member of N is printed before the* datum *members in the subtrees of N, and the* datum *members in the left subtree of N are printed before the* datum *members in the right subtree of N.* For example, if the strings in the tree in Fig. 5.27 are printed according to this rule, they will appear in this order (but on separate lines):

```
IDA    TOM    JAN    SAM    BOB    NAN    PAT    EVE    DON
GUS    LOU    ROY
```
We call this the "pre-order" output of the nodes in the tree.

Suppose we call the print_in_preorder function with a pointer to a tree containing n nodes and having height h. How much space and time will be required to execute the call?

The space requirements involve only the stack frames. Each stack frame has exactly the same size. The maximum number of stack frames that can be on the stack at any one time is equal to 1 plus the larger of the maximum number of frames for the first recursive call (on the left subtree) and the maximum number of frames for the second recursive call (on the right subtree). This is exactly the relationship that recursively defines the height of a binary tree. One difference, however, is that if $n = 0$ the maximum number of stack frames is 1 while the height of the tree in this

```
void print_in_preorder (node_ptr p)
{
  if (p != NULL)     // The base case is handled tacitly.
                     // If the tree pointed to by p is empty, the function
                     // executes a return immediately after testing p != NULL.
  {
    cout << p->datum << endl;
    print_in_preorder (p->left);
    print_in_preorder (p->right);
  }
}
```

Fig. 5.28 Printing a tree in pre-order

base case is -1, so the base cases differ by 2. Thus we have the following important fact:

The maximum number of stack frames that can be on the stack at any one time when the function in Fig. 5.28 is called with a pointer to a particular tree T of n nodes and height h is equal to $2 + h$.

In the worst case, when the tree has degenerated to a linear structure, $h = n - 1$, so the maximum number of stack frames on the stack at any one time is $n + 1$ in this unusual case. Thus the space requirements for this tree traversal are at worst a linear function of the number of nodes in the tree. In the best case, $h = \lfloor \lg(n) \rfloor$, so when the tree is as short as possible, the space requirement for the traversal is logarithmic in the number of nodes in the tree.

Now let's look at the amount of time that will be required when we call the function on a tree T with n nodes and height h. The function will be called once initially and $2n$ times recursively because it is called recursively on each of the two pointers stored in each of the n nodes. Our strategy for computing the total execution time will be to add up all the separate execution times for these $2n + 1$ calls. This is somewhat like the strategy used to analyze the execution time of a loop, where we attempt to count the number of times the body of the loop is executed and the amount of time required each time the body of the loop is executed.

Every call to the function requires some set-up time, some time to test p for NULL, and some return time. Those times are all constant. When a call finds that the pointer p it NULL, then that constant is the entire execution time for that call. If p is not NULL, however, additional execution time is required to print the datum value. Let's assume that time is bounded by constants (i.e., is $\Theta(1)$ as $n \to \infty$). When this is combined with the constant time for the other parts of the call, the execution time for the call is still $\Theta(1)$. [Note: we do not include here the time to make the two recursive calls because we are calculating the time of every call separately from all the other calls.] Since there are $2n + 1$ calls, each requiring $\Theta(1)$ time, we see that total execution time is $\Theta(2n + 1)$, or more properly, $\Theta(n)$ as $n \to \infty$.

It is worth noting here that the execution time is independent of the shape of the tree. Even if the tree is very lopsided and greatly strung out, the execution time depends only on the number of nodes in the tree. In particular, the execution time is not a function of the height of the tree.

```
int height (node_ptr p)  // p  is a pointer to a binary tree
{
  if (p == NULL)
    return -1;   // The base case of an empty binary tree.
  int left_height  = height (p->left);
  int right_height = height (p->right);
  if (left_height <= right_height)
    return 1 + right_height;
  else
    return 1 + left_height;
}
```

Fig. 5.29 The height of a binary tree

```
int height (node_ptr p)  // p  is a pointer to a binary tree
{
  if (p == NULL)
    return -1;   // The base case of an empty binary tree.
  if (height(p->left) <= height(p->right))
    return 1 + height(p->right);
  else
    return 1 + height(p->left);
}
```

Fig. 5.30 Inefficient version of the function height

More generally, if a call is made to a recursive function, and if the execution time for each call to the function is bounded by constants, *exclusive of any recursive calls that the function makes*, and if the total number of calls that take place as a result of the initial call is m, then the total execution time for the initial call and all its subsequent recursive calls is $\Theta(m)$. Compare this with the principle stated in Theorem 5.1.2 on p. 174 for loops.

When a recursive function makes a ***simple traversal*** of a binary tree in which the body of the traversal function contains exactly two recursive calls, one on the left subtree and one on the right, and all other parts of each call, exclusive of the recursive calls, require time bounded by constants, then the execution time for traversal of a tree with n nodes is $\Theta(n)$. The analysis would apply, for example, to the function in Fig. 5.29 that traverses the tree to calculate its height.

Figure 5.30 shows a differently coded version of the function that calculates the height of a binary tree. Note that the code is a little simpler (shorter) than the code in the version in Fig. 5.29. The code in Fig. 5.30 is *not* a "simple traversal" of the kind described above. Here is the reason: when recursive calls are made, exactly one of the recursive calls is *repeated*. Clearly then the total number of calls (initial and recursive) is not just $2n + 1$, where n is the number of nodes in the tree. Let's try to figure out the total number of calls that could be made when the second version of height is called on a tree T with n nodes.

Let $K(T)$ denote this total number of calls, and let L_T and R_T denote the left and right subtrees of T. Then we can write

$$K(T) = \begin{cases} 1 & \text{if } T = \emptyset \text{ (i.e. } n = 0) \\ 1 + K(L_T) + K(R_T) + K(\text{the taller of } L_T \text{ and } R_T) & \text{otherwise} \end{cases}$$

$$= \begin{cases} 1 & \text{if } T \text{ is empty} \\ 1 + K(L_T) + 2\,K(R_T) & \text{if } R_T \text{ is at least as tall as } L_T \text{ and } T \neq \phi \\ 1 + 2\,K(L_T) + K(R_T) & \text{otherwise} \end{cases}$$

For non-empty trees with n nodes, we can maximize the value of $K(T)$ by making the taller of L_T and R_T contain as many nodes as possible, so that the last term will add as much as possible to the value of $K(T)$. This involves putting all the nodes except the root into one of the two subtrees, and doing the same at every level below the root. This results in a tree that has maximum possible height $n - 1$. Suppose, for example we make every node (except the root) the right child of its parent. Let $F(n)$ denote $K(T)$ for this kind of tree T with n nodes (that is, $F(n)$ denotes the total number of calls that will be made on such a tree). Then our equations above can be turned into a recurrence problem of the form

$$F(0) = 1, \quad F(n) = 1 + F(0) + 2F(n - 1) = 2F(n - 1) + 2. \qquad (5.4)$$

This problem is easy to solve for $F(n)$, and the solution is $\Theta(2^n)$. That is, the second version of the `height` function has catastrophically bad execution time on degenerate binary trees of maximal height. This is the worst possible case for that algorithm.

Having identified the worst case for $K(T)$, let's now try to find the best case. Suppose we are given a positive integer n and asked which among all binary trees T with n nodes minimize $K(T)$. Let's call such a tree a *K-minimizing tree of size n*. Based on what we have just seen with trees that maximize $K(T)$, it is reasonable to conjecture that the way to build a K-minimizing tree of size is to make it as short as possible. Perhaps, one might guess, a binary tree is K-minimizing if and only if it is compact, as defined in Exercise 5.3.9. As it turns out, however, many compact trees are not K-minimizing, and many K-minimizing trees are not compact. In fact, it is surprisingly difficult to characterize the K-minimizing trees of a given size n, as can be seen by consulting (Vrajitoru and Knight 2011). What we'll do instead is prove that for a certain kind of well-balanced tree T of arbitrary size n, the value of $K(T)$ is much smaller than the $\Theta(2^n)$ we got for trees T that maximize $K(T)$. This will give us an upper bound for the growth rate of $K(T)$ for K-minimizing trees T as their sizes go to infinity.

Let's call a binary tree T with n nodes a *size-balanced* tree if and only if its left and right subtrees contain exactly $\lfloor (n - 1)/2 \rfloor$ and $\lceil (n - 1)/2 \rceil$ nodes respectively, and a similar partition of the descendants occurs at every node in the tree. Two examples of size-balanced trees are shown in Fig. 5.31. Note that for every node in a size-balanced binary tree, the subtree rooted at that node is, by our definition, size-balanced. Note also that for each positive integer n there is only one possible shape for a size-balanced tree with n nodes. Let $S(n)$ denote the value of $K(T)$ when T is

Fig. 5.31 Two size-balanced
trees, with 4 and 12 nodes
respectively

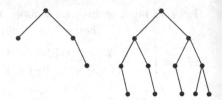

the size-balanced tree containing n nodes. That is, $S(n)$ is the total number of times
that the height function in Fig. 5.30 is called when the first call is to the size-balanced
tree of n nodes.

It is easy to prove by induction that if T_k and T_{k+1} are size-balanced trees having
k and $k + 1$ nodes respectively, then the height of T_k will be less than or equal to
the height of T_{k+1}. This means that at every node in a size-balanced tree, the height
of the left subtree of that node will be less than or equal to the height of the right
subtree of that same node. The height function in Fig. 5.30 is written in such a way
that for every call to the function on a size-balanced tree there will be one call on the
pointer to the left subtree and two calls on the pointer to the right subtree. Thus we
can write the following recurrence relation for $S(n)$:

$$S(n) = 1 + S\left(\left\lfloor \frac{n-1}{2} \right\rfloor\right) + 2S\left(\left\lceil \frac{n-1}{2} \right\rceil\right), \quad \text{which is valid for all } n \geq 1.$$

The initial value is $S(0) = 1$. Unfortunately, this is not a recurrence relation we know
how to solve. We can, however, use the recurrence relation and induction to prove
the inequality

$$S\left(\left\lfloor \frac{n-1}{2} \right\rfloor\right) \leq S\left(\left\lceil \frac{n-1}{2} \right\rceil\right), \quad \text{which is valid for all } n \geq 1.$$

This inequality can be combined with the recurrence relation for $S(n)$ to produce
two recurrence inequalities:

$$S(n) \leq 1 + 3S\left(\left\lceil \frac{n-1}{2} \right\rceil\right) \quad \text{and} \quad S(n) \geq 1 + 3S\left(\left\lfloor \frac{n-1}{2} \right\rfloor\right) \quad \text{for all } n \geq 1.$$

As will be shown in an exercise, these inequalities together with the initial value
$S(0) = 1$ imply that

$$S(n) \leq \frac{3^{\lfloor \lg(n) \rfloor + 2} - 1}{2} \quad \text{and } S(n) \geq \frac{3^{\lfloor \lg(n+1) \rfloor + 1} - 1}{2},$$

which imply that $S(n) = \Theta(n^{\lg(3)})$. Since $\lg(3) \approx 1.585$, it follows that the growth
rate of $S(n)$ is only a little greater than $\Theta(n\sqrt{n})$. Finally, remember that size-balanced
trees are not necessarily K-minimizing trees, and thus a K-minimizing tree T with n
nodes will satisfy $K(T) \leq S(n)$. From this it follows that $K(T) = O(n^{\lg(3)})$, where
n denotes the number of nodes in T.

5.4.1   Exercises

5.4.1 Each function below acts on a binary tree passed to it by means of a node pointer p. In each case, let n denote the number of nodes in the tree, and let h denote the height of the tree. If possible, express the execution time of the function as a single big-theta expression involving n and/or h. Where that is not possible, find big-theta expressions for the minimum and maximum execution times. Where it makes sense to do so, consider separately the cases where the function succeeds and the cases where it fails. Try to make use wherever possible of the principle stated on p. 222.

(a) This function deallocates all the nodes in a binary tree and makes the tree empty.

```
void destroy (node_ptr &p)
{
   if (p)  // if p != NULL
   {
      destroy (p->left);
      destroy (p->right);
      delete (p);        // Deallocates the node pointed to by p.
      p = NULL;          // Makes p NULL.
   }
}
```

(b) This function counts the number of leaves (childless nodes) in a binary tree.

```
int number_of_leaves (node_ptr p)
{
   if (!p)                        // One base case:  empty tree.
      return 0;
   else if (! p->left && ! p->right) // Another base case:  a leaf.
      return 1;
   else
      return number_of_leaves (p->left) + number_of_leaves (p->right);
}
```

(c) The following function replaces a binary tree by its mirror image.

```
void reverse (node_ptr p)
{
   if (p)   // if (p != NULL)
   {
      node_ptr temp;      // Swap the pointers in the root node
      temp = p->left;
      p->left = p->right;
      p->right = temp;

      reverse (p->left);  // Replace the subtrees by their mirror
      reverse (p->right); // images.
   }
}
```

(d) The following function determines whether a binary tree is "perfect" (Exercise 5.3.7).

```
bool is_perfect (node_ptr t)      // Driver function.  Non-recursive.
{
  int   junk;     // Define a variable to be passed to the helper function.
                  // The value that comes back is ignored.

  return test_perfect_and_height (t, junk);
}


// The following function determines whether the tree pointed to by p
// is perfect, and it also calculates the height of that tree and
// puts it in the "reference variable "height" if the tree is perfect.
bool test_perfect_and_height (node_ptr tp, int & height) // helper
{
  if (!p)           // The base case
  {
    height  = -1;   // The height of an empty tree is -1.
    return true;    // An empty tree is perfect.
  }

  else
  {
    int left_height, right_height;

    if ( ! test_perfect_and_height (p->left, left_height)
        || ! test_perfect_and_height (p->right, right_height) )

      return false;  // No need to give "height" a value.

    else if (left_height != right_height)
      return false;                    // No need to give "height" a value.

    else                              // Left and right heights are equal.
    {
      height = 1 + left_height;
      return true;
    }
  }
}
```

(e) The following function searches a binary tree for a specified target value stored in a node (it is assumed here that each node of the tree carries a "datum" member of type otype on which the == operator is defined). If the specified target value is found, the function returns a pointer to the node carrying the object with the target. If not, the function returns NULL.

```
template <class otype>
node_ptr location (node_ptr p, constant otype & target)
{
  if (p == NULL || p->datum == target) // two base cases
    return p;
  else
  { // First make a search of the left subtree.
    node_ptr left_location = location (p->left, target);
    if (left_location != NULL) // If the target is found, then
      return left_location;    // no need to search the right subtree
    else
      return location (p->right, target);
  }
}
```

5.5   Binary Search Trees

The binary trees we have looked at in the preceding two sections have been perfectly general. In this section we will review properties of *binary search trees*. These are trees in which each node contains a member datum of some otype on which the comparison operators are well defined. In particular, these operations should have the property that for any two otype objects x and y, if $x < y$ and $y < x$ are both false, then x and y are considered to be identical to each other. (This is the same assumption that we made in our binary search algorithm in Fig. 5.3 on p. 176.)

Definition 5.5.1 We say that a binary tree is a *binary search tree* provided that each node N in the tree has the following property: all nodes in the left subtree of N carry smaller datum values than the datum carried by N, and all nodes in the right subtree of N carry larger datum values than the datum carried by N.

In other words, the information in the tree has been stored in such a way that by starting at the root and going down the tree examining nodes, we can quickly determine whether an object with a specified target datum is stored in the tree. At most we search one "branch" of the tree (one path from root to leaf), not the entire tree. (Compare this with the function given in Exercise 5.4.1 (c) on p. 225, in which the entire tree may have to be searched to find a specified value). The binary tree shown in Fig. 5.32 with strings as datum values is a binary search tree under the usual alphabetical order relation on strings: for each node in the tree, all the nodes in its left subtree have alphabetically "smaller" labels and all the nodes in the right subtree have alphabetically "larger" labels.

A binary search tree has the property that the recursive function shown in Fig. 5.33 will output in increasing order all the datum values in a binary search tree pointed to by the parameter p. For example, the print_in_order function will output the strings in the tree in Fig. 5.32 in the order Ann, Beth, Chris, Ed, Jack, Judy, Ken, Lee, Lynn, Sandy, Tom (each on a separate line).

How can one find the smallest datum value in a non-empty binary search tree? The answer is simple: start at the root and follow left pointers down the tree until

Fig. 5.32 A binary search tree

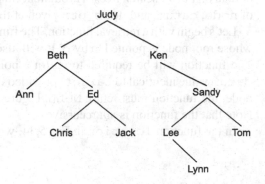

```
// This function outputs the datum values in a binary tree pointed to by p.
// For each node N in the tree it outputs the datum values in the left subtree of
// N, then the datum value in N, then the datum values in the right subtree of N.

print_in_order (node_ptr p)
{
  if ( p )    // if p is not NULL
  {
    print_in_order (p->left);
    cout << p->datum << endl;
    print_in_order (p->right);
  }
}
```

Fig. 5.33 Outputs datum values of a binary tree

you reach a node with a NULL left pointer. Similarly, the largest datum value is found by following right pointers down the tree. Here is a slightly harder question: how can one find the *inorder predecessor* of a datum value x in a node N of the tree, by which we mean the largest of all the datum values smaller than x in the tree? For example, in Fig. 5.32, Jack is the inorder predecessor of Judy, and Lynn is the inorder predecessor of Sandy, while Ann has no inorder predecessor in the tree, and the inorder predecessor of Chris is Beth. Finding the inorder predecessor of x is easy if the node N containing x has a non-empty left subtree; in that case you start at the root of the left subtree and go down to the right as far as possible. If, however, the left subtree of N is empty, then you must go back up the tree, one ancestor at a time, until you reach a node M such that N is in the right subtree of M. (This is a "visual" description of the search; searching for an inorder predecessor of a node is not easily programmed if there are no pointers from nodes to their parents, unless you start at the top of the tree.) Then the datum value in node M is the inorder predecessor of the datum value in N. For example, Lee is the inorder predecessor of Lynn, and Ken is the inorder predecessor of Lee. The notion of *inorder successor* of a datum value x in a binary search tree is similar: it is the smallest of all the datum values larger than x in the tree. For example, Chris is the inorder successor of Beth, and Ken is the inorder successor of Judy.

We are going to analyze functions that perform insertions, deletions, and retrievals of data on binary search trees. Throughout this discussion we assume the definitions of node, datum, and node_ptr given at the beginning of Sect. 5.4, p. 219.

Let's begin with a retrieval function. The function will be given a binary search tree whose root node is pointed to by p. It will also be given an otype value target. The function will be required to return a pointer to a node in our tree containing datum value identical to target, provided there is such a node. If there is no such node, the function must return NULL. Figure 5.34 shows code for such a function. Note that the function is *not* recursive.

In the function location in Fig. 5.34, when the loop ends, either

```
template <class otype>
node_ptr location (node_ptr p, const otype & target)
{
  bool found = false;              // Will be set to true if target is located.

  while ( !found & p )
  {
    if ( target < p->datum )       // Make p point to the left subtree of the
      p = p->left;                 // node that p currently points to.

    else if ( p->datum < target )  // Make p point to the right subtree of the
      p = p->right;                // node that p currently points to.

    else                           // p must be pointing to a node that contains
      found = true;                // a copy of target.
  }

  return p;
}
```

Fig. 5.34 Locating a target in a binary search tree

(1) found is true, in which case the loop stopped with p pointing to a node containing a copy of target; thus we should return p, OR
(2) found is false, in which case the loop stopped because p became NULL. This indicates that target is not in the tree. We can return p.

What are the space and time requirements for this function? Suppose the tree pointed to by p has n nodes. Then the memory requirement is $\Theta(1)$ as $n \to \infty$. For the analysis of execution times, let's assume that the comparison operation between two otype objects requires time bounded by constants. Then for a successful search, the minimum execution time is $\Theta(1)$, which occurs when the target is located at the root of the tree. The maximum execution time is proportional to the height of the tree, which is to say it is $\Omega(\log(n))$ and $O(n)$. Of course, in those cases where we already know the height, call it h, of the tree, then we can say the maximum execution time is $\Theta(h)$. For an unsuccessful search, the minimum execution time is roughly proportional to the level number of the highest empty subtree in the tree, i.e., the empty subtree closest to the root. Assuming the tree is non-empty, we know by Exercise 5.3.9 that this level number can be any integer between 1 and $1 + \lfloor \log(n) \rfloor$. Thus the minimum execution time is $\Omega(1)$ and $O(\log(n))$. The maximum time for an unsuccessful search is roughly proportional to the height of the tree, just like the maximum successful search time.

Since binary trees are defined recursively. and since we saw a number of examples of recursive functions on binary trees when we studied traversals (Sect. 5.4), you might wonder whether it would be appropriate to write the location function recursively. Certainly it is possible to do that, as Fig. 5.35 illustrates, and the code is perhaps more elegant than the code in Fig. 5.34.

```
template <class otype>
node_ptr location (node_ptr p, const otype & target)
{
  if ( !p )                         // base case
    return NULL;

  else if ( target < p->datum )
    return location ( p->left );

  else if ( p->datum < target )
    return location ( p->right );

  else                            // p->datum is identical with target
    return p;
}
```

Fig. 5.35 Recursively locating a target in a binary search tree

Is this recursive version more efficient than the iterative version in Fig. 5.34? The answer is that it is actually less efficient in every way than the iterative version. First, consider the memory requirement for a call to this function. The search proceeds by recursively calling the function at each level down the search path in the tree until the target is found or an empty subtree is reached. Each call puts a new stack frame on the run-time stack, so the maximum amount of memory required will be $\Theta(h)$, where h is the height of the tree. The execution time will have the same big-omega, big-oh, and big-theta sizes as the iterative version of the function, but the hidden constants of proportionality will be larger owing to the fact that each recursive function call requires the manufacture, and later the dismantling, of a stack frame for the call, so the execution time for a call to the recursive function may easily be several times as great as the·execution time for the iterative version of the function.

Each of the recursive calls in Fig. 5.35 is an instance of *tail recursion*, i.e. a recursive call followed immediately by a return. In the function in Fig. 5.35, the value returned by a recursive call is immediately returned to the next level up in the recursion. In any function that contains recursive calls, any instance of tail recursion can removed and replaced by iterative code (i.e., code that does its computation by means of a loop), and the resulting function will be more efficient in its space and time requirements. Illustrations of this can be found in the exercises.

Suppose we want to insert a copy of an otype object x into a binary search tree. The insertion must take place in such a way that the search property of the binary tree is not destroyed. For example, if we insert Helen into the tree shown in Fig. 5.32, she will have to be the left child of Jack. If, instead, we insert Karl, he will have to be the left child of Ken. Ben will go in as the right child of Ann. The code for such a function is given in Fig. 5.36.[2] A recursive alternative version of this function is

---

[2] Dynamic allocation can fail if not enough memory is available. Thus it is good programming practice to test whether the allocation operation succeeded. In our C++ code, however, we suppress almost all error-handling in order to avoid cluttering the code and obscuring the main ideas.

```
template <class otype>
inline void attach (node_ptr & p, const otype & x)
{
  p = new node; // Dynamically allocate a node
  p->datum = x;
  p->left = p->right = NULL;
}
template <class otype>
bool insert (node_ptr & p, const otype & x)
{
  node_ptr q;
  bool attached = false;
  if ( !p )    // if p is NULL
  {
    attach (p, x);
    attached = true;
  }
  else
  {
    q = p;     // Keep p pointed at the root, and let q move down the tree
    while ( !attached && q )
    {
      if ( x < q->datum )
      {
        if ( !q->left )   // if q->left is NULL
        {
          attach (q->left, x);
          attached = true;
        }
        else
          q = q->left;    // Move q into the left subtree.
      }
      else if ( q->datum < x )
      {
        if ( !q->right )    // if q->right is NULL
        {
          attach (q->right, x);
          attached = true;
        }
        else
          q = q->right;
      }
      else             // q is pointing to a node that contains a copy of x; we must
        q = NULL;      // not insert a duplicate datum so stop the while loop.
    }
    return attached;
}
```

Fig. 5.36 Inserting a new object in a binary search tree

shown in Fig. 5.37. Although the recursive version is not as efficient, it can be argued
that its simplicity makes it preferable. The function `attach` called in Fig. 5.37 is
the one in Fig. 5.36.

Both function return `true` if they succeed in inserting x into the tree. If either
function discovers that the tree already contains an object with the same `datum`

```
template <class otype>
bool recursive_insert (node_ptr & p, const otype & x)
{
  if (!p)      // if p is NULL
  {
    attach (p, x);
    return true;
  }

  else if (p->datum < x)
    return recursive_insert(p->right); // Try to insert into the right subtree

  else if (x < p->datum)
    return recursive_insert(p->left);  // Try to insert into the left subtree

  return false;  // We reach this point if and only if x == p->datum,
}                // in which case the insertion must fail.
```

Fig. 5.37 Recursive version of the insertion of a new object in a binary search tree

value as x, then it will not insert a copy of x and it will return the value `false`. The pointer parameter that points to the root of the tree must be a reference parameter in case the tree is empty, for in this case that pointer will be made to point to the node being inserted at root position.

What are the space and time requirements for a call to this function? The space requirement consists of one stack frame and – if the insertion is successful – one node that we dynamically allocate. To analyze the time requirement it is helpful to notice that the insertion algorithm is nearly the same as the retrieval algorithm in Fig. 5.34: we conduct what is essentially a search for a copy of the object x. If we find one, the insertion operation fails because we do not want any duplicate `datum` objects in the tree. If we don't find one, the search arrives at an empty subtree where the object x can properly be inserted. Thus the execution time for an unsuccessful insertion operation is the same as the execution time for a successful search, and the execution time for a successful insertion operation is only $\Theta(1)$ greater than the execution time for an unsuccessful search, provided that the objects of `otype` are of bounded size.

Now suppose we have a file containing some data objects in random order, and suppose we want to read these records into some data structure in a computer program so that individual objects can be accessed reasonably quickly by their keys, so that objects can be deleted from the data structure when they become obsolete, and so that new objects can be inserted into the data structure. Various data structures are possible: ordered arrays, linked lists, hash tables, and binary search trees. If we use a binary search tree, the algorithm for constructing the tree from the file might look like the one shown in Fig. 5.38.

To take some examples, what binary search trees would the algorithm in Fig. 5.38 construct from the following files? In each case, take the listed character strings to be the data objects.

```
// Pseudo-code for constructing a binary search tree from a data file
while unread data remain in the file
{
    read one data object from the file into a temporary variable;
    insert the object into the binary search tree;
    advance to the next unread data object in the data file;
}
```

Fig. 5.38 Constructing a binary search tree

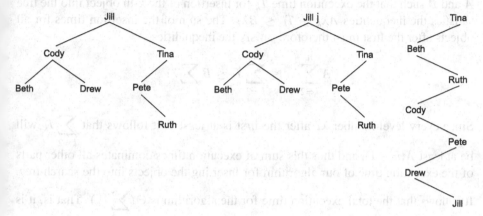

Fig. 5.39 Binary search trees

```
File 1:   Jill, Cody, Tina, Drew, Beth, Pete, Ruth
File 2:   Jill, Tina, Pete, Cody, Beth, Ruth, Drew
File 3:   Tina, Beth, Ruth, Cody, Pete, Drew, Jill
```

The answers are given in Fig. 5.39.

What are the space and time requirements for the tree-building algorithm outlined above?

Suppose we are given a file containing n otype objects. Assume that the objects are all different from each other so that every object in the file can be successfully inserted into the binary search tree. Also assume that the otype objects are of bounded size. Finally, assume that there is sufficient space in the run-time heap to dynamically allocate n new nodes. Then the space requirements will be as follows:

(1) one stack frame for the function that reads the file and inserts all the objects into the tree;
(2) one stack frame to be repeatedly created and destroyed for the n calls to the insert function;
(3) n dynamically allocated nodes, one for each copy of a file object.

Now let's analyze the execution time for a successful construction of the search tree. The total time required to execute the n read operations on the file will be $\Theta(n)$. How much time is required for the n calls to the insert function? The first call inserts the first object in the file into the empty tree at root position. Examination of the code shows that this requires $\Theta(1)$ time. (We assume here that dynamic allocation of a node requires only $\Theta(1)$ time.) Each of the remaining $n - 1$ objects in the file will cause the body of the `while` loop to be executed at least once. In particular, if the k-th object in the file is inserted at level λ_k in the search tree, then the body of the `while` loop will be executed exactly λ_k times. Since the execution time for the body of that `while` loop is easily seen to be $\Theta(1)$, it follows that there are constants A and B such that the execution time T_k for insertion of the k-th object into the tree satisfies the inequalities $A\lambda_k \leq T_k \leq B\lambda_k$. The sum of the insertion times for all objects after the first must therefore satisfy the inequalities

$$A \sum_{k=2}^{n} \lambda_k \leq \sum_{k=2}^{n} T_k \leq B \sum_{k=2}^{n} \lambda_k.$$

Since every level number λ_k after the first is at least 1, it follows that $\sum_{k=2}^{n} T_k$ will be at least $A(n - 1)$, and thus this sum of execution times dominates all other parts of the execution time of our algorithm for inserting the objects into the search tree. It follows that the total execution time for the algorithm is $\Theta(\sum_{k=2}^{n} \lambda_k)$. That is, it is roughly proportional to the sum of the level numbers of all the nodes in the tree that is produced by reading the file and inserting the objects into an initially empty search tree. (We say *all* the nodes, not *all the nodes after the first* because the first node is created at the root position, which has level number 0, which does not affect the sum.)

The sum of all the level numbers of the nodes in any binary tree (search tree or not) makes an appearance now and then in the analysis of tree algorithms, and it has been given the name *internal path length* of the binary tree. To give some examples, the internal path length of the binary tree in Fig. 5.20 on p. 212 is 26 ($= 0 + 1 + 1 + 2 + 2 + 2 + 2 + 3 + 3 + 3 + 3 + 4$), while the internal path length of each of the trees in Fig. 5.21 on p. 213 is 6 ($= 0 + 1 + 2 + 3$). The internal path lengths of the 3 trees in Fig. 30, p. 194, are 9, 7, and 6, and the internal path lengths of the 3 trees in Fig. 5.39, p. 233, are 11, 11, and 21. Our calculations in the preceding paragraph show that the execution time for the algorithm in Fig. 5.38 on p. 233 is big-theta of the internal path length of the resulting search tree. Naturally then we want to know the minimum and maximum possible values of the internal path length as a function of the number n of objects in the file we start with.

The maximum possible internal path length occurs when the tree has degenerated into a linked list, with exactly one node at each level from 0 to $n - 1$. The sum $0 + 1 + 2 + \cdots + (n - 1)$ is $n(n - 1)/2$, which is $\Theta(n^2)$.

The internal path length of a binary tree with n nodes is minimized by making the tree compact, as defined in Exercise 5.3.9. At level 0 there will be 1 node, at level 1 there will be 2 nodes, at level 2 there will be 2^2 nodes, and so on. If we let h denote the height of the perfect part of the tree, then the bottom row of the perfect part has level number h and will contain 2^h nodes. Thus the sum of the level numbers in the perfect part of the tree is

$$0 + 1 \cdot 2 + 2 \cdot 2^2 + 3 \cdot 2^3 + \cdots + h \cdot 2^h.$$

The total number of nodes in the perfect part of the tree is $2^{h+1} - 1$, so the number of nodes in the level below the perfect tree is $n - 2^{h+1} + 1$ (which may be 0), and they are all in level $h + 1$, so the internal path length of a compact tree with n nodes is

$$1 \cdot 2 + 2 \cdot 2^2 + 3 \cdot 2^3 + \cdots + h \cdot 2^h + (h + 1)(n - 2^{h+1} + 1).$$

Factoring 2 out of all terms except the last gives us

$$2 \left[1 + 2 \cdot 2^1 + 3 \cdot 2^2 + \cdots + h \cdot 2^{h-1} \right] + (h + 1)(n - 2^{h+1} + 1). \tag{5.5}$$

By Theorem 2.3.7 the sum in square brackets in (5.5) is

$$1 + h2^{h+1} - (h + 1)2^h = 1 + 2h2^h - h2^h - 2^h = 1 + h2^h - 2^h.$$

Substituting this expression into the square brackets in (5.5) yields

$$2 \left[1 + h2^h - 2^h \right] + (h+1)n - h2^{h+1} - 2^{h+1} + h + 1 = 3 + (h + 1)n - 2^{h+2} + h. \tag{5.6}$$

This is the internal path length of a compact binary tree containing n nodes. Exercise 5.3.9 shows that $h = \lfloor \lg(n + 1) \rfloor - 1$. From this it is not hard to show that the right side of Eq. (5.6) is $\Theta(n \log(n))$. This is the minimum execution time for the algorithm in Fig. 5.38 when processing a file of n distinct objects.

When a binary search tree is constructed using the algorithm in Fig. 5.38, without regard to the order in which the nodes are inserted, then it may or may not turn out to be reasonably well balanced. A well-balanced tree would be one whose height is close to the minimum possible height, which we know is $\lfloor \lg(n) \rfloor$ for a tree with n nodes. If we take no precautions, then the tree can become badly unbalanced, meaning that its height is close to the maximum possible height of $n - 1$.

Various schemes have been proposed for keeping binary search trees well-balanced while performing insertion and deletion operations. One of the best known is the "AVL scheme" [1, 12] named after Adelson-Velsky and Landis, two Russian computer scientists of the 1960s. Examples of alternative types of trees serving the same purpose are the 2–3 trees [14] or the red-black trees [3, 5, 18].

In the AVL scheme a binary search tree is forced at all times to satisfy the property of *height balance*, which is defined as follows:

Definition 5.5.2 A binary tree T is said to be *height balanced* provided that every node in T has the property that its left and right subtrees differ in height by at most 1.

Alternatively, we can define height balance recursively: a binary tree is height balanced if and only if it is empty or else its left and right subtrees are height balanced and differ in height by at most 1.

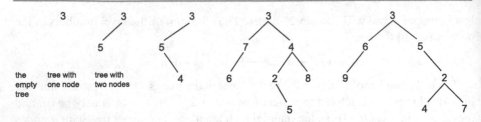

Fig. 5.40 Binary trees

Figure 5.40 shows some examples of binary trees. The first (i.e., the empty tree), second, third, and fifth ones are height balanced. Make sure you understand why. Also think about why the fourth and sixth are not height balanced. (Note: the trees in Fig. 5.40 are not binary *search* trees; the definition of height balance involves only the shape of the tree, not the labels on the nodes.) Notice that when checking a binary tree for height balance we need not check the leaves since both subtrees of a leaf have height -1.

Definition 5.5.3 A binary *search* tree that satisfies the property of height balance is called an *AVL tree*.

Adelson-Velsky and Landis showed that when an insertion or deletion of a node in an AVL tree destroys the property of height balance, the balance can be restored fairly easily by one or more tree rotations, which will not be described here. The interesting question for us is the following: *what are the minimum and maximum possible heights of a height balanced binary tree with n nodes?*

The minimum height will be $\lfloor \lg(n) \rfloor$ when $n \geq 1$ because a tree with n nodes and height $\lfloor \lg(n) \rfloor$ can be constructed in such a way as to fill all the rows except possibly the last, and this gives a height balanced tree. What is the maximum possible height? Let's use $H(n)$ to denote the maximum possible height of a height balanced tree containing n nodes. Then a little thought and trial-and-error show that $H(0) = -1$, $H(1) = 0$, $H(2) = 1$, $H(3) = 1$, $H(4) = 2$, $H(5) = 2$, $H(6) = 2$, $H(7) = 3$ (make the left subtree balanced with 4 nodes and height 2; make the right subtree balanced with 2 nodes and height 1). Then $H(n)$ remains at 3 for $n = 8, 9, 10, 11$. It jumps to 4 at $n = 12$, and stays 4 until n reaches 20.

A more systematic approach is to try to write a recurrence relation. Since the height of a tree with n nodes is equal to 1 plus the maximum of the heights of the left and right subtrees, and since the left and right subtrees in a height balanced tree can differ by at most 1, we can see that

$$H(n) = 1 + \max_{0 \leq i \leq n-1} \{H(i) : i \text{ is an integer such that } H(i) \text{ and } H(n-1-i) \text{ differ by at most 1}\}$$

$$(5.7)$$

which is similar to the recurrence relation (5.3) on p. 214. Unfortunately, this recurrence relation is rather complicated and does not have a form that we know how to solve. In this case it turns out to be useful to "invert the problem": instead of specifying the number n of nodes and asking which heights h are possible for a height balanced tree with n nodes, we can specify a height h and ask which numbers of nodes are possible for a height balanced tree of height h. In particular, we will be interested in the minimum number of nodes that can be used to build a height balanced tree of height h, because we can then turn that around into a relation that gives the maximum possible height for a given number of nodes.

Let $M(h)$ denote the minimum number of nodes that can be used to build a height balanced tree of height h. Then $M(0) = 1$, $M(1) = 2$, $M(2) = 1 + M(1) + M(0)$ (we build a "sparsest" height balanced binary tree of height 2 by making its left subtree a sparse balanced tree of height 1 and its right subtree a sparse balanced tree of height 0). In general we have the recurrence relation

$$M(h) = 1 + M(h-1) + M(h-2) \quad \text{for all } h \geq 2$$

because to build a height balanced binary tree of height h using as few nodes as possible we must have one of its subtrees be a height balanced binary tree of height $h-1$ containing as few nodes as possible, and then the other subtree is allowed to have height $h-2$, but it must also be height balanced and have as few nodes as possible.

This recurrence relation is second order linear, with constant coefficients. It is non-homogeneous, but the non-homogeneous term is a polynomial of degree 0. Solving the relation with the initial data $M(0) = 1$ and $M(1) = 2$ gives the formula

$$M(h) = \left(\frac{5+2\sqrt{5}}{5}\right)\left(\frac{1+\sqrt{5}}{2}\right)^h + \left(\frac{5-2\sqrt{5}}{5}\right)\left(\frac{1-\sqrt{5}}{2}\right)^h - 1 \quad \text{for all } h \geq 0.$$

Since $M(h)$ denotes the minimum number of nodes that can be in a height balanced tree of height h, it follows that in any height balanced binary tree with n nodes and height h, we have the inequality

$$n \geq \left(\frac{5+2\sqrt{5}}{5}\right)\left(\frac{1+\sqrt{5}}{2}\right)^h + \left(\frac{5-2\sqrt{5}}{5}\right)\left(\frac{1-\sqrt{5}}{2}\right)^h - 1 \quad \text{for all } h \geq 0.$$

Since $\dfrac{1-\sqrt{5}}{2}$ is a negative number whose absolute value is approximately 0.6180 (i.e., less than 1), the term $\left(\dfrac{5-2\sqrt{5}}{5}\right)\left(\dfrac{1-\sqrt{5}}{2}\right)^h$ oscillates between positive and negative values and "spirals" inward toward 0 as h grows toward infinity. More precisely, when plotted on a number line the values of this term look approximately like this:

(h = 1)	(h = 3)		(h = 2)	(h = 0)
−0.082	−0.031	0	0.050	0.132

We can definitely say that all these values are greater than -0.1, so

$$n \geq \left(\frac{5 + 2\sqrt{5}}{5}\right)\left(\frac{1 + \sqrt{5}}{2}\right)^h - 0.1 - 1 \quad \text{for all } h \geq 0,$$

and thus

$$n + 1.1 \geq \left(\frac{5 + 2\sqrt{5}}{5}\right)\left(\frac{1 + \sqrt{5}}{2}\right)^h \quad \text{for all } h \geq 0.$$

Taking logarithms yields

$$\lg(n + 1.1) \geq \lg\left(\frac{5 + 2\sqrt{5}}{5}\right) + h \lg\left(\frac{1 + \sqrt{5}}{2}\right) \quad \text{for all } h \geq 0,$$

which can be turned around to read

$$\lg\left(\frac{5 + 2\sqrt{5}}{5}\right) + h \lg\left(\frac{1 + \sqrt{5}}{2}\right) \leq \lg(n + 1.1) \quad \text{for all } h \geq 0.$$

Solving for h gives

$$h \leq \frac{\lg(n + 1.1)}{\lg\left(\frac{1+\sqrt{5}}{2}\right)} - \frac{\lg\left(\frac{5+2\sqrt{5}}{5}\right)}{\lg\left(\frac{1+\sqrt{5}}{2}\right)} \approx 1.44 \lg(n + 1.1) - 1.33 < 1.44 \lg(n) \quad \text{for all } n \geq 2$$

(for that last strict inequality, see Exercise 5.5.16).

The derivation above shows that the heights of height balanced binary trees are $O(\log(n))$, where n is the number of nodes. Earlier we established that for any binary tree (height balanced or not), $h \geq \lfloor \lg(n) \rfloor$. These inequalities prove that the heights of height balanced binary trees (and thus of AVL trees) are $\Theta(\log(n))$. What this means in terms of operations on AVL trees is that a search for a specified key can be carried out in time at most proportional to $\log(n)$, where n is the number of nodes in the tree. This is what makes AVL trees an important data structure for storage of large amounts of data in a computer program.

5.5.1   Exercises

5.5.4 In a binary search tree, if a datum value s is the inorder predecessor of a `datum` value t, then what is t to s?

5.5.5 In the first binary search tree in Fig. 5.39, p. 233, which name is the inorder predecessor of Jill? Of Tina? Which name is the inorder successor of Jill? Of Drew? Of Tina? Answer the same questions about the third binary search tree in Fig. 5.39.

5.5.6 Write a non-recursive C++ function that locates the inorder predecessor of a datum value x in a binary search tree pointed to by a pointer p. Refer to the discussion of the inorder predecessor on p. 228. The prototype for the function should be as follows:

```
void predecessor (node_ptr p, const otype & x,
node_ptr & q, bool & x_present);
```

The function should search down the tree for x, keeping track of what may turn out to be its predecessor. If x is not present in the tree, then the value parameter x_present should be set to false, and the value parameter q should be set to NULL. If x is present, then x_present should be set to true and q should be set to a pointer to the node containing the predecessor of x—provided there is a predecessor. If not, q should be set to NULL.

5.5.7 Suppose we want to delete a specified datum value x from a binary search tree. This operation turns out to be somewhat more complicated than inserting a new datum value into the tree. We first make a search for x, which is easy. Once we find it, however, the removal process must modify the tree in such a way that the binary search property is preserved. This is not hard if the node containing x is a leaf or has one empty subtree. A leaf can simply be deallocated, after which we set to NULL the pointer that pointed to the leaf. If the node containing x has one empty subtree, we store in a temporary location a pointer to the other (non-empty) subtree, deallocate the node containing x, and then attach the subtree to the parent of x. For example, if we want to delete Ken from the tree in Fig. 5.32, p. 227, we save the pointer to Sandy, deallocate the Ken node, and then set the right pointer of Judy so it points to Sandy. But what if the node containing x has two non-empty subtrees? For example, suppose we want to delete Sandy from the tree in Fig. 5.32. If we save copies of the pointers to the left and right subtrees of the node containing Sandy and then deallocate that node, we are stuck with two subtrees and no obvious way to re-attach them to the search tree. In this case, we use a different strategy: we replace the value x with its inorder predecessor or inorder successor, and then remove the lower node that contains the inorder predecessor or inorder successor. Returning to our example, if we want to delete Sandy from the tree in Fig. 5.32, we can overwrite Sandy with Lynn (the inorder predecessor of Sandy) and then delete the Lynn node below Lee. This is easy because the Lynn node below Lee is a leaf. After the operation is complete, Lynn has become the parent of Lee and Tom, each of which is now a leaf. Alternatively, we could overwrite Sandy with Tom (the inorder successor of Sandy), and then delete the lower Tom node.

(a) Write a *non-recursive* C++ function to delete a node with a specified datum value from a binary search tree. The prototype for the function should be
```
bool remove (node_ptr & p, const otype & x);
```
where p is a pointer to the tree and x is the datum value to be deleted.
(b) Write a *recursive* C++ function with the same prototype. You should be able to make the code somewhat shorter and more elegant than the code you wrote for part (a).

```
void print_in_preorder (node_ptr p)
{
  while ( p )      // while p is not NULL
  {
    cout << p->datum << endl;
    print_in_preorder (p->left);
    p = p->right;
  }
}
```

Fig. 5.41 Tail recursion removed

(c) Compare the efficiency of the functions you wrote in parts (a) and (b).

5.5.8 The `print_in_preorder` function in Fig. 5.27, p. 220, is recursive. The second recursive call (`print_in_preorder(p->right);`) is an instance of tail recursion because completion of that call is followed immediately by a return from the `print_in_preorder` function. The first recursive call (`print_in_preorder(p->left);`) is *not* an instance of tail recursion because something more occurs in the `print_in_preorder` function after the completion of that first call. Figure 5.41 shows how the tail recursion can be removed by using iteration (in this case a `while` loop). If the `print_in_preorder` function is called on a pointer to the tree in Fig. 5.32, then 22 recursive calls will be made as a result, one for each pointer within the tree (it will be called on each NULL pointer as well as on each non-NULL pointer). Suppose the function in Fig. 5.41 is called on the same tree. How many recursive calls will be made?

5.5.9 Is the recursive function call in Fig. 5.6, p. 183, an instance of tail recursion?

5.5.10 (a) Is there an instance of tail recursion in the `destroy` function of Exercise 5.4.1 (a) on p. 225 If so, show how the tail recursion can be removed and replaced by iteration.

(b) Is there an instance of tail recursion in the `number_of_leaves` function of Exercise 5.4.1 (b) on p. 225 If so, show how the tail recursion can be removed and replaced by iteration.

(c) Is there an instance of tail recursion in the `reverse` function of Exercise 5.4.1 (c) on p. 225 If so, show how the tail recursion can be removed and replaced by iteration.

(d) Is there an instance of tail recursion in the `test_perfect_and_height` function of Exercise 5.4.1 (e)? If so, show how the tail recursion can be removed and replaced by iteration.

(e) Is there an instance of tail recursion in the `location` function of Exercise 5.4.1 (d)? If so, show how the tail recursion can be removed and replaced by iteration.

5.5.11 Theorem 5.2.4 on p. 210 makes it tempting to write a recursive function to implement Euclid's algorithm for computing the greatest common divisor of two

```
      int g_c_d (int m, int n)  // m and n are assumed to be positive
      {
        int dividend = larger (m, n);   // code not shown for "larger"
        int divisor  = smaller (m, n);  // code not shown for "smaller"
        int remainder = dividend % divisor;

        if ( remainder == 0 )
          return divisor;
        else
          return g_c_d (remainder, divisor);
      }
```

Fig. 5.42 Euclid's algorithm for the greatest common divisor

positive integers. Such a function is shown in Fig. 5.42. Compare the efficiency of
this function with the efficiency of the one in Fig. 5.19, p. 206.

5.5.12 Compute the internal path length of the binary tree in Fig. 5.32 on p. 227.

5.5.13 Draw a binary tree with 7 nodes and internal path length 13. (There is more
than one correct solution.) Draw a binary tree with internal path length 1. Can you
draw one with internal path length 2? Can you draw one with internal path length 3?
And so on, at least up to 7.

5.5.14 Suppose binary tree T_1 contains n_1 nodes and has internal path length L_1,
while binary tree T_2 contains n_2 nodes and has internal path length L_2. Let's construct
a larger binary tree, call it T, by creating a root node and then making T_1 the left
subtree of T and T_2 the right subtree of T. Write an expression in terms of n_1, n_2,
L_1, and L_2, for the internal path length of the new tree T.

5.5.15 Suppose the definition of **height balance** for a binary tree is "relaxed" as
follows: a binary tree will now be called "nearly height balanced" if and only if for
each node N in the tree, the left and right subtrees of N differ in height by at most 2.
Let $M(h)$ denote the minimum number of nodes that can be used to build a nearly
height balanced binary tree. What are the values of $M(0)$, $M(1)$, $M(2)$, and $M(3)$?
Write a recurrence relation for $M(h)$ that's valid for all $h \geq 2$. DO NOT ATTEMPT
TO SOLVE IT.

5.5.16 Recall what happens when an attempt is made to insert a new object into
a binary search tree (code is given in Fig. 5.36 on p. 231). First a search is made
(recursively in Fig. 5.36) to determine whether and where the object can be inserted;
in the successful case, a new node is created and attached at a point where there was
an empty subtree. The execution time for such an insertion is roughly proportional
to the level number of the empty tree at which the newly inserted node is attached. In
the search tree in Fig. 5.32 on p. 227, insertion of string Kara would occur at level
2 (just to the left of Ken), while insertion of the string Moe would occur at level 5

(just to the right of Lynn). (Keep in mind that the level number of the root is 0, and level numbers increase as you go down the tree.)

When the search tree is height balanced (i.e., is an AVL tree), then the maximum height is $\Theta(\log(n))$, and thus the maximum execution time for an insertion is $\Theta(\log(n))$. What is the minimum execution time for a successful insertion into an AVL tree? The *minimum* time will be roughly proportional to the smallest level number of an *empty* subtree in the tree (see Exercise 5.3.10, p. 218 for the level number of an empty subtree). In the rest of this exercise, let's work on the problem of finding the smallest possible level number of an empty subtree in a *height balanced* tree (such as an AVL tree).

(a) What is the smallest possible level number of an empty subtree in a binary tree with only one node? (All such trees are height balanced.)
(b) What is the smallest possible level number of an empty subtree in a binary tree with exactly two nodes? (All such trees are height balanced.)
(c) What is the smallest possible level number of an empty subtree in a height balanced binary tree that contains exactly three nodes? *Hint:* look at various binary trees with three nodes and see which, if any, are height balanced.
(d) What is the smallest possible level number of an empty subtree in a height balanced binary tree that contains exactly four nodes?
(e) Let $L(n)$ denote the smallest possible level number of an empty subtree in a height balanced tree containing n nodes. Derive a good lower bound expression for $L(n)$. *Hint:* Although it is possible to write a recurrence relation for $L(n)$, the relation will not be one that we know how to solve. In this case, you might consider solving the inverted problem. That is, for a given level number λ, find the largest possible number of nodes in a height balanced binary tree in which the smallest level number of an empty subtree is λ. Introduce a symbol such as $M(\lambda)$ for this maximum number of nodes. You may want to begin by looking at special cases such as $M(1)$, $M(2)$, $M(3)$, which may help you figure out how to write a recurrence relation. This will not be a trivial recurrence relation to write down. You may find it helpful to review the table in Sect. 5.3 where a formula is given for the maximum number of nodes in a binary tree of height h.

5.5.17 A binary tree T is said to be **weight-balanced** if and only if for each node x in T, the following condition is met: the number of empty subtrees in the left subtree of x is at most twice the number in the right subtree of x, and vice versa (i.e., the number of empty subtrees in the right subtree of x is at most twice the number in the left subtree of x). To put it in another (equivalent) way, for each node x in T, the number of empty subtrees in the right subtree of x is at least half the number in the left subtree of x, and vice versa. Find an upper bound for the maximum possible height of a weight-balanced binary tree with n nodes. Keep in mind that the number of empty subtrees in a tree with k nodes is $k + 1$. *Hint:* while it is possible to derive a recurrence relation for the function $H(n)$ that denotes the maximum possible height of a weight-balanced tree with n nodes, the recurrence relation is somewhat complicated and does not have a familiar form. So you should "invert the problem" as we did on p. 236 for height-balanced binary trees.

5.5.18 Prove that $1.44 \lg(n + 1.1) - 1.33 < 1.44 \lg(n)$ for all integers $n \geq 2$.

Hint: $n + 1.1 = n \left(1 + \dfrac{1.1}{n}\right)$, so $\lg(n+1.1) = \lg(n) + \lg\left(1 + \dfrac{1.1}{n}\right)$. When $n \geq 2$, $\left(1 + \dfrac{1.1}{n}\right) \leq ?$ You may use a calculator.

5.5.19 On p. 235 it is asserted that the expression $3 + (h+1)n - 2^{h+2} + h$, in which $h = \lfloor \lg(n+1) \rfloor$, is $\Theta(n \log(n))$. Verify this assertion. For part of this exercise it can be helpful to note that $\lg(n) < \lg(n + 1) \leq \lg(n + n) = \lg(2n) = 1 + \lg(n)$.

5.6 Priority Queues and Binary Heaps

Let's start by defining the concept of a *priority queue*, which can be thought of as an ADT (abstract data type).[3] Each of the objects to be placed in a priority queue, call it PQ, must have some priority value associated with it. The priority values must be of some data type such as integers, real numbers, character strings, etc., on which an ordering is defined, so that we can talk about smaller and larger priority values. Objects can be inserted into PQ in any order, but when a "dequeue" operation is performed on PQ, the object that's removed from PQ is one with "highest" priority among the objects in PQ. (This means that a "priority queue" behaves quite differently from an ordinary "queue", which is a simple First-In-First-Out data storage structure.) The word "highest" here requires some interpretation. The object(s) with highest priority may be those with the smallest priority value (consistent with common usage, where we refer to tasks of "first priority", "second priority", and so on), or they may be those with the largest priority value. A *min-queue* is a priority queue in which objects with the smallest priority values are considered to have the highest priority; a *max-queue* is one in which larger priority values have higher priority.

There are various ways to implement a priority queue. The most common method uses the notion of a *binary heap*, by which we mean a (logical) binary tree, with high priority items at the top of the tree; more precisely, each node of the tree has priority at least as high as all of its descendants. An additional requirement for a heap is that all levels of the binary tree must be completely filled, except possibly the last, and the nodes at that level must be pushed to the left as far as possible. A binary tree having the property stated in the preceding sentence are said to be a *complete binary tree*

---

[3] An Abstract Data Type (ADT) is a set of objects together with a set of operations, both of which are mathematical abstractions. In the definition of an ADT, there is no mention of how the operations are implemented.

(see Exercise 5.3.8 on p. 218). A **min-heap** is a binary heap in which the smallest priority numbers are at the top of the tree, with larger priority numbers below them. The tree on the left in Fig. 5.43 below is a min-heap. A **max-heap** is one in which the larger priority numbers are at the top. The tree on the right in Fig. 5.43 below is a max-heap.

It is a delightful fact that a complete binary tree can be stored in an array in such a way that the parent-child relationships of the objects in the cells can be deduced from the positions of the objects in the array. For example, the two binary heaps shown in Fig. 5.43 can be implemented as follows:

0	1	2	3	4	5	6	7	8	9
3	7	12	20	9	15	18	21	26	17

0	1	2	3	4	5	6	7	8	9	10	11	12
44	26	15	25	10	6	11	22	24	1	8	2	5

The parent-child relationship is as follows: for a node at location k in the array, the children of that node are at locations $2k + 1$ and $2k + 2$, provided that node has children. Equivalently, for a node at location m in the array, the parent of that node is at location $\lfloor (m - 1)/2 \rfloor$, except, of course, for $m = 0$. Note that the subscripts on the arrays must always start at 1 to make this system work.

When a program has constructed a priority queue using some implementation (such as the binary heaps that we have just described), there are just two operations that can be performed on the priority queue:

(1) insertion of a new object (with its associated priority number) into the priority queue;
(2) deletion of an object from the priority queue; as mentioned in the definition, this deletion operation always removes and returns an object with highest priority in the queue at the moment when the operation was called; for a max-queue, this means that deletion returns an object in the max-queue with largest priority value; for a min-queue, this means that deletion returns the object in the min-queue with smallest priority value. (Note: we don't say "the object with highest priority" because a priority queue can contain objects with the same priority.)

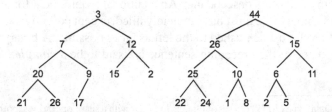

Fig. 5.43 A min-heap (*left*) and a max-heap (*right*)

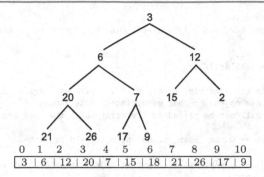

Fig. 5.44 Logical view of the min-heap and its array implementation

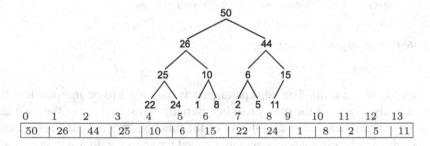

Fig. 5.45 The max-heap in Fig. 5.43 right after insertion of 50

Let's see how the operations of insertion and deletion are carried out when the priority queue is implemented as a binary heap. To take an example, suppose an object with priority value 6 is to be inserted in the min-heap shown in Fig. 5.43 (the "logical" view of the heap shows the tree with root 3; the actual physical implementation is the array with a 3 in cell 0). The simplest way known to carry out the insertion is to insert the new object (priority value 6) at the bottom of the tree (as the right child of node 9 in the tree diagram; this corresponds to cell 10 in the array), and then let it "percolate up the tree" to an appropriate position. When 6 is inserted below 9 in the min-heap, this violates the heap condition, so we swap the 9 with the 6 (swap the contents of cell 4 with cell 10). The 6 has percolated up one level. The min-heap property is still violated because 6 is less than its new parent 7, so we let 6 percolate up one more level by swapping it with 7. Now 6 is greater than its parent, so the binary tree has once again become a min-heap, as shown in Fig. 5.44.

Similarly, suppose we insert an object with priority number 50 into the max-heap shown in Fig. 5.43. First it would be made the left child of 11 (i.e., it would be placed in cell 13), but then the 50 would percolate up the tree, swapping places with the 11, then with the 15, then with the 44. These steps would restore the max-heap property of the tree, giving us the structure shown in Fig. 5.45.

Figure 5.46 shows some code for the insertion algorithm just described. The first parameter is the array that's being used to hold the binary heap, which is here assumed to be a max-heap. The second parameter is the number of data objects that

```
template <class otype>
void insert_into_max_heap (otype heap[], int & n, const otype & x)
{
  int child  = ++n,                    // Increment n by 1.
      parent = (child-1)/2;

  // "child" is the subscript of the cell in which we imagine
  // that the new object  x  has been placed (even though it
  // actually will not be placed in the array until the last moment)

  while (parent >= 0 && heap[parent].priority < x.priority)
  {
    heap[child] = heap[parent]; // parent object falls one level in the heap
    child = parent;
    parent = (parent-1)/2;
  }
  heap[child] = x;  // Copy the new object into the heap
}
```

Fig. 5.46 Insert an object into a max-heap

are currently in the heap. The third parameter is the object to be inserted into the heap (actually, a copy of the object will be inserted). For simplicity of the code and since our concern here is the complexity of the function, we make the assumption that the `otype` class has a public member called `priority`. In a standard object oriented implementation, this attribute would be declared as private and accessible through getter and setter functions.

Although the algorithm was described as if the new object is copied to the end of the array and then swapped with other objects as it percolates up, it is more efficient to hold the new object outside the tree and let the objects that it displaces fall to their new levels until the appropriate level for the new object is reached.

What are the space and time requirements of this function? The space requirement is trivial: one stack frame containing five numbers (in addition to the return address). The execution time, as in many earlier examples similar to this one, is big-theta of the number of times the body of the loop is executed, provided each individual priority comparison and object assignment only requires $\Theta(1)$ time. How many times is the body of the loop executed for a given value of n (the number of objects in the priority queue)? The answer depends on how far up the tree the object being inserted will percolate. The minimum number is zero, so the minimum execution time for a call to this function is $\Theta(1)$ as $n \to \infty$. The maximum number of times the body of the loop can be executed is exactly the same as the height of the tree *after* the new object has been (logically) inserted. This height is $\lfloor \lg(n + 1) \rfloor$. Thus the maximum execution time for an insertion operation is $\Theta(\log(n))$.

Now let's look at how the deletion operation can be performed on a priority queue implemented as a binary heap. First note that the object to be deleted (and returned) is precisely the root of the binary heap, i.e., the object in cell 0 of the array. Thus there is no need to search for the object to be deleted: it is immediately accessible. However, when we delete it, we have decapitated our logical binary tree, which must be re-formed into a binary heap. The best known way to do this is to remove the last object in the array, place it in the root position temporarily, and then (because it is likely to be out of place), let it "sift down" through the tree to an appropriate position.

To take an example, suppose we perform a delete on the max-heap shown in Fig. 5.43 (right) on p. 244. We begin by removing the object with highest priority 44, and replacing it with the object with priority 5, which is the "last" object in the heap. Now we let the 5 sift down the tree. The two children of 5 are 26 and 15. The 26 has higher priority than both 5 and 15, so it belongs above both of them. We swap 5 with 26. Continuing the sift-down operation, we note that the children of 5 are now 25 and 10. The 25 has higher priority than both 5 and 10, so we swap 5 with 25. Now the children of 5 are 22 and 24. Since 24 has higher priority than both 5 and 22, we swap 5 with 24. Now the 5 cannot fall any farther, so the sift-down operation is complete. The 44 we removed from the heap can be returned as the value of the deletion operation. The max-heap after the removal of 44 is shown in Fig. 5.47.

The sift-down operation does not always take an object all the way to the bottom of a heap. In the example in the preceding paragraph, if instead of 22 and 24 in the max heap in Fig. 5.45 the priorities had been 2 and 4, then when the object with priority 5 reached the level where it was the parent of 2 and 4, the sift-down operation would have halted.

Figure 5.48 on p. 248 shows some code to implement the deletion algorithm on a max-heap. It consists of two functions. The primary function moves the highest-priority object into a temporary location outside the array, copies the last (i.e., right-most) object into the root position, adjusts the size (number of objects) of the max-heap, and then calls a helper function to carry out a sift-down of the object at root position. Although the sift-down part of the algorithm was described in the preceding paragraph in terms of a sequence of object swaps, it is more efficient to hold the object being sifted down the tree in a temporary location and let higher priority "children" rise to their new positions until the appropriate level for the sift-down object is found.

When the delete_from_max_heap function is called on an array holding a max-heap consisting of n objects, the space requirements consist of one stack frame for the call to that function and one additional stack frame for the embedded call to the sift_down_in_max_heap function. Each of these frames has size $\Theta(1)$ as $n \to \infty$, so the total space requirement is $\Theta(1)$. The analysis of the time requirement

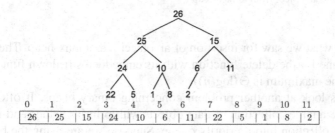

Fig. 5.47 The tree in Fig. 5.45 after deleting 44

```
template <class otype>
otype delete_from_max_heap (otype heap[], int & n)      // Assumes n >= 1.
{
  otype temp = heap[1];   // Hold highest priority object for the return.

  heap[1] = heap[n];      // Bring last object to root position.

  --n;                    // The heap will have lost one object.

  if ( n > 1 )
     sift_down_in_max_heap (heap, 0, n);
     // The argument 1 in this function call is the subscript of the cell
     // containing the object to be sifted down in the logical tree.

  return temp;
}

// The following function causes the object in cell k of the heap array to be
// sifted down to an appropriate level in the logical subtree rooted at cell k.
template <class otype>
void sift_down_in_max_heap (otype heap[], int k, int n)  // Assumes n >= 2.
{
  otype temp = heap[k];      // Make a copy of the object to be sifted down, so
                             // that a child of heap[k] can be moved into cell k.
  int parent = k;
  int child  = 2 * parent+1; // This is the subscript of the left child of heap[k].

  while ( child < n )        // This loop performs the sift-down operation.
  {
    if ( child + 1 < n &&
         heap[child].priority < heap[child+1].priority )
       ++child;

    if ( temp.priority < heap[child].priority )
    {
      heap[parent] = heap[child]; // Highest priority child rises a level.
      parent = child;
      child = 2 * parent+1;
    }
    else                     // The sift-down operation must be halted.
    {
      heap[parent] = temp;   // Insert the sifted-down object.
      n = 0;                 // Use an artificial way to terminate the loop.
    }
  }
}
```

Fig. 5.48 Delete an object from a max-heap

is similar to what we saw for insertion of an object into a max-heap. The minimum execution time for the delete function with its embedded sift-down function call is $\Theta(1)$, and the maximum is $\Theta(\log(n))$.

Now let's look at another problem concerning binary heaps. It often happens that we have a large collection of data objects with priority values and we need to convert the collection into a priority queue. Suppose we are using the binary heap implementation of a priority queue. How should the collection of objects (presumably in random order) be turned into a binary heap?

One method presents itself immediately. Create an array large enough to hold all n objects, and then call the insertion function on each separate object in the given collection. In the best case, each separate insertion will take only $\Theta(1)$ time, so the minimum execution time will be $\Theta(n)$. In the worst case, the insertion of the k-th object ($k = 1, 2, 3, \ldots, n$) requires time roughly proportional to $\log(k)$, so by Theorem 5.1.10 on p. 186, the maximum execution time for this simple algorithm of creating a heap of n objects will be

$$\Theta\left(\sum_{k=1}^{n} \log(k) \right) = \Theta(n \, \log(n)) \quad \text{(see Example 3.2.7, p. 75)}.$$

Can we do better? As it turns out, we can, although that is not obvious at this point. First let's review the algorithm we have just described. After k of the objects have been inserted, forming a tree of k nodes, the next object is inserted at the bottom of the heap and then allowed to percolate up. In the worst case, this takes $\lfloor \lg(k + 1) \rfloor$ steps, and since the overwhelming majority of the nodes in a complete binary tree are in the last few levels, most of the newly inserted nodes can end up rising through most of the levels of the final tree. Let's consider whether there might be some way of having the nodes *sift down* as they are inserted into the tree instead of percolating up, because then most nodes, even in the worst case, will fall only a few levels.

Suppose we begin by placing the n objects of the given collection into an array heap[0...n-1] in which a binary heap will gradually be formed. Now consider the objects that are in the positions that will be occupied by the leaves of the heap (when it has been constructed). The leaves make up the right half of the array (approximately), and we can consider each leaf to be a separate little binary heap of size 1 (height 0). Next, consider the parents of the leaves. These parents make up approximately one-fourth of the objects in the array. If a parent turns out to have lower priority than one or both of its children, then we can swap the parent with the child of highest priority. Now we have created a collection of separate little binary heaps of size 3 (or, in the case of the last node in the tree, of size 2). Each of these little heaps has height 1, so these parents can fall at most one level. Next, we consider the grandparents of the leaves and let them sift down the little trees of size 7 (or smaller). These trees are of height 2, so the grandparents can fall at most two levels. These grandparents make up approximately one-eighth of the nodes in the array, so already we have considered about 7/8 of the cells in the array. Continue this process until reaching the root node, which is just one node, and it can possibly sift down as many as $\lfloor \lg(n) \rfloor$ levels.

The algorithm for "heapifying" an existing array of objects with priority numbers is shown in Fig. 5.49. The assumption is that we will form the array into a max-heap. Code for a min-heap is similar.

Let's analyze the space and time requirements for this "heapifying" function. The space required is just two stack frames with a few numerical values stored. Thus the space requirement is independent of the size n of the array to be heapified.

```
template <class otype>
void form_max_heap (otype a[], int n)
{
    // As we work our way from right to left in a[0..n-1], thinking of
    // the nodes as forming a binary tree, we first reach a parent
    // node (i.e., a non-leaf) at cell number  (n-1)/2  (the floor of
    // the real number obtained by dividing n-1 by  2 ).

    int k;
    for (k = (n-1)/2; k >= 0; --k)
        sift_down_in_max_heap (a, k, n);
}
```

Fig. 5.49 Forming a max-heap in an unordered array of size n

Now consider the amount of time required. The best case occurs when the objects in the array already form a max-heap. In that case, each time the body of the loop is executed, the call to the sift-down function will require only constant time because no object will have to moved from its current position. The loop above has an index that runs from $\lfloor (n-1)/2 \rfloor$ back to 0, so the amount of time required in the best case is $\Theta(n)$. That is, the minimum execution time is $\Theta(n)$, where n is the size of the collection we started with.

What about the worst case? What is the maximum possible execution time for this "heapifying" function? The maximum execution time occurs when each call to the sift-down function requires as much time as possible. The maximum execution time for the sift-down function occurs when it makes as many object moves as possible, and the time it requires is approximately proportional to that maximum number of downward object moves. Thus the total execution time for the heapification function shown above is essentially proportional to the total number of downward object moves that occur during the entire heapification process.

What is the maximum number of downward object moves that can be made by an object that starts in location k in a heap of size n? We know that the whole tree has a height of $\lfloor \lg(n) \rfloor$ because it's a complete tree. By the same reasoning, a node of index k is on level $\lfloor \lg(k+1) \rfloor$ in the tree. The maximum number of movements is given by the difference between the height of the tree and the level number for the node k, which gives $\lfloor \lg(n) \rfloor - \lfloor \lg(k+1) \rfloor$. Using the fact that $\lfloor \lg(n) \rfloor \le \lg(n)$, we can show that $\lfloor \lg(n) \rfloor - \lfloor \lg(k+1) \rfloor \le \left\lfloor \lg\left(\dfrac{n}{k+1}\right) \right\rfloor$. Now let's sum over all the different values of k. The result is

$$\sum_{k=0}^{\lfloor (n-1)/2 \rfloor} \left\lfloor \lg\left(\frac{n}{k+1}\right) \right\rfloor = \sum_{j=1}^{\lfloor (n+1)/2 \rfloor} \left\lfloor \lg\left(\frac{n}{j}\right) \right\rfloor.$$

This sum represents the total number of downward object moves that can occur during heapification, and as we noted above, the maximum execution time for heapification will be big-theta of this number. Note that the sum above is a function of n only, not of the summation index k. Let's find the best possible upper bound approximation for the sum above.

$$\sum_{j=1}^{\lfloor(n+1)/2\rfloor} \lfloor\lg(n/j)\rfloor \leq \sum_{j=1}^{\lfloor(n+1)/2\rfloor} \lg(n/j) \qquad \text{by Theorem 2.1.4 (a),}$$

$$= \sum_{j=1}^{\lfloor(n+1)/2\rfloor} \left[\lg(n) - \lg(j)\right] \qquad \text{because } \log(a/b) = \log(a) - \log(b)$$

$$= \lfloor(n+1)/2\rfloor \lg(n) - \lg(\lfloor(n+1)/2\rfloor!) \qquad \text{see Theorem 2.3.2 on p. 32; also, } \sum_{j=1}^{m} \lg(j) = \lg(m!)$$

$$= \lfloor(n+1)/2\rfloor \lg(n) - C \ln(\lfloor(n+1)/2\rfloor!) \qquad \text{the constant } C \text{ converts from ln to lg}$$

$$< \lfloor(n+1)/2\rfloor \lg(n) - C \left[\lfloor(n+1)/2\rfloor \ln(\lfloor(n+1)/2\rfloor) - \lfloor(n+1)/2\rfloor + 1\right] \qquad \text{by Theorem 2.4.3, p. 54}$$

$$= \lfloor(n+1)/2\rfloor \lg(n) - \lfloor(n+1)/2\rfloor \lg(\lfloor(n+1)/2\rfloor) + C\lfloor(n+1)/2\rfloor + C$$

$$= \lfloor(n+1)/2\rfloor \lg\left(\frac{n}{\lfloor(n+1)/2\rfloor}\right) + C\lfloor(n+1)/2\rfloor + C$$

The fraction $\dfrac{n}{\lfloor(n+1)/2\rfloor}$ is approximately 2 when n is large. Certainly it is less than 3 for all large n (see Exercise 5.6.2). Thus the computations above show that

$$\sum_{j=1}^{\lfloor(n+1)/2\rfloor} \lfloor\lg(n/j)\rfloor \leq (\lg(3) + C)\lfloor(n+1)/2\rfloor + C = O(n).$$

It follows that the execution time for our "heapify" algorithm acting on an array of n objects is $O(n)$. We noted earlier that the minimum execution time is $\Theta(n)$, so now we can conclude that the execution time is always $\Theta(n)$.

5.6.1 Exercises

5.6.1 There is a well-known sorting algorithm that speeds up Selection Sort by exploiting the idea of a binary max-heap. (You may want to review Selection Sort in Example 5.1.11, p. 189.) The algorithm is known as **Heap Sort**. It works as follows. Suppose we are given an array a[0...n-1] of objects to be sorted. Assume that the objects can be compared directly using the < and > operators, so that there is no difference between an object and the priority of an object.

1. Call the form_max_heap function (Fig. 5.49 on p. 250) on the array; this rearranges the objects in the array so that they form a binary max-heap.
2. Swap the object in cell a[0], with the object in cell a[n-1]; this places the largest object in the cell where it belongs (at the right end of the array), so we need not consider it further.

3. Decrement n by 1.
4. Let the object in cell a[0] sift down in the shortened array a[0..n-1] (with n now smaller by 1); this restores the heap property of a[0..n-1].
5. Repeat steps (2), (3), and (4) until the array to be sorted is reduced to a single cell.

Here is the C++ version of Heap Sort:

```
template <class otype>
void heap_sort (otype a[], int n)    // Sorts a[0..n-1].
{
  form_max_heap (a, n);

  while (n > 0)
  {
    swap(a[0], a[n-1]);
    --n;
    sift_down_in_max_heap(a, 0, n-1);
  }
}
```

(a) Analyze the space and time requirements of Heap Sort on an array of n objects. As usual, assume that the "otype" objects are such that comparing two such objects or copying such an object from one place to another requires only $\Theta(1)$ time. This means that any assignment and any swap operation with these objects will require only $\Theta(1)$ time.

(b) A sorting algorithm is said to be an in-place sorting algorithm if it uses only $\Theta(1)$ extra memory space to carry out its work. Bubble Sort, Selection Sort, and Linear Insertion Sort are examples of in-place sorting algorithms that we have already seen in this textbook. Is Heap Sort an in-place sorting algorithm?

5.6.2 Show that for all integers $n \geq 2$, the fraction $\dfrac{n}{\lfloor (n+1)/2 \rfloor}$ is ≤ 3. Separate the proof into two cases:

(a) when n is even, $\lfloor (n+1)/2 \rfloor = n/2$, and thus $\dfrac{n}{\lfloor n/2 \rfloor} = \boxed{?}$;

(b) when n is odd, $\lfloor (n+1)/2 \rfloor = (n+1)/2$, and thus $\dfrac{n}{\lfloor (n+1)/2 \rfloor} = \boxed{?}$; show that the $\boxed{?}$ is ≤ 3.

5.7   Divide and Conquer: Merge Sorts

In this section we'll look at a well-known divide-and-conquer algorithm for sorting a list, namely Merge Sort, invented by J. von Neumann in 1945 according to Knuth

```
/********************  A R R A Y   M E R G E  ************************
This function assumes that the subarrays a[afirst..alast] and
b[bfirst..blast] contain objects of a data type on which the binary
comparison operator "<=" is defined. It also assumes that the objects
in each array are arranged in increasing order.  It begins by making
sure that the subarray c[cfirst..clast] is large enough to hold all
the objects from the other two arrays (if that is not the case, it
exits after setting the reference parameter "error" to true).  Then
all the objects from array  a  and  b  are copied into array c in
such a way that they form a single ordered list in  c.  Coded by
W. Knight, using a standard elementary merging algorithm. */

template <class otype>
void merge_arrays (const otype a[], int afirst, int alast,
                   const otype b[], int bfirst, int blast,
                   otype c[], int cfirst, int clast, bool &error)
{
  if (clast - cfirst + 1 < (alast - afirst + 1) + (blast - bfirst + 1))
  {
    error = true;
    return;
  }
  error = false;
  while (afirst <= alast && bfirst <= blast)   // While a and b both
    if (a[afirst] <= b[bfirst])                // have objects that
      c[cfirst++] = a[afirst++];               // are not yet copied,
    else                                       // merge them into
      c[cfirst++] = b[bfirst++];               // the array c.

  // When the loop above terminates, at most one of the following
  // two loops will have its loop condition true.
  while (afirst <= alast)        // Copy the remaining objects from
    c[cfirst++] = a[afirst++];   // array a into array c.
  while (bfirst <= blast)        // Copy the remaining objects from
    c[cfirst++] = b[bfirst++];   // array b into array c.
}
```

Fig. 5.50 Function merging two sorted arrays into a third array

(1998). This sorting algorithm makes use of the technique of merging two sorted lists. Thus, before we study Merge Sort, we'll begin by analyzing an array merge.

Example 5.7.1 (**Merging Two Sorted Arrays**): Consider the following *merging problem*. Suppose we are given two subarrays whose cells contain objects of a data type on which the relational operator $<=$ is defined. Suppose the objects in each of the separate arrays are arranged in increasing order. Let a[afirst..alast] be the first array and b[bfirst..blast] be the second. The objects from these two arrays are to be merged into a single, ordered list in a third array or subarray, call it c[cfirst..clast]. A version of the standard algorithm for accomplishing this is given in Fig. 5.50.

The space requirements for the function, as written, are the address and integer memory locations needed in a single stack frame for the arguments in the function call. The total extra space required by a call to this function is therefore $\Theta(1)$.

To compute the execution time for a call to this function, let's begin by looking at the "big picture" here: each of the m objects in a[afirst..alast] and each of the n objects in b[bfirst..blast] must be copied exactly once into the array c. Some of these $m + n$ copy operations are preceded by two subscript comparisons and one object comparison, while each of the remainder of these copy operations is preceded by exactly one subscript comparison. Let's assume (as we normally do) that each copy operation requires $\Theta(1)$ time, and also that each comparison between two objects requires $\Theta(1)$ time. Then each copy operation and its "accompanying" comparison operation(s) together require $\Theta(1)$ execution time. All remaining pieces of a call to this function (set-up time, initial test, return time) require $\Theta(1)$ time.

In summary, the number of assignments is always $n + m$. The least number of comparisons of elements of the array is $\min(n, m)$ when the elements of the smaller of the two arrays are less than the first element in the other array. The largest number of comparisons happens when a[alast-1] < b[blast] and a[alast] > b[blast], and in this case it is $n + m - 1$.

Thus the total execution time for a call to this function is $\Theta(n + m)$.

Example 5.7.2 (**Merge Sort**): This sorting algorithm uses a divide-and-conquer strategy. The idea of the algorithm is to break the array to be sorted into two subarrays of approximately equal size, to sort these *recursively*, and then to merge the two sorted subarrays. Figure 5.51 shows some C++ code to implement this idea.

The merge operation in the algorithm requires an auxiliary array. Thus the amount of additional memory space required by a call to this sorting function is proportional *at least* to the number of objects to be sorted. This is a huge amount of extra space, much more than what is needed for many other sorting algorithms. This form of Merge Sort is definitely not an in-place sorting algorithm.

Interestingly, however, the Merge Sort idea can be modified to work on linked lists, and in that context no extra space for an "auxiliary list" is needed for the merge (you can merge two linked lists simply by adjusting pointers). Two linked list versions of Merge Sort will be considered in the exercises.

The auxiliary array is dynamically allocated by the Merge Sort function. In order not to have to perform a memory allocation at every level in the array, an extra parameter has been introduced into the function that allows an auxiliary array to be allocated just once and then passed down through all the recursions. That extra parameter has a default value of NULL. When this function is called initially to sort some array, it should be called with just three arguments; no argument (or else a NULL value) should be supplied for the fourth parameter.

Aside from the auxiliary array, how much other additional memory space is required by a call to this function? Exercise 5.7.6 will ask you to compute the maximum number of stack frames that will be on a stack at any one time as a result of a call to merge_sort.

```
template <class otype>
void merge_sort (otype a[], int first, int last, otype *aux = NULL)
{
  if (last <= first) // a[first..last] has size <= 1.  If size is 1,
     return;          // then the array is already sorted.  This is
                      // the base case for the recursion.

  bool initial_call = !(aux); // Set to true if and only if aux
                              // is NULL.
  if (initial_call)
  {
     aux = new otype[last - first + 1]; // Allocate sufficient auxiliary space
                                        // to hold all the objects being sorted
  }

  int mid = (first + last) / 2;

  merge_sort (a, first, mid, aux);     // Sort left subarray.
  merge_sort (a, mid+1, last, aux);    // Sort right subarray.

  // Merge the two sorted subarrays in "a" into the aux array.

  bool error;  // Needed for the next line, but there is no need to initialize error.
  merge_arrays (a, first, mid, a, mid+1, last, aux, 0, last-first, error);
  // The variable "error" will be set to false because aux has adequate size.

  // Copy the sorted objects from aux back to "a".

  int i;
  for (i = first, j = 0;  i <= last;  ++i, ++j)
     a[i] = aux[j];

  if (initial_call)  // then the array pointed to by aux was
     delete [] aux;  // allocated during this call.  Deallocate it.
}
```

Fig. 5.51 Merge sort function

Now let's compute the amount of time required to execute the `merge_sort` function when the number of objects to be sorted is n. This recursive function has a different character from the recursive function in Fig. 5.6 on p. 183. That function contained only one recursive call, so that it was very much like a loop, whereas the `merge_sort` code contains two recursive calls, which makes the logical structure of its execution resemble a binary tree. Is it like the recursive functions we studied in Sect. 5.3, which act on binary trees? No, because in those examples the amount of time required by each call (exclusive of the time for the recursive calls) was $\Theta(1)$. In the `merge_sort` function, considerable work is done after the recursive calls. As it turns out, the best way to analyze this algorithm is to introduce a function that measures execution time on an array of n objects and then write a recurrence relation for that function.

Let $T(n)$, $n \geq 1$, denote the amount of time required by this function when it is called to sort an array of length n. Then $T(1) = A$ for some constant A because the very first instruction will detect that the length of the array is 1 and cause a return to be executed (this is the base case). Next consider the case where $n > 1$. Here we can decompose $T(n)$ into the following parts:

(a) the time required to execute all the simple instructions that are executed just once; *plus*
(b) the time required by the recursive calls on arrays of size $\lfloor n/2 \rfloor$ and $\lceil n/2 \rceil$; *plus*
(c) the time required by the call to the merge_arrays function; *plus*
(d) the time required to copy the data back into the array a.

Normally at this point we would analyze the best case and the worst case for the function by looking at the minimum and maximum number of basic operations required by each of these steps. As it turns out, each of these components has a time complexity described by a Θ expression. This means that we don't need to separate the best case from the worst case.

The amounts of time required for these various parts are as follows:

(a) $\Theta(1)$
(b) $T(\lceil n/2 \rceil) + T(\lfloor n/2 \rfloor)$;
(c) $\Theta(\lceil n/2 \rceil + \lfloor n/2 \rfloor) = \Theta(n)$ (see Example 5.7.1);
(d) $\Theta(n)$.

Putting all these pieces of $T(n)$ together and using $\lceil n/2 \rceil + \lfloor n/2 \rfloor = n$ gives us the following recurrence relation:

$$T(n) = T(\lceil n/2 \rceil) + T(\lfloor n/2 \rfloor) + \Theta(n).$$

By one of the formulas in Table 4.6, p. 161, we find that

$$T(n) = \Theta(n \log(n)). \tag{5.8}$$

It is important to note that since both the best case and the worst case for this function are $\Theta(n \log(n))$, we can conclude that the Merge Sort has a time complexity of $\Theta(n \log(n))$ in any situation.

Merge Sort is one of the few fast sorting algorithms that can be written so as to be *stable*. A sorting algorithm is stable provided it has the following desirable property: when two objects occur in a certain order in the original data and have the same key value, then they will remain in the same order after the sorting is completed. The merge_arrays and merge_sort functions have been written with stability in mind, so that the resulting merge_sort function is indeed a stable sort. The property of stability is useful when data objects are to be sorted on some "primary key", but where groups of objects that have the same primary key, the objects within each group are to be sorted on some secondary key. The way to achieve this kind of ordering is to sort first on the secondary key and then re-sort the data on the primary key using a stable sorting algorithm.

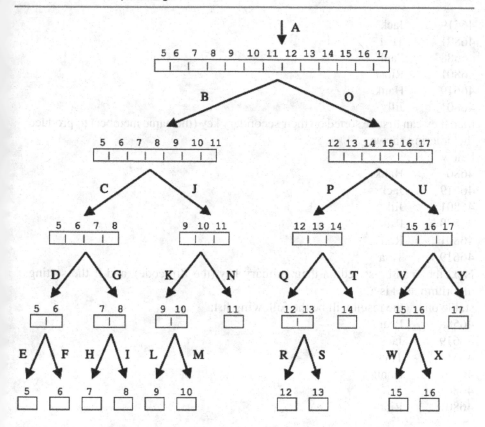

Fig. 5.52 An example of recursion tree for the merge sort

To take an example, suppose we are sorting data objects containing a Zip code as the primary key and a personal name as the secondary key. If the data are originally in the following random order shown on top of the next page.

Note that Jack comes before Tina in the arrangement before the second sort (the stable one), and it also comes before Tina after the second sort is finished.

You may object that if sorting is to be done on two keys, then we should overload the $<$ operator so it considers first the primary keys of two objects, and if those are identical, it considers the secondary keys. This is possible in C++ but not in all programming languages.

Another situation in which stability is important is when the data to be sorted on its primary key has already been sorted on a secondary key before its arrival. Then we must be careful not to disturb the ordering of the secondary keys within groups of objects having the same primary key.

The sequence of recursive calls that are generated by an initial call to Merge Sort can be usefully visualized as a binary tree in which the arrows represent calls to Merge Sort and the nodes to which they point represent the subarrays to be sorted by those calls. Figure 5.52 shows such a tree representing the action of Merge Sort

46619	Jack
46801	Tina
46588	Paul
46801	Rita
46619	Hank
46801	Jill

then they can first be sorted on their secondary key (the name member) to produce the ordering shown
below:

46801	Hank
46619	Jack
46801	Jill
46588	Paul
46801	Rita
46619	Tina

Next they can be sorted on their primary key (the Zip code), and if the sorting algorithm used is a
stable one,   the result will be the following list:

46588	Paul
46619	Jack
46619	Tina
46801	Hank
46801	Jill
46801	Rita

on an initial array of 13 objects located in cells 5 through 17. The upper case letters taken in alphabetical order show the order in which all the calls are made. Wherever there are two arrows (i.e., calls to Merge Sort) emanating from a node, a call to the Merge function will occur after the two recursive calls have finished sorting their separate subarrays. We call a tree of this type a *recursion tree*.

Small Array Improvement

   It is useful to note that a relatively simple strategy can substantially improve the efficiency of Merge Sort. The strategy takes advantage of the fact that on short arrays Merge Sort is slower than simpler sorting algorithms such as linear insertion sort, selection sort, or bubble sort. The reason for this is illustrated by the recursion tree in Fig. 5.52, which shows that an initial call to Merge Sort on an array of length 13 generates 24 recursive function calls, 13 of which are calls on subarrays of length 1, where no useful work at all is accomplished. Moreover there are 5 calls on arrays of length 2, and each of those 5 calls in turn calls the Merge function to combine two neighboring subarrays of length 1, a step which could have been more efficiently accomplished by one object comparison followed, when needed, by one swap. Similarly, the calls to merge neighboring pairs of subarrays of size 2 are inefficient compared with the time required by linear insertion sort to put 4 objects in order.

```
const CUT_OFF = 10;

if ( last - first + 1 <= CUT_OFF )        // Base case; arrays of length
{                                          // <= CUT_OFF will be sorted using the
    linear_insertion_sort (a, first, last);   // linear_insertion_sort.
    return;
}
```

Fig. 5.53 Merge sort base case where `linear_insertion_sort` is the one in Exercise 5.1.18 (**b**)

These observations suggest that when Merge Sort is called, the first step should be to check whether the array to be sorted is short, and if it is, then Merge Sort should turn the job over to some simpler sorting algorithm. That is, we could modify the code in Fig. 5.51 by replacing the base case there with the code shown in Fig. 5.53.

Where did the number 10 come from in Fig. 5.53? Experience accumulated over the years by programmers has shown that any number in the neighborhood of 10 will work well as the cut-off point for switching to a simpler algorithm. In the example given in Fig. 5.52, using 10 as the cut-off will "prune" away three levels of the tree, leaving just two recursive calls in place of 24. While this will not change the $\Theta(n \log(n))$ execution time for Merge Sort, it will make it noticeably more efficient.

Since linear insertion sort requires $\Theta(n^2)$ time in the worst case (see Exercise 5.1.18), you may be puzzled by the assertion that linear insertion sort will always be faster than Merge Sort on small arrays. After all, it is certainly true that $n \log(n) < n^2$ for all positive integers n. The resolution of this seeming contradiction lies in the fact that the multiplicative constants hidden in the Θ expression for Merge Sort are much larger than the constants in the Θ expression for linear insertion sort (or any of the other order n^2 sorting algorithms). When C is much larger than c, then $C n \log(n)$ is larger than $c n^2$ for small values of n.

One of the advantages of Merge Sort is that it is a *stable* sorting algorithm. Will it still be *stable* after we make the improvement suggested above? Yes. Linear insertion sort (properly written) is a stable sorting algorithm, so that property is preserved at every level. This would not be true if, for example, we used Selection Sort to sort the small subarrays.

5.7.1 Exercises

5.7.3 Let $S_{max}(n)$ denote the maximum number of stack frames that will be on the run-time stack at any one time as a result of calling the `merge_sort` function in Fig. 5.51 on p. 255 with a subarray of length n. Let's calculate the first few values of $S_{max}(n)$.

n = 1: It is easy to see that $S_{max}(1) = 1$ because a base case call makes no other function calls.

n = 2: First there is the stack frame for the call with the subarray of length $n = 2$. That call makes a recursive call and passes a subarray of length 1, so that recursive call will produce only one stack frame. When that stack frame is removed, the second recursive call is made, also with a subarray of length 1, so that recursive call will produce only one stack frame. When that's done, the non-recursive function that merges the subarrays is called, and it produces 1 stack frame. Thus we see that at any one time the maximum number of stack frames on the run-time stack as a result of a call with $n = 2$ is two. That is, $S_{max}(2) = 2$.

n = 3: First there is the stack frame for the call with the subarray of length $n = 3$. That call makes a recursive call and passes a subarray of length 2, so that recursive call will produce exactly two stack frames, as discussed in the case $n = 2$ above. When that recursive call is finished, a second recursive call is made, this time with a subarray of length 1, so that recursive call will produce only one stack frame. Then the function that merges the subarrays is called and produces 1 stack frame. Thus the maximum number of stack frames on the run-time stack at any one time as a result of a call with $n = 2$ is three. That is, $S_{max}(3) = 3$.

Write a recurrence relation for $S_{max}(n)$ for all $n \geq 2$ and use it (along with an appropriate table) to obtain a big-theta expression for $S_{max}(n)$.

5.7.4 Suppose that we have a linked list of objects to be sorted. Can we apply the Merge Sort strategy to a linked list? The answer is yes, and doing so is fairly straightforward. Assume the following C++ definitions:

```
struct node
{
  otype datum;   // Assume "otype" is some pre-defined object type
  node *next;
};
typedef node * node_ptr;
```

Various sorting techniques can be used to sort such a list. One possibility is to adapt the ideas of Merge Sort. As with arrays, we can write a function that merges two sorted linked lists, and then we can write a function that breaks a list into two lists, recursively sorts them, and calls the merge function to put them back together. The code for these functions is shown in Figs. 5.54 and 5.55.

(a) Analyze the time required to execute the function in Fig. 5.54 when it is passed pointers to two sorted, NULL-terminated linked lists, list1 and list2, containing m and n nodes respectively.
(b) Analyze the time required to execute the function in Fig. 5.55 when it is passed a NULL-terminated linked list, list, containing n nodes.
(c) Is this algorithm an in-place sorting algorithm?

```
node_ptr merge_lists(node_ptr list1, node_ptr list2)
{
  if (!list1)        // list1 is empty
    return list2;
  if (!list2)        // list2 is empty
    return list1;

  node_ptr front, back; // pointers to front & back of combined list

  if (list1->datum <= list2->datum)   // transfer smallest data item
  {
    front = back = list1;
    list1 = list1->next;
  }
  else
  {
    front = back = list2;
    list2 = list2->next;
  }
  while (list1 && list2)                  // merge the non-empty lists
    if (list1->datum <= list2->datum)
    {
      back->next = list1;
      back  = back->next;
      list1 = list1->next;
    }
    else
    {
      back->next = list2;
      back  = back->next;
      list2 = list2->next;
    }
  if (list1)                        // attach non-empty residue to back
    back->next = list1;
  else
    back->next = list2;
  return front;
}
```

Fig. 5.54 Merge two sorted linked lists

5.7.5 Figure 5.56 shows a different version of the merge_sort given in Exercise 5.7.4. This new version has no parameter to tell it the length of the list it is trying to sort, so whenever it is called it must first count the list. This requires extra time. Analyze the time required for execution of this function when it is passed a list containing n nodes.

5.7.6 Let $C(n)$ denote the total number of calls that will be made to the merge _sort function in Fig. 5.51 on p. 255 when it is passed a subarray of length n. Clearly $C(1) = 1$ because when $n = 1$ the initial call makes no recursive calls. A little thought shows that $C(2) = 3$. Write a recurrence relation for $C(n)$ valid for all $n \geq 2$ and use it to obtain a big-theta expression for $C(n)$.

```
void merge_sort(node_ptr & list, int n)
{
    if (n <= 1)  // This is the base case of the recursion.
      return;    // An empty list of a list of length 1 is already sorted.

    int count;
    node_ptr mid = list;

    // Advance the "mid" pointer from the front of the list to a point
    // half way down the list.
    for (count = 1; count <= n/2 - 1; ++count)
      mid = mid->next;

    node_ptr list2 = mid->next;      // Split off back half of the list.
    mid->next = NULL;                // NULL-terminate the front half.

    merge_sort (list, n/2);          // Front half length is floor(n/2)
    merge_sort (list2, n - n/2);     // Back half length is ceiling(n/2)

    list = merge_lists(list, list2);
}
```

Fig. 5.55 The merge sort function implemented on a linked list (for merge_list see Fig. 5.54)

```
void merge_sort(node_ptr & list)
{
    int      i, n;
    node_ptr mid;

    for (mid = list, n = 0; mid != NULL; ++n) // Use n to count the number
      mid = mid->next;                        // of nodes in the list.

    if (n <= 1) // Base case for the recursion; a trivial list is already sorted;
      return;

    // Advance "mid" half way down the list.
    for (i = 1; i <= n/2 - 1; ++i)
      mid = mid->next;

    node_ptr list2 = mid->next; // Split off back half of the list.
    mid->next = NULL;           // NULL-terminate the front half.

    merge_sort (list);      // Front half length is floor(n/2)
    merge_sort (list2);     // Back half length is ceiling(n/2)

    list = merge_lists(list, list2);
}
```

Fig. 5.56 Merge sort on a linked list without knowing the size, (for merge_list see Fig. 5.54)

5.7.7 An inventive programmer, having seen how well the divide-and-conquer strategy works in sorting arrays in random order (Merge Sort) and in searching ordered arrays (binary search), decides to try this strategy on the problem of finding the maximum object in an array of objects in random order (cf. Example 5.1.1, p. 170). She writes the code in Fig. 5.57.

```
template <class otype>      // Should not be called with last < first
int location_of_max (const otype a[], int first, int last)
{
    if (first == last)  // base case: the array contains just 1 object
        return first;
    int mid = (first + last) / 2;
    int left_best  = location_of_max (a, first, mid);
    int right_best = location_of_max (a, mid + 1, last);
    if (a[left_best] <= a[right_best])
        return right_best;
    else
        return left_best;
}
```

Fig. 5.57 Recursive version of the function locating the maximum element in an array

(a) Let $T(n)$ be the amount of time that this function will require when passed a subarray of size n. Clearly $T(1) = A$ for some constant A. Write a recurrence relation for $T(n)$ when $n \geq 2$. Solve the relation, and then give a big-theta expression for $T(n)$.

(b) Compare the execution time for this recursive version of location_of_max with the execution time for the iterative version on p. 169.

(c) Let $S_{max}(n)$ denote the maximum number of stack frames that will be on the run-time stack at any one time as a result of calling this recursive location_of _max function with a subarray of size n. Clearly $S_{max}(1) = 1$. Write a recurrence relation for $S_{max}(n)$ when $n \geq 2$, and solve it.

(d) Compare the space requirements of this recursive location_of_max function with the space requirements of the iterative version of the function in Example 5.1.1, p. 170.

(e) Relying on your computations in parts (a) through (d) of this exercise, write a brief advisory to our "inventive programmer" (referred to the first line of this exercise) telling her which of the two versions of location_of_max she should use, and why.

5.7.8 Exercises 5.1.19 and 5.1.20, pp. 197–198, asked you analyze two algorithms for solving the Maximum Subsequence Problem. The first algorithm was very naive and inefficient; it runs in $\Theta(n^3)$ time on sequences of length n. The second algorithm—which you wrote—improved that to $\Theta(n^2)$ time. Can we find an even better algorithm? What about trying to exploit the divide and conquer strategy? The idea (of course) is to split the array into two subarrays of equal, or nearly equal, length, solve the problem recursively on each of those subarrays, and then, if it is appropriate, join the two solutions into a single solution. Note, however, that the subsequence with maximum sum in the left subarray may not occur at the right end (i.e., may not be a *final* subsequence of the left subarray), and the subsequence with maximum sum in the right subarray may not occur at the left end (i.e., may not be an *initial* subsequence of the right subarray), so we may not be able to join the best subsequence in the left subarray with the best subsequence in the right subarray. Here is another possibility we must check for: the best subsequence in the entire array may be one that overlaps both subarrays, but the pieces of it in the two subarrays may not be the best in their subarrays. This means that the recursive function will also have to find the best *final* subsequence sum in the left subarray and the best *initial* subsequence sum in the right subarray, and see what happens when these sums are put together.

The code for a divide-and-conquer recursive algorithm is given on p. 264. Note that the code is substantially more complicated than the code you wrote for the $\Theta(n^2)$ algorithm. Analyze the space and time requirements of this new recursive algorithm when it is applied to an array of length $n = $ last - first + 1. NOTE: *it is not necessary to understand this recursive algorithm well in order to perform the analysis*. Just analyze the structure of the code, then write an appropriate recurrence relation (or more than one), and solve it (or them). Compare your results with those obtained for the simpler algorithms given in Exercise 5.1.19 and 5.1.20.

5.7.9 In Exercise 5.1.19 and 5.1.20, and 5.7.8 you analyzed several different algorithms for solving the Maximum Subsequence Sum Problem. On p. 265 you will find still another. It is iterative, not recursive. It is somewhat more subtle than the other iterative (non-recursive) versions, but can be understand by working through an example such as the sequence in the following array:

0	1	2	3	4	5	6	7	8	9
4.1	2.7	-9.9	3.8	6.0	-2.5	3.1	-7.9	-1.6	9.0

Analyze the space and time requirements of this algorithm as functions of the array length n. How does it compare with the algorithms that you saw in Exercises 5.1.19 and 5.1.20, and 5.7.8? [HINT: look at what happens to the variable j in the function.]

```
/********* M A X I M U M   S U B S E Q U E N C E   S U M  **************/
double max_subseq_sum (const double a[], int & first, int & last)
{
  if (first == last)        // base case
    if (a[first] > 0.0)
      return a[first];
    else
      return 0.0;           // The returned value will always be >= 0.
  int mid = (first + last)/2, left_first  = first, left_last   = mid,
      right_first = mid + 1, right_last = last;
  // Recursively find the max subseq sums in 2 halves of the array.
  double left_best  = max_subseq_sum (a, left_first,  left_last),
         right_best = max_subseq_sum (a, right_first, right_last);
  // Calculate the best final subsequence sum in left and right subarrays.
  double left_final_best = 0.0, right_initial_best = 0.0, sum = 0.0;
  int i, best_left_edge, best_right_edge;
  for (i = mid; i >= first; --i)          // Find best final sum
```

```
      if ((sum += a[i]) > left_final_best) // in the left subarray
      {
        left_final_best = sum;
        best_left_edge  = i;
      }
    for (sum = 0.0, i = mid + 1; i <= last; ++i) // Find best initial sum
      if ((sum += a[i]) > right_initial_best)    // in right subarray.
      {
        right_initial_best = sum;
        best_right_edge    = i;
      }
    double overlap_best = left_final_best + right_initial_best;
    if (left_best >= right_best && left_best >= overlap_best)
    {
      first = left_first;
      last  = left_last;
      return  left_best;
    }
    else if (right_best >= left_best && right_best >= overlap_best)
    {
      first = right_first;
      last  = right_last;
      return  right_best;
    }
    else  // overlap_best is the largest of the three quantities
    {
      first = best_left_edge;
      last  = best_right_edge;
      return  overlap_best;
    }
}


/********* M A X I M U M   S U B S E Q U E N C E   S U M ***********/
double max_subsequence_sum (const double a[], int & first, int & last)
{
    double max_so_far = 0.0;
    int best_first, best_last; // Not initialized if max seq sum is 0.0.
    int j;

    for (j = first; j <= last && a[j] <= 0.0; ++j)
      ;                          // Go past initial negative and zero values

    if (j > last)          // There are no positive numbers in the array.
      return max_so_far; // EXIT from the function and return 0.0

    max_so_far = a[j];   // This is 1st strictly positive number in a[].
    best_first = j;      // So far, the best subseq sum is just a[j].
    best_last  = j;

    // The following variables are used in the loop below to hold
    // various temporary values.

    double trial_sum  = max_so_far;
    int    trial_first = best_first;

    while (++j <= last)
    {
```

0	1	2	3	4	5	6	7	8	9	10	11	12	13	14	15	16	17	18	19	20	21	22	23	24	25

a: | 39 | 27 | 11 | 59 | 55 | 34 | 07 | 26 | 52 | 20 | 21 | 53 | 14 | 50 | 76 | 47 | 57 | 30 | 25 | 58 | 70 | 15 | 72 | 42 | 64 | 67 |

Fig. 5.58 An example of an array

```
    if (trial_sum <= 0.0  &&  a[j] > 0.0)
    {
      trial_sum  = a[j];  // Start a new trial sum.
      trial_first = j;
    }
    else
      trial_sum += a[j];

    if (max_so_far < trial_sum) // We've found a better subseq sum
    {
      max_so_far = trial_sum;
      best_first = trial_first;
      best_last  = j;
    }
  }

  first = best_first;
  last  = best_last;
  return max_so_far;
}
```

5.8   Quicksort

One of the best sorting methods is known as Quicksort. It was invented in the early 1960s by C.A.R. Hoare, who published his algorithm and a careful analysis of it in a research paper in 1962 [6]. Since that time there have been a number of small improvements on the algorithm, but the ideas are still substantially unchanged from Hoare's landmark paper. A non-recursive version can be found in (Sedgewick 2001) although it differs from the recursive function only by simulating the runtime frame stack.

Assume that we are given a (sub)array a[first..last] to sort. In the simple version of Quicksort that we will consider, the first object in the array is used to "partition" the remaining objects into those that are smaller than the first object and those that are larger than the first object. Those that are smaller are kept in the left part of the array, while those that are larger are kept in the right part of the array. This partitioning object is usually called the *pivot*. A C++ implementation is shown in Fig. 5.63.

Let's look at how the Quicksort in Fig. 5.63 would work on the array a[] shown in Fig. 5.58. The object here will be to sort a[0,25]. When the algorithm begins, i is set to 1 and j is set to 25. The pivot is the 39 in cell 0. The first while loop moves i to the right until it reaches the 59 (larger than 39) in cell 3. The second while loop moves j to the left until it reaches the 15 (smaller than 39) in cell 21. In the

0	1	2	3	4	5	6	7	8	9	10	11	12	13	14	15	16	17	18	19	20	21	22	23	24	25
a:	14	27	11	15	25	34	07	26	30	20	21	**39**	53	50	76	47	57	52	55	58	70	59	72	42	64	67

Fig. 5.59 The array after partitioning

0	1	2	3	4	5	6	7	8	9	10
a:	11	07	**14**	15	25	34	27	26	30	20	21	...

Fig. 5.60 The array for the *left* recursive call of the Quicksort after partitioning

third while loop the 59 and the 15 are swapped, and then the search for objects to swap begins anew. Now i moves right and stops at the 55 in cell 4. Then j moves left and stops at the 25 in cell 18. Since i < j the 55 and 25 are swapped. Then i moves right to the 52 in cell 8 and j moves left to the 30 in cell 17. Since i < j the 52 and 30 are swapped. Then i moves right to the 53 in cell 11 and j moves left to the 14 in cell 12. Since i < j the 53 and 14 are swapped. Then i moves right to the 53 in cell 12 and j moves left to the 14 in cell 11. This time i is *not* less than j, so execution jumps down to the instruction that swaps a[first] and a[j], that is, a[0] and a[11]. After the swap, the array is as shown in Fig. 5.59. The pivot 39 is now located so that it is at least as large as everything to its left (i.e., in subarray a[0..10]) and at least as small as everything to its right (i.e., in subarray a[12..25]). Thus it is exactly where it belongs and need not be moved again. We have completed what is usually called a "Quicksort pass" over the entire array a[0..25].

The algorithm will now make recursive calls to Quicksort the subarrays a[0..10] and a[12..25]. Figure 5.60 shows the subarray a[0..10] after the Quicksort pass in the first recursive call. The number 14 is the pivot, and it ends up in cell 2, so recursive calls to Quicksort will sort a[0..1] and a[3..10] (not a very even "split"). We won't work out the details of those recursive calls and of the calls that they make, etc. It would be tedious to work through all the recursions on smaller and smaller subarrays until we got down to the base case subarrays of lengths 0 and 1.

When the subarray a[0..10] has been completely sorted, execution will then move on to the recursive call on the subarray a[12..25] shown in Fig. 5.59. Figure 5.61 shows that subarray after the Quicksort pass over it. The number 53 is the pivot, and it ends up in cell 16, so recursive calls to Quicksort will sort a[12..15] and a[17..25]. Eventually, after many more recursive calls, the subarray a[12..25] will be completely sorted, at which point the entire array a[0..25] will have been sorted, as shown in Fig. 5.62. We omit the details of this process.

Quicksort is obviously a divide-and-conquer algorithm, but there is a significant difference between it and Merge Sort, our other divide-and-conquer sorting algorithm: when a[first] is used as the pivot, we cannot be sure that there will be nearly the same number of objects smaller than the pivot as there are objects larger

```
... 12 13 14 15 16 17 18 19 20 21 22 23 24 25
a: ...|52|50|42|47|53|57|55|58|70|59|72|76|64|67|
```

Fig. 5.61 The array for the *right* recursive call of the Quicksort after partitioning

```
  0  1  2  3  4  5  6  7  8  9 10 11 12 13 14 15 16 17 18 19 20 21 22 23 24 25
a:|07|11|14|15|20|21|25|26|27|30|34|39|42|47|50|52|53|55|57|58|59|64|67|70|72|76|
```

Fig. 5.62 The sorted array

than the pivot. By contrast, in Merge Sort we force the two subarrays on which recursion is performed to be of approximately equal size.

Most sorting algorithms run quite rapidly when they are given an array whose objects are already arranged in increasing order. Surprisingly, that is not true of Quicksort, as we shall now see. Suppose the objects in a[first...last] are all distinct and in increasing order when the Quicksort function is called. Let n denote the number of objects in this array. Let $T(n)$ denote the execution time for the function in this special case.

First consider the case where $n = 1$. Clearly $T(1) = A$ for some positive constant A. Next, consider what happens when $n \geq 2$.

- The first while loop stops after one iteration, so it requires $\Theta(1)$ time, provided we assume (as usual) that otype objects are of bounded size.
- The second while loop causes j to march to the left end of the array, so that j ends up with the value *first*. The time required for this is essentially a linear function of n. More precisely, it is $\Theta(n)$ as $n \to \infty$.
- The third while loop's test condition will be false immediately, so execution will jump down to the swap statement (just beyond the body of that while loop) and execute it. This will swap a[first] with itself. The test condition, the jump, and the swap will require $\Theta(1)$ time.
- Now we recursively call the function on a subarray of length 1 and then on a subarray of length $n - 1$. Note that the second of these two subarrays is still in increasing order because we have not moved any of the objects in its cells.

Adding together all the times above, we obtain the following recurrence problem:

$$T(1) = A, \quad T(n) = T(n-1) + \phi(n) \quad \text{for } n \geq 2, \text{ where } \phi(n) = \Theta(n).$$

By Example 4.5.1 on p. 153 and the solution that immediately follows it, we see that

$$T(n) = A + \sum_{k=2}^{n} \phi(k)$$

Since $\phi(n) = \Theta(n)$, it follows from Theorem 3.2.11 (e) that

$$\sum_{k=2}^{n} \phi(k) = \Theta(\sum_{k=2}^{n} k) = \Theta(n^2). \tag{5.9}$$

```
// The following code provides one of the simplest possible implementations
// of the basic ideas of the Quicksort method.  Better implementations will
// be described farther along in this section.

template <class otype>
void quicksort (otype a[], int first, int last)
{
    if (last <= first)    // base case; arrays of length <= 1 are sorted
        return;

    int i = first + 1,  j = last;     // Initialize the search subscripts.

    while (a[i] < a[first] && i < j)  // Move i to the right until either
        ++i;                          // a[i] >= a[first] or i == j (or both).

    while (a[j] > a[first])           // Move j to the left until finding an
        --j;                          // object at least as small as a[first].
                                      // It's possible that j ends up at first.
    while (i < j)
    {
        swap (a[i], a[j]);            // Move the large object to the right part
                                      // of the array and the small to the left.

        do                            // Resume the search for an object at
            ++i;                      // least as large as  a[first].
        while (a[i] < a[first]);

        do                            // Resume the search for an object at
            --j;                      // least as small as  a[first].
        while (a[j] > a[first]);
    }

    swap (a[first], a[j]);            // Place the partitioning object between
                                      // objects less than or equal to it and
                                      // objects greater than or equal to it.

    quicksort (a, first, j-1);        // Recursively sort the subarray of objects
    quicksort (a, j+1, last);         // less than or equal to the partitioning
                                      // object and the subarray of objects
}                                     // greater than or equal to it.
```

Fig. 5.63 Quicksort function

Thus the execution time for a call to the Quicksort function in Fig. 5.63 is $\Theta(n^2)$ *when the array to be sorted is already sorted and all the objects are distinct.*

What are the space requirements of our Quicksort when it is called on an array of n objects already in increasing order? The initial call to the function requires a stack frame of fixed size independent of the value of n. That call then makes a recursive call on an ordered array of $n - 1$ objects, which requires therefore a second stack frame of the same fixed size, while the first frame is still on the run-time stack. That call makes a call on an ordered array of $n - 2$ objects, which requires a third stack frame on the stack, and so on. The last of these recursive calls is made on an array of size 1, at which point there will be n stack frames on the stack. Thus the space requirement for a call to our Quicksort function is $\Theta(n)$ when the array is already in increasing order.

We have just seen that when the simple Quicksort function is applied to a pre-sorted array its performance is astonishingly bad. The running time is $\Theta(n^2)$, and the space requirement is $\Theta(n)$, which is far worse than the simple $\Theta(n^2)$ sorting algorithms like Selection Sort, Bubble Sort, and Insertion Sort, all of which are in-place sorting algorithms.

Is $\Theta(n^2)$ the worst possible execution time for Quicksort? Yes, it is, although we have not proved that. For all we know at this moment, there may be some arrangement of the objects in the array that can cause Quicksort to require $\Theta(n^3)$ time to sort the n objects. The proof that the maximum execution time is $\Theta(n^2)$ is discussed in Exercise 5.8.3.

If the worst case running time is so bad, why is Quicksort regarded as such a wonderful sorting algorithm? There are several reasons. First, the particular version of Quicksort given in Fig. 5.63 is a fairly naive implementation of the Quicksort idea. A few simple improvements in the code will lead to much better performance on pre-sorted arrays. For example, a standard improvement is to make a better choice for the pivot. Instead of always using a[first], we can use the median of the three objects a[first], a[mid], and a[last], where mid = (first + last)/2. The median of these three objects is swapped into cell a[first], and then the algorithm proceeds as already presented. Below and on the following page you will find an analysis of the execution time for this improved version when it is given a pre-sorted array.

The main reason that Quicksort is highly esteemed has to do with its performance on arrays in which the objects are in random order. As we will see later, its expected (i.e., average) execution time on such arrays is very good.

Median of 3 Partitioning

Suppose we insert the block of code shown in Fig. 5.64 into the function in Fig. 5.63, just after the "return;" statement in the base case. This block of code swaps the median of a[first], a[mid], and a[last] into cell a[first], where it will be used as the partitioning object for the remaining objects in the array. (Note: if there are only two objects in a[first..last], the block of code in Fig. 5.64 still works, but it accomplishes nothing useful.) This will almost always produce a more even partition of a[first..last] into two subarrays.

Let's see how Quicksort with median-of-three would act on the array shown back in Fig. 5.58. First we would calculate mid as the floor of $(0 + 25)/2$, which is 12. Then we would examine the three numbers 39, 14, and 67 located in cells 0, 12, and 25. The median of the three numbers is 39, so it remains in cell 0 and is used as the pivot in the pass over the array. This produces exactly the array shown in Fig. 5.59. As before, the pivot 39 ends up in cell 11.

Something new will happen in the recursive call on the subarray a[0..10]. We calculate mid = 5 and then examine the numbers 14, 34, and 21 in cells 0, 5, and 10. The median of these three numbers is 21, so it is swapped into cell 0 and used as a pivot during a pass over the subarray. That pass produces the subarray shown in

```
// The following code swaps the median of the objects a[first], a[mid], and
// a[last] into cell a[first], unless a[first] is already the median.
int mid = (first + last)/2;
if ( a[first] < a[mid] )
{
    if ( a[mid] < a[last] )      // In this case a[f] < a[m] < a[l], so a[mid]
        swap (a[first], a[mid]); // is the median of the three objects.
    else if ( a[first < a[last]) // In this case a[f] < a[l] <= a[m], so a[last]
        swap (a[first], a[last]); // can be taken to be the median.
    else                         // In this case a[l] <= a[f] <= a[m], so a[first]
        ; // Do nothing.         // can be taken to be the median.
}
else                             // In this case we know a[m] <= a[f].
{
    if ( a[last] < a[mid] )      // Then a[l] < a[m] <= a[f], so a[mid] can be
        swap (a[first], a[mid]); // taken to be the median.
    else if ( a[last] < a[first] // Then a[m] <= a[l] < a[f], so a[last] can be
        swap (a[first], a[last]) // taken to be the median.
    else                         // In this case a[m] <= a[f] <= a[l], so a[first]
        ; // Do nothing          // can be taken to be the median.
}
```

Fig. 5.64 Median of 3 partitioning strategy

	0	1	2	3	4	5	6	7	8	9	10	
a:	07	14	11	15	20	**21**	34	26	30	25	27	...

Fig. 5.65 The array for the *left* recursive call of the Quicksort after partitioning using the median of 3 strategy

		12	13	14	15	16	17	18	19	20	21	22	23	24	25
a:	...	52	50	42	47	53	**55**	57	58	70	59	72	76	64	67

Fig. 5.66 The array for the *right* recursive call of the Quicksort after partitioning using the median of 3 strategy

Fig. 5.65. Note that the partitioning object 21 has been swapped into cell 5, which is exactly where it belongs. Recursive calls will now be made to sort a[0..4] and a[6..10], which (in this case) are the same size. Let's skip the remaining details involved in completely sorting a[0..10].

After subarray a[0..10] has been completely sorted, a recursive call is made to sort the subarray a[12..25] in Fig. 5.59. We calculate mid = 18 and examine the numbers 53, 55, and 67 in cells 12, 18, and 25. The median of the three is 55, so it is swapped with the 53 in cell 12 and used as a pivot for a pass over a[12..25]. The result of that pass is shown in Fig. 5.66. Note that the pivot has been swapped into cell 17, so now there will be two recursive calls to Quicksort, one on the subarray a[12..16] and the other on the subarray a[18..25]. As usual, we will omit the details involved in completely sorting a[12..25].

Now suppose this modified Quicksort function is called on an array of *n* distinct objects that are already in increasing order. That is, initially we have these strict inequalities:

$$a[first] < a[first + 1] < a[first + 2] < \dots < a[last].$$

For such an array, the median of a[first], a[mid], and a[last] will be a[mid], and this will be swapped with a[first]. Then the initial while loop in Quicksort will move the subscript i to the position mid+1, because all the objects in a[first+1..mid] are smaller than a[first]. The second while loop will move the subscript j to the position mid because all the objects in a[mid+1..last] are larger than a[first]. Then the third while loop will terminate immediately because i is greater than j, and the pivot a[first] will be swapped back into its original position. Then recursive calls are made on the subarrays a[first..mid-1] and a[mid+1..last].

Let $T(n)$ denote the execution time for this modified Quicksort algorithm on a pre-sorted array of n distinct objects. Then $T(0) = T(1) =$ some positive constant A, and

$$T(n) = T(\lceil n/2 \rceil - 1) + T(\lfloor n/2 \rfloor) + \phi(n) \quad \text{for all } n \geq 2,$$

where $\phi(n)$ is $\Theta(n)$. To solve this we need to
(1) rewrite $\lfloor n/2 \rfloor$ as $\lceil (n-1)/2 \rceil$ (see Table 4.4, p. 157) and
(2) rewrite $\lceil n/2 \rceil - 1$ as $\lfloor (n-1)/2 \rfloor$ (see Table 4.4, p. 157: $\lceil n/2 \rceil - 1 = \lfloor (n+1)/2 \rfloor - 1 = \lfloor (n-1)/2 \rfloor$).
These substitutions give us the relation

$$T(0) = T(1) = A, \quad T(n) = T(\lfloor (n-1)/2 \rfloor) + T(\lceil (n-1)/2 \rceil) + \phi(n) \quad \text{for } n \geq 2.$$

As shown on p. 158, this is transformed by the substitution $T(n) = G(n+1)$ into the problem

$$G(1) = G(2) = C, \quad G(n) = G(\lfloor n/2 \rfloor) + G(\lceil n/2 \rceil) + \phi(n-1) \quad \text{for } n \geq 3.$$

where $\phi(n-1) = \Theta(n)$. By Table 4.6, p. 161, $G(n) = \Theta(n \log(n))$, from which it follows immediately that.

$$T(n) = \Theta(n \log(n)). \tag{5.10}$$

Small Array Improvement

Like Merge Sort, the Quicksort algorithm is slower than various simpler sorting algorithms when applied to a short array. This suggests that when Quicksort is called, the first step should be to check whether the array to be sorted is short, and if it is, then Quicksort should turn the job over to some simple sorting algorithm. That is, we could modify the base-case code in Fig. 5.63 along the lines shown in Fig. 5.67 (with median-of-three code added after the base case).

Note that this improved function does not simply replace the Quicksort with the insertion sort only for initial arrays of a small enough size. For arrays of a larger size, every recursive call made from the Quicksort eventually generates a call where the array is small enough, and so the insertion sort is called multiple times during the entire sorting process. The order of complexity of the function does not change, but the execution time is improved. The recursion tree is culled by about 9 levels, thus reducing the overhead generated by a large number of recursive calls.

There is, however, a slightly more efficient way to use linear insertion sort. It makes use of the important property noted in Exercise 5.1.18: *linear insertion sort is very efficient on nearly sorted arrays (i.e. arrays in which all the objects are close to the cell in which they belong)*. Let's see what would happen if we rewrote the Quicksort code so that whenever it was called on an array of length 10 or less, it refused to do any more work. That is, suppose we replaced the code in Fig. 5.67 with the code in Fig. 5.68. Then when Quicksort finished execution, it would have modified the order of the objects in such a way that no object would be farther than 10 cells from where it belongs when the array is completely ordered.

Let's illustrate this by applying this "incomplete" Quicksort (with median-of-three partitioning) to the example array in Fig. 5.58, the first pass would produce the array in Fig. 5.59, and then the two recursive calls on a[0..10] and a[12..25] produce the arrays in Figs. 5.65 and 5.66. No further recursions would take place because the subarrays a[0..4], a[6..10], a[12..16], and a[18..25] all have length less than the CUT_OFF value 10. Thus the incomplete Quicksort would produce the array shown in Fig. 5.69, in which the pivots that were used are shown in boldface. Note that all the numbers in a[0..4] are less than the pivot 21, which in turn is less than everything to its right, so all the numbers in a[0..4] belong in that subarray. Similarly with all the numbers in a[6..10], a[12..16], and a[18..25]. Thus no object anywhere in the array a[0..25] is more than 10 cells away from where it belongs. One function call will now sort the entire array more efficiently than the four calls that would be made if we used the code in Fig. 5.67. On a much longer array even more execution time would be saved.

Here's how we put together all the improvements on the simple Quicksort code we saw in Fig. 5.63.

(1) Change the name of the function to incomplete_quicksort.
(2) Replace the simple base case code with the code in Fig. 5.68.
(3) Next, insert the median-of-three code in Fig. 5.64.
(4) Create a "driver function" that first calls incomplete_quicksort. and then calls the version of linear_insertion_sort found in Exercise 5.1.18. See Fig. 5.70.

```
const CUT_OFF = 10;

if ( last - first + 1 <= CUT_OFF )       // Base case; arrays of length
{                                        // <= CUT_OFF will be sorted using the
    linear_insertion_sort (first, last); // linear_insertion_sort
    return;
}
```

Fig. 5.67 Quicksort base case where linear_insertion_sort is the algorithm in Exercise 5.1.18 (**b**)

```
        const int CUT_OFF = 10;

        if ( last - first + 1 <= CUT_OFF )         // Don't sort any short arrays.
            return;
```

Fig. 5.68 Arrays of size smaller than CUT_OFF are not sorted

```
     0  1  2  3  4  5  6  7  8  9  10 11 12 13 14 15 16 17 18 19 20 21 22 23 24 25
a: |20|0711|15|14|21|27|26|30|34|25|39|52|50|42|47|53|55|57|58|70|59|72|76|64|67|
```

Fig. 5.69 The array resulting from the incomplete Quicksort

```
            <class otype>
            void improved_quicksort (otype a[], int first, int last)
            {
                incomplete_quicksort (a, first, last);
                linear_insertion_sort (a, first, last);
            }
```

Fig. 5.70 Improved Quicksort, where incomplete_quicksort contains Fig. 5.68 as its base case and linear_insertion_sort is the one in Exercise 5.1.18 (b)

5.8.1 Exercises

5.8.1 Consider the Quicksort code given in Fig. 5.63. Suppose we pass to this function an array of length n in which the objects are distinct and arranged in reverse order, i.e., the largest is in cell a[first] and the smallest is in a[last], with the others in strictly decreasing order in between. Analyze the space and time requirements in this particular case. Be careful; it is easy to jump to incorrect conclusions on the basis of superficial analysis. HINT: when you introduce a time function $T(n)$, be very clear about what kind of array it describes.

5.8.2 Analyze the space and time requirements of the Quicksort function in Fig. 5.63 when it is passed an array of n identical objects.

5.8.3 Consider the naive Quicksort function given in Fig. 5.63. Suppose we pass it an array of length $n \geq 2$ in random order. Then we cannot predict with certainty where the pivot object in cell a[first] will be swapped to in the instruction

$$\text{swap(a[first], a[j]);}$$

just before the two recursive calls. All we can say is that the pivot will go into the k-th cell of a[first..last] for some integer k between 1 and n inclusive. In that case, the recursion will be called on a subarray of length $k - 1$ and a subarray of length $n - k$. An analysis similar to that on p. 268 shows that the execution time $T(n)$ will satisfy the inequality

$$T(n) \leq T(k-1) + T(n-k) + c\,n \tag{5.11}$$

for some positive constant c. Without loss of generality we can assume that c is at least as large as $T(0)$ and $T(1)$, both of which are equal to some positive constant A.

Use mathematical induction to prove that for all $n \geq 0$, $T(n) \leq c\,n^2 + A$. Begin by verifying that this is true when $n = 0$ and when $n = 1$. Then perform the inductive step on integers $n \geq 2$ for which we have the inequality (5.11) above. [HINT: if you produce a term of the form $c(n+1-k)^2$, then expand it as $c\,n^2 - 2\,c\,n(k-1) + c(k-1)^2$. This should simplify the remaining computations.]

When your proof is complete, you will have proved that the naive Quicksort function executes in $O(n^2)$ time on all arrays of length n. Since we have already seen one case in which an array of length n causes this function to run in $\Theta(n^2)$ time, we can now assert that the *maximum* execution time for naive Quicksort on an array of length n is $\Theta(n^2)$.

5.9 Comparison Based Sorting Algorithms

Consider any sorting algorithm that uses nothing but comparisons between objects in a collection in order to decide how to arrange them. This excludes algorithms such as "radix distribution sort" (or "bucket sort") that group objects based on the bits in the objects (Sedgewick 2001; Johnsonbaugh and Schaefer 2004). All the sorting algorithms that we have seen so far in this book base their decisions exclusively on pairwise comparisons. This includes Bubble Sort (p. 185), Selection Sort (p. 189), Linear Insertion Sort (p. 196), Heap Sort (p. 252), Merge Sort (p. 255), and Quicksort (p. 269). We will call such algorithms *comparison based sorting algorithms*.

Now consider the question of calculating the maximum number of object comparisons that can possibly be made when a comparison based sorting algorithm is applied to a collection of n objects. We know that for Selection Sort, Bubble Sort, and Quicksort this maximum is approximately proportional to n^2, and that for Merge Sort and Heap Sort, this maximum is approximately proportional to $n\lg(n)$. That is, the worst case running time in all the comparison based sorting algorithms we have studied so far is at least proportional to $n\lg(n)$.

This raises an interesting question. Is there a comparison based sorting algorithm whose worst case running time is proportional to, or bounded above by, some function that grows more slowly than $n\lg(n)$? For example, is there a comparison based sorting algorithm whose worst case running time is bounded above by some linear function of n? If so, this would be a great sorting algorithm for large values of n. Would it be worth our while to try to invent such an algorithm?

As it happens, investigation of this question is aided by the following observation: given any comparison based sorting algorithm and any given positive integer n, it is possible to draw a corresponding "binary decision tree" that illustrates all the "paths" that the algorithm could take when it sorts an array of length n. Each *non-leaf* node in the tree represents a particular object comparison that will be made at that stage of the execution of the algorithm. (The term "object comparison" does not include subscript

```
template <class otype>
void linear_insertion_sort (otype a[], int n)          // sorts a[0..n-1]
{
    int i, k;
    for (k = 1; k < n; ++k)
    {
        otype temp = a[k]; // Move a[k] to open a hole in the array.
        // Make a backward linear search, using a subscript i.
        for (i = k-1; i >= 0 && a[i] > temp; --i)
            a[i+1] = a[i]; // Slide a[i] to the right by one cell

        // Subscript  i  was decremented after correct position found
        a[i+1] = temp;  // Move old a[k] value to its correct position.
    }
}
```

Fig. 5.71 Linear insertion sort

comparisons.) Each two-way branch away from a "comparison node" corresponds to the two possible results of the comparison. Each leaf node in the tree corresponds to one logical possible arrangement of the objects when the algorithm has finished executing.

Figure 5.71 on p. 276 shows a version of the Linear Insertion Sort algorithm (seen earlier on p. 196). The object comparisons in this algorithm take place only in the expression a[i] > temp. Suppose that this algorithm is applied to an array of length $n = 3$. Let x, y, and z denote the actual objects that are stored in that order initially in the cells of an array a[0..2]. For simplicity, assume that x, y, and z are all distinct. Let's draw the binary decision tree for this algorithm, showing

1. the object comparisons that will be made (each comparison will represent an non-leaf node of the tree),
2. the contents of the array cells,
3. the contents of the variable temp,
4. the final arrangement of the objects x, y, and z in the array a (each such arrangement will be a leaf of the tree).

When an object is copied from one place to another, we'll show as empty the cell it was copied from.

The decision tree is shown in Fig. 5.72. Note that it has 6 leaves; each leaf corresponds to one of the possible correct orderings of the objects x, y, and z.

Each non-leaf node in such a decision tree corresponds to one particular object comparison. Each leaf of this decision tree corresponds to a possible arrangement of the objects we started with. In general, for a tree representing the sorting of n objects, there are $n!$ leaves in the tree. Each branch of the tree, i.e., each path from the root to a leaf node represents one particular "way" that the sorting algorithm can go. The length of such a branch is exactly the number of object comparisons that are made when the sorting algorithm is executed. Thus the *maximum* number of object comparisons that the algorithm can make is equal to the height of the tree.

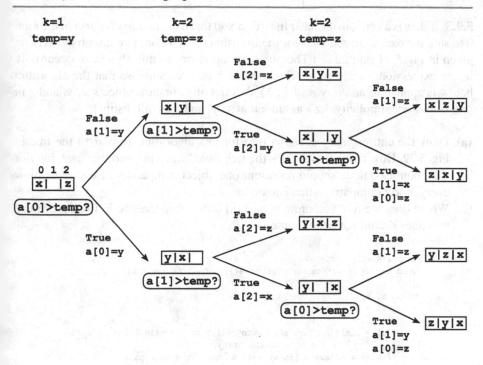

Fig. 5.72 Decision tree for the linear insertion sort of three objects

How big must that maximum be? Since the decision tree contains $n!$ leaf nodes, by Table 5.5 on p. 217, it must contain at least $2(n!) - 1$ nodes, and thus its height must be at least $\lfloor \lg(2(n!) - 1) \rfloor$, which is approximately $1 + \lg(n!)$. By Example 3.2.7 on p. 75, this quantity is $\Theta(n \log(n))$. We have therefore proved the following important theorem.

Theorem 5.9.1 *For every comparison based sorting algorithm and every collection of n distinct objects, there is a way of arranging the objects initially so that the number of object comparisons that will be made by the given algorithm while sorting the collection is at least* $\lfloor \lg(2(n!) - 1) \rfloor$. *Consequently, if* $T_{\max}(n)$ *denotes the maximum possible execution time for a comparison based sorting algorithm on an array of length n, then* $T_{\max}(n) = \Omega(n \log(n))$.

5.9.1   Exercises

5.9.2 Sketch out a small part of the binary decision tree for the linear insertion sorting algorithm in Fig. 5.71 on p. 276 when it is applied to an array a[1..4] that initially contains four distinct objects w, x, y, z in that order. How many leaves would the complete decision tree have?

5.9.3 Below is a version of Linear Insertion Sort that uses a *sentinel object* in location 0 to stop the backward searches for the insertion point. (Compare it with the version given in Fig. 5.71 on p. 276.) The object comparisons in this algorithm occur only in the expression a[i] > a[0] shown in boldface. Suppose that the algorithm below is applied to an array a[1..3] that initially contains objects x, y, and z *in that order*. For simplicity, let's assume that x, y, and z are all distinct.

(a) Draw the entire binary decision tree for this algorithm, similar to the tree in Fig. 5.72. How many leaves does the tree have? Keep in mind that each interior (i.e., non-leaf) node should represent one object comparison. Be sure to show every object comparison that can occur.

(b) Where does the tree you drew in part (a) differ from the tree in Fig. 5.72? (The two trees should not be the same.)

```
template <class otype>
void linear_insertion_sort (otype a[], int n) // sorts a[1..n]
{
  int i, k;
  for (k = 2; k <= n; ++k)
  {
    a[0] = a[k]; // Move a[k] into cell 0 as a sentinel and to open
                 // a hole in the array.
    // Make a backward linear search, using a subscript i.
    // The value in a[0] prevents i from going too far left.
    for (i = k-1; a[i] > a[0]; --i)
      a[i+1] = a[i]; // Slide a[i] to the right by one cell

    // Subscript i was decremented after correct position found
    a[i+1] = a[0]; // Move a[0] into its correct position.
  }
}
```

5.9.4 Figure 5.73 shows a version of the Selection Sort algorithm. Suppose the algorithm is applied to an array a[0..2] that initially contains objects x, y, and z *in that order*. For simplicity, assume that these three objects are all distinct. Half of the binary decision tree for this algorithm and $n = 3$ is shown in Fig. 5.74. Draw the other half of the binary decision tree. Keep in mind that each interior (i.e., non-leaf) node should represent one object comparison. The object comparisons in this algorithm occur only in the expression a[i] > a[max_loc]. Because Selection Sort often repeats object comparisons it has made earlier (it's not very smart), some comparisons that occur farther out in the tree can have only one logical value, not two.

5.9.5 Exactly one of the following statements is a correct conclusion that can be drawn from Theorem 5.9.1. Which one is the correct one?

```
template <class otype>
void selection_sort (otype a[], int n)          // sorts a[0..n-1]
{
  int i, k;
  for (k = n-1; k >= 1; --k)
  {
    int max_loc = 0;        // Location of largest object seen so far.

    for (i = 1; i <= k; ++i)
      if (a[i] > a[max_loc]) // If we find a larger object than the
        max_loc = i;         // prior one, "point" max_loc to that.

    swap (a[k],a[max_loc]);  // Code for swap not shown.  It does
  }                          // not make any object comparisons.
}
```

Fig. 5.73 Selection sort function

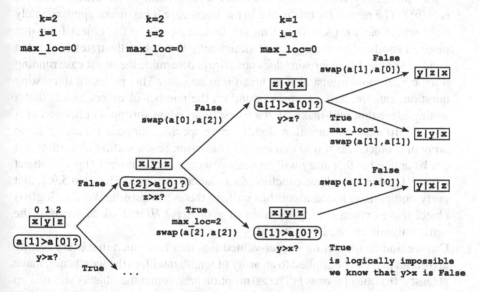

Fig. 5.74 Partial decision tree for the selection sort in Exercise 5.9.4

(a) If you sort n objects using a comparison based sorting algorithm, then the algorithm will always make at least $\lfloor \lg(2(n!) - 1) \rfloor$ object comparisons.

(b) If you sort n objects using a comparison based sorting algorithm, then the maximum number of object comparisons that can be made is $\lfloor \lg(2(n!) - 1) \rfloor$, which means that the algorithm will never make more than $\lfloor \lg(2(n!) - 1) \rfloor$ object comparisons.

(c) If you sort n objects using a comparison based sorting algorithm, then it is always possible that the algorithm will require $\lfloor \lg(2(n!) - 1) \rfloor$ or more object comparisons in order to finish the job.

(d) For any comparison based sorting algorithm, the average number of object comparisons that will be made when sorting n objects is at most $\lfloor \lg(2(n!) - 1) \rfloor$.

(e) For any comparison based sorting algorithm, the average number of object comparisons that will be made when sorting n objects is at least $\lfloor \lg(2(n!) - 1) \rfloor$.

5.9.6 The Binary Insertion Sort given in Fig. 5.18 on p. 204 is a comparison based sorting algorithm.

(a) Derive (mathematically) an estimate for the maximum number of object comparisons that it can make when sorting an array of length n. You may use an answer in Exercise 5.1.24 (b), p. 203: the maximum number of object comparisons that can be made during the binary search in that exercise on an array of length k is $\lceil \lg(k + 1) \rceil$). Theorem 2.3.8 on p. 37 may also be useful.

(b) We showed in Exercise 5.1.25 that Binary Insertion Sort is an "order-n-squared" algorithm because its maximum possible execution time on an array of length n is $\Theta(n^2)$. The reason for this is that in the worst case it can make approximately $n^2/2$ object *moves*. (An "object move" involves copying the object from one place to another by an assignment statement.) What this illustrates is that the number of object comparisons does not always determine the worst case running time: object moves must also be taken into account. This raises an interesting question: can we derive a lower bound on the number of object moves that a sorting algorithm will make, *in the worst case*, when sorting a collection of n objects? To make the question slightly more specific, suppose we are given an array of n objects. Is it true that every comparison based sorting algorithm that can be applied to this array will, in the worst case, make at least $\lfloor \lg(n!) \rfloor$ object moves? Or, can we at least conclude, in a manner similar to Theorem 5.9.1, that every comparison based algorithm will, in the worst case, make $\Omega(n \log(n))$ object moves when sorting an array of n objects? *Hint:* look at some of the sorting algorithms we have studied.

(c) Can we find an increasing integer-valued function $L(n)$ such that every sorting algorithm that can be applied to an array of length n will, in the worst case, make at least $L(n)$ object moves? (The assumption here is that the objects will end up in the same n cells in which they are given to the algorithm, but in sorted order.)

5.10 Pattern Matching Algorithms

A pattern matching algorithm can be explained in the simplest form as a function being called any time we do a search for a substring in a text document. This functionality is common to text editors, Internet browsers, and many other kinds of document viewers. The naïve algorithm accomplishing this task can be written by any beginner programmer, but the pervasive utility of the task requires us to employ a more efficient method if possible. Two known algorithms exist in the literature and in this chapter we will present and discuss them.

pattern:

0	1
i	n

text:

0 1 2 3 4 5 6 7 8 9 10 11 ...

T	h	e		b	e	s	t		t	h	i	n	g	s		i	n		l	i	f	e		a	r	e		f	r	e	e	.

Fig. 5.75 An example of text search

Definition 5.10.1 The *simple matching problem*: find the position of a given pattern (substring) within a given text (string, i.e. character array). The algorithm must return the index where the pattern was first found, or -1 if the pattern is not a substring of the text.

For example, given the pattern and the text shown in Fig. 5.75, a pattern matching algorithm should return the subscript value 11.

Definition 5.10.2 The *complex matching problem*: determine whether a given regular expression matches any substring of a given text, as for example "m*?[rt]", where '*' matches any substring (including an empty one), '?' matches a single character, and the expression within brackets is optional.

The algorithms for the complex matching problem can be adapted from the simple problem. A general description of such an algorithm can be found in (Johnsonbaugh and Schaefer 2004), as well as an algorithm for approximate pattern matching. For example, to search for the regular expression "ab*cde" in a text, we would do the following:

- Search for the substring "ab". Let i be the position returned by this search.
- If i is equal to -1, then return -1.
- Otherwise, search for the string "cde" in the original string, starting from position $i + 2$ (initial position plus the length of "ab", since '*' can match even an empty substring). Let j be the value returned by this function.
- If j is not -1, then return i.
- If j is -1, return -1.

For the remainder of the chapter, we shall focus on the simple matching problem. The brute force (naïve) approach shown in Fig. 5.76 solves the simple matching problem by attempting to match the characters of the pattern and of the text one by one for every valid position in the text. A *valid position* is defined as one where the number of characters from there to the end of the text is greater than or equal to the length of the pattern.

Let m be the size of the pattern and n the size of the text. The time complexity of this algorithm is in the worst case $\Theta((n - m + 1)m) = \Theta(n\,m)$, because for $n - m + 1$ positions in the text array, the algorithm could have to check whether m characters from the pattern match the characters in the text. The maximum value

```
// This function searches for the left-most occurrence of pattern[0..m-1]
// within text[0..n-1]. If there is no occurrence, the function returns -1.
int Search(char text[], char pattern[])
{
  bool found;
  int i, j, n = strlen(text), m = strlen(pattern);

  for (i = 0; i <= n-m; ++i)
  {
    found = true;                        // No mismatch has been detected yet.
    for (j = 0; j < m && found; ++j)
      if (text[i+j] != pattern[j])       // If a mismatch occurs here,
        found = false;                   // then terminate the inner loop.


    if (found)
      return i;
  }
  return -1;
}
```

Fig. 5.76 The brute force algorithm for the simple matching problem

of $(n - m + 1)m$, for a fixed value of n, occurs when $m = \left\lfloor \dfrac{n+1}{m} \right\rfloor$; the maximum value is $\left\lfloor \dfrac{n+1}{m} \right\rfloor \left\lceil \dfrac{n+1}{2} \right\rceil \approx \dfrac{n^2}{4} = \Theta(n^2)$. Such an example of worst case would be looking for the pattern "aaab" in the text "aaaaaaaaaa".

Next we'll see some better algorithms that have a complexity which is $O(n + m)$ at least on the average.

The Rabin-Karp Algorithm

This algorithm, first introduced in Karp and Rabin (1981), uses the idea that at each valid position a quick preliminary computation can be done to check whether the pattern could possibly match the corresponding characters in the text. This preliminary check often makes it unnecessary to go through the process of comparing pairs of corresponding characters.

The algorithm starts by computing the value of a carefully chosen numerical function, called the *fingerprint* function, based on the m characters in the pattern. Then, at each valid position in the text, the fingerprint function can be computed on m successive characters in the text. If the two fingerprint values are not equal, then it is impossible for the pattern to match the text at that position, and we need not initiate the process of directly comparing successive pairs of characters. A C++ implementation of this algorithm is shown in Fig. 5.77.

The efficiency of the Rabin-Karp algorithm depends on choosing the fingerprint function in such a way that its value can be computed in $\Theta(1)$ time when the algorithm moves from one position in the text to the next. The idea is to subtract the contribution of the first character in the old substring from the fingerprint, and to add the contribution of the last character in the next substring. An example will illustrate one way that this can be done.

```
// Searches for the left-most occurrence of pattern[0..m-1] in text[0..n-1]
// using a fingerprint test at each substring text[i..i+m-1] to quickly detect
// most mismatches.

int rabin_karp (char text[], char pattern[])
{
  int i, j, n = strlen(text), m = strlen(pattern);
  unsigned long int pfinger = fingerprint (pattern, m);
  unsigned long int tfinger = fingerprint (text, m);
  bool found;

  for (i = 0; i <= n-m; ++i)
  {                              // No mismatch has been detected yet.
    if (pfinger == tfinger) // then we must check individual characters.
    {
      found = true;
      for (j = 0; j < m && found; ++j)
        if ( text[i+j] != pattern[j] ) // If a mismatch occurs here,
          found = false;               // then terminate the inner loop.

      if (found)      // then the loop terminated without discovering a mismatch,
        return i;     // so the substring starting at text[i] matches pattern.
    }

    if (i+m <= n-1)   // then we'll try for a match with text[i+1..i+m].
      tfinger = update_fingerprint(tfinger, text[i], text[i+m]);
  }
  return -1; // This signals that no match could be found.
}
```

Fig. 5.77 Rabin-Karp algorithm searching for a pattern in a text

text: | T|h|e| |t|r|a|m|s| |a|r|e| |t|h|e| |s|m|a|r|t| |w|a|y| |t|o| |r|i|d|e|. |

Fig. 5.78 An example of a text array

Suppose we define a fingerprint function on character strings to be the sum of the ASCII values of the characters in a string (assuming that the characters are represented using ASCII codes). For example, the fingerprint of the string "bad" would be $98 + 97 + 100 = 295$ (the ASCII values of the lower case letters 'a' to 'z' of the English alphabet are the integers 97–122, and the ASCII values of the upper case letters 'A' to 'Z' are 65–90). Now suppose we use this fingerprint function when searching for the pattern "smart" within the text shown in Fig. 5.78. The fingerprint of "smart" is $115 + 109 + 97 + 113 + 116 = 550$. The fingerprint of "The t" (the initial 5-character substring of the text) is $84 + 104 + 101 + 33 + 116 = 438$. Since the fingerprint of the initial 5-character substring is not equal to the fingerprint of the pattern, the pattern cannot match that substring of the text. It would be pointless, therefore, to compare the individual characters of the pattern to the corresponding characters of the initial 5-character substring of the text.

Now the search moves one space to the right in the text. We want to know whether the pattern matches the 5-character substring "he tr", which is obtained from the previously considered substring by removing an initial 'T' and appending a final 'r'.

```
// Returns the sum of the ASCII values of the characters in str[0..m-1].

unsigned long int fingerprint (char str[], int m)
{
  int i;
  unsigned long int sum;

  for (i = 0, sum = 0; i < m; ++i)
    sum += str[i];   // str[i] will automatically be promoted to unsigned long

  return sum;
}

// Updates the fingerprint based on the previous value, the character that is dropped,
// and the character that is added.

unsigned long int update_fingerprint(int prior_finger, char old_char, char new_char)
{
  return prior_finger - old_char + new_char;
}
```

Fig. 5.79 The fingerprint and corresponding update functions for the sum of the ASCII values

We calculate the fingerprint of this new substring by subtracting the ASCII value of 'T' and adding the ASCII value of 'r':

$$438 - 84 + 114 = 468$$

This fingerprint does not match the 550 fingerprint of our pattern, so no match here is possible. Now the search moves to the next 5-character substring "e tra" obtained by removing an initial 'h' and adding 'a' to the previous 5-character substring. The fingerprint is obtained from the previous 468 by subtracting the ASCII value 104 for 'h' and adding the ASCII value 97 for 'a'. This gives 461, which does not match the fingerprint 550 of our pattern. No match here is possible.

After a few more steps, the algorithm will reach the 5-character substring "trams", which is exactly our pattern "smart" spelled backward. Obviously it will turn out to have the same fingerprint as our pattern, *but this does not mean there is necessarily a match*. What it means is that it is necessary to start the process of comparing the characters of the pattern to the corresponding characters of the 5-character substring. Immediately it will be discovered that there is no match here.

The functions necessary to implement this simple version of the Rabin-Karp algorithm are given in Fig. 5.79. The fingerprint function returns an unsigned long integer, which in C++ must be at least 32 bits, to make sure that in any practical example the sum of the ASCII characters in a pattern will not overflow.

For a second example, let's consider the fingerprint defined as the *character parity* (0 if the sum of all the ASCII values is an even number, 1 if it is odd) of the string. Suppose that we try to match a pattern of size 5 in the text below at the first two positions. Given the fact that the ASCII code for the letter 'a' is 97, an odd number, and that of 'b' is 98, an even number, the fingerprint of the 5 characters starting at the first position is 1.

```
previous string
fingerprint = 1
---------
|           |
a b b a a b a b
  |       |
  ---------
  next string
  fingerprint = 0
```

When we move to the second position, if we know that the fingerprint at the previous position is 1, then the new fingerprint can be computed as the previous fingerprint minus the parity of the ASCII code of the first character we removed ('a', 1) plus the parity of the character we added ('b', 0) modulo 2 (see Sect. 2.5). Thus, the fingerprint of the 5 characters starting at the second position is 0. Since this operation does not depend on the size of the pattern, its complexity is $\Theta(1)$. The efficiency of the Rabin-Karp algorithm depends on the `update_fingerprint` function being of complexity bounded by constants.

If we continue performing fingerprint updates on our text of length 8 at the valid positions for a pattern of length 5, then you can quickly check that we will obtain the fingerprints shown here:

```
fingerprint (parity for 5 chars)   1 0 1 1
                        text   a b b a a b a b
```

(when searching for a pattern of length 5 in a text of length 8, only the first 4 positions in the text are valid positions, so we compute exactly 4 fingerprints). The successive text computations would be performed after we had computed the fingerprint of the 5-character pattern we want to search for. Whenever we get a text fingerprint that does not match the pattern fingerprint we can move on immediately to the next valid position without comparing the pattern to the text.

For example, suppose we want to search the text above for the 5-character pattern "baabb", we would first compute its character parity to be 0. Then we would start across the text, computing the 5-character text fingerprints (1, 0, 1, 1). As you can see, there would be a fingerprint match only at the first 'b' in the text, so that's the only position at which we would compare "baabb" with the text. We would quickly find that there was no match.

On the average we can expect to eliminate about half of the positions in the text using this parity. The computational time is reduced by a factor of 2, but the algorithm is still quadratic in the worst case. Better functions for the fingerprint can make the algorithm $O(n + m)$ on average, but not in the worst case.

Figure 5.80 shows an example of the fingerprint function computed as the character parity.

Note. For the purpose of computing the parity, adding the old char has the same effect as subtracting it, because $(-n) \bmod 2 = n \bmod 2 = n\%2$ for all integers $n > 0$ (see Exercise 2.5.14). We are adding it because this way the result will always be positive and so the % operator will behave like the mathematical modulo function.

```
int fingerprint(char str[], int m)
{
  int i, sum;

  for (i = 0, sum = 0; i < m; ++i)
    sum += str[i];

  return sum%2;
}

int update_fingerprint(int prior_finger, char old_char, char new_char)
{
  return (prior_finger + (old_char % 2) + (new_char % 2)) % 2;
}
```

Fig. 5.80 The fingerprint and corresponding update functions for the character parity

To eliminate a more significant number of positions in the text array, we need a fingerprint function that can return more than just two values. Figure 5.81 shows a more sophisticated fingerprint function. The special feature of this new function consists of the different numerical "weights" given to the characters in the pattern. That is, it attaches various numerical coefficients to the ASCII values of the characters before summing them. This means that the contribution by a character such as 'A' to the fingerprint will depend not only on the ASCII value of 'A' but also on its position within a string. In this way two strings such as "smart" and "trams" are almost certain to have different fingerprints, even though they use the same characters.

As we will soon see, the fingerprint in Fig. 5.81 of a pattern p[0..m-1] turns out to be

$$(2^{m-1} \, p[0] + 2^{m-2} \, p[1] + \cdots + 2^1 \, p[m-2] + p[m-1]) \bmod q, \qquad (5.12)$$

where q is an appropriately chosen prime integer. (See Sect. 2.5 for the definition and implementation of $n \bmod q$.) Similarly, the fingerprint of a substring of length m starting at a position j in a text t[] will be

$$(2^{m-1} \, t[j] + 2^{m-2} \, t[j+1] + \cdots + 2^1 \, t[j+m-2] + t[j+m-1]) \bmod q. \quad (5.13)$$

The weights 2^{m-1}, 2^{m-2}, ... have been chosen, as we will see later, to make the *updates* of the fingerprints in the text array computable in $\Theta(1)$ time. But first we will look at the efficient step-by-step way that the fingerprint code in Fig. 5.81 calculates the fingerprint of the pattern p[0..m-1]. See Fig. 5.82, in which the single letter f is used as the value of the integer variable finger of Fig. 5.81.

Theorem 2.5.3 and Exercise 2.5.11 must be used to justify the intermediate formulas for f given at each stage of the loop execution. Note that the execution time for the loop, and thus for the entire fingerprint function, is $\Theta(m)$.

Now let's investigate what's required to update the fingerprints of substrings of the text as the matching algorithm moves across the text, computing successive fingerprints as it goes. We'll start with the first update between the substring text[0..m-1] and the next substring text[1..m]. Suppose we have already calculated the fingerprint of text[0..m-1], call it t_0, given by

$$t_0 = (2^{m-1} \, text[0] + 2^{m-2} \, text[1] + \cdots + 2^1 \, text[m-2] + text[m-1]) \bmod q,$$

```
int fingerprint(char str[], int m, const int q)
{
   int i, finger;

   for (i = 0, finger = 0; i < m; ++i)
      finger = mod( finger * 2 + str[i], q);

   return finger;
}

int update_fingerprint(int prior_finger, char old_char, char new_char, const int q, int r)
{
   return mod( (prior_finger - r * old_char) * 2 + new_char, q);
}

int improved_rabin_karp (char text[], char pattern[])
{
   const int q = 31321;   // A prime number near square root of MAX_INT;
   int i, j, r, n = strlen(text), m = strlen(pattern);
   int pfinger = fingerprint (pattern, m, q);
   int tfinger = fingerprint (text, m, q);
   bool found;

   for (i = 1, r = 1; i <= m-1; ++i)
      r = mod (2*r, q);               // Set r = (2 to the power m-1) mod q;

   for (i = 0; i <= n-m; ++i)
   {
      if ( pfinger == tfinger )    // then we may have a match, so compare
      {                            // character by character.
         found = true;
         for (j = 0; j < m && found; ++j)
            if ( text[i+j] != pattern[j] ) // then we have a mismatch,
               found = false;            // so we terminate the inner loop.

         if (found)     // then the loop terminated without discovering a mismatch,
            return i;    // so the substring starting at text[i] matches pattern.
      }
      if ( i+m <= n-1 ) // then we'll try for a match with text[i+1..i+m].
         tfinger = update_fingerprint(tfinger, text[i], text[i+m], q, r);
   }
   return -1; // This signals that no match could be found.
}
```

Fig. 5.81 A more elaborate Rabin-Karp algorithm

and we want to use that number to calculate the fingerprint of text [1..m], call it t_1:

$$t_1 = (2^{m-1} \, text[1] + 2^{m-2} \, text[2] + \cdots + 2^1 \, text[m-1] + text[m]) \bmod q.$$

To change t_0 into t_1 we need to perform these steps:

(a) subtract $2^{m-1} \, text[0]$ from t_0;
(b) multiply what remains by 2;

(c) add text [m] to the result;
(d) compute the residue of the sum modulo q.

Initialization: $f = 0$;

1st time through the loop: $f = (2f + p[0]) \bmod q$, which gives f the value p[0] mod q;

2nd time through loop: $f = (2f + p[1]) \bmod q$, so f is now $(2\,p[0] + p[1]) \bmod q$;

3rd time: $f = (2f + p[2]) \bmod q$, so f is now $(2^2\,p[0] + 2\,p[1] + p[2]) \bmod q$;

4th time: $f = (2f + p[3]) \bmod q$, so f is now $(2^3\,p[0] + 2^2\,p[1] + 2\,p[2] + p[3]) \bmod q$;

. . . . . .

m-th time: $f = (2f + p[m-1]) \bmod q$, so f ends up with the value in formula (41).

Fig. 5.82 Step by step execution of the fingerprint function in Fig. 5.81

Expressing this in mathematical symbols, we have

$$t_1 = ((t_0 - 2^{m-1}\ text[0]) \times 2 + text[m]) \bmod q.$$

The next update, between text[1..m] and text[2..m+1], will look like this:

$$t_2 = ((t_1 - 2^{m-1}\ text[1]) \times 2 + text[m+1]) \bmod q.$$

And so on. Each of these computations will require execution time $\Theta(1)$, provided we have calculated the quantity 2^{m-1} before any update is made.

The algorithm can function correctly for any prime number q. To ensure that the complexity of the algorithm is $\Theta(n+m)$ on the average, the number q must satisfy the requirement $q > m\,n^2$.

With this function, we can expect to eliminate on the average about $q-1$ out of every q positions. Since $q > n$, it can be proved that the number of positions for which the pattern and text fingerprints match is on the average $\Theta(1)$.

The following items must be taken into account to estimate the average complexity of this algorithm:

- We need $O(m)$ comparisons between the pattern and the text characters when a fingerprint match occurs.
- The fingerprint must be computed at the beginning for the pattern and for the print, both of which are $\Theta(m)$.
- For every position between 1 and $n-m$, the fingerprint must be computed again; each computation being $\Theta(1)$, this operation takes $\Theta(n-m)$.

When we put all of these together, the complexity of the function on the average can be shown to be $O(n+m)$.

For the worst case the complexity is still $O(n\,m)$ because even if it's very unlikely, it is possible for the pattern fingerprint to be equal to the fingerprint at every position in the text between 0 and $n-m$.

The Knuth-Morris-Pratt (KMP) Algorithm

The following algorithm was introduced by Knuth et al. (1977). Similar ideas are used by the Horspool and Boyer-Moore algorithms (Levitin 2007), with the difference that in those cases the search starts at the end of the pattern.

KMP is based on the idea that when we have a mismatch between the pattern and the text at a given position, we can eliminate a good number of adjacent positions based on the content of the pattern and on how far the characters in the text matched it before the mismatch occurred. The algorithm moves to the next position in the text where the pattern could eventually be matched again and uses any internal repetitions in the pattern.

For example, if we try to match "computer" in the text "computation", we find that the first 6 characters from the pattern are matched at the first six positions in the text, and a mismatch occurs at the seventh position.

```
index   | 0 1 2 3 4 5  6 7 8 9 10
text    | c o m p u t| a t i o n
pattern | c o m p u t| e r
next    |             c o m p u t e r
```

Since there is no 'c' in the text[1..5], it would not be possible for the pattern to be matched again starting from any of the characters that we have already checked. So we can directly skip 6 positions and start again at text[6].

For a second example, let us suppose that we search for the pattern "mermaid" in the text "mermelade" (which was purposefully misspelled for the sake of the explanation).

```
index   | 0 1 2 3  4 5 6 7 8
text    | m e r m| e l a d e
pattern | m e r m| a i d
next    |         m| e r m a i d
```

The first 4 characters of the pattern were matched in the text at position 0, and the mismatch occurred at text[4], of index 4. We can see that the 4th matched character is the same as the first letter in the pattern, so it is possible for the pattern to be matched starting at text[3], where the "m" occurred the second time. Furthermore, we need not check the first letter in the pattern again as we skip to this position, because we already know that we have a match in the text. With this reasoning we can hope to minimize the number of comparisons made for each character in the text. In the second example above, text[4] will be compared twice with a character in the pattern, but no more than that, and all the other characters in the text only once.

To speed up the computation, the algorithm starts by computing a table, called "shift", containing the number of positions to be skipped when a mismatch occurs, indexed by the last position in the pattern where a match occurred. It is computed based on repetitions in the pattern. More precisely, it is based on substrings from the beginning of the pattern that can be found again further inside the pattern. This table is also known as the *prefix* function [3].

Computing the shift array

Fig. 5.83 Function computing the shift array

```
int *compute_shift(char p[])
{
    int m = strlen(p), i=1, j=0;
    int *shift = new int[m+1];
    shift[-1] = 1; // this could be position m
    shift[0] = 1;
    while (i+j<m)
        if (p[i+j] == p[j])
        {
            shift[i+j] = i;
            j = j+1;
        }
        else
        {
            if (j == 0)
                shift[i] = i+1;
            i = i + shift[j-1];
            j = max(j-shift[j-1], 0);
        }
    return shift;
}
```

Let k be an integer such that pattern[0..k] has been matched in the text. By convention, if no character from the pattern has been matched in the text, we'll consider k to be -1.

The computation of the shift array, shown in Fig. 5.83, is using ideas very similar to the KMP algorithm itself. It starts by looking for positions in the pattern where the character matches the pattern[0], marked by the value of the variable i. From there on, while the substring of length j+1 starting from position i matches the substring of the same length starting from the beginning of the pattern, the shift array for the position $k = $ i+j will be assigned the value of i. This means that as long as a mismatch between the pattern and the text happens within this substring, the algorithm will try to match the pattern again starting from wherever the substring is in the text.

Below are some examples of the shift array:

```
          t o r t o i s e
          ------------------
k     -1 0 1 2 3 4 5 6 7
shift  1 1 2 3 3 3 6 7 8

          t w e e d l e d e e
          ----------------------
k     -1 0 1 2 3 4 5 6 7 8 9
shift  1 1 2 3 4 5 6 7 8 9 10

          p a p p a r
          --------------
k     -1 0 1 2 3 4 5
shift  1 1 2 2 2 3 6

          t a r t a r
```

Fig. 5.84 The Knuth Morris
Pratt algorithm searching for
a pattern in a text

```
int KMP(char text[], char pattern[])
{
    int n=strlen(text), m=strlen(pattern), i=0, j=0;
    int *shift = compute_shift(pattern);
    while (i <= n-m) {
        while (text[i+j] == pattern[j])
        {
            ++j;
            if (j >= m)
                return i;
        }
        i = i+shift[j-1];
        j = max(j-shift[j-1], 0);
    }
    return -1;
}
```

```
--------------
k      -1 0 1 2 3 4 5
shift   1 1 2 3 3 3 3
```

If `pattern[i]` does not match `pattern[0]` and is not part of a substring matching the beginning of the pattern, then `shift[i]` will be assigned the value of `i+1`. This means that in case of a mismatch at position `i+1` ($k = i$) in the pattern, the algorithm must skip all the positions in the text examined up to this point.

The KMP algorithm shown in Fig. 5.84 uses the `shift` array to skip a number of positions when a mismatch occurs. The index in the pattern from which the characters are compared with the text does not start from 0 every time, but uses the fact that the characters that are repeated in the pattern and that have already been checked need not be checked again.

Example. Let us suppose that we need to find the pattern "`tartar`" in the text "`tartans...`". The shift array has been computed on the previous page. On the next page is a breakdown of the execution of KMP step by step, with the values of the variables shown.

```
                     * *
text       t a r t a n s...
pattern    t a r t a r
i          0
j          0 1 2 3 4 5
pattern          t a r t a r
i                3
j                        2
pattern          t a r t a r
i                6
j                0
```

The * indicates a mismatch position. We start with `i` and `j` both being equal to 0. As long as we have a match, the value of `j` increases while the value of `i` doesn't change. So far the brute force algorithm would have done the same thing.

When the value of j becomes 5, we have a mismatch. Note that the value of shift[4] is 3. This means that we skip forward by 3 positions and attempt to match the pattern again in the text starting from the 4th position where we have the character 't'. This is accomplished by changing the value of i to 3. We know that we already have a match for the first two positions in the pattern, the 't' and the 'a', and we don't need to check them again. This is accomplished by changing the value of j to 2, which is the difference between its previous value (5) and the value of shift[4]. Thus at the next iteration we need to check the first character 'r' in the pattern against 'n' in the text.

At this point we have another mismatch. As shift[j-1] is equal to 3, we skip forward by 3 positions, taking us effectively beyond all the characters in the text that have been checked so far. This happens because in the set of characters that have been matched so far, there is no repetition of the beginning of the pattern, so we skip them altogether. The value of i becomes 6 and the value of j becomes negative if we subtract 3 from it, so it is reset to 0. The algorithm continues from the position of the character 's' if the text is longer than shown above.

Note. In a real implementation of this algorithm, the position shift[-1] is obviously not a valid element of the array shift. One must handle this element of the array with some special method, as for example, by shifting all positions in the shift array by 1 forward, or storing shift[-1] in a separate variable, or wrapping the shift array in a class that allows for a subscript of -1.

In C++ one can declare an array shift_base, then make the shift point to the first element of shift_base. That way shift[-1] would be the same element as shift_base[0] and the code does not have to change:

```
int shift_base[m+1];
int *shift = shift_base + 1;
```

In Python arrays are in fact circular lists and if shift is declared as an array of size $m + 1$, then shift[-1] will be the last element in the array.

Complexity of the KMP

The complexity of this algorithm is $O(n + m)$ in all cases. A proof of correctness of this algorithm can be found in [3]. The proof of the complexity is somewhat more involved, but it consists in the following observations.

(a) The computation of the shift is $\Theta(m)$.
(b) Most characters in the text will be compared only once or twice with characters from the pattern, both in cases of a match, and of mismatch.
(c) In some extreme cases, a character from the text might be compared with pattern characters m times—however, at most n/m of the characters from the text could be in that situation even in the worst case, and that still means $\Theta(n)$ comparisons on the whole.

To give such an extreme example, let us consider the pattern "aaaaa" in the text "aaaab". The shift array will be computed as

```
            a a a a a
            -------------
k        -1 0 1 2 3 4
shift     1 1 1 1 1 1
```

When the mismatch occurs between a and b, we shift forward by just one position and compare b with the previous a in the pattern. After each mismatch we shift forward one more position. In the end, the character b will be compared with 5 different characters a from the pattern. For this to occur, we still need 4 matches between the text and the pattern before that position, so only $n/5$ characters from the text can be compared 5 times with characters from the pattern.

5.10.1 Exercises

5.10.3 What is the complexity of any of the pattern matching algorithms in this chapter when $m > n$? Justify your answer.

5.10.4 How many comparisons of text and pattern characters (to each other) does the brute force search algorithm do when searching for the pattern "maze" in the text "amazing"? What is the value returned by the function?

5.10.5 Trace the Rabin-Karp search algorithm on pattern "ccc" and text "dccdcdd-ccddcccd" using the fingerprint function in Fig. 5.81 with $q = 5$. The ASCII code for the letters 'c' and 'd' are 99 and 100 respectively. Show the value of the fingerprint at each position in the text and mark the positions where there is a match with the fingerprint of the pattern. How many comparisons between the pattern and text characters are done?

5.10.6 (a) Compute the shift array for the Knuth-Morris-Pratt algorithm for the patterns "abracadabra" and "mathematics".
(b) Trace the KMP algorithm for the pattern "mathematics" in the text "mathematicians and mathematics" (a text composed of three words, not two different texts). How many comparisons of the text with pattern characters did the algorithm do?

Algorithms and Probabilities

6

In the preceding chapter we computed the minimum and maximum amounts of time and space that various algorithms require when they are run on a computer. In this chapter we will be concerned primarily with the "average" amounts of time that various algorithms require. We will also study some algorithms that use randomized procedures to achieve certain goals. Examples of such algorithms are "simulating random events", "randomizing the order of objects in a list", and "selecting a random sample from a population".

Throughout this chapter it is assumed that the reader has familiarity with the fundamental definitions and theorems of discrete probability theory. For readers who need to refresh their memories of that subject, there is an Appendix Chapter that summarizes the material needed. It defines the notions of statistical experiment, sample space, event, probability of an event, conditional probability, random variable, probability density function (p.d.f.), cumulative density function(c.d.f.), expected value of a random variable, and conditional expected value. The necessary theorems about these concepts are stated (but not proved) so that they can be cited in this algorithms chapter.

6.1   Simulation and Random Number Generators

Many computer applications require the **simulation** (i.e., computer modeling) of real-world systems for which at least part of the input is random in some way. For example, in a real-world queuing system such as a machine repair shop or a collection of grocery check-out lines, the arrivals of "customers" at the system occur unpredictably, but with a known probability distribution, and similarly the amount of time required to service one customer is variable in a way that depends on chance. Computer programs can be written that behave like queuing systems, and this makes it possible to study such systems and predict their behavior before they are actually built and put into service.

© Springer International Publishing Switzerland 2014   295
D. Vrajitoru and W. Knight, *Practical Analysis of Algorithms*,
Undergraduate Topics in Computer Science, DOI 10.1007/978-3-319-09888-3_6

Computer simulation of systems that have unpredictable inputs requires the use of **random number generators**. These are functions that, when called repeatedly, return a stream of numbers that appear to be randomly chosen from some range or interval. In reality, of course, the numbers returned by such a function are *pseudo-random* numbers since they are actually generated by specific recurrence relations that would allow us to calculate each value from one or more preceding values. It is nevertheless customary to refer to such numbers as random numbers, dropping the modifier "pseudo-", which means "fake".

Throughout this chapter we assume when convenient that we have access to a random number generator function in C/C++ with the prototype

```
long randint (long first, long last);
```

that returns random integers in the range from `first` to `last` inclusive. There are $(last - first + 1)$ integers in this range, and each will have probability $\dfrac{1}{last - first + 1}$ of being returned by the function.

We also assume that we have access to a random number generator function in C/C++ with the prototype

```
double randouble (void);
```

that returns random real numbers uniformly distributed in the range $[0.0, 1.0)$. Exercise 6.1.8 discusses some implementation details for these two functions.

The following examples illustrate how we can use a random number generator to simulate various statistical experiments (see Definition 3.3.1 in the Appendix). In each case, the solution given is just one of many possibilities.

Example 6.1.1 Suppose that a program we are writing needs to simulate the statistical experiment of making a single toss of a biased coin that turns up heads only 45 % of the time; that is, the probability of obtaining heads should be $45/100 = 9/20$. How can we use the `randint` function to help us simulate such a toss? The answer is easy: we place in our program an instruction of the form

```
r = randint (1, 20);
```

and observe that r has probability 9/20 of being between 1 and 9 inclusive. Thus we can have our program report that heads occurs if the r value that's returned is in the range 1–9, and that tails occurs if the r value is in the range 10–20.

Example 6.1.2 Suppose we want our program to simulate the statistical experiment of choosing an object at random from an array `a[first..last]` of objects of any kind. We place in our program an instruction of the form

```
r = randint (first, last);
```

and then choose `a[r]` from the array.

Example 6.1.3 Suppose we want to simulate the statistical experiment of throwing a biased die for which an ace (one spot) is twice as likely to turn up as any other face. We place in our program an instruction of the form

$$r = \text{randint}(0, 6);$$

and then if $r = 0$ or 1 is returned, the program can report that an ace has turned up, while if $r > 1$, the program can report that the face with r spots has turned up.

Example 6.1.4 Suppose we want to simulate the statistical experiment of drawing a card from a shuffled deck. A first step would be to have the program create an array deck[0..51] containing representations of the 52 cards in a standard playing deck. Then the program could execute the instruction

$$r = \text{randint}(0, 51)$$

and report deck[r] to be the card drawn. Even though the array deck[0..51] is in some fixed order, by making a random choice from the array we get the effect of drawing from a shuffled deck.

Second Option: This alternative does not require us to set up any array whatsoever. Instead, we make two calls to randint as follows:

$$\text{rank} = \text{randint}(1, 13) \quad \text{and} \quad \text{suit} = \text{randint}(1, 4).$$

Then a rank of 1 means an ace, and so on up to 11 which means jack, 12 which means queen, and 13 which means king. Similarly, if suit is 1 we call it a club, 2 is a diamond, 3 is a heart and 4 is a spade.

Third Option: We can be slightly more efficient by making only one call to randint, followed by a little arithmetic:

$$r = \text{randint}(0, 51),$$

$$\text{suit} = r/13 + 1 \quad \text{and} \quad \text{rank} = r\%13 + 1,$$

with the same interpretation of the numbers as in the Second Option. Calls to randint are likely to be significantly more time consuming than simple arithmetic operations.

Example 6.1.5 Suppose we want to simulate the statistical experiment of throwing a pair of fair dice and reporting the sum of the faces that turn up. Since the sum can be any integer between 2 and 12 inclusive, a naive programmer might place the instruction

$$t = \text{randint}(2, 12);$$

in the program and have the program report t to be the sum of the spots on the two faces. The reason this is wrong is that when actually rolling a pair of dice the sums of the spots are not equally likely: a sum of 7 is six times as likely as a sum of 2. The call randint(2,12) gives all sums from 2 to 12 an equal probability of occurring.

A correct way to simulate the throw is to make two calls to the random number generator, say

$$r = \text{randint}(1, 6); \quad \text{and} \quad s = \text{randint}(1, 6);$$

and return the sum of these two integers as the sum of spots on the faces of the two dice.

Example 6.1.6 Suppose we want to simulate the statistical experiment of tossing a fair coin 5 times. The most straightforward way to do this is to make five successive calls of the form `randint(0,1);` and report each 0 as heads and each 1 as tails.

6.1.1 Exercises

6.1.7 What is the probability that the C++ instruction

```
int rem = randint(1,12) % 5;
```

will assign to `rem` the value 1? The value 4?

6.1.8 (a) Consider the situation where the language only provides a function `rand()` returning a long unsigned integer in the range $[0, \text{RAND\_MAX}]$ where the constant `RAND_MAX` is provided by the same library as the function `rand`. How would you implement the function `randouble()`?

(b) Given a C++ function `rand()` returning a random long unsigned integer, consider the following implementation of the function `randint()`:

```
long randint(long first, long last)
{ return first + rand() % (last- first + 1); }
```

Suppose (for purposes of illustration) that `rand()` returns integers in the absurdly small range $0\ldots15$. Calculate the probability that the call `randint(1,9)` will return the value 4. Calculate the probability that the call `randint(1,9)` will return the value 8. Explain why the code given above for `randint` is biased.

(c) Starting from a uniform `randouble()` function, consider the following implementation of the function `randint()`:

```
long randint(long first, long last)
{ return first + int(floor(randouble() * (last - first + 1))); }
```

Show that this function is unbiased.

6.1.9 The solution to the simulation problem posed in Example 6.1.5 involves two calls to `randint()`. Describe a way to simulate the throw of a pair of fair dice using just one call to the random number generator followed by some computer arithmetic.

The outcome of your program must be the two numbers appearing on the pair of dice and not their sum. [Hint: see Example 6.1.4 where two random numbers rank and suit are generated with one call to randint() followed by some arithmetic.]

6.1.10 The solution to the simulation problem posed in Example 6.1.6 involves five calls to randint(). Describe a way to simulate five tosses of a fair coin using just one call to the random number generator followed by some computer computations. [Hint: think about the binary representation of non-negative integers.]

6.1.11 How could we simulate the experiment of drawing a marble at random from an urn that contains 12 identical red marbles, 19 identical white marbles, and 5 identical blue marbles? The result of the simulation should be one of the three possible colors.

6.2   Randomizing Arrays and Files

Suppose we want to write a C++ program that simulates the playing of various card games. We might conceivably make the definitions and declarations shown in Fig. 6.1.

Now suppose we want to write the code for the "shuffle" function. This function should simulate a *fair* shuffle of the deck, by which we mean that the shuffling process should give every one of the 52! possible arrangements of the deck an equal likelihood of occurring. To say it differently, a "fair shuffle" is an algorithm for putting the 52-card array in random order without giving any arrangement a higher chance than others. Figures 6.2 and 6.3 show two candidate algorithms for simulating a fair shuffle. Which (if either) of these algorithms produces a fair shuffle?

Each of these algorithms causes a subscript k to move across the deck array, and at each step a randomly chosen card is swapped with deck[k]. The two algorithms differ in the way the randomly chosen card is selected: in Algorithm 1, it can be any of the 52 cards in the deck; in Algorithm 2 the choice is restricted to cards in the "not-yet-randomized" portion of the deck.

Most people are surprised to learn that Algorithm 1 is biased, i.e., does not produce a fair shuffle, while Algorithm 2 is unbiased. It will be left as Exercise 6.2.1 to prove that Algorithm 1 does not give a fair shuffle.

Let's now prove that Algorithm 2 is unbiased. Here is what we must prove: given any arrangement $(c_1, c_2, c_3, \ldots, c_{52})$ of the 52 cards in the deck, the probability that Algorithm 2 will produce that particular arrangement is $\frac{1}{52!}$. Let A_k denote the event that card c_k ends up in cell deck[k]. Then we want to prove that

$$P(A_1 \cap A_2 \cap A_3 \cap \cdots \cap A_{52}) = \frac{1}{52!}.$$

Using the Chain Rule for conditional probability (Theorem 8.0.14), we can compute as follows: $P(A_1 \cap A_2 \cap A_3 \cap \cdots \cap A_{52}) = P(A_1) \times P(A_2|A_1) \times$

```
struct card_type
{
  int rank;
  int suit;
};

class deck_type
{
 public:

  enum suit_type {CLUB = 1, DIAMOND = 2, HEART = 3, SPADE = 4};

  enum rank_type {TWO   =  2, THREE = 3, FOUR = 4, FIVE =  5, SIX  =  6,
                  SEVEN =  7, EIGHT = 8, NINE = 9, TEN  = 10, JACK = 11,
                  QUEEN = 12, KING  = 13, ACE  = 14 };

  deck_type()           // Constructor
  {
    int i = 1, rank, suit;       // i will run along the deck array
    for (rank = TWO; rank <= ACE; ++rank)
      for (suit = CLUB; suit <= SPADE; ++suit)
      {
        deck[i].suit = suit;
        deck[i].rank = rank;
        ++i;
      }
  }

  void shuffle();      // Randomize the order of cards in a deck

 private:

  card_type deck[53]; // This allows subscripts to go from 1 to 52
};
```

Fig. 6.1 A class representing a deck of cards

```
Shuffling Algorithm 1:
int k, r;
for (k = 1; k <= 52; ++k)
{
  r = randint(1, 52); // Generate a random integer in the range  1... 52.
  swap(deck[r], deck[k]);
}
```

Fig. 6.2 The first shuffling algorithm

```
Shuffling Algorithm 2:
int k, r;
for (k = 1; k <= 51; ++k)
{
  r = randint(k, 52);  // Generate a random integer in the range  k...52.
  swap(deck[r], deck[k]);
}
```

Fig. 6.3 The second shuffling algorithm

$P(A_3|A_1 \cap A_2) \ldots \times P(A_{52}|A_1 \cap A_2 \cap \cdots \cap A_{51}) = \dfrac{1}{52} \dfrac{1}{51} \dfrac{1}{50} \cdots \dfrac{1}{1}$. It is quite obvious why $P(A_1) = 1/52$: when k is 1 , the call randint(k,52) gives each of the subscripts from 1 to 52 an equal probability of being chosen, and c_1 must be in one of those 52 cells. The reason that $P(A_2|A_1) = 1/51$ is that if A_1 does occur, then c_1 has definitely been swapped into cell deck[1], and so c_2 must be in one of the remaining 51 cells. Similarly, $P(A_3|A_1 \cap A_2) = 1/50$ because if A_1 and A_2 have indeed occurred, then c_1 and c_2 have been swapped into cells deck[1] and deck[2], and so c_3 must be in one of the remaining 50 cells etc.

Shuffling Algorithm 2 can be generalized to apply to any array a [first.. last]. You are asked to construct this generalization in Exercise 6.2.1. Thus from now on we can assume we are in possession of an algorithm for randomizing the order of the objects in a given array of length n, i.e., an algorithm for rearranging the objects in such a way that each of the $n!$ possible arrangements has probability $\dfrac{1}{n!}$ of occurring.

The problem of randomizing the order of a collection of objects also arises with files. Suppose we are given a sequential file on a disk or tape and asked to randomize the order of the objects in the file. (A "sequential" file is a file whose objects can be accessed only in the order in which they are arranged in the file; there is no "random access" to the objects as there would be if the objects were in an array.) This file randomization is easy to do if our program is able to allocate an array large enough to hold all the objects in the file. In this case we can simply read all the objects into the array, randomize the array, and then write the objects in their new order back to disk or tape. The problem becomes more difficult if the file is so large that its contents will not all fit into an array in the computer's memory. This problem is considered in Exercise 6.2.8.

6.2.1   Exercises

6.2.1 On p. 301 it is asserted that Shuffling Algorithm 1 on that page is biased, i.e., does not produce a fair shuffle of the deck. This exercise is designed to demonstrate that fact when we reduce the deck to just 3 cards.

(a) Suppose we have 3 cards, call them a, b, and c. Suppose they are placed in an array called deck so that deck[1] = a , deck[2] = b, and deck[3] = c initially. Now suppose we apply Algorithm 1, but with the number 3 in place of the number 52. Draw a tree diagram (see Example 8.0.15) showing all the arrangements that can be produced at every step along the way. Show that some final arrangements of a, b, and c have higher probability of occurring than others. (If the shuffle were fair, each of the 3! possible final arrangements would have probability $\dfrac{1}{3!}$ of occurring.)

(b) Now consider the case of a deck of size 52. Explain why it is impossible for all arrangements of the deck to have equal probability of being produced by

Shuffling Algorithm 1. Do this by proving that it is impossible for *any* arrangement to have probability $\frac{1}{52!}$ of being produced. [Hint: imagine drawing the same kind of tree diagram as in part (a), except that such a diagram would be HUGE.] How many leaves would that tree diagram have? What would be the probability of each of the paths from root to leaf in the tree?

(c) Some students note that there is a difference between the numbers of times the body of the loop in Algorithm 1 and the body of the loop in Algorithm 2 are executed. In Algorithm 1 the body of the loop is executed 52 times, while in Algorithm 2 the body of the loop is executed only 51 times. If we change the code for Algorithm 1 so that its loop stops at 51, will this make Algorithm 1 fair? Justify your answer.

6.2.2 Write a C++ function template that randomizes the order of the objects in a subarray a[first...last], where the objects can be of any data type. The prototype for the template should be as follows:

```
template <class otype>
void randomize (otype a[], int first, int last);
```

6.2.3 Here is an answer that has sometimes been given for Exercise 6.2.2:

```
template <class otype>
void randomize (otype a[], int first, int last)
{
  int k, r, s;
  for (k = first; k <= last; ++k)
  {
    r = randint(first, last);
    s = randint(first, last);
    swap(a[r], a[s]);
  }
}
```

(a) Show that if the length of the array is 2 (i.e., if last is first + 1), then this algorithm gives each of the two possible arrangements equal probability of occurring.
(b) Show that if the length of the array is 3 (i.e., if last is first + 2), then the algorithm is biased, i.e., it does *not* give each of the 3! = 6 possible arrangements equal probability of occurring. You may solve this problem either by drawing a tree diagram or by using a counting and divisibility argument.
(c) Show that for all arrays of length $n \geq 3$, the randomization algorithm above is biased.

Shuffling Algorithm 3:

```
int j, k;
for (k = 1; k <= 51; ++k)
{
    j = randint(k, 52);      // Produce a random integer i in the range  k...52.
    aux[k] = deck[j];        // Copy deck[j] into the auxiliary array.
    deck[j] = deck[k];       // Overwrite  deck[j]  location with the first card of the
}                            // subarray  deck[k...52], and now consider the deck
                             // to be reduced to the subarray  deck[k+1...52].
for (k = 1; k <= 51; ++k) // Copy the cards in the aux array back to deck.
    deck[k] = aux[k];
```

Fig. 6.4 The third shuffling algorithm

Shuffling Algorithm 4:
```
int j, k;
for (k = 1; k <= 52; ++k)
{
    j = randint(k+1, k+51);  // Produce a random integer in the range k+1... k+51.
    if (j > 52)              // If the  j  value is beyond the end of the deck,
        j = (j % 52);        // "wrap around" to the beginning of the deck.
    swap (deck[k], deck[j]);
}
```

Fig. 6.5 The fourth shuffling algorithm

6.2.4 Consider the algorithm in Fig. 6.4 for the "shuffle" function of the "deck_type" class. It uses an auxiliary array aux[1..51].

(a) Show that it produces a fair shuffle.
(b) Compare the number of object moves (assignment statements that copy a card from a cell to a cell) in Algorithm 3 above with the number of moves in Algorithm 2 in Fig. 6.3, p. 300. Note that a swap requires 3 object moves.
(c) Compare the number of calls to randint in Algorithm 3 with the number in Algorithm 2.
(d) Compare the space requirements of Algorithm 3 and Algorithm 2.
(e) Both Algorithm 3 and Algorithm 2 can be generalized in a trivial way to randomize arrays of length n instead of length 52. Express the running time for each of these generalized algorithms in big-theta notation. Assume that a swap requires $\Theta(1)$ time and $\Theta(1)$ space.

6.2.5 Algorithm 1 in Fig. 6.2, p. 300, allows a cell to be swapped with itself. Is it this property that causes it to be a biased algorithm? So consider the algorithm in Fig. 6.5 for the "shuffle" function of the "deck_type" class. The idea of this modified algorithm is that for each cell in the array "deck", the algorithm randomly picks a *different* cell and swaps the contents of those two distinct cells.

Shuffling Algorithm 5:

```
int r, k;
for (k = 2; k <= 52; ++k)
{
  r = randint(1, k);        // Produce a random integer in the range 1...k.
  swap(deck[k], deck[r]);
}
```

Fig. 6.6 The fifth shuffling algorithm

As an example of how this works, suppose the loop index k reaches the value 5. We want an integer j *different from* 5 to be selected at random, and then we'll swap the cards at locations k and j. The body of the loop sets j to a randomly chosen integer from among the 51 integers in the set 6, 7, 8, . . . , 52, 53, 54, 55, 56. The last four numbers in the set are outside the array limits, so if j has one of those values, we take its remainder after division by 52, which produces one of the number 1, 2, 3, 4. Thus a cell number between 1 and 52 is produced, but it is *not* 5.

(a) Determine whether this algorithm produces a fair shuffle on a deck of 3 cards. That is, replace the number 52 everywhere in Algorithm 4 with the number 3, and replace 51 with 2. Does the algorithm operate so as to give each possible final arrangement an equal probability of occurring?

(b) Is Algorithm 4 in Fig. 6.5 fair on a deck of 52 cards?

6.2.6 Consider the Shuffling Algorithm 5 in Fig. 6.6. Note that it differs from Algorithm 2 in that the index of the object swapped with the object at index k is less than or equal to k instead of greater than or equal to k. Prove that this algorithm also produces a fair shuffling.

6.2.7 Consider the C++ algorithm in Fig. 6.7 that randomizes the order of the nodes of a NULL-terminated, singly linked list, following the idea in Algorithm 5 in Fig. 6.6. Analyze the best and worst case running times for your algorithm for lists of length n assuming that the swap requires $\Theta(1)$ time and $\Theta(1)$ space.

6.2.8 Suppose we have a sequential file F so large that we cannot allocate an array large enough to hold all the objects in the file. Suppose, however, that we can create an array that holds at least half of the objects in F. How can we randomize the order of the objects in F? One way is to read the first half of F into our array, randomize the order of the objects in the array (see Exercise 6.2.2), write those objects out to a temporary file G, read the second half of F into the array, randomize, and write out those objects to a file H. Then we can open both G and H simultaneously and combine them into one output file, call it K, by a kind of "randomized merge" of G and H. Figure 6.8 shows a "naive" algorithm for implementing the randomized merge.

```
// This is a function that randomizes a NULL-terminated linked list of nodes.
// The algorithm follows the same idea as Shuffling Algorithm 5.

void randomize_linked_list (node_ptr list)
{
  node_ptr p, q;
  long k, r, i;

  if (! list || !list->next)     // If the given list is empty or of length 1,
    return;                      // there is no work to be done.
  else
  {
    p = list->next;              // we don't need to swap the first node
    k = 1;                       // index of the node p

    while (p)
    {
      r = randint(0, k);         // index of the node to swap p with
      q = list;                  // move q to the node to swap p with
      for (i=0; i<r; i++)        // move q forward r steps
        q = q->next;
      swap(p->datum, q->datum);  // swap the data in the nodes

      p = p->next;               // then advance p
    }
  }
}
```

Fig. 6.7 A list shuffling algorithm

```
void randomized_merge(istream &G, istream &H, ostream &K)
//Assumes that G and H are open for reading, K is open for writing
{
  while ("G and H are not empty")
  {
    int r = randint(1, 2); // "Toss a fair coin" to choose a file.
    if (r == 1)
      "read the next object from G and write it out to K";
    else // r must be 2
      "read the next object from H and write it out to K";
  }

  if ("H is empty")
    "copy the remaining objects from G to K";
  else
    "copy the remaining objects from H to K";
}
```

Fig. 6.8 Merges two files in a randomized fashion

(a) Use the special case where the number of objects in the file F is $n = 4$ to
show that this merge algorithm will bias the randomization process. Begin by
assuming that the objects in F are a, b, c, d in that order. Then G will get a, b in
one of two orders, and H will get c, d in one of two orders. Draw a tree diagram
that branches initially to the four possibilities for G and H at the instant at which

the merge algorithm above begins its work. Let further branches (based on the "coin tossing") show the possibilities for G, H, and K at each step. Calculate the probabilities of the various arrangements in K at the end of the process. Show that some arrangements are more likely than others.

(b) Consider the tree diagram in the solution for part (a). Suppose we change the probabilities on the "merging branches" so that at each step along the way the probability of choosing from each of the two intermediate files (G or H) is proportional to the number of unread objects remaining in that file. For example, when both G and H have the same number of unread objects remaining, the probability of choosing from G should be 1/2 and the same for H, but when G has only 1 unread object and H has 2, then the probability of choosing from G should be 1/3 and the probability of choosing from H should be 2/3. Show that in this case the randomization process is unbiased.

(c) Modify the pseudo-code in Fig. 6.8 so that at each step during the merge process the probability of choosing from each of the two intermediate files (G or H) is proportional to the number of unread objects remaining in that file. This can be shown to produce an unbiased randomization process. Use the following function prototype in which g and h are the initial sizes of (number of objects in) the files G and H.

```
//Assumes that G and H are open for reading, K is open for writing
void randomized_merge(istream &G, istream &H, ostream &K, int g, int h);
```

(d) Give a file randomization algorithm for taking care of the case where the file F is so large that *three* intermediate randomized files must be created and then merged. Your algorithm can *call* the function you wrote for part (c) if that is convenient.

6.2.9 (a) Suppose an unbiased randomization algorithm is applied to an array of length n (so that every possible arrangement of the objects in the array has equal probability $1/n!$ of occurring). Prove that each object in the original array has equal probability of being placed in any cell of the array when the algorithm is applied.

(b) Let's call that property the "any-object-can-go-anywhere" property. We have just noted that *if* a randomization algorithm is unbiased, *then* it must have the "any-object-can-go-anywhere" property. Some people assume that the converse must also be true: if a proposed randomization algorithm can be shown to have the "any-object-can-go-anywhere" property, then it must be unbiased. Consider, however, the algorithm in Fig. 6.9.

```
template <class otype>
void randomize (otype a[], int first, int last)
{
    int n = last - first + 1;    // Number of cells in a[first..last]
    otype temp[n];               // Need an extra storage array.
    int  r = randint(0, n-1);    // Generate a "shift distance."
    int  j, k;                   // j and k will run along the temp array
    for (j=0, k = first + r; k <= last; ++k)
        temp[j++] = a[k];        // Copy back part of "a" to front of "temp"
    for (k = first; k <= first + r - 1; ++k)
        temp[j++] = a[k];        // Copy front part of "a" to back of "temp"
    // Copy all of "temp" back to a[first..last]
    for (j = 0, int k = first; k <= last; ++j, ++k)
        a[k] = temp[j++];
}
```

Fig. 6.9 A function randomizing an array

To illustrate the algorithm with an example, suppose array a[first..last] initially looks like

4	5	6	7	8
a	b	c	d	e

If the random number generator returns $r = 3$, then the algorithm will copy the objects in cells 7 and 8 into the first two cells of temp and the objects in cells 4, 5, and 6 into the last three cells of temp to produce this arrangement:

	0	1	2	3	4
temp:	d	e	a	b	c

Then all five cells would be copied back to the original array. The effect is to produce a "3-cell right shift with wrap-around". As you can easily see, object a is equally likely to end up in any of the five cells of temp, and the same is true of the other four objects in the array. Thus in this example, and in general, the algorithm given above has the "any-object-can-go-anywhere" property. Explain why even so, the algorithm is badly biased.

6.3   Choosing a Random Sample from a Sequential File

Suppose we are given a large set of size N and asked to choose a random sample of size K from the set, i.e., a subset of size $K < N$. To be considered a random sample, the subset must be chosen by a process that gives every subset of size K an equal chance of being chosen. Since there are $\binom{N}{K}$ different subsets of size K in a

set of size N , each of these subsets must be given the probability $1/\binom{N}{K}$ of being

selected.

Why might someone want to choose a random sample of specified size from a large set, which we call a "population"? The answer generally is that a scientist or a commercial firm wants to obtain data about certain characteristics of the individuals or objects that make up the population, but the population is so large that it is impractical to study every member of the population. In such a case, an alternative is to choose as large a random sample as one can afford from the whole population, study the individuals of that sample, and then generalize the results to the entire population, using appropriate statistical techniques of estimation. Another situation, however, would be where a research team wants to select *randomly* half of a population (e.g., of cancer patients) on whom to try out a new and promising treatment.

Let's imagine that a scientist or marketing firm has come to us with a large file containing data records (perhaps names, addresses, and phone numbers) for all N individuals in the population to be studied. The data records in the file can be accessed sequentially only; that is, we do not have random access into the file. We are asked to write a program to select a random sample of K data records from the file and place them in another file where they will serve as the list of individuals to be studied as members of the sample. What is an efficient algorithm for choosing a truly random sample?

The first algorithm we'll examine assumes that the program is given the number N of data records in the file available as an input even before the file is read. That is, the program is told how many records the file contains before it begins reading the file. The algorithm chooses K distinct integers in the range from 1 to N and then reads the file, discarding all data records except those whose "number" was chosen. For example, if the file size is $N = 10$ (an unrealistically small size) and the required sample size is $K = 3$, and if the algorithm chooses the integers 2, 5, and 8, then the first 8 data records of the file will be read and the 2nd, 5th, and 8th records will be written to another file and will constitute the desired sample.

The algorithm we'll examine chooses the K integers by setting up a Boolean array with cells numbered from 0 to N and then generating random integers in the range from 1 to N, marking them in the Boolean array until K distinct integers have been marked. (Cell 0 is ignored in all this.) Code for the algorithm is given in Fig. 6.10. In the documentation for the algorithm we have used the phrase "data object" instead of the phrase "data record" (the word "object" is more general than "record" in computer science).

We have used the familiar file insertion « and extraction » operators from C++. The first question we should ask about Sample Select Algorithm 1 is whether it gives a valid random sample. That is, is the selection process unbiased, or do some subsets of size K have higher probability of being generated than do other subsets? The answer is that the process is unbiased.

Sample Select Algorithm 1

```
// This is a function template for selecting a random sample of K data objects
// from an open sequential file F known to contain N data objects.  The selected
// objects are written out to an open file G.  It is assumed that the stream
// insertion and extraction operators << and >> are overloaded for the otype
// class.  Error checking code has been omitted to avoid clutter.

template <class otype>
void select_sample (istream & F, int K, int N, ostream & G)
{
   bool in_sample[N+1];
   int i, r, count = 0;
   otype temp;

   for ( i = 1; i <= N; ++i )   // Initialize the in_sample array.
     in_sample[i] = false;

   while ( count < K )
   {
      r = randint(1, N);        // Randomly select the "file index" of an object
                                // in F. (The file index of the first object in F
      if ( ! in_sample[r] )     // is 1, the second object has file index 2, etc.
      {
         in_sample[r] = true;
         ++count;
      }
   }

   // When execution reaches this point, exactly K of the cells in the array
   // in_sample are marked true, and count has the value K.

   for (i = 1; count > 0; ++i)
   {
      F >> temp;                // Read the object with file index i from file F.
      if ( in_sample[i] )       // Was the i-th object in F selected for the sample?
      {
         G << temp;             // If so, write the i-th object into file G.
         --count;
      }
   }
}
```

Fig. 6.10 First algorithm for selecting a random sample from a file

Theorem 6.3.1 *Let* K *and* N *be positive integers, with* $K \leq N$. *Then for each subset* R *of size* K *of the set* $\{1, 2, 3, \ldots, N\}$, *Algorithm 1 has probability* $1/\binom{N}{K}$ *of choosing exactly the integers in the set* R. *Thus Algorithm 1 gives each subset of size* K *of the file* F *equal probability of being chosen.*

Proof Specify any particular subset R of size K of the set $\{1, \ldots, N\}$. Let A_i denote the event that the i-th number chosen by Algorithm 1 will be in R. We want to prove that

$$P(A_1 \cap A_2 \cap A_3 \cap \cdots \cap A_K) = 1/\binom{N}{K}.$$

We will do this by using the Chain Rule (Theorem 8.0.14): we will prove that

$$P(A_1)P(A_2|A_1)P(A_3|A_1 \cap A_2)\ldots P(A_K|A_1 \cap A_2 \cap A_3 \cap \cdots \cap A_{K-1}) = 1/\binom{N}{K}.$$

When the loop with control "while (count <K)" begins, the file index generated by the first call to randint(1,N) has probability K/N of being a member of our specified subset R. That is, $P(A_1) = \dfrac{K}{N}$.

The second time through the same loop, the call to randint(1, N) may produce the same file index that was returned by the first call, in which case that integer is ignored and another call is made, and if necessary another, and so on, until an integer different from the first is returned. What is the probability that this second integer will belong to R, given that the first chosen integer was in R? By Theorem 8.0.19, $P(A_2|A_1) = \dfrac{K-1}{N-1}$. Similarly, $P(A_3|A_1 \cap A_2) = \dfrac{K-2}{N-2}$. Etc. For the last number chosen, the probability that it will belong to R, given that the first $K-1$ integers chosen belong to R is $P(A_K|A_1 \cap A_2 \cap A_3 \cap \cdots \cap A_{K-1}) = \dfrac{K-(K-1)}{N-(K-1)} = \dfrac{1}{N-K+1}$. Multiplying all these probabilities together gives the desired probability:

$$P(A_1)\,P(A_2|A_1)\,P(A_3|A_1 \cap A_2)\ldots P(A_K|A_1 \cap A_2 \cap A_3 \cap \cdots \cap A_{K-1})$$
$$= \frac{K!}{N(N-1)(N-2)\ldots(N-K+1)} = \frac{K!\,(N-K)!}{N!} = \frac{1}{\binom{N}{K}}. \qquad \blacksquare$$

Algorithm 1 stops when it has read the r_K-th object of the input file, where r_K is the largest of the K random numbers marked by the algorithm. Usually r_K is smaller than, but close to, N, so the algorithm generally reads most but not all of its input file.

One disadvantage of Sample Select Algorithm 1 is that if N is large it will be necessary to create a large Boolean array. In some program execution environments, this may even be impossible.

A quick solution to this issue is to create an integer array of size K to hold the selected indexes (the value of r in Fig. 6.10). Since K is usually much smaller than N, this typically uses far less memory. This introduces a new difficulty: when generating a new file index to be selected, we need to check if it has been previously selected, to avoid repetition. While this was a trivial matter in the case of the Boolean array, with an index array, if we keep the selected indexes in a random order, we could have to check all of them for repetition for each new one that we introduce.

Thus, it is more efficient to keep the generated file indexes in order, and use binary search to check for repetition. The process of inserting a new element in a sorted array can be shown, however, to require $\Theta(K)$ operations on the average, so the algorithm has an expected time complexity that is $\Theta(K^2)$ in this version for the part

Sample Select Algorithm 2

```
// This is a function template for selecting a random sample of K data objects
// from an open sequential file F known to contain N data objects.  The selected
// objects are written out to an open file G.  It is assumed that the stream
// insertion and extraction operators << and >> are overloaded for the otype
// class.  This version uses less memory than Sample Select Algorithm 1.

template <class otype>
void select_sample_sort(istream & F, int K, int N, ostream & G)
{
    int sample[K+1];
    int pos, r, count = 0;
    bool found;

    while (count < K)
    {
        r = randint(1, N);

        binary_search(sample, r, 1, count, found, pos);

        if (!found)
        {
            // The following function call shifts each of the objects in the
            // subarray sample[pos, count] one cell to the right, opening up
            // a space into which the index r is then inserted.
            insert(sample, pos, count, r);
            ++count;
            // At this point, sample[1, count] contains the randomly chosen
            // array indexes, arranged in strictly increasing order.
        }
    }

    int i, j;
    for (i = 1, j = 1; i <= K; ++i)
    {
        for ( ; j <= sample[i]; ++j)
        {
            F >> temp;          // Read an object from input file F.
            G << temp;          // Write out the object to file G if the
        }                       // the object's index is in sample[1,K].
    }
}
```

Fig. 6.11 The second algorithm for selecting a random sample from a file

of selecting the K sample indexes. The process of reading the objects from the file F and writing them into the file G still has $\Theta(N)$ complexity on the average, just like for Algorithm 1. Sample Select Algorithm 2 in Fig. 6.11 presents an implementation of this idea, where the binary_search function is the one from Fig. 5.3 on p. 176. In terms of selected sample, though, the two algorithms are equivalent. This means that when given the exact same sequence of random numbers, they will produce the exact same sample from the file. Even with this optimization, a significant amount of memory is required for this algorithm to run.

Another disadvantage of Sample Select Algorithms 1 and 2 is that in the loop that selects K distinct integers, the random number generator may repeatedly "hit" file indexes that have been previously selected, which is a waste of time. This is not a serious drawback, however, if K is small relative to N, which is usually the case, because in this case the probability of duplicate "hits" is quite small. Later we will be able to calculate the average number of calls that will have to be made to the random number generator.

For these reasons it is important to know that there are algorithms that can operate "on-line" to select the objects of the random sample while objects are being read from the input file. The idea is to read the objects from the file one by one and use a random process to decide, as each is read, whether to retain it in the random sample. How is this decision made?

By Theorem 8.0.11, if a random sample of size k is selected from a population of size N, then each member of the population has the probability $\dfrac{K}{N}$ of being in the sample. If we want to read objects one by one from an input file of known size N and choose a random sample of size K as we go, then each object should have probability K/N of being selected. Thus, we give the first object read that probability of being selected. If it is selected, then we need a random sample of size $K - 1$ from the remaining $N - 1$ objects, so we give the second object the probability $(K - 1)/(N - 1)$ of being selected. However, if the first object is not selected, then we still need a random sample of size K from the remaining $N - 1$ objects, so we give the second object the probability $K/(N - 1)$ of being selected. At each remaining stage in the process, if M objects remain to be read from the input file, and if we still need J more objects for the sample, then we give the next object the probability J/M of being selected. Code for this algorithm is given in Fig. 6.12. In the code, we do not use the variables J and M. Instead, we vary N and K so that at every stage they tell us the number of objects remaining unread in the file and the number of objects that are still needed for the random sample.

Although it is possible that Sample Select Algorithm 3 will end up reading the entire file, the probability of that happening is quite small if K is much less than N. The question of what fraction of the file will be read, on the average, will be explored later.

Does Algorithm 3 give a valid random sample? That is, is the algorithm unbiased? Let's look at a particular numerical case. Suppose the file to be read is known in advance to contain $N = 12$ objects. Suppose we want a random sample of size $K = 3$. What is the probability that the 2nd, 5th, and 8th objects will be selected? (It should be $1/\binom{12}{3}$). The tree diagram in Fig. 6.13 will help us calculate this probability.

In the tree diagram in Fig. 6.13, only a part of the entire tree is shown. Enough of the tree is shown to allow us to calculate easily the probability that the 2nd, 5th, and 8th objects will be selected.

Let A_i denote the event that the i-th object in the file gets selected. Then we want to compute $P(A_1^c \cap A_2 \cap A_3^c \cap A_4^c \cap A_5 \cap A_6^c \cap A_7^c \cap A_8) = P(A_1^c) \cdot P(A_2|A_1^c) \cdot P(A_3^c|A_1^c \cap A_2) \cdot P(A_4^c|A_1^c \cap A_2 \cap A_3^c) \ldots P(A_8|A_1^c \cap \cdots \cap A_7^c) = \frac{9}{12} \frac{3}{11} \frac{8}{10} \frac{7}{9} \frac{2}{8} \frac{6}{7} \frac{5}{6} \frac{1}{5} = \frac{9 \cdot 8 \cdot 7 \cdot 6 \cdot 5 \cdot 3!}{12 \cdot 11 \cdot 10 \cdot 9 \cdot 8 \cdot 7 \cdot 6 \cdot 5} = \frac{9! \, 3!}{12!} = \frac{1}{\binom{12}{3}}$ as desired.

Sample Select Algorithm 3

```
// This is a function template for selecting a random sample of K data objects
// from an open sequential file F known to contain N data objects.  The selected
// objects are written out to an open file G.  It is assumed that the stream
// insertion and extraction operators << and >> are overloaded for the otype
// class.  Error checking code has been omitted to avoid clutter.
// The value parameters N and K will be modified inside the function.
// At all times N will tell us how many objects remain unread in file F,
// and K will tell how many objects are still needed for the sample.

template <class otype>
void select_sample (ifstream & F, int K, int N, ofstream & G)
{
  otype temp;
  int r;

  while (K > 0) // while we still need more objects for our sample
  {
    F >> temp;              // Read the next object from input file F.
    r = randint(1, N);
    if (r <= K)             // Give the object probability K/N of being chosen.
    {
      G << temp;            // Write the chosen object to file G.
      --K;                  // Decrease the count of objects needed for the sample.
    }
    --N; // Decrease the count of objects remaining unread in input file F.
  }
}
```

Fig. 6.12 The third algorithm for selecting a random sample from a file

The example given above does not constitute a *proof* that Algorithm 3 works correctly in all cases, but anyone who studies the example should be able to see why the algorithm is a correct one. Writing out all the details is tedious, however.

Algorithms 1, 2, and 3 require that the number N of objects in the input file be known before they start work. In many cases, that would mean that the entire input file would have to be read and counted before the select_sample function was called to read through it a second time. It is an amazing fact that it is possible to do the selection "on line" *without even knowing the size N of the file in advance!* All the algorithm needs to know is the desired sample size K. Here is a description of this wizard algorithm, known as *reservoir sampling* [11].

Begin by reading in the first K objects from the input file F and placing them in an array a, which we'll call our "sample array". (If it turns out that there are fewer than K objects in the file, report that it is impossible to take a sample of size K.) Consider these K objects to be the "initial sample".

Now read the next object, call it F_{K+1}, from file F. (If there is no next object, the initial sample is the only possible sample of size K.) Now we have $K + 1$ objects, which is too many. We must reject one of these $K + 1$ objects, and each must have an equal chance of being rejected. Thus we give each object of the initial sample and also the object F_{K+1} the probability $1/(K + 1)$ of being rejected. If F_{K+1} is not

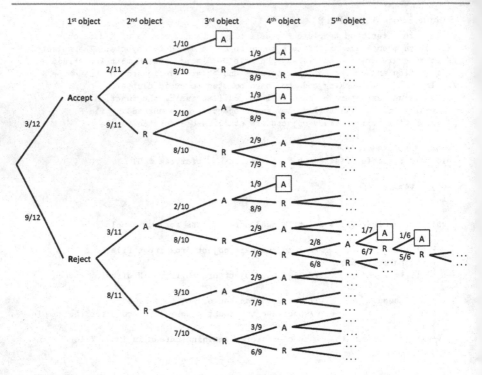

Fig. 6.13 Partial decision tree for the Algorithm 3

being rejected, then we overwrite the rejected object with F_{K+1}. The objects now in the sample array have not been rejected, and they form the new "current sample".

Note that each of the first $K + 1$ objects has been given probability $K/(K + 1)$ of being in the current sample. This is a special case of the more general case: if it turns out that there are N objects in the file, and if we are to choose a random sample of size K, then by Theorem 8.0.11, each object in the file must have a priori probability K/N of ending up in the sample. By the phrase "a priori probability", we mean a non-conditional probability, i.e., a probability, before the experiment has begun, of a particular event occurring.)

If file F is not completely read, then read the next object, call it F_{K+2}, from F. Now we must decide whether to keep F_{K+2} as part of our sample. By the preceding paragraph, we know that if the file turns out to have $K + 2$ objects (i.e., if N turns out to be $K + 2$), then we should give F_{K+2} the probability $K/(K + 2)$ of being chosen for the sample, and if it is chosen we will need to select one of the previously chosen K objects to be ejected from the sample. Each of those K objects should have an equal probability of being ejected, so we must give each one the probability $\frac{1}{K} \cdot \frac{K}{K+2}$ of being ejected, i.e., 1 chance in $K + 2$. Using this idea, select an object to reject, and if it is not F_{K+2}, then overwrite the object being rejected with F_{K+2}.

Sample Select Algorithm 4

```
// This is a function template for selecting a random sample of K data objects
// from an open sequential file F containing an unknown number of data objects.
// The selected objects are placed in an array a[1..K] that's dynamically
// allocated by the function.  The function returns false if there are fewer
// than K objects in F; otherwise it returns true. It is assumed that the
// stream extraction operator >> is overloaded on the class otype.

template <class otype>
bool select_sample (int K, istream & F, otype & a[])
{
    int M = 0;             // M counts the objects that have been read from F.
    a = new otype[K+1];    // Create an array in which to build the sample.

    while (M < K)          // Try to read K objects initially from F into a[1..K].
    {
        ++M;
        F >> a[M];
        if (F.eof())       // If the end of file F has been reached, exit from the
            return false;  // function because F contained fewer than K objects.
    }

    // If execution reaches this point, the array a[1..K] holds the first K
    // objects read from F, and M has the value K.

    F >> a[0];             // Try to read the (M+1)-st object into spare cell a[0].
    while (! F.eof())      // This loop will halt when an attempt to read an object
    {                      // fails because the end of file F has been reached.
        r = randint(1, M+1);
        if (r <= K)        // If r <= K we reject a[r] by overwriting it with a[0].
            a[r] = a[0];
                           // (If r > K we consider a[0] to be rejected.)
        ++M;               // Increase the count of objects already read from F.
        F >> a[0];         // Try to read the next object (if any) from F.
    }

    return true;           // The function succeeded in selecting a sample.
}
```

Fig. 6.14 The fourth algorithm for selecting a random sample, this time from a file of unknown size

In general, suppose we have read M objects from the file and have constructed a current sample in which each object had a priori probability K/M of being in the current sample. If the file has not been completely read, then read the next object, call it F_{M+1}. This object must be given probability $K/(M + 1)$ of being chosen for the sample, which is to say that with probability $K/(M + 1)$ some object of the current sample must be ejected. Giving each an equal probability of being ejected means that each object of the current sample must have probability $1/(M + 1)$ of being rejected. The algorithm is given in Fig. 6.14.

In those cases where $N \geq K$, does Sample Select Algorithm 4 give a valid random sample? That is, is the algorithm unbiased? Let's look at a specific example to give us some insight into the process. Suppose the size N of the file F is 12 objects, and suppose $K = 3$. That is, the algorithm is required to choose a random sample of size 3 from the file without knowing until reaches the end of the file that there are 12 objects in the file. Let's compute the probability that the set of file objects $\{F_2, F_5, F_8\}$ will be chosen.

The algorithm begins by reading file objects F_1, F_2, and F_3 into cells 1, 2, and 3 of the array a[0..3]. At this exer we can define the following events:

- let E_4 denote the event "F_2 will be in the sample after F_4 is read from the file and decided on"
- let E_5 denote the event "F_2 and F_5 will be in the sample after F_5 is read from the file and decided on"
- let E_6 denote "F_2 and F_5 will be in the sample after F_6 is read from the file and decided on"
- let E_7 denote "F_2 and F_5 will be in the sample after F_7 is read from the file and decided on"
- let E_8 denote "F_2, F_5, F_8 will be in the sample after F_8 is read from the file and decided on"
- let E_i denote "F_2, F_5, F_8 will be in the sample after F_i is read from the file", $i = 9, 10, 11, 12$.

We want to prove that $P(E_4 \cap E_5 \cap E_6 \cap \cdots \cap E_{12}) = 1/\binom{12}{3}$, which we can do by using the Chain Rule. We'll prove that

$$P(E_4)\, P(E_5|E_4)\, P(E_6|E_5 \cap E_4) \ldots P(E_{12}|E_4 \cap \cdots \cap E_{11}) = 1/\binom{12}{3}.$$

When F_4 is read from file F it is placed in array cell a[0]. Then a random number r is generated in the range 1–4 to determine whether F_4 will be selected or discarded. If r turns out to be ≥ 1 then we will overwrite a[r] with a[0], thereby putting F_4 into the sample and ejecting F_r; but if r is 0 we will do nothing, which will leave the sample unchanged. Thus the probability that F_2 will remain in the sample is 3/4. That is, $P(E_4) = 3/4$.

Now suppose E_4 occurs: F_2 remains in the sample when F_4 is read. The algorithm will go on to read F_5 into a[0] and then generate a random number r in the range 0...4 to determine whether F_5 will be selected or discarded. We now want to compute $P(E_5|E_4)$, which is the probability that if F_2 remains in the sample just before F_5 is read, then F_5 will be added to the sample. This occurs when r is either 1 or 3, which tells us that $P(E_5|E_4) = 2/5$.

Now suppose E_4 and E_5 have occurred. The algorithm will read F_6 into a[0] and generate r in the range 1...6 to determine whether F_6 will be selected or discarded. The event E_6 will occur if and only if $r \geq 4$ or r is the subscript of the cell containing neither F_2 nor F_5, so $P(E_6|E_4 \cap E_5) = 4/6$.

Similar reasoning yields the following values:
$P(E_7|E_4 \cap E_5 \cap E_6) = 5/7$
$P(E_8|E_4 \cap E_5 \cap E_6 \cap E_7) = 1/8$
$P(E_9|E_4 \cap E_5 \cap E_6 \cap E_7 \cap E_8) = 6/9$

$$P(E_{10}|E_4 \cap E_5 \cap E_6 \cap E_7 \cap E_8 \cap E_9) = 7/10$$
$$P(E_{11}|E_4 \cap E_5 \cap E_6 \cap E_7 \cap E_8 \cap E_9 \cap E_{10}) = 8/11$$
$$P(E_{12}|E_4 \cap E_5 \cap E_6 \cap E_7 \cap E_8 \cap E_9 \cap E_{10} \cap E_{11}) = 9/12$$

Multiplying all these values together gives

$$P(E_4)\,P(E_5|E_4)\,P(E_6|E_5 \cap E_4)\ldots P(E_{12}|E_4 \cap \cdots \cap E_{11})$$

$$= \frac{3\cdot2\cdot4\cdot5\cdot1\cdot6\cdot7\cdot8\cdot9}{4\cdot5\cdot6\cdot7\cdot8\cdot9\cdot10\cdot11\cdot12} = \frac{9!\,3!}{12!} = \frac{1}{\binom{12}{3}}.$$

Again, the calculations we have done in the example above do not constitute a proof of the correctness of Algorithm 4, but the ideas for the proof can be extracted from the example.

6.3.1   Exercises

6.3.2 Compare the four sample select algorithms in terms of the minimum and maximum number of objects they need to read from the file F, and the minimum and maximum number of times the function `randint` is called.

6.3.3 Analyze the minimum and maximum execution times for Algorithms 1, 2, 3, and 4 for selecting a random sample. Express your answers in terms of K and/or N.

6.3.4 Suppose we have a sequential file containing $N = 5$ objects a, b, c, d, and e in that order. Suppose we want to select a random sample of size $K = 3$. There are $\binom{5}{3}$ different possible samples.

(a) List all the various possible samples.
(b) Draw the decision tree for Algorithm 3 in this case, and label its branches with appropriate probabilities. Verify that each of the possible samples you listed in part (a) has probability $1/\binom{5}{3}$ of being chosen by Algorithm 3.
(c) Draw the decision tree for Algorithm 4 in this case, and label its branches with appropriate probabilities. (Each node in the tree should represent a "sample so far". If K were equal to 2, for example, initially the "sample so far" would consist of objects a and b. After another object is read and processed, there would be three possible "samples so far": $\{a, b\}$, $\{a, c\}$, $\{b, c\}$ etc.) Verify that each of the possible samples you listed in part (a) has probability $1/\binom{5}{3}$ of being chosen by Algorithm 4.

6.3.5 Suppose we have a sequential file containing $N = 4$ objects a, b, c, d in that order. Suppose we want to select a random sample of size $K = 2$. There are $\binom{4}{2}$ different possible samples.

(a) List all the various possible samples.

(b) Suppose Algorithm 1 is used to choose the random sample. What is the probability that only two calls will be made to the random number generator? What is the probability that exactly three calls will be made? What is the probability that exactly four calls will be made? That exactly n calls will be made?

(c) Draw the decision tree for Algorithm 3 in this case, and label its branches with appropriate probabilities. Verify that each of the possible samples you listed in part (a) has probability $1/\binom{4}{2}$ of being chosen by Algorithm 3.

(d) Draw the decision tree for Algorithm 4 in this case, and label its branches with appropriate probabilities. (Each node in the tree should represent a "sample so far". Initially, for example, the "sample so far" consists of objects a and b. After another object is read and processed, there are three possible "samples so far": $\{a, b\}$, $\{a, c\}$, $\{b, c\}$ etc.) Verify that each of the possible samples you listed in part (a) has probability $1/\binom{4}{2}$ of being chosen by Algorithm 3.

6.3.6 Suppose a random sample of size 2 is to be selected from a population of 10 objects using Algorithm 3. Show using a (partial) tree diagram how to compute the probability that the 2nd and 7th objects in the file will be the ones selected for the sample. Is the probability what it ought to be? Explain.

6.3.7 Suppose that the data objects for a population from which a random sample is drawn are held in an array instead of a sequential file. This means that any algorithm for choosing the random sample will have "random access" into the set of data objects. Devise an algorithm similar to Algorithm 1 for choosing the random sample, but without using an auxiliary Boolean array and without the drawback of having some random numbers "wasted" by duplicate "hits". Draw a decision tree for your algorithm when the population size is 5 and the sample size is 2, and use the tree to determine whether your algorithm is fair or biased in this special case.

6.3.8 Suppose a sequential file of size N is known to be in random order. Suppose we wish to select a random sample of size K from the file, where $K \leq N$. Prove that if we simply take the first K objects from the file, then we have a random sample.

6.3.9 It is not hard to see that in the first half of Algorithm 1, the repeated calls to the random number generator eventually produce a random sample of K integers from the set $\{1, 2, 3, \ldots, N\}$. (If you are skeptical of that idea, imagine that the file containing the population consists of the integers $1, 2, 3, \ldots, N$ in that order. Then the integers r_i chosen by the random number generator will select "themselves" out of the population file.) Thus we know that each of the $\binom{N}{K}$ possible K-sized subsets of the set $\{1, 2, 3, \ldots, N\}$ are equally likely to be chosen during execution of this algorithm.

(a) What is the probability that the largest integer chosen in this way will be K?
(b) What is the probability that the largest integer chosen in this way will be $K + 1$?
(c) What is the probability that the largest integer chosen in this way will be $K + 2$?

(d) What is the probability that the largest integer chosen in this way will be N?
(e) Let A_x denote the event that the largest integer chosen by Algorithm 1 will be x, where x is an integer in the range $K \leq x \leq N$. Compute $P(A_x)$ for all such integers x. If your formula for $P(A_x)$ is correct, you should be able to show that the sum $\displaystyle\sum_{x=K}^{N} P(A_x)$ is equal to 1. Use Exercise 2.3.51, p. 52, to help you show that this sum is indeed equal to 1.

6.3.10 Recall that when an unbiased sampling algorithm is applied to a population of size N to select a sample of size K, every subset of size K must be given equal probability $\dfrac{1}{\binom{N}{K}}$ of being selected. Theorem 8.0.11 implies that if a sampling algorithm in unbiased, then when it is applied to a population of size N to select a sample of size K, each member of the population will have probability $\dfrac{K}{N}$ of ending up in the sample. Some people mistakenly assume that the converse must also be true: if a proposed sampling algorithm can be shown to give each member of the population of size N the probability $\dfrac{K}{N}$ of being selected property for a sample of size K, then it must be unbiased. Consider, however, the algorithm in Fig. 6.15 for choosing a random sample of size $K < N$ from an array a[0,N-1].

To illustrate the algorithm with an example, suppose array a[0..6] initially looks like

0	1	2	3	4	5	6
a	b	c	d	e	f	g

Here $N = 7$. Suppose the function above is called with $K = 3$. If the random number generator returns $r = 2$, then the algorithm will select objects c, d, and e to be written to the output file. If, instead, the random number generator returns $r = 5$, then the algorithm will select objects f, g and a to be written to the output file. It is easy to see that in this example, each object will have probability $\dfrac{3}{7}$ of being selected for the random sample. The same is true in general for the algorithm above. Explain why even so, the algorithm is badly biased when $2 \leq K \leq N - 2$.

6.4 Simulating Observations of a Discrete Random Variable

Let X denote the sum of the two faces that turn up when a pair of fair dice is thrown. Then X is a random variable, as described in Definition 8.0.26. Suppose we are asked to write a C++ function that returns simulated observations X. The most "natural"

```
template <class otype>
void select (otype a[], int N, int K, file F)
{
    int  r = randint(0, N-1), i;      // Generate a ``starting point"
    for (i = r; i <= N-1 && K > 0; ++i)
    {
        F << a[i] // Write a[i] to the file F.
        --K;
    }
    if (K > 0)    // Wrap around; get remaining objects from front.
        for (i = 0; K > 0; ++i)
        {
            F << a[i]; // Write a[i] to the file F.
            --K;
        }
}
```

Fig. 6.15 A seriously bad sample selection algorithm

```
int sum_of_faces()
{
    int r = randint(1, 6);
    int s = randint(1, 6);
    return  r + s;
}
```

Fig. 6.16 Simulating a pair of fair dice

way to do this is to have the function make two calls to a random number generator to simulate the numbers on the two faces and then return the sum of those two values:

Calls to random number generators with parameters, for example our `randint` function, are somewhat time-consuming because of the amount of arithmetic involved and the fact that they call other generators. For this reason, when writing a function that involves randomness, programmers often try to use algorithms that minimize the number of calls to random number generators. To illustrate how this can sometimes be accomplished, we're going to replace the algorithm for the `sum_of_faces` function in Fig. 6.16 with one that makes just one call instead of two to the `randint` function. The technique uses the values of the c.d.f. of the random variable X. (See Definition 8.0.22 for c.d.f., the cumulative distribution function, for which we have the notation $F_X(x)$.

To see how this is going to work, look at the graph of the c.d.f. in Fig. 6.17. The values of the c.d.f. of X are plotted along the vertical axis. The gap between 0 (c.d.f. of 2) and 1/36 (c.d.f. of 3) is exactly the probability that $X = 2$, the gap between 1/36 (c.d.f. of 3) and 3/36 (c.d.f. of 4) is the probability that $X = 3$, and so on. The gap between 35/36 (c.d.f. of 11) and 1 (c.d.f. of 12) is the probability that $X = 12$. This suggests the following strategy: generate a random real number u in the interval $[0.0, 1.0) = \{t : 0.0 \le t < 1.0\}$. If u lies in the interval $[0.0, 1/36)$, i.e., if $0.0 \le u < 1/36$, then interpret this as the simulated observation "$X = 2$". If u lies in the interval $[1/36, 3/36)$, i.e., if $1/36 \le u < 3/36$, interpret this as "$X = 3$" etc.

To make a C++ function do this, we make it first set up the following static arrays:

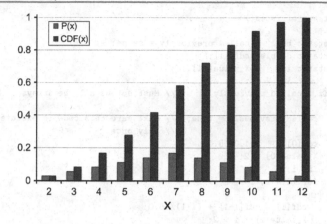

Fig. 6.17 Probability and c.d.f. for the sum of a pair of dice

	0	1	2	3	4	5	6	7	8	9	10
cdf:	1/36	3/36	6/36	10/36	15/36	21/36	26/36	30/36	33/36	35/36	36/36
	0.0278	0.0833	0.1667	0.2778	0.4167	0.5833	0.7222	0.8333	0.9167	0.9722	1.0

X_value:| 2 | 3 | 4 | 5 | 6 | 7 | 8 | 9 | 10 | 11 | 12 |

Then whenever the function is called it can generate u in the interval $[0.0, 1.0)$, search the array cdf for the left-most cell containing an entry larger than u, look up the corresponding value of X in the second array, and return that value. For example, if the value 0.714 is generated for u, then a linear search of cdf starting at the left end would reveal that 26/36 is the first number in the array larger than 0.714. Using the subscript 6 discovered during the linear search, the corresponding number in the X_value array would be found to be 8, and so 8 would be returned as the simulated value of X on that call to the function. Some code to do all this is shown in Figs. 6.18 and 6.19.

We can generalize the ideas in the preceding example to simulate observations of any discrete random variable X with a prescribed set of probabilities. We compute and store the possible values of X in one array and the corresponding values of $F_X(x)$ in a parallel array. Suppose the possible values of X are $x_0 < x_1 < x_2 < x_3 < \cdots < x_{n-1}$. Then the arrays would look like

	0	1	2	3	...	n − 1
X_value:	x_0	x_1	x_2	x_3	...	x_{n-1}
cdf:	$F_X(x_0)$	$F_X(x_1)$	$F_X(x_2)$	$F_X(x_3)$	...	1.0

If X can have infinitely many different discrete values, then we must, of course, make the array finite, but make it sufficiently long that all values of $F_X(x_i)$ are very nearly equal to 1.0 when $x_i > x_{n-1}$. Also, it is critical to make sure that the last cell contains the value 1.0.

```
int sum_of_faces()
{
  static bool    called_previously = false;
  static double  cdf[11];
  static int     X_value[11];
         int     i;
  if (!called_previously)       // Must set up all the arrays.
  {
    called_previously = true;  // Make sure this code is executed
                               // only once.
    cdf[0]      = 1.0/36.0;
    X_value[0] = 2;
    int i;
    for (i = 1; i <= 5; ++i)
    {
      cdf[i] = cdf[i-1] + (i+1)/36.0;
      X_value[i] = i + 2;
    }
    for (i = 6; i <= 9; ++i)
    {
      cdf[i] = cdf[i-1] + (11-i)/36.0;
      X_value[i] = i + 2;
    }
    cdf[10] = 1.0;  // Make sure the last cell contains 1.0.
    X_value[10] = 12;
  }
  return select_event(cdf, X_value);
}
```

Fig. 6.18 Simulating the sum of the faces of two dice using the c.d.f.; the function select_event is shown in Fig. 6.19

```
// Note that we do not need to know the size of the cdf array because the last
// element will always be equal to 1. The X_value array has the same size.
int select_event(double cdf[], int X_value[])
{
  double u = randouble();  // Generate real number in [0.0,1.0).
  int i = 0;
  while (u >= cdf[i])      // Linear search for first cell containing
    ++i;                   // a c.d.f. value greater than u.
  return X_value[i];
}
```

Fig. 6.19 Function selecting a simulated event based on a pre-calculated c.d.f. array

Once the arrays are constructed, we can generate one simulated observation of X by carrying out the following steps:

(1) Use a random number generator to generate a value u for the uniform random variable U on the interval [0.0, 1.0).
(2) Find the smallest integer i such that $u < F_X(x_i)$.
(3) Return the number x_i as the simulated observation of X.

Example 6.4.1 Consider the experiment of tossing a fair coin until it comes up heads. Let X denote the number of tosses required to produce the first heads outcome. Then X has infinitely many possible values, namely $x_0 = 1, x_1 = 2, x_2 = 3, x_3 = 4, x_4 = 5, \ldots$ Suppose we want to use the computer to simulate observations of the random variable X. An inefficient way to do this would be mimic the coin tossing by repeatedly calling `randint(1,2)` and treating an outcome of 1 as heads and an outcome of 2 as tails. Thus one "run" of the experiment might generate the numbers 2, 2, 2, 1. The first three of these "tosses" are regarded as tails and the fourth is regarded as heads, so the simulated observed value of X for this run would be 4.

The method described in the preceding paragraph is very slow compared with the discrete random variable simulation method outlined in this section of the notes. Using the method outlined, we should set up two parallel arrays:

	0	1	2	3	$\ldots$	$n-1$
X_value:	1	2	3	4	$\ldots$	n
cdf:	$F_X(1)$	$F_X(2)$	$F_X(3)$	$F_X(4)$	$\ldots$	1.0

Since this random variable X can assume infinitely many possible values, and since the cdf array must be finite, we choose n so large that $F_X(n)$ is extremely close to 1.0, and then we explicitly put 1.0 into cell $n - 1$ in place of the true value $F_X(n)$, which means that the simulation will never generate a value greater than n. How large should we take n to be? A good choice might be to take n so large that the difference between $F_X(n)$ and 1.0 is less than one-billionth. How can we find the smallest integer n such that $1.0 - F_X(n) < 10^{-9}$ (one billionth)?

We begin by writing the general formula for $F_X(k), k = 1, 2, 3, 4, \ldots$ The values for the p.d.f. (probability density function; see Definition 8.0.26) are given by $f_X(1) = \dfrac{1}{2}$, $f_X(2) = \dfrac{1}{4}$, and in general $f_X(k) = \dfrac{1}{2^k}$. Thus the c.d.f. is given by

$$F_X(k) = P(\text{``}X \le k\text{''}) = \frac{1}{2} + \frac{1}{4} + \frac{1}{8} + \cdots + \frac{1}{2^k}$$

$$= \frac{1}{2} \cdot \left[1 + (1/2) + (1/2)^2 + \cdots + (1/2)^{k-1}\right]$$

$$= \frac{1}{2} \cdot \frac{1 - (1/2)^k}{1 - (1/2)} = 1 - (1/2)^k.$$

Now we can see that finding the smallest integer n for which $1.0 - F_X(n) < 10^{-9}$ is equivalent to finding the smallest integer n for which $1.0 - (1 - (1/2)^n) < 10^{-9}$, which simplifies to $(1/2)^n < 10^{-9}$. This is equivalent to $n \lg(1/2) < -9 \lg(10)$, which in turn is equivalent to $n > \dfrac{-9 \lg(10)}{\lg(1/2)}$. [Note: the direction of the inequality was reversed because we divided both sides of the preceding inequality by the *negative* number $\lg(1/2)$.] A fairly easy computation shows that $\dfrac{-9 \lg(10)}{\lg(1/2)} \sim 29.89$. The smallest integer n satisfying $n > 29.89$ is $n = 30$. Thus we can create a cdf array containing 30 cells indexed by the integers 0, 1, 2, 3, ..., 29, and in the last cell (cell 29) we would put the value 1.0 instead of the actual value of $F_X(x_{29})$. The parallel arrays would look like this:

	0	1	2	3		...	29
X_value:	1	2	3	4		...	30
cdf:	0.5	0.75	0.875	0.9375		...	1.0

Suppose we set up the cdf array and then call to a uniform random number generator on the interval [0.0, 1.0). Suppose that call produces the floating exer value 0.802, what simulated value of X would that correspond to? It would be the smallest integer i such that $0.802 < \text{cdf}[i]$. Looking at the numbers we calculated in above, we see that the smallest such integer i is 2. Thus a randomly generated floating point value of 0.802 would produce the simulated value $x_2 = 3$ for the random variable X.

In a situation like this, where the values of the random variable are successive integers in some particular range, it is easy to see that we can dispense with the X_value array. When our random number generator generates a particular floating point number u, we search the cdf array to find the smallest subscript i such that $u < \text{cdf}[i]$, and then we simply return $i + 1$ as our value of the random variable X.

Finally, note that the cdf array is an *ordered* array of 30 numbers. In such a case it would be possible to use a binary search instead of a linear search to locate the smallest integer i such that $0.802 < \text{cdf}[i]$. This requires a slight modification of the usual binary search function in which a specific target value is passed to the search function. We leave the details to the reader.

6.4.1 Exercises

6.4.2 Consider the statistical experiment in which a fair die is thrown repeatedly until one of the faces appears for the second time. An outcome of the experiment is a list of the faces that are thrown. Here are some possible outcomes of this experiment: (3, 6, 2, 6) ; (5, 5) ; (1, 4, 3, 6, 2, 4). Let Y denote the random variable that tells how many throws were necessary to produce a repetition of a face. For the three outcomes listed above, the corresponding values of Y would be 4, 2, and 6. Describe two different algorithms for simulating an observation of Y. The first algorithm should be the "naïve" one that makes repeated calls to a random number generator to represent the separate throws of the die. The second algorithm should be one that makes only one call to a random number generator and uses an array containing the c.d.f. values of Y, as described in this section. Calculate the p.d.f. and c.d.f of Y and answer this question: what value of Y will be produced if the call to randouble() returns the value $u = 0.6184$?

6.4.3 Suppose that a family with 5 children has a rule that says that every day the child to do the dishes will be chosen randomly with a probability directly proportionate to the number of hours they have spent playing games on the computer. Suppose that on one particular day we have the following distribution of hours: Joe 2 h, Bob 3.2 h, Sandy 1.5 h, Kim 2.5 h, Sue, 1.8 h.

(a) Calculate the probability function for the child to be chosen to do the dishes.
(b) Compute the c.d.f. from this function.
(c) Suppose that the function `select_event` in Fig. 6.19 is called to select the child to do the dishes, and that the value of the variable u is 0.65. Which child will be assigned the chore that day?

6.5   Randomized Algorithms

In this section we will discuss a category of algorithms relying on pseudo-random numbers to find the solution to a problem. The difference between these algorithms and the simulation algorithms that we've seen in the previous sections is that for this category of algorithms the answer is deterministic, while for the simulation algorithms, it is not.

More precisely, for a simulation or array shuffling algorithm, two separate executions of an algorithm on the same input data will likely result in a different outcome, which makes the answer non-deterministic. For randomized algorithms, for a specific problem, there is, at least theoretically, a single correct answer. The probabilistic aspects from one execution of the algorithm to the next are whether this solution is found or not, the precision of the solution, or the time it takes to reach this solution.

There are two major categories of randomized algorithms: Monte Carlo and Las Vegas. Monte Carlo algorithms are always fast, but they give the correct answer only with a given probability. Las Vegas algorithms will always give the correct answer, but they are not guaranteed to always be fast.

6.5.1   Monte Carlo Algorithms

Monte Carlo algorithms are guaranteed to be fast, but they may or may not find the correct solution. What makes them interesting for the users is that the probability that the correct answer is found can be computed and controlled through the parameters of the algorithm. In some cases, the probability of error can be so low, even within efficient execution time, that it can be considered as negligible for practical purposes. Thus, the execution time for these algorithms is deterministic, but the result may be wrong with a small probabilistic error.

The most common examples of Monte Carlo algorithms are for decision problems. These can be described as questions for which the answer is true or false, yes or no. For this type of problem, randomized algorithms can be true-biased or false-biased. If the answer given by a *true-biased* algorithm is *true* or *yes*, then this answer is surely correct. If the answer is false, then the answer given may be the correct answer with

```
// This function tests whether it is likely that n is prime. It does this by
// testing k positive integers a to determine whether they satisfy the
// equation a^(n-1) mod n = 1 of Fermat's Little Theorem. The boolean value
// returned by the function may be incorrect. If k is large, the probability
// of an incorrect answer is extremely small.

bool is_prime(int n, int k)
{
  int i;
  for (i=0; i<k; i++)
  {
    a = randint(2, n-1);
    if (power(a, n-1) % n != 1)
      return false;
  }
  return true;
}
```

Fig. 6.20 Monte Carlo Primality Test algorithm

a given probability. For *false-biased* algorithms, an answer of *false* or *no* will always be correct, while the opposite is correct only with a given probability.

Primality Test. For an example of such an algorithm, Fig. 6.20 shows a randomized algorithm that tests whether a number is prime. Here the function power is the common function found in many languages, such as the one provided by the cmath library in C++. This algorithm is based on Fermat's Little Theorem.

Theorem 6.5.1 (Fermat 1640). *If the integer p is prime, then for every integer a satisfying* $1 \le a < p$,

$$a^{p-1} \bmod p = 1.$$

In other words, if the value n of the parameter n of the algorithm in Fig. 6.20 is a prime number, then any number a between 1 and $n-1$ raised to the power $n-1$ will yield the remainder 1 when divided by n. The algorithm selects a number of candidates a for the test, and checks if the property holds for each of them. If we find any such number a for which the property is *not* satisfied, then it is certain that the number n is not a prime. Thus, this algorithm is *false-biased*.

What is important now is to figure out is how accurate a *true* answer is. In other words, if the algorithm returns the value true, stating that the number n is prime, how much confidence can we have that this is indeed the case? A second theorem related to prime numbers will provide the answer to this question.

Theorem 6.5.2 *If the integer p is not a prime, then at most half of the integers a from 1 to p − 1 satisfy the equation stated in* Theorem 6.5.1.

What this second theorem tells us is that if we run the test once ($k = 1$) with the number n not being prime, we have at least 50 % probability that we will find one of the numbers that do not satisfy the property, thus getting the correct answer. This means that in general, if the algorithm returns `true`, then the probability of error is at most 50 %.

Now let's consider the case where we run the test with $k = 2$. Since the two random numbers a are chosen independently of each other, the chances that we find one that satisfies the equation in Theorem 6.5.1 twice if the number n is not prime are reduced to 25 %. We can simply multiply the probabilities of the two independent events to get to this result. Thus, the probability of error in the case of a `true` answer decreases to $1/4$. By generalization, for a given value of the parameter k, the probability of error in the case where the algorithm returns the value `true` is $1/2^k$. Thus, the error can easily be made exponentially low, and even for $k = 10$, it is negligible.

This is a remarkable result that allows us to avoid testing whether the number n is divisible by any number between 2 and its square root, an operation that would be a lot more costly. Even though an efficient deterministic primality test algorithm has been discovered, the Monte Carlo primality test is still the one most used for this purpose in cryptography.

6.5.2 Las Vegas Algorithms

Las Vegas algorithms are guaranteed to give the correct answer in all the cases, but their execution time is probabilistic. They are generally fast, and the probability of an efficient execution time can be computed and in some cases even controlled through the parameters of the algorithm. Thus, even though they are generally expected to be fast, and will always give the correct answer, it can happen (with a low probability) that they take a long time to give the answer.

For an example, consider the case of a Quicksort choosing the pivot for partitioning randomly. This method is more likely to yield the expected complexity of $\Theta(n \lg(n))$ than the standard deterministic version, where n is the size of the array to be sorted. The worst case complexity of $\Theta(n^2)$ can still occur, but its probability is much smaller. Thus, this algorithm will be fast with a high probability.

Another example would be a randomized search for a given target in an array of the form a[0.. n-1], shown in Fig. 6.21. This algorithm chooses an element of the array randomly until either it exhausts all possibilities and returns failure, or until it finds the target. This type of search can be shown to be faster than the linear search on the average in the case where the array contains multiple occurrences of the target.

One of the most popular Las Vegas algorithms is related to randomized hashing functions for hash tables. This algorithm can be shown to be more efficient than binary search trees on the average.

```
bool las_vegas_search(int a[], int n, int target)
{
  int test;
  for (i=0; i<n; i++)
  {
    test = randint(0, n-1);  // Make sure that no repeating indexes are generated.
    if (a[test] == target)
      return true;
  }
  return false;
}
```

Fig. 6.21 Las Vegas Randomized Search algorithm

6.5.3 Exercises

6.5.3 Verify Theorem 6.5.1 for $p = 5$. Find a number a that does not satisfy the equation in Theorem 6.5.1 for $p = 10$. You may use a calculator for this.

6.5.4 Write a Monte Carlo algorithm that searches for a target in an array; it could be similar but not identical to the one in Fig. 6.21. Is this algorithm true-biased or false-biased? Calculate the probability of error of your algorithm as a function of the prescribed number of trials.

6.6   Expected Behavior of Algorithms

In this section we'll investigate the "theoretical average behavior" of a variety of algorithms. Recall the following definition from your study of probability theory.

Definition 6.6.1 Given a random variable X with the possible values $\{a_1, a_2, \ldots, a_n\}$, the *expected value* of X (informally, the *theoretical average* of X) is denoted by $E(X)$ and is defined by

$$E(X) = \sum_{i=1}^{n} a_i \, P(X = a_i),$$

where $P(X = a_i)$ is the probability that X will assume the value a_i.

Example 6.6.2 Suppose a linear search must be made for a target object stored in an unordered array a[first..last] using the algorithm in Fig. 6.22 (previously seen in Fig. 5.2 on p. 175). Assume that otype is a data type on which the non-equality operator != is defined.

Let n denote the number of cells in the array to be searched; i.e., $n = last - first + 1$.

```
template <class otype>
int location_by_linear_search (const otype a[], const otype &target,
                               int first, int last)
{
   while (first <= last && a[first] != target)
      ++first;      // Go to the next cell if target not found.
   return first;    // first will be last+1 if target is not present.
}
```

Fig. 6.22 Location of a target in an array

(a) Suppose a copy of the target object is present in the array, and suppose it is equally likely to be in any of the n locations. What is the *expected* number of times that the body of the loop will be executed during the search? What is the *expected* search time required by a successful search?

(b) Suppose the target value is not in the array (of course, this is not known in advance of the search). What is the *expected* number of times that the body of the loop will be executed during the unsuccessful search? What is the *expected* search time required by an unsuccessful search?

Solutions.

(a) Let X denote the number of times the body of the loop is executed during a successful search.

Possible values of X : $x =$	0	1	2	3	...	$n-1$
Values of the p.d.f.: $f_X(x) =$	$\frac{1}{n}$	$\frac{1}{n}$	$\frac{1}{n}$	$\frac{1}{n}$	...	$\frac{1}{n}$

$$E(X) = 0 \cdot \frac{1}{n} + 1 \cdot \frac{1}{n} + 2 \cdot \frac{1}{n} + 3 \cdot \frac{1}{n} + \cdots + (n-1)\frac{1}{n}$$
$$= \frac{1}{n}[0 + 1 + 2 + 3 + \cdots + (n-1)] = \frac{1}{n}\frac{(n-1)n}{2} = \frac{n-1}{2}.$$

On average, we have to search approximately half of the array to find the target when it is present.

The search time, which is a random variable Y, is the sum of two components: the time, call it T_1 for the "function overhead", which is $\Theta(1)$, and the time, call it T_2, required to execute the loop. Since the body of the loop requires $\Theta(1)$ time each time it is executed, and each loop control operation requires $\Theta(1)$ each time it is executed, $T_2 = \Theta(X)$. That is, there exist positive constants c_1 and c_2 such that $c_1 X \leq T_2 \leq c_2 X$. By the properties of the expected value of a variable, $c_1 E(X) \leq E(T_2) \leq c_2 E(X)$. Since $E(X) = \Theta(n)$, it follows that $E(T_2) = \Theta(n)$. Then $E(Y) = E(T_1) + E(T_2) = \Theta(n)$.

(b) Let Z denote the number of times the body of the loop is executed during an unsuccessful search. Then Z is a constant random variable, with fixed value n.

```
template <class otype>
void binary_search (const otype a[], const otype & target, int first,
                    int last, bool & found, int & subscript)
{
  int mid;

  found = false;  // Will remain false until target is found.

  while (first <= last && !found)     // The value parameters "first"
  {                                   // and "last" are modified
    mid = (first + last)/2;           // during loop execution.
    if (target < a[mid])
      last = mid - 1;
    else if (a[mid] < target)
      first = mid + 1;
    else // Only remaining logical possibility: a[mid] matches target
      found = true;
  }

  if (found)
    subscript = mid;   // The location of "target".
  else
    subscript = first; // This is the appropriate subscript to
                       // return if "target" is not present.

}
```

Fig. 6.23 Binary search function

Thus $E(Z) = nP(\text{"}Z = n\text{"}) = n \cdot 1 = n$. By an argument similar to the one in part (a), it follows that the expected search time required by an unsuccessful search is $\Theta(n)$.

Example 6.6.3 Suppose we have an ordered array of 10 objects. Suppose a binary search is to be made in the array to locate an object that's in the array. The binary search algorithm is shown in Fig. 6.23 (which appeared earlier in Fig. 5.3, p. 176).

If the target is in the array and is equally likely to be in any of the 10 locations, what is the expected number of times that the body of the loop will be executed? What is the expected number of otype *object comparisons* that will be required to find the target?

Solution. Let X denote the number of times the body of the loop will be executed. Let Y denote the number of object comparisons that will be made. For concreteness, assume that initially first = 0 and last = 9. Then the search will begin with mid = 4. If the target is in cell a[4], then this will be discovered the first time the body of the loop is executed; two object comparisons ("target <a[4]" and then "a[4] <target") will be made, both of which will return false. Thus in this case X will be 1 and Y will be 2. If, instead, it turns out that "target <a[4]" is true, then mid will be re-calculated to the value 1. If the target is in cell a[1], then this will be discovered with 1 more execution of the body of the loop, which will make two more object comparisons. In this case X will be 2 and Y will be 3 (one

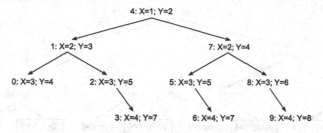

Fig. 6.24 Execution tree for a successful binary search

object comparison when `mid` is 4 and two more when `mid` is 1). And so on. The *logical* search tree in Fig. 6.24 gives the entire story. The label "6:X=4; Y=7" on a node means that if the algorithm finds the target in the cell `a[6]`, then the number of times the body of the loop is executed is 4, and the number of object comparisons required to make that discovery is 7.

x (possible values of X)	1	2	3	4
$f_X(x) = P(\text{"}X = x\text{"})$	$\dfrac{1}{10}$	$\dfrac{2}{10}$	$\dfrac{4}{10}$	$\dfrac{3}{10}$

$$E(X) = 1 \cdot \frac{1}{10} + 2 \cdot \frac{2}{10} + 3 \cdot \frac{4}{10} + 4 \cdot \frac{3}{10} = \frac{29}{10} = 2.9.$$

y (possible values of Y)	2	3	4	5	6	7	8
$f_Y(y) = P(\text{"}Y = y\text{"})$	$\dfrac{1}{10}$	$\dfrac{1}{10}$	$\dfrac{2}{10}$	$\dfrac{2}{10}$	$\dfrac{1}{10}$	$\dfrac{2}{10}$	$\dfrac{1}{10}$

$$E(Y) = 2 \cdot \frac{1}{10} + 3 \cdot \frac{1}{10} + 4 \cdot \frac{2}{10} + 5 \cdot \frac{2}{10} + 6 \cdot \frac{1}{10} + 7 \cdot \frac{2}{10} + 8 \cdot \frac{1}{10} = \frac{51}{10} = 5.1.$$

When we have more powerful techniques for computing probabilities, we will solve this binary search problem for arrays of arbitrary size n, not just $n = 10$.

Example 6.6.4 In the preceding problem, suppose the target is NOT in the array. What is the expected number of times that the body of the loop will be executed? What is the expected number of `otype` object comparisons that will be required to discover that the target is not in the array? Assume that the target object has equal probability of belonging at any "cell boundary" in the array, i.e., between any two objects in the array or at the ends.

Solution. Again, for concreteness, assume that initially `first = 0` and `last = 9`. When the target is not in the array, then the search will have to narrow down the subarray in which it searches until that subarray is of length 0. This will determine which of the 11 "cell boundaries" is the spot where the target belongs. In the logical search tree, this corresponds to going down some path in the tree until an empty subtree is encountered. Let X denote the number of times the body of the loop is executed during the search, and let Y denote the number of object comparisons required. Then we have the logical search tree shown in Fig. 6.25:

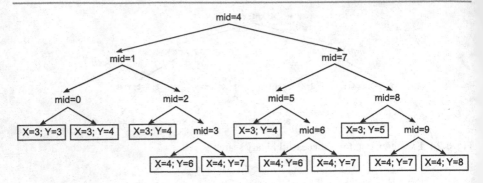

Fig. 6.25 Execution tree for an unsuccessful the binary search

$$\begin{array}{c|cc} x \text{ (possible values of } X) & 3 & 4 \\ \hline f_X(x) = P(\text{``}X = x\text{''}) & \dfrac{5}{11} & \dfrac{6}{11} \end{array}$$

$$E(X) = 3 \cdot \frac{5}{11} + 4 \cdot \frac{6}{11} = \frac{39}{11} = 3.5.$$

$$\begin{array}{c|cccccc} y \text{ (possible values of } Y) & 3 & 4 & 5 & 6 & 7 & 8 \\ \hline f_Y(y) = P(\text{``}Y = y\text{''}) & \dfrac{1}{11} & \dfrac{3}{11} & \dfrac{1}{11} & \dfrac{2}{11} & \dfrac{3}{11} & \dfrac{1}{11} \end{array}$$

$$E(Y) = 3 \cdot \frac{1}{11} + 4 \cdot \frac{3}{11} + 5 \cdot \frac{1}{11} + 6 \cdot \frac{2}{11} + 7 \cdot \frac{3}{11} + 8 \cdot \frac{1}{11} = \frac{61}{11} = 5.5.$$

Example 6.6.5 (This example assumes acquaintance with the concept of a hash table.) The diagram in Fig. 6.26 shows a small hash table in which collision resolution was performed by separate chaining of unordered lists. Each node in a list contains a string that was hashed to that array location. For example, the hash function that was used to create the table hashed the name "Chris" to location 8. (The hash function is not given here because it is not relevant to the questions we want to consider.) A list node was dynamically at location 8 and "Chris" was copied into the node. Later the name "Juan" was hashed to location 8 as well, so a list node was dynamically allocated, the name was copied into the node, and the node was inserted at the front of the existing list.

(a) What is the expected number of string comparisons that will be made during a successful search of the table if each string has equal likelihood of being the target of the search?
(b) What is the expected number of string comparisons that will be made during an unsuccessful search of the table if the target string is equally likely to be hashed to any of the 13 addresses in the table?

Solutions.

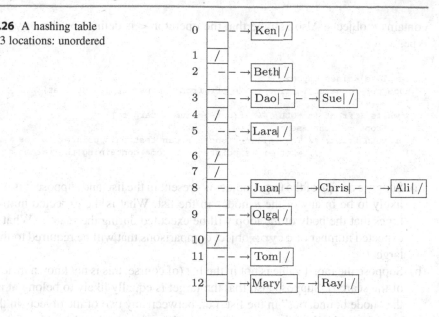

Fig. 6.26 A hashing table with 13 locations: unordered chains

(a) There are 12 strings in the table, so each has probability 1/12 of being the target of the search. Let X denote the number of string comparisons that will be made during a successful search. Then the 8 strings that are in the front nodes of the lists will require only one string comparison, which means that $P(“X = 1”) = 8/12$. The 3 strings that are in second position in their lists will require two string comparisons, which means that $P(“X = 2”) = 3/12$. Only 1 string (“Ali”) requires three comparisons, so $P(“X = 3”) = 1/12$. Thus

$$E(X) = 1 \times \frac{8}{12} + 2 \times \frac{3}{12} + 3 \times \frac{1}{12} = \frac{17}{12} \approx 1.4 .$$

(b) Let Y denote the number of string comparisons that will be made during an unsuccessful search. If the target string hashes to one of the 5 addresses that has an empty list, then the value of Y will be 0, so $P(“X = 0”) = 5/13$. If the target string hashes to one of the 5 addresses that has a list of length 1, then Y will be 1, so $P(“Y = 1”) = 5/13$. If the target string hashes to one of the 2 addresses that has a list of length 2, then Y will be 2, so $P(“Y = 2”) = 2/13$. Finally, if the target string hashes to the address with a list of length 3, then Y will be 3, so $P(“Y = 3”) = 1/13$. Thus

$$E(Y) = 0 \times \frac{5}{13} + 1 \times \frac{1}{13} + 2 \times \frac{2}{13} + 3 \times \frac{1}{13} = \frac{8}{13} \approx 0.62 .$$

6.6.1   Exercises

6.6.6 Suppose a search of an *ordered* linked list is going to be made for some specified target object using the function below. Assume that the list is NULL-terminated and contains n objects. Also assume that the operator $<$ is defined on the otype data type.

```
template <class otype>
node_ptr location_in_list (node_ptr front, const otype & target)
{
  while ( front != NULL  &&  front->datum < target )
    front = front->next;
  return front; // The calling function can test this pointer to see
                // whether it points to a node containing the target.
}
```

(a) Suppose a copy of the target object is present in the list, and suppose it is equally likely to be in any of the n nodes in the list. What is the expected number of times that the body of the loop will be executed during the search? What is the expected number of otype object comparisons that will be required to find the target?

(b) Suppose the target value is not in the list (of course, this is not known in advance of the search). Suppose also that the target is equally likely to belong at any of the "node boundaries" in the list, i.e., between any two of the objects in the list or at the ends. What is the expected number of times that the body of the loop will be executed during the (unsuccessful) search? Keep in mind that the objects are in increasing order in the list. Read the code above with care so that you do not fall into the error of thinking this is just like Example 6.6.2.

(c) (Continuation of part (b).) What is the expected number of otype object comparisons that will be required to discover that the target is not in the list? This last question is tricky. Begin by examining all 3 possibilities when the list is of length $n = 2$.

6.6.7 Suppose we have a table maintained as an array or linked list, and suppose the objects in the table obey Zipf's Law, which says that the k−th most common word in natural language text seems to occur with a frequency inversely proportional to k. Suppose we arrange the objects in the table in order of decreasing frequency of access, so that the most frequently accessed object is at the front and the least frequently accessed is at the end. Find a simple expression that approximates the expected number of object comparisons (i.e., tests of equality between two objects) that will be made during a successful linear search of the table if there are n objects in the table and n is large. The search algorithm is exactly the one used in Example 6.6.2 (but now the objects are *not* in random order).
Hint: if X denotes the number of comparisons, then the p.d.f of X will involve the n-th harmonic sum $H(n)$.

6.6.8 Suppose that in Example 6.6.3 on p. 330, the order of the two object comparisons is interchanged. That is, suppose the code reads this way:

```
    ...
    if (a[mid] < target)
```

```
    first = mid + 1;
  else if (target < a[mid])
    last = mid - 1;
  else...
```

Compute the expected number of `otype` object comparisons that will be made during a successful search of an array of 10 objects under the assumption that the target is equally likely to be in any of the 10 cells. Is the answer better or worse than the answer we obtained in Example 6.6.3? Offer a reason why your answer makes sense.

6.6.9 Suppose a binary search using the algorithm in Example 6.6.3, p. 330, is made on an array of 13 `otype` objects arranged in increasing order. For concreteness, suppose that the cells of the array are numbered from 0 to 12.

(a) If a copy of the target is present in the array, what is the *exact* expected number of `otype` object comparisons that will have to be made to find the target? Assume that all 13 objects in the array are equally likely to be the target. (You are more likely to get the right answer if you draw the logical search tree.)
(b) If the target is not present, what is the *exact* expected number of `otype` object comparisons that will have to be made to discover that the target is not there? Assume that the target is equally likely to belong at any one of the 14 cell boundaries of the array.

6.6.10 Repeat Exercises 6.6.9 (a) and (b) using the binary search algorithm given in Fig. 5.15b on p. 201. Compare your answers with the answers in 6.6.9. (Note: there is a difference between the successful and unsuccessful searches here. In the *successful* case, if the search arrives at a point at which `mid` is 12, then it is not logically possible, for `a[mid]` to be less than `target`.)

6.6.11 Figure 6.27 shows an AVL tree, i.e., a height-balanced binary search tree. The integers shown at the nodes are the keys of the data objects stored at those nodes. Now suppose a search is about to be made for an object with a specified "target" key. Code for the search algorithm is shown above the tree.

(a) If the target key is actually present in the tree, and if the target is equally likely to be any one of the keys in the tree, then what is the expected number of key comparisons (i.e., tests of inequalities of the form `p->key <target` and `p->key >target`) that will be required to find the object containing the target key?
(b) If the target key is not in the tree, and if the key is equally likely to belong in any of the empty subtrees of the tree, then what is the expected number of key comparisons that will be required to find that the target is not in the tree? (As an

example, the key 35 is not in the tree; it "belongs" in the empty subtree to the left of 40 because that's where we would place it if we now inserted it.)

```
node_ptr key_location (node_ptr p, int target)
{
  bool found = false;
  while (p && !found)
    if (p->key < target)
      p = p->right;
    else if (p->key > target)
      p = p->left;
    else
      found = true;
  return p;
}
```

6.6.12 Suppose the strings in Example 6.6.5 are placed in a hash table of size 13 using *linear probing* instead of separate chaining. (Recall that in linear probing, when a collision occurs during insertion, the insertion algorithm moves down the array, one cell at a time, with wrap-around, until it finds an empty cell into which it can place the object being inserted.) We can tell by looking at Fig. 6.26 exactly which addresses the strings hash to: for example, the string "Lara" hashes to address 5. Suppose the strings are inserted into the table in the following order (the numbers in parentheses show the hash addresses): Ali (8), Lara(5), Ken(0), Olga(9), Sue(3), Chris(8), Ray(12), Tom(11), Juan(8), Mary(12), Beth(2), Dao(3). The result will be the array shown below.

0	1	2	3	4	5	6	7	8	9	10	11	12
Ken	Juan	Mary	Sue	Beth	Lara	Dao		Ali	Olga	Chris	Tom	Ray

(a) What is the expected number of string comparisons that will be made during a successful search of the table if each string has equal likelihood of being the target of the search? (To take one example, suppose the string "Mary" is the target of the search. Then 4 string comparisons will be made during the search for that target: "Ray" in cell 12 (the address to which "Mary" hashes), "Ken" in cell 0, "Juan" in cell 1.)

(b) What is the expected number of string comparisons that will be made during an unsuccessful search of the table if the target string is equally likely to be hashed to any of the 13 addresses?

Note: those who remember how hash tables should be operated will see that this table is badly over-loaded. When a hash table is implemented using linear (or quadratic) probing, the load factor on the table should never be allowed to go above 50%. Load factors higher than that cause the performance of the table to degrade, as we can see in the calculations above. You should compare your answers here to the numbers we derived in Example 6.6.5.

6.6.13 (For the mathematically gifted.) Suppose we partition an array a[0...n-1] of *distinct* objects in random order into two subarrays, say a[0..m-1] and a[m..n-1], where $1 \le m < n$. Suppose that each subarray is then sorted using some sorting algorithm (which algorithm is irrelevant here). Next, suppose the objects in these sorted subarrays are merged into a single sorted array c[0...n-1] using the following algorithm (slightly modified from Fig. 5.50):

```
template <class otype>
void merge_array(const otype a[], otype c[], int m, int n)
{
    int afirst = 0;      // Make afirst ''point'' to the 1st cell of a[0..m-1] and
    int bfirst = m;      // bfirst ''point'' to the 1st cell of a[m..n-1] and
    int cfirst = 0;      // cfirst ''point'' to the 1st cell of c[0..n-1].
    while (afirst < m  && bfirst < n)  // Don't go outside of subarrays.
        if (a[afirst] <= a[bfirst])
            c[cfirst++] = a[afirst++];  // Copy from left subarray into c.
        else
            c[cfirst++] = a[bfirst++];  // Copy from right subarray into c.
    // When the loop above stops, exactly one of two things will be true:
    // afirst will be < m and bfirst will be = n, in which case we must
    // copy the remaining objects from a[afirst..m-1] into c[cfirst..n-1];
    // OR bfirst will be < n and afirst will be = m, in which case we
    // must copy the remaining objects from a[bfirst..n-1] into c[first..n-1].
    while (afirst < m) // This loop or the one following it will be executed.
        c[cfirst++] = a[afirst++];
    while (bfirst < n)
        c[cfirst++] = a[bfirst++];
}
```

(a) Derive a summation formula in the variables m and n for the expected number of object comparisons of the form "a[afirst] <= a[bfirst]" that will occur during the first "while" loop above. (Note that we are ignoring subscript comparisons such as afirst <m.) A useful observation is that when the first loop above is executed, one of two things must occur: *either* the "while" loop will stop because afirst reaches the value m, which occurs if and only if the largest object in a[0..m-1] is smaller than one or more of the objects in a[m..n-1], *or else* the loop will stop because bfirst reaches n, which occurs if and only if the largest object in a[0..m-1] is larger than all the objects in a[m..n-1].

(b) (HARD) Prove that the summation formula derived in part (a) can be reduced to the closed form

$$\frac{m(n-m)(n+2)}{(m+1)(n-m+1)}$$

(c) Show that if m is $\lfloor(1+n)/2\rfloor$, then the formula in part (b) lies between $n-2$ and $n-1$ (and is therefore asymptotic to n). Keep in mind that $1 \le m < n$, so $n \ge 2$. (In the Merge Sort in Fig. 5.51 on p. 225 the number

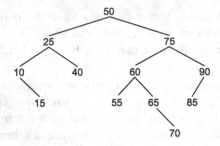

Fig. 6.27 An AVL tree

```
template <class otype>
void simple_bubble_sort (otype a[], int n)
{
  int j, k;
  for (k = n-1; k >= 1; --k)
    for (j = 0; j <= k-1; ++j)
      if (a[j] > a[j+1])              // then these 2 objects are out of order
        swap (a[j], a[j+1]);
}
```

Fig. 6.28 Simple Bubble Sort function

mid = (first + last)/2 plays the role that m is playing in this exercise. We'll use this exercise later to calculate the expected number of object comparisons made during a run of Merge Sort.)

6.7   Applications of Expected Value Theorems to Analysis of Algorithms

This section contains two examples and several exercises that illustrate how standard theorems about expected values can be put to work to calculate the average (i.e., expected) behavior of some well known elementary algorithms.

Example 6.7.1 In Fig. 5.9, p. 185, we looked at a simple version of Bubble Sort (reproduced in Fig. 6.28) and calculated the minimum and maximum execution times for the algorithm. Now let's look at its average behavior. Assume that all the objects in the array are distinct and are arranged initially in random order. Calculate the expected number of object comparisons (this does not include subscript comparisons) that will be made during execution of this function when it is applied to an array of n objects. Also calculate the expected number of object swaps.

As it turns out, the number of object comparisons is a deterministic function of n: the first time the body of the outer loop (controlled by variable k) is executed, the inner loop variable j will satisfy the condition $j < k-1$ exactly $n-1$ times, so there will be exactly $n - 1$ object comparisons. We call this the "first pass" over the array. On the second pass, the inner loop body will make $n - 2$ object comparisons. Etc. Altogether, the number of object comparisons is $(n-1)+\ldots+2+1 = \dfrac{(n-1)n}{2}$. If we let X denote the random variable that counts the number of object comparisons, then X is constant and $E(X) = \dfrac{(n-1)n}{2}$ (see Theorem 8.0.29).

Now let Y denote the number of object swaps that will take place. Then Y is very much dependent on the initial arrangement of the objects in the array. If by chance the objects are in increasing order initially, then $Y = 0$, whereas if the objects are in decreasing order initially, you can verify that $Y = \dfrac{(n-1)n}{2}$. These are the extreme possible values of Y. Calculating the expected value of Y is not especially easy.

It turns out to be convenient to introduce some auxiliary random variables that are related to Y. For each integer i in the range $0 \le i \le n - 1$ let L_i denote the random variable that counts the number of objects that are *larger* than a[i] but that lie to the *left* of a[i] in the initial arrangement of the objects in the array. For example, if the array is initially

0	1	2	3	4	5	6	7	8	9
a: Ken	Nan	Ida	Lee	Pat	Cal	Gus	Ray	Joy	Moe

then $L_0 = 0$, $L_1 = 0$, $L_2 = 2$, $L_3 = 1$, $L_4 = 0$, $L_5 = 5$, $L_6 = 5$, $L_7 = 0$, $L_8 = 5$, $L_9 = 3$. Now at some stage in the Bubble Sort, the object Moe will have to be swapped to the left with each of the 3 objects that are larger than it because they need to move to the right of Moe. A similar statement is true about all the other objects in the array: the i-th object will have to be swapped to the left with the L_i objects that are larger but lie to its left. Thus the total number of "left swaps" (which is the same as the total number of swaps) that will be made, which we call Y, can be expressed as $Y = L_0 + L_1 + \cdots + L_{n-1}$. By Theorem 8.0.30 in the Appendix, $E(Y) = 0 + E(L_1) + E(L_2) + \cdots + E(L_{n-1})$. We have thus reduced the problem to calculating $E(L_i)$ for each $i = 1, 2, 3, \ldots, n - 1$.

So now consider, for a fixed integer i in the range $1 \le i \le n - 1$, the random variable L_i. Its possible values are $0, 1, 2, 3, \ldots, i$. The event "$L_i = 0$" occurs if and only if a[i] is initially larger than all the objects to its left. The probability of this is $\dfrac{1}{i+1}$. The event "$L_i = 1$" occurs if and only if a[i] is initially the second-largest object in the subarray a[0..i], and the probability of this is also $\dfrac{1}{i+1}$ (see Theorem 8.0.12). In fact, for each of its possible values, the probability that L_i will assume that value is $\dfrac{1}{i+1}$, and thus

$$E(L_i) = \frac{1}{i+1}[0 + 1 + 2 + \cdots + i] = \frac{1}{i+1} \frac{i(i+1)}{2} = \frac{i}{2}.$$

Now we can return to $E(Y)$. As shown above, $E(Y) = E(L_1) + \cdots + E(L_{n-1})$,

$$\text{so } E(Y) = \frac{1}{2} + \frac{2}{2} + \cdots + \frac{n-1}{2} = \frac{1}{2}[1 + 2 + \cdots + (n-1)] = \frac{(n-1)n}{4}.$$

Example 6.7.2 In this example we will make use of Theorem 8.0.27.

Review Algorithm 1 on p. 309 for choosing a random sample of size K from a population of size N. The method involves initializing a Boolean array of length N to false everywhere and then using a random number generator to choose integers in the range $1 \ldots N$ until K distinct integers have been chosen. What is the expected number of calls to the random number generator required to produce the sample of size K? The answer should be expressed in terms of K and N.

Let X_2 denote the number of calls, after the first call, necessary to produce a second integer different from the first. Let X_3 denote the number of calls, after the appearance of the second integer, necessary to produce a third integer different from the first two. Etc. to X_K. Let X denote the total number of calls necessary to produce K distinct integers. Then

$$X = 1 + X_2 + X_3 + \cdots + X_K, \text{ so } E(X) = 1 + \sum_{i=2}^{K} E(X_i). \text{ By Theorem 8.0.27,}$$

$$E(X_i) = \frac{1}{\frac{N-(i-1)}{N}} = \frac{N}{N-i+1}, \text{ so}$$

$$E(X) = 1 + \sum_{i=2}^{K} \frac{N}{N-i+1} = 1 + N\left(\frac{1}{N-1} + \frac{1}{N-2} + \cdots + \frac{1}{N-K+1}\right)$$

$$= N\left(\frac{1}{N} + \frac{1}{N-1} + \frac{1}{N-2} + \cdots + \frac{1}{N-K+1}\right)$$

If K is small relative to N, then each of the K fractions in the sum in parentheses is approximately equal to $\frac{1}{N}$, so N times that sum is approximately K, which is what common sense tells us should be the approximate expected value. If K is not small relative to N, then we can note that the sum in parentheses above is the difference between two harmonic sums, provided $K < N$:

$$E(X) = N[H(N) - H(N-K)] \approx N[\ln(N) - \ln(N-K)] = N \ln \frac{N}{N-K},$$

where $H(n)$ denotes the n-th harmonic sum.

6.7.1 Exercises

6.7.3 Suppose we use the following algorithm (taken from Fig. 5.1, p. 170) to find the largest object in an array a[first..last].

```
template <class otype>
int location_of_max (const otype a[], int first, int last)
{
    int max_loc = first;                    // The first cell of the subarray will
                                            // contain the ''largest seen so far''.
```

```
    for (++first; first <= last; ++first) // Start at the second cell.
      if (a[first] > a[max_loc])          // The value paramtr ''first''
         max_loc = first;                 // can be modified since its
                                          // initial value need not be
    return max_loc;                       // preserved.
}
```

We know that if there are n objects in the array, then exactly $n - 1$ object comparisons will be made. The assignment statement max_loc = first inside the loop body may never be executed, or it may be executed $n - 1$ times, or it may be executed some number of times between 0 and $n - 1$. What is the *expected* number of times that it will be executed if all the objects are distinct, and in random order? **Hint:** Express the random variable here as the sum of a bunch of indicator random variables.

6.7.4 Let W denote the number of swaps that will be made during the first pass of the Bubble Sort algorithm on p. 339 when applied to an array of n distinct objects in random order. (By "first pass" we mean the complete execution of the inner loop controlled by the index j during the first execution of the body of the outer loop.)

(a) Compute the expected value of W as a function of n. **Hint:** an object a[j] will be swapped to its right if and only if what is true? Use indicator random variables (see Definition 8.0.21 and Theorem 8.0.39).

(b) At the end of the first pass, what is the probability that a[1] will be less than a[2]?

6.7.5 Below is code for a version of Linear Insertion Sort.

```
template <class otype>
void linear_insertion_sort (otype a[], int n)  // sorts a[1...n]
{
    int i, k;
    for (k = 2; k <= n; ++k)
    {                          // Move a[k] into cell 0 where it can act
        a[0] = a[k];  // as a sentinel and to open a hole in the array.
        // Make a backward linear search, using a subscript i.
        // The value in a[0] prevents  i  from going too far left.
        for (i = k-1; a[i] > a[0]; --i)
          a[i+1] = a[i]; // Slide a[i] to the right by one cell
        // Subscript  i  was decremented after correct position found
        a[i+1] = a[0];     // Move a[0] into its correct position.
    }
}
```

Assume that all n objects in a[1..n] are distinct and that they are arranged in random order initially. Calculate the expected number of object comparisons (a[i] >a[0]) and the expected number of object moves (assignments of one data object to another).

Hint: Let X_2 denote the number of object comparisons that will be made when k has the fixed value 2; let X_3 denote the number of comparisons that will be made when k has the value 3; and so on up to X_n when k has the value n. Let X denote the total number of object comparisons altogether, so that $X = X_2 + X_3 + \cdots + X_n$. What are the possible values of X_2? The possible values of X_3? What are the possible values of X_k, where $2 \le k \le n$? Start by calculating the probability of each of the values of X_2. Of each of the values of X_3. Etc. for each X_k, $2 \le k \le n$. Use these to compute $E(X_k)$ for $2 \le k \le n$, and then compute $E(X)$, i.e., the expected total number of object comparisons. To deal with object moves, let Y_2 denote the number of object moves when $k = 2$, etc. Then note that Y_k is related in a simple way to X_k.

6.7.6 In Exercise 6.7.4 you computed the expected number of swaps that will be made during the first pass of the Bubble Sort algorithm on Example 6.7.1 when applied to an array of length n *in random order*. The answer should have been $\dfrac{1}{2} + \dfrac{2}{3} + \dfrac{3}{4} + \dfrac{4}{5} + \ldots + \dfrac{n-1}{n}$. This can be written as

$$(1 - \frac{1}{2}) + (1 - \frac{1}{3}) + (1 - \frac{1}{4}) + (1 - \frac{1}{5}) + \cdots + (1 - \frac{1}{n})$$

$$= (n-1) - \left(\frac{1}{2} + \frac{1}{3} + \frac{1}{4} + \frac{1}{5} + \cdots \frac{1}{n} \right) = n - H(n),$$

where $H(n)$ denotes the n-th harmonic sum. Now suppose we decide to apply this to the analysis of the *complete* Bubble Sort Algorithm when it acts on an array of length n in random order. Let W_n denote the number of swaps that will be made during the first pass over the array of length n; let W_{n-1} denote the number of swaps that will be made during the second pass over the reduced array of length $n - 1$; etc. Then the total number of swaps during the execution of the entire algorithm will be $W_n + W_{n-1} + W_{n-2} + \cdots + W_2$ (the last pass is over an array of length 2). It follows that the expected number of swaps during the execution of the entire algorithm will be $E(W_n) + E(W_{n-1}) + E(W_{n-2}) + \cdots + E(W_2)$. By Exercise 6.7.4, $E(W_n) = n - H(n)$. On the next pass, the array we are working with is of length $n - 1$ so we ought to have $E(W_{n-1}) = (n - 1) - H(n - 1)$. Similarly, we ought to have $E(W_{n-2}) = (n - 2) - H(n - 2)$ etc. Putting all these together will give the following formula for the expected number of swaps during the execution of the entire algorithm:

$$n + (n - 1) + (n - 2) + \cdots + 2 - [H(n) + H(n - 1) + H(n - 2) + \cdots + H(2)].$$

This analysis of Bubble Sort is simpler than the one used in Example 6.7.1. Note, however, that it gives a different answer! (You can verify in a simple case such as $n = 3$ that the answer here does not match the answer in Example 6.7.1.) As it turns out, there is an error of reasoning in this simpler analysis. Find it.

Hint: it has something to do with the italicized phrase at the beginning of this exercise.

6.7.7 Look back at Algorithm 1, p. 300, for choosing a random sample of size K from a file of size N. A collection of K distinct random integers is chosen, and then the file is read and the file records corresponding to those K integers are selected for the random sample. Generally only a portion of the file needs to be read. More precisely, if L is the largest of the K integers chosen in the first part of the algorithm, then L records must be read from the file, which is to say that the fraction L/N of the file will have to be read. Compute the expected number of records that will be read from the file.

Hint: use Exercise 2.3.51 on p. 52. Also use one of the formulas from Exercise 2.3.51 on p. 52. Be sure to reduce your answer algebraically to as simple a form as possible (a lot of factorials should cancel out).

Note: before doing this problem, you may want to predict the answer based on the following intuitive notion: the K chosen integers should partition the remaining $N - K$ integers into $K + 1$ segments having average size $\dfrac{N - K}{K + 1}$. The largest of the K chosen integers should be located just before the final one of these segments. Thus the largest of the K chosen integers should be what?

6.7.8 Look at Algorithm 3, p. 313, for choosing a random sample. Explain carefully why, for a given pair N and K, the expected number of records that will be read from the file by Algorithm 3 is exactly the same as the expected number that will be read by Algorithm 1 (see Exercise 6.7.7). You may use the fact that Algorithm 3 is known to be unbiased.

6.7.9 Compute the expected number of iterations for the linear search algorithm seen in Fig. 5.2, p. 175, with `first = 0` and `last = n - 1`, when the array contains exactly two occurrences of the target placed at random in the array.

Hint: The linear search will find a target at position k in the array if neither target value is present from 0 to $k - 1$ in the array, and one of the two target values is at position k.

6.8   Applications of Conditional Expected Value to Analysis of Algorithms

This section contains several examples and exercises that apply theorems about conditional expected values to analysis of familiar algorithms. See Definition 8.0.34 and Theorems 8.0.35 and 8.0.36 in the Appendix.

Example 6.8.1 Suppose we have a table of 50 objects maintained as an array in random order. Suppose the table is static, and that frequent searches are made in the table using the algorithm in Fig. 6.23 on p. 330. If 80 % of the searches are unsuccessful, then what is the expected number of times the body of the loop will be executed during a single search of the table?

Solution. Let X denote the number of object comparisons that will be made during a search of this table. We are asked to compute $E(X)$. Since the number of comparisons surely depends on whether the target is present or not, it makes sense to introduce the following events: let A_1 denote the event "the target will be in the table" and let A_2 denote the event "the target will not be in the table". Then A_1 and A_2 make up a partition of the sample space of possible targets, so by Theorem 8.0.36 we have

$$E(X) = P(A_1)E(X|A_1) + P(A_2)E(X|A_2).$$

We are told in the problem that $P(A_1) = 0.20$ and $P(A_2) = 0.80$. We can express the results derived in Example 6.6.2 on p. 328 this way: $E(X|A_1) = \dfrac{50-1}{2}$ and $E(X|A_2) = 50$. It follows that

$$E(X) = 0.20 \cdot \frac{49}{2} + 0.80 \cdot 50 = 4.9 + 40 = 44.9$$

Example 6.8.2 (**Analysis of Successful Binary Search**): Suppose we have a table of n objects maintained as an array a[first..last] in sorted order. Suppose we are about to make a binary search of the array using the algorithm given in Example 6.6.3 on p. 330. Assume that target is in the array and is equally likely to be in any of the n cells of the array. What is the expected number of object comparisons that will be made during the search?

Solution. Let X_n denote the number of object comparisons that will be made during a successful binary search of an ordered array of n objects. Let A_1 denote the event that target <a[mid] will be true on the first probe of the search ("probe" here means an examination of the contents of a[mid]; a probe will involve either one or two object comparisons). Let A_2 denote the event that a[mid] <target will be true on the first probe of the search. Let A_3 denote the event that a[mid] == target will be true on the first probe of the search. Using the Fig. 2.1 on p. 14, we can see that

$$P(A_1) = \frac{\lfloor (n-1)/2 \rfloor}{n}, \quad P(A_2) = \frac{\lfloor n/2 \rfloor}{n}, \quad P(A_3) = \frac{1}{n} \quad \text{for all } n \geq 1.$$

We can write X_n in the form

$$X_n = 1 + I_{A_2 \cup A_3} + Z_n,$$

where Z_n denotes the number of object comparisons that will be made in a[first.. last] after the first probe (i.e., after the first time through the loop body). The expression $I_{A_2 \cup A_3}$ denotes the indicator random variable for the event $A_2 \cup A_3$. Its value is 1 if A_2 or A_3 occurs (i.e., two object comparisons are made on the first time through the loop), while the value is 0 if A_1, the complement of $A_2 \cup A_3$, occurs (i.e., 1 object comparison is made). Then for all $n \geq 1$ we have

$$E(X_n) = 1 + P(A_2 \cup A_3) + E(Z_n)$$
$$= 1 + P(A_2 \cup A_3) + P(A_1)E(Z_n|A_1)$$
$$+ P(A_2)E(Z_n|A_2) + P(A_3)E(Z_n|A_3)$$
$$= 1 + \frac{\lfloor n/2 \rfloor + 1}{n} + \frac{\lfloor (n-1)/2 \rfloor}{n} E(X_{\lfloor (n-1)/2 \rfloor}) + \frac{\lfloor n/2 \rfloor}{n} E(X_{\lfloor n/2 \rfloor}) + 0$$

provided we interpret $E(X_0)$ as denoting 0 (when $n = 1$, $E(Z_n|A_1) = E(Z_n|A_2) = 0$, and when $n = 2$, $E(Z_n|A_1) = 0$). In the equation above, multiply on both sides by n to get

$$nE(X_n) = n + (\lfloor n/2 \rfloor + 1) + \lfloor (n-1)/2 \rfloor E(X_{\lfloor (n-1)/2 \rfloor})$$
$$+ \lfloor n/2 \rfloor E(X_{\lfloor n/2 \rfloor}) \quad \text{for all } n \geq 1.$$

Let $F(n)$ denote the product $nE(X_n)$. Then $F(0) = 0$, and the equation above takes the form

$$F(n) = n + \lfloor n/2 \rfloor + 1 + F(\lfloor (n-1)/2 \rfloor) + F(\lfloor n/2 \rfloor) \quad \text{for all } n \geq 1.$$

This is a recurrence relation we can solve. It requires a slight transformation, however, along the lines shown in Table 4.4 on p. 157. We note that $\lfloor n/2 \rfloor = \lceil (n-1)/2 \rceil$, so the equation can be rewritten as

$$F(n) = n + \lfloor n/2 \rfloor + 1 + F(\lfloor (n-1)/2 \rfloor) + F(\lceil (n-1)/2 \rceil) \quad \text{for all } n \geq 1.$$

Now we apply the transformation $F(n) = G(n+1)$ to obtain (again see Table 4.4, p. 157)

$$G(n) = (n-1) + \left\lfloor \frac{n-1}{2} \right\rfloor + 1 + G(\lfloor n/2 \rfloor) + G(\lceil n/2 \rceil) \quad \text{for all } n \geq 2,$$

and $0 = F(0) = G(1)$. Using the fact that $\lfloor (n-1)/2 \rfloor = \lceil n/2 \rceil - 1$, we can now write

$$G(1) = 0, \qquad G(n) = G(\lfloor n/2 \rfloor) + G(\lceil n/2 \rceil) + n - 1 + \lceil n/2 \rceil \quad \text{for all } n \geq 2.$$

By Table 4.1 on p. 147,

$$G(n) = \alpha n + \phi_1(n) - (-1) + \phi_2(n), \quad \text{where } \phi_1(n) \sim n \lg(n) \text{ and } \phi_2(n) \sim \frac{1}{2} n \lg(n).$$

By Theorem 3.3.8 (e) on p. 90 and Theorem 3.3.6 on p. 90, $G(n) \sim \frac{3}{2} n \lg(n)$. Now we return to $F(n) = G(n+1)$, which gives $F(n) \sim \frac{3}{2}(n+1) \lg(n+1)$, or more simply, $F(n) \sim \frac{3}{2} n \lg(n)$. Finally, we recall that $F(n) = nE(X_n)$, so $E(X_n) = \frac{1}{n} F(n)$, which gives us our final answer:

$$\boxed{E(X_n) \sim \frac{3}{2} \lg(n)}$$

Example 6.8.3 (**Successful Search in Hash Table with Separate Chaining**): Suppose we are going to construct a hash table named T with size M using separate chaining for collision resolution. This means that T will be an array with cells numbered $0, 1, 2, \ldots, M - 1$, and each cell $T[i]$ will contain a pointer to a (possibly empty) linked list. We'll assume that when an object is inserted into the hash table, it is simply placed at the front of the list at the cell to which its key hashes. The hash function will be assumed to be a good one: any given key value is equally likely to be hashed to any of the M locations. Figure 6.29 shows the code for placing a copy of an object x in the table T.

Figure 6.30 shows the code for searching the table for an object having a specified key value k.

How well can the hash table be expected to perform under a load of size n, that is, after n objects have been inserted? To find out, we'll count the expected number of key comparisons as a measure of the expected time required to perform one operation on the table. In this example we'll look at the case of a successful search for a specified key k. The exercises will look at the case of an unsuccessful search and of an insertion operation.

Suppose then that a key value k is specified and (although we don't know it before we make the search) there is an object with that key in the table T. Then that object is equally likely to be anywhere in the hash table. Let X denote the number of times that the expression "temp->info.key == k" will be evaluated during the successful search. Then X could theoretically take any value from 1 to n because the chain containing the target key could contain as many as n nodes, and the target key could be anywhere in that chain. Thus we know the best and worst cases possible for X. We now calculate $E(X)$. Our approach will use conditional expected values based on the possible lengths of the chain containing k. Let A_λ denote the event that the chain containing k will be of length λ for $\lambda = 1, 2, 3, \ldots, n$. Then by Theorem 8.0.31 and a calculation similar to that of Example 6.6.2 on p. 328,

$$E(X) = \sum_{\lambda=1}^{n} P(A_\lambda)E(X|A_\lambda) = \sum_{\lambda=1}^{n} P(A_\lambda)\frac{\lambda+1}{2}.$$

Let $h(k)$ denote the address to which the key k hashes. The event A_λ occurs when $\lambda - 1$ of the other $n - 1$ keys hash to $h(k)$. These $n - 1$ individual hashing actions can be viewed as independent binary trials (each key either does or does not hash to $h(k)$) with probability $1/M$ of success on each trial, so $P(A_\lambda) = b(\lambda - 1; n - 1, 1/M)$

```
bool insert (otype &x, nodeptr T[]) // Returns true if insertion is successful.
{                                   // Returns 0 if T already contains an
   int i = hash(x.key);             // object whose key matches x.key
   nodeptr temp = T[i];             // Create a temporary hash node pointer.
   while (temp != NULL)             // This works even if T is empty.
     if (temp->info.key == x.key)
        return false;               // RETURN from function. Insert failed.
     else
        temp = temp->next;
   temp = new node;                 // Allocate.
   temp->info = x;                  // Copy object x into node.
   temp->next = T[i];               // Place the new node at the front
   T[i] = temp;                     // of the chain at cell T[i].
   return true;                     // Indicate that the insertion operation was successful.
}
```

Fig. 6.29 Inserting an object in a hash table

```
otype* search(nodeptr T[], key_type k)// Returns pointer to the unique
{                                      // object in T with key k if such an
   int i = hash(k);                    // object exists. Else returns NULL.
   nodeptr temp = T[i];                // Create a temporary hash node pointer.
   while (temp != NULL)
      if (temp->info.key == k)
         return &(temp->info); // EXIT from function if search succeeds.
      else
         temp = temp->next;
   return NULL;                        // Search was unsuccessful. Return NULL.
}
```

Fig. 6.30 Searching for an object in a hash table

(see Definition 8.0.34 and Theorem 8.0.35). Thus

$$E(X) = \sum_{\lambda=1}^{n} \frac{\lambda+1}{2} b\left(\lambda - 1; n - 1, \frac{1}{M}\right) \text{ [Shift index of summation by letting}$$

$$x = \lambda - 1, \lambda = x + 1.]$$

$$= \sum_{x=0}^{n-1} \frac{x+2}{2} b\left(x; n - 1, \frac{1}{M}\right)$$

$$= \frac{1}{2} \sum_{x=0}^{n-1} x\, b\left(x; n - 1, \frac{1}{M}\right) + \sum_{x=0}^{n-1} b\left(x; n - 1, \frac{1}{M}\right)$$

where $b(j; k, p)$ denotes the probability of j successes in k independent trials of a binary random variable, with probability p of success on each trial. By Definition 8.0.34 and Theorem 8.0.36 the equation above simplifies to

$$= \frac{1}{2}(n-1)\frac{1}{M} + 1.$$

Let's write L for the "load index" of the table, which is defined by $L = \dfrac{n}{M}$. Then if you are planning to create a separate chaining hash table with load index L, you can expect that successful searches will require

$$roughly \quad \frac{L}{2} + 1$$

key comparisons on the average. Note that if each cell of the table had a chain of the same length as all the other cells, then the length of each chain would be exactly L.

The point of view we have adopted in the foregoing discussion is that we are doing our calculations before the table is constructed. We are trying to predict how the "average" table will perform. After the table is actually constructed, its particular performance may be better or worse than the predicted, a priori expected value. Thus, for example, if by some stroke of good luck, the table we construct has all its chains of exactly equal length L, then in such a table the expected number of key comparisons during a successful search will be $\dfrac{L+1}{2}$. If, instead, by some dreadful misfortune, the table we construct has only a single chain (all objects happen by chance to hash to the same cell), then in such a table the expected number of key comparisons during a successful search will be $\dfrac{n+1}{2}$.

Example 6.8.4 (**Probabilistic Analysis of Quicksort**): When we analyzed the simple Quicksort algorithm given in Fig. 5.63, we looked only at the best and worst cases. We found that a worst case occurs when the objects to be sorted are already in correct order or in reverse order from the desired order. In these cases the running time for Quicksort is $\Theta(n^2)$. We did not study the question of how Quicksort can be expected to perform when given an array of objects in random order. An intuitive consideration of this case can be found in [3].

Refer back to the Quicksort function on p. 269. The largest part of the work in the function is done during the loops where two objects are compared each time the loop condition is tested. Object swaps are also performed, but the number of swaps is less than the number of object comparisons. So let's compute the expected number of object comparisons that will be made when this function is called with an array of n distinct objects. To do this, we must introduce an appropriate random variable. We'll use X_n to denote the number of object comparisons that will be made when the Quicksort function is called with an array of n objects in random order. Clearly X_n is a random variable. It can be as small as $n \lg(n)$ (approximately) or as large as $n^2/2$ (approximately). Also note that $X_0 = 0$ and $X_1 = 0$ (these fall under the base case test at the beginning of the function). What we want to compute is $E(X_n)$ for all $n \geq 0$.

Since the Quicksort function is recursive, it is natural to seek a recurrence relation involving $E(X_n)$ when $n \geq 2$. The idea is to decompose X_n into the number of comparisons that are made during the non-recursive part of the function body plus the number of comparisons that are made during the two recursive calls. Let Y_n denote the number of comparisons that will be made during the recursive call on the part of the array to the left of the final position of the partitioning object, and let Z_n denote the number of comparisons that will be made during the recursive call on the right part of the array. Then $X_n = $ (number of object comparisons during the non-recursive part) $+ Y_n + Z_n$ for all $n \geq 2$.

Every object in the array except the partitioning object is compared at least once with the partition object that's at the left end of the array. This means there are at least $n - 1$ object comparisons. Are there any more comparisons? Yes. When the loop subscripts i and j stop moving, it is because they have "crossed over each other" (this is guaranteed by the fact that the objects in the array are all different from each other), so the loop controlled by the condition i <j ends by having two objects compared for a second time against the partitioning object. Thus the total number of object comparisons made during the loops is exactly $(n - 1) + 2 = n + 1$. (If you are not certain about this, take a very small example such as an array of length 5 and look at all the various possibilities for where i and j might stop.)

Now we are able to write our equation for X_n this way:

$$X_n = n + 1 + Y_n + Z_n \quad \text{for all } n \geq 2.$$

It follows that

$$E(X_n) = n + 1 + E(Y_n) + E(Z_n) \text{ for all } n \geq 2.$$

The problem we encounter at this point is that Y_n and Z_n will depend on how the array a[first..last] "splits" into two subarrays to be sorted recursively. We need to account for all the different possibilities, which are

- the subarray on the left is of length 0 and the subarray on the right is of length $n - 1$;
- the subarray on the left is of length 1 and the subarray on the right is of length $n - 2$; etc.
- the subarray on the left is of length $n - 1$ and the subarray on the right is of length 0.

Let A_k denote the event that the subarray on the left is of length k, where k is an integer in the range $0 \leq k \leq n - 1$. Then by Theorem 8.0.39,

$$E(Y_n) = P(A_0)E(Y_n|A_0) + P(A_1)E(Y_n|A_1)$$
$$+ \cdots + P(A_{n-1})E(Y_n|A_{n-1}) \quad \text{for all } n \geq 2.$$

The event A_0 occurs if and only if the partitioning object in cell a[first] is the smallest object in the array. Since the objects in the array are in random order, $P(A_0) = 1/n$. Similarly, the event A_1 occurs if and only if the partitioning object is the next-to-smallest object in the array, so $P(A_1) = 1/n$. And so on. Thus

$$E(Y_n) = \frac{1}{n}[E(Y_n|A_0) + E(Y_n|A_1) + \cdots + E(Y_n|A_{n-1})] \quad \text{for all } n \geq 2. \quad (6.1)$$

Now note that if either A_0 or A_1 occurs, then the recursion on the left subarray encounters a base case, so the recursive call on the left returns with 0 object comparisons. It follows that $E(Y_n|A_0) = 0 = E(Y_n|A_1)$. For $k \geq 2$, if A_k occurs, then the recursion on the left subarray is a Quicksort on an array of k distinct objects in random order (you need to think a little to see that the left array really will be in random order). Thus $E(Y_n|A_k) = E(X_k)$ when $k \geq 2$. Thus

$$E(Y_n) = \frac{1}{n}[0 + 0 + E(X_2) + E(X_3) + \cdots + E(X_{n-1})] \quad \text{for all } n \geq 2.$$

In the special case where $n = 2$, it will be understood that this sum is 0 (to see this, look at Eq. (6.1)).

Now that we have an expression for $E(Y_n)$, let's go back and look at $E(Z_n)$, which is the expected number of object comparisons during the recursion on the right subarray. By arguments entirely symmetric with those for Y_n, we can derive exactly the same formula for $E(Z_n)$ that we have derived for $E(Y_n)$, although the terms in the sum will appear in the opposite order. Thus $E(Z_n) = E(Y_n)$. Putting together all the equations we have derived, we find that

$$E(X_n) = n + 1 + 2E(Y_n) = n + 1 + \frac{2}{n}[E(X_2) + E(X_3)$$
$$+ \cdots + E(X_n - 1)] \quad \text{for all } n \geq 2.$$

This is a recurrence relation in the quantity $E(X_n)$. To make it look more familiar, write $F(n)$ for $E(X_n)$. Also note that $F(0) = E(X_0) = 0$ and $F(1) = E(X_1) = 0$. Thus we have this problem:

$$F(0) = 0, \quad F(1) = 0, \quad F(n) = n + 1 + \frac{2}{n}[F(2) + F(3)$$
$$+ \cdots + F(n-1)] \quad \text{for all } n \geq 2. \tag{6.2}$$

To try to solve it we might begin by multiplying the recurrence relation through by n:

$$nF(n) = n^2 + n + 2[F(2) + F(3) + \cdots + F(n-1)] \quad \text{for all } n \geq 2. \tag{6.3}$$

To get rid of all those low order terms we'll use a little trick. Replace n by $n-1$ throughout:

$$(n-1)F(n-1) = (n-1)^2 + (n-1) + 2[F(2) + F(3) + \cdots + F(n-2)] \quad \text{for all } n \geq 3. \tag{6.4}$$

Subtracting the left and right sides of (6.4) from the sides of (6.3) gets rid of many terms on the right:

$$nF(n) - (n-1)F(n-1) = n^2 - (n-1)^2 + n - (n-1) + 2F(n-1) \quad \text{for all } n \geq 3.$$

Rearrangement of terms and some algebraic simplification transforms this into the equation

$$nF(n) = (n+1)F(n-1) + 2n \quad \text{for all } n \geq 3.$$

What are the initial values for this problem? We know that $F(0) = F(1) = 0$, but for the problem above we need $F(2)$. We can get this from Eq. (6.2). We have $F(2) = 2 + 1 + \frac{2}{2}[0] = 3$.

So we are trying to solve

$$F(2) = 3, \quad nF(n) = (n+1)F(n-1) + 2n \quad \text{for all } n \geq 3.$$

Dividing through by both n and $n+1$ gives this problem:

$$F(2) = 3, \quad \frac{F(n)}{n+1} = \frac{F(n-1)}{n} + \frac{2}{n+1} \quad \text{for all } n \geq 3.$$

Now it is easy to spot a pattern for substitution: let $G(n) = \frac{F(n)}{n+1}$. This transforms the problem into

$$G(2) = \frac{3}{3} = 1, \quad G(n) = G(n-1) + \frac{2}{n+1} \quad \text{for all } n \geq 3.$$

We can solve this by the technique we used in Example 4.5.1 on p. 153.

$$G(3) = G(2) + \frac{2}{3+1} = 1 + \frac{2}{4}$$
$$G(4) = G(3) + \frac{2}{4+1} = 1 + \frac{2}{4} + \frac{2}{5}$$
$$G(5) = G(4) + \frac{2}{5+1} = 1 + \frac{2}{4} + \frac{2}{5} + \frac{2}{6}$$

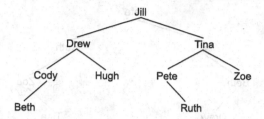

Fig. 6.31 A random binary search tree

etc.

In general,

$$G(n) = 1 + \frac{2}{4} + \frac{2}{5} + \frac{2}{6} + \cdots + \frac{2}{n+1} = 1 + 2\left(\frac{1}{4} + \frac{1}{5} + \frac{1}{6} + \cdots + \frac{1}{n+1}\right)$$

for all $n \geq 3$.

The sum in parenthesis in the formula above is the harmonic sum $H(n)$ defined on p. 33 missing the first 3 terms. Recalling the definition of $G(n)$ in terms of $F(n)$, we can write

$$\frac{F(n)}{n+1} = 1 + 2\left[H(n+1) - 1 - \frac{1}{2} - \frac{1}{3}\right]   \text{for all } n \geq 3.$$

This yields

$$F(n) = 2(n+1)H(n+1) - \frac{8}{3}(n+1)   \text{for all } n \geq 3.$$

Now recall that $E(X_n) = F(n)$, so we have shown that $E(X_n) \sim 2n\ln(n)$. If we want to put this in terms of the logarithm base 2, we can get

$$E(X_n) \sim 2n\frac{\lg(2)}{\lg(e)} \approx 1.39\, n \lg(n).$$

Example 6.8.5 (**Random Binary Search Trees**): Suppose we are given a file containing n objects, each having some key (distinct from all the other keys in the file). Suppose further that we write a program that reads the file and creates a binary search tree by repeatedly inserting each newly read object into the binary search tree, with no re-balancing of the AVL kind. (Cf. pp. 227–236.) Then the resulting tree may have a variety of shapes, and its height can be any number from $\lfloor \lg(n) \rfloor$ to $n - 1$. If the objects in the file are in random order, then we'll call a binary search tree built by this method a random binary search tree.

Now suppose we want to calculate the number of nodes that will be examined during a successful search for a specified key in a random binary search tree with n nodes. This number is a random variable, and its value might be anything from 1 (if the specified key happens to be located at the root) to $h + 1$, where h is the height of the tree. For example, consider the random search tree generated by a file containing names in this order: Jill, Tina, Pete, Drew, Ruth, Cody, Zoe, Hugh, Beth. The resulting tree is shown in Fig. 6.31.

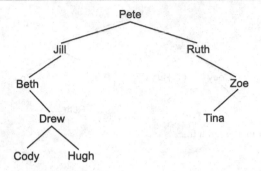

Fig. 6.32 Another random binary search tree

1 node will be examined if the specified key is Jill;
2 nodes will be examined if the specified key is Drew or Tina;
3 nodes will be examined if the specified key is Cody, Hugh, Pete, or Zoe;
4 nodes will be examined if the specified key is Beth or Ruth;

If X denotes the number of nodes that will be examined during a successful search for a specified key in this particular tree, and if each of the 9 keys is equally likely to be specified, then

$$E(X) = \frac{1}{9}[1 \cdot 1 + 2 \cdot 2 + 3 \cdot 4 + 4 \cdot 2] = \frac{25}{9} = 2\frac{7}{9}.$$

Of course, the tree might have turned out differently if the names in the file had been in a different order (although this is not necessarily true). Thus, for example, if the names in the file had been in the order Pete, Jill, Ruth, Zoe, Beth, Drew, Cody, Tina, Hugh then the tree would have looked like the one in Fig. 6.32.

If we let Y denote the number of nodes that will be examined in a successful search for a specified key in this particular tree (Fig. 6.32) and if each of the 9 keys is equally likely to be specified, then

$$E(Y) = \frac{1}{9}[1 \cdot 1 + 2 \cdot 2 + 3 \cdot 2 + 4 \cdot 2 + 5 \cdot 2] = \frac{29}{9} = 3\frac{2}{9}.$$

As we can see from these examples, the expected number of nodes that will be examined during a successful search for a specified key in a random binary search tree depends on the order of the objects in the file from which the tree will be built.

In each of the two cases we have just examined, we considered the tree to be already in existence, and we calculated the expected number of nodes that will be examined in a successful search. The underlying "statistical experiment" then consists of being given a randomly selected key from the set of keys in the tree and asked to make a search for that key in the tree. Now let's back up one step and consider the statistical experiment in which

(1) we will be given a file of n keyed records in random order;

(2) we will build the search tree by reading the file and inserting the records one by one, without rebalancing;

(3) we will then be given a randomly selected key from the set of keys in the tree and asked to make a search for that key in the tree. Each of the n keys will be equally likely to be the target key.

Let X_n denote the number of nodes that will have to be examined during the search. Let's calculate the expected value of X_n.

The difference between this problem and the two problems we looked at involving Figs. 6.31 and 6.32 is that we must now take into account (i.e., must "average over") all the different possible orderings of the records in the file and (therefore) all the different trees that could be built.

Since a search in a binary search tree is somewhat similar to a binary search in an ordered array, it is reasonable to approach this problem along those lines: we can look separately at the case where the search goes into the left subtree, the case where the search goes into the right subtree, and the case where the search stops at the root because the target key is there. Let A_1 denote the event that the search will go into the left subtree, A_2 the event that it will go to the right, and A_3 the event that the search will stop at the root. Also note that X_n can be written as $1 + Y_n$, where Y_n is the number of nodes that will be examined after the root node has been examined. Then since A_1, A_2, and A_3 form a partition of the sample space of X_n, it follows that

$$E(X_n) = 1 + E(Y_n) = 1 + P(A_1)E(Y_n|A_1) + P(A_2)E(Y_n|A_2) + P(A_3)E(Y_n|A_3).$$

Note, however, that $P(A_1)$ is not easy to compute directly because it seems to depend on how the tree is shaped. The first record in the file will determine what goes into the left subtree and what goes into the right (all keys smaller than the first will go left, all larger right). (This should remind you of what happens in Quicksort, where the first object in the array partitions the rest of the array.) Thus it will be easier to work this out the numbers above if we introduce an additional collection of events that partition the sample space in a different way: let B_0 denote the event that the left subtree will be empty; this is exactly the same as saying that the smallest key in the random file is in the first record of the file. Let B_1 denote the event that the left subtree will contain only one node; this is exactly the same as saying that the next-to-smallest key in the file comes first. More generally, for $i = 0, 1, 2, \ldots, n-1$ let B_i denote the event that the left subtree will contain exactly i nodes. Then we can think of the sample space of X_n as partitioned as shown in Fig. 6.33.

Now we can decompose $E(X_n) = 1 + E(Y_n)$ using all the intersections of the B_i's and A_j's:

$$E(X_n) = 1 + \sum_{i=0}^{n-1} [P(B_i \cap A_1)E(Y_n|B_i \cap A_1) + P(B_i \cap A_2)E(Y_n|B_i \cap A_2) + 0],$$

where the 0 at the end of the sum comes from the obvious fact that $E(Y_n|B_i \cap A_3) = 0$ for all i.

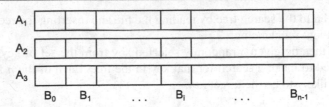

Fig. 6.33 Event partitioning

Now we can use the Chain Rule for Conditional Probability to compute $P(B_i \cap A_1)$:

$$P(B_i \cap A_1) = P(B_i)P(A_1|B_i) = \frac{1}{n} \cdot \frac{i}{n} = \frac{i}{n^2} \quad \text{for all } i,$$

because if there are i nodes in the left subtree of the search tree, then the probability is $\frac{i}{n}$ that one of those nodes will contain the target key. Similarly,

$$P(B_i \cap A_2) = P(B_i)P(A_2|B_i) = \frac{1}{n} \cdot \frac{n-1-i}{n} = \frac{n-1-i}{n^2} \quad \text{for all } i.$$

Also note that $E(Y_n|B_i \cap A_1) = E(X_i)$ and $E(Y_n|B_i \cap A_2) = E(X_{n-1-i})$, so the expression for $E(X_n)$ above now takes the following form:

$$E(X_n) = 1 + \left[\frac{0}{n^2}E(X_0) + \frac{n-1}{n^2}E(X_{n-1}) + \frac{1}{n^2}E(X_1) + \frac{n-2}{n^2}E(X_{n-2}) \right.$$
$$\left. + \frac{2}{n^2}E(X_2) + \frac{n-3}{n^2}E(X_{n-3}) + \cdots + \frac{n-1}{n^2}E(X_{n-1}) + \frac{0}{n^2}E(X_0) \right]$$

Note that every term of the form $\frac{i}{n^2}E(X_i)$ appears twice in this sum, so it reduces to

$$E(X_n) = 1 + \frac{2}{n^2}[1E(X_1) + 2E(X_2) + 3E(X_3) + \cdots + (n-1)E(X_{n-1})].$$

This formula is valid for all $n \geq 2$. Note also that $E(X_1) = 1$, and thus from the sum above,

$$E(X_2) = 1 + \frac{2}{4}E(X_1) = \frac{3}{2}.$$

To simplify the recurrence relation above, we first multiply through by n^2 to get

$$n^2 E(X_n) = n^2 + 2[1E(X_1) + 2E(X_2) + 3E(X_3) + \cdots + (n-1)E(X_{n-1}]$$
$$\text{for all } n \geq 2. \tag{6.5}$$

Then we replace n by $n-1$ everywhere to obtain the relation

$$(n-1)^2 E(X_{n-1}) = (n-1)^2 + 2[1E(X_1) + 2E(X_2) + 3E(X_3) + \cdots + (n-2)E(X_{n-2})] \tag{6.6}$$

for all $n \geq 3$. Subtracting the parts of Eq. (6.6) from parts of (6.5) gives

$$n^2 E(X_n) - (n-1)^2 E(X_{n-1}) = 2n - 1 + 2(n-1)E(X_{n-1}) \quad \text{for all } n \geq 3.$$

Moving $E(X_{n-1})$ to the right and combining terms gives us the rather simpler recurrence relation

$$n^2 E(X_n) = 2n - 1 + (n^2 - 1)E(X_{n-1}) \quad \text{for all } n \geq 3.$$

Here we can see the pattern $nE(X_n)$ and $(n-1)E(X_n - 1)$, but with extra nuisance factors. Dividing by $n(n+1)$ however gives the relation

$$\frac{nE(X_n)}{n+1} = \frac{2n-1}{n(n+1)} + \frac{(n-1)E(X_{n-1})}{n} \quad \text{for all } n \geq 3.$$

If we let the left side be denoted by $F(n)$ we now have

$$F(n) = \frac{2n-1}{n(n+1)} + F(n-1) \quad \text{for all } n \geq 3. \tag{6.7}$$

The initial values of $F(n)$ are $F(1) = \frac{1 \cdot 1}{1+1} = \frac{1}{2}$ and $F(2) = \frac{2 \cdot 3/2}{2+1} = 1$.

While this recurrence problem can be solved exactly, at this point we may be content to estimate $F(n)$. Note that $\frac{2n-1}{n(n+1)} < \frac{2n}{n(n+1)} = \frac{2}{n+1}$, so we have the recurrence inequality

$$F(1) = \frac{1}{2}, \quad F(2) = 1, \quad F(n) < \frac{2}{n+1} + F(n-1) \quad \text{for all } n \geq 3.$$

Writing out the first few instances of this inequality gives us

$$F(3) < \frac{2}{4} + 1$$
$$F(4) < \frac{2}{5} + \frac{2}{4} + 1$$
$$F(5) < \frac{2}{6} + \frac{2}{5} + \frac{2}{4} + 1 \text{ etc.}$$

Clearly we have

$$F(n) < 2H(n+1) - \left(\frac{2}{3} + \frac{2}{1}\right) = 2H(n+1) - \frac{8}{3} \quad \text{for all } n \geq 3.$$

This shows that $F(n) = O(\lg(n))$.

We've now found an upper bound for $F(n)$. Can we get a lower bound as well? Returning to relation (6.7) we see that $\frac{2n-1}{n(n+1)} > \frac{n}{n(n+1)}$ for all positive integers n, and so

$$F(1) = \frac{1}{2}, \quad F(2) = 1, \quad F(n) > \frac{1}{n+1} + F(n-1) \quad \text{for all } n \geq 3.$$

Writing out the first few instances of the inequality will convince you that

$$F(n) > H(n+2) - \left(\frac{2}{4} + \frac{2}{3} + \frac{2}{2}\right) = H(n+2) - \frac{22}{3} \quad \text{for all } n \geq 3.$$

Combining this with the upper bound we derived for $F(n)$ gives us

$$2H(n+2) - \frac{22}{3} \leq F(n) < 2H(n+1) - \frac{8}{3}$$

It is easy to show that both $H(n+1)$ and $H(n+2)$ are asymptotic to $H(n)$, which is asymptotic to $\ln(n)$. Thus $F(n) \sim 2\ln(n)$.

Now let's return to $E(X_n)$. From the equation $F(n) = \dfrac{nE(X_n)}{n+1}$ we get $E(X_n) = \dfrac{n+1}{n}F(n)$. Since $\dfrac{n+1}{n} \to 1$ as $n \to \infty$, we can conclude that

$$E(X_n) \sim 2\ln(n) \approx 1.39\ln(n).$$

A warning is in order here: files in the "real world" often arrive for processing with their objects already partially sorted. Just because you know nothing of the way in which a file of keyed objects was constructed is not a good reason to assume that the objects are in random key order. When the objects from a partially sorted file are put into a binary search tree, the result is almost always a collection of long chains of nodes. As a result, the expected search times may not remain logarithmic in the number of nodes. If you must build a binary search tree from a file about which you know nothing, you would be wise to "shuffle" its objects into random order before starting the tree building process, or else use re-balancing as the tree is constructed, as for example with AVL trees.

6.8.1 Exercises

6.8.6 In Example 6.8.2, p. 344, we calculated an asymptotic formula for the expected number of object comparisons that will be made during a successful binary search of an ordered array of n objects. Now do a similar calculation for the expected number of object comparisons that will be made during an unsuccessful binary search of an ordered array of n objects. Use the same binary search algorithm as in Example 6.8.2. Assume that the target object has equal probability of belonging at any "cell boundary" in the array, i.e., between any two objects in the array or at the ends.

6.8.7 Suppose we use the binary search algorithm given in Fig. 5.15b, p. 201 to make a search of an ordered array of n objects.

(a) Calculate the expected number of object comparisons that will be made during a search when the target of the search is not in the array (which, of course, is not discovered until the search ends). Assume that the target object has equal probability of belonging at any "cell boundary" in the array, i.e., between any two objects in the array or at the ends (as in Exercise 6.8.6 above).
(b) Calculate the exact number of object comparisons that will be made if the target is larger than every object of the array. (This is not an "expected value" problem; it can be solved with a recurrence relation.)
(c) Let X_n denote the number of object comparisons that will be made during a search when the target of the search is in the array (which will be discovered only when the search loop terminates). Assume that the target object is equally

likely to be in any of the n cells. Using the answer for part (b) above, write a recurrence relation whose solution would provide a formula for $E(X_n)$. You are not required to solve the recurrence relation, but see if you can get some idea about the asymptotic behavior of $E(X_n)$.

6.8.8 Suppose we are planning to create a separate chaining hash table with load index L. The insertion and search algorithms will be as given in Example 6.8.3 on p. 346, so the chains are unordered. What is the expected number of object comparisons that will be made in such a table during an unsuccessful search for a given key value k?

6.8.9 Suppose we are planning to create a separate chaining hash table of size M with *ordered* linked lists. The table will be initialized so that each chain consists of a single "dummy" hash node containing a "plus infinity" key value, i.e., a key value so large that no actual key can exceed it. The initialization, insertion, and search algorithms are as shown in Fig. 6.34. Suppose we plan to place n objects in the table.

(a) What is the expected number of key comparisons that will be required during a successful search of the table for a given key value k?
(b) What is the expected number of key comparisons that will be required during an unsuccessful search? Assume that the hash function will be a good one. You may use the answer for Exercise 6.6.6 on p. 334 if you have solved it.

6.8.10 Suppose we plan to use the Sample Select Algorithm 3 in Fig. 6.12 on p. 313 to choose a random sample of size K from a file known to contain N records, where $K \leq N$. Let $X_{N,K}$ denote the number of objects that will have to be read from the file to obtain the sample. Then $X_{N,K}$ is a random variable whose smallest possible value is K (the case where the first K records happen by chance to be chosen) and whose largest possible value is N (the case where the final, i.e., K-th, record is not chosen until the last record of the file is reached. Let's calculate $E(X_{N,K})$ in terms of N and K. In the totally trivial case where $K = 0$, we will not read any records from the file, so we can say that $E(X_{N,0}) = 0$ for all positive integers N. Also note that in the special case where $K = N$, we will have to read every record in the file, so we can say that $E(X_{N,N}) = N$ for all positive integers N. Now consider the case where $0 < K < N$. We will certainly have to read the first record from the file, so let's introduce the random variable $Y_{N,K}$ to stand for the number of records that will have to be read after the first one. Then $X_{N,K} = 1 + Y_{N,K}$.

(a) Use Theorem 8.0.38 on p. 461 to derive a recurrence relation for $E(X_{N,K})$ in terms of $E(X_{N-1,K})$ and $E(X_{N-1,K-1})$, valid for all integers N and K satisfying $0 < K < N$.
   Hint: express $E(Y_{N,K})$ in terms of events that say whether the first record read from the file is kept or rejected.

```
// Initializes all the elements of the hash table with an "unused" flag +infinity.
void initialize (list_node_ptr T[])
{
  int i;
  for (i = 0; i < M; ++i)
  {
    T[i] = new list_node;               // Dynamically allocate a node.
    T[i]->info.key = "plus infinity";   // Genuine code will require us to
  }                                     // know the value of +infinity.
}


// Returns true if insertion is successful.
// Returns false if T already contains an object whose key matches x.key.
bool insert (otype &x, list_node_ptr T[])
{
  int i = hash(x.key);
  list_ node_ptr temp = T[i];          // Create a temporary hash node pointer.
  while (temp->info.key < x.key)
     temp = temp->next;                // Search the linked list. Loop must halt.
  if (temp->info.key == x.key)
     return false;                     // EXIT from function. Insertion failed.
  else
  {                                    // Insert copy of x into ordered chain.
    list_node_ptr p = new list_node;
    p->info = temp->info;              // Copy the bigger object into new node.
    temp->info = x;                    // Copy x into old node; overwrite bigger
    p->next = temp->next;              // Splice new node into the list following
    temp->next = p;                    // the copy of x.
  }
  return true;                         // Indicate that the insertion operation
}                                      //  was successful.


// Returns pointer to the unique object in T with key k if such an object exists.
// Otherwise it returns NULL.
otype* search(list_node_ptr T[], key_type k)
{
  int i = hash(k);
  list_node_ptr temp = T[i];           // Create a temporary hash node pointer.
  while (temp->info.key < k)
     temp = temp->next;                // Search the linked list. Loop must halt.
  if (temp->info.key == k)             // Decide what to return.
     return &(temp->info);
  else
     return NULL;
}
```

Fig. 6.34 Functions for a hash table with separate chaining using ordered linked lists

(b) Let's try to guess the solution for the recurrence relation derived in part (a). We already have the initial values $E(X_{N,0}) = 0$ and $E(X_{N,N}) = N$. On average, the K records to be chosen should be spread out "evenly" among the $N - K$ records that will not be chosen. This means that the $N - K$ non-chosen records will, on average, be split into $K + 1$ equal parts, each of size $\dfrac{N - K}{K + 1}$. One of

```
// Searches for a target key in a binary search tree. Returns a pointer to the
// node containing it if found, NULL otherwise.

template <class otype, class key_type>
tree_node_ptr key_location (tree_node_ptr p, const key_type * target)
{
  while (p)
    if (key(p->datum) < target)        // go into right subtree
      p = p->right;
    else if (key(p->datum) > target)  // go into left subtree
      p = p->left;
    else
      return p;                       // target key has been found

  return NULL;                        // could not find target key
}
```

Fig. 6.35 Search in a binary search tree

these parts will precede the first chosen record, one will follow the last (K-th) chosen record, and the other parts will be in between successive chosen records. Since we will have to read to the last chosen record, this will, on average, leave just $\dfrac{N - K}{K + 1}$ records unread (the ones that follow the last chosen record). Thus we can expect that $N - \dfrac{N - K}{K + 1} = \dfrac{NK + N - (N - K)}{K + 1} = \dfrac{(N + 1)K}{K + 1}$ records will be read. That is, our conjecture is that $E(X_{N,K}) = \dfrac{(N + 1)K}{K + 1}$. Verify that this formula satisfies all the initial conditions we have stated and also satisfies the recurrence relation derived in part (a).

Note: This problem was solved in a different way earlier in this chapter, in Exercises 6.7.7 and 6.7.8.

6.8.11 Consider the experiment in which a file of n distinct keys in random order is formed into a binary search tree without rebalancing.

(a) Find an asymptotic expression for the expected number of nodes that will have to be examined in an unsuccessful search for a specified key. Assume that the target key is equally likely to lie between any two keys in the file or at either "end" of the ordered list of keys. (There are $n + 1$ such locations where it might belong, each with equal probability.)

(b) Find an asymptotic expression for the expected number of key comparisons that will be examined in a successful search for a specified key if the search algorithm in Fig. 6.35 is used. Note the order in which the comparisons are made. Assume that all n keys are equally likely to be the target of the search.

6.8.12 If we want to solve the recurrence relation (6.7) on p. 355 exactly, then it is helpful to decompose the fraction into two separate ones:

$$F(1) = \frac{1}{2}, \quad F(2) = 1, \quad F(n) = \frac{2}{n+1} - \frac{1}{n(n+1)} + F(n-1) \quad \text{for all } n \geq 3.$$

(a) By computing the values of sums of the form

$$\frac{1}{1 \cdot 2}$$

$$\frac{1}{1 \cdot 2} + \frac{1}{2 \cdot 3}$$

$$\frac{1}{1 \cdot 2} + \frac{1}{2 \cdot 3} + \frac{1}{3 \cdot 4}$$

obtain (by guesswork) a closed form for the general sum

$$\frac{1}{1 \cdot 2} + \frac{1}{2 \cdot 3} + \frac{1}{3 \cdot 4} + \cdots + \frac{1}{n(n+1)}.$$

The proof of this closed form uses mathematical induction.

(b) Now solve for $F(n)$ exactly.

Finite Graph Algorithms

7

In this chapter we are going to study various algorithms for solving certain classical problems in graph theory. Before we can do that we need to have a precise definition of the concept of a finite graph, and we need an efficient way to implement graphs within computer programs.

7.1 General Definitions

Definition 7.1.1 A *finite graph*, call it G, consists of a finite set, call it V, of *vertices*,[1] and a finite set, call it E, of pairs of vertices from V. We call each pair an *edge* of the graph G. The number of vertices in V is denoted by $|V|$, and the number of edges in E is denoted by $|E|$.

If each edge in E is an *ordered* pair (i.e. there is definite first vertex of the pair, and a definite second vertex), then we say that the graph is a *directed graph*, or *digraph*. If all the edges in E are unordered pairs (i.e. sets of size 2), then we say that G is *non-directed*, or *undirected*. If each edge in G is assigned a numerical value, then we call G a *weighted graph*, and the numbers assigned to the edges are the *weights* in G.

If v_1 and v_2 are vertices in V, then we say that there is *an edge from v_1 to v_2* if and only if the ordered pair (v_1, v_2) is in the edge set E (in the case of a digraph) or the unordered pair $\{v_1, v_2\}$ is in the edge set E (in the case of an undirected graph); in an undirected graph we also speak of an edge being *between* v_1 and v_2. A vertex v_2 is said to be *adjacent to* a vertex v_1 if and only if there is an edge from v_1 to v_2. In this case we say that v_2 is a *neighbor* of v_1.

---

[1] The word *vertices* is the plural of the noun *vertex*.

© Springer International Publishing Switzerland 2014
D. Vrajitoru and W. Knight, *Practical Analysis of Algorithms*,
Undergraduate Topics in Computer Science, DOI 10.1007/978-3-319-09888-3_7

Note that we are using the standard notation of set theory in which an ordered pair is indicated by ordinary ("round") parentheses, while an unordered pair is indicated by braces ("curly brackets").

Under Definition 7.1.1, for any two distinct vertices v_1 and v_2 in a graph there can be at most one edge from v_1 to v_2. The reason for this is that a single pair cannot belong to a set twice. In a digraph it is possible to have an edge from a vertex to itself (such an edge is called a "loop"), but except in examples where we state otherwise, we will assume that our digraphs contain no loops. An undirected graph cannot have a loop because an unordered pair must contain two different elements to be a pair.

Finite graphs can be used to represent such things as

- power line connections in a community;
- road systems in a state;
- flows of information (data);
- dependencies among functions in programs;
- finite automata (e.g. lexical analyzers);
- circuits on a microchip;
- course prerequisites in an academic setting;

and so on. The variety of applications is limitless.

Example 7.1.2 Let G be the *digraph* whose vertex set is $V = \{v_1, \ v_2, \ v_3, \ v_4\}$ and whose edge set is $E = \{(v_1, \ v_2), \ (v_1, \ v_3), \ (v_3, \ v_1), \ (v_3, \ v_2), \ (v_2, \ v_4), \ (v_4, \ v_3)\}$. Figure 7.1 left shows a diagram that represents this graph. Each arrow represents an edge from one vertex to another. Figure 7.1 right shows a different diagram that represents this same graph G. For any graph with more than one vertex there will be many different diagrams that can be drawn to represent the graph.

Note that in this graph G the vertex v_4 is adjacent to vertex v_2, but v_2 is not adjacent to v_4.

We could make G a weighted graph by assigning weights to its edges. For example, we could define a weight function W on the edges as follows: $W(v_1, \ v_2) = 27$, $W(v_1, \ v_3) = 11$, $W(v_3, \ v_1) = 8$, $W(v_3, \ v_2) = 14$, $W(v_2, \ v_4) = 20$, $W(v_4, \ v_3) = 9$.

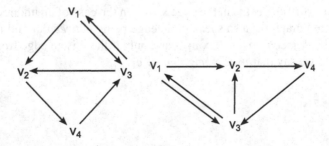

Fig. 7.1 Diagrams for the graph in Example 7.1.2

Fig. 7.2 A diagram for the weighted graph in Example 7.1.2

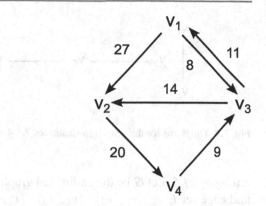

Fig. 7.3 *Two* different diagrams for the graph in Example 7.1.3

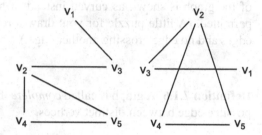

Figure 7.2 shows the graph with the edges labeled with their weights. Note that in this example the weight assigned to the edge (v_1, v_3) is not the same as the weight assigned to (v_3, v_1).

Example 7.1.3 Let G be the *undirected* graph with vertex set $V = \{v_1, v_2, v_3, v_4, v_5\}$ and edge set $E = \{\{v_1, v_3\}, \{v_2, v_3\}, \{v_2, v_5\}, \{v_5, v_4\}, \{v_2, v_4\}\}$. Figure 7.3 left shows a diagram that represents this graph. Note that in this graph the vertex v_2 is adjacent to v_4, and v_4 is adjacent to v_2 (cf. Example 7.1.2). Figure 7.3 right shows a different diagram for G. In the second diagram, some of the edges are shown crossing each other. This is permitted. Indeed, in many cases it is impossible to draw a graph without at least one crossing point. The crossing points are not vertices of the graph. Generally when we draw a representation of a graph we try to minimize the number of crossing points of the edges.

Example 7.1.4 Let G be the undirected graph with vertex set $V = \{v_1, v_2, v_3, v_4, v_5\}$ and edge set $E = \{\{v_1, v_2\}, \{v_3, v_5\}, \{v_4, v_5\}\}$. Figure 7.4 left shows a diagram representing this graph. Note that the graph consists of two separate pieces. This is allowed. The most extreme case of this would be a graph with n vertices and no edges (i.e., the edge set E is empty). A diagram of such a graph would consist of n isolated vertices sprinkled about on the page.

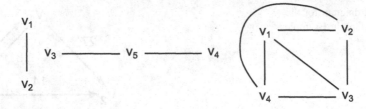

Fig. 7.4 Diagrams for the graphs in Examples 7.1.4 and 7.1.5

Example 7.1.5 Let G be the undirected graph with vertex set $V = \{v_1, v_2, v_3, v_4\}$ and edge set $E = \{\{v_1, v_2\}, \{v_1, v_3\}, \{v_1, v_4\}, \{v_2, v_3\}, \{v_2, v_4\}, \{v_3, v_4\}\}$. Figure 7.4 right shows a diagram representing this graph. Note that one of the edges of the graph is shown as curved instead of being a straight line segment. This is permitted. (A little puzzle for you: draw a representation of G that has no curved edges and no edge crossing another edge.)

Definition 7.1.6 A graph is called *complete* if and only if its edge set contains every possible edge between distinct vertices.

The undirected graph in Example 7.1.5 is a complete graph.

Suppose a digraph G has n vertices and is complete. How many edges are there in its edge set E? That is, what is the value of $|E|$? To put it differently, in how many distinct ways can we construct an edge of G? The answer is easy: there are n ways to choose the first vertex in the ordered pair that represents an edge, and for each such choice of first member, there are $n - 1$ ways to choose the second (necessarily different) vertex. Thus there are $n(n-1)$ edges in a complete digraph with n vertices.

How many edges are there in an undirected graph G with n vertices? To get the answer, imagine converting G into a digraph by replacing each edge $\{v_i, v_j\}$ of G with the two ordered pairs (v_i, v_j) and (v_j, v_i). The resulting digraph is complete and has n vertices (same as G), so it has $n(n-1)$ edges. This number is twice the number of edges in the original complete undirected graph G, so G has $\dfrac{n(n-1)}{2}$ edges.

The foregoing discussion shows that the number of edges in a finite graph—directed or undirected—with n vertices is $O(n^2)$, and the number of edges in a complete finite graph with n vertices is $\Theta(n^2)$.

Definition 7.1.7 Let G be a finite graph, and let v and w be vertices in this graph. A *path* in G from v to w is a finite sequence of edges, say (v_0, v_1), (v_1, v_2), (v_2, v_3), ..., (v_{k-1}, v_k), in a digraph, or $\{v_0, v_1\}$, $\{v_1, v_2\}$, $\{v_2, v_3\}$, ..., $\{v_{k-1}, v_k\}$, in an undirected graph, such that $v_0 = v$ and $v_k = w$. We call such a sequence the *edge sequence* of the path. It is easy to see that we can equally well specify a path by specifying the *vertex sequence* of the path, i.e., the list of vertices that are

Fig. 7.5 Graph for Example 7.1.8

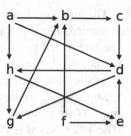

successively encountered along the path: v_0, v_1, v_2, ..., v_k. The *length of the path* is the number of *edges* that make up the path, which is k in the cases above. For any vertex v, we'll consider the empty set of edges to constitute a path of length 0 from v to itself.

Example 7.1.8 In the digraph shown in Fig. 7.5, the edges (a, d), (d, g), (g, b), (b, c), (c, d), (d, h), (h, e) form a path from a to e. Typically we use the vertex sequence because it is more compact: a, d, g, b, c, d, h, e. The length of the path is 7.

Definition 7.1.9 A path in a finite graph is called a *simple path* if and only if no vertex is repeated in the vertex sequence of the path. A path is called a *cycle* (or *circuit*) if and only if the first and last vertices in the vertex sequence are the same. A *simple cycle* (or *simple circuit*) is a cycle such that when the last vertex is removed from the vertex sequence, the remaining sequence is a simple path. A graph is called *acyclic* if and only if it contains no cycles.[2]

In the digraph in Example 7.1.8, the path given there is not simple, nor is it a cycle. The path specified by the vertex sequence b, e, c, h, g is simple. The path specified by the vertex sequence a, d, g, b, c, d, h, e, a is a cycle, but not a simple cycle. The path specified by the vertex sequence b, e, c, h, g, b is a simple cycle.

Definition 7.1.10 An undirected graph is called *connected* if and only if for every pair of vertices x and y in the graph there is a path from x to y (and since the graph is undirected, the "reverse" path would be a path from y to x). A directed graph is called *strongly connected* if and only if for every pair of vertices x and y in the graph there is a path from x to y and also a path from y to x. A directed graph is called *weakly connected* if and only if the undirected graph derived from it by ignoring the directions on the edges is connected.

---

[2] *Note* The prefix a- on words of Greek origin often means something like "without": amoral (without morals), asymmetric (lacking symmetry), amorphous (formless), atheistic (godless), arrhythmic (out of rhythm).

The undirected graph in Fig. 7.3 is connected. The digraph in Fig. 7.2 is strongly connected. The digraph in Fig. 7.5 is weakly connected but not strongly connected. The undirected graph shown in Fig. 7.4 is not connected, but it has two "connected components". The undirected graph shown in Fig. 7.6 is also not connected. We can define this notion in terms of *equivalence relations*.[3]

Suppose we create a binary relation, call it C, on the vertex set V of any finite graph G as follows: xCy if and only if there exists a path in G from x to y. (The letter 'C' was chosen to suggest the reading "can be connected to".) It is easy to verify that *if G is undirected, then the relation C is an equivalence relation on V*.

Definition 7.1.11 Let G be an undirected graph with vertex set V. Let C denote the equivalence relation defined on V as follows: $x \, C \, y$ if and only if there exists a

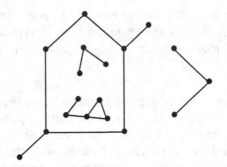

Fig. 7.6 An undirected graph with 4 connected components

---

[3] An *equivalence relation* on a non-empty set S is a set, say R, of ordered pairs of elements of S, with the following properties for R:

(a) (reflexivity) for every x in S the pair $(x, \, x)$ belongs to R;
(b) (symmetry) for every x and y in S, if $(x, \, y) \in R$, then $(y, \, x) \in R$;
(c) (transitivity) for every x, y, and z in S, if $(x, \, y) \in R$ and $(y, \, z) \in R$, then $(x, \, z) \in R$.

  Suppose R is an equivalence relation on a set S. Then it is customary to write $x \, R \, y$ in place of $(x, \, y) \in R$. For each x in S the set $\{y \in S : y R x\}$ is called the *equivalence class of x* and is denoted by $[x]$. Using properties (a), (b), (c) above, it is easy to prove the following assertions for all x and y in S:

(d) $x \in [x]$;
(e) if $x \in [y]$, then $y \in [x]$;
(f) if $[x] \cap [y]$ is non-empty, then $[x] = [y]$.

  Here is one of the most important theorems about equivalence relations:

  If R is an equivalence relation on a non-empty set S, then the set of all equivalence classes of the elements of S forms a *partition* of S into disjoint non-empty subsets of S.

  The proof follows fairly quickly from assertions (d),(e), and (f) above.

path in G from x to y. Then the equivalence classes of the relation C are called the *connected components* of the graph G.

It is possible to define the notion of connected component of an undirected graph in a different way, as a "maximal connected subgraph" of G. The following definition and theorem provide this alternative way of looking at connected components.

Definition 7.1.12 A graph H with vertex set W and edge set F is a *subgraph* of a graph G with vertex set V and edge set E if and only if $W \subseteq V$ and $F \subseteq E$.

Theorem 7.1.13 *A graph H is a connected component of an undirected graph G if and only if*

(1) *H is a subgraph of G, and*
(2) *H is connected, and*
(3) *there is no other connected subgraph K of G such that H is a subgraph of K.*

Proof The proof is not deep, but it's not very interesting to check all the details. ∎

Here are some frequently occurring finite graph problems that programmers are often called on to solve.

Connectedness problems Is a graph connected?

Tours In a connected graph, find a path that moves along each edge in the graph exactly once. Alternatively, in a connected graph, find a path that visits each vertex exactly once.

Shortest route problems Given a weighted graph in which the weights are interpreted as "distances", and given an "origin" (starting vertex) and a "destination" (goal vertex), find a shortest path from origin to destination, provided such a path exists.

Traveling salesman problems Given a weighted graph in which the weights are interpreted as distances, find a shortest path that visits every vertex.

Maximal flow problems Given a weighted graph in which each weight is interpreted as a "capacity" for that edge, and given a "source" vertex and a "sink" vertex, find a way of assigning "flows" to the edges to maximize the throughput from source to sink.

Task sequencing problems Given a directed graph in which each node represents a task to be done and each edge (v, w) represents a restriction specifying that task v must be completed before w can be started, find a way of listing all the tasks to be done in such a way that all the restrictions are met.

Minimal spanning tree problems Given a weighted graph in which each weight is interpreted as a "cost", find a minimal-cost set of edges that connect (directly or indirectly) all the vertices.

Isomorphism problems [4] Given two graphs, determine whether they have identical structure.

We will look at algorithms for solving most of these problems. We will practice these algorithms by carrying out the computations on rather small graphs. You should keep in mind, however, that when graph problems are solved in real world applications, the graphs may very well have thousand of vertices and tens or hundreds of thousands of edges. Any practical algorithm for solving a problem in graph theory will have to run efficiently on very large graphs. An algorithm that may seem straightforward when used on a small graph may not be as efficient, and therefore not as useful, as a somewhat more complicated algorithm.

7.1.1 Exercises

7.1.14 In each case below, draw a diagram representing the graph whose vertex set V and edge set E are given. Try to minimize the number of edge crossings. (Both graphs can be drawn with no edge crossing.)

(a) $V = \{M, N, P, Q, R, S, T, U\}$,
$E = \{(P, N), (R, T), (Q, M), (T, P), (R, U), (S, P), (U, N),$
$(M, S), (T, Q)\}$
(b) $V = \{M, N, P, Q, R, S, T, U\}$,
$E = \{\{P, N\}, \{R, T\}, \{Q, M\}, \{R, Q\}, \{U, P\}, \{N, U\}, \{M, S\},$
$\{R, S\}\}$

7.1.15 In each case below, draw a diagram representing the graph whose vertex set V and edge set E are given. Try to minimize the number of edge crossings. (Both graphs can be drawn with no edge crossing.)

(a) $V = \{A, B, C, D, E\}$,
$E = \{(A, B), (A, D), (A, E), (B, C), (D, A), (D, B), (E, C),$
$(E, D)\}$
(b) $V = \{A, B, C, D, E\}$,
$E = \{\{A, B\}, \{A, D\}, \{A, E\}, \{B, C\}, \{D, B\}, \{E, C\}, \{E, D\}\}$

7.1.16 Find all paths from R to N in the graph in Exercise 7.1.14 (a). Is that graph strongly connected? Is it weakly connected? Does the graph contain any cycles, or is it acyclic?

7.1.17 Find all simple paths from A to C in the graph in Exercise 7.1.15 (a). Give an example of a non-simple path from A to C. Explain why there are infinitely

---

[4] "Iso-", same; "morph", form.

many non-simple paths from A to C. Is that graph strongly connected? Is it weakly connected? Does the graph contain any cycles, or is it acyclic?

7.1.18 Find all simple paths from T to S in the graph in Exercise 7.1.14 (b). Is that graph connected? If not, identify its connected components. Does the graph contain any cycles, or is it acyclic?

7.1.19 Draw the digraph whose vertices are the nineteen integers from 2 to 20 and whose edge set is $\{(k, n) : k$ is a divisor of n but $k \neq n\}$. For example, the graph contains an edge from 5 to 15, but no edge from 4 to 14. (It is possible to draw this graph with no edge crossing.)

7.1.20 Draw the undirected graph whose vertices are the eleven integers from 20 to 30 inclusive, and whose edge set is $\{\{m, n\}: m$ and n have at least one common prime divisor but $m \neq n\}$. For example, the graph will contain an edge between 21 and 28 because those vertices have 7 as a common prime divisor, but the graph will not contain an edge between 22 and 25 because they are "relatively prime", i.e., their only common divisor is the non-prime integer 1.

7.2 Computer Representations of Finite Graphs

Now that we know the formal definitions for finite graphs, let's look at ways in which graphs can be represented in computer programs that solve graph problems. The goal here is to create graph data structures that support efficient graph algorithms. We'll call these data structures *adjacency structures* because they will hold the information that tells which vertices are adjacent to other vertices.

As you will soon see, computer computations on a graph are made much simpler by assuming that the vertex set of the graph has the form $\{0, 1, 2, \ldots, n - 1\}$, where n is the number of vertices in the graph. If the vertex set is not of this form but instead consists of, say, character strings such as city names, then a program can always enumerate the vertices, starting with the number 0, and then work with the assigned numbers in place of the actual vertex names. The program can construct a table that translates between the actual vertex names and their assigned numbers. This will allow the program to express the final results of the graph computation in terms of the original vertex names. See [18] for details.

Let's begin with a simple example to illustrate a common adjacency structure for a graph. Consider the digraph given in Example 7.1.2 and Fig. 7.1. We replace the vertices v_1, v_2, v_3, v_4 by the integers 0, 1, 2, 3, respectively. Then the edges in the example are replaced by (0, 1), (0, 2), (2, 0), (2, 1), (1, 3), (3, 2). Figure 7.7 shows this graph with its new vertex enumeration and an adjacency structure for the graph. The subscripts of the array labeled vertex are exactly the vertices 0, 1, 2, 3. For each vertex i the array cell vertex[i] contains a pointer to a

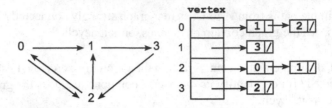

Fig. 7.7 A small digraph and its adjacency list representation

NULL-terminated linked list of all the vertices adjacent to vertex i. For example, the pointer in the cell vertex[2] points to a list containing the vertices 1 and 0, indicating that there is an edge from 2 to 1 and a separate edge from 2 to 0. (*Caution: nothing in that list should be interpreted as saying there is an edge from 1 to 0 in the graph.*) The linked lists shown in Fig. 7.7 are called *adjacency lists*, the nodes that make up the lists are called *edge nodes*, and the structure as a whole is called an *adjacency list representation* of the graph, or sometimes an *adjacency list structure*.

If a graph is undirected, then for every edge {i, j} in the graph, i is adjacent to j and j is adjacent to i . This means that the list pointed to by vertex[i].edge_list contains an edge_node carrying the number j, and the list pointed to by vertex[j] contains an edge_node carrying the number i. Thus every edge in the graph is represented by an edge_node in each of two adjacency lists. This turns out to cause no difficulties so long as we remain aware of this fact. Figure 7.8 shows an undirected graph and an adjacency list representation for it. Note that we could interpret this structure as representing a special kind of digraph in which for every edge (i, j) in the graph, the edge (j, i) is also in the graph.

Some graph algorithms require storing pieces of information "at" (or "in", or "together with") the vertices of the graph. For example, when a program needs to visit all the vertices of the graph, it will probably want to "check off" each vertex when it is visited. This can be done by adding a Boolean field named visited to each cell of the vertex array, initializing all these fields to false, and then changing

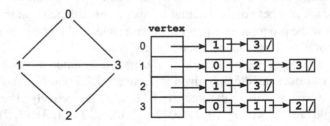

Fig. 7.8 A small undirected graph and its adjacency list representation

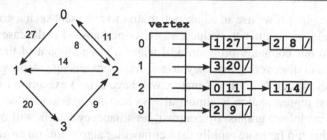

Fig. 7.9 A weighted digraph and the corresponding adjacency structure

$$
\begin{array}{c c}
\begin{array}{cccc}
 & 0 & 1 & 2 & 3 \\
0 & F & T & T & F \\
1 & F & F & F & T \\
2 & T & T & F & F \\
3 & F & F & T & F \\
\end{array}
&
\begin{array}{cccc}
 & 0 & 1 & 2 & 3 \\
0 & -1 & 27 & 11 & -1 \\
1 & -1 & -1 & -1 & 20 \\
2 & 8 & 14 & -1 & -1 \\
3 & -1 & -1 & 9 & -1 \\
\end{array}
\end{array}
$$

Fig. 7.10 Adjacency matrices for the digraphs in Figs. 7.7 and 7.9

them, one by one, to `true` as the corresponding vertices are visited. Alternatively, this can be accomplished by allocating a Boolean array "parallel" to the `vertex` array in which to keep the information as the search proceeds. Recall that some graphs have weights assigned to the edges. How can we accommodate these extra pieces of data in the adjacency structure for the graph? In the linked-list adjacency structure we can specify that each list node has an extra field (data member) that can store the weight of the edge. Figure 7.9 shows a weighted graph, identical to the one in Fig. 7.2 except for the vertex labels, and its modified adjacency structure. There are alternatives to using a linked-list adjacency structure to represent a graph in a computer program. One possibility is to use what programmers call an *adjacency matrix* for a graph. Given a graph with vertex set $\{0, 1, 2, \ldots, n-1\}$, we dynamically allocate an $n \times n$ Boolean array. Then in each row i and column j we place a `true` if j is adjacent to i; otherwise we place a `false` in that location. Figure 7.10 left shows the adjacency matrix for the digraph in Fig. 7.7.

If the graph has edge weights, a modification of this matrix representation must be used. For example, suppose we know that in a particular case all the weights are going to be non-negative real numbers. Then the adjacency matrix can be allocated as an $n \times n$ array of `float` or `double` numbers. In row i and column j we place the weight of the edge if j is adjacent to i, but otherwise we place a sentinel value such as -1 in that location. Figure 7.10 right shows an adjacency matrix for the digraph in Fig. 7.9.

Suppose we want a computer program to solve a graph problem on graphs that are expected to be sparse. (A "sparse graph" is one whose edge set is far smaller than the edge set of the complete graph on the same vertices; there is no precise definition of "sparse graph".) If we use an adjacency matrix to represent such a graph, most of the matrix cells will contain the value `false`, or perhaps -1 in the case of weighted graphs. Then our computer program will waste a large amount of time accessing matrix cells and discovering that they do not represent an edge. A program that has to examine every cell of an $n \times n$ matrix will have $\Omega(n^2)$ execution time. Thus an adjacency list representation is almost always best for sparse graphs. For "dense" (i.e., nearly complete) graphs, by contrast, an adjacency matrix will often support algorithms that run far more rapidly than competing algorithms on an adjacency list structure.

7.2.1   A Graph Class in C++

Let's look at one possible way of writing C++ code for adjacency list structures representing graphs. To avoid complications that interfere with our focus on algorithm performance, we will assume that every vertex set will consist of integers $0, 1, 2, \ldots, n-1$ for some positive integer n. Figure 7.11 exhibits a declaration of a

```
class Graph {
protected:
  struct edge_node
  {
    int neighbor;
    // There may be other data members, e.g. a weight member.
    edge_node *next;
  }

  struct vertex_record
  {
    edge_node *edge_list;
    // There may be other data members to hold computational results.
  }

  void insert_at_front (int i, edge_node* &p);
  vertex_record *vertex;  // The array that represents vertices 0,1,2,...,n-1.

  int  num_vertices;      // The "n" in the line above.
  int  num_edges;
  bool directed;

public:
  Graph(bool is_directed = false, int n = 0);   // Constructor has default values.
  ~Graph();                       // Destructor.
  void make_empty();              // Turns an existing graph into an empty graph.
  void add_edge (int i, int j);   // Adds an edge from vertex i to vertex j.
  void add_vertices (int m);      // Creates m new vertices in the graph.
  void print();                   // Outputs a description of the graph.
  //Additional member functions may be present.

} // End of Graph class definition.
```

Fig. 7.11 A possible C++ definition of a graph class

```
// This constructor creates an adjacency list graph structure with n vertices
// but zero edges.  By default, it is undirected.  Other class methods can be
// used to add edges and even to add additional vertices.
Graph::Graph(bool is_directed, int n)
{
  num_vertices = n;
  num_edges = 0;
  directed = is_directed;
  vertex = NULL;

  if ( n > 0 )
  {
    vertex = new vertex_record[n];  // Allocate the vertex array.
    for ( n = 0; n < num_vertices; ++n)
    {
      vertex[n].edge_list = NULL;   // Initialize all edge-lists to empty.
      // If there are other data members, they may need to be initialized also.
    }
  }
}


// The call to make_empty in this destructor will deallocate all dynamically
// allocated memory in the adjacency list structure for the graph.
Graph::~Graph()
{
  make_empty();
}


// The make_empty function deallocates all edge_nodes and the vertex array
// of the graph.  The number of vertices will be set to zero.
// The graph will remain directed or undirected as created initially.
void Graph::make_empty()
{
  int       i;
  edge_node *p;

  for ( i = 0; i < num_vertices; ++i)
    // Deallocate all edge_nodes in the NULL-terminated vertex[i].edge_list.
    for ( p = vertex[i].edge_list; p != NULL; p = vertex[i].edge_list)
    {
      vertex[i].edge_list = p->next;
      delete p;
    }
  num_edges = 0;
  delete [] vertex;  // Deallocate the vertex array.
  num_vertices = 0;
}
```

Fig. 7.12 Constructor, destructor, and utility function for the Graph class in Fig. 7.11

graph class. Figures 7.12, 7.13 and 7.14 continue with the implementation of some
of the class methods.

```
// This utility function inserts an integer into the "neighbor" field of a newly
// allocated edge_node and then attaches the edge_node to the front of a list of
// edge_nodes pointed to by p.
void Graph::insert_at_front (int i, edge_node* &p);
{
  edge_node *q = new edge_node;
  q->neighbor = i;
  q->next = p;
  p = q;
}

// This function adds existing vertex j to the front of the edge_list of existing
// vertex i in the graph.  If the graph is undirected, then in addition i will be
// added to the edge_list of j.
void Graph::add_edge (int i, int j)
{
  insert_at_front (j, vertex[i]);

  if ( !directed )
    insert_at_front (i, vertex[j]);

  ++num_edges;
}

// This function increases the number of vertices in the graph by m.
// It does not create any edges among the new vertices.
void Graph::add_vertices (int m)
{
  int i;
  vertex_record *p = new vertex_record[num_vertices + m];

  for ( i = 0; i < num_vertices; ++i)      // Has no effect if num_vertices is 0.
    p[i].edge_list = vertex[i].edge_list;

  for ( i = num_vertices; i < num_vertices + m; ++i)  // Initialize the edge-lists
    p[i].edge_list = NULL;                            // for the new vertices as empty.

  num_vertices += m;  // Increase the number of vertices.
  delete [] vertex;   // Deallocate the old vertex array.
  vertex = p;         // Make vertex point to the newly allocated array.
}
```

Fig. 7.13 Member functions of the Graph class in Fig. 7.11

7.2.2 Exercises

7.2.1 Draw a diagram of the digraph whose adjacency list structure looks like the one in Fig. 7.15.

7.2.2 Draw a diagram of the undirected graph whose adjacency list structure looks like the one in Fig. 7.16.

7.2.3 Draw the adjacency list structure of the digraph with vertex set $V = \{0, 1, 2, 3, 4, 5\}$ and edge set $E = \{(5, 4), (1, 0), (5, 3), (1, 2), (3, 2), (0, 5), (4, 3), (5, 1)\}$.

```
// This function outputs the essential information about a Graph.
void Graph::print()
{
  int i;
  edge_node *p;

  if (directed)
    cout << "The graph is directed." << endl;
  else
    cout << "The graph is undirected." << endl;

  cout << "It contains " << num_vertices << " vertices and " << num_edges
       << " edges."

  if ( num_vertices > 0 )
  {
    cout << "Here are the adjacency lists: " << endl;
    for (i = 0; i < num_vertices; ++i)
    {
      cout << i << " ---> ";
      for (p = vertex[i].edge_list; p != NULL; p = p->next)
        cout << p->neighbor << " ";
      cout << endl;
    }
  }
}
```

Fig. 7.14 An output function for the Graph class of Fig. 7.14

Fig. 7.15 An adjacency structure for a digraph

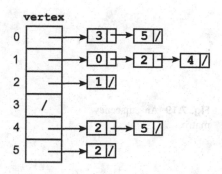

7.2.4 Draw the adjacency list structure of the undirected graph with vertex set $V = \{0, 1, 2, 3, 4, 5\}$ and edge set $E = \{\{3, 4\}, \{2, 0\}, \{4, 2\}, \{0, 3\}, \{1, 0\}, \{4, 0\}\}$.

7.2.5 Draw the weighted digraph represented by the adjacency structure in Fig. 7.17. Use the sequence numbers to label the vertices of the graph.

7.2.6 Draw the undirected graph represented by the adjacency structure in Fig. 7.18. Use the sequence numbers to label the vertices of the graph.

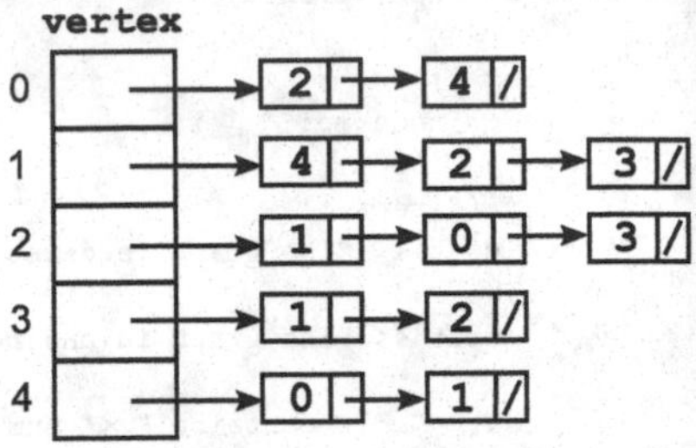

Fig. 7.16 An adjacency
structure for an undirected
graph

Fig. 7.17 An adjacency
structure

Fig. 7.18 An adjacency
matrix

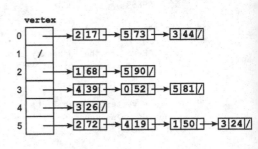

Fig. 7.19 An adjacency
matrix

$$
\begin{array}{c}
\\
0 \\
1 \\
2 \\
3 \\
4 \\
5
\end{array}
\begin{array}{cccccc}
0 & 1 & 2 & 3 & 4 & 5
\end{array}
\left(
\begin{array}{cccccc}
F & F & F & F & T & F \\
T & F & F & T & T & F \\
T & T & F & T & F & T \\
F & T & T & F & F & F \\
T & F & T & F & F & T \\
T & F & F & T & T & F
\end{array}
\right)
$$

7.2.7 Draw a diagram of the digraph whose adjacency matrix is shown in Fig. 7.19.

7.2.8 How can we tell, just by examining the adjacency matrix in Fig. 7.19, that it
is not the adjacency matrix of any undirected graph?

7.3   Breadth-First Search and Depth-First Search

Most algorithms that we perform on finite graphs involve searching the graphs in a systematic manner and processing the information that we find as we search. Almost all graph searches employ one of the following two search strategies: *breadth-first search* and *depth-first search*. For both of them the idea is to start from an origin vertex and to explore all the edges and vertices that can be reached from the origin by "traveling" along the edges. As the search proceeds, data developed during the search may be stored alongside the vertices and made available to the rest of the program when the search ends. To avoid running into an endless loop by traversing a cycle over and over, the algorithms will visit every vertex at most once and every edge at most one in directed graphs and at most twice in undirected ones (once in each direction).

7.3.1   Breadth-First Search

A *breadth-first search* starts with the origin, then explores all the vertices adjacent to it (its neighbors), then all vertices adjacent to the neighbors, and so on. The algorithm explores the graph in the manner of a wave moving away from a starting point in concentric circles of increasing radius. To put it differently, a breadth-first search strategy processes some initial vertex v, then processes all vertices to which there is a path of length 1 from v, then processes all vertices to which there is a path of length 2 from v, and so on.

To implement a breadth-first search, we keep a list of vertices that need to be processed. The list also helps us process them in the correct order. The kind of list we must keep is a First-In-First-Out (FIFO) list, which is to say, a standard *queue*.

The pseudo-code implementation for a breadth-first search in a graph G starting from a prescribed vertex v is shown in Fig. 7.21.

Example 7.3.1 As a simple illustration of a breadth-first search algorithm, consider Fig. 7.20. It shows a function named bfs_print that outputs all vertices that can be reached from a specified vertex v. The function is intended to be added as a member of the Graph class in Fig. 7.11, p. 372. Thus bfs_print assumes that the graph is implemented using an adjacency list representation. The function outputs the vertices in the order in which they are reached during the breadth-first search.

Here is what occurs when bfs_print(0) is called on the graph shown in Fig. 7.20:

- An array reached[] is created, "parallel" to the vertex array, and initialized to false everywhere.
- reached[0] is set to true and is placed in Q to initialize that queue.
- Execution enters a loop that continues until Q becomes empty.

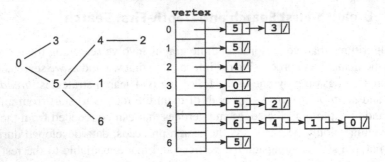

Fig. 7.20 A graph and its adjacency structure

- 0 is removed from the front of Q; its `edge_list` is traversed so that it "sees" its neighbors 5 and 3, neither of which has previously been reached; each of 5 and 3 gets marked as reached, printed out, and placed at the back of Q.
- 5 is removed from the front of Q; its `edge_list` is traversed so that it "sees" its neighbors 6, 4, 1, and 0; 6, 4, and 1 get marked as reached, printed out, and placed at the back of Q; 0 is found to have been reached already, so nothing is done with 0.
- 3 is removed from the front of Q; its `edge_list` is traversed so that it "sees" 0, which has already been reached, so nothing is done with 0.
- 6 is removed from the front of Q; its `edge_list` is traversed so that it "sees" 5, which has already been reached, so nothing is done with 5.
- 4 is removed from the front of Q; its `edge_list` is traversed so that it "sees" 5 and 2; vertex 5 has been reached already, but vertex 2 has not, so 2 gets marked as reached, printed out, and placed at the back of Q.
- 1 is removed from the front of Q; its `edge_list` is traversed so that it "sees" 5, which has already been reached, so nothing is done with 5.
- 2 is removed from the front of Q; its `edge_list` is traversed so that it "sees" 4, which has already been reached, so nothing is done with 4.
- Q is now empty, so the function halts.

The order in which the vertices were printed was 0, 5, 3, 6, 4, 1, 2. Here are "snapshots" of the queue Q after each vertex is inserted or removed. (empty) → (0) → (empty) → (5) → (5 3) → (3) → (3 6) → (3 6 4) → (3 6 4 1) → (6 4 1) → (4 1) → (1) → (1 2) → (2) → (empty).

When given a diagram of a finite graph and a list adjacency structure for it, it is easy with pen and paper to figure out how a breadth-first search will traverse the graph. Once the idea of the search is understood, it is not necessary work through the code in Fig. 7.21.

It is useful to note that the adjacency list representation of the graph in Fig. 7.20 is not unique. We can rearrange the order of the edge_nodes in the lists and still have a correct representation. If we do that, then the vertices will be printed in a different

```
// This function uses breadth-first search to traverse a Graph, starting from
// a specified vertex v, and printing out along the way the vertices that can
// be reached from vertex v in the graph.  It prints v initially. The algorithm
// uses a queue of integers.  Code for a queue class template is not given, but
// is widely available.
// "bool *reached" must be added as data member to the class Graph.
void Graph::bfs_print (int v)
{
  reached = new bool[num_vertices];     // An array parallel to the vertex array.
  queue<int> Q;
  int x, y;
  edge_node * p;

  for (x = 0; x < num_vertices; ++x)    // Initialize the cells of "reached".
    reached[x] = false;                 // We haven't reached any vertex yet.

  reached[v] = true;
  cout << v << endl;
  Q.enqueue(v);                         // Initialize Q by inserting v.

  while (! Q.is_empty())                // We may still have some vertices to visit.
  {
    x = Q.dequeue();
    for (p = vertex[x].edge_list; p != NULL; p = p->next);
    {
      y = p->neighbor;
      if (! reached[y])                 // This is the first time we encounter y.
      {
        reached[y] = true;              // Mark the vertex to avoid visiting it again.
        cout << y << endl;
        Q.enqueue(y);                   // Add it to the queue so we can visit
      }                                 // its neighbors later.
    }
  }
}
```

Fig. 7.21 Breadth-First Search function for graph traversal

order during the breadth-first search. Eventually, however, all vertices reachable from vertex 0 will be printed. In this example, every vertex in the graph is reachable from 0.

What would happen if we made a breadth-first search of the graph shown in Fig. 7.22, starting at vertex 0? (The fact that the graph is directed makes no difference in the strategy.)

As you can see, not every vertex of the graph would end up marked "reached". For example, vertex 7 cannot be reached along a path from 0. If we wanted to print out all vertices of the graph, we would have to scan down the array reached[] until we came to a vertex v for which reached[v] is false. Then we could perform another breadth-first search starting at v. When we finished, we would again continue our scan down the array. In this way we would eventually conduct enough breadth-first searches to print all vertices of the graph.

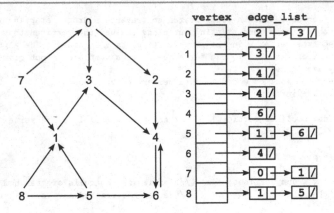

Fig. 7.22 A graph and its adjacency list structure

7.3.2 Depth-First Search

Now let's look at the other search strategy: *depth-first search*. This algorithm starts with the origin and explores connected vertices on one path going away from it, as far as it can reach without vertex repetition. When the search reaches a vertex whose neighbors have all been visited already, it *backtracks* on the path to the first vertex going backward that still has an unseen neighbor. At that point the search will continue on a new path starting from this neighbor and will explore it as far as possible, and so on.

Backtracking is useful in many applications and is covered at length in [15].

How can we make a function keep track of what path it followed during a "forward search" so that it can backtrack easily whenever that becomes necessary. Naturally the function must keep a list of the vertices reached while going forward, but during backtracking the function will return to and discard vertices in the list in the opposite order from that in which the vertices were placed there. Such a list is, of course, a *stack*, a Last-In-First-Out (LIFO) structure. As it turns out, the function can operate the stack explicitly, as was done with a queue in breadth-first search (see Fig. 7.21), or the function can use recursion, which lets invisible run-time support routines operate the stack using stack frames behind the scenes.

If a depth-first function operates the stack explicitly, then it turns out that an extra item has to be stored in each level of the stack. The reason for this is that when the function backtracks to a vertex w, it needs some way of knowing which neighbor of w needs to be reached next. For this reason, every time we push a vertex w onto the stack, we also push a pointer to the edge_node of the neighbor of w that will need to be reached at some future point during the search.

Example 7.3.2 As a simple illustration of a depth-first search algorithm, consider Fig. 7.23. It shows a function named dfs_print that outputs all vertices that can be reached from a specified vertex v. The function is intended to be added as a

```
// This function uses depth-first search to traverse a Graph, starting
// from a specified vertex v, and printing out along the way the vertices
// that can be reached from vertex v in the graph. It prints v initially.
// The algorithm uses a stack of integer-pointer pairs. Code for a stack
// class template is not given, but is widely available.
// "bool *reached" must be added as data member to the class Graph.
void Graph::dfs_print (int v)
{
  reached = new bool[num_vertices];    // An array parallel to the vertex array.
  stack<int, edge_node*> S;            // An empty stack of integer-pointer pairs.
  int x, y;                            // Will be vertex numbers.
  edge_node * p;

  for (x = 0; x < num_vertices; ++x)   // Initialize the cells of "reached".
    reached[x] = false;

  reached[v] = true;                   // Mark the specified initial vertex v.
  cout << v << endl;                   // Print it (send it to standard output).
  S.push(v, v.edge_list);              // Initialize S by pushing v and a pointer
                                       // to its edge_list onto S.
  while (! S.is_empty())
  {
    S.pop(x, p);                       // Pop the integer-pointer pair off the top
                  // of S into the variables x and p.
    while (p != NULL)
    {
      y = p->neighbor;                 // The search will go next to vertex y
      p = p->next;
      if (! reached[y])
      {
        reached[y] = true;
        cout << y << endl;
        S.push(x, p);
        x = y;
        p = vertex[x].edge_list;
      }
    }
  }
}
```

Fig. 7.23 Depth-First Search algorithm for graph traversal, iterative version

member of the Graph class in Fig. 7.11, p. 372. Thus dfs_print assumes that the graph is implemented using an adjacency list representation. The function outputs the vertices in the order in which they are reached during the depth-first search.

Although we can work our way through the algorithm as we have done it for the function bfs_print(), it remains somewhat unclear why it should work. There is a better way to write the algorithm. It takes advantage of the fact that after printing the first vertex and moving on to the second, we are essentially starting over on a depth-first search in the graph. This suggests that the algorithm can be written recursively, and that is indeed the case. A recursive version of the algorithm in Fig. 7.23 is given

```
// This function is a driver for a function that uses recursion to perform depth-
// first search on a Graph G, starting from a specified vertex v, and printing
// out along the way the vertices that can be reached from v.
void Graph::dfs_print (int v)
{
  bool reached [num_vertices];        // An array parallel to the vertex array.
  int i;

  for (i = 0; i < num_vertices; ++i)
    reached[i] = false;

  recursive_dfs_print (v, reached);
}

void Graph::recursive_dfs_print (int v, bool reached[])
{
  reached[v] = true;
  cout << v << endl;
  p = vertex[v].edge_list;
  while (p != NULL)                   // Move across the edge_list of v,
  {                                   // performing depth-first searches on all
    w = p->neighbor;                  // unreached neighbors of v.
    if (! reached[w])
      recursive_dfs_print(w, reached); // Perform a depth-first search on the
    p = p->next;                       // part of G that has not been reached.
  }
}
```

Fig. 7.24 Depth-First Search algorithm for graph traversal, recursive version

in Fig. 7.24. If you work through the example in Fig. 7.22, starting at vertex $v = 0$ and tracing through the recursive calls and their returns, you will find that the operations on the adjacency structure are carried out in exactly the same order as they are when we use the non-recursive version with its explicit stack.

We encounter a small difficulty as soon as we begin coding the recursive version of our depth-first search algorithm. The array "reached[]" cannot be a local array in each separate call when the recursion is in progress. We must provide one "reached[]" array that can be shared by all the separate calls. We do this by adding an array parameter to the heading of the function to enable sharing. To get the array created initially, we also create a "driver" function that calls the recursive function.

Let's look at what occurs when dfs_print(0) in Fig. 7.24 is called on the graph shown in Fig. 7.20.

- An array reached[] is created, "parallel" to the vertex array, and initialized to false everywhere.
- The function recursive_dfs_print(0) is called. The vertex 0 is printed and marked as reached.
- The while loop is started with w equal to 5, the first neighbor of 0 in the adjacency list, not yet reached.

- A recursive call is made from 5, which is printed and marked as reached. The `while` loop is started with w being 6, not yet reached.
- A recursive call is made from 6, which is printed and marked as reached. The `while` loop is started with w being 5.
- The node 5 has been previously marked as reached. Thus, the algorithm does not make another recursive call from it. As 6 does not have any other neighbors, the `while` loop terminates, which causes the recursive call with 6 as argument to complete.
- The code execution returns to the recursive call on 5. This is an example of the backtracking operation.
- Back in the call where v is 5, we move to the next neighbor in its `edge_list`, which is 4, not yet reached.
- A recursive call is made with argument 4, and so 4 is printed and marked as reached. The `while` loop is started with w equal to 5. Since 5 was reached before, we skip the recursive call and proceed to the next iteration, where w is 2, not yet reached.
- A recursive call is made with argument 2, which is printed and marked as reached. The only neighbor 2 has is 4, which has been reached before. Thus, the call with argument 2 completes. Returning to the call with argument 4, we have also reached the end of its adjacency list, so we backtrack to 5.
- Back in the call where v is 5, we move to the next neighbor in its edge-list, which is 1, not yet reached.
- A call is made with v equal to 1, so 1 is printed and marked as reached. No unreached neighbors are available, so we backtrack to 5 again.
- From 5 the algorithm has only 0 left in the `edge_list`, and 0 has been reached. This call is also completed, and we backtrack to 0.
- From 0 we move forward to the vertex 3, not yet reached. A last recursive call happens where 3 is printed and marked as reached. After this, all the remaining calls complete and the original call terminates.

The order in which depth-first search prints the vertices for the list adjacency structure in Fig. 7.20 is 0, 5, 6, 4, 2, 1, 3. As was mentioned in connection with breadth-first search, the list adjacency structure in Fig. 7.20 is not unique. If the order of the edge_nodes is changed, that will change the order in which the vertices are printed.

Again, when we are given a diagram of a finite graph and a list adjacency structure for it, it is easy with pen and paper to figure out how a depth-first search will traverse the graph. Once the idea of the search is understood, it is not necessary to work through the code in Fig. 7.24.

7.3.3 Complexity of the Breadth-First and Depth-First

To analyze the time complexity of the breadth-first and depth-first functions we presented, we start by noticing that both functions will only print each vertex that can be reached from the origin of the search once and only once. Furthermore, both algorithms use each edge on any path going out from the origin of the search once for directed graphs and twice for undirected graphs (once in each direction). All the other operations necessary for the search require $\Theta(1)$ time.

In the best case, the origin vertex is not connected to any other in the graph. In this case, the algorithms visit a single vertex and use no edge. Thus, the required time is $\Theta(1)$.

In the worst case, the origin vertex is connected to all the others, which means that the algorithms will visit all n nodes and use all m edges in the process. This gives us a complexity of $\Theta(n + m)$.

To sum up the analysis, both the breadth-first and the depth-first (in both versions) requires $\Omega(1)$ and $O(n + m)$ execution time. As the number of edges is at most $n(n - 1)$ for a directed graph and half as much for an undirected one, we can say that these algorithms are $O(n^2)$.

We can use methods described in Chap. 6 to show that on the average these algorithms require $\Theta(n^2)$ time. We can also say that is b is the average branching factor in a connected graph with n vertices, then the traversal function will require $\Theta(bn)$ execution time.

Let's examine the space complexity. This time we need to look at each presented algorithm separately.

For the breadth-first algorithm, the largest piece of extra space is required by the queue Q. This queue will hold vertices that have been printed already, but whose edge_lists have not been visited yet. We make the observation that a vertex is only enqueued right after it is marked as reached, and so it cannot be enqueued more than once. This means that the largest number of vertices that can be present in the queue at any time is n. Everything else requires $\Theta(1)$ space, so we can conclude that the algorithm has a space complexity which is $\Omega(1)$ and $O(n)$.

For the iterative depth-first algorithm, the largest piece of extra space is required by the stack S. For the same reason as for the queue, the stack cannot store a vertex more than once. In each step of the algorithm, the stack will contain the path from the origin to the vertex being examined. Thus, this algorithm also has a space complexity of $\Omega(1)$ and $O(n)$.

For the recursive depth-first algorithm, the extra space is given by the number of stack frames in the runtime stack. At any moment, the values of the argument v in each stack frame together compose the path from the origin of the search to the vertex being examined. Thus, the content of the runtime stack is parallel to the stack S for the iterative version. This means that this algorithm has the same order of space complexity as the iterative one.

7.3.4 Exercises

7.3.3 Consider the digraph whose adjacency list structure is shown in Fig. 7.25 (repeated from Exercise 7.2.5, p. 376). If we use this adjacency structure to conduct a breadth-first search, starting at vertex 0, in what order will the vertices be reached? Will the search mark all of them? In what order will the vertices be reached if we make a depth-first search, starting at vertex 0?

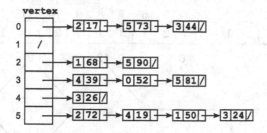

Fig. 7.25 An adjacency structure

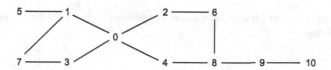

Fig. 7.26 An undirected graph

7.3.4 Create an adjacency list structure for the graph shown in Fig. 7.26. Suppose a breadth-first search is made on this graph, starting at vertex 0 and using your adjacency structure. In what order will the vertices be reached? In what order will the vertices be reached if you make a depth-first search, starting at 0?

7.4 Numbering the Connected Components of an Undirected Graph

Suppose we are given an adjacency structure for an undirected graph G and asked to determine whether the graph is connected. This is an easy problem to solve. We simply make a breadth-first search of the graph, starting at any vertex, and see whether this marks all the vertices. If it does, the graph is connected. If it doesn't, the graph is not connected. A depth-first search will work just as well: either type of search will mark all the vertices that can be reached from the vertex we started with.

Now let's make the problem more interesting. When an undirected graph is NOT connected, then it has more than one *connected component*. Is there an algorithm that "sorts" the vertices into their respective components? More precisely, can we find an algorithm that assigns numerical values to the vertices is such a way that all vertices having the same assigned number belong to the same connected component?

This is actually not hard at all. Figure 7.28 shows a function that can do the job. The function starts with vertex 0 and performs a breadth-first search of the graph, assigning the component number 1 to each vertex reachable from 0. When the search is finished, the function scans through the vertices to determine whether there are any that have not yet received a component number (and thus were not reached by the

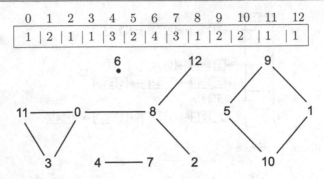

Fig. 7.27 An undirected graph with 4 connected components (*bottom*) and the component number for each vertex (*top*)

breadth-first search). If such a vertex, call it v, can be found, a breadth-first search from v is initiated, and all vertices reachable from v will be assigned the component number 2. This process is repeated until every vertex has been assigned a component number. The function returns the component numbers of the vertices in an array that it has dynamically allocated.

As an example, consider the undirected graph in Fig. 7.27. If the function "number_the_components()" is called on that graph, the function will return (a pointer to) the array

This is actually not very hard at all. Figure 7.28 shows some pseudo-code to do the job. It assumes that in the adjacency structure for a graph G, each cell of the vertex array contains a field (i.e., member) named comp_number, as well as a pointer to an edge-list.

Although breadth-first search is specified in the algorithm above to set the value of the component, depth-first search works just as well.

7.4.1 Exercises

7.4.1 Figure 7.29 below shows the adjacency structure for an undirected graph. *Without actually drawing the graph*, perform the algorithm given on the preceding page and determine how many components the graph has and which vertices belong together in which components.

7.5   Shortest Path Problems

Let's begin with an easy version of the classical shortest path problem. Suppose we are given a finite graph G (directed or undirected) and two vertices, one of which is specified as an "origin" and the other of which is specified as a "destination". How can we find a path in G from the origin to the destination with the *fewest possible*

```
// This function identifies the connected components of an undirected graph
// and assigns sequence numbers, starting at 1, to those components.  It
// returns an array, dynamically allocated by the function, that shows,
// for each vertex v, the sequence number of the connected component that
// contains v.

int* Graph::component_numbers()
{
    int v, comp_count;
    int* component;                      // Will point to a dynamically allocated
                                         // array parallel to "vertices[]".

    component = new int[num_vertices];   // Will hold the component numbers.

    for (v = 0; v < num_vertices; ++v)   // Set the component number of each vertex v
        component[v] = -1;               // to the sentinel value -1, indicating that
                                         // that v has not been reached or numbered.
    comp_count = 1;                      // The vertices of the first connected
                                         // component will be assigned the number 1.

    for (v = 0; v < num_vertices; ++v)
        if (component[v] == -1)          // Checks whether v is not yet numbered.
        {
            // The following function call assumes existence of a method very close
            // to the method Graph::bfv_print(v), except that in place of a "reached[]"
            // array, this method uses the "component[]" array.  For each vertex w
            // reachable from v, it assigns the parameter value "comp_counter" to
            // "component[w]".  It does not output the vertex numbers.

            bfs_set_component(v, comp_count, component);

            ++comp_count;
        }
    return component;
}
```

Fig. 7.28 Algorithm numbering the connected components of a graph

edges? Of course, if it turns out that there is no path at all in G from origin to destination, we'll want to discover that also.

While it would be possible to solve this problem by repeated depth-first searches in G starting from the origin, that is not likely to be an efficient way to find a shortest path, especially if the destination is near the origin. A little thought about how a breadth-first search works will convince you that you are likely to find a shortest path more quickly by using a breadth-first search, which first "marks" all the vertices separated by 1 edge from the origin, then all vertices separated by 2 edges from the origin, and so on. Figure 7.30 shows some code that implements this idea.

The algorithm in Fig. 7.30 uses a queue of vertex numbers in much the same way as the breadth-first algorithm in Fig. 7.21, p. 379. However, the algorithm in Fig. 7.30 is more complicated. It employees two arrays parallel to the vertex[] array, called distance[] and predecessor[] (Fig. 7.31). For each vertex v that's reached during the search, the cell distance[v] is given the number of edges along the path that's been discovered from the origin to v, and the cell predecessor[v] is

Fig. 7.29 An adjacency
structure for an undirected
graph and the component
number array

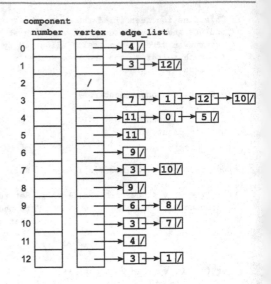

given the number of the vertex that immediately precedes v on that path. As a simple
example, if the function in Fig. 7.23 is applied to the list adjacency structure shown
in Fig. 7.22, with origin 4 and destination 1, then at the point where the destination
1 is reached, we'll have the following values in the arrays: distance[4] is 0 and
predecessor[4] is −1 (a sentinel value to indicate no predecessor on the path),
distance[5] is 1 and predecessor[5] is 4, and distance[1] is 2 and
predecessor[1] is 5. At this point the function will print out the vertex numbers
1, 5, 4 in a column, which means that 4, 5, 1 is a shortest path from 4 to 1.

We could improve the function so that it printed the vertices along a shortest path
in the "natural" order from origin to destination. The way to do that is to push the
vertices onto a stack instead of printing them, then print them as they are popped off
the stack. This would be especially desirable if the graph were directed.

Note that we do not speak of "the" shortest path, since there may be two entirely
different shortest paths from a specified origin to a specified destination. We will not
deal with the problem of finding *all* shortest paths, but it is not difficult to modify
the algorithm in Fig. 7.30 to produce an algorithm that finds them all.

Now let's make the problem more challenging. Suppose now that we are considering a *weighted* graph, that is, a graph G in which each edge has been assigned a
non-negative number, called the "cost" of that edge. In many applications, each cost
is simply the distance along some road or air route from one place to another. The
problem to be considered is this: given a vertex specified as the "origin" and another
specified as the "destination", find a path in G from the origin to the destination such
that the sum of the costs of the edges along the path is as small as possible; if there
is no path in G from the origin to the destination, discover and report this fact.

```
void Graph::print_shortest_path (int origin, int destination)
{
  int x, y;
  int distance[num_vertices];        // Two arrays parallel to the vertex array
  int predecessor[num_vertices];     // for recording paths and distances.
  queue<int> Q;
  edge_node *p;
  for (x = 0; x < num_vertices; ++i)  // Load arrays with sentinel -1
    distance[x] = predecessor[x] = -1; // to show no vertices reached.
  distance[origin] = 0;
  Q.enqueue (origin);                 // Initialize the queue.

  while (Q is not empty && distance[destination] == -1)
  {
    x = Q.dequeue();
    for (p = vertex[x].edge_list; p != NULL; p = p->next)
    {
      y = p->neighbor;
      if (distance[y] == -1)          // then y was not reached earlier.
      {
        distance[y] = 1 + distance[x];
        predecessor[y] = x;
        Q.enqueue(y);
      }
    }
  }
  if (distance[destination] == -1)    // then Q is empty; destination not found
    cout << "There is no path from the origin " << origin
         << " to the destination " << destination " in the graph." << endl;
  else
  {
    cout << "Here are the vertices on a shortest path from vertex "
         << origin << " to vertex " << destination << ", printed "
         << "in reverse order:" << endl;
    y = destination;
    cout << y << endl;
    while (y != origin)
    {
      y = predecessor[y];
      cout << y << endl;
    }
  }
}
```

Fig. 7.30 Algorithm for finding the path with fewest edges from an origin vertex to a destination vertex

The best known algorithm for solving this *Least Costly Path Problem* was invented in 1959 by the famous Dutch computer scientist Edsger Dijkstra.[5] It employs a modi-

---

[5] (DIKE-struh) In case you haven't heard of him before, he became an object of heated controversy because of a letter he wrote in 1968 to the Communications of the ACM. The letter was printed under the title "Go To Statement Considered Harmful". A goto instruction in a programming language is an instruction that allows execution to be directed from any place in a program to any other specified

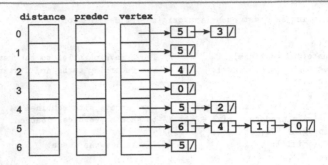

Fig. 7.31 A graph given by its adjacency list structure

fication of the breadth-first search method that we have just examined for unweighted graphs. It is not exactly a breadth-first search, however, because it is a "greedy algorithm": it attempts to follow low cost paths before pursuing higher cost paths. In order to accomplish this, it uses a *priority queue* in place of the simple FIFO queue. Priority queues are implemented efficiently using binary heaps. They have been discussed in detail in Sect. 5.6.

In addition to maintaining a priority min-queue, the Dijkstra algorithm stores and repeatedly updates three pieces of information about each vertex v in the graph. These are

- `total_cost[v]`, which shows the sum of the costs along the "best path to v known so far"; when a better (i.e., less costly) path to v is discovered during the search, the `total_cost` is updated with the smaller value;
- `predecessor[v]`, which shows the vertex from which v is reachable along the "best path to v known so far";
- `finalized[v]` (boolean), which shows whether the "best path to v known so far" is an actual best.

How do we initialize the variables listed above? In every `total_cost[v]` we place a "plus infinity", a floating point number so large that it will exceed any possible actual sum of costs along any path in the graph (generally `FLT_MAX` will work). Then right away we lower the `total_cost` value of the origin to 0, since the empty path

---

(Footnote 5 continued)

place (the place is specified by a label). In assembly languages the JUMP and BRANCH instructions are goto instructions. In languages such as old FORTRAN and old BASIC, the GOTO is indispensable for control-flow. Dijkstra argued that availability of a goto instruction in high level languages was bad because it encouraged promiscuous transfers of execution that made programs hard to read and debug. He and several colleagues proved that in languages that include the now familiar control-flow instructions such as "if... else...." and "while", no goto statement is logically necessary. Dijkstra's letter generated a storm of letters arguing for and against the proposal he had made. Today most high level languages still have the goto instruction available, but programmers are strongly discouraged from ever using this instruction, since it creates "unstructured" code.

```
// Initializes the parallel arrays used by Dijkstra's algorithm. The pointers
// predecessor, total_cost, and finalized must be added as data members
// to the Graph class.

void Graph::dijkstra_init()
{
  int x;

  // Allocate and initialize the parallel arrays.
  predecessor = new int[num_vertices];
  total_cost  = new float[num_vertices];
  finalized   = new bool[num_vertices];

  for (x = 0; x < num_vertices; ++x)
  {
    predecessor[x] = -1;        // sentinel value
    total_cost[x]  = FLT_MAX;   // "plus infinity"
    finalized[x]   = false;
  }
}
```

Fig. 7.32 Initialization of data structures for Dijkstra's algorithm

from the origin to the origin has the least cost. For every predecessor[v] we use the same sentinel value that we used in Fig. 7.7, namely −1. We set finalized[v] to false for every v, and then switch the value to true for the origin.

Figures 7.32 and 7.33 exhibit a mixture of pseudo-code and actual code for the Dijkstra algorithm. The pseudo-code assumes the availability of a priority min-queue class containing these methods:

```
void priority_min_queue();        // Constructor for empty
min-queue.void insert             // Insert a pair (i, f) into the min-queue,
(int i, float f);                 // using f for comparing with other pairs.
void delete_min(int &i, float&f); // Remove a pair with smallest second
                                  // component and set i to the first
                                  // component and f to the second component.
bool is_empty();                  // Use this before calling delete_min.
```

In addition, we'll assume that we have a function report_path doing the following. If finalized[destination] is still false, it reports that there is no path in this graph from the origin to the destination. Otherwise, it prints out the vertices along the least costly path that has been discovered in the graph (see the code in Fig. 7.30). It also prints out the total cost of the least costly path.

The Dijkstra algorithm proceeds by marking a vertex as "finalized" when a least cost path to it is known, and then "updating" the distance members of the non-finalized neighbors of the newly finalized vertex. All the updated members are put into the priority queue.

Dijkstra's algorithm often inserts a vertex and its new total_cost into the priority queue even though that same vertex is already in the priority queue with a larger total_cost. Don't worry about that. Careful mathematical analysis (not given here) has shown that this duplication is a small price to pay for simplicity in the code.

```
// This function implements the Dijkstra algorithm for finding a least costly
// path in a weighted graph from a specified origin to a specified definition.
// It assumes that each edge_node of the graph contains an extra field named
// "cost", which is of type "float". When the function has found a least
// costly path, it outputs the vertices along that path in reverse order,
// provided there is at least one path from origin to destination. If there
// is none, the function prints a message to that effect.

void Graph::dijkstra_algorithm (int origin, int destination)
{
  int   x, y;
  float c;
  edge_node * p;
  priority_min_queue pq;

  dijkstra_init(origin);                 // Initialize the parallel arrays.

  total_cost[origin] = 0.0;
  pq_insert (origin, 0.0);               // Initialize the priority min-queue.

  while (! pq.is_empty() && ! finalized[destination])
  {
    pq.delete_min(x, c);                 // Remove a pair with least second component.

    if (! finalized[x])
    {
      finalized[x] = true;

      // This loop traverses the edge_list of vertex x, updating the total_cost
      // fields of the neighbors of x.
      for (p=vertex[x].edge_list; p!=NULL; p = p->next)
      {
        y = p->neighbor;
        if (!finalized[y])
        {
          c = total_cost[x] + p->cost; // p->cost is the cost of edge x to y.
          if (c < total_cost[y])       // A better path to y has been found,
          {                            // and x precedes y on that path.
            total_cost[y] = c;
            predecessor[y] = x;
            pq.insert(y, c);
          }
        }
      }
    }
  }     // End of "while" loop;  time to report result of the computation.
  report_path(destination);
}
```

Fig. 7.33 Dijkstra's algorithm for finding the least costly path from the origin to the destination

Let's practice the Dijkstra algorithm on the undirected, weighted graph shown in Fig. 7.34. Take 0 to be the origin and 3 to be the destination.

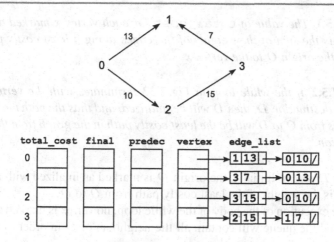

Fig. 7.34 A graph and the data structures for the Dijkstra algorithm

- Initialize `total_cost[]`, `predecessor[]`, and `finalized[]`; change `total_cost[0]` to 0.0 and insert the pair (0, 0.0) into the priority min-queue `pq`.
- Since `pq` is not empty and `finalized[3]` is false, delete (0, 0.0) from `pq`, which sets $x = 0$ and $c = 0.0$; set `finalized[0]` = true.
- Set $y = 1$ (the first non-finalized neighbor of 0); set $c = 0.0 + 13.0 <$ FLT_MAX and `total_cost[1]` = 13.0; insert (1, 13.0) into `pq`.
- Set $y = 2$ (the second non-finalized neighbor of 0); set $c = 0.0 + 10.0 <$ FLT_MAX and `total_cost[2]` = 10.0; insert (2, 10.0) into `pq`.
- Return to the top of the `while` loop; `pq` is not empty and `finalized[3]` is false, so delete (2, 10.0) (the pair with least cost) from `pq`, which sets $x = 2$ and $c = 10.0$; set `finalized[2]` = true.
- Set $y = 3$ (the only non-finalized neighbor of 2); set $c = 10.0 + 15.0 <$ FLT_MAX and `total_cost[3]` = 25.0; insert (3, 25.0) into `pq`.
- Return to the top of the `while` loop; `pq` is not empty and `finalized[3]` is false, so delete (1, 13.0) (the pair with least cost) from `pq`, which sets $x = 1$ and $c = 13.0$; set `finalized[1]` = true.
- Set $y = 3$ (the only non-finalized neighbor of 1), set $c = 13.0 + 7.0 < 25.0$ and `total_cost[3]` = 20.0; insert (3, 20.0) into `pq`.
- Return to the top of the `while` loop; `pq` is not empty and `finalized[3]` is false, so delete (3, 20.0) (the pair with least cost) from `pq`, which sets $x = 3$ and $c = 20.0$; set `finalized[3]` = true.
- There are no non-finalized neighbors of 3, so return to the top of the `while` loop. Although `pq` is not empty, the destination 3 has been finalized, so the `while` loop ends and the vertices 3, 1, 0 are printed, along with to total cost 20.0 of that path.

It's far from obvious that the Dijkstra algorithm in Fig. 7.33 will work correctly in all cases. A proof requires a useful loop invariant, which Theorem 7.5.1 provides.

Theorem 7.5.1 *The value of* `total_cost` *for each vertex x marked as finalized in Fig. 7.33 is the sum of the weights of the edges along a least costly path in the graph from the origin O to the vertex x.*

Corollary 7.5.2 *If the while loop in Fig. 7.33 terminates with the vertex x being equal to the destination D, then D will be finalized, and thus the path marked by the predecessors from O to D will be the least costly path in the graph from the origin to the destination.*

Proof of the Theorem Initially, the origin O is marked as finalized with a total cost of 0, which is the weight of the least costly path from O to O.

After one execution of the body of the while loop, no vertex is marked as finalized except O, and the queue will contain all the neighbors of O in order of the weight of the edges from O to them.

The next iteration of the while loop, the vertex x deleted from the priority queue will be the neighbor of O with edge of minimum weight from O to x. This represents a least costly path from O to x, because any other path will contain an initial edge having weight at least as great.

The proof of the induction step uses the following additional loop invariants:

(a) For every finalized vertex, its neighbors are either finalized or in the priority queue pq.
(b) For every vertex in pq, its predecessor is already finalized.
    and the following property:
(c) If $O\ x_1\ x_2 \ldots x_k$ is a least costly path from O to x_k, then $O\ x_1 \ldots x_i$ is a least costly path from O to x_i, for all i satisfying $1 \leq i \leq k-1$.

We will use proof by contradiction.

Let us suppose that the invariant stated in Theorem 7.5.1 is true when we test that pq is empty. Suppose that we execute the body of the while loop again. Let x be the next vertex that we delete from pq.

Suppose by contradiction that there is another path from O to x that costs less than the current total cost for x. Let v be the finalized vertex in the second path that is the closest to x. See Fig. 7.35 for a reference.

If there is an edge from v to x, then `total_cost[x]` should be equal to the cost of the second path because all of the neighbors of v have been added to the priority queue before. Since x is a neighbor of v in this case, `total_cost[x]` cannot reflect a number larger than a known path from the origin to it.

If there is no edge from v to x, let w be the next vertex in the path from v to x. Then w must be in pq with the total cost being equal to the cost of the path from O to v plus the weight of the edge from v to w. Since the cost on this path from O to x is lower than `total_cost[x]`, we must deduce that `total_cost[w]` < `total_cost[x]`, which contradicts the fact that x should have the lowest total cost in pq in order for it to be the one extracted by the `delete_min` operation. ■

Fig. 7.35 Reference for the loop invariant for the Dijkstra algorithm

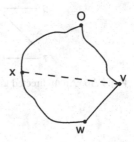

What are the time and space complexities of Dijkstra's algorithm? For the space complexity, the algorithm requires the parallel arrays `finalized`, `predecessor`, and `total_cost` and the priority queue. All three arrays are of size n, which the priority queue will contain at most m entries of type (vertex, total cost). Thus, the space complexity is $\Theta(n + m)$.

For the time complexity, initializing the parallel arrays requires $\Theta(n)$ operations. In the best case, the destination could be equal to the origin, in which case, the algorithm would complete with only a constant number of operations following the initialization.

Unlike the breadth-first algorithm, Dijkstra's algorithm might visit each vertex more than once. However, we know that it will visit each *edge* in the graph at most once. For some of the edges, the vertex y will be added to the min-queue with a new value for the total cost. We know that for each edge, we add at most one new vertex to pq, so the number of vertices in pq is at most m. Using the heap implementation introduced in Sect. 5.6, the insert and delete operations require $O(\log(m))$ operations. Thus, in the worst case the complexity is $\Theta(n + m \log(m))$ which is also $O(n^2 \log(n))$. Overall, we can say that the algorithm is $\Omega(n)$ and $O(n + m \log(m))$ or $O(n^2 \log(n))$.

A final comment on terminology. In the foregoing discussion, the problem that Dijkstra's algorithm was invented to solve has been referred to as the "Least Costly Path Problem". In many places, however, it is referred to by the name "Shortest Path Problem", which, in these notes, has been used only in reference to the problem of finding a paths with the fewest possible edge. It is important, however, to be aware that in the wider world the phrase "Shortest Path Problem" is often used in place of "Least Costly Path Problem".

7.5.1 Exercises

7.5.3 Using the graph shown in Fig. 7.36 (repeated from Exercise 7.3.4, p. 384), run the simple algorithm in Fig. 7.30 for finding a shortest path (path with fewest edges) from vertex 8 to vertex 5. Be sure to set up the adjacency structure that a computer program would work with, and work from that structure, not from the picture of the graph. When the algorithm is complete, list the vertices "backward" along the path from the destination to the origin.

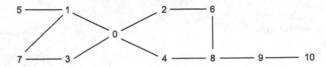

Fig. 7.36 An undirected graph (repeated)

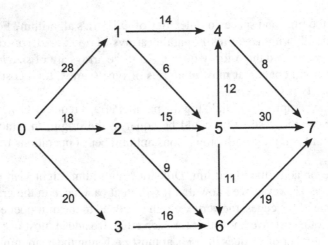

Fig. 7.37 Graph for Exercise 7.5.5

7.5.4 What happens when we run the shortest path algorithm in Fig. 7.30 on the graph in Exercise 7.4.1, p. 386, using 0 as origin and 1 as destination?

7.5.5 Set up an adjacency structure for the graph in Fig. 7.37. Use it to run Dijkstra's least costly path algorithm of Fig. 7.33 on this digraph using 0 as origin and 7 as destination.

7.5.6 Dijkstra's algorithm stops when it finalizes the vertex that it has been told is the destination. What minor modification could we make in the code for Dijkstra's algorithm in Fig. 7.33 to make it find, for *every* vertex v in G, a least costly path to v from the origin? In other words, when the modified algorithm stops, every vertex reachable from the origin should have been labeled with its distance along a least costly path from the origin, and it should be possible to read off (backward) a least costly path from the origin to any specified vertex.

7.5.7 Dijkstra's algorithm works equally well on directed and undirected graphs. Run the Dijkstra algorithm on the digraph in Fig. 7.38. Take the origin to be vertex 1 and the destination to be vertex 7.

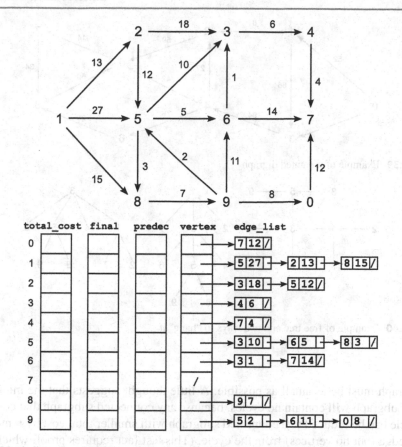

Fig. 7.38 A digraph and the data structures for the Dijkstra algorithm

7.6 Minimum Spanning Trees

Suppose a cable TV company is contemplating providing service to a rural area consisting of some widely separated residences. Each residence must be connected to the "grid" in some way. Direct connections between some pairs of residences are possible, while such connections are impossible for other pairs of residences. An installation cost for each connection that's possible can be calculated. If we were given the data about which connections are possible and how much they cost, how could we calculate the least expensive way of providing the desired service? For example, suppose the residences and the *possible* direct connections, together with their costs, are as shown in Fig. 7.39.

What we would be seeking in the graph above is a *subgraph* with two properties: the subgraph must be connected, and the sum of the weights of the edges in the

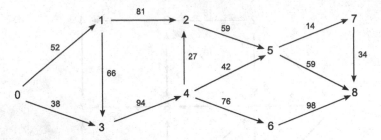

Fig. 7.39 Example of weighted digraph

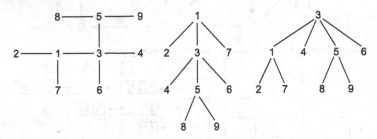

Fig. 7.40 Example of free tree and two ways to "hang" it

subgraph must be as small as possible. A little thought suggests that the minimum cost subgraph will contain no cycles, because any connected subgraph that contains a cycle can be reduced to a connected subgraph with smaller total cost by removing one edge (but no vertices) from the cycle. (This last fact requires proof, which will be provided.)

The problem we have just considered arises in many other contexts as well, and we can state it simply as a problem about graphs with weighted edges. Before doing so, it will be convenient to have available some additional vocabulary in which to talk about the problem.

Definition 7.6.1 A *free tree* (or *non-rooted tree*) is an undirected, connected, acyclic graph. A *spanning tree* for an undirected graph G is a subgraph T of G with these two properties: (1) T has the same vertex set as G, and (2) T is a free tree.

The term "free tree" comes from the fact that if we take any undirected, connected acyclic graph and choose any vertex arbitrarily ("freely"), we can "hang" the graph from that vertex and make it look like a (not necessarily binary) tree. Figure 7.40 shows an example of a free tree and two ways to re-draw it so that it "hangs" from a single vertex.

Figure 7.41 shows two undirected graphs. You can quickly verify that one of them contains a spanning tree, while the other does not.

We are ready now to state the graph theoretic problem suggested by the example involving the TV cable company.

Fig. 7.41 Two examples of graphs, each with 5 vertices

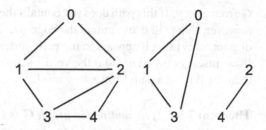

The Minimum Spanning Tree Problem: Let G be an undirected graph with weighted edges. Find a spanning tree for G having the least possible sum of edge weights. Such a tree is called a minimum (or minimal) spanning tree for G.

Before attacking this problem, we're going to look at some theorems about connectivity and free trees and spanning trees. These will help us think more clearly about what it is we are looking for when seeking a minimum spanning tree.

Theorem 7.6.2 *If a graph (directed or undirected) contains a path from a vertex x to a different vertex y, then the graph contains a* simple *path from x to y.*

Proof Suppose a path from x to y is not simple and (thus) has a vertex list of the form

$$x, \ldots, v, \ldots, v, \ldots y.$$

Then we can remove the vertices following the first occurrence of v up to and including the last occurrence of v and still have a path from x to y. If this path is not simple, we can remove more vertices from its vertex list. Continuing in this way we will eventually obtain a path from x to y with no repetition of vertices in the vertex list, because the original list is of finite length.   ∎

Theorem 7.6.3 *If a graph G (directed or undirected) is acyclic, then all subgraphs of G are acyclic.*

Proof The contrapositive of this "if... then..." statement says the following: If there exists a subgraph of G that contains a cycle, then G contains a cycle. This is obviously true, so the statement of the theorem must also be true.   ∎

Theorem 7.6.4 *If an undirected graph is connected and contains a cycle, then the subgraph obtained by removing any edge (but no vertex) from the cycle is connected.*

Proof Let G be an undirected graph that's connected and contains a cycle. Let $\{a, b\}$ be any edge in that cycle, and consider the subgraph H obtained by removing this edge from the edge set of G (but keeping the same vertex set). It is easy to see (and tedious to prove by induction) that there is still a path between a and b in the subgraph H. To prove that H is connected, take any vertices x and y of H. We must prove that there is a path in H from x to y. Since G is connected, there is a path in

G from x to y. If this path does not contain the edge $\{a,\ b\}$, then it is a path in H. If, however, this path does contain the edge $\{a,\ b\}$, then we can suppose (without loss of generality) that it appears in the path vertex list this way: $x,\ \ldots,\ a,\ b,\ \ldots,\ y$. If we insert between a and b the vertices along a remaining path in H from a to b, then we'll have a path from x to y in H.   ∎

Theorem 7.6.5 *If an undirected graph G is connected and contains two vertices a and b but does not contain the edge between them, then the graph H obtained by adding the edge $\{a,\ b\}$ to the edge set of G is connected and contains a cycle, one of whose edges is $\{a,\ b\}$.*

Proof The connectedness of H is obvious: since any two vertices of G can already be connected by edges in G, the two vertices can be connected by the same edges in H. To see that there is a cycle in H, observe that a can already be connected to b by a path in G. Adding the undirected edge $\{a,\ b\} = \{b,\ a\}$ to the end of that path gives a cycle that starts and finishes at a.   ∎

Theorem 7.6.6 *Every undirected connected graph contains at least one spanning tree.*

Proof Take any undirected connected graph G. If G is acyclic, then it contains a spanning tree, namely itself. If G contains a cycle, then by Theorem 7.6.4 we can remove an edge from the cycle to obtain a connected subgraph with the same vertices. If this subgraph contains a cycle, then we can remove another edge to obtain a connected subgraph with the same vertices. We can repeat this process only finitely many times because G has finitely many edges. Thus we eventually obtain a connected subgraph with the same vertices but no cycles. This subgraph is a spanning tree for G.   ∎

Theorem 7.6.7 *Every free tree with exactly n vertices has exactly $n - 1$ edges.*

Proof We'll prove this by induction. The statement in the theorem is clearly true when $n = 1$.

Now take any k such that the theorem statement is true for all integers n less than or equal to k. Is the theorem statement true when $n = k + 1$? To prove that it is, take any free tree T with $k + 1$ vertices. We must prove that T has k edges. Choose any vertex v of T. Let $w_1,\ \ldots,\ w_r$ denote the vertices to which v is connected in T (it is connected to at least one other vertex because T is connected and has at least 2 vertices). Remove from T the vertex v and all the edges out of v to produce a subgraph T^*. Let $T_1,\ \ldots,\ T_r$ denote the connected components of T^* containing the vertices $w_1,\ \ldots,\ w_r$, respectively. There are three things to observe about these components.

(1) Every vertex in T^* belongs to one of these components. To see this, take any vertex w in T^*. Then w is connected to v by some *simple* path in T (see Theorem 7.6.2), and the next-to-last vertex on that path is one of the w_i's, so w is in the connected component of that w_i.

(2) The components $T_1, \ldots, T_r$ are disjoint from each other. To see this, suppose for purposes of contradiction that w_i and w_j were different but belonged to the same connected component of T^*; then the free tree T would contain a cycle consisting of the path from w_i to w_j in T_i and the edges $\{w_j, v\}$ and $\{v, w_i\}$. This contradicts the definition of free tree.

(3) Each of the components T_i is a free tree, because it is connected (by its very definition) and is acyclic because T is acyclic (see Theorem 7.6.3).

Let n_i denote the number of vertices in the free tree T_i. Then by the inductive hypothesis, T_i contains exactly $n_i - 1$ edges. Also notice that by observation (2) above, the number of vertices in T^* is $n_1 + \ldots + n_r$. Since T^* contains one less vertex than T, it follows that $n_1 + \ldots + n_r = k$. Now we can write the following equations:

$$\text{number of edges in } T = (\text{number of edges in all the } Ti's)$$
$$+(\text{number of edges from } v \text{ to the } u_i's)$$
$$= [(n_1 - 1) + \ldots + (n_r - 1)] + r$$
$$= (n_1 + \ldots + n_r) - r + r$$
$$= k,$$

which is what we said we wanted to prove.   ∎

Corollary 7.6.8 *Every undirected connected graph with n vertices has at least $n - 1$ edges.*

Proof You will be asked to prove this in an exercise.   ∎

Theorem 7.6.9 *If a connected undirected graph with exactly n vertices has exactly $n - 1$ edges, then it must be acyclic (and thus it must be a free tree, since it's connected and acyclic).*

Proof You will be asked to prove this in an exercise.   ∎

Theorem 7.6.10 *Let G be an acyclic undirected graph with exactly n vertices. Let k denote the number of connected components of G. Then G has exactly $n - k$ edges.*

Proof Let $G_1, \ldots, G_k$ denote the connected components of G. Since G is acyclic, we know by Theorem 7.6.4 that each G_i is acyclic. Since each G_i is connected (by definition), it follows that each G_i is a free tree. Let n_i denote the number of elements of G_i. Then $n_1 + \ldots + n_k = n$. By Theorem 7.6.7, the number of edges in G_i is $n_i - 1$. Since the edges in the connected components make up all the edges of G, the number of edges in G is

$$(n_1 - 1) + \ldots + (n_k - 1) = (n_1 + \ldots + n_k) - k = n - k$$ ∎

Theorem 7.6.11 *If an acyclic undirected graph with exactly n vertices has exactly n − 1 edges, then it must be connected (and thus it must be a free tree, since it's connected and acyclic).*

Proof Let G be any acyclic undirected graph with exactly n vertices and exactly $n − 1$ edges. By Theorem 7.6.10 the number of edges in G is $n − k$, where k is the number of connected components of G. Since G has $n − 1$ edges, it follows that $k = 1$. Thus there is only one connected component in G, which means that G is connected.   ∎

We can summarize Theorems 7.6.7, 7.6.9, and 7.6.11 in one corollary.

Corollary 7.6.12 *Let G be an undirected graph with exactly n vertices.*

(a) *If G is connected and acyclic, then G has exactly n − 1 edges.*
(b) *If G is connected and has exactly n − 1 edges, then G is acyclic.*
(c) *If G is acyclic and has exactly n − 1 edges, then G is connected.*

Now let's begin looking at connected, undirected, weighted graphs and see if we can find *minimum* spanning trees in such graphs. Figure 7.42 shows some examples. It is easy to check that removing edges {C, D} and {A, C} from the first graph produces a minimum spanning tree. (It is not unique.) Similarly, removing edge {K, L} from the second graph produces a minimum spanning tree.

Theorem 7.6.13 *Every connected, undirected, weighted graph contains at least one minimum spanning tree.*

Proof Take any connected, undirected, weighted graph G. By Theorem 7.6.6, G contains at least one spanning tree. Since there are only finitely many edges in G, there are only finitely many possible spanning trees. By looking at the sum of the weights of the edges in each spanning tree, we can select a tree of least total edge weight. This is a minimum spanning tree.   ∎

Fig. 7.42 Two examples of graphs

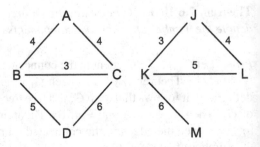

Theorem 7.6.13 guarantees the existence of a minimum spanning tree in a connected, undirected, weighted graph, but it doesn't give us an efficient method for finding one. In general, the task of finding all the possible spanning trees in a connected undirected graph G is Herculean. We need something less exhausting. Our next theorem will give us a clue for a very efficient algorithm for finding minimum spanning trees.

Theorem 7.6.14 *Let G be a connected, undirected, weighted graph, and let e be an edge of minimal weight among all the edges of G. Then there is a minimum spanning tree for G that contains e.*

Proof Take any minimum spanning tree T^* for G (we know that one exists by Theorem 7.6.13). If T^* already contains edge e then there is nothing to prove. Suppose, however, that T^* does not contain e. Then we'll construct a different minimum spanning tree that does contain e. Begin by adding the edge e to T^* to produce a graph H that's a subgraph of G having the same vertex set as G. By Theorem 7.6.5, H is connected and contains a cycle. Choose any edge e^* other than e in the cycle. By Theorem 7.6.4, we can remove e^* and still have a connected graph, call it T. Then T has the same number of vertices and edges as T^* (so the same vertices as G). By Theorem 7.6.9, T must be a free tree, and thus a spanning tree for G. Now let's look at the sum of the weights of the edges in T. Since e has minimal weight among all edges in G, the cost of e is less than or equal to the cost of e^*. Since T^* and T are identical except that edge e^* in T^* is replaced by e in T, the sum of the edge weights in T must be less than or equal to the sum of the edge weights in T^*. But we know that T^* is a minimum spanning tree for G, so T cannot have a smaller sum of edge weights than T^*, and thus T has the same sum, and must be a minimum spanning tree like T^*. (Incidentally, it follows that e^* has the same weight as e, although we do not need that fact here.) ∎

Theorem 7.6.14 suggests that if we want to build a minimum spanning tree in a connected, undirected, weighted graph G, then we can begin by picking out an edge of G having minimal weight, because at least one minimum spanning tree contains the edge we have picked. Then we might consider picking a second edge of minimal weight among the remaining edges and asking whether there is a minimum spanning tree that contains both of the edges we have picked. Indeed, there will be, and if we continue in this way, making sure never to choose an edge that would create a cycle, then we'll eventually have enough edges to make a spanning tree. This idea was first published by Kruskal [13]. It is often found in textbooks paired with Prim's algorithm [18] which is only slightly different. Although they have the same order of complexity, Kruskal's algorithm is faster for sparse graphs, while Prim is recommended for dense graphs. Both of them have several applications, the most popular being random maze generation.

7.6.1   Kruskal's Minimum Spanning Tree Algorithm (1956)

Suppose we are given an undirected, weighted graph $G = (V, E)$ with n vertices. Then the following algorithm will construct a minimum spanning tree $T = (V, E_T)$ for G if G is connected, and if G is not connected, it will detect this fact.

- Initialize the graph T so that its vertex set is V but its edge set E_T is empty. That is, T starts out as the "totally disconnected" graph with vertex set V.
- Let C denote the collection of connected components of T (so that initially C consists of n singleton sets).
- Repeat the following step until $|E_T| = n - 1$ or until the edge set E is exhausted:
- Remove a lowest cost edge e from E;
- if the endpoints of e belong to different connected components of T (i.e., different subsets in C), then
- add e to the set E_T and
- form the union of the two components containing the endpoints of e, creating a single component of the (now modified) collection C.

Claim: If G is connected, then $|E_T|$ will be equal to $n - 1$ when the Repeat loop above ends, and (V, E_T) will be a minimum spanning tree; but if G is not connected, then $|E_T|$ will be less than $n - 1$ when the Repeat loop ends.

The following two theorems prove the two halves of the claim made just above.

Theorem 7.6.15 *If G is connected, then Kruskal's Algorithm does construct a minimum spanning tree.*

Proof Assume that G is connected and has n vertices. We know already that if we choose an edge e_1 of smallest weight from E there will be a minimal spanning tree for G that contains e_1. Since the endpoints of e_1 will be in different connected components of G initially, the algorithm will allow us to add e_1 to the set E_T, and to put the two endpoints of e_1 into a single connected component. Now $T = (V, \{e_1\})$, and the number of connected components in the graph T has decreased by 1 to $n - 1$. If $n = 2$, then the algorithm will stop with the correct number of edges to make T a minimum spanning tree.

Suppose $n > 2$. Since G is connected, it has at least 2 edges (see Corollary 7.6.8), so we can pick a minimal weight edge e_2 from those that remain in E. At least one of the endpoints of e_2 will be different from the endpoints of e_1, so the endpoints of e_2 will belong to different connected components of T. Obeying Kruskal's algorithm we add e_2 to the set E_T and form the union of the two components of T containing the endpoints of e_2. This decreases the number of connected components of T by 1 to $n - 2$.

Now let's prove that G has a minimum spanning tree that contains both e_1 and e_2. We already know that G has a minimum spanning tree, call it T_1 that contains e_1. If e_2 is in T_1, then there is nothing more to prove. If e_2 is not in T_1, then add it to T_1 to create a connected subgraph of G having a cycle containing e_2. Then an argument similar to the one in Theorem 7.6.13 will show that we can remove another edge from that cycle to obtain a minimum spanning tree. We need not remove e_1 if that is part of the cycle, because e_1 and e_2 cannot by themselves form a cycle in an undirected graph.

Now $T = (V, \{e_1, e_2\})$. If $n = 3$, then Kruskal's algorithm will stop with the correct number of edges to make T a minimum spanning tree.

If $n > 3$, then by Theorem 7.6.10 the current number of connected components of T is $n - 2$, which is greater than 1. Since G is connected there must be at least one edge remaining in E whose endpoints are in different connected components of T. Remove minimal cost edges from E until arriving at such an edge (its endpoints are in different components of T), and call this edge e_3. Add this edge to the set E_T and form the union of the two connected components of T containing the endpoints. This reduces the number of connected components of T by 1 to $n - 3$. Now let's prove that G has a minimum spanning tree that contains e_1, e_2, and e_3. We've proved already that G has a minimum spanning tree, call it T_2 that contains e_1 and e_2. If e_3 is in T_2, then there is nothing more to prove. If e_3 is not in T_2, then add it to T_2 to create a connected subgraph of G having a cycle containing e_3. Then we can remove another edge from that cycle to obtain a minimum spanning tree containing e_3. We need not remove e_1 or e_2 if they are part of the cycle, for if the cycle consisted of just e_1, e_2, and e_3, then the endpoints of e_1 and e_2 would have belonged to the same connected component of T before we added e_3, and e_3 would have had both its endpoints in this connected component (which we were careful to avoid).

Now $T = (V, \{e_1, e_2, e_3\})$. If $n = 4$, then Kruskal's algorithm stops with the correct number of edges to make T a minimum spanning tree. If $n > 4$, we can continue on as in the preceding paragraph. The graph T keeps growing in this way until it becomes a minimum spanning tree. ∎

Theorem 7.6.16 *Let G be an undirected graph with n vertices. If G is not connected, then Kruskal's algorithm stops with $|E_T| < n - 1$.*

Proof We'll prove the contrapositive: If Kruskal's algorithm stops with $|E_T| \geq n-1$, then G is connected. Suppose Kruskal's algorithm stops with $|E_T| \geq n - 1$. By the specification of the algorithm, it must then stop with $|E_T| = n - 1$. Since the algorithm never permits T to add an edge that would create a cycle, T is always acyclic, and so when the algorithm stops, T is an acyclic graph with exactly $n - 1$ edges. By Theorem 7.6.11, T must be connected, and since it is a subgraph of G, it follows that G is connected. ∎

Kruskal's Algorithm poses two interesting computer implementation problems for us.

(1) How will we make a program keep track of which edges remain in the set E and efficiently locate the one with smallest edge weight when that is required?

(2) How will we make a program keep track of the connected components of the growing graph T in such a way that given any edge of G we can quickly determine whether its endpoints are in the same component?

The answer to the first question is not hard. We put all the edges of G into a priority queue initially; this should be a min-queue because we want each delete operation on the queue to give the edge with *smallest* edge weight among those still in the queue. It is possible to construct the priority queue in such a way that we do not have to copy all the information in the edge nodes of the graph. We can simply put pointers to the edge nodes into the priority queue, and then follow the pointers whenever we want to examine an edge.

There is one extra thing we'll have to store in each edge node of our adjacency structure for the graph G: both vertices that make up the endpoints of the edge must be present in order for a program to be able to "see" the endpoints when we remove an edge (actually a pointer to an edge) from the priority queue.

The second question about making a program keep track of connected components of T requires a digression on the problem of forming the unions of disjoint sets and determining which set a given element belongs to. The general problem can be stated this way: suppose a program contains a collection of n data objects of some kind, call them $s_1, s_2, \ldots, s_n$. Suppose initially we want the program to treat each object as the sole element of a singleton set, so that initially the program is working with n sets $\{s_1\} \{s_2\} \ldots \{s_n\}$. Suppose the program is required to perform a sequence of union operations on pairs of sets in this collection, so that after a number of such union operations the collection consists of disjoint sets such as

$$\{s_7, s_3, s_{12}, s_4\} \quad \{s_5, s_8\} \quad \{s_6\} \quad \{s_2, s_1, s_{11}, s_9, s_{10}\} \cdots \qquad (7.1)$$

How can the program keep track of these sets, and, for a given object s in the original collection, how do we answer the question "Which set does s belong to?"? This is known as the Union/Find Problem in algorithm theory.

The best known solution to this problem can be found in a data structures textbook, as for example, [18]. First consider the Find Problem: the program is given an object s and asked what set the object belongs to. We handle this problem by having the program select arbitrarily an object from each set to serve as the "representative object" of that set. Then when the program is asked to "find" the set to which s belongs, it returns the representative object of the set containing s. This can be done by making the other objects in the set point either to the representative object of the set or else to some other object in a chain leading to the representative object. Thus, for example, the sets (7.1) might be represented in the way shown in Fig. 7.43 (among many possibilities).

Then when the program is asked to find the set containing some particular s, the program follows a chain of pointers to the representative object of the set, and returns that object.

Now suppose the program is required to form the union of two of these sets (the Union Problem). This is easy to take care of: the program makes the representative object of one of the sets point to the representative object of the other set. To avoid

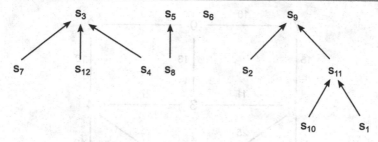

Fig. 7.43 Objects arranged in sets

producing long chains during the formation of unions, we practice *balancing*, which requires us to keep a "size" field in the representative object of each set. The size field tells the number of objects in that set. When a union operation is performed on two sets, we make the representative object of the smaller set point to the representative object of the larger set, and then update the "size" field in the representative object of the combined set. In case of a tie, either can be made to point to the other. If we consistently follow this balancing rule for deciding which root points to the other during union operations, then it is a fact that the height of each tree T in the collection is bounded by $\log_2(n_T)$, where n_T denotes the number of objects in the tree T. You will be asked to prove this fact in Exercise 7.6.24.

There is another technique for shortening the lengths of chains in the disjoint sets. It is called *path compression*, and it is used during Find operations. We'll neglect path compression in what follows, but be aware that path compression can improve the performance of the Kruskal algorithm.

To implement the union and find operations on disjoints sets of these data objects, we require two extra fields in each cell of the array: a "parent" field for pointing to a parent in the tree of data objects making up a set, and a "size" field for keeping track of the size of the set represented by a data object. We initialize all the "parent" fields to the sentinel value -1, and we initialize all the "size" fields to 1 because initially each data object is considered to be in a singleton set by itself.

For a C++ implementation of this algorithm, we recommend the use of the Standard Template Library `set` class and of the `set_union` function.

Now let's practice Kruskal's Minimum Spanning Tree Algorithm on the undirected graph in Fig. 7.44. Suppose that when we read the graph data from a file we end up with the adjacency structure in Fig. 7.45.

To make the algorithm easier to carry out, here is a list of the edges in increasing order by weight:

{2, 4} {1, 3} {4, 6} {0, 3} {5, 8} {1, 7} {0, 7} {4, 5} {5, 6} {0, 2} {1, 8} {1, 5} {3, 4}.

(We would insert these into a priority queue initially if we wanted to do this in the most efficient possible way.)

The first 6 edges in this list in the order of weight can be added to the spanning tree. Then the edge {0, 7} would create a cycle (0, 3, 1, 7, 0), and thus is discarded. {4, 5} can be added, but not {5, 6}. The next one, {0, 8}, is the last one to be added because

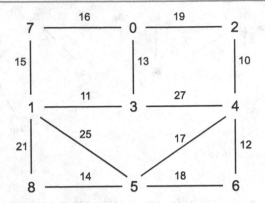

Fig. 7.44 Example of undirected weighted graph

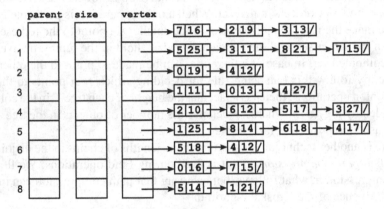

Fig. 7.45 Adjacency structure for the graph in Fig. 7.44

at this point the tree is completely connected. The resulting minimum spanning tree is shown in Fig. 7.46.

7.6.2 Prim's Algorithm (1957)

In 1957, Robert C. Prim provided an alternative algorithm for solving this problem. The idea is to build the free tree incrementally starting with a single vertex and expanding it in each step by adding an unconnected vertex to it. The vertex to be added will be chosen from the list of unconnected vertices that have an edge towards any vertex in the tree. The set of all the edges in the graph that connect a vertex in the tree to one that is not in the tree is called the *frontier*. The algorithm selects the edge of minimal weight from the frontier and adds the edge and the unconnected vertex on it to the tree. When all the vertices in the graph have been added to the tree, the algorithm stops.

Fig. 7.46 Spanning tree obtained by Kruskal's algorithm from the graph in Fig. 7.44

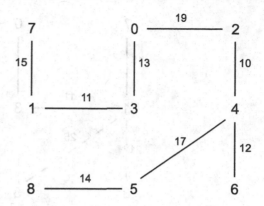

Here are the steps of this algorithm for an undirected graph with n vertices:

- Start with the tree T containing a single arbitrary vertex v_0.
- Initialize the *Frontier* edge set as the edge-list of v_0.
- Repeat the following steps until $|E_T| = n - 1$ or until *Frontier* is empty:
- Select an edge of minimal weight from *Frontier*. Let v_1 be the vertex on this edge belonging to T and v_2 the vertex not belonging to T.
- Add v_2 to T.
- Remove all the edges in *Frontier* that contain v_2.
- For every edge $\{v_2, v_3\}$ in the edge-list of v_2:
  if v_3 is not in T, add the edge to *Frontier*.

In terms of data structures, we can assume that T will be stored as an object of the Graph class. For the *Frontier*, we need a container type of data structure that allows us to find the object of minimum weight. We can either store it as a priority min-queue, or as a sorted linked list.

The priority queue will make the extraction of the edge of minimum weight of complexity $O(\log(m))$ where m is the number of edges in the graph. However, searching for edges containing v_2 will be linear over m, and removing each of them will require a number of operations that is $O(\log(m))$. Thus, removing all the edges containing v_2 from *Frontier* would require $O(m \log(m))$ operations. Inserting a new edge into *Frontier* is $O(\log(m))$ in this case. As we have at most $n - 1$ such edges and we know that for any connected graph $n - 1 \leq m$, the complexity of iteration of the loop in the algorithm would be $O(m \log(m))$. The loop will require precisely $n - 1$ iterations, which means that the complexity of this algorithm is $O(nm \log(m))$ in this case.

With a sorted list, the operation of removing the edge of minimal weight will be bounded by constants. Searching the list and removing all the edges containing v_2 is a linear operation. Inserting an edge into the frontier would take linear time over m for every edge. Thus, the complexity of every step would be $O(nm)$. Since $m \leq n(n-1)$ for any graph, this implementation is less efficient than using a priority queue.

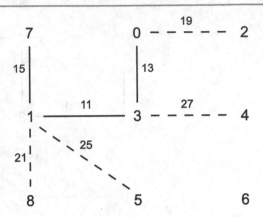

Fig. 7.47 Example of tree T and the $Frontier$ set (dotted lines) after 3 steps of Prim's algorithm applied to the graph in Fig. 7.44

Assuming that we use a priority queue data structure to represent the $Frontier$, the entire algorithm has a complexity $O(nm \log(m))$. Since m is no larger than $n(n-1)$, we can also say that the complexity is also $O(n^3 \log(n))$.

Let's examine a few steps of Prim's algorithm on the graph in Fig. 7.44. Let's assume that the random initial vertex v_0 is the one of label 3.

Step 1. We start with $T = (V_T = \{3\}, E_T = \emptyset)$ (an empty edge set) and $Frontier$ $= \{\{1, 3\}, \{3, 4\}, \{0, 3\}\}$. Of these three edges, $\{1, 3\}$ has the lowest weight (11), so this is the chosen one. Thus, 1 will be added to T, the edge $\{1, 3\}$ is removed from $Frontier$, and the edges $\{1, 7\}$, $\{1, 8\}$, and $\{1, 5\}$ are added to it.

Step 2. Now $T = (V_T = \{1, 3\}, E_T = \{\{1, 3\}\})$ and $Frontier = \{\{3, 4\}, \{0, 3\}, \{1, 7\}, \{1, 8\}, \{1, 5\}\}$. The edge of minimal weight in $Frontier$ is $\{0, 3\}$ with a weight of 13. Thus, the vertex 0 is added to the tree, the edge $\{0, 3\}$ is removed from $Frontier$, and the edges $\{0, 7\}$ and $\{0, 2\}$ are added to it.

Step 3. Now $T = (V_T = \{0, 1, 3\}, E_T = \{\{1, 3\}, \{0, 3\}\})$ and $Frontier = \{\{3, 4\}, \{1, 7\}, \{1, 8\}, \{1, 5\}, \{0, 7\}, \{0, 2\}\}$. The edge of minimal weight in $Frontier$ is $\{1, 7\}$ with a weight of 15. Thus, the vertex 7 is added to the tree and both the edges $\{1, 7\}$ and $\{0, 7\}$ are removed from $Frontier$ because they connect the newly added vertex to one that is already in T. No new edges are added to $Frontier$ because the vertex 7 is not connected to any vertex that is not in T.

Figure 7.47 shows T after these 3 steps, with $Frontier$ represented by dotted lines.

After a few more steps, Prim's algorithm also terminates with T being the graph in Fig. 7.46.

Prim's algorithm is a frequent choice for maze generation, which has direct application to games. A labyrinth can be described as a two-dimensional table where each

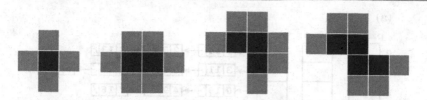

Fig. 7.48 Example of a few steps of Prim's algorithm building a maze with space cells drawn in black and the frontier represented by gray cells

cell represents a location in the arena, and can be either a space or a wall. A maze is a labyrinth with a special property: that each space cell is connected to all of the others by a unique simple path.

Thus, we can represent a labyrinth as a graph. Every space cell of the table becomes a vertex of the graph. We add an edge in the graph for any two space cells that are adjacent in the labyrinth. Thus, a path in the graph translates to a path that can be walked in the labyrinth.

To generate a maze, we can imagine that we are building a randomized spanning tree in an initial graph representing a labyrinth with no walls and where all the weights are 1. We can apply either Prim's algorithm or Kruskal's, but practically Prim's is used more often. Such an algorithm starts with a random cell in the table that is transformed into a space. The frontier initially contains all the walls adjacent to it. For each step, a random wall is chosen from the frontier to be converted to a space. The frontier is then updated to remove all the walls that are neighbors to more than one space cell, and to add all the walls adjacent only to the newly added space. When the frontier becomes empty, the algorithm stops. The result is a maze (Fig. 7.48).

7.6.3   Exercises

7.6.17 Suppose a computer program has 15 objects in an array, in locations 0 through 14. Let the objects be referred to by the index of the cell in which they are located. Using the technique described on pp. 407 and 408, show how the program could perform the following sequence of operations: Union(2, 8), Union(14, 5), Union(3, 11), Union(10, 2), Union(8, 3), Union(6, 7), Union(12, 14), Union(9, 14), Union(3, 5), Find(11), Find(9), Find(4).

7.6.18 Using Kruskal's and Prim's Algorithms, find (if possible) a minimum spanning tree for graphs having the adjacency structures in Fig. 7.49a, b.

7.6.19 Prove Corollary 7.6.8, using theorems that preceded it.

7.6.20 Prove Theorem 7.6.9 by the method of contradiction. Your proof should begin with words like these: "Take any connected undirected graph G having exactly n vertices and exactly $n - 1$ edges. Suppose (for purposes of contradiction) that G

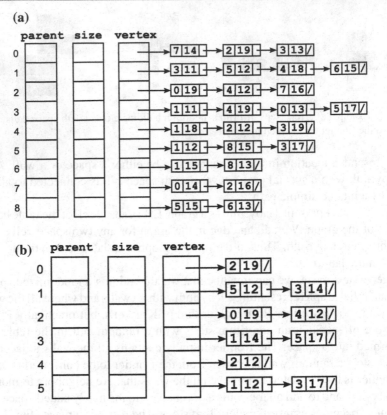

Fig. 7.49 Graphs for Exercise 7.6.18 **a** (top) and **b** (bottom)

contains a cycle." The proof will need to use some of the theorems that precede Theorem 7.6.9.

7.6.21 Prove that every acyclic undirected graph having exactly n vertices has at most $n - 1$ edges. Use the theorems proved in this section.

7.6.22 Let G be a connected, undirected graph with exactly n vertices. Prove that if G has more than $n - 1$ edges, then G has more than one spanning tree.

7.6.23 Let G be a connected, undirected, weighted graph. Suppose no two edges of G have the same weight. Prove that there is exactly one minimum spanning tree for G.

7.6.24 Suppose we begin with a collection of singleton sets, each implemented as a tree with just one node, and we perform a sequence of union operations on these sets, being careful at each stage to follow the rule described on p. 407: make the root of the tree with the smaller number of nodes point to the root of the tree with the larger number of nodes. Prove that for every tree T produced in this way, the height of T, call it h_T, and the number of nodes in T, call it n_T, satisfy the inequality $2^{h_T} \le n_T$. (From this it follows that $h_T \le \log_2(n_T)$, as stated on p. 438.) HINT: Use weak induction to prove that the following predicate is true for all positive integers m. $S(m)$: at the m-th stage (after $m - 1$ union operations have been performed), every tree T in the collection satisfies the inequality $2^{h_T} \le n_T$.

7.7   Topological Sorting of Digraphs (Task Sequencing)

Suppose we are given a collection of tasks that need to be performed. Suppose, moreover, that some of the tasks must be completed before others can be started. Finally, suppose that only one task can be done at a time, and once begun, that task must be carried to completion before another is begun. A very natural problem in such a situation is to find, if possible, a non-repetitive listing of all the tasks in such an order that for every pair of tasks x and y, if x must be completed before y is begun, then x precedes y in the list. A description of this problem and an outline of an algorithm to solve it can be found in [19].

One way of visualizing the situation just described is to represent the tasks as vertices of a directed graph in which an edge from a vertex x to a vertex y represents a requirement that task x be completed before task y is begun. Then we have transformed the problem into an instance of the following general graph problem:

Definition 7.7.1   The Topological Sorting Problem: Given a digraph G, find, if possible, a non-repetitive listing of all its vertices in such an order that for every pair of vertices x and y, if the edge $(x, \ y)$ is in the graph G, then x precedes y in the list. Any listing of the vertices with these properties is called a *topological ordering* of the vertices, and finding such a listing is called *sorting the vertices into a topological order*.

For the four small graphs in Fig. 7.50 we can solve the topological sorting problem simply by inspection. In the first, 0,2,1,3 and 2,0,1,3 are topological orderings, as are 0,1,2,3 and 0,1,3,2. In the second graph, 0,1,2,3 and 0,2,1,3 are the only topological orderings. In the third graph, 0,2,1,3 is the only topological ordering. The fourth graph contains a cycle, which makes solving the topological problem impossible for that graph.

Note that when an edge (x, y) belongs to the digraph G, we do not require that the vertex x immediately precede the vertex y in a topological ordering. All that we require is that x be somewhere in the list ahead of vertex y.

Now let's attack the problem of constructing an algorithm for determining whether a topological ordering of the vertices is possible and finding such an ordering when one can exist. Under what conditions is a topological ordering impossible? The fourth example in Fig. 7.50 illustrates what happens if there is a cycle in the graph: a

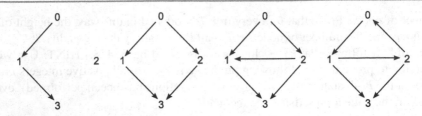

Fig. 7.50 Examples of graphs for the topological sorting problem

topological ordering is impossible because no matter which vertex one picks in the cycle, all the vertices in the cycle—including itself—must follow it in a topological ordering. Thus, we can say that if a digraph contains a cycle, then it cannot be topologically ordered. Contrapositively, if a graph can be topologically ordered, then it does not contain a cycle.

We have just seen that a *necessary* condition for a digraph to admit a topological ordering is that the graph be acyclic. Is this also a *sufficient* condition? That is, if a digraph is acyclic, then can we be sure that it will be possible to give it a topological ordering? Yes, and the proof will be by mathematical induction. We will need the following lemma and its contrapositive.

Lemma 7.7.2 *If each vertex in a digraph has at least one edge that goes to some other vertex, then the digraph contains at least one cycle.*

Proof Let G be a digraph with the property that *for every vertex x in G*, there is an edge of the form (x, y) in G. Pick any vertex v_1 in G. Then there exists at least one vertex y in G such that (v_1, y) is in the graph. Pick such a vertex and call it v_2. Similarly, pick a vertex v_3 such that (v_2, v_3) is in the graph. If v_3 is the same as v_1, then we've found a cycle. If not, pick a vertex v_4 such that (v_3, v_4) is in the graph. If v_4 is the same as v_1 or v_2, then we've found a cycle. If not, keep going. Since the graph contains only finitely many vertices, eventually this process must lead to a repetition of some vertex, which will then give us a cycle. ∎

Corollary 7.7.3 *If a digraph is acyclic, then the graph contains at least one vertex that has no vertices adjacent to it (i.e., no edge emerging from it).*

Proof This is simply the contrapositive of the statement of the lemma above. ∎

In a digraph a vertex that has no vertices adjacent to it (i.e. has no outgoing edges) is called a *sink*.

Theorem 7.7.4 *If a digraph is acyclic, then it can be topologically ordered.*

Proof The proof will be by weak induction on the number of vertices in the graph. Let $S(n)$ denote the following predicate:

"Every acyclic digraph with n vertices can be topologically ordered."

The statement is trivially true when $n = 1$. For the inductive step of the proof, take any positive integer k for which $S(k)$ is true, i.e., for which the following is true:

"Every acyclic digraph with k vertices can be topologically ordered."

We'll prove that $S(k + 1)$ must be true as well. $S(k + 1)$ is the proposition

"Every acyclic digraph with $k + 1$ vertices can be topologically ordered."

Take any acyclic digraph G with $k + 1$ vertices. By Corollary 7.7.3, G has at least one sink, i.e., a vertex that has no edge going to another vertex. Pick such a vertex and call it x. Then consider the subgraph H obtained by eliminating from G the vertex x and all the edges (if any) that go to x. This digraph H has only k vertices. Certainly H contains no cycle, for such a cycle would also be a cycle in G. By the inductive hypothesis, H can be topologically ordered. Having listed its vertices as $v_1, v_2, \ldots, v_k$, we can now add the sink x to the end of the list and obtain thereby a topological ordering of G. The reason for this is that any vertex v for which (v, x) is in the graph G must precede x in the augmented list, and there are no edges of the form (x, y) in G. ∎

A pleasant consequence of having proved the three preceding propositions is that the proofs give us a clue for creating an algorithm for solving the topological sorting problem: we can begin by searching the digraph for a sink. If we cannot find one, we know that the digraph will not admit a topological ordering. If we do find a sink, this does not yet guarantee that there is a topological ordering of the digraph (there may be a cycle that we have not yet detected), but at least we know that the sink can be the last vertex in a topological ordering of the vertices. We can start up an empty "topological list" (a separate data structure) and place the vertex number of the sink at the end of it. Then we can mark the sink as "removed" from the digraph (conceptually, without actually altering the graph), and then search for a sink in the reduced digraph. If we find one, we can place its vertex number in the topological list in front of the first sink and mark it as "removed". Continuing in this manner, we can reduce the digraph to empty and build a list that gives a topological ordering of its vertices, provided there are no cycles in the graph.

Using the standard list adjacency structure, it is easy to spot a sink or determine that there is none: we just start at the top of the vertex array and scan down looking for an empty edge list. If we find one, it is a sink. But this method does not work well when searching for sinks in successively reduced graphs. As it turns out, there is a much more efficient way to find sinks (or cycles) in reduced graphs. Start at any vertex x and mark it as "reached". Follow an edge out of x to some vertex y and mark that as "reached". Follow an edge out of y to some vertex z. etc. If we reach a vertex with no edge out of it, that's a sink and we mark it as "removed" and put its vertex number at the front of the list that will become the topological ordering. Then we can backtrack to the previous vertex, call it v, and re-start the forward search along a different edge out of v. If there is none, backtrack again and re-start the forward search. A forward search should never be allowed to go to a vertex that's been marked as "removed". If a forward search goes to a non-removed vertex that been previously reached, that indicates the presence of a cycle.

If the process described above eventually backtracks all the way to the vertex from which the searches began, that vertex can be marked as "removed", and then a scan down the vertex array for a non-reached vertex can be made. If one is found, a new search can be started from that vertex.

It should be obvious now that the process described above consists of a sequence of depth-first searches for sinks in successively reduced graphs. Figures 7.51 and 7.52 give an implementation of these depth-first searches using recursion. The driver (Fig. 7.51) for the recursion (Fig. 7.52) has the job of scanning down the vertex array looking for non-reached vertices from which to launch the recursive searches. The functions are written in a mixture of code and pseudo-code.

Example 7.7.5 Let's use the algorithm in Figs. 7.51 and 7.52 to search for a topological ordering of the vertices in the digraph having the adjacency structure shown in Fig. 7.53.

Solution We begin in Fig. 7.51 by initializing all cells of the arrays `reached[]` and `removed[]` to `false`. We also initialize `cycle_found` to `false` and make the `topolist` empty. We mark 0 as reached and start a depth-first search from vertex 0 (see Fig. 7.52). Vertex 4 in the edge-list of 0, and it is neither removed nor reached, so we mark 4 as reached and continue the depth-first search from 4. Vertex 6 is at the front of the edge list of 4, and it is neither removed nor reached, so we mark 6 as reached and continue the depth-first search from 6. Vertex 9 is a neighbor of 6, and it is neither removed nor reached, so we mark 9 as reached and continue the depth-first search from 9. Vertex 8 in the edge list of 9, and it is neither removed nor reached, so we mark 8 as reached and continue the depth-first search from 8. The edge list of 8 is empty, so we've reached a sink. We mark 8 as removed and place the number 8 in the empty `topolist`. We backtrack to vertex 9 and discover it has no more neighbors. Thus 9 is a sink in the reduced graph. We mark it removed and insert 9 at the front of `topolist`. We backtrack to vertex 6 and discover it has no more neighbors, so it is now a sink. We mark it removed and insert 6 at the front of `topolist`. We backtrack to vertex 4 and find its next neighbor 7. Since 7 is neither removed nor reached, we mark it reached and make a depth-first search from 7. Its only neighbor is 8, which has been removed, so we backtrack to 4, which has no more neighbors. We mark 4 as removed and insert a 4 at the front of `topolist`. We backtrack to 0, mark it as removed, and insert it into `topolist`. We backtrack, and this moves execution of the code back into the driver (Fig. 7.51). The for loop increments v to 1,

```
// The functions below assume a definition of a struct data type named "node"
// with two members, one of type int and the other of type node*.  The first
// function is a driver for the second, which is recursive.  The first function
// returns a NULL-terminated linked list of nodes containing a topological
// ordering of the vertices of the digraph, or NULL if the digraph has a cycle.
// reached and removed must be added as data members to the class Graph.

node * Graph:: topological_ordering ()  // to be used only for digraphs
{
    reached = new bool[num_vertices];
    removed = new bool[num_vertices];
    bool cycle_found = false;
    node * topolist = NULL;
    int  v;

    Initialize all the cells of the arrays reached[] and removed[] to false.

    for (v = 0; v < num_vertices && ! cycle_found; ++v)
    {
      if (! reached[v])
      {
        reached[v] = true;
        dfs_topological_order(v, cycle_found, topolist);   // Call recursive function.
        if (cycle_found)
           Deallocate all the nodes in topolist and set topolist to NULL.
      }
    }
    return topolist;
}
```

Fig. 7.51 Driver algorithm ordering the vertices of a graph in topological order

```
// This recursive function is always called with cycle_found false. The
// vertex v will have been marked as reached immediately before the call, and
// removed[v] will be false.  If this function returns with cycle_found still
// false, then vertex v, and possibly many other vertices, will have been marked
// as "removed", and copies of them will have been placed in the topolist.

void Graph::dfs_topological_order (int v, & cycle_found, node * & topolist)
{
  node * p;

  for (p = vertex[v].edge_list; p != NULL && ! cycle_found; p = p->next)
  {
    if (removed[p->neighbor])    ;  // Do nothing; go to the next neighbor of v.
    else if (reached[p->neighbor])
      cycle_found = true;
    else
    {
      reached[p->neighbor] = true;
      dfs_topological_order (p->neighbor, cycle_found, topolist);
    }
  }

  if (! cycle_found)
    Mark v as "removed" and attach a new node, containing v, to the front of  topolist.
}
```

Fig. 7.52 Recursive algorithm ordering the vertices of a graph in topological order

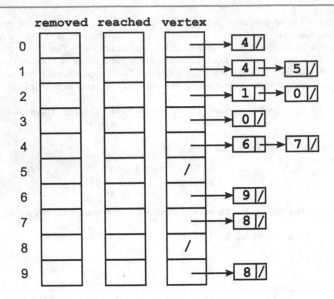

Fig. 7.53 A digraph given by its adjacency list structure

which has not been reached, so we mark 1 as reached and start up a new depth-first search. Neighbor 4 is removed. Neighbor 5 is neither removed nor reached, so we mark 5 as reached and continue the depth-first search from 5. We see that 5 is a sink, so we mark 5 as removed and insert a 5 at the front of `topolist`. We backtrack to 1, which has no other neighbors. The for loop in Fig. 7.51 increments v to 2, which has not been reached, so we mark 2 as reached and start up a new depth-first search. The neighbors of 2 have already been reached, so we mark 2 as removed and insert a 2 at the front of `topolist`. Execution moves back to the driver and the for loop increments v to 3 and marks it as reached. A depth-first search finds its neighbor 0 has been reached. Execution returns to the driver. All vertices of the graph have now been removed. The driver returns a pointer to the `topolist` (3,2,5,1,0,7,4,6,9,8).

7.7.1 Exercises

7.7.6 (a) Find, if possible, a topological ordering for the vertices in the digraph represented by the structure in Fig. 7.54.

(b) Find, if possible, a topological ordering for the vertices in the digraph in Fig. 7.55.

7.7.7 Find, if possible, a topological ordering for the vertices in the digraph whose adjacency structure is shown in Fig. 7.56.

7.7.8 Give pseudo-code for an algorithm that searches any given digraph just for the purpose of determining whether the graph is acyclic. Also give such an algorithm for undirected graphs.

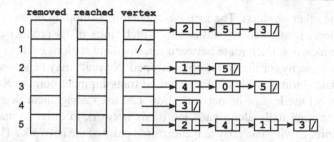

Fig. 7.54 Digraph given by its adjacency list structure

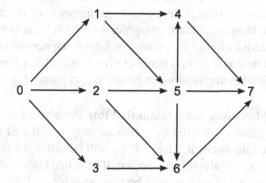

Fig. 7.55 A digraph given by its adjacency list structure

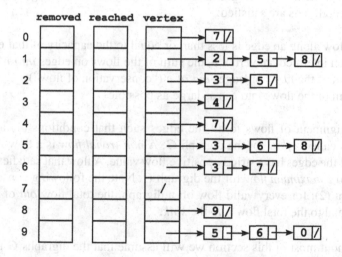

Fig. 7.56 Graph given by its adjacency list

7.8   Maximum Flow in Weighted Digraphs

Suppose a production firm needs to make daily shipments of as many units as possible of its product to some location at which the product is consumed (or sold, or used in making some other product). The firm has available a shipping network consisting of a collection of intermediate stations to which units of its product can be sent daily on some carrier. Each route between intermediate stations of this network has a fixed daily capacity for the units being shipped. No units may be stored overnight at intermediate stations (which are also called transshipment points). Knowing the capacities of all the legs of its network, how can the management determine how many units to send daily along each leg of its network in order to maximize the number of units arriving each day at the terminal point of the network? This problem is, from a graph theory point of view, the same as many other problems involving the flow of goods or material from an origin to a destination. Such problems occur frequently in practical settings, often with huge numbers of transshipment points, so it is important to have an efficient computer algorithm for solving them. Detailed examples of applications to airline control or image segmentation can be found in [9]. The maximum flow algorithm is connected to the simplex algorithm and to linear programming, which has applications in business and games [4].

Definition 7.8.1 Maximum (or Maximal) Flow Problem: Let G be a weighted digraph with one vertex, s, having no edges coming into it and another vertex, t, having no edges coming out of it. The vertex s will be called the *source*, the vertex t will be called the *sink*, and all other vertices will be called *intermediate vertices*. The weights of the edges, all of which must be non-negative, will be called *capacities*. Find an assignment of *flows* (non-negative numbers) to all the edges such that the following conditions are satisfied:

(1) each flow along an edge is less than or equal to the capacity of that edge;
(2) for each intermediate vertex v, the sum of the flows on edges *into* v is equal to the sum of the flows on edges *out of* v ("conservation of flow");
(3) the sum of the flows into t is as large as possible.

Any assignment of flows to all the edges such that conditions (1) and (2) are satisfied, is called a *flow* for the digraph G. A *non-trivial flow* is a flow in which at least one of the edges has a strictly positive flow value. A flow that satisfies condition (3) is called a *maximum flow* for the digraph G. Note the following consequence of requirement (2): for every valid flow on a digraph, the total flow *out* of the *source* must be equal to the total flow *into* the *sink*.

Throughout most of this section we will assume that the digraphs G that we are considering have at most one edge between each pair of vertices. That is, if there is an edge from a vertex x to a vertex y in G, then there is no edge from y to x. Toward the end of this section we will see how to deal with digraphs that do not satisfy this restriction.

Let's try to get some intuition about the Maximum Flow Problem by looking at a small example. In the digraph in Fig. 7.57, the vertex 0 is the source and 3 is the sink. One flow for the graph is shown in the list to the right of the diagram. Note that the conservation of flow property is satisfied.

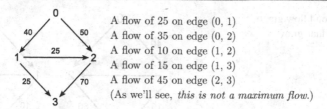

A flow of 25 on edge (0, 1)
A flow of 35 on edge (0, 2)
A flow of 10 on edge (1, 2)
A flow of 15 on edge (1, 3)
A flow of 45 on edge (2, 3)
(As we'll see, *this is not a maximum flow*.)

Fig. 7.57 A weighted graph and a flow assigned to it

Fig. 7.58 First flow graph
(*left*) and residual graph
(*right*)

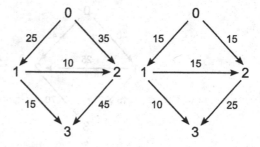

When a flow has been found for such a digraph, the graph obtained by replacing
the capacities by the flows assigned to the edges is called a *flow graph* for the given
problem. The flow graph for the flow listed in Fig. 7.57 is shown on the left in
Fig. 7.58. The edge (1, 2), which has capacity 25, has been assigned a flow of 10,
which leaves a *residual capacity* of 15. The *residual graph* for a flow on a digraph is
the graph obtained by replacing the original capacities of the edges by their residual
capacities. The residual graph for the flow listed in Fig. 7.57 is shown on the right in
Fig. 7.58.

When a non-trivial flow F^* can be found in the residual graph for a flow F, then the
flow F is not a maximum flow because we can add the flow values of F^* to the flow
values for F to get a larger total flow. How might we go about finding a non-trivial
flow in the residual graph? One method is to search (perhaps using breadth-first or
depth first methods) for a path from the source to the sink such that the residual
capacity on each edge of the path is greater than zero. A path having that property
is called an *augmenting path* in the residual graph. When such a path is found, the
smallest capacity along that path serves as a limiting value on the amount of extra
flow that can be pushed along that path. We can add that amount to each edge on the
path to produce an improved *flow* graph, and we can subtract that amount from each
edge on the path in the *residual* graph, reducing to zero the residual capacity on at
least one edge. When the residual capacity on an edge is reduced to zero, we regard
the edge as removed from the residual graph.

Let's return to the example we were considering. In the residual graph shown
in Fig. 7.58, the edges (0, 1), (1, 2), (2, 3) form an augmenting path. The smallest
residual capacity on that path is 15, so we can add 15 to the flow on each of the edges
of that path. This gives us the flow graph and residual graph shown in Fig. 7.59.

Fig. 7.59 Second flow graph
(*left*) and residual graph
(*right*)

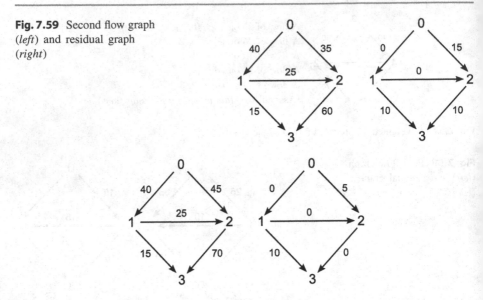

Fig. 7.60 Third flow graph (*left*) and residual graph (*right*)

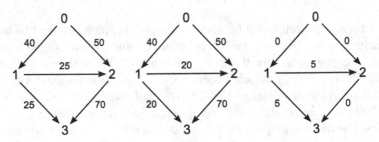

Fig. 7.61 Original graph (*left*), flow graph (*center*) and residual graph (*right*)

There is an augmenting path in this new residual graph. The edges (0, 2), (2, 3) form an augmenting path with smallest residual capacity 10. If we add 10 to the flow on each of these edges, we obtain the flow and residual graphs shown in Fig. 7.60.

Examination of the new residual graph shows that there are no longer any paths from the source to the sink. It appears to be impossible to find a better flow than the one we have found, and so it is tempting to report that we have found a maximum flow for our weighted digraph. The total number of units we can send from source to sink appears to be at most $15 + 70 = 85$. Interestingly enough, however, there is a better flow. It involves sending 5 more units along the edge (0, 2), "canceling" 5 units of flow along edge (1, 2), and sending 5 more units along the edge (1, 3). The resulting flow and residual graphs are shown in Fig. 7.61, and illustrate the fact that we can ship more than 85 units from source to sink.

The total flow out of the source is now 90 (which is also the total flow into the sink, of course). Do we now have a maximum flow in our digraph? Certainly we must, since it is impossible to ship more than 90 units out of the source.

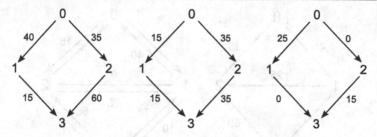

Fig. 7.62 Digraph (*left*), flow graph (*center*), and residual graph (*right*)

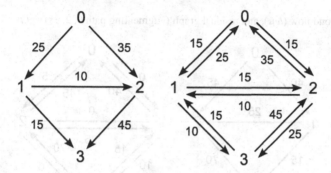

Fig. 7.63 Initial given flow (*left*), residual graph (augmenting path 0, 1, 2, 3) (*right*)

Suppose we have a flow F on a weighted digraph G. Suppose further that the total flow out of the source is less than the total capacity of the edges out of the source, and the total flow into the sink is less than the total capacity of the edges going into the sink. This was the situation for the flow shown in Fig. 7.58. Do these conditions mean that a better flow than F can always be found on G? Not always. The digraph and flow diagram shown in Fig. 7.62 show an example in which these conditions are met but no improved flow can be found.

In general, we must solve the problem of determining whether a given flow F on a weighted digraph G is a maximum flow. One way to find out is to introduce into the residual graph for F a collection of fictitious "push-back edges" in the opposite directions from edges having positive flow. The "capacity" of any such push-back edge is the flow in the direction opposite to that edge. If we had introduced these edges when we started working with our graph in Fig. 7.57, we would have obtained the following flow and residual graphs shown in Figs. 7.63, 7.64, 7.65 and 7.66.

Now the residual graph has no path from source to sink because we regard an edge with zero capacity as removed from the graph. Thus, it certainly cannot have an augmenting path. This is the test for determining whether a given flow is maximal.

How can we implement these ideas in a computer program? It turns out that a slight modification of the usual adjacency structure works best. For each directed edge (v, w) we create an edge node that carries the following information:

• the vertex v from which a flow can occur;

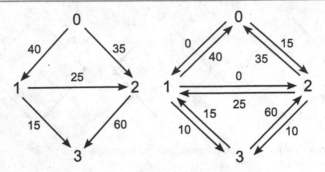

Fig. 7.64 Second flow (*left*), and residual graph (augmenting path 0, 2, 3) (*right*)

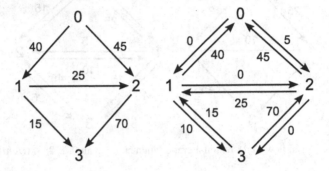

Fig. 7.65 Third flow (*left*), residual graph (augmenting path 0, 2, 1, 3) (*right*)

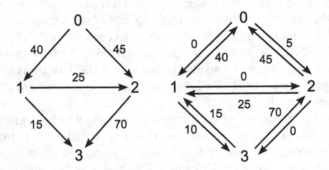

Fig. 7.66 Fourth flow (*left*), and residual graph (no augmenting path) (*right*)

- the vertex w to which the flow can occur;
- the residual capacity of the edge (v, w); initially this will be the capacity of the edge;
- the flow that has been assigned so far to the edge.
  This node is then placed *simultaneously in the edge-list of v and the edge-list of w*. Since the node is in two lists at the same time, we require *two pointers* to the other parts of the two lists; that is, the node will also carry the following two fields:
- a pointer to the remaining edge-list of the vertex v;

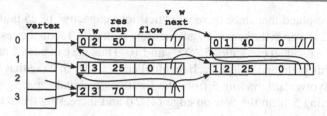

Fig. 7.67 Data structure for the weighted graph and the flow graph in Figs. 7.57 and 7.58

• a pointer to the remaining edge-list of the vertex w.

| v | w | resid-capac v to w | flow v to w | v next | w next |

As an example, let's return to the directed weighted graph given in Fig. 7.58 on p. 421. Suppose the edges are given to us in the following order. Let's see how the maximum flow adjacency structure would be constructed for this graph.
Edge from 0 to 1 with capacity 40.
Edge from 0 to 2 with capacity 50.
Edge from 1 to 2 with capacity 25.
Edge from 1 to 3 with capacity 25.
Edge from 2 to 3 with capacity 70.
The source is vertex 0 and the sink is vertex 3.

Now suppose we take the maximum flow adjacency structure we have just constructed and enter into it the flows that we were given initially in Fig. 7.58. (Don't worry yet about where these flows came from.) The result is shown in Fig. 7.67.

With a little thought you should now be able to use the structure shown in Fig. 7.67 to visualize the flow graph and the residual graph in Fig. 7.58.

Now let's follow the same steps we did on pp. 421–424 in which we assign ("push") units of flow along augmenting paths in the residual graph until no greater flow is possible out of the source 0.

First we looked at the augmenting path 0, 1, 2, 3. In the structure in Fig. 7.67 we can see that this is an augmenting path (don't worry yet about how that path was obtained). We can also see that the maximum *additional* number of units that can be pushed along this path is 15 (the smallest of the residual capacities on the edges (0, 1), (1, 2), (2, 3)). We can modify Fig. 7.67 by adding 15 to the flow on each of these three edges, and reducing the residual capacity on each of those edges by 15. You should now be able to use the modified structure to visualize the flow graph and residual graph shown in Fig. 7.59.

Next we looked at the augmenting path 0, 2, 3. In Fig. 7.67 (modified) we can see that this is an augmenting path and that the maximum *additional* number of units that can be pushed along this path is 10 (the smallest of the residual capacities on the edges (0, 2) and (2, 3)). In the structure above we add 10 to the flow on both of these edges and subtract 10 from their residual capacities. Now you should be able to use Fig. 7.67 see the flow graph and residual graph shown in Fig. 7.60.

Finally, we noted that since there is a "fictitious capacity" of 25 units backward from vertex 2 to vertex 1, there is an augmenting path 0, 2, 1, 3 in the residual graph. Its edges have residual capacities 5, "25", and 10. Thus we can push 5 more units of flow along this path, and reduce each residual capacity by 5. Note that for the edge (2, 1) this involves *subtracting* 5 from the fictitious residual capacity of that edge (i.e., subtracting 5 from the *flow* on edge (1, 2)) and increasing the actual residual capacity of the edge (1, 2).

At this point a search of the adjacency structure shows that there is no augmenting path from the source to the sink, not even one that uses a fictitious residual capacity. Thus we have found a way to have a maximum flow on the graph:

Ship 50 units from vertex 0 to vertex 2.

Ship 40 units from vertex 0 to vertex 1.

Ship 20 units from vertex 1 to vertex 3.

Ship 20 units from vertex 1 to vertex 2.

Ship 70 units from vertex 2 to vertex 3.

It is easy to check that the flow into each intermediate vertex is equal to the flow out of that vertex, and that the flow out of the source is equal to the flow into the sink. The total maximum flow is 90.

It is apparent that we are following a kind of algorithm on the maximum flow adjacency structure. The steps are as follows:

(1) Search for an augmenting path in the residual graph from the source to the sink, keeping track at all times of the minimum residual capacity of the edges along the path. If such a path can be found, go to step (2); otherwise, go to step (3). Keep in mind that a flow from the first vertex to the second can be regarded as a residual capacity in the opposite direction.

(2) In each edge along the augmenting path, increase the flow by the minimum capacity found in step (1), and decrease the residual capacity by the same amount. Now go back to step (1).

(3) A maximum flow in the graph has been found. Print out each edge and the flow to be assigned to that edge.

The algorithm just described was proposed by L. R. Ford and D. R. Fulkerson in 1962. Since it increases the total flow at every stage, it might appear that the algorithm is bound to terminate eventually with a maximum flow. That is, in fact, true if all the capacities of the edges are integers, or even if they are rational numbers. There are examples, however, that show that when some of the capacities of the edges are irrational numbers, the algorithm may fail to terminate. The proofs of these assertions will be omitted, since they are surprisingly complicated.

The Ford-Fulkerson algorithm is actually not a genuine algorithm because it does not specify in a precise way how the searches for augmenting paths should be conducted. This oversight can allow for extremely inefficient solutions to the problem. To take a famous example, suppose we are given the weighted digraph described below:

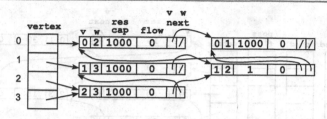

Fig. 7.68 Data structure representing a flow graph

edge from 0 to 1 with capacity 1000;
edge from 0 to 2 with capacity 1000;
edge from 1 to 2 with capacity 1;
edge from 1 to 3 with capacity 1000;
edge from 2 to 3 with capacity 1000.
The source is vertex 0 and the sink is vertex 3.

When we build a maximum flow adjacency structure for this graph, it might look like the structure in Fig. 7.68.

Now let's suppose we run the Ford-Fulkerson algorithm in the following way: each time we begin a new search, let's choose an edge out of the source different from the one we chose on the previous search. Also, whenever we're at vertex 1 let's try to go to vertex 2, and whenever we're at vertex 2 let's try to go to vertex 1. It is not hard to see that this algorithm for finding the augmenting paths pushes 1 additional unit of flow along each newly found augmenting path, and thus the algorithm requires 2000 paths to be found. A better algorithm would first find augmenting path 0, 2, 3 and push 1000 units along it, and then find augmenting path 0, 1, 3 and push 1000 units along it, and terminate.

The preceding example illustrates in a very simple case that if we choose augmenting paths badly, it may take much longer for the algorithm to terminate than it should. This can be overcome to a large extent by choosing our augmenting path at each stage to be the *shortest path* in the residual graph, as measured by number of edges. This heuristic was proposed by J. Edmunds and R. Karp in 1972. They proved that when the breadth-first search given in Fig. 7.21 is used to find the shortest path at each stage, then the running time for the algorithm is $O(n \cdot m^2)$, where n is the number of vertices and m is the number of edges.

Let's use the Edmunds-Karp algorithm to find the maximum flow in the following weighted digraph:
edge from 0 to 1 with capacity 30;
edge from 0 to 2 with capacity 10;
edge from 1 to 4 with capacity 20;
edge from 2 to 3 with capacity 15;
edge from 2 to 4 with capacity 40;
edge from 3 to 5 with capacity 50;
edge from 4 to 5 with capacity 25;
the source is vertex 0 and the sink is vertex 5.

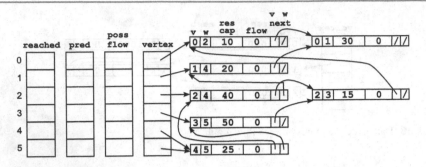

Fig. 7.69 Initial flow graph

If we use the data above to build a maximum flow adjacency structure, it might look like the one shown in Fig. 7.69.

We begin with a breadth-first search starting from the source 0 with destination the sink 5. We initialize the search by marking 0 as reached and putting 0 into an empty queue Q.

- Remove 0 from Q and see what can now be reached from 0 along edges of positive residual capacity.
- We can reach 2 (not yet reached) with a residual capacity of 10; mark 2 as reached; set its predecessor field to 0; set its "possible flow" field to 10; enqueue 2.
- We can reach 1 (not yet reached) with a residual capacity of 30; mark 1 as reached; set its predecessor field to 0; set its "possible flow" field to 30; enqueue 1.
- There are no more vertices that can be reached from 0 along edges with positive residual capacity.
- Dequeue 2 and see what can now be reached from 2 along edges of positive residual capacity.
- We can reach 4 (not yet reached) with a residual capacity of 40; mark 4 as reached; set its predecessor field to 2; set its "possible flow" field to 10 (not 40, because we know that we can push only 10 units to 2); enqueue 4.
- We can reach 3 (not yet reached) with a residual capacity of 15; mark 3 as reached; set its predecessor field to 2; set its "possible flow" field to 10 (not 15, because we know that we can push only 10 units to 2); enqueue 3.
- Following the edge-list of vertex 2 farther brings us to the node representing the edge from 0 to 2; but 0 has already been reached, so we need not consider it further.
- There are no more unreached vertices that can be reached from 2 along edges with positive residual capacity.
- Dequeue 1 and see what can now be reached from 1 along edges of positive residual capacity.
- We can reach 4 but it has already been reached.
- Following the edge-list of vertex 1 farther brings us to the node representing the edge from 0 to 1; but 0 has already been reached.

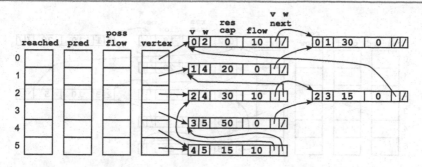

Fig. 7.70 Flow graph after adding the augmenting path 0, 2, 4, 5

- There are no more unreached vertices that can be reached from 1 along edges with positive residual capacity.
- Dequeue 4 and see what can now be reached from 4 along edges of positive residual capacity.
- We can reach 5 (not yet reached) with a residual capacity of 25; mark 5 as reached; set its predecessor field to 4; set its "possible flow" field to 10 (because the possible flow to predecessor 4 is only 10); since 5 is the sink, the breadth-first search stops.
- Going backward through predecessors we discover that we have the following augmenting path: 0, 2, 4, 5 and we can push 10 units along this path. When we do so we obtain the modified structure shown in Fig. 7.70.

Now we reinitialize the `reached` and `predecessor` and `possible_flow` arrays and start a new breadth-first search for a shortest augmenting path. This time we get the path 0, 1, 4, 5, along which we can push 15 additional units. We make the adjustments in the structure above. (We won't reprint the newly modified structure here.)

Again we start up a new breadth-first search for a shortest augmenting path. This time we have to use an artificial residual capacity. We are able to go from vertex 0 to vertex 1, then from vertex 1 to vertex 4, and then—by treating the flow from vertex 2 to vertex 4 as a residual capacity from 4 to 2—we can go from 4 to 2, then from 2 to 3, then from 3 to 5. The maximum number of additional units we can push along this path is 5. After making those adjustments we have the graph in Fig. 7.71 in which there are no more augmenting paths (a breadth-first search will fail to reach the sink).

Here is the maximum flow we have found for this weighted digraph.

Ship 10 units from vertex 0 to vertex 2.

Ship 20 units from vertex 0 to vertex 1.

Ship 20 units from vertex 1 to vertex 4.

Ship 5 units from vertex 2 to vertex 4.

Ship 5 units from vertex 2 to vertex 3.

Ship 5 units from vertex 3 to vertex 5.

Ship 25 units from vertex 4 to vertex 5.

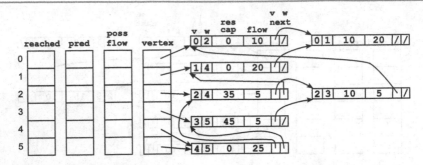

Fig. 7.71 Flow graph after adding the augmenting paths 0, 1, 4, 5 and 0, 1, 4, 2, 3, 5

It is easy to check that the flow into each intermediate vertex is equal to the flow out of that vertex, and that the flow out of the source is equal to the flow into the sink. The total maximum flow is 30.

A still more complicated method for choosing the augmenting paths is to find, at each stage, the augmenting path along which the greatest possible amount of flow can be sent. Abstractly, at each stage the problem is to find in a weighted digraph a path from one specified vertex to another such that the smallest weight along this path is as large as possible. It is not hard to see that straightforward modification of Dijkstra's Least Costly Path Algorithm will give an algorithm for finding such a path. The effort one expends in programming this more complex method for choosing the augmenting paths is well rewarded by an algorithm that solves most large maximum flow problems more quickly than the Edmunds-Karp algorithm.

In the late 1980s a new method of attacking the maximum flow problem was invented by A. V. Goldberg. His "preflow-push" algorithm has been modified and refined by a number of researchers, and there are now some algorithms that run in roughly $O(|V| \cdot |E|)$ time, which most people suspect is about as fast as we'll ever be able to solve the maximum flow problem. Goldberg's methods are somewhat complicated, and will not be described here.

Throughout this entire discussion we have been tacitly assuming that for every pair of vertices there is at most one edge between them. But now let's consider how to deal with the case in which the digraph may have an edge from a vertex x to a vertex y and also an edge from y to x. When this is possible, then the adjacency structure must be constructed in a slightly different manner. When an edge from x to y with capacity c is read from the input file, the construction algorithm must check to see whether there is already a node in the structure representing an edge from y to x. (This involves searching the edge-list of vertex y.) If there is, the capacity c is simply entered into a "residual $x \rightarrow y$ capacity" field in the existing node. If not, then a node is allocated and initialized as shown in the following example.

Suppose we read an edge from a to b with capacity 25 from the input file. Suppose a search of the b edge-list does not find a node representing an edge from b to a. Then a node should be allocated, placed in the edge-list for a, and initialized as shown in Fig. 7.72.

Fig. 7.72 Data structure
representing a flow on an edge

		actual $a \to b$ capac	resid $b \to a$ capac	resid $a \to b$ capac		
a	b	25	25	0		

Fig. 7.73 This node represents a flow of 0 from a to b

		actual $a \to b$ capac	resid $b \to a$ capac	resid $a \to b$ capac		
a	b	25	25	15		

Fig. 7.74 Represents a flow
of 20 from a to b

		actual $a \to b$ capac	resid $b \to a$ capac	resid $a \to b$ capac		
a	b	25	5	35		

Fig. 7.75 Represents a flow
of 5 from a to b

		actual $a \to b$ capac	resid $b \to a$ capac	resid $a \to b$ capac		
a	b	25	30	10		

Suppose that we later read an edge from b to a with capacity 15 from the input
file. Since a search of the edge-list of a will turn up the node shown in Fig. 7.72, we
will simply enter the capacity 15 into the "resid b→a capac" field, as shown
in Fig. 7.73.

Now suppose that we start up an algorithm for finding the maximum flow, and at
some point we decide to assign a flow of 20 from a to b. We will modify the node
above as shown in Fig. 7.74.

Later we may decide to assign a flow of 25 from b to a. We will modify the node
to look like Fig. 7.75.

If we later decide to increase the flow from b to a by 10, we will modify the node
as shown in Fig. 7.76.

The difference between the first two fields represents at all times the "signed flow"
from a to b.

Fig. 7.76 Represents a flow
of 15 from *a* to *b*

	actual $a \to b$ capac	resid $b \to a$ capac	resid $a \to b$ capac	
a | b |	25	40	0 |	|

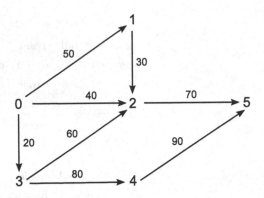

Fig. 7.77 A weighted digraph

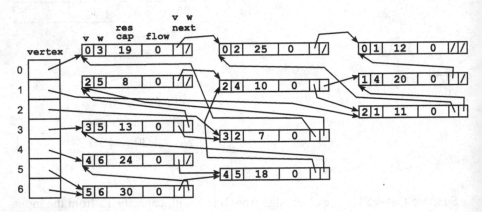

Fig. 7.78 Data structure corresponding to Fig. 7.77

7.8.1   Exercises

7.8.2 Use the Edmunds-Karp version of the Ford-Fulkerson method to find a maximum flow in each of the following graphs. Use the adjacency structure given below the graph. Show the queues that you use to find the augmenting paths and flows along the paths. When you have found the maximum flow, list the flow that must be assigned to each edge to produce this maximum flow.

(a) See Figs. 7.77 and 7.78. The source is vertex 0. The sink is vertex 5.
(b) See Figs. 7.79 and 7.80. What is the source and what is the sink?

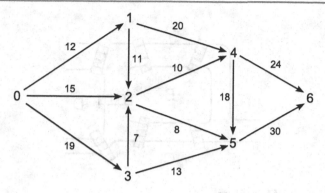

Fig. 7.79 A weighted digraph

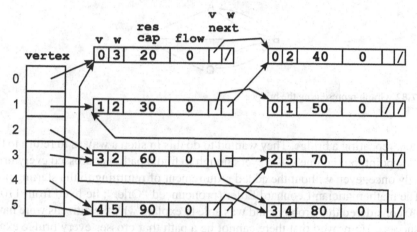

Fig. 7.80 Data structure corresponding to Fig. 7.79

7.8.3 Explain how the Dijkstra Shortest Path Algorithm can be modified to produce an algorithm for finding a path from source to sink with the largest possible minimum residual capacity along the path.

7.9 Tours

The city of Kaliningrad now lies in Russia, but in the 18-th century it lay in eastern Prussia (Germany) and had the name Königsberg. The river Pregel flows through the city, and in the middle of the river are two islands. At the time of this story, six bridges had been built from the banks of the river to the islands, and a seventh bridge connected the two islands directly. Figure 7.81 shows the general shape of things there.

Tradition has it that the citizens of Königsberg amused themselves on pleasant Sunday afternoons by strolling across the various bridges, trying to cross them all

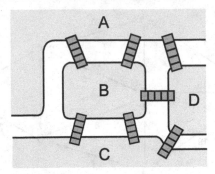

Fig. 7.81 The bridges of Königsberg

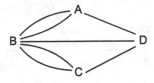

Fig. 7.82 Graph representing the bridges

without repeating a bridge. They wanted to do this in such a way as to return to their starting point, but no one was clever enough to find a path that crossed every bridge exactly once, even without the added requirement of returning to the starting point.

The mathematician Leonhard Euler (pronounced "Oiler"; he lived from 1707 to 1783) considered this problem and was able to explain why the citizens were having no success. He proved that there cannot be a path that crosses every bridge exactly once. His discoveries about this problem and ones similar to it are considered to be the first significant results anyone ever proved about finite graphs, so Euler is sometimes referred to as the "father of graph theory". He did many other beautiful and profound things in mathematics and is universally regarded as one of the most innovative and productive mathematicians of all time. A translation of his paper on this particular problem can be found in [2].

How did Euler tackle the problem of the bridges? He considered the two banks and two islands as forming what we would now call the vertices of a finite, undirected graph, and he viewed the bridges as edges between those vertices. This gave him the finite graph in Fig. 7.82.

Now he reasoned as follows: suppose there is a path P that crosses each edge (bridge) exactly once. Then, we can see that the path P must either start at vertex A or end up there, because it if doesn't start at A, then P must eventually cross one of the 3 edges into A, then must leave along another edge, and later cross over the remaining edge, arriving at A, where it cannot depart. The crucial point here is that vertex A has *odd degree*, which simply means that the number of edges out of A is odd. Now notice that vertices B, C, and D also have odd degree. The same reasoning that we applied to vertex A can be used to argue that path P must either start or end

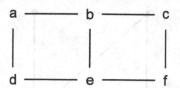

Fig. 7.83 Graph having a non-simple Eulerian path

at B, at C, and at D. Of course, this is impossible for a single path. It follows that P cannot exist.

Definition 7.9.1 Let G denote an undirected, connected graph. An *Eulerian path* in G is a path that includes every edge in G exactly once. An *Eulerian circuit* (or *Eulerian cycle*, or *Eulerian tour*) is an Eulerian path that ends at the same vertex at which it started.

Note that if a graph G has an Eulerian circuit, then any vertex in the graph can be considered to be the starting and ending point of the circuit.

Also note that an Eulerian path need not be a simple path. The path b, e, d, a, b, c, f, e in Fig. 7.83 is Eulerian, but since it visits vertices b and e twice, it is not simple..

You might wonder why Definition 7.9.1 requires the graph G to be connected. Surely an undirected graph that contains a path passing through every edge must be connected! Or will it? Not necessarily. A graph consisting of a triangle and an isolated point is not connected, but it has a path that contains each edge exactly once. We prefer not to call such a path Eulerian, so it is customary to consider only connected graphs when looking for the Eulerian property.

Definition 7.9.2 The *degree* of a vertex v in an undirected graph is the number of edges that touch v (i.e., have v as one of their endpoints).

Theorem 7.9.3 *Let P denote a path in an undirected graph G, and let v denote a vertex on P. Suppose moreover that P passes exactly once over every edge that touches v.*

(a) *If the degree of v is odd, then P must either start or stop at v, but cannot do both.*

(b) *If the degree of v is even, then P must both start and stop at v or else must neither start nor stop at v.*

Proof The argument for part (a) is exactly the one Euler used for the Königsberg bridges. The argument for part (b) is very similar. ∎

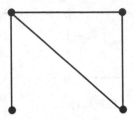

Fig. 7.84 An example of an undirected graph

Theorem 7.9.4 *Let G be a undirected, connected graph. If G contains more than two vertices with odd degree, then G cannot contain an Eulerian path. If G contains exactly two vertices with odd degree, then any Eulerian path in G must start at one of these vertices and end at the other (so it cannot be an Eulerian circuit). If G contains no vertices with odd degree, then any Eulerian path in G must be an Eulerian circuit.*

Proof This depends in a straightforward way on Theorem 7.9.3.   ∎

Theorem 7.9.4 does not tell us anything about Eulerian paths in undirected graphs having exactly one vertex of odd degree. And with good reason! There is no such thing. The explanation for this lies in the following simple theorem.

Theorem 7.9.5 *The sum of the degrees of all the vertices in an undirected graph $G = (V, E)$ is equal to twice the number of edges in G. That is, $\sum_{v \in V} degree(v) = 2(|E|)$.*

Proof Think of going from vertex to vertex in G, computing the sum of all the degrees by counting all the edges out of each vertex and marking each edge as it is counted. Then every edge would be marked exactly twice during the counting process. (It helps to look at a specific example. Try this counting process on the graph shown in Fig. 7.84.)   ∎

Theorem 7.9.6 *There are always an even number of vertices of odd degree in an undirected graph.*

Proof If there were an odd number of vertices of odd degree in some undirected graph G, then the sum on the left side of the equation in Theorem 7.9.5 would be odd, which is impossible because the right side of the equation is even.   ∎

Look again at Theorem 7.9.4. A superficial reading may suggest that it claims that if an undirected, connected graph has exactly two vertices of odd degree, then it definitely must contain an Eulerian path. Close reading, however, shows that the theorem makes no such claim. Thus the following theorem is of interest and will require a new proof.

Theorem 7.9.7 *Let G be a connected, undirected graph. If G contains no vertices of odd degree, then G has an Eulerian circuit. If G contains exactly two vertices of odd degree, then G has an Eulerian path.*

Proof The proof uses mathematical induction on the number of edges in G. It also depends on the next theorem. We omit the details.   ∎

Figure 7.85 shows an algorithm, expressed primarily in pseudo-code, that determines whether a given undirected graph contains an Eulerian path starting at a given vertex v. If the graph is not connected or if it has more than two vertices of odd degree, an error message is printed (see Theorem 7.9.6). If the graph is connected and has no vertices of odd degree, the algorithm will print an Eulerian path starting and ending at v. If the graph is connected and has two vertices of odd degree, the algorithm ignores v and prints an Eulerian path (which may or may not start with or end at v).

The algorithm uses recursion, and, as is often the case, a driver function is needed to perform some preliminary tasks before the initial recursive call can be made. The driver determines whether the given graph is connected, which it does by a breadth-first search similar to the one in Fig. 7.27. It also sets up an array named "degree", parallel to the vertex array. During the breadth-first search the driver counts the number of edges in the edge-list of each vertex v and stores that number in degree[v]. This allows the driver to determine whether there are too many vertices of odd degree, and if there not, to decide which vertex to pass to the recursive function.

The recursive function in Fig. 7.85, when traversing the graph and printing out an Eulerian path, must keep track of which edges it has already used at each step of the traversal. This requires that an extra data member, of boolean type, be declared in the edge_node struct in the definition of the Graph class (Fig. 7.11, p. 372). In Fig. 7.85 this boolean data member is called used. The driver initializes all the used members in the edge-lists to false ("unused") during its breadth-first search.

A slight complication occurs when the recursive function in Fig. 7.85 is required to mark an edge $\{v, w\}$ as "used" (i.e., set the used field to true). Recall that in the usual adjacency list representation of an undirected graph, each edge $\{v, w\}$ in the graph is represented by two edge_nodes, one in the edge-list of v and the other in the edge-list of w. When an edge must be marked as "used", this must occur in two different edge-lists. We can avoid lengthy searches by declaring another data member, let's call it twin, of pointer type edge_node*, in the edge_node struct in the definition of the Graph class. Then, when the graph is constructed originally, each edge_node can have its twin pointer set to point to the other edge_node that represents the same edge.

```
// This function is a driver for the recursive function "print_eulerian".
// It searches the graph to determine whether an Eulerian path can be found, and
// during the search it performs various initializations.
// It assumes that the "edge_node" struct type in the Graph class has two extra data
// members: "used" of type bool, and "twin" of pointer type edge_node*. For every
// edge {x, y} in the graph, the edge_node carrying y in the edge-list of x has
// "twin" point to the edge_node carrying x in the edge-list of y, and vice versa.

void Graph:: eulerian_path (int v) // An algorithm for undirected graphs only.
{
    int degree[num_vertices];        // Will record the degree of each vertex.

  Make a breadth-first search in the graph, starting at vertex 0, that performs
      the following tasks for each vertex w encountered during the search:
      For each pointer y to a node in the edge-list of w:
        y->used = false;
        count the edges in this list;
      degree[w] = count of edges in the edge-list of w;

    For each vertex w in the graph:
        if (degree[w] == 0)          // Indicates w is not reachable from vertex 0.
        print an error message saying the graph is not connected and exit;
        else if (degree[w] %2 == 1)  // Contains an odd integer.
        keep track of how many and which they are;

    if there are more than two vertices of odd degree:
      print a message saying there is no Eulerian path;
    if there are exactly two vertices of odd degree, say x and y:
      print_eulerian(x);
    if there are no vertices of odd degree:
      print_eulerian(v);
}

// The following recursive function is called only if its driver has determined
// that there is an Eulerian path ending at vertex v in the given graph.

void Graph::print_eulerian (int v)
{
  For each unused edge {v, w} in the edge-list of v,
  {
    Mark {v, w} as used in the edge-list of v;
    Using the "twin" pointer, mark {v, w} as used in the edge-list of w;
    print_eulerian (w);
  }
  cout << v << " ";   // Output v followed by a blank space.
}
```

Fig. 7.85 Algorithm for finding Eulerian paths in undirected graphs

The proof that the functions in Fig. 7.85 correctly search for an Eulerian path in a given graph G uses mathematical induction on the number of edges in G, and makes use of Theorem 7.9.8.

Theorem 7.9.8 *Let G be an undirected, connected graph, and let $\{v, w\}$ be any edge in G. Let G^* denote the subgraph obtained by removing this edge from the*

edge set of G (this does not remove the endpoints of the edge from the vertex set). Then G* is either connected or else contains exactly two connected components, one containing v, and the other, w.

Proof See the Exercises. ∎

Let's see how our algorithm for finding Eulerian paths would work on the undirected graph shown in Fig. 7.86. Let's assume that when the adjacency structure is built initially, the edges appear in the edge-lists in decreasing order by sequence number. Thus, for example, the edge-list out of vertex 8 would contain nodes representing edges to vertices 16, 15, 14, 13, 10, 9, 7, and 6, in that order.

The driver for the function in Fig. 7.85 begins with a set of initializations in the list adjacency structure for the given graph, call it *G*. Then it conducts a breadth-first search from vertex 0 to find out whether *G* is connected. Each time it arrives at a new edge it increments an edge counter for each of the two endpoints. When the breadth-first search ends, the driver scans down the vertices to see whether there is an edge counter with value 0 (indicating a vertex that was never reached, and thus a non-connected graph) and whether there are any vertices of odd degree. The graph in Fig. 7.86 will be found to be connected and to have exactly two vertices of odd degree, namely 0 and 12. Thus the recursive `print_eulerian` function can be called with either 0 or 12 as its argument. Let's suppose the driver calls `print_eulerian(0)`. In the list that follows, we'll use the abbreviation "PE(v)" for a function call `print_eulerian(v)`. It will be easier to follow the steps below if you draw a stack of the function calls as they are made, and mark them off as the calls end.

- PE(0) marks edge {0, 6} as used and calls PE(6);
- PE(6) marks edge {6, 10} as used and calls PE(10);
- Similarly, PE(10) calls PE(11), which calls PE(12);
- PE(12) finds no unused edge out of 12, so it outputs 12 and returns (backtracks);

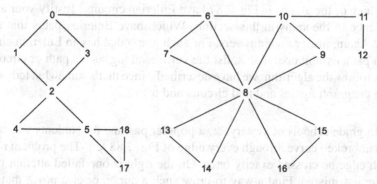

Fig. 7.86 An example of graph

- PE(11) is re-activated; it finds no unused edge out of 11, so it outputs 11 and returns;
- PE(10) is re-activated; it calls PE(9), which calls PE(8), which calls PE(16);
- PE(16) calls PE(15), which calls PE(8), which calls PE(14), which calls PE(13);
- PE(13) calls PE(8), which calls PE(10);
- PE(10) finds no unused edge out of 10, so it outputs 10 and returns; the most recent PE(8) call is re-activated; it calls PE(7), which calls PE(6), which calls PE(8);
- PE(8) finds no unused edge out of 8, so it outputs 8 and returns;
- PE(6) is re-activated; it finds no unused edge out of 6, so it outputs 6 and returns;
- PE(7) is re-activated; it finds no unused edge out of 7, so it outputs 7 and returns;
- PE(6) is re-activated; it finds no unused edge out of 8, so it outputs 8 and returns; (NOTE: vertex 8 is going to be printed several times, which is allowed in an Eulerian path);
  etc.

The following list of vertices representing an Eulerian path from 12 to 0 will be printed:

12 11 10 8 6 7 8 13 14 8 15 16 8 9 10 6 0 1 2 4 5 17 18 5 2 3 0

One last question: how efficient is our algorithm? The answer is that the algorithm consists of one breadth-first search in the driver function. Each vertex reached is marked, and each edge reached is initialized and tallied. As we discussed earlier, this straightforward process requires $\Theta(n + m)$ amount of time, where n is the number of vertices and m is the number of edges in the graph. Then the function that prints the Eulerian path is precisely a depth-first search function, so the time it requires is also $\Theta(n + m)$. Thus the entire algorithm runs in $\Theta(n + m)$ amount of time.

7.9.1 Exercises

7.9.9 Which of the graphs in Fig. 7.87 have Eulerian circuits? Justify your answers by reference to theorems in this section. Which have Eulerian paths that are not circuits? Again, justify your answers. For each graph that has an Eulerian circuit or Eulerian path, exhibit one; that is, list the vertices along such a path or circuit. You need not follow the algorithm we have described, since that's somewhat tedious. Just mark up the graph figures and find circuits and paths.

7.9.10 In grade schools of yesteryear, a popular pastime for students was to try to draw an unbroken curve through every edge of Fig. 7.88 left. The problem required that each edge be crossed exactly once. On the right is one failed attempt because one edge was missed. Find a way to draw such a curve, or else prove that such a curve is impossible.

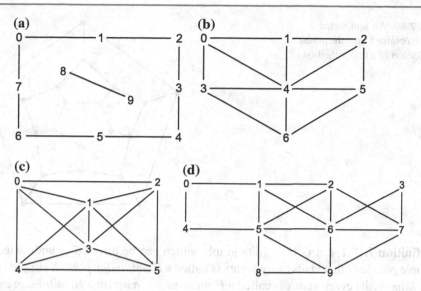

Fig. 7.87 Exercise 7.9.9. **a, b, c** and **d**

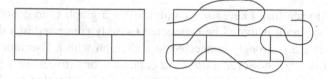

Fig. 7.88 Exercise 7.9.10: the puzzle (*left*) and an attempted solution (*right*)

7.10 Hamiltonian Paths and Circuits

In the Eulerian path problem we are required to find a path that travels across every edge exactly once in an undirected, connected graph. We were able to find an algorithm for solving this "tour" problem, and we saw that the algorithm runs in "linear time" in the number of vertices n and edges m. That is, the running time is $\Theta(n+m)$ time, which is quite efficient.

Now let's look at another tour problem that appears to be quite similar. Its history begins with the Irish mathematician William Hamilton, who lived from 1805 to 1865. In 1859 A puzzle that he had invented was marketed by an Irish toy maker. The puzzle was "played" on a regular dodecahedron, a solid with 12 pentagonal faces, 30 edges, and 20 corners. Each of the corners was labeled with the name of a different city, and the player was challenged to find a path that stayed on the edges and passed through every city exactly once, returning to the point where the path had started. This solid can be projected onto the plane to form the image in Fig. 7.89, where one face is hidden behind all the faces shown. In the language of graph theory, the player was being challenged to find a simple cycle that passes through every vertex in the graph.

Fig. 7.89 An undirected
graph obtained from the planar
projection of a dodecahedron

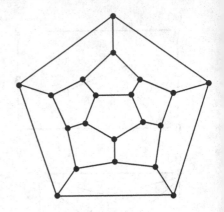

Definition 7.10.1 Let G be a finite graph, which can be directed or undirected. A simple path in G that visits every vertex is called a *Hamiltonian path*. A simple cycle in G that visits every vertex is called a *Hamiltonian circuit* (or a *Hamiltonian cycle*, or a *Hamiltonian tour*).

It is easy to see that a *necessary* condition for a graph G to contain a Hamiltonian path or circuit is that G be connected (weakly connected in a digraph with a Hamiltonian path, strongly connected in a digraph with a Hamiltonian circuit). Connectedness is not, however, a *sufficient* condition for G to contain a Hamiltonian path or circuit. The simplest example of a connected undirected graph having no Hamiltonian path is the graph consisting of 4 vertices and forming the uppercase letter T. A little thought will convince you that any graph having three or more vertices of degree 1 cannot have a Hamiltonian path.

Here are some questions whose purpose is to get you thinking about what a Hamiltonian path or circuit is, and what properties a graph may have that determine whether it can or cannot have such a path.

1. Does a *complete* undirected graph with three or more vertices have a Hamiltonian circuit? (See Definition 7.1.6, p. 364.)
2. Does a Hamiltonian path or circuit in a graph have to travel along every edge of the graph?
3. Is an Eulerian circuit in a graph always a Hamiltonian circuit?
4. If a graph has a Hamiltonian path, and if we add new edges between some of the existing vertices, will the resulting graph have a Hamiltonian path?
5. If a graph with n vertices has a Hamiltonian path, how many edges are there in the path? Answer the same question about Hamiltonian circuits.
6. If a connected, undirected graph has a vertex of degree 1, does this imply anything about whether the graph has a Hamiltonian path? About whether it has a Hamiltonian circuit?

7. Suppose the vertices of a connected, undirected graph all have degree exactly 2. Does this imply anything about whether the graph has a Hamiltonian path? A Hamiltonian circuit?
8. Suppose every vertex in a connected, undirected graph has degree at least 2. Must the graph have a Hamiltonian path? A Hamiltonian circuit?

Here are answers for the questions above.

1. Such a graph contains many Hamiltonian circuits. If the vertices are the integers $0, 1, \ldots, n - 1$, then you can visit the vertices in that order and return to 0, because every edge is present in the graph. In fact, you can visit the vertices in any order and return to the first one.
2. No. Draw the complete graph on four vertices, and you can easily find a Hamiltonian circuit that travels on just four of the six edges, as well as a Hamiltonian path that travels on just three edges.
3. No. An Eulerian path or circuit will visit every vertex, but quite often it will visit some vertices more than once, which is not permitted for a Hamiltonian path and is permitted for a Hamiltonian circuit only at the end.
4. The Hamiltonian path or circuit of the smaller graph will still be present in the larger graph, which has the same vertices as the smaller one.
5. Start at one end of the Hamiltonian path and travel along it. For each of the n vertices except the last, you will travel away from the vertex on just one edge, so there are $n - 1$ vertices along the path. A Hamiltonian circuit will consist of exactly n edges.
6. If the graph has a vertex of degree 1, it may or may not have a Hamiltonian path, but it cannot have a Hamiltonian circuit, because every vertex in a circuit must have at least two edges, one to arrive on and another to depart along.
7. The graph must have a Hamiltonian circuit. To see this, start at any vertex and choose an edge to depart along. When you reach its neighbor, there will be only one edge to depart along, and similarly for the next vertex, etc. At each vertex you have only one possible next neighbor. You cannot return to the initial vertex until you have visited every vertex, because if this process were to leave a vertex unvisited, the graph would not be connected. When every vertex has been visited, the edge out of the last vertex must take you back to the initial vertex, for otherwise some intermediate vertex would have degree at least 3.
8. Figure 7.90 shows a connected, undirected graph in which every vertex has degree at least 2, but the graph has neither a Hamiltonian circuit nor a Hamiltonian path.

In Sect. 7.9 we found a simple set of conditions for the existence of an Eulerian path or circuit in any *undirected* graph. We simply check that the graph is connected and has at most two vertices of odd degree. Moreover, we saw a highly efficient algorithm for constructing an Eulerian path or circuit once we determine that one is present in the graph. Since the problem of finding a Hamiltonian path or circuit resembles the problem of finding an Eulerian path or circuit, we might reasonably expect to be able to find a simple solution for the Hamiltonian problem, at least in

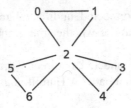

Fig. 7.90 A connected, undirected graph with no Hamiltonian circuit or path

undirected graphs. Surprisingly, no simple and efficient general solution has been found.

Some special cases have been discovered. For example, a theorem proved in 1960 by the Norwegian mathematician Øystein Ore states that a graph with n vertices ($n \geq 3$) has a Hamiltonian cycle if, for every pair of non-adjacent vertices, the sum of their degrees is at least n. That's a sufficient condition, but far from a necessary one, for the existence of a Hamiltonian cycle. Moreover, it gives no hint on how to find the Hamiltonian cycle whose existence it posits.

It is always possible to solve the Hamiltonian problem by a *brute force search* (also called an *exhaustive search*), which involves looking at all possible paths in the graph that never visit a vertex twice and seeing whether any of them visit every vertex in the given graph (and, if looking for a circuit, checking whether the final vertex of a Hamiltonian path is adjacent to the initial vertex). As an example, consider the graph in Fig. 7.91. We can illustrate a brute force search for a Hamiltonian path by drawing a tree (called a *logical search tree*) that shows all possible paths, starting with any vertex in the graph, as shown in Fig. 7.92. The possible initial vertices are shown in the row just beneath the root of the tree. The circled vertices at the bottom of the tree are the final vertices of Hamiltonian paths. We can read off four such paths: (1,0,3,2,5,4), (1,0,3,2,4,5), (4,5,2,1,0,3), and (4,5,2,3,0,1). None of these can be extended to Hamiltonian circuits. The vertices that are shown underlined mark the points at which attempts to create a Hamiltonian path ended unsuccessfully. The dashed vertical columns (as for example, under vertex 5) indicate deliberate omissions of possible paths based on symmetry. Since the graph in Fig. 7.91 is symmetric across its central vertical axis, all paths that would start with 5 are simply mirror images of the paths that start at vertex 4, so to save space on the page they are not shown. If we had shown those paths, we would see four additional Hamiltonian paths, two of them starting at vertex 3 and two more starting at vertex 5.

Drawing by hand and eye the logical search tree for Hamiltonian paths in a graph is not difficult, but it requires uncommon patience, especially if the graph has more than just a few vertices. Happily, the task can be turned over to a computer. Let's look at the problem of writing an algorithm to search for a Hamiltonian *path* in a graph G, and print such a path if one can be found. We can begin by making a pass over the adjacency list structure to initialize an "included" field in each vertex to false. Later, when we are building a path, each vertex that gets added to the path will have its "included" field changed to true. During the initialization pass we can also

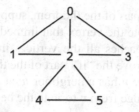

Fig. 7.91 An undirected graph

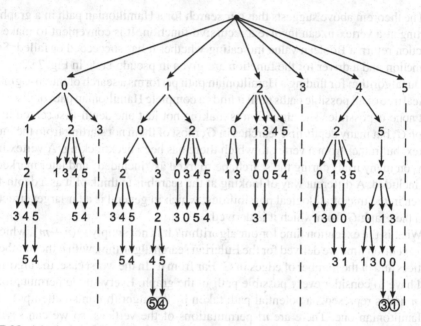

Fig. 7.92 A logical search tree for Hamiltonian paths in Fig. 7.91

examine each edge-list to find any vertices with degree 0 or 1. A vertex of degree 0 allows us to stop the search because the graph G will not be connected (unless, of course, G has only one vertex). Similarly, if we discover more than two vertices of degree 1 we can stop immediately, since such a graph cannot contain a Hamiltonian path. If we find one or two vertices of degree 1 we can start our search at such a vertex. If every vertex has degree at least 2, then our algorithm will (potentially) try all vertices as starting points in searches for a Hamiltonian path.

The key observation for writing a search function for a Hamiltonian *path* is the following theorem.

Theorem 7.10.2 *Let G be a finite graph with at least two vertices, and let v be a vertex in G. Let G^* denote the graph obtained by removing from G the vertex v and all edges that touch v. Then G contains a Hamiltonian path that starts at v if and only if there exists a vertex w adjacent to v such that G^* contains a Hamiltonian path that starts at w.*

Proof To prove the "only if" part of the theorem, suppose that G has a Hamiltonian path starting at v. Let w denote the vertex that immediately follows v on this path. The remainder of the path reaches all the vertices in G^* exactly once, so it is a Hamiltonian path in G^*. To prove the "if" part of the theorem (the converse of what we have just proved), suppose v has a neighbor w at which a Hamiltonian path in G^* begins. Then adding the edge from v to w to the beginning of that path produces a Hamiltonian path in G starting at v.   ∎

The theorem above suggests that our search for a Hamiltonian path in a graph G, starting at a vertex v, can involve a recursive function. It is convenient to make the function return a Boolean value indicating whether it has succeeded or failed. Such a function and a driver for the function are given in pseudo-code in Fig. 7.93.

Our algorithm for finding a Hamiltonian path performs a search of the (imaginary) logical tree of all possible paths until it finds a complete Hamiltonian path or discovers that none is possible. The algorithm is making not just one depth-first search in the graph G, but many depth-first searches in G, most of them not starting from the initial vertex, but rather from a vertex to which there has been backtracking. A vertex in G may, on many trials during the search, be marked as "included" and later marked as not included. A different way of looking at the search is to think of it as a depth-first search in the tree of all logical possibilities, which in general is a far larger structure than the graph G from which it is derived.

What is the execution time for our algorithm? It is not simply $\Theta(n + m)$, which is the execution time we derived for the Eulerian search algorithm, with n the number of vertices and m the number of edges in G. Far from it! In the worst case, the algorithm will have to consider every possible path in the graph. Every single permutation of the n nodes represents a potential path taken by the algorithm in an attempt to find a Hamiltonian one. There are $n!$ permutations of the vertices, so we can say that our algorithm is $O(n!)$. But can we be sure that there exists a graph for which the algorithm requires a constant times $n!$ operations? While we cannot provide such an example, we can show that there is a type of graph with n vertices for which the algorithm requires $\Theta(2^n)$ operations.

Let us consider a directed graph where every vertex i has an edge towards all the vertices j in the graph such that $j < i$. Let us also suppose that the edges are placed in the adjacency list in ascending order. Figure 7.94 shows an example of the graph and the adjacency list structure for $n = 5$. The structure forces the algorithm to consider every possible path in the graph. The last call of the recursive function with the vertex $n - 1$ returns true and the Hamiltonian path is $(n - 1, n - 2, \ldots, 0, 1)$.

Let's count the recursive calls made by the function in Fig. 7.93 on such a graph with n nodes. Let $C(n)$ be the number of function calls. Then the number of calls generated by starting the search with the vertices from 0 to $n - 1$ is equal to $C(n - 1)$. When we call the function with the parameter v having the value n, we traverse the adjacency list, and for each vertex on it, we make a function call. Because of the symmetry in the graph, each of these calls is equivalent to running the whole algorithm on a graph of smaller size. Thus, we can sum this up in the recurrence

```
// Driver function for the recursive function that searches for a Hamiltonian path
// in any graph, directed or undirected.

bool Graph::hamiltonian_driver ()
{
  for each vertex v in the graph:  // initialization loop
    vertex[v].included = false;

  for each vertex v in the graph:
    if ( create_ham_path (v, num_vertices) )
      return true;
  return false; // if cannot find a vertex that permits a H. path
}

/***********************************************************************************
The following recursive function searches the logical tree of all possible paths in
the undirected graph G, starting from vertex v, to try to find a Hamiltonian path in G.
Before this function is called intially, the "included" field of each vertex in G
should be assigned the value false to indicate that the vertex has not yet been added
to a path. The initial call to this function should pass the argument n to the
parameter "num_vertices_needed", where n is the number of vertices in G.
When the function is called with num_vertices_needed equal to 1, this indicates that a
Hamiltonian path starting with v has been found, so the vertex v is printed, and then
each prior recursive call prints the vertex that was passed to it. Thus the vertices
along the path are printed in reverse order.
***********************************************************************************/

bool Graph:: create_ham_path (int v, int num_vertices_needed)
{
  if (num_vertices_needed == 1) // base case of the recursion
  {
    print v;
    return true;
  }
  vertex[v].included = true;     // Now v is included in a
                                 // partial path.

  for each neighbor w of v such that vertex[w].included == false,
    if (create_ham_path (w, num_vertices_needed - 1))
    {
      print v;
      return true;               // EXIT having found a hamiltonian path.
                                 // DO NOT examine remaining neighbors of v.
    }

  vertex[v].included = false;
  return false;                  // EXIT having failed to find a hamiltonian path.
}
```

Fig. 7.93 Function searching for a Hamiltonian path with a given number of vertices

relation

$$C(1) = 1, \quad C(n) = 1 + C(n-1) + C(1) + C(2) + \ldots + C(n-1)$$

Writing this recurrence relation for $n-1$, we have

$$C(n-1) = 1 + C(n-2) + C(1) + C(2) + \ldots + C(n-2)$$

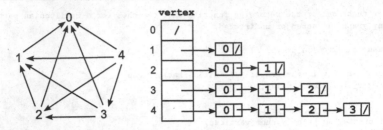

Fig. 7.94 A digraph and its adjacency list structure

By subtracting each side from the original recurrence relation, we obtain
$$C(n) - C(n-1) = C(n-1) - C(n-2) + C(n-1)$$
which becomes
$$C(1) = 1 \quad C(n) = 3C(n-1) - C(n-2)$$
The characteristic equation $r^2 = 3r - 1$ gives us the roots $r_1 = 2$ and $r_2 = 1$. By adding $C(2) = 3$ to the recurrence relation, we can solve it completely and obtain $C(n) = 2^n - 1$. Thus, the algorithm requires $\Theta(2^n)$ time for this family of graphs.

While more efficient algorithms than the one in Fig. 7.93 do exist, no one has yet invented an algorithm for the Hamiltonian problem that executes in $O(P(n, m))$ time, where $P(n, m)$ is a polynomial in n and m. At the present time, no one knows whether it is possible to find a polynomial time algorithm for searching for a Hamiltonian path. Most people who have studied the problem intensively suspect that someday it will be shown that a polynomial time algorithm for the problem cannot exist.

7.10.1 Exercises

7.10.3 (a) Give an example, if it is possible, of an undirected graph that contains a Hamiltonian path but no Hamiltonian circuit.

(b) Give an example, if it is possible, of an undirected graph that contains a Hamiltonian circuit but no Hamiltonian path.

7.10.4 By making an exhaustive search of the logical tree of all possible paths (i.e., logical search tree), prove that the graph in Fig. 7.95 does not contain a Hamiltonian path. Use symmetry, where possible, to reduce the amount of work involved. For example, if you show there is no Hamiltonian path starting at 6, then by symmetry there cannot be a Hamiltonian path starting at 7.

7.10.5 Find a Hamiltonian path in the graph in Fig. 7.96. Explain why we cannot have a Hamiltonian circuit.

7.10.6 Find all Hamiltonian paths in the digraph in Fig. 7.97. Hint: in this graph, where must such a path begin?

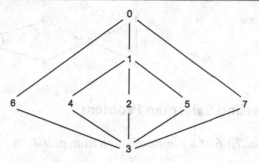

Fig. 7.95 An undirected graph

Fig. 7.96 An undirected graph

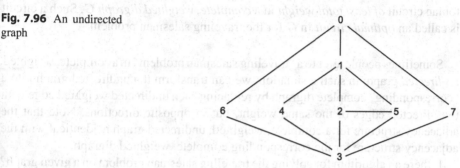

Fig. 7.97 Digraph with a Hamiltonian path

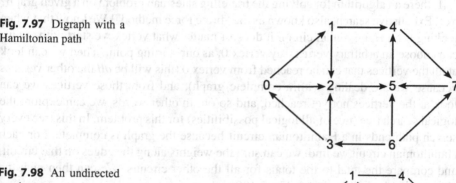

Fig. 7.98 An undirected graph

7.10.7 Find a Hamiltonian circuit in the graph in Fig. 7.98.

7.10.8 Give a convincing argument for the fact that a connected graph of the form shown in Fig. 7.99 cannot contain a Hamiltonian circuit.

Fig. 7.99 An undirected
graph

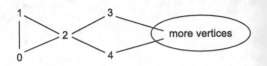

7.11 The Traveling Salesman Problem

Recall the Definition 7.1.6 of a complete graph from p. 364.

Definition 7.11.1 The *traveling salesman problem* is the problem of finding a Hamiltonian circuit *of least total weight* in a *complete, weighted digraph G*. Such a circuit is called an *optimal circuit* in *G* for the traveling salesman problem.

Sometimes people refer to a "traveling salesman problem" in a complete, weighted, *undirected* graph; in such a situation, we can transform the undirected graph into a "corresponding" complete digraph by replacing each undirected weighted edge with two directed edges of the same weight, but in opposite directions. Note that the adjacency structure for a complete, weighted, undirected graph is identical with the adjacency structure for the corresponding complete, weighted digraph.

Is there an algorithm for solving the traveling salesman problem on a given graph? Yes. Exhaustive search, also known as the "brute force method"! We know that when looking for a Hamiltonian circuit it doesn't matter what vertex we start with, so we can choose an arbitrary vertex, say vertex 0, as our starting point. Then we can look at all the vertices that can be reached from vertex 0 (this will be *all* the other vertices because we are dealing with a complete graph), and from those vertices we can look at the vertices not yet reached, and so on. In other words, we can explore the logical search tree (tree of all logical possibilities) for this problem. In this tree every search path ends in a Hamiltonian circuit because the graph is complete. For each Hamiltonian circuit we find, we can sum the weights along the edges on that circuit, and compare the total to the totals for all the other circuits. We can then pick the circuit with the smallest total (Fig. 7.100).

How many search paths (and therefore how many different Hamiltonian circuits) are there that start at vertex 0? If there are n vertices in the complete graph, then there are $n - 1$ branches from vertex 0 to the other $n - 1$ vertices. From each of those vertices there are $n - 2$ branches to the remaining $n - 2$ vertices, giving us $(n - 1)(n - 2)$ possibilities so far. There are $(n - 1)(n - 2)(n - 3)$ possibilities by the time we reach level 3 in the tree. Continuing in this way, we find that there are $(n - 1)(n - 2)(n - 3) \ldots (1) = (n - 1)!$ distinct possible Hamiltonian circuits starting at 0 in a complete graph on n vertices.

A simpler way to explain this is to remark that any permutation of the vertices 1 to $n - 1$, attached to the starting vertex 0, represents a valid path in the graph. The number of such permutations is $(n - 1)!$. This factorial is unimaginably large even when n is a moderate size number like 100. Clearly the brute force method of

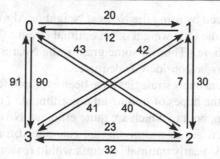

Fig. 7.100 A complete weighted directed graph

solving the traveling salesman problem is not feasible when n is larger than about 20 (roughly speaking).

Is there a more efficient algorithm for solving TSP (as it is often known), something along the lines, say, of Kruskal's minimum spanning tree algorithm? Recall that Kruskal tells us to select an edge of least weight, then another of least weight among the remaining edges, and so on, always being careful to discard edges that would produce a cycle. Kruskal's Algorithm is a "greedy algorithm", by which we mean that at each stage where a choice must be made, the algorithm makes its choice on the basis of what seems best immediately, in the short run, without attempting to take a longer view.

There are a number of greedy algorithms for trying to generate low cost circuits in a complete, weighted digraph. Unfortunately, none of these algorithms is guaranteed to give an optimal circuit. They simply produce circuits that—in most cases—are "fairly close" to optimal.

One such greedy algorithm is the Nearest Neighbor Algorithm: starting at 0, mark it as "included", examine all edges $(0, w)$, and choose the edge of least weight, call it $(0, A)$. This first phase can be carried out using $n - 1$ steps involving the $n - 1$ edges out of vertex 0. Next, starting at vertex A, mark it as "included", examine all edges (A, w) to non-included vertices w, and choose the edge of least weight, call it (A, B). This second phase can be carried out using $n - 1$ steps. Keep on going in this manner, until you have marked all the vertices, and then go back to vertex 0 from the last marked vertex.

The Nearest Neighbor Algorithm has the unfortunate feature that the last two edges traveled will be completely determined, with no choices possible, and these edges may have tremendously large weights, swamping the small weights obtained by the earlier "greedy" choices. It is possible to prove, however, that if

(1) the weights on the edges satisfy the "triangle inequality" (by which we mean that for every triple of vertices x, y, and z, the weight of the edge (x, y) plus the weight of the edge (y, z) is greater than or equal to the weight of the edge (x, z)), and

(2) the weights are symmetric (the weight on (x, y) is always equal to the weight on (y, x)),

then the circuit produced by using the Nearest Neighbor Algorithm has total weight no greater than twice the total weight of an optimal circuit. (The proof is not deep, but will not be given here.) Thus on some graphs, the Nearest Neighbor Algorithm gives a circuit that may be considered adequate.

Over the past 60 years many strategies have been explored for solving the traveling salesman problem in the hopes of finding an algorithm akin to Dijkstra's algorithm or Kruskal's algorithm, both of which are quite efficient. No one has yet discovered such an algorithm. There are algorithms that are guaranteed, under certain restrictions on the weights, to find "nearly optimal" circuits within reasonable amounts of time. Special "approximation" algorithms such as these are very valuable for practical problems, but they do not give us that ultimate satisfaction of allowing us to find actual optimal solutions in reasonable amounts of time.

7.11.1 Exercises

7.11.2 Solve the traveling salesman problem for the graph in Fig. 7.99. Show that no optimal circuit includes the edge of least weight (cf. Theorem 7.6.14 related to the minimum spanning tree problem). What circuit is produced by the Nearest Neighbor Algorithm starting at 0?

Appendix: Probability Theory

This appendix is provided so that various theorems of probability theory can be cited where needed in the material on probabilistic analysis of algorithms. Except in one case (tree diagrams in conditional probability calculations), examples illustrating the theorems are not provided. The assumption is that the reader will be familiar with probability theory and can knowledgeably consult these definitions and theorems to be reminded of the terminology and useful facts.

In a few places expressions of the form $\binom{n}{k}$ will appear. This expression, read "n choose k", denotes the binomial coefficient $\dfrac{n!}{k!(n-k)!}$. This fraction gives the number of distinct subsets of size k in a set of size n. It also gives the number of distinguishable character strings containing exactly k characters a and $n - k$ characters b.

Definition 8.1 A *statistical experiment* is a repeatable experiment with (usually) more than one possible outcome, where the particular outcome on any trial of the experiment cannot (generally speaking) be predicted with certainty. A *sample space* for the experiment is a set consisting of representations of all the possible outcomes of the experiment. Each separate outcome in the sample space is called a *sample point* of the space. When the experiment is actually performed, we obtain an *observation* (i.e. one of the sample points).

Definition 8.2 An *event* is any describable subset of a sample space.[1] An event A in a sample space is said to *occur* when the experiment is performed when the outcome of the experiment corresponds to one of the sample points in the set A. In any sample space S the empty subset $\emptyset$ is called the *impossible event*, and the entire space S is called the *certain event*.

---

[1] For the expert in probability, Definition 8.2 lacks the precision that comes with defining an *event* to be a member of a σ-ring of subsets of the sample space. The less formal approach we take is adequate for all applications in this text.

© Springer International Publishing Switzerland 2014
D. Vrajitoru and W. Knight, *Practical Analysis of Algorithms*,
Undergraduate Topics in Computer Science, DOI 10.1007/978-3-319-09888-3_8

Definition 8.3 The *complement* of an event A in a sample space S is the event consisting of all sample points of S that do not belong to A. We will denote the complement of A by A^c. The *intersection* of two events A and B in a sample space is denoted and defined by $A \cap B = \{x : x \in A \text{ and } x \in B\}$. Two events A and B are said to be *mutually exclusive* or *mutually disjoint* iff $A \cap B = \emptyset$; i.e., when the experiment is performed, A and B cannot both occur. The *union* of two events A and B is denoted and defined $A \cup B = \{x : x \in A \text{ and/or } x \in B\}$.

Definition 8.4 A *probability space* consists of a sample space S for a statistical experiment and a function P, called a *probability function*, which is defined on the events in S in such a way that the following axioms are satisfied:

1. For every event A we have $0 \le P(A) \le 1$.
2. $P(\emptyset) = 0$ and $P(S) = 1$.
3. For every finite sequence $A_1, A_2, \ldots, A_n$ of pairwise mutually exclusive events,

$$P(A_1 \cup A_2 \cup \ldots \cup A_n) = P(A_1) + P(A_2) + \cdots + P(A_n) \quad \text{(the Additivity Rule)}.$$

Theorem 8.5 (Complementarity) *For any event A in a probability space we have*

$$P(A) = 1 - P(A^c).$$

Theorem 8.6 (Inclusion-Exclusion Principle) *For every pair of events A and B in a probability space we have*

$$P(A \cup B) = P(A) + P(B) - P(A \cap B).$$

Theorem 8.7 *For every pair of events A and B in a sample space, if $(A \supseteq B)$ (i.e., if every sample point in B also belongs to A), then $P(A) \ge P(B)$.*

When speaking of the probabilities of an elementary event $\{x\}$, where x is a sample point in a sample space, it is customary to refer informally to "the probability of the outcome x" or "the probability that x occurs" instead of using the more precise language "the probability that the event $\{x\}$ occurs. Similarly, it is customary to write $P(x)$ in place of the more precise notation $P(x)$. In this appendix, we often follow this convention. We do so in the following theorem.

Theorem 8.8 (Equally Likely Outcomes) *Suppose a statistical experiment has n possible outcomes, and suppose it is desired to make all outcomes equally likely, by which we mean that for every possible pair of sample points x and y we want $P(x) = P(y)$. To achieve this, each singleton event must be assigned the probability $1/n$, and any event that contains exactly k distinct outcomes must be assigned the probability k/n.*

Theorem 8.9 *Let A be a non-empty set of size n, and let x be any particular element of A. If a subset of A of size k is to be chosen at random from A, then the probability that x will be in the chosen subset is k/n.*

(The proof uses the fact that there are $\binom{n}{k}$ equally likely subsets of A of size k, and of these, exactly $\binom{n-1}{k-1}$ contain the element x.)

Theorem 8.10 *Suppose n distinct objects are to be inserted in random order into an array* a[0...n−1]. *(By this we mean that the insertion is to be carried out in such a way that each of the n! possible arrangements of the objects will have probability 1/n! of occurring.) Suppose also that the objects have an order relation on them (i.e., for every pair of the objects, one of them is larger than the other). Then for any integers i and j satisfying $0 \le j < i < n$, the probability that exactly j of the objects in the subarray* a[0...i−1] *are greater than* a[i] *is* $1/(i+1)$.

(The proof uses these facts:

(a) there are $\binom{n}{i+1}$ ways to choose the $i+1$ objects to be placed in a[0...i];
(b) there is exactly one way to place in cell a[i] the unique object that's smaller than exactly j of these $i+1$ objects;
(c) there are i! ways to distribute the other i objects over a[0...i−1]; and
(d) there are $(n-i-1)!$ ways to distribute the $n-i-1$ non-chosen objects over the subarray a[i+1...n−1].)

Definition 8.11 Let A and B be events in a probability space, and suppose $P(A) > 0$. Then the *conditional probability of B given A* is denoted and defined as follows:

$$P(B|A) = \frac{P(A \cap B)}{P(A)}.$$

If $P(A) = 0$, then $P(B|A)$ is not defined.

$P(B|A)$ is the fraction of the time that B occurs in those cases where A occurs. It is important to keep in mind, when calculating $P(B|A)$ from its definition in the equation above, that the probabilities in the numerator and denominator are probabilities in the original sample space of the experiment. Sometimes we refer to $P(B)$ as the a priori *probability of B* or the *absolute probability of B*, and $P(B|A)$ may be called the a posteriori *probability of B given A*. Note that there is no *event* called "B given A" denoted by "B|A". When we write $P(B|A)$ we are not writing the probability of an event, but rather an abbreviation for a combination of probabilities of events in the original sample space, i.e., a combination of a priori probabilities.

The following theorem is indispensable in almost all applications of probability theory.

Theorem 8.12 (Chain Rule) *For any events A, B, C, A_1, A_2, ..., A_m in any probability space,*

$$P(A \cap B) = P(A) \times P(B|A) \quad \text{provided } P(A) > 0,$$

$$P(A \cap B \cap C) = P(A) \times P(B|A) \times P(C|A \cap B) \quad \text{provided } P(A \cap B) > 0,$$

and more generally,

$$P(A_1 \cap A_2 \cap A_3 \cap \ldots \cap A_m) = P(A_1) \times P(A_2|A_1) \times P(A_3|A_1 \cap A_2) \ldots$$
$$P(A_m|A_1 \cap A_2 \cap \ldots \cap A_{m-1})$$

provided $P(A_1 \cap A_2 \cap \ldots \cap A_{m-1}) > 0.$

Example 8.13 A *tree diagram* can be a valuable aid in solving probability problems in which the underlying statistical experiment consists of a sequence of actions. To illustrate this idea and show how the Chain Rule can be used in combination with the tree, let's suppose we have an urn containing 6 marbles, indistinguishable except for color: 1 is blue, 2 are green, and 3 are red. Marbles will be drawn from the urn, one after another, until a red marble is drawn. Assume we want to compute the probabilities of all possible ways the drawing might go. The sample points of the sample space can be strings such as "gbgr", which denotes the outcome in which green is drawn first, then blue, then green, then red.

Figure 8.1 shows all the possible outcomes of the statistical experiment. The root of the tree at the left edge represents the moment before the first marble is drawn. Its children in the column to the right of the root show the color of the first marble drawn, with the probabilities of each of the three possible colors shown on the branches. The colors in the second column are the possibilities for the second marble, with *conditional probabilities* shown on the branches. The boxed colors indicate the points at which the successive draws terminate.

For an example of how to use this tree, let's suppose that we want to find out the probability of getting the sequence green, blue, red as the outcome of the experiment. We would use the chain rule and multiply the probability of the individual event in each drawing conditioned by the previous ones. Thus, we would have 1/3 for the first ball being green, followed by 1/5 for the second one being blue given that the first one was green, and 3/4 for the third one being red given that the first two were green and blue. This gives us 1/20 for the intersection of the three events.

Theorem 8.14 *Let S be the sample space in a probability space. Suppose there are events A_1, A_2, ..., A_m, none having probability zero, that form a partition of S (i.e., the A_i's are pairwise disjoint, and their union is S). Then for any event B in S we have*

$$P(B) = P(A_1 \cap B) + P(A_2 \cap B) + \cdots + P(A_m \cap B)$$
$$= P(A_1)P(B|A_1) + P(A_2)P(B|A_2) + \cdots + P(A_m)P(B|A_m).$$

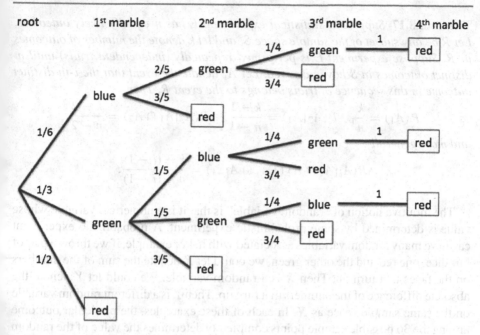

Fig. 8.1 Complete tree diagram for Example 8.13

Theorem 8.15 *Let A, B, and C be events in any probability space.*

(a) (Complementarity) If $P(A) > 0$, then $P(B^c|A) = 1 - P(B|A)$.
(b) (Inclusion-Exclusion) If $P(A) > 0$, then

$$P(B \cup C|A) = P(B|A) + P(C|A) - P(B \cap C|A).$$

Suppose A and B are events in a probability space, and suppose that knowing that A has occurred does not influence your estimate of the probability that B has occurred. In other words, suppose that $P(B|A) = P(B)$. Then the occurrence of B is "independent" of the occurrence of A. The equation $P(B|A) = P(B)$ can be written in the form $\dfrac{P(A \cap B)}{P(A)} = P(B)$, provided $P(A) > 0$, and then rewritten as $P(A \cap B) = P(A) \times P(B)$. It is customary to take this last equation as the mathematical definition of independence of two events because it is defined even if $P(A) = 0$.

Definition 8.16 Events A and B in a probability space are said to be *(stochastically) independent (of each other)* iff $P(A \cap B) = P(A) \times P(B)$. More generally, a collection C of events in a probability space is said to be a *stochastically independent collection* if and only if for every finite set of events $\{A_1, A_2, \ldots, A_n\}, n \geq 2$, drawn from the collection C we have

$$P(A_1 \cap A_2 \cap \ldots \cap A_n) = P(A_1) \times P(A_2) \times \cdots \times P(A_n).$$

Theorem 8.17 *Suppose a statistical experiment E has n equally likely outcomes. Let R be any subset of the sample space S, and let k denote the number of outcomes in R. Suppose experiment E is performed repeatedly (independent trials) until m distinct outcomes in S have occurred. Let A_i denote the event that the i-th distinct outcome in this sequence of trials belongs to the event R. Then*

$$P(A_1) = \frac{k}{n}, \quad P(A_2|A_1) = \frac{k-1}{n-1}, \quad P(A_3|A_1 \cap A_2) = \frac{k-2}{n-2},$$

and more generally

$$P(A_i|A_1 \cap A_2 \cap \ldots \cap A_{i-1}) = \frac{k-(i-1)}{n-(i-1)}.$$

The intuitive notion of "random variable" is that it is a numerical variable whose value is determined by some probabilistic experiment. A probabilistic experiment can have many random variables associated with it. For example, if we throw a pair of fair dice, one red and the other green, we could let X denote the sum of the numbers on the faces that turn up. Then X is a random variable. We could let Y denote the absolute difference of the numbers that turn up. Then Y is a different random variable on the same sample space as X. In each of these examples, the particular outcome among the 36 possible sample points completely determines the value of the random variable. To put it differently, to each outcome (sample point), the random variable assigns a numerical value according to some rule. That is, a random variable is a function on a sample space.

Definition 8.18 A *random variable* is a function that assigns a real number to each sample point in a sample space. If X is a random variable on a sample space S, then X is said to *assume a value x* if and only if there exists a sample point s in S such that $X(s) = x$, in which case we say that X *assumes the value x at s*. The set of values that X can assume is sometimes called the *range* of X. A random variable is said to be *discrete* if and only if the set of values that it can assume is either a finite set or is a countably infinite set of isolated values. It is said to be *continuous* iff the set of values it can assume consists of one or more entire intervals.

Definition 8.19 Let A denote any event in a probability space S. Then the *indicator random variable* for the event A is the function I_A defined on all sample points s by

$$I_A(s) = 1 \text{ if } s \in A \quad \text{and by} \quad I_A(s) = 0 \quad \text{if } s \notin A.$$

Definition 8.20 Suppose X is a discrete random variable. The *probability density function of X, abbreviated p.d.f. of X*, is the function f_X defined by the formula

$$f_X(x) = P(\text{"}X = x\text{"}) \quad \text{for all real numbers } x.$$

(The reason for the quotation marks in "$X = x$" is that this is an informal way of denoting the event consisting of all sample points for which the value of the random variable X is the real number x. The subscript on f_X is often omitted when there can be no confusion about which random variable is under discussion.)

Theorem 8.21 *Let f_X denote the probability density function of a discrete variable X. Then*

(a) *for every real number x we have $f_X(x) \geq 0$;*
(b) *$\Sigma f_X(x) = 1$. (Here the summation is over all x such that $f_X(x) > 0$.)*

Definition 8.22 The *cumulative distribution function (c.d.f.)* of a random variable X is the function $F_X(x)$ defined by the formula

$$F_X(x) = P(\text{"}X \leq x\text{"}) \quad \text{for all real numbers } x.$$

When X is discrete, then

$$F_X(x) = \Sigma_{x_i \leq x} \, f_X(x_i),$$

where the summation is taken over all the possible values x_i of the random variable X.

Theorem 8.23 *Every c.d.f. has all four of the following properties:*

(a) *$F_X(x)$ is monotone increasing on $(-\infty, +\infty)$.*
(b) *$\lim_{x \to -\infty} F_X(x) = 0$ and $\lim_{x \to +\infty} F_X(x) = 1$.*
(c) *$P(\text{"}a < X \leq b\text{"}) = F_X(b) - F_X(a)$ for all real numbers a and b satisfying $a \leq b$.*
(d) *Let x_{i-1} and x_i be two successive values that the random variable X can have (that is, $P(x_{i-1} < X < x_i) = 0$). Then $P(\text{"}X = x_i\text{"}) = f_X(x_i) = F_X(x_i) - F_X(x_{i-1})$.*

Definition 8.24 Let X be any discrete random variable with probability density function $f_X(x)$. Then the *expected value of X* (or *theoretical average value of X*, or *theoretical mean value of X*) is denoted by $E(X)$ or μ_X (or simply μ if X is well understood) and is defined to be the real number

$$E(X) = \mu_X = \mu = \Sigma \, x f_X(x),$$

where the sum is over all values of x such that $f_X(x) > 0$. That is, if $a_1, a_2, a_3, \ldots$ are the possible different values that X can assume, then

$$E(X) = \mu_X = \mu = a_1 P(\text{"}X = a_1\text{"}) + a_2 P(\text{"}X = a_2\text{"}) + a_3 P(\text{"}X = a_3\text{"}) + \cdots$$

Note that the "expected value" of a random variable X is often not a number that X can actually assume. For example, if X denotes the number of spots that turn up when a fair die is thrown, then $E(X) = 1(1/6) + 2(1/6) + 3(1/6) + 4(1/6) + 5(1/6) + 6(1/6) = 3.5$, which is not a possible value for X.

Theorem 8.25 (Repeated Trials Until Success) *Suppose a certain experiment has just two outcomes, one of which can be labeled "success", the other "failure". Suppose that on any one trial of the experiment the probability of success is some* *fixed positive number $p < 1$. Now suppose we decide to make repeated, independent trials of the experiment until we obtain one success. Let T denote the number of such independent trials. Then $E(T) = \dfrac{1}{p}$.*

Theorem 8.26 (Symmetric Probability Functions) *Let X be a discrete random variable whose p.d.f. is symmetric about some point μ on the real axis, by which we mean that for all real numbers t we have $f_X(\mu + t) = f_X(\mu - t)$. Then $E(X) = \mu$.*

Theorem 8.27 *If a random variable is a constant (i.e., it can assume only one value, so that it hardly deserves the name "random variable"), then its expected value is its constant value.*

We sometimes abuse notation slightly by writing Theorem 8.27 this way: $E(b) = b$ when b is a constant.

Theorem 8.28 *The expectation "operator" is linear on discrete random variables. That is, for all discrete random variables X, X_1, and X_2, and for all real numbers c,*

$$E(cX) = cE(X) \quad and \quad E(X_1 + X_2) = E(X_1) + E(X_2).$$

More generally, for all random variables $X_1, \ldots, X_n$ and X, and for all real numbers $a_1, \ldots, a_n$, and b,

$$E(a_1 X_1 + \cdots + a_n X_n) = a_1 E(X_1) + \cdots + a_n E(X_n);$$
$$E(X_1 - X_2) = E(X_1) - E(X_2);$$
$$E(X + b) = E(X) + b.$$

Theorem 8.29 *Let I_A denote the indicator random variable for some event A in a probability space (see Definition P.18). Then*

$$E(I_A) = P(A).$$

Theorem 8.30 *Let X and Y be discrete random variables defined on the same sample space. If $X < Y$ at every sample point, then $E(X) < E(Y)$. If $X \leq Y$ at every sample point, then $E(X) \leq E(Y)$. In particular, if there is are constants a and b such that $a \leq X \leq b$ at every sample point, then $a \leq E(X) \leq b$.*

Theorem 8.31 *Suppose the range of a random variable X is the set $\{1, 2, 3, \ldots, n\}$. Then*

$$E(X) = 1 + \sum_{x=1}^{n-1} [1 - F_X(x)] = \sum_{x=0}^{n-1} P(``X > x") = n - \sum_{x=1}^{n-1} F_X(x),$$

where $F_X(x)$ is the c.d.f. of X at x (see Definition 8.22).

Suppose we have a statistical experiment that has just two outcomes, one of which can be labeled "success", the other "failure". Let p denote the probability of success and q the probability of failure (so $q = 1 - p$, of course). We call such an experiment a *simple binary experiment*. Now suppose we design an experiment that consists of carrying out a specified number, call it n, of successive independent trials of this simple binary experiment. Then a good sample space for this experiment is the set of all character strings of length n consisting solely of s's and f's, where s stands for success and f for failure. There are 2^n such sample points, but they should not be considered to be equally likely unless $p = q = 0.5$. Instead, if a sample point consists of k s's and (therefore) $n - k$ f's, then by the independence of each trial from the trials that precede and follow it, that sample point should be assigned the probability $p^k q^{n-k}$.

Definition 8.32 Let X denote the number of successes that will be observed during a predetermined number n of independent trials of a simple binary experiment, with probability p of success on each separate trial. Then X is called a *binomial random variable with parameters n and p*. Its possible values are $0, 1, 2, \ldots, n$, and the values of the p.d.f. of X are denoted by $b(x; n, p)$ for $x = 0, 1, 2, \ldots, n$ by Theorem 8.21 and Definition 8.24 we must have

$$\sum_{x=0}^{n} b(x; n, p) = 1 \quad \text{and} \quad \sum_{x=0}^{n} x b(x; n, p) = E(X).$$

Theorem 8.33 *The p.d.f. of a binomial random variable with parameters n and p is given by the formula*

$$b(x; n, p) = \binom{n}{x} p^x q^{n-x} \text{ for } x = 0, 1, 2, \ldots, n, \quad \text{where } q = 1 - p.$$

Theorem 8.34 *Let X be a binomial random variable with parameters n (prescribed number of trials) and p (probability of success on each separate trial). Then $E(X) = np$. That is,* $\sum_{x=0}^{n} x b(x; n, p) = np$.

Definition 8.35 Let X denote a discrete random variable, and let A denote an event in its sample space. If $P(A) > 0$, then the *conditional expected value of X given A* is defined by

$$E(X|A) = \sum_{x} x P(\text{``}X = x\text{''}|A),$$

where as usual the expression "$X = x$" denotes the event consisting of all sample points at which X has the value x, and the summation is taken over all possible values x of the discrete random variable X.

Theorem 8.36 *Let X and Y denote discrete random variables defined on some sample space, and let A denote any event satisfying $P(A) > 0$ in that sample space. Then*

(a) $E(X + Y|A) = E(X|A) + E(Y|A)$;

(b) $E(cX|A) = cE(X|A)$ for all real numbers c;

(c) $E(X + b|A) = E(X|A) + b$ for all real numbers b.

In this text we make frequent use of the following theorem.

Theorem 8.37 Let $A_1, \ldots, A_m$ be events having non-zero probabilities and forming a partition of a sample space S. Let X be a discrete random variable on S. Then

$$E(X) = \sum_{i=1}^{m} P(A_i) E(X|A_i)$$

(cf. Theorem 8.14 on p. 456).

References

1. Adelson GM, Landis EM (1962) An algorithm for organization of information. Soviet Math Doklady 3:1259–1263
2. Biggs NL, Lloyd EK, Wilson RJ (1986) Graph theory 1736–1936, 2nd edn. Clarendon Press, Oxford
3. Cormen TH, Leiserson CE, Rivest RL, Stein C (2002) Introduction to algorithms, 2nd edn. The MIT Press, Cambridge
4. Dasgupta S, Papadimitriou C, Vazirani U (2008) Algorithms. McGraw Hill, Boston
5. Goodrich MT, Tamassia R, Mount D (2004) Data structures and algorithms in C++. John Wiley & Sons Inc., New York
6. Hoare CAR (1962) Quicksort. Comput J 5(1):10–15
7. Johnsonbaugh R, Schaefer M (2004) Algorithms. Pearson Education/Prentice Hall, New York
8. Karp RM, Rabin MO (1981) Efficient randomized pattern-matching algorithms. Technical report TR-31-81, Aiken Computation Laboratory, Harvard University.
9. Kleinberg J, Tardos E (2005) Algorithm design. Pearson / Addison Wesley, Boston
10. Knuth DE, Morris JH, Pratt VR (1977) Fast pattern matching in strings. SIAM J Comput 6(2):323–350
11. Knuth DE (1981) The art of computer programming. In: Seminumerical algorithms, vol 2, 2nd edn. Addison-Wesley, Massachusetts.
12. Knuth DE (1998) The art of computer programming. In: Sorting and searching, vol 3, 3rd edn. Addison-Wesley, Massachusetts.
13. Kruskal JB (1956) On the shortest spanning subtree of a graph and the traveling salesman problem. In: Proceedings of the American mathematical society, 1 February 1956, pp 48–50.
14. Levitin A (2007) Introduction to the design and analysis of algorithms, 2nd edn. Pearson/Addison Wesley, London
15. Neapolitan R, Naimipour K (2004) Foundations of algorithms, 4th edn. Jones and Bartlett Publishers, Sudbury
16. Sedgewick R (2001) Algorithms in C++, 3rd edn. Addison-Wesley, Upper Saddle River
17. Vrajitoru D, Knight W (2011) On the k-optimality of a family of binary trees. Indiana University South Bend, Technical report
18. Weiss MA (2006) Data structures and algorithm analysis in C++, 3rd edn. Pearson Addison-Wesley, Massachusetts

© Springer International Publishing Switzerland 2014
D. Vrajitoru and W. Knight, *Practical Analysis of Algorithms*,
Undergraduate Topics in Computer Science, DOI 10.1007/978-3-319-09888-3

Index

A
Adjacency matrix, 371
Adjacency list, 369
Adjacency structure, 369
Adjacent vertex, 361
Ancestor node, 212
Asymptotic functions, 89
AVL tree, 236

B
Big-omega notation, 74
Big-theta notation, 75
Binary insertion sort, 204
Binary search, 176, 200–202, 330
Binary search tree, 227, 358
Binary tree, 212
Binary tree height, 213, 222
Binary tree level, 213
Breadth-first search, 377, 379
Bubble sort, 186, 199, 338

C
c.d.f., 322
Ceiling, 9
Chain rule, 456
Characteristic equation, 108
Child node, 212
Compact binary tree, 218
Complete binary tree, 218
Complete graph, 364
Conditional probability, 455
Connected components, 366, 387
Connected graph, 365
Cycle, 365

D
Depth-first search, 380
Descendant node, 212
Digraph, 361
Dijkstra's algorithm, 391, 392
Division theorem, 58

E
Edge, 361
Euclid's algorithm, 206, 240
Euler's formula, 35
Eulerian circuit, 438
Eulerian cycle, 435
Eulerian path, 435
Event, 453
Expected value, 328, 459

F
Factorial, 52
Fingerprint function, 282
Finite graph, 361
Floor, 9
Free tree, 398
Fundamental strategy, 186

G
Geometric sum, 32
Graph, 361
Graph cycle, 365
Graph class, 372
Graph edge, 361
Graph vertex, 361

H
Hamiltonian circuit, 442, 447
Hamiltonian path, 442

© Springer International Publishing Switzerland 2014
D. Vrajitoru and W. Knight, *Practical Analysis of Algorithms*,
Undergraduate Topics in Computer Science, DOI 10.1007/978-3-319-09888-3